Causation and Counterfactuals

Representation and Mind
Hilary Putnam and Ned Block, editors

Causation and Counterfactuals

edited by John Collins, Ned Hall, and L. A. Paul

A Bradford Book
The MIT Press
Cambridge, Massachusetts
London, England

This book was set in Times New Roman on 3B2 by Asco Typesetters, Hong Kong, and was printed and bound in the United States of America.

Library of Congress Cataloging-in-Publication Data

Causation and counterfactuals / edited by John Collins, Ned Hall, and L. A. Paul.
    p.   cm. — (Representation and mind)
"A Bradford book."
Includes bibliographical references and index.
    ISBN 978-0-262-03317-6 (hc. :alk.paper)—ISBN 978-0-262-53256-3 (pb. :alk.paper)
    1. Causation. 2. Counterfactuals (Logic). I. Collins, John David. II. Hall, Edward J.
(Edward Jonathan), 1966– . III. Paul, L. A. (Laurie Ann), 1966– . IV. Series.
BD541.C192   2004
122—dc22   2003060612

10 9 8 7 6 5 4 3 2

To the memory of David Lewis

Contents

      Igal Kvart

16   A Counterfactual Analysis of Indeterministic Causation   387
      Murali Ramachandran

17   Do All and Only Causes Raise the Probabilities of Effects?   403
      Christopher Hitchcock

18   Causation, Counterfactuals, and the Third Factor   419
      Tim Maudlin

**19   Going through the Open Door Again: Counterfactual versus Singularist
      Theories of Causation**   445
      D. M. Armstrong

      References   459
      General Index   469
      Index of Examples   479

Contributors

D. M. Armstrong is Emeritus Professor of Philosophy at the University of Sydney.

Helen Beebee is Senior Lecturer in Philosophy at the University of Manchester.

David Coady is Lecturer in Philosophy at the University of Tasmania.

John Collins is Associate Professor of Philosophy at Columbia University.

Ned Hall is Associate Professor of Philosophy at the Massachusetts Institute of Technology.

Christopher Hitchcock is Professor of Philosophy at the California Institute of Technology.

Igal Kvart is Professor of Philosophy at the Hebrew University of Jerusalem.

David Lewis was the Class of 1943 University Professor of Philosophy at Princeton University.

Cei Maslen is Assistant Professor of Philosophy at Florida State University.

Tim Maudlin is Professor of Philosophy at Rutgers University.

D. H. Mellor is Emeritus Professor of Philosophy at Cambridge University.

Peter Menzies is Associate Professor of Philosophy at Macquarie University.

L. A. Paul is Associate Professor of Philosophy at the University of North Carolina at Chapel Hill.

Murali Ramachandran is Senior Lecturer in Philosophy at the University of Sussex.

Jonathan Schaffer is Assistant Professor of Philosophy at the University of Massachusetts, Amherst.

Stephen Yablo is Professor of Philosophy at the Massachusetts Institute of Technology.

1 Counterfactuals and Causation: History, Problems, and Prospects

John Collins, Ned Hall, and L. A. Paul

Among the many philosophers who hold that causal facts[1] are to be explained in terms of—or more ambitiously, shown to reduce to—facts about *what happens*, together with facts about the *fundamental laws* that govern what happens, the clear favorite is an approach that sees *counterfactual dependence* as the key to such explanation or reduction. The paradigm examples of causation, so advocates of this approach tell us, are examples in which events *c* and *e*—the cause and its effect—both occur, but: Had *c* not occurred, *e* would not have occurred either. From this starting point ideas proliferate in a vast profusion. But the remarkable disparity among these ideas should not obscure their common foundation. Neither should the diversity of opinion about the prospects for a philosophical analysis of causation obscure their importance: Even those philosophers who see these prospects as dim—perhaps because they suffer post-Quinean queasiness at the thought of *any* analysis of *any* concept of interest—can often be heard to say such things as that causal relations between events are somehow "a matter of" the patterns of counterfactual dependence to be found in them.

It was not always so. Thirty-odd years ago, so-called regularity analyses (so-called, presumably, because they traced back to Hume's well-known analysis of causation as constant conjunction) ruled the day, with Mackie's *Cement of the Universe* embodying a classic statement. But this sort of view fell on hard times, both because of internal problems—which we will review in due course—and because dramatic improvements in philosophical understanding of counterfactuals made possible the emergence of a serious and potent rival: a counterfactual analysis of causation resting on foundations firm enough to repel the kind of philosophical suspicion that had formerly warranted dismissal. One speculates at peril about the specific intellectual and social forces driving trends in philosophy. Still, it is a safe bet that Lewis's groundbreaking paper "Causation" (1973a) helped to turn the tide. Elegant, concentrated, and compelling, this paper contained a forceful condemnation—much quoted, by this point—of the incumbent view:

It remains to be seen whether any regularity analysis can succeed in distinguishing genuine causes from effects, epiphenomena, and preempted potential causes—and whether it can succeed without falling victim to worse problems, without piling on the epicycles, and without departing from the fundamental idea that causation is instantiation of regularities. I have no proof that regularity analyses are beyond repair, nor any space to review the repairs that have been tried. Suffice it to say that the prospects look dark. I think it is time to give up and try something else.

A promising alternative is not far to seek. (1973a, p. 160)

At the time, the sentiment Lewis expressed in this passage was entirely fitting.

Whether—and to what extent—that sentiment continues to be fitting is a judgment that this volume aims to inform. Here we bring together some of the most important recent work connecting—or in some cases, disputing the connection between—counterfactuals and causation. Some of these essays (chapters 2–4, 7, and 8) appeared previously in a special issue (April 2000) of the *Journal of Philosophy* devoted to this topic; the rest are published here for the first time, or in new and updated forms. (Lewis's groundbreaking "Causation as Influence"—chapter 3—has been greatly expanded for this volume.) Our aim in this introductory chapter is to set the stage for the essays that follow by providing a map of the main features of the philosophical terrain that our authors are navigating. Accordingly, we will discuss the work on the semantics of counterfactuals that set the stage for counterfactual analyses of causation (section 1), review the early successes and more recent challenges to such analyses (sections 2 through 4), probe some important points of methodology that play a significant but often tacit role in philosophical investigations of causation (section 5), and review (in sections 6 and 7) two topics of general interest that work in the counterfactual tradition has shed a great deal of light on, and that many of our contributors are concerned to address: the transitivity of causation, and the nature of the causal relata.

For those who come to our topics for the first time, our overview should provide you with the background you need to appreciate the often subtle and intricate dialectical interplay featured in the remaining contributions; for seasoned veterans, we hope nevertheless to reveal unnoticed connections within and novel perspectives on what may have seemed boringly familiar material. (Those of you who are impatient can skip ahead to section 8, where we give capsule summaries of the contributions in this volume.)

Let us begin by rehearsing the first half of our topic: counterfactuals.

1 Counterfactuals

A *counterfactual* is a conditional sentence in the subjunctive mood. The term "counterfactual" or "contrary-to-fact" conditional carries the suggestion that the antecedent of such a conditional is false. Consider, for example: "If this glass had been struck, then it would have shattered." The implication is that the glass was actually not struck and did not shatter. Yet these conditionals do not appear to differ in kind from those in which the truth value of the antecedent is an open question (e.g., "If this glass were struck, then it would shatter"). While this suggests that the expression "subjunctive conditional" might more appropriately delineate the topic, the term "counterfactual" is by now so well entrenched that it will suffice to stipulate that counterfactuals may have true antecedents.

The philosophical significance of counterfactuals is apparent from the way in which they have figured so prominently in recent discussions of many other philosophically important concepts: knowledge, perception, and freedom of the will, to name just a few. An attractive thought is that this conceptual connection is best understood as being mediated by the concept of *cause*. Thus, for example, counterfactuals are relevant to discussions of perception because the most promising theories of perception are causal theories, and counterfactuals are fundamental to any philosophical understanding of causation.

The thought from which counterfactual theories of causation proceeds is this. A certain glass is struck, and shatters. To say that the striking of the glass caused the shattering of the glass is to say that if the glass had not been struck then it would not have shattered. The striking caused the shattering in virtue of the fact that the shattering was *counterfactually dependent* on the striking. The papers in the present volume are devoted to exploring the prospects of an account of causation based on that simple idea. But before turning to that discussion, we shall review some of the basic semantic features of counterfactuals.

Counterfactual conditionals themselves pose a problem that must be solved before such conditionals are recognized as a fit tool for further philosophical analysis. The problem, first raised in the recent philosophical literature by Chisholm (1946) and Goodman (1947), is to provide noncircular truth conditions for the general counterfactual conditional with antecedent A and consequent C. We shall abbreviate this conditional as "$A \mathbin{\square\!\!\rightarrow} C$," to be read: "If it were the case that A, then it would be the case that C."

Observe first of all that the counterfactual must be distinguished from both the material conditional and strict entailment. The material conditional's truth conditions are too weak; not every subjunctive conditional with a false antecedent is true. But on the other hand, the strict conditional is too strong; the shattering of the glass is not logically entailed, or metaphysically necessitated, by the striking of the glass.

The right account is, presumably, located somewhere between these extremes. A natural next thought is that "$A \mathbin{\square\!\!\rightarrow} C$" is true if and only if C is entailed not by A alone, but by A in conjunction with some other truths: these might include, for example, fundamental truths about the laws of nature. The problem with this suggestion is that no single set of fixed truths will do the job for all A and C. As Lewis (1973b) notes, specifying such a set would incorrectly include strengthening the antecedent among the valid forms of inference for counterfactuals, yet counterfactuals are clearly *nonmonotonic*. For example, from the fact that a particular match would light if it were struck, it does not follow that if the match were struck *and there were no oxygen present*, then it would light.

Counterfactuals are variably strict conditionals. In evaluating a counterfactual we see what is entailed by the antecedent along with some other truths, but the set of truths to be held fixed varies from case to case in a way that is determined by the antecedent A. In Goodman's phrase: We hold fixed everything that is *cotenable* with the truth of the antecedent. The threat of circularity should now be apparent, for what could it mean for a proposition to be "cotenable" with A, other than that the proposition is one that would still be true if A were true? One can hardly explain counterfactuals in terms of the notion of cotenability and then proceed to give a counterfactual analysis of "cotenable."

A way out of this circle was presented in the work of Stalnaker (1968) and Lewis (1973b), inspired by the development of possible worlds semantics in modal logic. Central to the Stalnaker–Lewis approach is the assumption that possible worlds can be ordered with respect to their similarity to the actual world. Since the relation of comparative similarity to the actual world is assumed to be a weak order (i.e., a connected and transitive relation) we may usefully think of it as a relation of comparative "closeness." Call a world at which the proposition A is true an "A-world." Then the counterfactual "$A \mathbin{\Box\!\!\rightarrow} C$" is true if and only if C is true at the closest A-world to the actual world. If, following Lewis (1973b), we want to allow that there may not be a single A-world, or even any set of A-worlds, closest to the actual world, the truth condition is more appropriately given like this:

"$A \mathbin{\Box\!\!\rightarrow} C$" is true if and only if some $(A\&C)$-world is more similar to the actual world than any $(A\&{\sim}C)$-world is.

It is worth noting how much of the logic of counterfactuals follows simply from the assumption that the similarity relation is a weak order. We can see immediately, for example, the particular logical form of the fallacy of strengthening the antecedent. It is a fallacy analogous to the mistake made by someone who infers from "There is no hardware store in the closest town to here that has a bank" that "There is no hardware store in the closest town to here that has a bank and a restaurant." Further exercise of the analogy between similarity and closeness leads to the correct prediction that contraposition is also invalid, and that counterfactuals fail to be transitive. Appreciation of these points will be key to the discussion that follows.

Although much of the logic of counterfactuals follows just from the assumption that any reasonable relation of comparative similarity will be a weak ordering, we will need to say something more substantial about the notion of similarity if our hope is to provide an account of counterfactuals on which a theory of causation can be based. The problem is that similarity is multidimensional. If two worlds are each similar to the actual world in a different respect, which is most similar to the actual world all things considered?

We might in general be content to consign the weighing of respects of similarity and difference to the pragmatic rather than the semantic part of the theory. So we might say: In one context it is appropriate to assert that Caesar would have used the atom bomb had he been in command in Korea; in another that he would have used catapults (example from Quine 1960, p. 222). One of the contributors to this volume (Maslen, chapter 14) is happy to allow that because of this feature of counterfactuals, the causal relation itself is context dependent—that whether or not it is correct to describe one event as a cause of another is relative to the contrast situation one has in mind. But those who hope for a *context-independent* counterfactual account of causation must confront the issue of respects of similarity head on.

The issue arises most sharply in connection with temporal considerations. Causes precede their effects. A defender of a counterfactual theory of causation will likely think that this temporal asymmetry in causation reflects an asymmetry in counterfactual dependence: Whereas the future depends counterfactually on the past and present, the past is not counterfactually dependent on the present and future.

Admittedly, we are sometimes willing to talk about how things would have been different in the past, had they been different now. ("If I had pulled the trigger just now, there would have to have been no one in the line of fire. I'm not a homicidal maniac!") But as Lewis (1979a) notes, such *backtracking conditionals* are typically "marked by a syntactic peculiarity"—note the "have to have been" construction in the above example. Backtracking conditionals will have to be set aside if we want to defend a counterfactual theory of causation. And they will have to be ruled out in some principled way. This provides a clue to the problem of weighing respects of similarity.

It is clear, as we noted above, that similarities with respect to the laws of nature (*nomological* similarities) should generally outweigh similarities with respect to accidental matters of fact in the all-things-considered evaluation of similarity. But apparently this cannot be an invariable rule. That's one of the lessons of temporal asymmetry: If the actual laws of nature are deterministic toward both past and future, then any world that shares these laws yet differs from the actual world in some particular present matter of fact will have not only a different future from the actual world, but a different past as well. We then have backtracking on a massive scale.

So we must allow that certain minor violations of the laws of nature ("small miracles") may be compensated for by agreement in past matters of particular fact.

Yet it would hardly do to secure this agreement by stipulation. That would incorrectly (to our minds) deem backward causation an a priori impossibility. (Later in this section we will see that this issue is more complicated than the present remarks suggest, as accommodating backward causation turns out to be trickier than it might seem.) Nor, in the present context, is it an attractive option to appeal to *causal* notions—requiring, for example, that in a counterfactual situation in which some (actually occurring) event c does not occur, everything either causally antecedent to or causally independent of c be held fixed. Such a stipulation might guarantee the right truth values for the counterfactuals that feature in a counterfactual analysis of causation, but it would do so at too high a price in circularity.[2] The challenge for the Stalnaker–Lewis account of counterfactuals is to provide criteria for weighing respects of comparative similarity that yield temporal asymmetry without doing so by fiat.

The challenge has been pressed most vigorously in connection with what is known as the "future similarity objection" (see Fine 1975, and references in Lewis 1986a, 43 to seven more published versions of the objection). We may suppose the following counterfactual is true:

If Nixon had pressed the button, there would have been a nuclear holocaust.

But it seems as though according to the Stalnaker–Lewis theory it will come out false. Suppose a nuclear war never actually takes place; then any world in which no nuclear war takes place will be more similar to the actual world than any world in which a nuclear war does take place. A nuclear war would, after all, make things very different from the way they actually are. Hence, given any world in which the antecedent and consequent are both true, it is easier to imagine a closer world in which the antecedent is true and the consequent false. Just imagine some minor change that prevents the nuclear disaster from occurring.

In response Lewis says:

The thing to do is not to start by deciding, once and for all, what we think about similarity of worlds, so that we can afterwards use these decisions to test [the analysis].... Rather, we must use what we know about the truth and falsity of counterfactuals to see if we can find some sort of similarity relation—not necessarily the first one that springs to mind—that combines with [the analysis] to yield the proper truth conditions. (Lewis 1979a, p. 43)

By pursuing this strategy of "reverse engineering" the similarity ordering from our intuitions about particular conditionals, Lewis obtains a set of criteria (1979a, pp. 47–48) that, he argues, suffice to rule out backtracking in worlds like ours without making backward causation a conceptual impossibility. In brief, Lewis argues as follows: Take some event c that occurs at time t. Assuming determinism—and assuming that the world displays certain de facto temporal asymmetries that Lewis attempts to characterize (it is this assumption that is supposed to leave the door open for backward causation)—the only way to construct a counterfactual scenario in which (i) c does not occur at t, and (ii) there are no gratuitous departures from actuality, is to insert, shortly before t, a "divergence miracle": a localized violation of actual (though not counterfactual) law that throws history off course just enough to make it the case that c does not occur. Thus, we get a counterfactual situation in which history until shortly before t is exactly as it actually is, but whose history after t diverges substantially from actual history; moreover, only during a relatively short interval of time, and in a relatively localized region of space, do the events of this world fail to conform to the actual laws. Lewis argues that we cannot do things in reverse: There is no similar way to insert a single localized "reconvergence miracle" so as to arrive at a counterfactual scenario whose past before t differs from the actual past, but whose future from shortly after t onward is exactly like the actual future. It is in this way that his truth conditions secure a nonbacktracking reading of the conditional.

But worries remain on this score. For example, it is not clear whether future similarity should count for absolutely *nothing* in the ordering, or whether it should merely have relatively little weight. Here it helps to think about examples that are not deterministic, but which involve some genuine chance process. For simplicity, suppose that a certain coin toss is genuinely chancy. If I haven't tossed the coin yet, and the coin is fair, it seems wrong to say that "If I were to toss the coin, then it would land heads." It seems wrong to say this even if, as a matter of fact, the coin actually does land heads when I get around to tossing it. This suggests that worlds in which the coin will land tails when tossed are as close to the actual world as any world in which the coin will land heads. This means that there are nonactual worlds that are as similar to the actual world as the actual world is to itself. And of course that's just what one would expect to be the case if a certain respect of similarity or difference is to count for nothing.

But the interplay between counterfactuals and chance involves some subtlety. As Sid Morgenbesser reminds us, if I offer to bet you that the coin will land tails and you decline the wager, then I can say later, after the coin lands heads, "Look, you would have won!" How can the Stalnaker–Lewis account reconcile these conflicting intuitions?

A second and quite serious difficulty has recently been pressed by Adam Elga (2000).[3] Elga argues, very persuasively, that Lewis's attempt to provide truth conditions for a nonbacktracking reading of the counterfactual runs afoul of statistical mechanics. Recall the dialectic: For any event c occurring at time t in world w, there are worlds w' whose histories match that of w *exactly* until shortly before t, but which then exhibit a small "divergence miracle" that throws history off course just enough to guarantee c's nonoccurrence. But, Lewis claims (and *must* claim), provided w exhibits the appropriate de facto temporal asymmetries, there are *no* worlds w' in which (i) c does not occur; (ii) history from shortly *after* t on matches w's history exactly; and (iii) this perfect match comes about as a result of a small "reconvergence miracle."

Elga shows that this last claim is false—at least, it is false for many typical choices for c, in any world that displays the global entropic features of our own. Suppose, to borrow his example, that Suzy cracks an egg into a hot pan, and it cooks. Let c be her cracking of the egg. Pick a time t shortly after it has cooked. Now look at what happens from t *backward*: A cooked egg sits in a pan, gradually *un*cooking; it coalesces into a raw egg and leaps upward; a shell closes around it, forming a perfect seal. Surprisingly, the kind of time-reversibility that the laws of our world apparently exhibit allows that this entropy-diminishing process (flipped over in time, and run from past to future) is *possible* (see Albert 2000 for details); but they also guarantee that it is highly *unstable*, in the sense that a slight change in the initial conditions will upset the delicately timed processes that result in the uncooking and sealing of the egg (it is in establishing this result that statistical mechanics comes into play). Make such a slight change—say, by altering the positions of the molecules in one corner of the pan—and the egg will just sit there, slowly growing colder.

But, as Elga points out, such a slight change, inserted at t in the *actual* world, accomplishes exactly what is required of a "reconvergence miracle." That is, we construct a possible world by holding history beyond t fixed, making a slight, localized change in the state of the world at t, and running the laws backward: In such a world, the egg is never cracked, and so c does not occur. The needed asymmetry between divergence and reconvergence miracles vanishes. There is a real irony here: Lewis closes his famous paper by observing, "I regret that I do not know how to connect the several asymmetries I have discussed and the famous asymmetry of entropy" (1986a, p. 51).

Though serious, this problem should not be overstated. It is not just that some way might be found to amend Lewis's account in response to Elga's challenge (for example, one might construct standards of similarity that give significant weight to the global entropic profile of a world).[4] It is also that the philosopher who desires a nonbacktracking reading of the counterfactual *solely* to serve the purposes of her counterfactual analysis of causation—and not also, as in Lewis (1986a), to provide an account of the asymmetry between past and future—can fall back on a recipe for evaluating counterfactuals that guarantees, more or less by stipulation, that they will have the needed nonbacktracking reading. This can be done as follows:

The first step is to require that causes must *precede* their effects. (More, in a moment, on whether this requirement carries too high a price.) Then the counterfactual analyst need only consider conditionals of the form "$\sim O(c) \mathbin{\square\!\rightarrow} \sim O(e)$" where c and e both occur, and c before e. ("$O(c)$" is short for "c occurs," etc.) Suppose we are given such a conditional. To construct the relevant counterfactual situation, focus first on the time t at which c actually occurs. Consider the complete physical state of the world at that time. (Or: the complete state on some spacelike hypersurface that includes the region of c's occurrence.) Make changes to that state localized to the region in which c occurs, and just sufficient to make it the case that c does not occur. (These are the changes that Lewis's account would have brought about by a "miracle.") Evolve the new state forward in time in accordance with the actual laws, and check to see whether e occurs. If it does, the conditional is false; if it doesn't, true.

Matters might be more complicated: Perhaps there are many equally minimal ways to change the given state, or an infinite succession of ever-more-minimal ways. If so, we employ the obvious sophistication: the conditional "$\sim O(c) \mathbin{\square\!\rightarrow} \sim O(e)$" is true just in case *some* $\sim O(c)$-state that yields a $\sim O(e)$-future is "closer" to the actual state (i.e., involves a more minimal change from the actual state) than is any $\sim O(c)$-state that yields an $O(e)$-future.

Notice that in following this recipe we have implicitly replaced a similarity metric on *worlds* with a similarity metric on *states*, or if you like, worlds-at-times. Not a problem—but it does make clear (what was perhaps obvious anyway) that the recipe is limited in scope, working best (perhaps only) when the antecedent of the conditional is a proposition entirely about a particular time or narrow interval of time.[5] The counterfactual analyst should not worry: After all, she is doing the metaphysics of causation, and not the semantics of some fragment of English. And her counterfactual conditional evidently has enough in common with the ordinary language one still to deserve the name.

But two other problems plague the counterfactual analyst who takes our suggestion for responding to Elga's challenge. She has stipulated that causes must precede their effects. Has she not thereby ruled out—a priori—both simultaneous causation and backward causation? But both are surely possible. As to the first, we have, for example, the situation in which the particle's presence at a certain location in the force field at time t causes its acceleration with a certain magnitude at time t. As to the second, we have any of a number of seemingly perfectly consistent time-travel stories, for example, the following: A billiard ball subject to no forces flies freely through space; call this ball "Bill." Off to the left is the Time Travel Exit

Portal. Off to the right is the Time Travel Entrance Portal. At time 0, a billiard ball —call it "Sue"—emerges from the Exit Portal, flies toward Bill, and strikes it. Bill goes careening off toward the Entrance Portal, and crosses it at time 1—and, of course, leaves the Exit Portal at time 0: Bill and Sue are one and the same.[6]

Examples such as these appear to depict genuine possibilities, but if causes must precede their effects then it seems that this appearance is illusory. In fact, however, we think matters are not nearly so simple. For reasons of space we will forgo a full discussion; but we will try to say enough to make it clear that these two problems should not prevent one from taking seriously the method we have suggested for guaranteeing the asymmetry of causation.

As to simultaneous causation, one promising strategy is to deny that the examples allegedly depicting it in fact succeed in doing so. Consider the example we gave, where the effect supposedly contemporaneous with its cause is the acceleration of a particle at time t. We suggest that the example gains its intuitive appeal only so long as we remain naive about the underlying physics: what it *is* for a particle to be accelerating with a certain magnitude at time t is for its motion—*in an interval of time extending forward from t*—to display a certain character.[7] Put another way, it is *not* an intrinsic property of the state of the particle—or indeed of the world—as it is at time t that the particle has the given acceleration, then; rather, it is a *relational* property, where the relatum is the trajectory of the particle in the immediate future of t. We could properly insist, then, that when we loosely speak of the particle's position in the force field at time t causing its acceleration at that time, what we *mean* is that its position in the field causes a certain aspect of its *subsequent* motion. But then any conflict with the stipulation that causes must precede their effects disappears. Indeed, the example begins to look like the following example of "simultaneous causation": Say that a window is "doomed" at time t just in case it will shatter within ten seconds of t. Suzy throws a rock at a window at noon—instantaneously causing the event of its being doomed at noon. That is silly, the kind of example about which no competent philosopher would think twice. We think that careful reflection exposes the example of the particle in the force field as being equally silly. And, while we will not pursue the matter here, we suspect that other alleged cases of simultaneous causation can be given a similar exposé.

Backward causation requires, we think, a different treatment, for unlike some authors (e.g., Mellor 1998, chapter 12), we do not wish to deny its possibility. Accordingly, we suggest a much more defensive maneuver, which is to point out that the need to accommodate backward causation provides, surprisingly, no reason whatsoever to return to Lewis's miracle-based account of the truth conditions of the counterfactual.

To see why, return to our example of the collision of Bill/Sue with itself. Focus on a time moments before the ball crosses the Time Travel Entrance Portal. Let c be the event of its flying toward the Entrance, at that time; let e be the earlier event of its flying out of the Exit. Clearly, c causes e. But whether e counterfactually depends on c is not at all clear, and that is because it is not at all clear what is going on in a counterfactual situation in which c does not occur. Try first to construct this situation in a flat-footed way, by inserting a "divergence miracle" into the actual course of events just before c occurs, a miracle just sufficient to guarantee that c doesn't occur. You will quickly find that limiting yourself to just one such miracle cannot possibly do, for remember that the *rest* of what goes on—the totality of events that follow your miracle, and the totality of events that precede it—must *conform* to actual law. Suppose for illustration that your miracle makes the ball vanish, just before it reaches the Entrance. Then, by law, it cannot leave the Exit—not at time 0, nor at any other time. And there are no other balls in the picture. So *no* ball ever leaves the Exit. So no ball ever collides with Bill/Sue. So Bill/Sue continues on its original course. So, far from vanishing just before it reaches the Entrance at time 1, the ball is nowhere near it, then. Contradiction.

We could try to fix matters by inserting a second localized miracle: Let the ball (miraculously) leave the Exit at time 0, even though it does not cross it at time 1. Then we have a consistent story, *most* of which is compatible with the actual laws: The ball is flying through space; a ball (miraculously) flies out of the Exit at time 0; the two collide, sending the original ball toward the Entrance; just before time 1, it (miraculously) vanishes. But e occurs, in this scenario. So if this is what would have happened, had c not occurred, then e does not depend on c. So the counterfactual analysis gets the causal structure of our case wrong.

We could also try to fix matters by insisting that the counterfactual situation in which c does not occur is simply one in which nothing ever leaves the Exit or crosses the Entrance: instead, the ball just flies through space, unmolested. So e does not occur; so—if this is what would have happened—e depends on c, after all. True, we do not reach this situation by inserting a miracle into the actual course of events. But Lewis's official criteria for similarity of worlds do not *require* miracles: One is supposed to introduce them only if doing so is necessary to secure widespread and perfect match of particular fact.

The problem should now be obvious, for securing such a perfect match is exactly what we accomplish by introducing a second miracle, whereby the ball leaves the Exit, even though it does not cross the Entrance. In fact, the first counterfactual situation we described matches the actual situation perfectly, *everywhere*, except for a tiny interval before time 1, in a small region of space near the Entrance. By Lewis's own criteria, it should therefore win out over the second situation. So the account of the truth conditions for counterfactuals in which these criteria feature does not, after all, seem so clearly preferable to the "asymmetry by fiat" account sketched above.

There is an important open question here, which we must simply note and pass over: How exactly can any sort of reductive account of causation—counterfactual or otherwise—accommodate backward causation? We strongly suspect that the best answers will end up treating backward causation as a kind of special case. If so, that may prove to be more good news for our suggested truth conditions for the counter-factual, for it may be to their credit that they allow for no straightforward treatment of backward causation within the context of a counterfactual analysis. At any rate, those truth conditions evidently provide the ingredients necessary for pursuing a counterfactual account of less exotic varieties of causation. Let us now consider the prospects for such an account.

2 Reductionism about Causation

It will be helpful to begin by situating counterfactual approaches to causation within the much larger constellation of philosophical accounts of causation quite generally. Probably the most useful distinction to make at the outset is that between accounts that do and accounts that do not attempt to *reduce* causal facts to facts about what happens, together with facts about what the laws are that govern what happens. (We have a permissive sense of "what happens" in mind: It is to include facts about what objects exist where and when, and what categorical properties and relations they instantiate.) Immediately, two questions arise, which we will not pursue in any detail: First, can facts about the laws themselves be reduced to the totality of categorical facts? Some—notably, Lewis (e.g., 1983b)—will say "yes," others "no." We wish merely to note that with respect to the aims of the essays in this volume, almost nothing hangs on this dispute. (For example, Lewis's account of causation could be adopted wholesale by one who disagreed with him about whether the laws them-selves reduce to categorical facts.) Second, is there in fact a legitimate distinction to be drawn between categorical and noncategorical facts about the world? Put another way, is it possible to specify, in *noncausal* terms, the facts about "what happens" that form part of our reduction base? The facts about the laws? We will simply proceed under the assumption of an affirmative answer; but see Shoemaker (1980) and Cart-wright (1999) for influential statements of contrary views.

We will henceforth label "reductionist" any position according to which causal facts can be reduced to categorical plus nomological facts, and label "antireductionist" any position that denies this claim. Most of the essays in this volume are written from a reductionist perspective—or at any rate, from a perspective entirely congenial to reductionism. (Armstrong, chapter 19 of this volume, "Going through the Open Door Again," is a notable exception.) It is useful to add, however, that some antireductionists find strong motivation for their view in certain key thought experiments. Here, for example, is one provided by Michael Tooley (1990, p. 228, italics in the original):

Given [the assumption that there is nothing incoherent in the idea of an uncaused event], one can consider a world where objects sometimes acquire property Q without there being any cause of their doing so, and similarly for property R, and where, in addition, the following two statements are true:

(1) It is a law that, for any object x, x's having property P for a temporal interval of length Δt either causes x to acquire property Q, or else causes x to acquire property R;

(2) It can *never* be the case, for any object x, that x's having property P for a temporal interval of length Δt causes x to acquire both property Q *and* property R.

Suppose, finally, that an object a in such a world, having had property P for the appropriate interval, acquires both Q and R. In view of the law described in statement (1), either the acquisition of Q was caused by the possession of P for the relevant interval, or else the acquisition of R was so caused. But, given statement (2), it cannot be the case that the possession of P for the relevant interval caused *both* the acquisition of Q *and* the acquisition of R. So once again, it must be the case that one of two causal states of affairs obtains, but the totality of facts concerning, first, the non-causal properties of, and relations between, events, secondly, what laws there are, and thirdly, the direction of causation in all potential causal processes, does not suffice to fix which causal state of affairs obtains.

In section 5 below, where we take up a number of tricky methodological issues, we will briefly touch on the question of how much probative value thought experiments like this have (to anticipate: not much). Let us now proceed to draw further distinctions between reductionist approaches to causation.

Once again, a particular distinction stands out as especially helpful: that between what we will call "physical connection" accounts of causation and what we will call "nomological entailment" accounts. Examples will work better than definitions to give the idea.

Physical connection accounts, although reductionist, appeal to the fundamental laws only indirectly—typically, in the specification of some quantity whose "transfer" is thought to constitute the causal relation.[8] Thus, we might say, with Fair (1979), that causation consists in the transfer of *energy*. Or, with Ehring (1997), that it occurs in the transfer of a *trope*; or, with Dowe (1992) and Salmon (1994), in the transfer of some *conserved quantity*—where appeal is made to fundamental physics for an inventory of such quantities. This last example shows most clearly how the fundamental laws can have a place in such accounts.

We think such accounts suffer from a lack of ambition, twice over: First, however successful they are at limning the features of causation, as it relates events in the purely *microphysical* realm, there seems little hope that they can succeed in doing so in the messy macroscopic realm. Suzy kisses Billy, causing him to flush; are we to suppose that the causal relation between these two events is to be mapped out by looking at how energy, or some other fundamental physical quantity, is transferred? Well, it might be romantic to say so. But it is not, we think, particularly enlightening.

Second, assuming, as seems reasonable, that it is a contingent matter what the fundamental laws are, physical connection accounts cannot (because they are not designed to) tell us anything about causation as it might have been—in particular, as it is in worlds with laws very different from our own. That limitation seems not merely unfortunate but deeply misguided; for it seems clear that although the fundamental laws play an essential role in fixing the causal facts, they do not do so in so *specialized* a manner. Put another way, it seems both reasonable and worthwhile to try to specify the way in which the fundamental laws fix the causal facts in terms that *abstract away* from the gory details of those laws—thereby to produce an account that has a hope of proving to be not merely true, but necessarily so.

That is what nomological entailment accounts attempt to do. As a simple example—one that shows where the label "nomological entailment" comes from— consider the view that takes c to be a cause of e just in case it follows, from the proposition that c occurs, together with the proposition that encapsulates the fundamental laws, that e occurs (where the "following" relation could be spelled out in terms of deductive entailment, or in terms of some notion of metaphysical necessity: more on this in the next section). Or we might go the other way: c is a cause of e just in case it follows, from the proposition that e occurs, together with the proposition that encapsulates the fundamental laws, that c occurs. Or we might go both ways at once. (Lesson: do not take the "entailment" in question invariably to proceed from cause to effect.) The defects in these accounts are perfectly obvious, but it is *also* obvious that they do not suffer from the two kinds of constriction that made physical connection accounts so disappointing.

(The distinction between physical connection accounts and nomological entailment accounts does not exhaust the range of *reductionist* accounts of causation. Maudlin's "Causation, Counterfactuals, and the Third Factor" [chapter 18] provides an excellent illustration of this point: He argues that our ability to apply any discriminating notion of cause is parasitic on our ability to analyze the *laws* governing the situation in question into, on the one hand, laws that specify how things will behave if left undisturbed, and, on the other hand, laws that specify the exact consequences of particular disturbances.)

Of course, more sophisticated and correspondingly more interesting nomological entailment accounts are easy to find. For example, we might side with Mackie (1965): c is a cause of e iff, from the proposition that c occurs, together with the proposition that encapsulates the fundamental laws, together with some suitably chosen proposition about conditions that obtain at the time of c's occurrence, it follows that e occurs, where the premise that c occurs is essential to the entailment. Or we might try building on the idea that c is a cause of e just in case the conditional probability that e occurs, given that c occurs, is greater than the unconditional probability that e occurs. (For a sophisticated version, see Eells 1991.) Note that in calling this a "nomological entailment" account, we are, in the first place, assuming that the relevant probabilities are somehow determined by the laws (i.e., they are not subjective probabilities); and, in the second place, we are permissively counting probability-raising as a kind of "entailment." No matter: consider this a small sacrifice of accuracy for the sake of having a handy label.

More to the point, we might endorse the simplest counterfactual analysis: c is a cause of e iff, had c not occurred, e would not have occurred—where this entailment relation between the proposition that c does not occur and that e does not occur counts as "nomological" because of the central role played by the fundamental laws in fixing the truth conditions of the counterfactual (see section 1). Or we might hold some more sophisticated counterfactual analysis that builds on the core idea contained in the simple version. Indeed, many philosophers hold out such firm hope for some sort of counterfactual analysis precisely because they are convinced, in the first place, that some sort of *nomological entailment* account must be correct; and, in the second place, that no rival to the counterfactual approach has a prayer. (See Lewis's "Causation as Influence," chapter 3 in this volume, for a particularly forceful defense of this motivation.) Be that as it may, in attempting such an analysis one should certainly come armed with a clear view of the major obstacles, a host of which have emerged over the course of the last twenty-five years. We will now briefly survey the most important of them.

3   The Original Lewis Analysis

Let us first take stock of the principal *advantages* of the counterfactual approach. Focus on one of the simplest counterfactual analyses: Lewis's original (1973a) analysis. He took causation to be the ancestral of counterfactual dependence: c causes e iff

c and e both occur, c and e are distinct, and there is a (possibly empty) set of events $\{d_1, d_2, \ldots, d_n\}$ such that if c had not occurred, d_1 would not have occurred; and if d_1 had not occurred, d_2 would not have occurred; ... and if d_n had not occurred, e would not have occurred.

The analysis is attractively simple and extremely intuitive, given how obvious it seems that there must be *some* intimate connection between causation and counterfactual dependence. To be sure, the connection need not be explained by supposing that causation must be given a counterfactual analysis; see Maudlin's contribution (chapter 18) for a rival explanation. But the prima facie plausibility of a counterfactual analysis is sufficiently clear that no one can reasonably doubt that exploring its prospects is worthwhile.

Next, the account makes it exquisitely clear what role the laws of nature play in fixing the causal facts—and moreover, it makes it clear that this role does not require *too much* of the laws. Let us explain what we mean by this by contrasting the Lewis analysis with a Davidsonian account of causation. According to this latter kind of account, what distinguishes a true causal claim of the form *"c is a cause of e" as such* is that, when the names *"c"* and *"e"* are replaced by suitable uniquely identifying descriptions of the respective events, the resulting sentence can be seen to be a deductive consequence of some universal generalization or generalizations that hold with lawful necessity (together with additional premises specifying that the given events in fact occur). Morton White (1965, pp. 56–104) presents a clear statement of this sort of approach.[9]

This Davidsonian account faces a number of difficulties, but for our purposes the one to focus on is that it places severe constraints on an account of laws that can meet its needs. Are we to suppose, for example, that the lawful universal generalizations come directly from fundamental physics—so that the uniquely identifying descriptions have to be descriptions in the language of fundamental physics? Or is it rather that we can pick out higher-level laws tailored to any domain where we can find true causal claims? But then as good reductionists, we should want to know how these higher-level laws themselves reduce to facts about what happens, together with facts about the *fundamental* laws. Even if we are *not* good reductionists, we should want to know this—for unless we are told, we should view with serious skepticism the claim that there even *are* such suitable higher-level laws (enough of them, anyway).

Our simple counterfactual analysis elegantly avoids these issues: As we saw in section 1, all we need by way of an account of laws is an account of which worlds are *nomologically possible*. Put another way, that is all that the laws need to contribute to the truth conditions for the relevant counterfactual conditionals. We do not need what the Davidsonian requires: for each causal relation, a law that will directly "cover" it, at least when the relata are described appropriately. (In hindsight, the crucial mistake the Davidsonian committed here was to require a deductive relation between *sentences* rather than a kind of metaphysical entailment relation between *propositions*.)

Next, if we remember that the semantics used for the kind of counterfactual conditional appropriate to counterfactual analyses will guarantee a *nonbacktracking* reading of that conditional, then we can appreciate how the Lewis analysis neatly avoids three problems that were thorns in the side of earlier regularity analyses. First, in many cases where c is a cause of e, it will turn out that e is lawfully necessary and/or sufficient for c (at least, in the circumstances); on a number of regularity analyses, it will follow that e is a cause of c. More generally, those analyses tend to face a serious problem in explaining the asymmetry of the causal relation. One way to guarantee such asymmetry is to insist that causes must precede their effects, thus piggybacking causal asymmetry on the asymmetry between past and future. But doing so seems to rule out rather hastily the possibility of either simultaneous or backward causation.

Still, our discussion at the end of the last section may show that simultaneous causation need not be taken too seriously, and that backward causation is everyone's problem. So observe that this maneuver is of no help in solving the second problem, which arises from cases in which an event c causes two events d and e along different and independent causal routes. As an illustration, consider figure 1.1. Here, **c** fires, sending a stimulatory signal to **d**, causing it to fire. (Circles represent neurons; arrows represent stimulatory connections; shaded circles represent neurons that are firing; the time order of events is left-to-right. In the text, **bold** letters name neurons, *italicized* letters the events of their firing.) In addition, **c**'s firing causes **e** to fire, by way of the intermediate neuron **b**. Now, given a suitable specification of the circumstances (e.g., which neurons are connected to which other neurons), it follows from the fact that **d** fires, together with the laws, that **e** fires; and likewise vice versa. Moreover, the

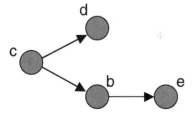

Figure 1.1

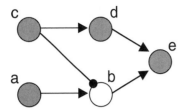

Figure 1.2

firing of **d** precedes the firing of **e**. But the one is not a cause of the other—trouble, once again, for any of a number of regularity analyses of causation. And stipulating that causes must precede their effects helps not at all.

For the third problem, consider figure 1.2. Here, the line with a blob at the end represents an inhibitory signal. Thus, **c** fires, stimulating **d** to fire, which in turn stimulates **e** to fire. Meanwhile, **a** fires, but the stimulatory signal it sends to **b** is blocked by an inhibitory signal from **c**, so **b** does not fire. Again, given a suitable specification of the circumstances, it follows from the fact that **a** fires, together with the laws, that **e** will fire. But to conclude from this fact, together, perhaps, with the fact that the firing of **a** precedes the firing of **e**, that **a** is a cause of **e** is simply to confuse *guaranteeing* an outcome with *causing* that outcome.

Thanks to the stipulation that the counterfactual conditional is to be given a non-backtracking reading, Lewis's analysis cleanly avoids each of these three problems (bracketing, for the moment, the reservations voiced in section 1 about some of the principal attempts to provide the needed truth conditions for nonbacktracking counterfactuals). If the effect had not occurred, we are not entitled to conclude that it must have been the case that the cause did not occur: for to do so would be to impose the forbidden backtracking reading of the conditional. In figure 1.1, in evaluating what would have happened if **d** had not fired, we hold fixed the occurrence of other events contemporaneous with **d**—in particular, the firing of **b**—and hence conclude that it still would have been the case that **e** fired. Likewise in figure 1.2, if **d** had not fired, we do not conclude that it must (or even might) have been the case that **b** fired (on the basis that it must have been the case that **c** did not fire, and so must have been the case that no signal from **c** prevented **b** from firing), so that **e** would (or might) have fired all the same. Rather, we hold fixed the nonfiring of **b**, and so endorse the conditional that if **d** had not fired, **e** would not have fired. (This last example, by the way, shows that the prohibition on backtracking is needed not merely to secure the sufficiency of the Lewis analysis, but also to secure its necessity: See Hall, "Two Concepts of Causation," chapter 9, pp. 233–234.)

Thus, confronted with a suite of extraordinarily simple and straightforward examples that nevertheless proved stubbornly resistant to the regularity analyst's treatment, the counterfactual analysis appears to succeed quite effortlessly. What's more, the Lewis analysis appears to have the resources to handle quite naturally both causation by omission and causation under probabilistic laws. For the first, observe that we can take the failure of c to occur (or perhaps better: the failure of an event of type C to occur) to cause event e just in case, had c occurred (or: had an event of type C occurred), e would not have occurred. (Causation *of* omission can be given a similar treatment.) For the second, the counterfactual analyst can build on the idea that even under probabilistic laws, causes typically make a positive difference to the chances of their effects. That is, what distinguishes c as a cause of e, in the first instance, is that if c had not occurred, the chance of e's occurring would have been much less than in fact it was (Lewis 1986b). Note that in the deterministic case, this condition reduces to the condition that had c not occurred, e would not have occurred (since the only chances available are 0 and 1). Many have therefore viewed its apparent ability to provide a uniform analysis of causation under both determinism and indeterminism to be a signal advantage of the counterfactual analysis.

The successes of the Lewis analysis are impressive; little wonder that Lewis's original paper had the influence it did. Still, further developments quickly showed the need to revise his proposal. We will focus now on the principal sources of pressure for revision, beginning with problems well known for quite some time, and moving to problems that have only recently cropped up in the literature.

4   Problems, Old and New

Some problems take the form of clean, simple counterexamples to the Lewis analysis. Others take the form of challenges to lay out its foundations more precisely. We will begin with three problems of the latter variety.

First, for reasons already addressed, one might doubt whether an adequate semantics for the counterfactual can be produced that will yield the needed non-backtracking reading of that conditional. Observe that insofar as the Lewis analysis aims to be *reductive*, the project of giving such a semantics becomes especially difficult. We cannot say, for example, that we are to arrive at the nonbacktracking reading of "if c had not occurred, then e would not have occurred" by considering a counterfactual situation in which c does not occur, but in which all of its *causes* do (and then checking to see whether, in this situation, e occurs).

Waiving this problem, one might worry, second, that we do not really have a handle on what sort of counterfactual situation we are supposed to be envisioning.

That is, we are told that we must consider what would have happened if a particular event c had not occurred. To see how difficult it might be to do so, consider a simple example: Billy and Suzy converse, say, between noon and 12:30 one day. Let c be their conversation. What would have happened if c—that very conversation—had not occurred? Offhand, it is extremely difficult to say, simply because it is extremely difficult to discern where the boundary lies between those possible worlds in which that very conversation occurs, and those possible worlds in which it does not. After all, to map this boundary we need answers to the following sorts of questions: Would c have occurred if Billy and Suzy had conversed, but about an entirely different topic? Would it have occurred if they had conversed about the same topic, but an hour later? A day later? A few yards away from where they in fact conversed? A hundred miles? Could c have involved entirely different people—or was it essential to it that it be a conversation between Billy and Suzy? Could their conversation c have been, in fact, a race they were running together? Presumably not—but *why* not? To answer these and other questions, we should need an account of which features of it are essential to their conversation, and which accidental. Without such an account, it seems that we are at sea with respect to evaluating the very conditionals that form the heart of the Lewis analysis.

Unfortunately, this problem has tended to get overlooked in the literature. (See Bennett 1988 for a notable and welcome exception.) Part of the reason, no doubt, is that in the sorts of simple "neuron world" examples that often drive discussion in the literature, it is clear enough what counterfactual situation the author has in mind: letting c be the firing of some particular neuron, the counterfactual situation in which c does not occur is a situation in which that neuron doesn't fire, but rather remains idle. More generally, if event c consists in the φ-ing of some particular x at some time t, then we might naturally construe the counterfactual situation in which c does not occur as simply a situation in which x does not φ at time t. That does not yet solve the problem, for it is not necessarily clear how we decide what x would be doing *instead*. But here too, there might be a natural choice. Thus, if a neuron were not firing at a certain time, it would be idle instead. (It would not be glowing pink, or have turned into a dove, or have disappeared, etc.) Similarly, if Billy and Suzy had not conversed between noon and 12:30, they would have done some other activity normal for them instead (played, read books, sat quietly, etc.).

But to say that some such rough and ready rules guide our understanding of the counterfactuals that appear in the Lewis analysis does not *help* that analysis, so much as make more vivid one crucial shortcoming in its foundations (namely, that no clear and precise rules have been laid down for evaluating the counterfactuals)—unless, of course, the analysis is amended to explicitly incorporate these rules (in, one would hope, a much less rough and ready form). Note, finally, that although Lewis is aware of this problem, his own remarks are not particularly helpful. Here is what he says, in "Causation as Influence," chapter 3 (p. 90, italics added):

What is the closest way to actuality for C not to occur?—It is for C to be replaced by a very similar event, one which is almost but not quite C, one that is just barely over the border that divides versions of C itself from its nearest alternatives. But if C is taken to be fairly fragile, then if C had not occurred and almost-C had occurred instead, very likely the effects of almost-C would have been much the same as the actual effects of C. So our causal counter-factual will not mean what we thought it meant, and it may well not have the truth value we thought it had. When asked to suppose counterfactually that C does not occur, we don't really look for the very closest possible world where C's conditions of occurrence are not quite sat-isfied. Rather, we imagine that C *is completely and cleanly excised from history*, leaving behind no fragment or approximation of itself.

We leave it to the reader to try to figure out what it means to "cleanly excise" an event. (Fill the spacetime region in which it occurs with vacuum?) That an answer will likely prove elusive reinforces the suspicion that this issue needs to be taken more seriously by advocates of counterfactual analyses.

A third and related challenge for the counterfactual analyst—and, to be fair, for almost anyone who wishes to come up with a philosophical account of causation that treats events as the primary causal relata—is to provide some sort of account of what events *are*. Without such an account it may be difficult to fend off various annoying counterexamples. For instance:

Suppose that Suzy shuts the door, and in fact slams it. We may have two events here—a shutting and a slamming—distinguished because the first could have hap-pened without the second (if, for example, Suzy had shut the door softly). But if she hadn't shut the door, she couldn't (and so wouldn't) have slammed it—so it seems that the analysis wrongly tells us that the shutting is a cause of the slamming.

Another case: Suzy expertly throws a rock at a glass bottle, shattering it. The shattering consists at least in part of many smaller and more localized events: first the glass fractures, then one shard goes flying off this way, another that way, and so on. If the shattering hadn't happened then none of its constituent events would have happened—so it seems that the analysis wrongly tells us that the shattering is a cause of them all.

A third case: far away, Billy throws another rock, shattering a different glass bottle. Suppose there is a "disjunctive" event c that, necessarily, occurs if and only if either Suzy's throw or Billy's throw occurs. If c hadn't occurred, neither bottle would have shattered—so it seems that, according to the analysis, we have discovered a fairly immediate common cause of these widely separated events.

A final case: Suppose there is a type of extrinsically specified event that, necessarily, has an instance occurring at time t if and only if Suzy sends an email message exactly two days before t. Let c be such an instance, and let e be the reply (from Billy, of course), occurring at, say, a time one day after Suzy sent the given email (and so a day *before* c). Since e would not have happened if c hadn't, it seems that, according to the analysis, we have backward causation very much on the cheap.

Each case deserves a different diagnosis. In the first case, we should say that the events fail to be distinct—and so are not eligible to stand in a causal relationship—because of their logical relationship (some would prefer: because there is only *one* event, differently described). In the second case, we should say that the shattering is not distinct from its constituents, because of their mereological relationship. In the third case, we should say that the disjunctive event is not an event at all, hence not apt to cause (or be caused). In the final case, we should say that genuine events cannot have such extrinsic "essences." We should say all these things, and it's up to a philosophical theory of events to tell us why we are justified in doing so.

Still, it is hardly a peculiarity of the counterfactual analysis that it needs this sort of supplementing. Suppose, following Mackie (1965), that we analyze a cause of an event as a distinct event that is sufficient, given the laws and relevant circumstances, for that first event's occurrence. This analysis can be "refuted" in an equally trivial fashion by noting the following "consequences": The slamming causes the shutting; the shattering's constituent events jointly cause it (and, perhaps, it causes them as well); there is still a fairly immediate common cause of the two widely separated shatterings (namely, the "conjunctive" event that, necessarily, occurs iff both Suzy's and Billy's throws occur); and the "emailed two days ago" event **c** still causes the earlier reply **e**. So we do not think that these (admittedly challenging) issues involving the nature and individuation of events pose any problem for counterfactual analyses of causation *in particular*. (For discussion, see Kim 1971.) Contrast the earlier problem about evaluating the relevant counterfactuals: that problem *does*, offhand, seem idiosyncratic to counterfactual analyses.

Let us turn now to the simple counterexamples, both old and new, that have forced those pursuing a counterfactual analysis to add successive refinements to Lewis's original version. It will in fact be helpful to rewind slightly, and consider a version even simpler than Lewis's, namely, the analysis that says that c is a cause of e if and only if c and e both occur, but had c not occurred, e would not have occurred. Figure 1.2 already showed why this analysis won't work; for if **c** had not fired, **e** would have fired all the same, as a result of the "backup" process initiated by the firing of **a**. Hence Lewis's decision to take causation to be the *ancestral* of counter-

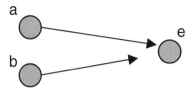

Figure 1.3

factual dependence: Although the firing of **e** does not depend on the firing of **c**, we can trace a chain of stepwise dependence via the firing of **d**.

But there are two problems with the simple fix. The first is that it automatically commits the analysis to the view that causation is transitive—a view that, however intuitive, has recently come under suspicion, thanks to a range of purported counterexamples (see section 6 below). These counterexamples can, perhaps, be resisted. But a second and more serious problem is that there are simple ways to tweak the example depicted in figure 1.2 that render Lewis's fix inapplicable. For instance, consider figure 1.3. Here, **a** and **b** fire at the same time, both sending stimulatory signals to **e**. However, the signal from **b** is a bit slower (a fact represented by drawing its arrow so that it does not quite connect with **e**). Hence the signal from **a**, arriving first, is what causes **e** to fire. Countless real-world examples duplicate this structure, for example: Billy and Suzy both throw rocks at a window; each throw would be enough, by itself, to break the window; but Suzy's rock gets there first, and hence it is her throw, not Billy's, that is a cause of the subsequent shattering.

Pick the firing of **a**—or indeed, any event in the sequence constituting the passage of the stimulatory signal from **a** to **e**—and consider what would have happened if it had not occurred. Answer: **e** would have fired all the same, as a result of the signal from **b**. There is no hope, then, of tracing a chain of stepwise dependence from the firing of **a** to the firing of **e**.

The literature has dubbed this the problem of "late preemption" (as contrasted with the problem of "early preemption" exhibited, for example, by figure 1.2). A natural enough response to it is to focus attention on the *timing* of **e**'s firing, pointing out that if **a** had not fired, **e** would have fired moments later, whereas if **b** had not fired, **e** would have fired at exactly the same time. The literature has seen a number of attempts to leverage this feature of the case into a solution to the problem of late preemption. We won't try to review these here (but see the extended version of Lewis's "Causation as Influence," chapter 3, for a valuable and comprehensive discussion); we do, however, want to suggest that the pursuit of this kind of solution may

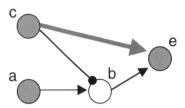

Figure 1.4

be misguided. Suppose, for example, that the signal from **a** exerts a retarding force
on the signal from **b**, slowing it down slightly. Suppose that the exact strength of this
force is such that, had **a** not fired, the signal from **b** would have arrived at **e** at exactly
the same time that the signal from **a** in fact arrives. Then not only does the firing of **e**
not depend on the firing of **a**, but nothing *about* the firing of **e**—not its timing, nor
any other feature of its manner of occurrence—depends on the firing of **a**. (We can
further suppose that the retarding force is of just the right strength that, for exactly
the same reason, *e* exhibits a total lack of dependence on each of the events that
consist in the passage of the stimulatory signal from **a** to **e**.)

At any rate, it is safe to say that the problem of late preemption has proved quite
stubborn and has provoked vigorous discussion in the literature. Several of the contributions in this volume give up-to-the-minute treatments of it.

There is another way to tweak the example of figure 1.2 so as to foil Lewis's original fix. It involves the controversial assumption that there can be action at a temporal distance. Suppose, as in figure 1.4, that one effect of **c**'s firing is to cut off the
stimulatory signal from **a**, as before; but suppose further that when **c**'s firing causes **e**
to fire, it does so not by way of any intermediate events, but rather by acting *directly*
on **e** (albeit at a spatial and temporal distance; we represent this direct action by a
thick, shaded arrow). Once again, the situation provides no materials for tracing a
chain of dependence from *c* to *e*. We leave it to the reader to consider whether this
sort of example is more stubbornly resistant to treatment than the kind of late preemption depicted in figure 1.3.

We noted above that one of the features of the Lewis analysis that made it appear
particularly promising was that it could give a clean and uniform account not only of
ordinary causation under determinism, but of causation by omission, and of causation under indeterminism. But serious complaints have been raised with respect to
these latter two points. About causation by omission—and, more generally, other
kinds of causal fact that seem to involve omissions (such as prevention)—two problems call for particular attention.

First, the typical counterfactual condition deemed necessary and sufficient for causation of event *e* by the omission of an event of type *C*—namely, that no event of type *C* occurs, that *e* occurs, and that had an event of type *C* occurred, *e* would not have occurred—has struck many as wildly permissive. Suzy and Billy plan to meet for lunch, but Billy doesn't show up; consequently, Suzy becomes sad. So far, no problem: Billy does not show up (i.e., no event of the Billy-showing-up type occurs); Suzy becomes sad; and, if Billy had shown up (i.e., if an event of the omitted type had occurred), Suzy would not have become sad. But something *else* that doesn't happen is Bill Gates's showing up to present Suzy with a $10 million check. And, if he had, she would certainly not have become sad (she doesn't like Billy *that* much). Are we to conclude that his failure to show up with the check likewise caused her to become sad? Once you see the trick, the embarrassing examples quickly proliferate. In general, for any event *e* there will typically be a vast multitude of ways that it could, in principle (and compatibly with the laws), have been prevented. Are we to say that for each such would-be preventer, its failure to occur was among *e*'s causes? The counterfactual analyst seems committed to a "yes" answer here; but again, to many, that answer seems absurd.

So posed, the challenge invites the response that it is really everyone's problem—that is, that given modest assumptions, it follows that there is either a whole lot of causation by omission (much more than we would ordinarily feel comfortable admitting), or that there is none at all. For example, what principled basis is there for distinguishing Billy's failure to show up for lunch from Bill's failure to show up with a check? That Billy promised to, whereas Bill did not? But how could that sort of normative consideration have any place in a proper account of *causation*? Beebee's contribution (chapter 11: "Causing and Nothingness") presses this argument, and both she and Lewis (chapter 3: "Causation as Influence," and especially chapter 10: "Void and Object") endorse this disjunctive "either an awful lot or none at all" conclusion, albeit for different purposes. (See also McGrath 2002 for a sophisticated treatment of this issue.)

For the second problem, consider how a counterfactual analyst might analyze the notion of *prevention*. A natural approach is to say that event *c* prevents event *e* from occurring (or perhaps better: prevents an event of type *E* from occurring) just in case *c* occurs, *e* does not (or: No event of type *E* does), and if *c* had not occurred, *e* (or: An event of type *E*) would have occurred. Thus, Billy throws a baseball at the window, and Suzy prevents the window from breaking by catching it: That is, her catch occurs, the window does not break (no event of the window-breaking type occurs), but if she hadn't caught the baseball, the window would have broken.

Figure 1.5

So far, so good. But now tweak the example so that it becomes an instance of what is commonly called "preemptive prevention": Suzy's friend Sally stands behind her, ready and able to catch the ball if Suzy does not. In fact, because Suzy catches the ball, Sally doesn't have to do anything. With that change, we have lost the dependence of the window's failure to break on Suzy's catch; but for many, the intuitive verdict that Suzy's catch prevents the window from breaking still holds. After all, Sally just stood there, doing nothing—and since *something* obviously prevented the window from breaking, it had to be Suzy (or rather, her catch). On the other hand, many find that Sally's presence undermines the original verdict—or if Sally is not enough, then substitute in her place the presence of a high, thick, sturdy brick wall. After all, how can Suzy get credit for preventing the window from breaking, when it was never in any danger from Billy's throw? The issues here are subtle, for it is a difficult matter to tease out exactly what is guiding our intuitions in such cases. (For discussion, see the contributions by Maudlin [chapter 18: "Causation, Counterfactuals, and the Third Factor"] and Collins [chapter 4: "Preemptive Prevention"]; we will briefly return to this kind of case in section 5, below.)

Still, if, with Sally present, the intuitive verdict that Suzy's catch prevents the window's breaking *stands*, then that is trouble for the counterfactual analysis. It is not at all clear how any of the standard tools for handling *ordinary* cases of preemption can be applied to get Suzy's catch—and *only* Suzy's catch (not also Sally's presence, or the presence of the wall, etc.)—to connect up in the right way with the window's failure to break.

A serious problem has also emerged for the standard counterfactual treatment of causation under probabilistic laws. Recall the key idea: c is a cause of e if c and e occur, but if c had not occurred, then the chance of e's occurring would have been much lower than in fact it was. (We then add various refinements to extend that sufficient condition for causation into a full-blown analysis of causation.) As an example, consider figure 1.5. Here, **a** fires, sending a stimulatory signal to **e**, which fires. Let the laws state that **e** is certain to fire if it receives such a signal, but has a tiny chance—say, 0.01—of firing spontaneously, even if it receives no signal. So far, so good: our sufficient condition correctly classifies **a**'s firing as a cause of **e**'s firing, in this case.

Figure 1.6

(Some would object, wanting to insist that it remains up in the air whether **e**'s firing was caused by the signal from **a**, or rather was one of those rare instances of a spontaneous firing. But no reductionist can endorse this objection, for what difference—either in categorical facts, or in the laws—could distinguish the two situations? Note, in this regard, the close parallel between the example depicted in figure 1.5 and Tooley's antireductionist thought experiment discussed above.)

But now consider a variant: We allow that there is some small chance—again, say, 0.01—that the signal from **a** will die out shortly before it reaches **e**. Suppose, as in figure 1.6, that it does so. But **e** fires all the same. Then the trouble is that even though it is clear that **a**'s firing is not a cause of **e**'s firing, it still seems that the sufficient condition is met: **a** fires, **e** fires, and if **a** had not fired, then the chance of **e**'s firing would have been much lower (0.01 instead of slightly greater than 0.99).

A possible fix is to be more careful about the time at which we evaluate the chance of **e**'s firing. In the depicted scenario, it is true that immediately after **a** fires, the chance that **e** will fire when it does is close to 1. But, letting time t be a time immediately before **e** fires but *after* the signal from **a** has fizzled out, it is also true that the chance, at t, of **e**'s firing is a mere 0.01—exactly what it would have been, if **a** had not fired. So the t-chance of **e**'s firing does not depend counterfactually on **a**'s firing. It remains to be seen whether this fix could be extended into a proper counterfactual treatment of causation under probabilistic laws; in particular, it is not clear how the original sufficient condition should be modified, in order to be able correctly to classify some cases of causation as such, and not merely avoid misclassifying some cases of noncausation. See the contributions by Kvart (chapter 15: "Causation: Probabilistic and Counterfactual Analyses"), Ramachandran (chapter 16: "A Counterfactual Analysis of Indeterministic Causation"), and Hitchcock (chapter 17: "Do All and Only Causes Raise the Probabilities of Effects?") for highly sophisticated treatments of causation under indeterminism.

Turn now to more novel counterexamples. The first of these has come to be called "trumping" preemption. As an illustration, consider figure 1.7. Let us suppose, here, that neurons can fire with different intensities, and with different polarities ("positive" and "negative"). Suppose further that a neuron that receives a single stimulatory signal fires in the polarity of that signal (although with an intensity independent of the intensity of the stimulating signal). Finally, when, as here, a neuron

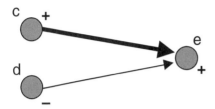

Figure 1.7

Figure 1.8

receives two stimulatory signals simultaneously, it fires in the polarity of the more intense signal: in this case, the signal from **c** (its greater intensity being represented by a thicker arrow). No problem yet—or at least, no serious problem: as long as we are willing to assert that the positive firing of **e** that in fact occurs would not have occurred if **e** had fired negatively, then we can safely conclude that the firing of **e** depends on the firing of **c**.

But now tweak the example in the obvious way, so that **c** and **d** fire with the same (positive) polarity; but as before, let **c** fire more intensely. Many consider it just as intuitive that in figure 1.8 *c* alone—and not *d*—is a cause of *e*. But if **c** had not fired, **e** would have fired in exactly the same manner; and the same is true if we focus not on **c**, but rather on any event in the passage of the stimulatory signal from **c** to **e**. (For detailed discussion—which shows how wide is the range of counterfactual analyses that this example threatens—see Schaffer, "Trumping Preemption," chapter 2 in this volume.)

For the next novel counterexample, consider "double prevention." We will borrow Hall's example. In figure 1.9, neurons **a**, **b**, and **c** all fire simultaneously; **c**'s firing prevents **d** from firing. Figure 1.10 depicts what would have happened, had **c** not fired. Evidently, **e**'s firing depends counterfactually on **c**'s firing; for that reason, almost every counterfactual analysis will count *c* a cause of *e*.

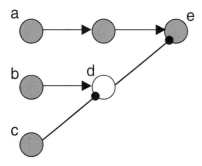

Figure 1.9

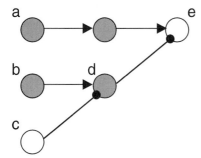

Figure 1.10

Some would consider that result a counterexample as it stands, since it strikes them as intuitively wrong that c is a cause of e, here—the idea being that c is not connected up to e in the right sort of way. Hall (in "Two Concepts of Causation," chapter 9 in this volume) argues in favor of this intuition by drawing what he takes to be three damaging conclusions from the claim that c is a cause of e: first, that the counterfactual analysis will lose the ability to distinguish genuine from ersatz action at a distance (for c and e are not connected by a spatiotemporally continuous causal chain); second, that the analysis will be forced to give up the idea that, roughly, the causal structure of a process is intrinsic to that process (for the fact that e depends on c can easily be made to be extrinsic to the processes depicted); and third, that it will be forced to deny that causation is transitive (for reasons we will take up in section 6, below). Whether this last consequence is really so devastating is controversial, for the recent literature has also seen a spate of counterexamples to transitivity itself—and not merely to the conjunction of transitivity with one or another counterfactual analysis.

Let us now turn our attention away from the prospects and problems for a successful counterfactual analysis of causation, and consider a number of broader issues in the philosophy of causation. As will be apparent, tight connections remain: Almost every topic we will discuss in the sections ahead has been illuminated in myriad and interesting ways by work in the counterfactual tradition. We begin with a brief look at methodology.

5   Methodology

Work on philosophy of causation is, not surprisingly, heavily driven by intuitions about cases. Standard procedure often seems to be the following: A philosopher proposes a new analysis of causation, showing how it delivers the intuitively correct results about a wide range of cases. But then novel cases are proposed, and intuitions about them exhibited that run counter to the given theory—at which point, either refinements are added to accommodate the recalcitrant "data," or it's back to the drawing board.

It's worth taking time out to consider some methodological questions concerning this procedure. That is what we will do in this section.

One obvious and extremely difficult methodological question is this: What sort of project are philosophers of causation engaged in, that consulting intuitions about cases would be an appropriate way to pursue it? We won't have much to say about that question, not merely because it is so difficult, but also because it does not have much to do with work on causation per se. The methodology in question is so widespread in philosophy that the question should really be asked of the field as a whole. Still, it will be useful to distinguish two quite different aims that a philosopher working on causation might have. On the one hand, she might, like Lewis, take herself to be providing a good old-fashioned conceptual analysis of causation—a detailed explanation, that is, of how our ordinary concept works (see especially section 1.1 of Lewis's "Causation as Influence," chapter 3 of this volume). (Note that in doing so, she need not take on the extra commitment to a *reductive* account—reductionism is an optional, if natural and attractive, extra.) On the other hand, she might view her account as at least partially stipulative—that is, as providing a cleaned up, sanitized version of some causal concept that, though it may not track our ordinary notion of causation precisely, nevertheless can plausibly be argued to serve some useful theoretical purpose. (Or one might fall somewhere in between: certainly, the distinction admits of plenty of gradations.)

Obviously, someone who pursues this latter aim ought to say at some point what such purposes might be. But we think that she is under no obligation to make this clear at the outset. On the contrary, it strikes us as a perfectly appropriate strategy for a philosopher working on causation to try to come up with a clean, elegant, theoretically attractive account of causation (or of some causal concept), in the reasonable expectation that such an account will serve some, possibly as-yet undisclosed, philosophical or perhaps even scientific purpose. And that expectation can be reasonable even if it is clear—because of recalcitrant intuitions about certain cases— that the account does not earn its keep by providing an explanation of how our *ordinary* concept works. This tolerant methodological perspective gains further support from the observation that causal concepts are used all over the place, both in philosophy and in the sciences; indeed, just sticking to philosophy, it often seems that for any philosophically interesting X, there is at least one "causal theory of X" on the market. It would be hasty to assume that the causal concept or concepts at work in any such theory is just our plain old ordinary one. In short, then, there is good reason to think that there is plenty of work available for those philosophers of causation who take themselves to be in the business of, as it were, "conceptual synthesis," rather than old-fashioned conceptual analysis.

It is clear enough—at least, for present purposes—why someone interested in providing a conceptual analysis of our ordinary notion of causation should attend carefully to intuitions about cases. What we wish to emphasize is that even someone interested in "synthesizing" a new and potentially useful causal concept needs to heed these intuitions, else she risks cutting her project free of any firm mooring. More specifically, a reasonable and cautious approach for her to take is to treat intuitions about cases as providing a guide to where interesting causal concepts might be found. Thus, although the account can selectively diverge from these intuitions, provided there are principled reasons for doing so, it should not diverge from them wholesale.

It is particularly clear that one should pay attention to intuitions about cases if the stipulative element in one's analysis consists only in resolving various ambiguities or indeterminacies in our ordinary notion of "cause," or in some other way refining or precisifying that notion. For example, one might think that our ordinary notion is context sensitive in its application in various ways; and one might be interested in looking for a closely related notion from which such context-sensitivity has been expunged. Or one might suspect that our ordinary notion of causation involves an unsupportable element of antireductionism—as witness the intuitive pull (such as it is) of thought experiments like Tooley's; one might therefore try to produce a sanitized, reductionist-friendly surrogate for our ordinary notion. More provocatively, one might hold with Hall ("Two Concepts of Causation," chapter 9) that there is no way to provide a univocal analysis of our ordinary notion of causation, and that therefore the best thing for a philosopher to do is to break it up into two or more distinct concepts—distinct, at least, in the sense that they deserve radically different analyses. The list goes on: Indeed, even a cursory survey of work in philosophy (as well as in the conceptual foundations of other disciplines) will reveal numerous precedents for the view that there can be legitimate philosophical studies that do not count as conceptual analysis of some ordinary concept, but that still require close attention to intuitions involving the application of such a concept.

It is not always clear in the literature what a given author's aim is: conceptual analysis, conceptual synthesis, or perhaps something else entirely. But it is important to be aware of the options, for otherwise it can be quite difficult to assess the cogency of certain typical responses philosophers make when confronted with recalcitrant intuitions. Above, we observed that *one* typical response—the most obvious one—is to go back and revise the theory. But that is hardly the only response. In addition, philosophers will often try to argue that the recalcitrant intuitions need not be respected. There are a number of strategies for doing so, and philosophers are not always careful to make explicit which strategy or combination of strategies they are pursuing. So we think it useful to list, and briefly comment on, some of the most prominent ones. As we will see, in several cases the effectiveness of the strategy depends crucially on whether or not the theory being defended is offered as a conceptual analysis of our ordinary concept of causation.

Suppose, then, that we have some philosophical theory of causation T that issues some verdict about some case, and that ordinary intuition about the case runs counter to the verdict. Then there are at least eight distinct ways that we might try to fend off the recalcitrant intuition.

First way: The intuitions in question are really not so firm—so the case is an example of "spoils to the victor."

Lewis has provided a particularly nice statement of the idea behind this strategy:

When common sense delivers a firm and uncontroversial answer about a not-too-far-fetched case, theory had better agree. If an analysis of causation does not deliver the common-sense answer, that is bad trouble. But when common sense falls into indecision or controversy, or when it is reasonable to suspect that far-fetched cases are being judged by false analogy to commonplace ones, then theory may safely say what it likes. Such cases can be left as spoils to the victor, in D. M. Armstrong's phrase. We can reasonably accept as true whatever answer comes from the analysis that does best on the clearer cases.   (1986b, p. 194)

As an example, consider a case of perfectly symmetrical overdetermination: Suzy and Billy both throw rocks at a window; the rocks strike at the same time, with exactly the same force; the window shatters. Furthermore, each rock strikes with sufficient force to shatter the window all by itself. There is some intuition here that both Suzy's and Billy's throws are causes of the shattering. But this intuition is far from firm. Hence, when a counterfactual analysis says—as it likely will—that neither Suzy's nor Billy's throw was a cause of the shattering (because it depended on neither, etc.), then that verdict can perhaps be considered one of the "spoils" to which the analysis is entitled (provided, of course, that it emerges victorious in its competition with its rivals).

But Lewis's claim makes little sense if one is pursuing a genuine *conceptual analysis* of our ordinary notion of "cause." A successful such analysis will show how our concept works; so if our concept goes indeterminate in a particular case, then the analysis had better show that and why it does so. (Obviously, such an expectation is *not* appropriate if one's aim is to refine, precisify, or in some other way modify our ordinary conception of causation.) For comparison, suppose that we offered an analysis of "bald" according to which anyone with fewer than 500 hairs on his or her head counted as bald, and anyone with 500 or more hairs counted as not bald. Never mind the many other reasons why the analysis is inadequate (it matters how the hair is distributed, etc.): The one to focus on is that it leaves it completely opaque why there should ever be a borderline case of "bald." That would be reason enough to count it a failure, *if* we had offered it as an account of our *ordinary notion* of "bald."[10]

At any rate, the example of symmetrical overdetermination also illustrates an important if unrelated point: Whereas we might happily reject whatever intuition there is to the effect that each of Billy's and Suzy's throws is a cause of the shattering, we should *not* be happy with the conclusion that the shattering lacks causes altogether—and on the face of it, counterfactual analyses threaten to yield this conclusion. (Some, e.g., Lewis 1986b, try to defend the view that the *mereological sum* of the two throws causes the shattering.) Our point is not to press this problem on those analyses, but simply to observe that, to handle a difficult case, it may not always be enough simply to argue away the recalcitrant intuitions about it.

Second way: The case is misleading, because it is easily confused with other, unproblematic cases.

As an example of a case where this strategy might apply, consider the instance of action at a temporal distance depicted in figure 1.4. One might try to argue that in forming intuitive judgments about this case—in particular, the intuitive judgment that c is a cause of e—it is extremely hard not to let one's intuitions be guided by the thought that there is some faint, indetectable signal transmitted from **c** to **e** that is responsible for establishing the causal connection between the firings of the two neurons.

Or again, consider the example of trumping depicted in figure 1.8. One might argue that, in judging any such case, it is very hard not to presuppose that the trumping pattern is present in virtue of some unspecified and hidden physical mechanisms. (And when that is the case, examples of trumping become much less problematic; for further discussion see Schaffer, "Trumping Preemption," chapter 2.)

Third way: The case is misleading, because it is misleadingly presented.

As an example, let us return to Tooley's antireductionist argument. Observe that in setting up that argument, he invites us to consider a possible world in which it is a law that when an object has property P, its possession of this property causes it to acquire either property Q or property R—but never both. Note that the word "causes" is crucial to the specification of the content of the laws, for we are *also* invited to believe that in this possible world an object can, consistently with the laws, acquire both Q and R after coming to possess P. Thus we cannot consistently replace "causes" by "is followed by." But to describe the relevant laws in this way prejudices matters enormously. After all, a good reductionist about causation will hold that the content of the fundamental laws can, in principle, be specified in *noncausal* terms— indeed, can perhaps be identified simply with a set of nomologically possible worlds. (And it is well to remember that insofar as we wish to look to the physics of our day for paradigm examples of fundamental laws, this reductionist position is by far the more sensible: Schrödinger's equation, for example, makes no mention of *causal* relations between physical states.) Tooley's thought experiment presupposes a very different conception of laws; it seems to us that the reductionist is well within her rights to reject this conception. She should insist that Tooley has either mischaracterized the content of the laws, or has not succeeded in describing a genuine possible world.

Fourth way: The example is misleading, because it naturally draws our attention to other, related concepts; we therefore mistake the conditions appropriate for applying these other concepts with the conditions appropriate for applying the concept of causation.

Beebee's contribution ("Causing and Nothingness," chapter 11) provides an excellent case study of this strategy at work. She argues that there is no such thing as causation by omission, but that we can perfectly well explain the occurrence of some ordinary event by citing the failure of some other kind of event to occur, where an occurrence of that kind of event would have prevented the explanandum event. Beebee goes on to argue that the reason that we often mistakenly think that there is causation by omission is that it is easy for us to confuse causation with explanation.

As another example—one where this strategy should have been applied, but wasn't—consider the following passage from Lewis (1986d, p. 250):

It is one thing to postpone an event, another to cancel it. A cause without which it would have occurred later, or sooner, is not a cause without which it would not have occurred at all. Who would dare be a doctor, if the hypothesis under consideration [that an event's time is essential to it] were right? You might manage to keep your patient alive until 4:12, when otherwise he would have died at 4:08. You would then have caused his death. For his death was, in fact, his death at 4:12. If that time is essential, his death is an event that would not have occurred had he died at 4:08, as he would have done without your action. That will not do.

The case is a bad one, because it is very easy to confuse the question of whether the doctor's action is a *cause* of the patient's death with the question of whether, by so acting, the doctor *killed* the patient. The answer to the latter question is quite clearly "no"; confuse it with the former, and you will think that the answer to that question is "no" as well. But once the questions are firmly separated, it is no longer so clear that it is unacceptable to count the doctor's action as among the causes of the patient's death. (Certainly, the doctor's action was one of the things that helped cause it to be the case that the patient died at 4:12.) At any rate, what *is* clear, given the manifest possibility of confusion, is that it is unwise to use this case to generate substantive conclusions about the metaphysics of causation or of events.

Fifth way: The recalcitrant intuitions conflict with sacrosanct general principles about causation, and so ought to be dismissed.

One such principle commonly appealed to is, roughly, that like cases be treated alike. Thus, in "Causation as Influence," Lewis has us imagine a case where it is intuitively correct to say that someone's birth is a cause of his death; by appeal to the foregoing principle, he uses this case to argue against the oft-cited complaint that counterfactual analyses have the unacceptably unintuitive consequence that births cause deaths. The example also illustrates how more than one general principle might be brought into play, for one can certainly appeal to transitivity to connect up an agent's birth with his death, as well.

Or again, one might respond to alleged counterexamples to transitivity simply by refusing to give up that principle, perhaps on the basis that its intuitive appeal out-weighs the intuitions driving the counterexample, or on the basis that it plays too essential a role in one's analysis. (For example, one might think that only by an appeal to transitivity can an analysis handle certain kinds of preemption cases.)

Someone who pursues this strategy—insisting that an intuition, however firm, be rejected for the sake of some sacrosanct general principle—will help her case im-measurably if she can add some explanation for why intuition has been so misled. Thus, this strategy is most effectively combined with one or more of the other strat-egies being discussed here. (As a nice example, consider Beebee's case, in "Causing and Nothingness" [chapter 11], that there is no causation by omission: She supports this counterintuitive position in part by appeal to the general principles that causation must relate events, and that omissions cannot be thought of as a species of event, and in part by providing the explanation already discussed for why our intuitions about alleged cases of causation by omission should not be considered trustworthy.) But observe that it may be far less urgent to provide such an explanation if one is not engaged in conceptual analysis: then one may be able to argue that the given divergence from intuition is the price one must pay for synthesizing a concept that is clean, theoretically attractive, and so on.

Sixth way: The unintuitive verdict issued by the theory is not false—it's just odd to say, for pragmatic reasons.

Here, for example, is Lewis, responding to a worry about his account of causation by omission:

One reason for an aversion to causation by absences is that if there is any of it at all, there is a lot of it—far more of it than we would normally want to mention. At this very moment, we are being kept alive by an absence of nerve gas in the air we are breathing. The foe of causation by absences owes us an explanation of why we sometimes do say that an absence caused something. The friend of causation by absences owes us an explanation of why we sometimes refuse to say that an absence caused something, even when we have just the right pattern of dependence. I think the friend is much better able to pay his debt than the foe is to pay his. There are ever so many reasons why it might be inappropriate to say something true. It might be irrelevant to the conversation, it might convey a false hint, it might be known already to all concerned.... (Lewis, "Causation as Influence," chapter 3 in this volume)

We think that care must be taken in executing this gambit. In general, solid reasons should be given why certain judgments should be explained away by appeal to pragmatics while others should be incorporated into the analysis. (Observe, in this regard, how silly it would be to offer as a theory of causation the following: Every event causes every later event; it is just that in many cases, it is odd to say so, for pragmatic reasons.) What's more, it is one thing to wave one's hands toward some pragmatic account—as Lewis does here—and quite another to provide the specifics (including: an account of exactly *which* of the many principles governing the pragmatics of communication should be appealed to). We think that unless they are provided— or unless it is fairly clear how they can be provided—the reader deserves to be suspicious of such appeals.

Still, there are other problem cases to which the "pragmatic" treatment seems exactly what is needed. Suzy is in a room with a match. She strikes the match, lighting it. Intuitively, it is perfectly clear that among the causes of the lighting is the striking. It is much less intuitive—but a consequence of most every analysis of causation, all the same—that among the causes of the lighting is the presence of oxygen next to the match. But we think it a serious mistake to count this a counterexample—at least, without first investigating the possibility that for straightforward pragmatic reasons, reports of causes are typically expected to be reports of *salient* causes. Compare the following scenario: Until recently, all air had been pumped out of the room; only shortly before Suzy entered it with her match was air pumped back in. Now, when asked about the causes of the lighting, we find it quite appropriate to cite the presence of oxygen. Are we to expect this shift in intuitive judgments about what is appropriate to say to reflect a shift in the *truth* of the claim that the presence of oxygen is a cause of the lighting? That strikes us as foolish. Much better to suppose that in altering this scenario, we have altered which features of it are especially salient—and to remember that considerations of salience will weigh heavily on our judgments about what is appropriate to report as a cause.

Seventh way: Intuitions about the case are too easily buffeted about to be taken seriously.

As an example of how such buffeting can work, consider again the case of preemptive prevention in which Billy throws a rock at a window, Suzy blocks it, but Sally was waiting behind Suzy to block the rock, if necessary. Emphasize Sally's idleness, and you can easily secure the intuitive judgment that Suzy prevented the window from breaking. But as Maudlin notes in his contribution ("Causation, Counterfactuals, and the Third Factor," chapter 18), there are other ways to describe such cases. In particular, think of the window and Sally as constituting a single system, remembering that Sally is perfectly able and willing to block the rock. We might then describe this system as a "protected window"—which, because of the state it is in, is not under *any* threat of damage from the rock. Conceived that way, the case prompts a very different intuitive judgment: Suzy does not prevent the window from breaking, because, after all, the window was never under any threat of being broken.

It seems to us a fascinating phenomenon—worth much more attention than it has been given in the literature—that some cases evoke intuitions that are easily subject to such buffeting, whereas others do not. For example, when Suzy and Billy both throw rocks at the window, and Suzy's gets there first, no amount of redescription of the case will reverse the intuitive judgment that only Suzy's throw is a cause of the shattering. If one is engaged in conceptual analysis, then, this strategy surely backfires, for one thing we should expect from any successful such analysis is an explanation of what distinguishes cases that are subject to buffeting from cases that are not. But if one is engaged in something more like conceptual synthesis, then this strategy might well be appropriate.

Eighth way: The case is too outré for intuitions about it to be of much concern.

As examples, one might want to dismiss from consideration any intuitions about cases that involve action at a temporal distance, or backward causation, or indeterminism at the level of the fundamental laws. We have already seen several reasons why one might set aside such cases: intuitions about them might not be very firm; or there might be reason to suspect that our intuitive judgments cannot easily distinguish such cases from other, less problematic cases; or the judgments about these outré cases might conflict with sacrosanct general principles about causation; and so on. But we have in mind something different here, which is that these cases be dismissed *simply* because they are outré in some readily recognizable respect.

To see what this amounts to, observe that the conceptual analyst has no business whatsoever pursuing this strategy. If, for example, we construct a case involving action at a temporal distance—and the case passes all other reasonable methodological tests—then any decent account of how our ordinary concept of causation works must respect the data concerning its application to the given case. On the other hand, someone who constructs an account of causation with the aim of precisifying, reforming, or in some other way altering or replacing our ordinary concept can perfectly well insist, at the outset, that she only intends her account to cover causation under determinism, or under the assumption that there is no backward causation, or action at a temporal distance, and so on. Imagine that her account succeeds brilliantly within its intended domain, and then consider how foolish it would be to reject it out of hand because it had not been extended to cover a broader domain of possible laws. We do not mean to suggest that there would be no interest in trying to extend the account; of course there would. But even if there were in principle obstacles to doing so, this would not rob the account of its philosophical interest or utility.

There is, in addition, a second point to make—one that, though modest, is often overlooked, with unfortunate results. When a philosopher sets out to give an account of causation, and it is clear at the outset that there will be great difficulty in extending the account to cover a certain range of cases (causation under indeterminism, backward causation, etc.), it is all too tempting to simply fix on this limitation as a reason to dismiss the account out of hand. We consider that attitude mistaken, and urge, in opposition to it, a modest methodological pluralism: the topic of causation is difficult enough that it is worth pursuing avenues of investigation even when, at the outset, it seems clear that they will not give us everything we want (i.e., will not give us an account that covers a range of cases that fall outside certain well-defined limitations). A philosopher can therefore reasonably dismiss outré cases from consideration simply because she means—at least for the moment—to limit her ambitions. She is guilty of no philosophical error in doing so. (As an example in this volume, Kvart's contribution, "Causation: Probabilistic and Counterfactual Analysis" [chapter 15], lays out an account of causation under indeterminism that he quite forthrightly observes would be difficult to extend to the deterministic case; it strikes us as no less interesting and important for all that.)

Let us move away now from methodological concerns and back to properly metaphysical concerns, focusing in the next section on two questions that confront any account of causation, counterfactual or otherwise: is causation transitive? And what exactly are the causal relata?

6   Transitivity

We normally think of the causal relation as a *transitive* relation: if c causes d, and d causes e, then c causes e. The simplest analyses of causation based on sufficiency under laws generate a transitive causal relation immediately: When c, together with the right laws, is sufficient for d, and d, together with the right laws, is sufficient for e, then c, together with the right laws, is sufficient for e. Analyses of causation based on counterfactual dependence typically need to guarantee transitivity by taking causation to be the ancestral of the dependence relation, as dependence relations (e.g., straightforward counterfactual dependence, or the kind of counterfactual covariation that figures in Lewis's new "influence" account) are typically not transitive.

Some (e.g., Hall: See chapter 7, "Causation and the Price of Transitivity") suggest that the claim that causation is transitive should be treated as a sort of "bedrock datum"; but that strikes us (Hall now included) as hasty. Certainly the claim has a great deal of intuitive appeal; but rather than simply endorse it unquestioningly, we ought to investigate the source of that appeal. Although we have nothing decisive to offer on this score, we think it suggestive that the way in which causal claims are often justified seems to *presuppose* transitivity. Someone claims that c causes e. Why? Because c causes d, which in turn causes e.

This kind of reasoning is commonplace. But if we could not assume that the causal relation were always transitive, then it is not clear why we would ever be entitled to it. It would seem, rather, that to determine whether c causes e, for any c and e that are not directly linked (i.e., for any c and e that are causally related, if at all, only *by way of* intermediate events) we would have to determine of every link in the causal chain whether it prevented or allowed for transitivity—whether it was the sort of c–d–e link that licensed the inference from "c causes d" and "d causes e" to "c causes e." This would be a serious problem indeed, since (a) it is not clear that we could always distinguish between the types of causal connections that were transitive and the types that were not, and (b) we would, on the face of it, need to have a detailed account of *every* link in the causal chain. Providing such an account would apparently require us to determine the minimal units of the causal chain in question—which, among other things, would involve a fuller specification of the causal relata (usually taken to be events) than theorists have been able to develop.

Hence, it appears that if the causal relation were not transitive, many of our everyday causal claims would be unjustified. (For related discussion, see Lewis, chapter 3, "Causation as Influence," sections 2.2 and 2.3.)

Unfortunately, there are some compelling examples that suggest that causation is *not* transitive. The examples often exhibit the following abstract structure: c does something that threatens to prevent e. However, c also causes d, which in turn helps bring about e in spite of the threat.[11] For example, a train rushes toward a fork in the tracks. If a switch is flipped, the train will take the left track, and if the switch is left in its original position, the train will take the right track. Further on, the left and the right tracks merge, and just after they meet, a damsel in distress is tied to the tracks. If Jill flips the switch, and the train runs over the damsel, should we say that Jill's flip is a cause of the death of the damsel? Obviously not, says intuition. But if the flipping of the switch is a cause of the train taking the left track, and the train running on the left track is a cause of the train's merging back on the main track, and the train's being on the main track is a cause of the death of the damsel—and, finally, if causation is transitive—then Jill's flip is a cause of the death. Notice the abstract structure: the flip threatens to prevent the death—by diverting the train from a track that would have led it to the damsel—but simultaneously does something that helps "undo" the threat—by diverting it *onto* another track leading to the damsel.

A similar kind of example[12] discussed by several of the papers in this collection involves a bomb that is placed in front of someone's door. The bomb is set to explode in five minutes. But just before it explodes, a friend comes along and defuses it. As a result, the intended victim continues to live. The presence of the live bomb is a cause of its being defused, and the bomb's being defused is a cause of the intended victim's continued existence. If transitivity holds here, then the presence of the live bomb is a cause of the intended victim's continued existence. Note again the abstract structure: The presence of the live bomb threatens to cut short the victim's life, but simultaneously "undoes" this threat by attracting the attention of the friend.

The manifest similarity in structure between these two cases should not make us overlook one difference—a difference that *may* be crucial. In the case of Jill's flip, there is, straightforwardly, a spatiotemporally continuous causal chain running from the flip to the damsel's death; it is "causal" in the sense that each constituent event is,

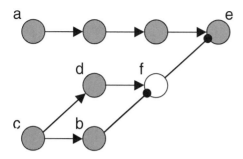

Figure 1.11

unproblematically, a cause of the immediately subsequent events. The question is only whether being linked by such a sequence of causes is enough for the endpoints to count as causally related. By contrast, in the case of the bomb there is no such spatiotemporally continuous causal chain linking its presence to the continued life of the intended victim. Rather, the case is much more like Hall's "inert neuron network" (figure 1.11).

Here **a** fires, stimulating **e** to fire. Meanwhile, **c** fires, stimulating both **b** and **d** to fire. The firing of **b** prevents the signal from **d** from stimulating **f** to fire, thereby safeguarding the firing of **e**—for if **b** had not fired, **e** would not have fired. If such dependence by "double prevention" suffices for causation, then *b* is a cause of *e*. And, obviously, *c* is a cause of *b*. So if, in addition, causation is transitive, then *c* is a cause of *e*: the neuron-world analogue of the bomb's presence "causing" the intended victim to continue living. As in the bomb example, no spatiotemporally continuous causal chain connects *c* to *e*. (Unless, perhaps, it is a chain partially constituted by *omissions*. But even if so, that fact does not erase the distinction between this kind of case and the "switching" cases of which Jill's flip is an instance. And see Hall 2002a for doubts that one can always interpolate an appropriate sequence of omissions.)

This distinction might matter, because there is some reason—albeit far from decisive—to hold that dependence by double-prevention does not suffice for causation. If so, then a whole class of alleged counterexamples to transitivity—namely, those that exhibit the structure of figure 1.11—can be dismissed. Pursuing a "divide and conquer" strategy in defense of transitivity, one could then try to find grounds for dismissing the remaining counterexamples. Hall's "Causation and the Price of Transitivity" (chapter 7) takes this approach.

But there are other strategies one can employ to address the problems. David Lewis, in his "Causation As Influence," chapter 3, denies that these cases are counterexamples to transitivity. Lewis argues that as long as the requisite dependence relations hold between links in the chain, transitivity holds, prima facie intuitions to the contrary. Lewis traces our mistaken rejection of transitivity to misgivings we might have about accepting preventers as causes, accepting events that initiate deviant or unusual paths to their effects as causes, or to a residual inclination to think that for c to cause e, e must depend counterfactually on c.

Stephen Yablo, taking the opposite tack, takes the cases that raise problems for transitivity to be so important as to justify acceptance of a strikingly novel counterfactual account of causation. In his "Advertisement for a Sketch of an Outline of a Prototheory of Causation," chapter 5, Yablo defends an analysis of causation that tells us the flip, the bomb or the neuron that initiates the inert neuron network can't count as causes merely because they bring about threats to the effect but simultaneously cancel those threats. There are deeper requirements (such as the effect's depending on the putative cause under conditions that are suitably natural) that an event must meet in order to be a cause.

Cei Maslen, in "The Context-Dependence of Causation," chapter 14, argues that causation is a three-place relation between a cause, an effect, and a contrast event: when c causes e, c is a cause of e relative to a contrast event c^*. Maslen argues that in cases where contexts (which fix the contrast events) are incompatible, causation is not transitive. She considers several cases that seem to cause problems for transitivity and resolves them under the contrast account.

There is a very different kind of example that needs discussing. Here is an instance (thanks to Judith Thomson for providing it): Suzy lights a firework, which shoots up in the air and explodes in a brilliant shade of red. The light triggers a nearby photodetector that is sensitive to that particular shade of red. Meanwhile, young Zeno, a boy in the crowd, covers his ears in response to the loud explosion. Plausibly, Suzy's lighting the firework counts as a cause both of Zeno's action and of the triggering of the photodetector. But now let us complicate matters: Earlier in the day, Billy added a chemical to the firework that would guarantee that it would explode in the given shade of red; if he hadn't, the explosion would have been yellow. What did Billy's action help cause? Well, the triggering of the photodetector, certainly. But, intuitively, *not* Zeno's action: Billy had nothing to do with that. The problem is this: How are we to secure the first result without undermining the second?

Billy's action does not help bring about the triggering in any mysterious, action-at-a-temporal-distance manner. Rather, there is an ordinary causal chain of events leading from one to the other—by way of the explosion. It therefore seems that, to count as a cause of the triggering, Billy's action must *also* count as a cause of the *explosion*, since it was only *by way of* the explosion that he helped bring about the triggering. But the explosion also caused Zeno to put his hands over his ears. So why must we not therefore conclude that by adding the chemical, Billy likewise was a cause of Zeno's action?

Looked at a certain way, the case can seem to be another counterexample to transitivity: Billy's action was a cause of the explosion—it had to be, else we could not get it to come out a cause of the triggering of the photodetector. The explosion, in turn, was a cause of Zeno's action. But Billy's action was not a cause of Zeno's action. So perhaps we have, here, yet another reason to give up transitivity.

If so, it is an entirely different kind of reason from that which applied, say, to the inert neuron network: Billy's action does not both initiate a threat to Zeno's action and simultaneously do something to cancel that threat. Moreover, we cannot in good philosophical conscience stop with a denial of transitivity, for a thorny puzzle remains: why is it that *Suzy's* action counts as a cause of Zeno's, by way of the explosion, but Billy's does not?

Some will be impatient for what they consider the obvious response: There is not just *one* explosion, but at least *two*—distinguished by the fact that it is somehow constitutive or essential to one of them, but not the other, that it be an explosion in the given shade of red. Call these explosions "*e*" and "*e+*," the latter being the one that is constitutively or essentially red in the given shade. Then we have what seems a transitivity-preserving solution: Billy's action causes *e+* but not *e*; Suzy's action causes both *e* and *e+*; *e+* causes the triggering but not Zeno's action.

An attractive story, perhaps, although many will find the ontological inflation of events *un*attractive. We should not accept it without taking several steps back, and considering with more care than we have so far the question of what, exactly, the causal relation *relates*. That is what L. A. Paul does in "Aspect Causation," chapter 8. She discusses a case[13] that appears to create problems for transitivity, and she argues that this appearance is illusory—closer inspection shows that in such cases, transitivity fails to apply. Causation may well be transitive; it is, rather, an underlying tension between extant theories of events coupled with reductive analyses of causation that gives rise to these seeming counterexamples. Here is the example that Paul considers: Suzy breaks her right wrist, which causes her to write her philosophy paper with her left hand. The paper is then sent off to a journal, which accepts it. If the breaking causes the event of the left-handed paper-writing, and the paper writing causes the acceptance, and if causation is transitive, it seems—contrary to intuition—that the breaking caused the acceptance.

Paul shows that none of the major contenders for a theory of events coupled with a theory of causation succeeds against such examples, and she argues that this makes trouble for theories of event causation. She exploits this trouble in order to argue in favor of taking *property instances* (what she calls "aspects") rather than events to be the causal relata. (We discuss related issues involving the nature of the causal relata below.) Observe how this maneuver will handle the forgoing case of the loud, colorful explosion: Billy's action causes the explosion to have a certain aspect—namely, to be an explosion in that particular shade of red. This aspect in turn is responsible for the triggering—but not for Zeno's covering his ears. Transitivity is preserved. Still, as Hall points out in his "Causation and the Price of Transitivity," chapter 7, making room for aspects is not enough to resolve what he calls the "hard cases" for transitivity, so even if a different account of the causal relata helps, serious problems remain. We will nevertheless set them aside, and focus squarely on the question Paul's paper brings to the fore: what does causation relate?

7   The Causal Relata

Most contemporary analyses of causation hold that causation is a relation between *events*, where these are taken to be particulars, entities that occupy spatiotemporal regions. But unless we are prepared to take events as unanalyzable primitives, an acceptable (reductive) analysis of the causal relation as a relation between events requires an acceptable theory of eventhood. The theory of events thus counts as a subtheory of a complete theory of causation.

By wide agreement, such a theory will broaden the category of event to include items never ordinarily so-called. When Suzy throws a rock at the window, breaking it, we naturally tend to think that there is just *one* sequence of events—the one initiated by Suzy's throw—converging on the effect. But it is far better, at least for the purposes of systematic metaphysics, to see this effect as standing at the intersection of *two* sequences of events: There is the interesting sequence just mentioned, and then there is the quite boring sequence consisting in the continued presence of the window, up to the moment it shatters. More generally, a proper theory of events almost certainly must count as such things that we would ordinarily classify as states, or standing or background conditions.

Next, there is widespread agreement that a theory of events must have the resources to tell us when two events, though nonidentical, fail to be wholly distinct—for example, because one is part of the other, or they have a common part, or they stand in some sort of intimate logical relationship. As we saw in section 4, a theory unable to draw such distinctions will almost certainly leave the account of causation that makes use of it easy prey for various counterexamples, in the form of not wholly distinct events that stand in relations of counterfactual dependence.

But within these broad parameters, there is no consensus as to which theory of eventhood is the correct one. This lack of consensus traces in part to conflicting intuitions—in particular, about when we have just one event, and when (and why) we have more than one. You walk to class. As you walk, you talk to your companion. Is your walking one event and your talking a numerically distinct event? Or are they the same event? There are considerations on both sides. On the one hand, the walking and the talking occurred at the same time and were performed by the same person, so common sense might dictate that they are the same event. On the other hand, the walking and the talking seem to stand in different causal relations to subsequent events: your walking made your legs tired, while your talking gave you a sore throat.

In general, we can characterize the individuation conditions put forward in different theories of events along a continuum from *coarse grained* to *fine grained*. Roughly, the more fine grained a theory takes event identity to be, the more events exist according to the theory. So a theory that held that the walking and talking were one and the same would be more coarse grained than a theory that distinguished them; this theory in turn would, if it recognized but *one* talking, be more coarse grained than a theory that distinguished your talking *loudly* from your talking *simpliciter*.

It's one thing to insist on such distinctions; it's another to explain them. Among those who want to draw them, probably the most popular explanation appeals to differences in the possible conditions of occurrence—or "essences"—of events.[14] You could have walked without talking, and vice versa; so your walking and talking are distinct events. More ambitiously, perhaps your talking *loudly* is a different event from your *talking*, because the latter, but not the former, would have occurred if you had been talking softly. If so, then the two events are alike in all categorical respects: Not only do they occupy the same region of spacetime, but they are both loud (one essentially, one accidentally so), both energetic, and so on. Notice that once the door is open to events that differ *only* along such modal dimensions, it will be difficult to close it; that is, the number of events that one must recognize as being perfectly categorically coincident will probably be enormous. There is the talking, the talking that is essentially not quiet, the talking that is essentially loud, the talking that is essentially exactly *that* loud, and so on—and we have been drawing only crude distinctions, about only one of the many aspects of these events. This ontological proliferation leads to trouble, as we will shortly see.

Theories of events that do not draw distinctions in this way—because they draw them either in some other way,[15] or not at all—still face an important question concerning essences. Consider your walking: what are the possible conditions under which *it*—and not just some event very much like it—could have occurred? To the extent that these conditions are very restrictive, your walking is modally *fragile*—unable, as it were, to survive in all but a few alternate possible worlds.

It is important to recognize that the question of how fragile events are cross-cuts the question of how many there are. For example, one could hold a highly coarse-grained theory—say, one according to which there is at most one event per region of spacetime—without committing oneself as to how modally fragile these events are. Or one could hold a highly fine-grained theory while remaining uncommitted. Of course, the questions *can* intersect: The account just considered, one that distinguishes a multitude of perfectly coincident events by their differing conditions of occurrence, is highly fine grained in a way that automatically commits it to the existence of plenty of events that are extremely modally fragile—and, for that matter, plenty of events that are not fragile at all, and plenty of events that are somewhere in between. (For example, your talking *loudly* is more fragile than your talking *simpliciter*, etc.)

Among theories that hold that (all) events are fragile, toward one extreme is a view according to which *any* difference in time, place, or manner of occurrence would make for a numerically different event.[16] Why adopt such a position? We can recognize one important reason—and also an unfortunate consequence—if we return to late preemption. Recall our paradigm example: Billy and Suzy throw rocks at a window, with Suzy's reaching it first, breaking it. How can we secure the result that Suzy's throw, and not Billy's, causes the breaking? Perhaps by insisting that the actual breaking is quite fragile: Had the window broken a few moments later, that would have been a numerically different breaking. Then, arguably, the breaking that actually occurs counterfactually depends on Suzy's throw, but not on Billy's.

Many people find this view compelling until they realize that tightening the individuation conditions for events in this way results in a landslide of causal connections, too many of them unwanted. (It should also be remembered that variations on late preemption yield examples immune from this treatment.) Your sore throat occurred at precisely 4 P.M., but if you had not stopped by your office to pick up your bag before you commenced your walk (and thus your discussion), you would have had a sore throat at 3:59 P.M. Under the fragility account, that sore throat would be a *numerically distinct event* from the sore throat at 4 P.M. Hence, standard regularity and counterfactual accounts of causation will count picking up your bag from your office a cause of the sore throat that actually occurred.

Although defenders of fragility accounts recognize that many more events will count as causes and effects than untutored intuition will be comfortable with, they believe the cost is worth the benefit. David Coady, in "Preempting Preemption" (chapter 13), argues that a counterfactual analysis of causation employing fragile events will solve a number of problems, and along the way he gives an able defense of the fragility strategy.[17]

Notice that the advantages that accrue to this strategy do not obviously extend to an account that, while recognizing the existence of a highly fragile window-breaking, also recognizes less fragile (and perfectly coincident) breakings, all differing in their essences. On such an account, there is a window-breaking that necessarily occurs just when it does; perhaps that breaking counterfactually depends on Suzy's throw alone. But there is also a breaking that could have occurred as much as a few moments later. What caused *it*? It's not even intuitively clear what the answer is, but at any rate it would be an embarrassment for an account of causation if it held that *nothing* caused this event (e.g., because no event could be found on which it depends, etc.). What reason could there be for admitting such uncaused events into one's ontology?

In fact, the reason standardly given is that we need such events as effects (and causes). More precisely, perfectly coincident events differing only in their essences are supposed to help us draw certain causal distinctions. For example, suppose Billy's throw makes a slight difference to the way in which the window shatters, perhaps by way of the gravitational pull his rock exerts on Suzy's. We would like to say: Billy's throw doesn't cause the breaking, but it *does* help cause that breaking to happen in just the way it does. Or, returning to the example considered toward the end of last section, Billy's action does not cause the firework's explosion, but it *does* cause it to be the color it is. Distinguishing a breaking that necessarily happens in just the way it does provides us with an event to be an effect of Billy's throw; distinguishing an explosion that is essentially red provides us with an event to be an effect of Billy's earlier action (and, by the way, to be a *cause* of the subsequent triggering of the photodetector).

Of course, this reason for drawing purely modal distinctions between events provides no ingredients for solving the problem posed by late preemption; the theorist needs to turn elsewhere for such a solution. There is a worse problem. Consider a simple situation, in which Suzy, all alone, throws a rock at a window, breaking it. The following sentence is true—and *determinately* so: "Suzy's throw is a cause of the breaking." But to what do the expressions "Suzy's throw" and "the breaking" refer? There are far too many eligible candidates for it to be at all plausible that their reference is *determinate*. So what? Why not just recognize a (large) number of admissible assignments of referents to each expression? Well, because doing so leaves it obscure how our sentence gets to have a determinate truth value. Suppose we assign a comparatively fragile event to "Suzy's throw" and a comparatively robust one to "the breaking"; then our effect will in all likelihood not depend on our cause. Nor is this trouble just for a counterfactual analysis: reverse matters, assigning a fragile event to "the breaking" and a robust one to "Suzy's throw," and a typical regularity account will have trouble making the latter out to be a cause of the former. The upshot is that on standard accounts of causation, there will be admissible assignments of referents that make our sentence *false*. And so even if there are admissible assignments that make it *true*, the sentence will not come out—as it should—*determinately* true.[18]

Why not opt for a more parsimonious account of events—holding, for example, that events are individuated by the spatiotemporal regions they occupy? But such a seemingly attractive theory itself has unwelcome consequences. If we had a metal sphere that as it rotated also heated up, we would have to identify the event of the rotating of the sphere with the event of the heating up of the sphere—they are the same event because they occur in the same spatiotemporal region. But our earlier reasons for wanting occasionally to distinguish coincident events remain in full force, for it seems easy to imagine a situation in which the sphere's rotation has different effects from its heating.

A different approach to causal relata bypasses at least some of these problems by holding that the causal relata are not events after all. (Or at least, the causal relation can be said to hold between events only in virtue of holding between something else.) Various alternative accounts of the causal relata have been put forward, the most plausible of which take them to be property instances, facts, states of affairs, or propositions.

Those who hold that the causal relata are property instances often argue that causation obtains between instantiations of universals or between tropes. A different but related view holds that causation obtains between states of affairs, where states of affairs consist in particulars having properties. Such views can still accept that events are causal relata in a derivative sense, since events may well be constructed from property instances or states of affairs.

In "Aspect Causation," chapter 8, Paul argues that we should take the causal relata to be property instances (*aspects*), as this can help resolve some outstanding problems with transitivity and allows us to bypass the need to provide individuation conditions for events. If the causal relata are property instances, then we can construct a reductive analysis of causation independently of an analysis of events—a result that, given the lack of consensus over what counts as a satisfactory theory of events, philosophers of causation should welcome.

There is a quite different motivation for abandoning or at least qualifying the default position that events are the primary causal relata. It stems from the need to accommodate causation involving *omissions*: prevention, causation by omission, and (arguably) causation by double prevention. (See the contributions by Lewis, Beebee, Menzies, Mellor, and Armstrong.) Focus just on causation by omission, as when Billy's failure to show up for their lunch date causes Suzy to become disappointed. The possibility of this kind of causation creates an immediate difficulty for those who would hold that causation must relate events. On the face of it absences (omissions) are not particulars at all, and so not events; what are we to make, then, of causation "involving" them? We seem to find ourselves with a causal relation that is missing a relatum. D. H. Mellor, in his "For Facts as Causes and Effects" (chapter 12), responds by defending the view that *most* causes and effects are not particulars, but rather *facts*. Mellor takes facts to be states of affairs expressed by true sentences, statements or propositions.[19] An advantage of Mellor's position is that it allows him to handle cases involving negative causation quite naturally. It is an unhappy philosopher who is forced to believe in negative *events*, but Mellor by contrast can quite serenely grant that there are negative *facts*.

Lewis's response, in "Causation as Influence" (chapter 3), and especially "Void and Object" (chapter 10), is to insist that when there *are* causal relata, they are invariably events—but to go on to assert that in cases of causation by omission or prevention, one of the relata is missing: "So I have to say that when an absence is a cause or an effect, there is strictly speaking nothing at all that is a cause or effect. Sometimes causation is not a relation, because a relation needs relata and sometimes the causal relata go missing" ("Causation as Influence," p. 100). Nevertheless, he claims, in all such cases there will be an appropriate pattern of counterfactual dependence—not between two events, but, say, between an event and the fact that no event of some specified type occurs. (Thus, Suzy's sadness depends counterfactually on the fact that no event of the Billy-showing-up type occurs.) Why this relation of dependence does not qualify the foregoing fact as a *cause* is, to our minds, left a bit unclear.

Beebee responds to problems involving absences by rejecting causation by omission. For Beebee, causation always relates particulars; hence, there can be no causation involving absences. She argues that commonsense intuitions about causation by omission make trouble both for those who defend causation by omission and those who reject it. For example, she must deny that Billy's absence causes Suzy's disappointment. But those who disagree typically hold that mere counterfactual dependence suffices for causation by omission; consequently, they must hold that the failure of Bill Gates to show up with a fat check for Suzy also causes her disappointment (since if he had shown up, she would not have become disappointed). Such parity leads Beebee to seek other desiderata on an account of causation in order to settle whether absences can cause; she thinks that the attractiveness of the view that causation invariably relates events tells against this position. Finally, Beebee accounts for the central role that causation by omission can play in our ordinary causal claims by arguing that common sense fails to discriminate between causation and explanation.

Menzies takes a new approach to the problem of how our intuitions about omissions seem to generate conflicting results, arguing that we can develop an account of causation based on relevant difference-making that distinguishes between absences as causes and absences as "mere conditions." (The distinction between causes and conditions is relative to a field of normal conditions generated by a causal model.) Menzies's account is constructed so as to avoid the sorts of spurious causes that Beebee cites and that make trouble for a nondiscriminating counterfactual account of causation by omission.

Recognizing the special challenges that causation involving absences presents suggests that it might be helpful to distinguish kinds of causation. There is garden-variety causation, as when Suzy's throw causes the window to break. There is causation by omission, as when Billy's failure to stop her likewise causes the breaking. There is prevention, as when (this time) Billy stops the rock midflight, preserving the window. There is double prevention, as when Sally knocks Billy aside before he can block the rock, thus contributing to the window's breaking. And perhaps there are still more exotic varieties of omission-involving causation.

It may well be that the different kinds of causation require different explications. (Both Hall, in "Two Concepts of Causation," chapter 9, and Armstrong, in "Going through the Open Door Again," chapter 19, argue as much.) If so, then it comes as no surprise that uniform analyses of causation are vulnerable to counterexamples and inadequate for complicated examples where different kinds of causation are combined. Here it is well to recall some of the problems involving transitivity discussed in the previous section, where omissions played a central role in the structure of the case (the inert network is a good example). Hall in particular argues that such cases threaten transitivity only if we hold that transitivity must apply to the kinds of causation—in particular, causation by double prevention—featured in them.

The problem of explaining causation by and of omission, and hence by extension explaining what it is to prevent events from occurring or to allow events to occur, is an area of continuing research. The importance of the problem is highlighted by the special roles that preventing and allowing seem to play in related areas of inquiry, for example, accounts of our ascriptions of moral and legal responsibility.

8 Summaries of the Contributions

Here we provide capsule summaries of the contributions that follow.

Chapter 2: Jonathan Schaffer, "Trumping Preemption"

Schaffer develops a novel kind of example that poses trouble for most existing accounts of causation. So-called *trumping preemption* occurs when two (or more) processes, each sufficient to bring about some effect, go to completion. But unlike cases of symmetric overdetermination, there is an asymmetry: One of the processes is such that variation in it would have been followed by corresponding variation in the effect, whereas the same is not true of the other. For short, the first process *trumps* the second. As an example, Schaffer imagines a sergeant and a major simultaneously shouting orders to their troops. In cases of conflict, the troops obey the major; but this time the order is the same. Schaffer argues, first, that in cases like this the "trumping" event (e.g., the major's shout) is the sole cause of the effect (the troops' response), and, second, that existing counterfactual accounts of causation cannot accommodate this fact.

Chapter 3: David Lewis, "Causation as Influence"

Lewis replaces the old idea that causation is, at heart, counterfactual dependence between events, with the thesis that causation is, at heart, counterfactual *covariation* between events. He first defines a relation of "influence"—which is, roughly, the relation an event c bears to an event e just in case the manner of occurrence of e depends counterfactually in a suitably systematic way on the manner of occurrence of c. Lewis then takes causation to be the ancestral of influence. As an illustration, Lewis's solution to the problem of late preemption—as exhibited, say, in the example of Suzy, Billy, and the broken window—is that Suzy's throw exerts much more influence on the shattering of the window than does Billy's: counterfactually varying Suzy's throw in any of a number of ways will result in corresponding changes in the shattering, whereas the same is not true of Billy's throw—or at least, not nearly to the same extent. For that reason, Suzy's throw, and hers alone, counts as a cause of the shattering. En route to developing this account, Lewis treats a number of central methodological and metaphysical issues, discussing transitivity, causation involving omissions, the varieties of preemption, and the reasons for pursuing an analysis of causation at all.

Chapter 4: John Collins, "Preemptive Prevention"

You catch a ball headed for a window. Common sense credits you with preventing the window from breaking, even though I leapt behind you ready to take the catch if you missed. Your catch was an act of preemptive prevention. My leap was a dependence preventer; it prevented the window's not breaking from depending on your catch. Yet if a brick wall had stood between you and the window, we are now reluctant to say that your catch caused the window to remain unbroken. Collins suggests that our ambivalence here is governed by how far-fetched it is to assume the absence or failure of the dependence preventer. This suggests the possibility of an account of causation in terms of would-be dependence. The analysis falls to Schaffer's examples of trumping preemption. Collins goes on to argue that cases of "masking" and "finkish" trumping pose new problems for a counterfactual analysis of dispositions.

Chapter 5: Stephen Yablo, "Advertisement for a Sketch of an Outline of a Prototheory of Causation"
Yablo argues that we should return to the original, spartan idea that causation is counterfactual dependence—but understand that dependence to be something he calls "de facto dependence." The idea is, roughly, that e de facto depends on c just in case, had c not happened—and had suitably chosen other factors been held fixed—then e would not have happened. As an illustration, Yablo would say that the shattering of the window de facto depends on Suzy's throw because, had Suzy not thrown—and had it still been the case that Billy's rock never struck the window—then the window would not have broken. Obviously, the success of this proposal depends heavily on being able to pick out, in a principled way, which factors should be held fixed; much of Yablo's paper is devoted to this question.

Chapter 6: Peter Menzies, "Difference-making in Context"
Menzies argues that Lewis's counterfactual analysis of causation is insensitive to the various context-relative ways in which commonsense distinguishes between causes and background conditions. Menzies develops the conception of a cause as something that makes a difference with respect to an assumed background or causal field by giving a detailed analysis of an account of difference-making in terms of context-sensitive counterfactuals.

Chapter 7: Ned Hall, "Causation and the Price of Transitivity"
Various purported counterexamples to the transitivity of causation have recently appeared in the literature. Hall argues that these fall into two types. On the one hand, there are examples that only seem to serve as counterexamples to transitivity: Their intuitive status as such can, in fact, be resisted on a principled basis. On the other hand, there are examples with much greater intuitive force, but that function as counterexamples to transitivity only if one endorses the controversial thesis that counterfactual dependence suffices for causation. Hall suggests that it is better to abandon the controversial thesis than to give up transitivity.

Chapter 8: L. A. Paul, "Aspect Causation"
Paul shows that reductive analyses of causation that take events to be the causal relata face counterintuitive consequences with respect to the transitivity of causation, and she proposes an analysis of causation where aspects, or property instances, are

the causal relata. Aspect causation combines elements of regularity theories with influence (patterns of counterfactual covariation) and takes property instances to be the causal relata. Paul argues that changing the causal relata to property instances resolves some outstanding problems with transitivity and allows the development of a theory of causation that is not held hostage to a theory of event individuation.

Chapter 9: Ned Hall, "Two Concepts of Causation"
Hall argues that philosophers seeking to analyze causation should distinguish two fundamentally different concepts of causation: dependence, which can to a first approximation simply be identified with counterfactual dependence, and production, which requires a very different analysis more in the spirit of Mackie's original "INUS conditions" account. The case for the distinction turns on examples that reveal systematic tensions between two sets of theses that might be thought to characterize causation. On the one hand, causation seems to be a transitive, intrinsic, local relation (local in the sense that there is no causation at a temporal distance). On the other hand, counterfactual dependence seems to suffice for causation, and omissions seem capable of standing in causal relations (to ordinary events and to each other). Hall argues that it is impossible to provide an account of causation that does justice to both sets of theses, but that the tensions can be resolved if we take the first set to characterize production and the second to characterize dependence.

Chapter 10: David Lewis, "Void and Object"
Lewis argues that the possibility of causation by omission requires an analysis that can handle cases of causation without causal relations. (For an instance of causation to be an instance of a causal relation, there must be relata for the relation. But an absence cannot be a relatum, for an absence is nothing at all.) A counterfactual analysis of causation can provide an analysis of causation that includes an analysis of causation by omission, because it can define causation without a causal relation: Causation is (somehow) a matter of counterfactual dependence of events (or absences) on other events (or absences). Lewis also argues that the project of defining a functional analysis of familiar instances of the causal relation ("biff") to serve as a basis for defining an (unrestricted) conceptual analysis of causation fails.

Chapter 11: Helen Beebee, "Causing and Nothingness"
Against Lewis, Beebee defends the view that there is no such thing as causation by absence. We do often speak as though absences are causes. Thus: If Smith fails to water her office plants, and the plants die, we might say that her failure to water them caused them to die. Yet common sense balks at the judgment that, for example,

Queen Elizabeth's failure to water Smith's plants was also a cause of their death. The problem is that commonsense assertions and denials of causation by absence seem to be guided by normative considerations that have no place in a metaphysical account of causation. Beebee suggests that the key to solving this problem lies in the distinction between causation and causal explanation. We can admit, she argues, that there are causal explanations that invoke facts about absences without allowing that absences are causes. Absences and omissions can causally explain, without being the causes of what they explain.

Chapter 12: D. H. Mellor, "For Facts as Causes and Effects"

Mellor argues that facts, rather than particulars such as events, are causes and effects. For Mellor, singular causal claims are best rendered in the form "E because C," where C and E are sentences and "because" is a sentential connective; "E because C" is interpreted as equivalent to "the fact that C causes the fact that E." Mellor argues that there is no reason to take causation to be a relation, much less a relation between events, and that this perspective enables negative facts to be causes and effects. For Mellor, facts are superior to events as causes and effects because fact causation can handle causation of or by negative facts much more easily than event causation can handle causation of or by omission.

Chapter 13: David Coady, "Preempting Preemption"

Coady defends what he calls the "naive counterfactual analysis of causation," that c causes e if and only if, if c had not occurred, e would not have occurred. This analysis is widely believed to be refuted by the possibility of preemption, which is a species of redundant causation. Through a careful consideration of the different kinds of events related in paradigmatic examples, Coady argues that there are in fact no cases of preemption: All such cases are either cases of symmetrical overdetermination or are not cases of redundant causation after all.

Chapter 14: Cei Maslen, "Causes, Contrasts, and the Nontransitivity of Causation"

Maslen develops an account according to which events cause other events only relative to contrast situations. For Maslen, causation in the world is an objective, *three*-place relation between causes, contrasts, and effects, and the truth and meaning of causal statements depend on the context in which they occur (for it is this context that helps determine the relevant contrast situation). Maslen also argues that her contrast theory of causation makes the intransitivity of the causal relation intuitively plausible, and she gives compelling analyses of several counterexamples to the transitivity of (binary) causation.

Chapter 15: Igal Kvart, "Causation: Probabilistic and Counterfactual Analyses"

Kvart presents a probabilistic analysis of (token) causation. He argues that an account of causal relevance must play a crucial role in any such analysis. Cases of preemption will then be handled by the fact that the preempted cause is causally irrelevant to the effect. Causal irrelevance is established by identifying a "neutralizing" event that screens off the effect in a stable way. Kvart argues that the resulting account can deal with cases of probability-lowering causes. In the final sections of the essay it is argued that since any adequate account of counterfactuals must be based on causal notions, the counterfactual analysis of causation will turn out to be circular. Philosophers have been too quick to abandon the probabilistic analysis of causation, Kvart suggests.

Chapter 16: Murali Ramachandran, "A Counterfactual Analysis of Indeterministic Causation"

Ramachandran develops a counterfactual analysis of causation intended to work under the assumption of indeterminism. He argues that three core problems for Lewis's probabilistic theory and his latest "causation as influence" theory (given in this volume) are: (i) it (mistakenly) takes causation to be transitive; (ii) it precludes the possibility of backward causation; and (iii) it cannot handle certain cases of overdetermination. Ramachandran tackles these problems by way of three special notions: (a) a notion of time-invariant overall world chance of an event's occurring already present in the notion of background chance; (b) a notion of accumulative (counterfactual) chance-raising that discriminates between causal and noncausal chance-raising chains; and (c) a notion of potential chance-raisers (as in "c would have raised the chance of e but for the occurrence of certain other events").

Chapter 17: Christopher Hitchcock, "Do All and Only Causes Raise the Probabilities of Effects?"

According to probabilistic theories of causation, causes raise the probabilities of their effects. Critics of these theories have tended to concentrate on putative examples of non-probability-raising causes. Here Hitchcock focusses attention on the possibility of probability-raising noncauses. These cases turn on fundamental questions about the nature of indeterministic causation. Probabilistic theories usually presuppose that indeterministic causes bring about their effects only via their contributions to a total "probability pool," there being no causal facts of the matter extending beyond these probabilistic contributions. We can construct cases in which it is stipulated that there are such further facts, but then there is no reason to think that the probabilities in question are irreducible. The problem, Hitchcock suggests, is that the only cases in which we do have reason to think that the probabilities are irreducible are cases involving microphysics, where our ordinary causal intuitions are no longer reliable.

Chapter 18: Tim Maudlin, "Causation, Counterfactuals, and the Third Factor"
Maudlin argues that the key to understanding much of our thought about causation lies in distinguishing laws of inertia—laws that, roughly, specify how things behave if left alone—from laws of deviation—laws that "specify in what conditions, and in what ways, behavior will deviate from the inertial behavior." The primary notion of cause, according to Maudlin, is the notion of an event that figures in some law of deviation. He suggests further that the content of this distinction between laws—and indeed whether such a distinction is even possible—will depend significantly on the level of description of the phenomena under consideration.

Chapter 19: D. M. Armstrong, "Going through the Open Door Again: Counterfactual versus Singularist Theories of Causation"
Armstrong criticizes the counterfactual analysis put forward by David Lewis and defends a singularist theory. Armstrong's singularist theory holds that causation is a two-term relation—a universal—holding between cause and effect (where causes and effects are states of affairs). For Armstrong, causation is conceptually primitive. He cites several reasons why we can take ourselves to have observational access to singular causal facts: ordinary language, experiences such as the perception of pressure on one's body, our awareness of the operation of our will, and psychological experimental evidence. Armstrong also discusses the treatments he favors for several issues concerning causation, including causation by omission, action at a distance, probabilistic causation, and the connection between causation and laws.

Notes

1. Let us be clear from the outset that by "facts" here we mean nonlinguistic items.

2. But see Woodward (2003) for a sophisticated development and defense of such an approach. Woodward grants the circularity, but argues persuasively that the resulting account of causation is nevertheless highly informative.

3. Albert (2000) also discusses the problem.

4. There is one other lesson from physics that is not so easily avoided, however. Here is an illustration: Suppose you have before you a glass of hot water. What would happen were you to put an ice cube in it? We would like to answer: The ice cube would melt. But statistical mechanics, together with the time-reversibility of the fundamental dynamical laws that appear to govern our world, tells us that there would be some *extremely tiny* (but nonzero) probability that the ice cube would grow, while the water heated up. (Time-reversibility tells us that such an occurrence is nomologically possible, statistical mechanics that it is extremely unlikely.) If so, then the answer we would like to give is *false*—since it *might* be that the ice cube would *not* melt. As far as we know, there is no decent way to construct truth conditions for the counterfactual that avoids this result. But the counterfactual analyst need not be greatly concerned: She need

merely grant that her account of causation must be built on conditionals of the form "if c had not occurred, then the probability that e occurred would have been extremely close to zero." We will ignore this complication henceforth.

5. See Maudlin (forthcoming) for discussion of how to extend this recipe to counterfactuals with more complicated antecedents.

6. Observe that if backward causation is possible, and if causation is transitive, then simultaneous and indeed *self*-causation are possible: e.g., Bill/Sue's collision with itself causes that very same collision. Still, there is a distinct kind of simultaneous causation whose possibility cannot be secured in this way, where the causal relationship between c and its contemporaneous effect e is *direct*, involving the action of no causal intermediates. We intended the example of the particle in the force field to illustrate this sort of simultaneous causation.

7. Here are the technical details: Let $f(T)$ be a function that gives the particle's position for each time T (specified relative to some inertial frame of reference). We assume that the function is continuous, but not that it is everywhere differentiable. But suppose further that for some open interval extending forward from time $T = t$, the second derivative $f''(T)$ is well defined and continuous; then the particle's instantaneous acceleration at t, "taken from the future," can be defined as the limit as T approaches t "from above" of $f''(T)$. (For a well-behaved particle, this will equal the limit "from below," and we can speak simply of the acceleration at t, simpliciter.)

8. Typically, but not always: Ducasse (1926), for example, takes causation to be essentially nothing more than spatiotemporal contiguity plus temporal priority. (That is, c causes e just in case c and e are spatiotemporally contiguous, and c precedes e.) We view this as a kind of limit case of physical connection accounts.

9. See also Davidson (1967). Note that Davidson does not treat the word "cause" in the way one might expect—namely, by providing it with an explicit definition that would allow for the deduction of the target sentence from sentences that did not themselves contain the word "cause." Rather, he includes the word "cause" in the statement of the laws themselves, a move that is both bizarre (given that the paradigm examples of laws provided by fundamental physics never make use of this notion) and that inexplicably ruins the chances for providing a reductive analysis of causation.

10. Given that Lewis quite explicitly takes himself to be providing a conceptual analysis of causation, it is therefore mysterious to us why he continues thus: "It would be still better, however, if theory itself went indecisive about hard cases. If an analysis says that the answer for some hard case depends on underdescribed details, or on the resolution of some sort of vagueness, that would explain nicely why common sense comes out indecisive." Lewis nowhere explains why he thinks it would merely be "better," as opposed to crucial, to explain "why common sense comes out indecisive" when it does.

11. Note that this cannot be the *whole* story, for ordinary cases of preemption such as that exhibited in figure 1.2 likewise exhibit this structure.

12. Suggested by Hartry Field, who learned it from Ellery Eells.

13. The case appears in McDermott (1995a).

14. See Lewis (1986d). For a closely related essentialist theory, see Yablo (1992a,b, 2000).

15. See for example Kim (1973a, 1980). According to Kim, each event corresponds to a triple of a "constitutive" time, particular, and property. It is not entirely clear what it means for such elements to be constitutive. But Kim explicitly distances himself from the view that they are constitutive in the sense that it is essential to the event's occurrence that the given particular has the given property at the given time.

16. *Toward* one extreme, but not all the way to the end: One could add, for example, that any difference in causal origins would make for a different event.

17. Lombard (1986) also holds that events are fragile with respect to time, and so could not have occurred at any time other than the time they actually did.

18. See Bennett (1988) for an expert statement of this problem.

19. Others have also defended the idea that the causal relata are facts; e.g., Jonathan Bennett gives a well-argued defense of the view that causes and effects are facts in his (1988).

2 Trumping Preemption

Jonathan Schaffer

Extant *counterfactual accounts of causation* (CACs) still cannot handle preemptive causation. I describe a new variety of preemption, defend its possibility, and use it to show the inadequacy of extant CACs.

Imagine that it is a law of magic that the first spell cast on a given day match the enchantment that midnight. Suppose that at noon Merlin casts a spell (the first that day) to turn the prince into a frog, that at 6:00 P.M. Morgana casts a spell (the only other that day) to turn the prince into a frog, and that at midnight the prince becomes a frog. Clearly, Merlin's spell (the first that day) is a cause of the prince's becoming a frog and Morgana's is not, because the laws say that the first spells are the consequential ones. Nevertheless, there is no counterfactual dependence of the prince's becoming a frog on Merlin's spell, because Morgana's spell is a dependency-breaking backup. Further, there is neither a failure of intermediary events along the Morgana process (we may dramatize this by stipulating that spells work directly, without any intermediaries), nor any would-be difference in time or manner of the effect absent Merlin's spell, and thus nothing remains by which extant CACs might distinguish Merlin's spell from Morgana's in causal status.

1 Trumping Preemption

In order to establish the possibility and relevance of trumping scenarios such as the wizards case, I rebut the following imagined objections: that the causal judgments evoked are unclear, that the laws involved are question-begging, and that the case invoked is unrealistic, either in the sense that it is empirically implausible, given what we know about our world, or in the sense that it is pretheoretically implausible, given what we habitually assume about our world. I conclude that delivering the right verdict in trumping cases is an adequacy condition on an account of causation.

Objection: It is not intuitively clear that Merlin's spell is a cause and Morgana's not of the prince's becoming a frog. The judgment of an otherwise successful theory (assuming CACs are otherwise successful) ought to overrule the judgment of unclear intuition. The wizards case, and trumping preemptions in general, should be left (to use David Armstrong's phrase) as spoils to the victor.

Originally published in a special issue of the *Journal of Philosophy* (April 2000): 165–181. Minor revisions have been made for consistency.

Reply: To my mind, the judgment that Merlin's spell is a cause and Morgana's not is intuitively clear (and so, to my mind, any account that cannot accommodate this judgment just is not an account of *causation*). But no matter. To the philosopher who does not share my intuitions, or does not attribute as much clarity to these intuitions, I reply that any account of causation which hopes to respect the central connotations of the causal concept had better agree that Merlin's spell is a cause and Morgana's not. To treat trumping preemptions as spoils to the victor is to risk spoiling the point of having a causal concept.

The concept of causation lies in a web of concepts including (most centrally) those of law, explanation, counterfactual implication, agency, and evidence. To a crudest approximation, (1) causes and their effects are subsumed under the laws; (2) causes explain their effects; (3) causes, were they different, would counterfactually imply different effects; (4) causes are means to their effects; (5) causes provide evidence both to and from their effects. Some or all of these relations may need to be refined or even ultimately abandoned. I submit, however, that any pair of events that satisfies *all* these relations deserves to be considered clearly causally related, while any pair of events that satisfies *none* deserves to be considered clearly not causally related.[1]

Consider the relation between causes and laws. Since the law is that the first spell cast on a given day match the enchantment that midnight, and since Merlin's spell is first that day, his spell satisfies the antecedent conditions of the magic law, and so calling his spell a cause of the enchantment that midnight respects the subsumption of causal structure by nomic structure. Morgana's spell, in contrast, does not satisfy the antecedent conditions of the magic law, and so her spell has no relevant lawful consequences. Thus, calling the spell a cause of the enchantment posits causation not covered by law.

Now, consider the relation between causes and explanations. Intuitively, if you want to know why the prince became a frog that midnight, Merlin's spell is part of a good answer. The deductive account of explanation vindicates this intuition:

(1) At noon, Merlin cast a spell to turn the prince into a frog.

(2) No other spells were cast that day prior to or contemporaneous with Merlin's.

(3) It is a law that the first spell cast on a given day match the enchantment that midnight.

Therefore,

(4) The prince became a frog at midnight.[2]

Thus, treating Merlin's spell as a cause respects the connection between causes and explainers. Morgana's spell, in contrast, intuitively explains nothing about the prince's fate, and the deductive account vindicates this intuition:

(1) At 6:00 P.M., Morgana cast a spell to turn the prince into a frog.

(2) ...

(3) It is a law that the first spell cast on a given day match the enchantment that midnight.

Therefore,

(4) The prince became a frog at midnight.

There is no way to fill in (2) so as to get a deductively valid argument without rendering (1) superfluous, since the argument will be deductively valid (in a way that makes essential use of the laws in (3)) only when a first spell is specified, at which point Morgana's spell need not be.[3] Thus, calling Morgana's spell a cause invents causes that explain nothing.

Next, consider the relation between causes and counterfactual variance. Had Merlin's spell been different, such as a spell to turn the prince into a goat, then the prince's fate would have been different: He would have become a goat.[4] Thus, the prince's fate counterfactually varies with Merlin's magic, just as the barometer reading counterfactually varies with the atmospheric pressure, in that in both cases the noncompossible family of propositions representing differences in the former counterfactually depends on the noncompossible family of propositions representing differences in the latter—a relation that David Lewis[5] points out is typical of such intuitively causal processes as measurement, perception, and control. Not so for Morgana's spell: Had she cast a spell to turn the prince into a goat, to protect his humanity, or even to make the sky the color of gold, come midnight all that would happen would be the prince's becoming a frog (because we are holding fixed Merlin's prior spell as well as the laws). To call her spell a cause would be to countenance causes whose alleged effects were counterfactually oblivious to them.

Next, as to the relation between causes and agency, it is widely agreed that "If an effect is an end, its causes are means to it."[6] This is usually spelled out decision-theoretically: if E is a desired end and C a prospective means, C will be effective if and only if the probability of E given C is greater than the probability of E given $\neg C$. One way to spell this idea out in more detail is to use agent probabilities (on which actions are assumed free in having no causal antecedents), so that C will be effective if and only if $p^A(E|C) > p^A(E|\neg C)$.[7] On this test, Merlin's spell is an effective means for (E) the prince's becoming a frog, since $p^A(E|\text{Merlin-casts-his-spell}) = 1$, while $p^A(E|\text{Merlin-does-not-cast-his-spell}) < 1$ (Morgana is assumed free, so she might not cast her spell). Morgana's spell, on the other hand, is ineffective, since $p^A(E|\text{Morgana-does-not-cast-her-spell}) = 1$ as Merlin has already acted to determine the prince's fate. Thus, treating Merlin's spell as a cause and Morgana's as a noncause of the prince's becoming a frog respects the agential connotations of causes as means.

Finally, consideration of the relation between causes and evidence will converge on the same conclusion, namely, that Merlin's spell is a cause of the prince's metamorphosis and Morgana's not. Intuitively, causes provide (epistemically valuable) evidence both to and from their effects: If I see someone fire a bullet at Jones's heart, I am licensed to infer that Jones will die; and, conversely, if I see Jones supine with a bullet-shaped entry wound left of his sternum, I am licensed to infer that he was shot. There is typically a relation of scale in both directions: The more details I know about the cause, the more details I have license to predict concerning the effect; and the more details I know about the effect, the more details I have license to retrodict concerning the cause.

Suppose that all I know about Merlin's spell is that it is the first one cast that day; then all I have license to predict is that there will be some enchantment at midnight. If I learn more detail, such as that it targets the prince, then I can predict the resulting enchantment in more detail, namely, that it will concern the prince. And so on. This relation of scale also holds in reverse. If I know that the prince became a frog, I may infer that a spell of the form "Presto, prince to frog!" was first that day. And if I then learn that Merlin's spell was first that day, I can come to know its intimate details, though I never witnessed it. Merlin's magic fits the prince's fate as the gun its bullet.

Morgana's spell, once again, fails the test of causes. If I know that hers is not the first that day, I can infer nothing about what will happen at midnight from the details of her performance. If I do not know that hers is not the first that day, any inferences I make based on her performance will be, if true, merely accidentally so (and so not licensed).[8] In reverse, if I know what enchantment has befallen the prince that midnight, I have no license for inferring the details of later spells cast that day, and any inferences I make concerning Morgana's spell out of ignorance as to the fact that Merlin's came earlier will be at best accidentally true.

In summary, Merlin's spell is nomically antecedent for, explanatory of, counterfactually variant with, a means to, and evidence both to and from, the prince's becoming a frog at midnight, while Morgana's spell is none of these. So every individual measure of causeworthiness converges on the result that Merlin's spell is a cause of the prince's becoming a frog, whereas Morgana's spell is not.

Objection: The arguments that Merlin's spell is a cause and Morgana's not of the prince's metamorphosis all turn on the stipulated law that the first spells cast match midnight enchantments. But such stipulation begs the question against those (such as Lewis, the leading proponent of CACs) who hold that laws supervene on occurrent facts. Why not stipulate that last spells cast match midnight enchantments, or that at least they do when first and last spells agree, since in any case the result is the same: the prince becomes a frog at midnight? If these stipulations represent genuine possibilities, then the supervenience of laws on facts is lost.

Reply: Even if the wizards scenario were incompatible with the supervenience of laws on facts, this would still show (surprisingly) that the success of CACs is tied to the supervenience of laws. Those who would deny supervenience in the manner of Fred Dretske, Michael Tooley, and Armstrong[9] (who hold that laws are contingent necessitation relations between universals) could not avail themselves of this objection, since on their view there may well be a contingent necessitation relation between the universals "first spell cast on day x" and "midnight enchantment on day x"; those who would deny supervenience in the manner of John Carroll and Tim Maudlin[10] (who hold that laws are primitive) could not avail themselves of this objection either, since on their view there is no barrier at all to the existence of a primitive lawful relation between the first spells and midnight enchantments. But no matter. To the philosopher who is willing to tie the success of CACs to the supervenience of laws on facts, I reply that the existence of laws favoring the first spells even when first and later spells agree (as per the wizards) is fully compatible with the supervenience of laws on facts, and is actually entailed by leading supervenientist accounts of laws, given certain facts in the world's history.

Suppose laws supervene on facts, and suppose for the sake of definiteness that (1) laws supervene as per the Mill–Ramsey–Lewis[11] (MRL) account: L is a law of nature if and only if L is a theorem of the axiomatization of the facts that best balances simplicity and strength. Now (2) let the world history contain "decisive competitions" between spells, where first and later spells disagree, and where the first spell cast always wins (that is, you try first to turn the queen into a frog, I try later to turn her into a goat, and she becomes a frog). Finally (3), let the laws summarizing the nonmagical remainder of the world history be independent of the magical laws (say, the world is otherwise Newtonian). This suffices to fix the laws as per the wizards case: When first and later spells agree, it will be simpler (and just as strong) to regard these cases as extensions of the same overall pattern of first-spell dominance found in (2), rather than as new examples of a second pattern of later-spell dominance or first-and-later-spell equality; this gain in simplicity will not compromise the simplicity/ strength of the other laws since they are assumed independent by (3), and so this local and not-compromised-elsewhere gain in simplicity without loss in strength will by (1) entail laws favoring the first spells even when first and later spells agree.

Somewhat more precisely, consider how the laws of a world in which the first spells dominate when first and later spells disagree might cover cases in which first and later spells agree:

(a) *Asymmetric* in allowing only the first spells to satisfy their antecedents (as per the wizards): for all spells x and days y, if x is first on y, then the x-matching enchantment obtains that midnight.

(b) *Symmetric* in allowing both first and later spells to satisfy their antecedents: for all spells x and days y, if x is first on y or there is a spell z which is first on y and which agrees with x, then the x-matching enchantment obtains that midnight.

(c) *Asymmetric* in allowing only later spells to satisfy their antecedents: for all spells x and days y, if (x is first on y and there is no spell z which is later on y and which agrees with x) or (there is a spell z which is first on y and which agrees with x and there is no z' which is both later than x and which agrees with x), then the x-matching enchantment obtains that midnight.

(d) *Silent* in these cases: for all spells x and days y, if x is first on y and there is no spell z which is later on y and which agrees with x, then the x-matching enchantment obtains that midnight.

Now, it is apparent that (a) is simpler than (b), (c), or (d): (a) subsumes all cases under one pattern/clause, that of first-spell dominance, while (b)–(d) require multiple clauses to accommodate multiple patterns;[12] it is especially revealing that (d), which is silent on first-later agreements, is actually more complicated than (a)—to get the laws not to say anything about first-spell dominance, you need to add a silencing clause. Further, it is obvious that (a) is as strong as (b) or (c) and stronger than (d): (a)–(c) have identical consequences as to which events are entailed, and how informatively described each event is; whereas (d) is as strong but for cases of first-later agreement under which no events are entailed. So, on the MRL account, given that laws are the theorems of the maximally simple and strong deductive system (I have been supposing that the laws of magic are independent of the other laws), it follows that the laws of magic say that the first spells entail matching enchantments.

Generalizing away from the MRL account, the above result shows that any account of laws which rules simplest laws at least possible (which I consider an adequacy condition on an account of lawhood, given the role of simplicity in scientific practice) must deliver at least some worlds with laws as per the wizards. So even someone who thinks laws are contingent necessitation relations between universals in the manner of Dretske, Tooley, and Armstrong, or who thinks laws are primitive in the manner of Carroll and Maudlin, should accept that there are at least some worlds with laws as per the wizards (they will presumably add that there are other worlds, factually identical to the wizards with laws as in (b), (c), and (d), and maybe with no laws at all). Thus, the laws invoked should be unproblematic on reflection.[13]

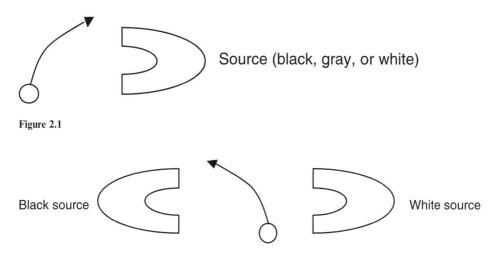

Figure 2.1

Figure 2.2

Objection: Causation is an empirical concept, and an account that mishandles fairy-tale cases like the wizards will be no less empirically adequate. Even if the wizards case is a conceptual possibility, it involves magic and action-at-a-distance, and so is too far-fetched to worry about.

Reply: I think accounts of causation need to be not just empirically but conceptually adequate. Without prior conceptual analysis, how could we tell whether an empirical investigation had hit its mark? But no matter. To the philosopher who scorns such "merely conceptual possibilities" as those involving magic and action-at-a-distance and demands empirically plausible scenarios, I reply that there exist empirically plausible trumping scenarios.

Imagine a world whose laws of physics are very much like our own, but for recognizing types of fields, "black," "gray," and "white," which do not superpose. Whenever a particle is subject to just one of these fields (assume for simplicity that no further forces are present), the particle will accelerate along a curved trajectory (fig. 2.1). Whenever a particle is subject to multiple fields, the particle will accelerate as if subject only to the darkest field, for example (fig. 2.2).[14] Thus, the laws of physics at this world would include a color-field law, most simply formulated as: The intensity of the darkest fields on a given object = the color force on that object. Although this world does not have the physics we now believe our world to have, it is relatively easy to imagine actual physicists discovering further types of fields, performing the experiments represented above, and supplementing our laws of physics in accord.

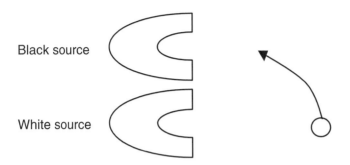

Figure 2.3

Moreover, this world is free of magic, action-at-a-distance, and other types of "far-fetched" causal connections. It is in this sense that it is empirically plausible.

Now, if a particle is subject to both a black and a white field that "pull in the same direction" with the same magnitude, it is still only the black field that causes the resultant acceleration (fig. 2.3). Here, we have an empirically plausible trumping scenario: replace Merlin with the black source, Morgana with the white source, the prince's fate with the particle's acceleration, spells with fields, and laws favoring earlier spells with laws favoring darker fields—the arguments from cause-worthiness all carry over.

The fields case shows that all that is needed for trumping are three events, $C1$, $C2$, and E, where E would be produced by $C1$ alone or by $C2$ alone (redundant causation), but where the laws render $C1$ the exclusive factor in the entailment of E (trumping preemption). This is why the causal exotica of the wizards case is inessential. Nothing empirically implausible remains.

Objection: Causation is a folk concept, and an account of causation which mishandles fairy-tale cases like the wizards and faux-physical cases like the fields will be no less useful in our everyday dealings with people, rocks, and the like. Even if the wizards case is a conceptual possibility and the fields case an empirical possibility, both involve behaviors so unlike those typical of local middle-sized dry objects that both cases are too removed from our habitual assumptions about the world for us to expect our concept of causation to be adequate to them.

Reply: I think the objector is overly pessimistic about the viability of our concepts in unfamiliar scenarios. The intuitive clarity of a judgment in a given case strikes me as strong evidence for the viability of the judged concept in that case (I hope to have already convinced the reader of the intuitive clarity of causal judgments in trumping cases). But no matter. To the philosopher skeptical of judgments in unfamiliar scenarios who requires scenarios that accord with the world we habitually take ourselves to inhabit, I reply that there exist pretheoretically plausible trumping scenarios.

Imagine that in a world that could well be our own, the major and the sergeant stand before the corporal, both shout "Charge!" at the same time, and the corporal decides to charge.[15] Orders from higher-ranking soldiers trump those of lower rank. I hope you agree that the major's order, and not the sergeant's, causes the corporal's decision to charge (for the same reasons as in the wizards and fields cases: Ranking orders are like the first spells and darkest fields). The soldiers case shows that everyday scenarios can stand in the pattern constitutive of trumping preemption. Nothing pretheoretically unfamiliar is needed.

The sophisticated philosopher might presume that the soldiers (unlike the wizards and the fields) must be a case of standard preemption, by presuming that, as the major's and sergeant's orders engage the corporal's mental mechanisms en route to his decision module, there must be some (at least unconscious) intermediate filter through which the major's order is passed but the sergeant's order blocked. But those who would reject the wizards and fields cases on the grounds that causation is a folk concept are not entitled to such sophisticated presumptions. Perhaps the corporal decides to charge via some such unconscious intermediate filter (as in standard preemption), or perhaps he decides to charge because his training has simply made his decision module exclusively sensitive to ranking orders (as in trumping preemption). The folk do not know how the mind is wired here, and from the point of view of attributing causation, they do not care.

In conclusion, trumping preemptions are intuitively clear, unproblematic in their assumptions, and fully realistic in being both empirically and pretheoretically plausible. Pending further objections, I take the above to show that delivering the right verdict in trumping cases is an adequacy condition on an account of causation.

2   Counterfactual Accounts of Causation

CACs, developed especially by Lewis, in their simplest form claim that: C causes E if and only if (i) C and E are actual, distinct events, and (ii) if C had not occurred, E would not have occurred.

Preemptions show that simple counterfactual dependence is not necessary for causation, because, in evaluating the counterfactual implications of C's not occurring, we hold the presence of the backup fixed, and so still get E. In response, defenders of CACs have refined the counterfactual-dependence relation. The leading extant refinements (Lewis's ancestral dependence, fragility, and quasi-dependence; Peter Menzies's continuous processes; Michael McDermott's minimal-counterfactual sufficiency; Murali Ramachandran's minimal-dependence sets)[16] all rely on failed intermediaries along the backup process or on would-be differences in the effect absent the main process to distinguish preempting causes from preempted backups. For this reason, none has the resources to distinguish trumping causes from trumped backups.

Ancestral dependence, quasi-dependence, continuous processes, and minimal-dependence sets all rely on failed intermediaries along the backup process to distinguish preempting causes from preempted backups. According to ancestral dependence (suggested by Lewis to transitivize simple counterfactual dependence and handle preemption cases in one swoop), C may cause E even though E does not counterfactually depend on C, as long as there is an event D (or some finite set of Ds) such that E counterfactually depends on D and D on C. Thus, where there are two gunmen C and C' but only C shoots, the death E does not counterfactually depend on either C or C', but does presumably depend on the bullet-flying D, which in turn depends on C. Ancestral dependence works only if there are failed intermediaries on the backup process prior to the effect (early), since these failures are what create counterfactual dependence of the effect on some post-failure intermediary D along the main process, by spoiling the dependency-breaking redundancy. For this reason, ancestral dependence miscounts the trumping cause as a noncause. There is no intermediary along the trumping process such that the effect depends on it, either because the causation is direct (no intermediaries), as in the wizards, or because the trumped process is fully intact, as with the white field that propagates all the way to the particle, and with the sergeant's order that remains with the corporal throughout the decision process, breaking the dependency of the effect on all intermediaries along the entire trumping process.

According to quasi-dependence (tentatively adopted by Lewis at the end of post-script E to "Causation"), C may cause E even though E does not counterfactually depend on C, as long as C and E are part of a process that is intrinsically such as typically to induce counterfactual dependence (this relation of counterfactual or quasi-dependence is then transitivized by taking the ancestral). Thus, where there are two gunmen C and C' but only C shoots, the C to E process will still be intrinsically such as typically to induce counterfactual dependence, because the presence of a backup gunman is presumably atypical. What about the C' to E process? The only reason I can see why this process (understood, for example, as the sequence of events $\langle C'$ armed and malevolent, E dead$\rangle$) is intrinsically not such as typically to induce counterfactual dependence is that there are failed requisite intermediaries along this process, such as a failure of C' to pull the trigger.[17] For this reason, quasi-dependence miscounts the trumped backup as a cause. If Merlin's spell is to count as a cause because the great majority of intrinsic duplicates of the sequence ⟨Merlin casts prince to frog, prince turns to frog⟩ exhibit counterfactual dependency, then Morgana's spell must count as a cause as well, since the great majority of intrinsic duplicates of ⟨Morgana casts prince to frog, prince turns to frog⟩ will exhibit just as much dependency, since in both cases we abstract away from the atypical presence of a rival spell caster; likewise for the field-process and soldier-process duplicates. Trumping cases show that the intuition that motivates quasi-dependence—namely, that causation is determined by the intrinsic character of events (plus the laws)—is hasty, since the laws may well be sensitive to extrinsic characteristics, such as which spell is earlier.

The continuous-process refinement (suggested by Menzies as a solution to "making it the hard way" preemption cases) requires that C and E be connected by a temporally continuous chain of counterfactual dependencies. Here, failed intermediaries function as discontinuities in the dependency chains from the backup. Without these discontinuities, the backup will spoil the final dependency of effect on the immediately prior event along the causal process. Thus, because the trumped backup runs continuously in the fields case, the final dependency of the particle's acceleration on the black source is spoiled by the continued propagation of the white field, and so the continuity requirement miscounts the trumping cause as a noncause. Worse, requiring temporal continuity rules out by brute stipulation the intuitive possibility of action-at-a-distance and so could not count Merlin's spell as a cause even if Morgana had not cast a spell at all.[18]

According to minimal-dependence sets (devised by Ramachandran), preempter C counts as a cause of E because the C-process involves only actual events, while backup C' is not a cause because the C'-process includes failed events. First, Ramachandran defines an M-set for E as a nonempty set of events S such that:

(i) E is not a member of S, (ii) if no members of S had occurred, E would not have occurred, and (iii) no proper subset of S meets (ii).

He then shows that M-sets will contain exactly one event, actual or not, from each process, preempted or not, leading to E, and concludes that C causes E if and only if:

(iv) C and E are actual events, (v) C is in an M-set for E, and (vi) there are no two M-sets for E which differ only in having one or more nonactual events in place of C.

The failed-intermediaries idea is implemented in (vi), since given that M-sets contain exactly one event from each process, C will be replaceable by a nonactual event (and thus not a cause) only if there is a nonactual event on its process. Ramachandran is fully explicit in his reliance on the failed-intermediaries idea:

It seems true in all genuine cases of causal pre-emption ... that the pre-empted processes do not run their full course.... For any pre-empted cause *x*, of an event, *y*, there will be at least one possible event ... which fails to occur in the actual circumstances *but which would have to occur in order for x to be a genuine cause of y*.... All genuine causes, on the other hand, *do* seem to run their full course; indeed, they presumably count as genuine precisely because they do so. (1997a, p. 273)

Thus, minimal-dependence sets miscounts the trumped backup as a cause, because it runs its full course. In the wizards case, {Merlin's spell, Morgana's spell} will be an *M*-set for the prince's metamorphosis, but there will be no nonactual event substitutable for Morgana's spell, since there is no nonactual event along the process from Morgana's spell to the effect; likewise for the fields and soldiers cases.

Thus, ancestral dependence, quasi-dependence, continuous processes, and minimal-dependence sets cannot distinguish trumper from trumped. It is important to see that this failure is due, not to the mere details of each refinement, but to the underlying assumption they share (call this the cutting assumption) that backup processes are such because they have failed intermediaries. Trumping preemptions show that the root idea of these refinements is inadequate.

Both fragility and minimal-counterfactual sufficiency add the strictest standards of event individuation to the failed-intermediaries idea. According to fragility (proposed though tentatively rejected by Lewis on grounds of spurious causation), the above ancestral-dependency analysis is to be implemented on the understanding that events have their times and manners of occurrence essentially.[19] Fragility-based approaches are intended to handle late preemption cases in which the failed intermediaries on the backup process occur at or after the time of the effect (since it then follows, assuming no simultaneous/backward causation, that had the backup been left to produce the effect, the effect would have been delayed) and are no help at all with trumping. In the wizards case, for instance, the prince's metamorphosis, absent Merlin's spell, would still take place at exactly midnight, and in precisely the same manner; the analogous point applies to the fields and soldiers cases. Thus, the fragility refinement miscounts the trumping cause as a noncause.

According to minimal-counterfactual sufficiency (due to McDermott 1995a), the root causal notion is of counterfactual sufficiency between strictly individuated events, where a set of actual events *C* is counterfactually sufficient for *E* if and only if:

There is no set of actual events *D*, where *E* is not a member of *D*, such that (if the members of *C* had all occurred and the members of *D* had all not occurred, then *E* would not have occurred).[20]

Now, *C* is minimally counterfactually sufficient for *E* if and only if:

(i) C is counterfactually sufficient for E, (ii) no proper subset of C is counterfactually sufficient for E, and (iii) there is no actual event D (distinct from E and the members of C) such that for some proper subset C' of C, $C' \cup \{D\}$ is counterfactually sufficient for E, and for some proper subset C'' of C, $C'' \cup \{\neg D\}$ is counterfactually sufficient for E.

McDermott equates direct causation with minimal-counterfactual sufficiency, and claims that, "a part of a minimal sufficient condition is always a cause" (1995a, p. 535). He denies the converse, and so supplements his account by defining processes via chains of minimally counterfactually sufficient conditions, relativizing causes to processes, and distinguishing between realizing the real as opposed to nominal essence of an event. I need not spell out these (considerable) complications here, since the trumped backup disproves the claim that a part of a minimally counterfactually sufficient condition is always a cause, and since these complications merely countenance more causes. Consider the set {Morgana's spell}. It is a sufficient condition, according to the strictly individuated counterfactual-based definition, since its occurrence by itself would still lead to the prince's becoming a frog exactly as and when he actually does. It is clearly minimal, since (i) it is sufficient, (ii) its only proper subset, { }, is not sufficient for the prince's becoming a frog, and (iii) there is no actual event D such that both { } $\cup \{D\}$ as well as { } $\cup \{\neg D\}$ are sufficient for the prince's becoming a frog (in particular Merlin's spell fails the latter). But Morgana's spell, despite being part of a minimally counterfactually sufficient condition, is not a cause of the prince's becoming a frog.[21]

Thus fragility and minimal counterfactual sufficiency cannot distinguish trumper from trumped. This failure is due to the underlying assumption they share (call this the *precision assumption*), namely that backup processes are such that had they run to completion the effect would have been somewhat different in time or manner. Trumping preemptions show that the root idea of these refinements is inadequate.

In conclusion, extant CACs still cannot handle preemptive causation. Trumping preemptions show that the failed intermediary and would-be differences strategies that extant CACs use are inadequate as general solutions to the preemption problem.[22] Of course there may yet be some new strategy for CACs which will prove adequate, but at this point the prospects look dark.

Notes

1. Compare D. H. Mellor (1995, pp. 58–66), who argues for the viability of indeterministic causation as fitting "the connotations of causation."

2. The main extant accounts of explanation are (a) deductive, (b) causal, and (c) pragmatic accounts. While (b) and (c) are not helpful here, because with regard to (b) the cause of the prince's metamorphosis

is currently at issue, and with regard to (c) these accounts yield (by design) no objective fact, account (a) proves helpful. I take it that most will concede that, whether or not deductive accounts are ultimately viable, they at least provide reasonable codifications of our intuitions in most cases.

3. There are tricks around this, such as by filling in (2) with some sort of disjunction, such as: either Morgana's spell was first that day, or it was not but what was first agreed with Morgana's in the enchantment it called for. But these are just the tricks which a deductive account of explanation must rule out as implausible anyway, and so in using the deductive account to justify our intuitions, we may assume (though we may not even be able to say how) such tricks are excluded.

4. This follows on such leading accounts of counterfactual implication as David Lewis's in his (1973b). According to Lewis, we evaluate the implications of the counterfactual supposition that Merlin had cast a spell to turn the prince into a goat by postulating a minimal "divergence miracle" on which Merlin says "Presto, prince to goat!" instead of "Presto, prince to frog!" while holding fixed the course of history up to Merlin's conjuring (so holding fixed the absence of any prior or contemporaneous spells that day) as well as the laws (so presumably keeping the magic laws intact) to the extent compossible with the miracle; all this results in Merlin's casting the first spell that day to turn the prince into a goat, where the first spells cast match midnight enchantments, and so all this results in the prince's becoming a goat that midnight.

5. In his 1973a. Since I shall show that Lewis's counterfactual account of causation fails to accommodate this variational type of counterfactual dependence in trumping cases, one way to read this result is that Lewis's account of causation as counterfactual dependence between event occurrences fails to capture his own intuitions about the general relation between counterfactual variation and causation.

6. See Mellor (1988), p. 230.

7. The main versions of decision theory are (a) evidential, and (b) causal (turning on whether "the probability of E given C" is interpreted as (a) $p(EC)/p(C)$, or (b) $p(C$ will cause E)). While (b) is not helpful since whether C causes E is currently at issue, (a) proves helpful, and since (a) and (b) agree on non-Newcomb cases, (a) can be used neutrally in the case at hand. (See Harper and Skyrms, eds., 1988.) The point of introducing agent probabilities is to free evidentialism from the spurious correlations of Newcomb cases. For further discussion, see Menzies and Price (1993).

8. In a sense, Morgana's spell is evidence for the prince's becoming a frog, since given certain (plausible) prior probability distributions, one may assign a greater subjective probability to the prince's becoming a frog given Morgana's spell. But this is not a sense of "evidence" relevant here, since in this sense, given certain prior probability distributions, anything may count as evidence for anything (in particular the increased probability that the conditionalizer may assign prince-to-frog given Morgana's spell is exactly parallel to the increased probability assignable victim's death given backup shooter's presence; Morgana's spell carries exactly as much and as little evidence of the effect as any preempted process). The sense of "evidence" relevant here, which typically holds between cause and effect, which holds between Merlin's spell and the prince's becoming a frog, and fails between Morgana's spell and the prince's becoming a frog, is evidence with *epistemic value*: that which may confer knowledge.

9. See Dretske (1977a); Tooley (1987); Armstrong (1983).

10. See Carroll (1994); and Maudlin (forthcoming).

11. See Lewis (1973b); also Earman (1984).

12. We could, of course, be more precise, or employ different vocabulary, but no added precision or shift of (natural) vocabulary should alter the greater simplicity of (a) as compared to (b)–(d). Of course, sufficiently "gruesome" predicates would alter this verdict, but the MRL account of lawhood, which I am presently assuming, is viable only to the extent that our similarity judgments, based in part on our vocabulary, have objective bite; so for purposes of showing that the wizards laws beg no questions against supervenientists like Lewis, we may assume what the MRL advocate must.

13. Perhaps some will balk at the laws invoked, not because of worries about supervenience, but because of disbelief in the possibility of laws projecting extrinsic properties, such as being first cast on a given day. I see no grounds for such disbelief (moreover none of the leading accounts of lawhood provides grounds for such disbelief). Further, I take worlds such as the wizards world, in which there is perfect covariance between events with the extrinsic property of being-the-first-spell-cast-on-day-x and events of midnight

enchantments, and in which there may well be no such covariance between events merely-intrinsically-described and midnight enchantments, to show exactly why such disbelief is unwarranted.

14. This does not mean that white fields in general are always trumped: there may be times when no black fields exist, or the black fields might have finite spatial extent, or the black fields might trump only insofar as they exceed a certain threshold. Nor does it mean that this particular white field is completely epi-phenomenal: it might trump on other types of particles, or trigger a white flag in the distance, or have any number of other effects as long as they are not manifest on this particle. More interestingly, there might be a functional law on which the ratio of darker field to lighter field influences cycles through the epochs, with the relevant experiments done in a 1:0 epoch. This raises the empirically open possibility that our world is such a world (with respect to, say, types of electromagnetic force): our epoch just happens to be 1:1, so we do not notice.

15. This particular case is a variant of one due to Bas van Fraassen, though the discovery of this type of case is Ned Hall's. A variant of one of Hall's cases illustrates just how common these cases are: the Bradys are deciding where to vacation, and Cindy and Bobby both plead "Hawaii!" Since Ma and Pa always do what Cindy wants, the Bradys decide on Hawaii. Trumping is everywhere.

16. These accounts are offered, respectively, in Lewis (1973a) and (1986b); Menzies (1989a); McDermott (1995a); Ramachandran (1997a).

17. Jonardon Ganeri, Paul Noordhof, and Ramachandran come to the same understanding of quasi-dependence in their (1996), p. 220.

18. Menzies (1996) has recently moved to a theoretical definition of causation on which causation is that intrinsic relation between actual, distinct events which typically induces counterfactual dependence be-tween them. This definition is still troubled by trumping, since it takes as platitudinous that causation is an intrinsic-to-its-pairs relation between events. Take different-day duplicates of the pair ⟨Merlin's spell, prince's metamorphosis⟩. Whether a given duplicate is causal will depend, inter alia, on whether there was a Morgana spell at 9:00 A.M. Thus, trumping refutes Menzies's central assertion that, "The distinc-tive mark of our intuitive concept of causation ... is that it takes causal relations to be determined by the natural properties of the relata and the natural relations holding between them, taken in isolation from everything else happening in the world" (ibid., p. 100).

19. We may distinguish temporal fragility from fragility of manner, and fragility of effects from fragility of events generally. All Lewis needs (for his reply to *late* preemption) is the temporal fragility of effects. In fact, all that is needed is the stipulation that the effect not be delayed, as L. A. Paul has shown (1998b). Nothing here will turn on the details of how the fragility proposal is implemented.

20. This is a questionable use of counterfactuals. It is difficult enough to say what would happen on the counterfactual supposition that one event not occur, and almost completely indeterminate what would happen had most of the rest of the world other than C and E not occurred: Spacetime might simply col-lapse. And the strict individuation of events which McDermott adds only makes things worse, because it tightens the standards for saying that E still occurs.

21. Adding the rest of McDermott's machinery: the set P of all events involved in the process is {Morga-na's spell, the prince becoming a frog}, the set Pi of intermediate events is { }, and the set Pc of primary causal factors is {Morgana's spell}. Now, it is clear that Morgana's spell is counterfactually sufficient rel-ative to P, and minimally so, and so vis-à-vis realizing the nominal essence of E, which is just the prince's becoming a frog. The added machinery will not help with the fields or soldiers, either. In the fields case (the analogous points will hold for the soldiers), the process is something like {the insertion of the white source, the propagation of the white field, the white field hitting the particle, the particle accelerating along a curved trajectory}. The set Pc is {the insertion of the white source}. Now, all the intermediaries in the process are held fixed, and so the insertion of the white source now counts as counterfactually sufficient relative to P, and minimally so, and so vis-à-vis the nominalization "the particle's accelerating along a curved trajectory," and thus the presence of the white source is miscounted as a cause.

22. One solution to trumping is to analyze causation via nomic subsumption rather than counterfactual dependence, since Merlin's spell is subsumed under the magic law while Morgana's is not (likewise for the fields, and likewise presumably for the soldiers given that the corporal's decision module works as described). But this is a whole other story.

3 Causation as Influence

David Lewis

1 Lecture I

My second paper in my first philosophy course defended a counterfactual analysis of causation. I've been at it, off and on, ever since. But it's obvious that the simplest counterfactual analysis breaks down in cases of redundant causation, wherefore we need extra bells and whistles. I've changed my mind once more about how those bells and whistles ought to work.

This paper mostly presents the latest lessons I've learned from my students. Under the customs of the natural sciences, it should have been a joint paper, the coauthors being (in alphabetical order) John Collins, Ned Hall, myself, L. A. Paul, and Jonathan Schaffer. But under the customs of philosophy, a paper is expected to be not only a report of discoveries, but also a manifesto; and, happily, the five of us have by no means agreed upon a common party line. So, while I'm much more than usually indebted to the work of Collins, Hall, Paul, and Schaffer, they cannot be held responsible for the position I have reached.

1.1 Why Seek a Counterfactual Analysis?

The best reason to persist in trying to make a counterfactual analysis of causation work is that the difficulties that confront rival approaches seem even more daunting.

It is not a foregone conclusion that causation requires analysis at all. Is there, perhaps, an unanalyzable relation of singular causation, which we know by perceptual acquaintance, and which we are therefore in a position to refer to and think about? It might indeed turn out that this relation can be identified with some relation already familiar to us either from physics or from metaphysical speculation; but if so, that identification would be a physical or metaphysical hypothesis, not a matter for a priori conceptual analysis.[1]

Hume, of course, taught that we never perceive causation, but only repeated succession. But it's famously difficult to draw the line between what's true according to perceptual experience all by itself and what's true according to a system of beliefs shaped partly by perceptual experience and partly by previous beliefs. The boot comes forward and touches the ball, and straightway the ball flies off through the goalposts. Do I see that the one thing causes the other? Or do I infer it from what I do see, together with my background knowledge about the ways of the world? I don't

Originally published in a special issue of the *Journal of Philosophy* (April 2000). Minor revisions have been made for consistency.

know, and I don't know how to find out. So I'm in no position to deny that in such a case I'm perceptually acquainted with an instance of a causal relation; and thereby acquainted as well with the relation that is instantiated.[2]

I'm acquainted with *a* causal relation—not with *the* causal relation. Causal relations are many and various, and no amount of watching the footy will acquaint me with all the causal relations there are, let alone all the causal relations there might have been. And yet I seem to have picked up a *general* concept of causation, applicable to all different kinds of causation, and applicable even to kinds of causation never found in our own world. That's the real problem, even if I concede *pace* Hume that I sometimes perceive causation.

If ever I perceive causation, I perceive it when I watch the footy; or, to take the customary example, if I watch the motions of billiard balls. But the causal mechanism whereby a dinner too low in carbohydrate causes low blood sugar is utterly different. The causal mechanism whereby our former congressman helped cause his own defeat by literally singing the praises of Kenneth Starr is different again. And so on, and so forth; not quite ad infinitum if we limit ourselves to actuality. But we should not limit ourselves to actuality, given that we can perfectly well understand fantasies, or theologies, in which causation works by magical mechanisms entirely alien to the world of our acquaintance. We are not perceptually acquainted with each and every one of all these different actual and possible causal relations. If there is a single causal relation, either it is a far from natural relation, a gruesomely disjunctive miscellany, and so not the sort of relation we can become acquainted with by being acquainted with some few of its disjuncts; or else the many disjuncts have something in common. I think conceptual analysis is required to reveal what it is that all the actual and possible varieties of causation have in common.

A parallel objection applies to the "Canberra plan" for causation. The plan is that we first elicit, Meno-fashion, the folk theory of causation that we all implicitly hold. That done, we can define causation as whatever it is that comes closest, and close enough, to occupying the role specified by our folk-theoretical platitudes. We require conceptual analysis of the job description, so to speak; but not of the actual occupant of the role specified thereby.[3,4] We leave it open that the role may be occupied by different relations in different possible worlds, thereby explaining how our concept of causation applies to causation by possible mechanisms alien to actuality. But the problem of the many diverse actual causal mechanisms, or more generally of many diverse mechanisms coexisting in any one world, is still with us. If causation is, or might be, wildly disjunctive, we need to know what unifies the disjunction. For one thing the folk platitudes tell us is that causation is one thing, common to the many causal mechanisms.

The problem becomes especially acute when we remember to cover not only causation of positive events by positive events, but also causation by absences, causation of absences, and causation via absences as intermediate steps. The most fundamental problem is that absences are unsuitable relata for any sort of causal relation, by reason of their nonexistence. This is everyone's problem. It is not to be dodged by saying that causation involving absences is really "causation*," a different thing from genuine causation—call it what you will, it still needs to be part of the story. It is my problem too, and I shall return to it; but in the meantime, let the missing relata objection join the miscellany objection as reasons to think that acquaintance with "the" causal relation, or characterization of "it" as the occupant of a role, are not workable rivals to a conceptual analysis of causation.

If we are convinced of that, one rival to the counterfactual analysis remains standing. That is the analysis that says, roughly, that a cause is a member of a set of conditions jointly sufficient, given the laws of nature, for the effect (or perhaps for a certain objective probability thereof). (See White 1965, pp. 56–104; and Mackie 1965.) This deductive-nomological analysis is descended from Hume's constant conjunction theory, just as our counterfactual analysis is descended from Hume's offhand remark that "if the first object had not been, the second never had existed."[5]

However, we don't want to count C as a cause of E just because C belongs to some sufficient set or other for E: A sufficient set remains sufficient if we add irrelevant rubbish, and C might be exactly that. C should belong to a *minimal* sufficient set, and that is not easy to define. It won't work just to say that no condition in the set may be deleted without rendering the remainder insufficient: that can be circumvented by mingling relevant and irrelevant information in such a way that each item in the set contains some of each. I might suggest appealing to a counterfactual: we want our sufficient set to consist of items without which the effect would not have occurred. (That doesn't work as it stands, but it's at least a step in the right direction.) But now we have departed from the deductive-nomological analysis in the direction of a counterfactual analysis.

Another difficulty is that it can perfectly well happen that an effect is a member of a minimal jointly sufficient set for its cause; or that one effect of a common cause is a member of a minimal jointly sufficient set for another. The falling barometer supposedly causes the low pressure; or the falling barometer supposedly causes the storm. Even if we were willing to declare a priori that no cause ever precedes its effect, that would be no solution. The falling barometer *does* precede the storm. I know of no solution to these familiar difficulties within the confines of a purely deductive-nomological analysis of causation.

The final rivals to a satisfactory counterfactual analysis of causation are the *un*satisfactory counterfactual analyses. Long, long ago, I thought it would suffice to say that event C is a cause of event E iff E depends counterfactually on C; iff, if C had not occurred, E would not have occurred. But this turns out to need qualifications before we have even a sufficient condition for causation.

First. We need the right kind of relata. C and E must be distinct events—and distinct not only in the sense of nonidentity but also in the sense of nonoverlap and nonimplication. It won't do to say that my speaking this sentence causes my speaking this sentence; or that my speaking the whole of it causes my speaking the first half of it, or vice versa; or that my speaking it causes my speaking it loudly, or vice versa. Nor should C and E be specified in an overly extrinsic way; it won't do to say that events a third of a century ago caused me to speak this sentence in the place where once I was a student. (Though those events did cause my speaking simpliciter.) See Kim (1973b) and Lewis (1986d).

Second. We need the right kind of counterfactual conditionals. Why can't we say, given the laws connecting barometer readings and air pressure, that if the barometer hadn't fallen, that would have been because the pressure wasn't low? Why can't we then conclude that if the barometer hadn't fallen, there wouldn't have been a storm? Yet if we say such things, why doesn't our counterfactual analysis fail in just the same way that the deductive-nomological analysis did?—I agree that we're within our linguistic rights to assert these backtracking, or back-and-then-forward, counterfactuals. But they are out of place in the context of establishing causal connections. Here the much-bemoaned flexibility of counterfactual conditionals is our friend. When we imagine Caesar in command in Korea, we have a choice: We can hold fixed Caesar's military knowledge, or we can hold fixed the weaponry of the Korean war. Likewise when we imagine the barometer not falling, we have a choice: we can hold fixed the previous history, or we can hold fixed the lawful connections between that history and what the barometer does. For purposes of analyzing causation, our policy in all such cases must be to prefer the first choice to the second. If need be, we hold history fixed even at the price of a miracle (see my 1979a).

Now I think our oversimple counterfactual analysis succeeds in characterizing one kind of causation. But other kinds are omitted. We have a sufficient, but not a necessary, condition for causation.

For one thing, we usually think that causation is transitive: if C causes D, which in turn causes E, it follows that C causes E. That is why we can establish causal connections by tracing causal chains. But we have no guarantee that the relation of counterfactual dependence will be invariably transitive. (Shortly we shall see how its transitivity can fail.) So we need to provide for causation not only by direct dependence, but by chains of stepwise dependence. We can do so by defining causation as the ancestral of dependence (see my 1986b).

But that still does not suffice to capture all cases of causation. We have at least three items of unfinished business. Probabilistic causation, preemptive causation, and causation by, or of, absences are not yet fully covered. Here I shall mostly be discussing the second and third topics.

1.2 Probabilistic Causation

I have little to say about probabilistic causation. Not because I don't believe in it: More likely than not, our world is so thoroughly indeterministic that most or all of the causation that actually takes place is probabilistic. Whether our world is governed by indeterministic laws is settled neither by the Moorean fact that we make free choices nor by a priori principles of sufficient reason. Rather, it is a contingent question of theoretical physics. If the best explanation of quantum phenomena requires spontaneous collapses of the wave function, then we should believe in widespread indeterminism. If Bohmian mechanics is a better explanation, we should believe that our world is deterministic after all. Either way, there is plenty of causation in the world. Those who believe in widespread indeterminism still ascribe causal connections. It would be preposterous to deny that the connections they ascribe deserve the name they are given. Therefore chancy events can be caused. They can be caused even when their causes do not make them inevitable, and do not even make them highly probable. They can be caused even when they have some slight chance of occurring spontaneously.

The probabilistic counterpart of the simplest sort of counterfactual dependence is, roughly, probability-raising. C occurs, E has a certain chance (objective single-case probability) of occurring, and as it happens E does occur; but without C, E's chance would have been less. Likewise, the more complicated patterns of counterfactual dependence that I shall be discussing later also come in probabilistic versions.

I used to think (substantial) probability-raising could simply take the place of all-or-nothing counterfactual dependence in an analysis of causation (see my 1986b, pp. 175–180). But there is a problem: Not all probability-raising counts. One terrorist places an unreliable bomb—a genuinely indeterministic device—on Flight 13; another terrorist places an unreliable bomb on Flight 17. As it happens, the bomb on Flight 13 goes off and the bomb on Flight 17 doesn't. The *Age* runs a headline: "Airline bomb disaster." The headline would have been just the same if it had been the bomb on Flight 17 that went off, or if it had been both. So the bomb on Flight 17 raised the probability of the headline, but certainly didn't cause it. We want to say that the raising that counts is the raising of the probability of the causal chain of events and absences whereby the effect was actually caused. Raising the probability of some unactualized alternative causal chain leading to the same effect doesn't count. But it would be circular to say it that way within an analysis of causation. I hope there is some noncircular way to say much the same thing, but I have none to offer.[6]

That said, let us set aside the probabilistic case. The proper treatment of causation in a deterministic world will give us difficulties enough. Those same difficulties would reappear for causation under indeterminism, and I hope the same solutions would apply.

1.3 Preemption Revisited

It sometimes happens that two separate potential causes for a certain effect are both present; and either one by itself would have been followed by the effect (or at least by a raised probability thereof); and so the effect depends on neither. Call any such situation a case of *redundant causation*. (For short: *redundancy*.) Some cases of redundancy are symmetrical: Both candidates have an equal claim to be called causes of the effect. Nothing, either obvious or hidden, breaks the tie between them. It may be unclear whether we ought to say that each is a cause or whether we ought to say that neither is a cause (in which case we can still say that the combination of the two is a cause). But anyway it is out of the question to say that one is a cause and the other isn't. Because it's unclear what we want to say, these symmetrical cases are not good test cases for proposed analyses of causation. Set them aside.

Other cases are asymmetrical. It's very clear what we want to say: One of the two potential causes did cause the effect, the other one didn't. Call the one that did the causing a *preempting* cause of the effect. Call the other one a *preempted* alternative, or *backup*.

When our opinions are clear, it's incumbent on an analysis of causation to get them right. This turns out to be a severe test. The simplest sort of deductive-nomological analysis flunks: The preempted alternative is a member of a minimal jointly sufficient set for the effect, yet it is not a cause. The simplest sort of counterfactual analysis likewise flunks: The preempting cause is not a condition without which the effect would have been absent, yet it is a cause. Both these attempts fail because they treat the preempting cause and its preempted alternative alike, whereas we know very well that one is a cause and the other is not. A correct analysis will need to discern the source of the difference.

1.4 Trumping

I used to think that all cases of preemption were cases of *cutting*: cases in which, first, there is a completed causal chain (often, but not necessarily, spatiotemporally continuous) running from the preempting cause all the way to the effect; but, second, something cuts short the potential alternative causal chain that would, in the absence of the preempting cause, have run from the preempted alternative to the effect.[7] Some think so still, but I have learned better.[8]

The Sergeant and the Major are shouting orders at the soldiers. The soldiers know that in case of conflict, they must obey the superior officer. But, as it happens, there is no conflict. Sergeant and Major simultaneously shout "Advance!"; the soldiers hear them both; the soldiers advance. Their advancing is redundantly caused: If the Sergeant had shouted "Advance!" and the Major had been silent, or if the Major had shouted "Advance!" and the Sergeant had been silent, the soldiers would still have advanced. But the redundancy is asymmetrical: Since the soldiers obey the superior officer, they advance because the Major orders them to, not because the Sergeant does. The Major preempts the Sergeant in causing them to advance. The Major *trumps* the Sergeant.

We can speculate that this might be a case of cutting. Maybe when a soldier hears the Major giving orders, this places a block somewhere in his brain, so that the signal coming from the Sergeant gets stopped before it gets as far as it would have done if the Major had been silent and the Sergeant had been obeyed. Maybe so. Or maybe not. We don't know one way or the other. It is epistemically possible, and hence it is possible simpliciter, that this is a case of preemption without cutting.

If we forsake everyday examples, we become free to settle by stipulation that we have no cutting. We can stipulate, for instance, that the causal process in question works by action at a distance. Nothing goes missing when the process is preempted, because ex hypothesi there are no intermediate events to go missing. Here is such an example. Suppose the laws of magic state that what will happen at midnight must match the first spell cast on the previous day. The first spell of the day, as it happens, is Merlin's prince-to-frog spell in the morning. Morgana casts another prince-to-frog spell in the evening. At midnight the prince turns into a frog. Either spell would have done the job, had it been the only spell of the day; but Merlin's spell was first, so it was his spell that caused the transmogrification. Merlin's spell trumped Morgana's. Merlin's spell was a preempting cause, Morgana's was the preempted backup. But we stipulate also that the causal process from spell to transmogrification has no intermediate steps.[9]

1.5 Commonplace Preemption

Trumping shows that preemption does not require the cutting of a causal chain. Nevertheless, the most familiar variety of preemption does work by cutting. The causal chain from the preempting cause gets in first: it runs to completion, and the effect happens, while the chain from the preempted alternative is still on its way. The preempted chain is cut. The effect itself is what prevents its final steps.

Billy and Suzy throw rocks at a bottle. Suzy throws first, or maybe she throws harder. Her rock arrives first. The bottle shatters. When Billy's rock gets to where the bottle used to be, there is nothing there but flying shards of glass. Without Suzy's throw, the impact of Billy's rock on the intact bottle would have been one of the final steps in the causal chain from Billy's throw to the shattering of the bottle. But, thanks to Suzy's preempting throw, that impact never happens.

I used to call such cases as this "late preemption." (In hindsight, "late cutting" would have been a better name.) I meant to contrast them with "early preemption": easy cases in which we have, if not direct counterfactual dependence of the effect itself on the preempting cause, at least stepwise dependence. The effect depends on some intermediate event, which in turn depends upon the preempting cause. (Or we may have stepwise dependence through a longer chain of intermediates.) These are cases in which dependence is intransitive, but we get the right answer by defining causation as the ancestral of dependence.

There is a small industry devoted to solving the preemption problem under the presupposed premise that preemption always works by cutting (see, e.g., Ramachandran 1997a). However well such solutions may (or may not) work in the cases they were made for, they are not general solutions because they do not deal with trumping. We may have to rest content with a patchwork of solutions, different ones for different cases, but let us hope for something more ambitious.

1.6 Quasi-dependence Rejected

I used to think that late preemption (and maybe early preemption as well) could be handled by appealing to the intuitive idea that causation is an intrinsic relation between events[10] (except insofar as being subject to such-and-such laws of nature is an extrinsic matter, as I believe it to be). Take another case, actual or possible, which is intrinsically just like the case of Suzy throwing her rock at the bottle (and which occurs under the same laws), but in which Billy and his rock are entirely absent. In this comparison case, we have a causal chain from Suzy's throw to the shattering which *does* exhibit counterfactual dependence and which is an intrinsic duplicate of the actual chain from Suzy's throw with Billy present. (Near enough. Doubtless the presence of Billy and his rock makes some tiny difference to the gravitational force on Suzy's rock, and therefore some negligible difference to that rock's trajectory.) I thought: If being a causal chain is an intrinsic matter, then both or neither of the two chains that are intrinsic duplicates (and occur under the same laws) must be causal; but the comparison chain, which exhibits dependence, surely is a causal chain; so the actual chain, even though thanks to Billy it does not exhibit dependence, must be a causal chain too. I said that the actual chain exhibited *quasi-dependence*: it qualified as causal by courtesy, in virtue of its intrinsic resemblance to the causal chain in the comparison case.

Quasi-dependence was a bad idea, for five reasons.

First. Imagine that Suzy's and Billy's rock-throwing takes place in a world with laws just a little different from what we take to be the laws of our actual world: laws under which flying objects sometimes make little random jumps. Imagine also that Suzy's rock is an intrinsic duplicate of Billy's. Now consider the chain of events consisting of Billy's throw, the flight of Billy's rock up to but not including the time when it reaches the place where the bottle used to be, plus the impact of Suzy's duplicate rock on the bottle and the shattering of the bottle. Compare this chain with another chain of events in which Suzy is absent, Billy throws, his rock takes a little jump just before impact, it hits the bottle, and the bottle shatters. The original chain and the comparison chain are intrinsic duplicates (or near enough) under the same laws. The comparison chain exhibits counterfactual dependence. But now we're forced to conclude that the shattering quasi-depends on *Billy's* throw! (As well as on Suzy's.) And that's the wrong answer: just as in the original case, Billy's throw is not a cause of the shattering, but rather a preempted alternative.[11]

Second. The intrinsic character of causation is, at best, a parochial feature of our own possible world. It does not apply, for instance, to an occasionalist world in which God is a third party to all causal relationships whatever between natural events. And yet occasionalism certainly seems to be a genuine possibility. So if we aim at conceptual analysis, not just a contingent characterization of the causal connections that are found in this world of ours, we cannot assume a priori that causation is an intrinsic matter.

Third. Quasi-dependence gives the wrong answer in cases of trumping preemption. The trumped causal chain runs to completion; therefore it is an intrinsic duplicate (near enough) of an *un*trumped causal chain in a comparison case (under the same laws) which exhibits counterfactual dependence. This reinforces our previous conclusion that quasi-dependence fails in some other possible worlds, for instance the world in which Merlin's spell trumps Morgana's. But worse, it may mean that the intrinsic character of causation is an overhasty generalization even about the causation that happens in our own world. It may be, for all we know, that our case of the soldiers obeying the Major is a trumping case that actually happens.

Fourth. There is another kind of causal connection to which the intuition that causation is an intrinsic matter does not apply. This is *double prevention*: a cause prevents something which, had it not been prevented, would have prevented the

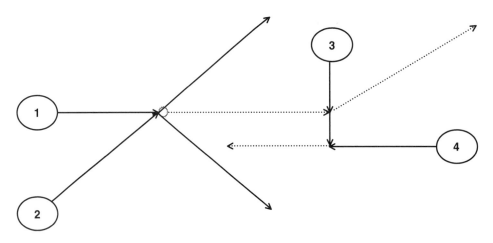

Figure 3.1

effect. The collision between billiard balls 1 and 2 prevents ball 1 from continuing on its way and hitting ball 3 (fig. 3.1). The collision of 1 and 3, had it occurred, would have prevented the subsequent collision of balls 3 and 4. But since in fact the collision of 1 and 3 was prevented, the collision of 3 and 4 was *un*prevented. That is how the collision of 1 and 2 causes the collision of 3 and 4. It's a straightforward case of counterfactual dependence: Without the collision of 1 and 2, the collision of 3 and 4 would not have occurred. But notice that this counterfactual dependence is an extrinsic matter. Had there been some other obstruction that would have stopped ball 1 from hitting ball 3, the collision of 3 and 4 would not have depended on the collision of 1 and 2. So even in this very ordinary thisworldly case, the causal connection is extrinsic.

Two more examples. Michael McDermott's: A crazed American President is about to launch a nuclear attack on Russia; that attack would have provoked a counterstrike, which would have prevented Joe Blow from eating breakfast the following day. Luckily, the President's assistant intervenes to stop the attack. Joe Blow's breakfast depends counterfactually upon that intervention. But the dependence is an extrinsic matter: Had Russia been uninhabited or unarmed, there would have been no such dependence (McDermott 1995a).

Ned Hall's: Billy, the pilot of the escort fighter, shoots down the interceptor that would otherwise have shot down the bomber. Therefore the successful bombing of the target depends counterfactually on Billy's action. But again the dependence is extrinsic. If the interceptor had been about to receive a radio order to return to base without attacking the bomber, then the successful bombing would not have depended on Billy's action.[12]

Fifth. Besides the overhasty intuition of the intrinsic character of causation, there is another presupposition of the method of quasi-dependence that also breaks down in cases of double prevention. That is the presupposition that we have a chain of events that runs from the preempting cause to the effect. We need this chain of events so that we can say what chain of events in the comparison case is its intrinsic duplicate. But when we have causation by double prevention, there is often no continuous chain of events running from cause to effect. Between the collision of balls 1 and 2 and the collision of balls 3 and 4, or between the intervention by the President's assistant and Joe Blow's breakfast, or between the shooting down of the interceptor and the bombing of the target, nothing much happens. What matters, of course, is what *doesn't* happen. Sometimes maybe we can assign definite locations to the prevented intermediates, and thereby locate a chain of events *and absences*. Sometimes not. If a preempting cause happens to work by double prevention—and, once we watch for them, cases of double prevention turn out to be very common—and if we cannot assign any definite location to the relevant absences, there is no saying what the intrinsic character of the comparison chain is required to match.

Put another way, the method of quasi-dependence breaks down when we have causation at a distance; and causation at a distance, rather than being the far-fetched possibility we might have thought it was, turns out to be a feature of commonplace cases of double prevention. What *is* far-fetched—though it may nevertheless turn out to be the truth about the collapse of spatially spread-out wave functions—is *action* at a distance; and that is only one variety of causation at a distance.[13,14] If, for instance, one body exerted a force on a distant body without any field or any particle going from one to the other, *that* would be action at a distance. Our billiard-table example of double prevention, however, exhibits quite a different kind of causation at a distance.

1.7 Fragility Corrected

There is an obvious solution to cases of late preemption. Doubtless you have been waiting impatiently for it. Without Suzy's preempting rock, the bottle would still have shattered, thanks to Billy's preempted rock. But this would have been a *different* shattering. It would, for instance, have happened a little later. The effect that actually occurred *did* depend on Suzy's throw. It did not likewise depend on Billy's. Sometimes this solution is just right, and nothing more need be said. Suppose it were alleged that since we are all mortal, there is no such thing as a cause of death. Without the hanging that allegedly caused Ned Kelly's death, for instance, he would sooner or later have died anyway. Yes. But he would have died a different death. The event which actually was Kelly's death would never have occurred.

The case of Suzy's preempting throw is different, however. It's not just that without it the bottle would have shattered somehow, sooner or later. Without it, the bottle would have shattered at very nearly the same time that it actually did shatter, in very nearly the same way that it actually did. Yet we're usually quite happy to say that an event might have been slightly delayed, and that it might have differed somewhat in this or that one of its contingent aspects. I recently postponed a seminar talk from October to December, doubtless making quite a lot of difference to the course of the discussion. But I postponed it instead of canceling it because I wanted *that very event* to take place.

So if we say that the shattering of the bottle was caused by Suzy's throw, because without it that very shattering would not have occurred, we are evoking uncommonly stringent conditions of occurrence for that event. We are thinking that it would take only a very slight difference to destroy that event altogether, and put a different substitute event in its place. We are supposing the shattering to be modally *fragile*. This is not something we would normally suppose. We have no business first saying as usual that the very same event might have been significantly delayed and changed, and then turning around and saying that it is caused by an event without which it would have been ever so slightly delayed and changed, and then saying that this is because it takes only a very slight delay or change to turn it into a different event altogether.

How much delay or change (or hastening) *do* we think it takes to replace an event by an altogether different event, and not just by a different version of the same event? An urgent question, if we want to analyze causation in terms of the dependence of whether one event occurs on whether another event occurs. Yet once we attend to the question, we surely see that it has no determinate answer. We just haven't made up our minds; and if we speak in a way that presupposes sometimes one answer and sometimes another, we are entirely within our linguistic rights. This is itself a big problem for a counterfactual analysis of causation, quite apart from the problem of preemption.[15]

At least, it is a problem so long as we focus on whether–whether counterfactual dependence. But there are other kinds of dependence. There is, for instance, when-on-whether dependence: When one event occurs depends counterfactually on whether another event occurs. And that is only the beginning. But even this beginning is enough to rehabilitate the obvious solution to late preemption, at least in very many commonplace cases. Let us by all means agree that Suzy's throw caused the shattering of the bottle because, without her throw, the shattering would have been slightly delayed. But let us not go on to say that if it had been slightly delayed, that would have turned it into a different event altogether. Let us rather say that Suzy's throw caused the shattering of the bottle in virtue of when-on-whether dependence. When the shattering occurred depended on Suzy's throw. Without Suzy's throw, it would not have occurred exactly when it actually did occur.

L. A. Paul has proposed an emended analysis of causal dependence: event E depends causally on a distinct actual event C if and only if "if C had not occurred, then E would not have occurred at all *or would have occurred later than the time that it actually did occur*" (Paul 1998b).[16] (Causation itself is the ancestral: C causes E iff there is a chain of such dependencies running from C to E.) This proposal does not abandon the strategy of fragility, but corrects it. Instead of supposing that the event itself is fragile—which would fly in the face of much of our ordinary talk—we instead take a tailor-made fragile proposition about that event and its time. The negation of that fragile proposition is the consequent of our causal counterfactual. Now we get the right answer to commonplace cases of late preemption. Suzy's throw hastens the shattering, Billy's doesn't. So Suzy's throw causes the shattering, Billy's doesn't.

If we stopped here, we would be building into our analysis an asymmetry between hasteners and delayers. We would be saying that an event without which the same effect would have happened later is a cause, whereas an event without which the same effect would have happened earlier is not.[17] For that reason, among others, we should not stop here. We should admit delayers as causes, even when the delayed event is the very same event that would otherwise have happened earlier—or at least, to acknowledge our indecision about such questions, not clearly *not* the same event.

We're often ambivalent about the status of delayers. Perhaps that is because a delayer often works by double prevention. It causes a later version of the event by preventing an earlier version, which, had it happened, would have prevented the later version. Then if we ask whether the delayer prevented the event or caused it, and we overlook the possibility that it might have done both, we have to say "prevented" (see Mackie 1992). To restore symmetry between hastening and delaying, we need only replace the words "or would have occurred later than the time that it actually did occur" by the words "or would have occurred at a time different from the time that it actually did occur." I favor this further emendation. (As does Paul.) But I think we should go further still. What's so special about time? When we thought that without the actual causes of his death, Ned Kelly would have died a different death, we were thinking not just that he would have died at a different time, but also that he would have died in a different manner. According to the uncorrected strategy of fragility, which supposes that events have very stringent conditions of occurrence, a difference either of time or of manner would suffice to turn the effect into a numerically different event. And if, imitating Paul's correction, we relocate the fragility not in the event itself but rather in a tailor-made proposition about that event, that will be a proposition about whether and when and how the effect occurs. We could further emend our analysis to require dependence of whether and when and how upon whether: Without C, E would not have occurred at all, or would have occurred at a time different from the time that it actually did occur, or would have occurred in a manner different from the manner in which it actually did occur. (And we could redefine causation as the ancestral of this new kind of dependence.)

This formulation still distinguishes the case that event E occurs differently from the case that E does not occur at all. The distinction has been made to not matter, but we're still presupposing that there is a distinction. If we're as indecisive about such questions as I think we are, it would be better to avoid that presupposition.

Let an *alteration* of event E be either a very fragile version of E or else a very fragile alternative event which may be similar to E, but is numerically different from E. One alteration of E is the very fragile version that actually occurs: the *unaltered* alteration, so to speak. The rest are unactualized. If you think E is itself very fragile, you will think that all its unactualized alterations are alternatives, numerically different from E itself. If you think E is not at all fragile, you will think that all its alterations are different versions of one and the same event. Or you might think that some are alternatives and others are versions. Or you might refuse to have any opinion one way or the other, and that is the policy I favor. Now we may restate our current analysis of causal dependence. We can return to whether–whether counterfactual dependence, but with alterations of the effect put in place of the event itself: Without C, the alteration of E which actually did occur would not have occurred. However indecisive we may be about how fragile an event itself is, its actual alteration is by definition fragile.

Now we say that Suzy's throw caused the shattering of the bottle and Billy's preempted throw did not because, without Suzy's throw, the alteration of the shattering which actually did occur would not have occurred, and a different alteration would have occurred instead. And here we are considering not only the slight delay before Billy's rock arrived but also any differences to the shattering that might have been made because Billy's rock differs from Suzy's in its mass, its shape, its velocity, its spin, and its aim point.[18]

1.8 Spurious Causation

We have dealt with one objection against the fragility strategy: that it conflicts with what we normally think about the conditions of occurrence of events. But there is a second objection, and it applies as much to the corrected strategy as to the strategy in its original form. All manner of irrelevant things that we would not ordinarily count among the causes of the effect can be expected to make some slight difference to its time and manner. I once gave this example: If poison enters the bloodstream more slowly when taken on a full stomach, then the victim's death, taken to be fragile—we might better say, the actual alteration of the victim's death—depends not only on the poison but also on his dinner.[19] If we heed still smaller differences, almost everything that precedes an event will be counted among its causes. By the law of universal gravitation, a distant planet makes some minute difference to the trajectory of Suzy's rock, thereby making a tiny difference to the shattering of the bottle. So by adopting the fragility strategy, whether in corrected or uncorrected form, we open the gate to a flood of spurious causes.

Among the spurious causes that should have been deemed irrelevant is Billy's rock, the preempted alternative. For one thing, it too exerts a minute gravitational force on Suzy's rock. We wanted to say that (the actual alteration of) the shattering depended on Suzy's throw and not on Billy's, but that turns out to be not quite true.

Well—these differences made by spurious causes are negligible, so surely we are entitled to neglect them? Just as it's right to say that a box contains nothing when, strictly speaking, it contains a little dust, so likewise we are within our linguistic rights to say that Billy's throw made no difference to the shattering when, strictly speaking, its gravitational effects made an imperceptibly minute difference. And if for some strange reason we chose to attend to these negligible differences, would we not then put ourselves in an unusual context where it is right, not wrong, to count all the things that make negligible differences as joint causes of the effect?

That would be a sufficient reply, I think, but for the fact that sometimes the difference made by a preempting cause is also minute. Imagine that Suzy's throw precedes Billy's by only a very short time; and that the masses, shapes, velocities, spins, and aim points of the two rocks also differ very little. Then without Suzy's throw we might have had a difference equal to, or even less than, some of the differences made by causes we want to dismiss as spurious.

But even so, and even if Billy's rock makes a minute difference to the shattering by way of its gravitational effects on Suzy's rock, yet Suzy's throw may make much *more* of a difference to the effect than Billy's. The alteration that would have occurred without Suzy's throw, though not very different from the actual alteration, may differ from it in time and manner much more than the alteration that would have occurred without Billy's. Though the difference made by Billy and the difference made by Suzy may both count as small by absolute standards, yet the difference made by Billy may be small also in comparison to the difference made by Suzy. That would be enough to break the symmetry between Suzy and Billy, and to account for our judgment that Suzy's throw and not Billy's causes the shattering. We speak of the asymmetry as if it were all-or-nothing, when really it is a big difference of degree, but surely such linguistic laxity is as commonplace as it is blameless.

If, on the other hand, Billy's throw does somehow make roughly as much difference to the effect as Suzy's, that is a good reason to judge that Billy's throw is not after all a mere preempted alternative. Rather it is a joint cause of the shattering. So in this case too we get the right answer.

2 Lecture II

2.1 Alterations of the Cause

Because we're so indecisive about the distinction between alterations that are different versions of the very same event and alterations that are different but similar events, we ought to make sure that this distinction bears no weight in our analyses. So far, we're obeying that maxim only one-sidedly. The distinction doesn't matter when applied to the effect, but it still matters when applied to the cause. What it means to suppose counterfactually that C does not occur depends on where we draw the line between C not occurring at all and C occurring differently in time and manner.

That makes a problem. What is the closest way to actuality for C not to occur?— It is for C to be replaced by a very similar event, one which is almost but not quite C, one that is just barely over the border that divides versions of C itself from its nearest alternatives. But if C is taken to be fairly fragile, then if C had not occurred and almost-C had occurred instead, very likely the effects of almost-C would have been much the same as the actual effects of C. So our causal counterfactual will not mean what we thought it meant, and it may well not have the truth value we thought it had.[20] When asked to suppose counterfactually that C does not occur, we don't really look for the very closest possible world where C's conditions of occurrence are not quite satisfied. Rather, we imagine that C is completely and cleanly excised from history, leaving behind no fragment or approximation of itself. One repair would be to rewrite our counterfactual analysis, or add a gloss on its interpretation, in order to make this explicit (Lewis 1986b, p. 211).

But there is another remedy. We could look at a range of alterations of C, not just one. As on the side of effects, we need not ever say which of these are versions of C and which if any are alternatives to C. These alterations may include some in which C is completely excised, but we need not require this. They may include some which are almost but not quite C, but nothing is to be said that restricts us to the closest possible alterations. Then we look at the pattern of counterfactual dependence of alterations of the effect upon alterations of the cause. Where C and E are distinct actual events, let us say that C *influences* E iff there is a substantial range $C_1, C_2, \ldots$ of different not-too-distant alterations of C (including the actual alteration of C) and there is a range $E_1, E_2, \ldots$ of alterations of E, at least some of which differ, such that if C_1 had occurred, E_1 would have occurred, and if C_2 had occurred, E_2 would have occurred, and so on. Thus we have a pattern of counterfactual dependence of whether, when, and how on whether, when, and how. (As before, causation is the ancestral: C causes E iff there is a chain of stepwise influence from C to E.) Think of influence this way. First, you come upon a complicated machine, and you want to find out which bits are connected to which others. So you wiggle first one bit and then another, and each time you see what else wiggles. Next, you come upon a complicated arrangement of events in space and time. You can't wiggle an event: it is where it is in space and time, there's nothing you can do about that. But if you had an oracle to tell you which counterfactuals were true, you could in a sense "wiggle" the events; it's just that you have different counterfactual situations rather than different successive actual locations. But again, seeing what else "wiggles" when you "wiggle" one or another event tells you which ones are causally connected to which.

A process capable of transmitting a mark, in the sense of Reichenbach and Salmon, is a good example of influence (Reichenbach 1928, sections 21 and 43; Salmon 1994). We have some sort of process extending along a continuous spatio-temporal path. We can mark the process at one stage, and that mark will persist at later stages. Or rather—since it is irrelevant whether there is actually anything around that can make a mark—if the process *were* somehow marked at one stage, that mark *would* persist at later stages. That is, we have patterns of influence whereby alterations of later stages depend counterfactually on alterations of earlier stages.[21] The process capable of transmitting a mark might, for instance, be a flow of energy, matter, momentum, or some other conserved quantity: if there were a little more or less of the quantity at an early stage, there would be correspondingly more or less of it at later stages (Fair 1979; Dowe 1992).

But transmission of a mark is only one special case of a pattern of influence. In general, we do not require that the alterations of E resemble the alterations of C that map onto them. Nor do we require that sufficiently similar alterations of C map onto similar alterations of E. Nor do we require a process along a spatiotemporally continuous path; we could have influence of C upon E even if these were two separated events with nothing relevant between them. And we do not require a many–many mapping; the simplest sort of whether–whether dependence, with only two different alterations of E, still qualifies as one sort of pattern of influence. Recall Hall's example of causation by double prevention: The shooting down of the interceptor causes the destruction of the target by preventing the shooting down of the bomber. The shooting down of the interceptor does not much resemble the destruction of the target; there was no continuous process linking cause and effect; and alterations of the cause would in some cases have prevented the effect and in some cases not, but in no case would they have made a (more than negligible) difference to the effect without preventing it altogether.[22]

Influence admits of degree in a rough and multidimensional way. How many different C_is are there? How distant are the rest of them from the actual alteration of C, and from one another? How much do the E_is differ from one another: How many different ones are there, and when two of them do differ, how distant (on average, or at maximum) are they? Plainly there are many ways in which something can be more of a cause of some effect than something else is, even if it is not an all-or-nothing difference of influence versus no influence.

Now we are in a better position than before to say that Suzy's throw is much more of a cause of the bottle's shattering than Billy's. Even if the throws are so much alike that removing Suzy's throw altogether would make little difference to the shattering, it's still true that altering Suzy's throw while holding Billy's fixed would make a lot of difference to the shattering, whereas altering Billy's throw while holding Suzy's fixed would not. Take an alteration in which Suzy's rock is heavier, or she throws a little sooner, or she aims at the neck of the bottle instead of the side. The shattering changes correspondingly. Make just the same alterations to Billy's preempted throw, and the shattering is (near enough) unchanged.[23]

(Although Billy's throw does not influence the shattering, Billy's *not* throwing before the time of Suzy's throw does. This is a typical example of a delaying cause. The doctors who treated Ned Kelly's wounds lest he cheat the hangman by dying prematurely were the hangman's accomplices: joint causes, along with the judge and the hangman, of the death Ned actually died. Likewise Billy's earlier nonthrow and Suzy's throw were joint causes of the shattering that actually occurred.)

Thanks to this latest emendation of the counterfactual analysis, cases of trumping are covered along with commonplace preemption. Sergeant and Major both shout "Advance!" The soldiers advance. Altering the Major's command while holding the Sergeant's fixed, the soldiers' response would have been correspondingly altered. If the Major had said "Take cover!" they would have taken cover, if he had said "Retreat!" they would have retreated, and so on. Altering the Sergeant's command while holding the Major's fixed, on the other hand, would have made (near enough) no difference at all. If we look only at the whether–whether dependence of the soldiers' response on the actual commands of the two officers, we miss exactly the sort of counterfactual dependence that breaks the symmetry between the two.[24]

Likewise for the two wizards. If Merlin's first spell of the day had been not prince-to-frog, but rather king-to-kangaroo, the transmogrification at midnight would have been correspondingly altered. Whereas if Morgana's trumped spell had been, say, queen-to-goanna (holding fixed Merlin's earlier spell and the absence of any still earlier spell) what happened at midnight would have been exactly the same as it actually was: The prince would have turned into a frog, and that would have been all.

(Simon Keller has objected as follows. Suppose the soldiers are not perfectly obedient, and they know that the Sergeant is better placed than the Major to spot approaching danger. The Sergeant and the Major both shout "Retreat!" The soldiers infer from the Sergeant's order that they are in danger, so they retreat. The Sergeant's order causes the retreat. Yet if the Sergeant's order had been anything else, they would not have inferred danger, so they would have obeyed the Major.—Reply: the soldiers think "This is one of those exceptional times when it's best to obey the Sergeant." There is a range of alterations of the Sergeant's order, namely the range of alterations in which this thought is held fixed, for which we would have corresponding alterations of the soldiers' response. True, if the Sergeant's order had been different, this thought would not have been there. But even when it's true that if P, it would not have been that Q, we can still entertain the counterfactual supposition that P and Q.[25] And we have not restricted ourselves to the alterations that are closest to actuality.)

2.2   Transitivity of Causation

Causation, I previously said, is the ancestral of causal dependence. Event C causes event E iff there is a chain of dependencies running from C to E. That part of my analysis has remained untouched, even as my definition of causal dependence evolved from simple whether–whether dependence between events to a pattern of influence. Is it still necessary to take the ancestral? Or does our improved definition of causal dependence as a pattern of influence allow us just to identify causation with dependence?—No. Influence is not invariably transitive. If we want to ensure that causation is invariably transitive, we still have to take an ancestral.

You might think that intransitivities of influence could arise from intransitivities of the counterfactual conditional itself. We know that it can be true that if P, it would be that Q, and true also that if Q, it would be that R, yet false that if P, it would be that R (see my 1973b, pp. 32–33; Stalnaker 1968). But that is not the problem. Though counterfactual transitivity itself is fallacious, a closely related inference

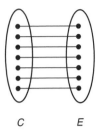 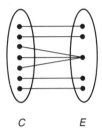 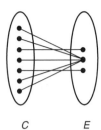

C   E   C   E   C   E

Figure 3.2

pattern is valid: from the premise that if P, it would be that Q, and the premise that if *both* P and Q, it would be that R, it does follow that if P, it would be that R (Lewis 1973b, p. 35). Let the counterfactual from C_i to D_i be part of a pattern of influence of C on D; let the counterfactual from D_i to E_i be part of a pattern of influence of D on E; then it would seem that if both C_i and D_i, it would be that E_i; so we do indeed have the counterfactual from C_i to E_i, and likewise for the other counterfactuals that constitute a pattern of influence of C on E.

The real problem with transitivity is that a pattern of influence need not map *all* the not-too-distant alterations of C onto different alterations of D, or all the not-too-distant alterations of D onto different alterations of E. Transitivity of influence can fail because of a mismatch between the two patterns of influence.

In figure 3.2 I picture three possible patterns of influence of C on E. The first is nice and simple: it maps several alterations of C one–one onto alterations of E. But less nice patterns will still qualify. Let the actual alteration be at the center, and imagine that distance from the center somehow measures closeness to actuality. (There's no need to make this distinction of inner and outer precise. Its only point is to make the cases easier to picture.) We might have a pattern of influence that maps the outer alterations of C one–one onto different alterations of E, but funnels all the inner alterations alike onto a single point (second picture). Or we might have a pattern that maps the inner alterations of C one–one onto different alterations of E, but funnels all the outer alterations alike onto a single point (third picture).

Now suppose C influences D by a pattern that funnels all the inner alterations onto a single point, while D influences E by a pattern that funnels all the outer alterations onto a single point (leftmost picture in fig. 3.3); or vice versa (middle picture). Or we might have more complicated cases (rightmost picture). In each case, the two patterns of influence that take us from C to D to E are mismatched: The values of the first pattern do not coincide with the arguments of the second. So C influences D and D influences E, but C does not influence E. If we nevertheless want to say

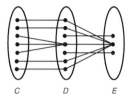 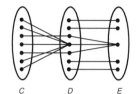 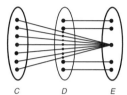

Figure 3.3

that C causes E, we have to take the ancestral and say that causation outruns direct influence.

How might such a case arise? Here is a famous example (from Frankfurt 1969; see also Heinlein 1951). The Neuroscientist knows exactly how she wants Jones to behave. She hopes that Jones, left to himself, will behave just as she wants him to. By reading his brain, she can predict what he will do if left to himself. She reads that he will do what she wants, so she does nothing further. But if instead she had read that he would stray from the desired path, she would have taken control. She would have made him a puppet, manipulating his brain and nervous system directly so as to produce the desired behavior. The initial state of Jones's brain is a preempting cause of his behavior; the idle Neuroscientist is a preempted backup. The moral of the story is that preemptive causation, without dependence, suffices to confer ownership and responsibility for one's actions.

Let C be Jones's initial brain state; let E be the desired behavior. Consider a time after the Neuroscientist has read Jones's brain, but before she would have seized control if the reading had been different. Let D combine Jones's brain state at that time with the Neuroscientist's decision not to intervene. C influences D. D in turn influences E, since at the time of D it's too late for the Neuroscientist to intervene. So we have a two-step chain of influence from C to D to E. But C does not influence E: any alteration of Jones's initial brain state would have led to the same behavior in the end, one way or the other.

The actual alteration of C is the one (assume it to be unique) that leads to exactly the desired behavior. The actual alteration of E consists of the desired behavior; the other alterations of E consist of different behavior. The actual alteration of D is the one that leads to the desired behavior, and that includes the Neuroscientist's decision not to intervene. The "inner" alterations of D are those that would not lead to the desired behavior, but that include the Neuroscientist's decision to intervene in one or another way. The "outer" alterations of D are those that would not lead to the desired behavior, but that nevertheless include the Neuroscientist's decision not to intervene.[26] These are arguments of the pattern of influence from D to E, and without them it would not be a pattern of influence at all. But they are not among the values of the pattern from C to D. The pattern of influence of C on D maps the actual alteration of C onto the actual alteration of D, and all other alterations of C onto inner alterations of D. The pattern of influence of D upon E maps all the inner alterations of D onto the actual alteration of E, and the outer alterations of D onto different alterations of E. Feeding the first pattern into the second, we get a pattern which maps all alterations of C onto the actual alteration of E. Thus the patterns are mismatched in the way shown in the rightmost picture in figure 3.3. Transitivity of influence fails.

This is an easy case of early preemption—just the sort of case that my strategy of taking the ancestral was originally made for. If we'd tried to make do without the ancestral, and get by with influence alone, it would remain unsolved—provided that we insist, as of course we should, that, with no intervention at all by the Neuro-scientist, Jones's initial brain state is indeed a cause of his behavior.

2.3 Transitivity Defended

Some will say that by making causation invariably transitive, our strategy of taking the ancestral makes more trouble than it cures. It collides with a flock of alleged counterexamples to transitivity of causation. Thus I've incurred an obligation to deal with these examples.

The alleged counterexamples have a common structure, as follows. Imagine a conflict between Black and Red. (It may be a conflict between human adversaries, or between nations, or between gods striving for one or another outcome, or just be-tween those forces of nature that conduce to one outcome versus those that conduce to another.) Black makes a move that, if not countered, would have advanced his cause. Red responds with an effective countermove, which gives Red the victory. Black's move causes Red's countermove, Red's countermove causes Red's victory. But does Black's move cause Red's victory? Sometimes it seems not.

One of the best known of these Black–Red counterexamples comes from Jonathan Bennett (1987). *Forest fire*: Let Black be those forces of nature that want the forest to survive; let Red be those forces of nature that want it to burn. Black protects the forest from the May lightning by raining all over it in April. Red dries the forest off again before more lightning comes. The forest burns in June. The April rain caused there to be an unburnt forest in June, which in turn caused the June fire. If causation is invariably transitive, we must conclude that the rain caused the fire.

Two more come from Michael McDermott (1995a). *Shock C*: Black is C's friend, Red is C's foe. C will be shocked iff the two switches are thrown alike. Black, seeing that Red's switch is initially thrown to the left, throws his switch to the right. Red, seeing this, responds by throwing his switch also to the right. C is shocked. Black's throwing his switch caused Red to throw his switch, which in turn caused C to be shocked. Thus Black's attempt to protect C is thwarted. If causation is invariably transitive, Black's failed attempt to prevent the shock is actually among the causes of the shock.

Dog-bite: Red wants to cause an explosion; Black (nature) wants him not to. Black's move: a dog bites off right-handed Red's right forefinger. Red's counter-move: with difficulty, he uses his left hand to set off the bomb. The bomb explodes. The dog-bite caused Red to set off the bomb with his left hand, which in turn caused the explosion. If causation is invariably transitive, the dog-bite was a cause of the explosion.

Another comes from Hartry Field (unpublished lecture). *The bomb outside the door*: Black wants Red dead, so he leaves a bomb outside Red's door. Red finds it and snuffs out the fuse. Red survives. Placing the bomb caused Red to snuff out the fuse, which in turn caused Red's survival. If causation is invariably transitive, placing the bomb was a cause of Red's survival.

Three more examples come from Ned Hall ("Two Concepts of Causation"). *The deadly double dose*: Black endangers Billy by giving him half of the deadly double dose on Monday. Red counters by withholding the second half on Tuesday. Billy survives. Monday's dose caused Tuesday's withholding, which in turn caused Billy's survival. If causation is invariably transitive, Monday's dose was a cause of Billy's survival.

The alarm clock: The ringing of the alarm clock summons the Black champion forth into battle, where he is slain by the Red forces. Without him, Black's cause is lost. Red wins. The ringing clock caused the champion to be slain, which in turn caused Red's victory. If causation is invariably transitive, the ringing clock was a cause of Red's victory.

The inert network (fig. 3.4): Red wants neuron F to fire, Black wants it not to. Since F is extraneously stimulated, it will fire unless it is somehow inhibited. Black's move: Fire C, which has a stimulatory connection to D, which in turn has a stim-ulatory connection to E, which in turn has an inhibitory connection to F. Red's countermove (made in advance): Provide another stimulatory connection from C to B, which in turn has an inhibitory connection to E. So E doesn't fire, F is uninhib-ited, and F does fire. The neural network consisting of $C, D, B,$ and E is inert, so far as F is concerned; there's no way it could have prevented F from firing. Yet the firing of C caused the firing of B; which in turn caused the *non*firing of E, which in turn caused the firing of F. If causation (including causation by double prevention) is invariably transitive, then the firing of C was a cause of the firing of F.

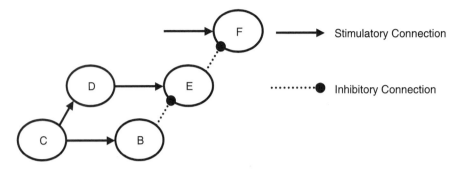

Figure 3.4

My last example is suggested by a familiar saying, *Damned if you do, damned if you don't*: Black tries to do what God has commanded, but the Red Devil interferes so that he messes it up. There ain't no justice: God accepts no excuses. So Black is damned. Black's failed attempt at pious obedience caused the Devil to interfere, which in turn caused Black to be damned. If causation is invariably transitive, Black's pious conduct caused him to be damned. In all these cases, there are two causal paths the world could follow, both leading to victory for Red. The two paths don't quite converge: Victory may come in one way or in another, it may come sooner or it may come later, but Red wins in the end. Black's thwarted attempt to prevent Red's victory is the switch that steers the world onto one path rather than the other. That is to say, it is because of Black's move that Red's victory is caused one way rather than the other. That means, I submit, that in each of these cases, Black's move does indeed cause Red's victory. Transitivity succeeds.

That is my considered opinion, but I do admit to feeling some ambivalence. Insofar as I can conjure up any inclination to accept the counterexamples, I think my inclination has three sources, all of them misguided.[27]

First. In many of these cases Red's victory would have come sooner, or more directly, without Black's move. Black's move prevents Red's victory as well as causing it: It causes one version but it prevents another. If we thought we had to choose, we would wrongly infer that since it is a preventer it cannot be a cause. (We've already noted this ambivalence in the case of delaying causes generally.)

Second. Moves such as Black's are in general conducive to victory for Black, not for Red. If we mix up questions of what is generally conducive to what with questions of what caused what in this particular case, we may think it just a bit of good common sense to say that Black's moves advance Black's cause, not Red's.[28]

Third. We note that Black's move didn't matter; Red would have won all the more easily without it. The effect doesn't depend on the cause. The idea that causation requires whether–whether dependence may retain some grip on us. But if you *ever* accept preemptive causation, you must have learned to resist that grip. Why yield to it now? It's true that Black's move didn't matter. But that's because the choice Black faced (whether he knew it or not) was whether to have his defeat caused in one way or in another; and, either way, Black's defeat is *caused*.

In rejecting the counterexamples, and accepting that Black's move is a cause of Red's victory, I think I am doing what historians do. They trace causal chains, and, without more ado, they conclude that what comes at the end of the chain was caused by what went before. If they did not, they could say little about historical causation; because, over intervals of any length, historical counterfactuals become so very speculative that nothing much can be known about the dependence of any event on its causal ancestors. And every historian knows that actions often have unintended and unwanted consequences. It would be perfectly ordinary for a move by Black to backfire disastrously.

I've assumed so far that the Black–Red examples are genuine test cases: We really do have an event C that causes an event D that in turn causes an event E. But unless the examples are carefully formulated, perhaps with the aid of somewhat artificial stipulations, that may not be so. It may rather be that C causes D_1 and D_2 causes E; and D_1 and D_2 are different, even though perhaps we may refer to them by the same name. If so, the example is not a test case, and if it turns out (contrary to my opinion) that C does not cause E, that is no problem for the thesis that causation is invariably transitive.

D_1 and D_2 might, for instance, be two different aspects of the same event: *D-qua*-event-of-kind-*A* and *D-qua*-event-of-kind-*B* (see Paul, "Aspect Causation," chapter 8 in this volume). Or D_1 and D_2 might be D taken with two different contrasts: *D*-rather-than-*X* and *D*-rather-than-*Y* (see Maslen, "The Context-Dependence of Causation," chapter 14 in this volume; Hitchcock 1996b). The contrast might be supplied tacitly by contextual clues, or it might be explicit. I think the aspect proposal and the contrast proposal don't differ much: The aspect *D-qua*-event-of-kind-*A* pretty much amounts to the contrasted event *D*-rather-than-a-version-of-*D*-that-is-not-of-kind-*A*. I'd suggest that aspects and contrasts alike are best understood as constraints on the range of relevant alterations.

2.4   Causation by Absences

Alterations, I said, are very fragile events. That was not quite right: Some of them are absences. Absences can be causes, as when an absence of food causes hunger.

Absences can be effects, as when a vaccination prevents one from catching a disease. And absences can be among the unactualized alterations of a cause or effect that figure in a pattern of influence.

Absences are not events. They are not *anything*: Where an absence is, there is nothing relevant there at all.[29] Absences are bogus entities. Yet the proposition that an absence occurs is not bogus. It is a perfectly good negative existential proposition. And it is by way of just such propositions, and only by way of such propositions, that absences enter into patterns of counterfactual dependence. Therefore it is safe to say with the vulgar that there are such entities as absences, even though we know better. If there is no more beer in the fridge, it is a fiction that the beer has been replaced by something else, something called an "absence of beer." We can say that there's an absence of beer, sure enough; and it's part of the fiction that this proposition is made true by the existence of the absence. But the sober truth is rather that this proposition is true because the proposition that there is some beer is false. That said, I also insist that the fiction is harmless, and we are within our linguistic rights to indulge in it. Accordingly, I shall carry on make-believedly quantifying over absences without apology.

(Should we conclude, then, that when we say that absences are causes, really it is true negative existential propositions that do the causing?—No; in other cases we distinguish between the cause itself and the true proposition that describes it. For instance, we distinguish the explosion from the proposition that an explosion occurred at so-and-so place and time. The explosion caused the damage; the proposition is a necessary being, "abstract" in one sense of that multifariously ambiguous term, and doesn't cause anything. On absences, as also on the aspects of events, I have met the friends of "fact causation" more than halfway; but I refuse to concede that facts—true propositions—are literally causes.[30] So I have to say that when an absence is a cause or an effect, there is strictly speaking nothing at all that is a cause or effect. Sometimes causation is not a relation, because a relation needs relata and sometimes the causal relata go missing [see my "Void and Object," chapter 10 in this volume]. But often, when one genuine event causes another, there are relata, and a causal relation that holds between them. So if we ignore all causal judgments except those framed by putting a "because" between clauses that express propositions, we overlook part of our topic.)

One reason for an aversion to causation by absences is that if there is any of it at all, there is a lot of it—far more of it than we would normally want to mention. At this very moment, we are being kept alive by an absence of nerve gas in the air we are breathing. The foe of causation by absences owes us an explanation of why we sometimes do say that an absence caused something. The friend of causation by absences owes us an explanation of why we sometimes refuse to say that an absence caused something, even when we have just the right pattern of dependence.[31] I think the friend is much better able to pay his debt than the foe is to pay his. There are ever so many reasons why it might be inappropriate to say something true. It might be irrelevant to the conversation, it might convey a false hint, it might be known already to all concerned, and so on (Grice 1975).

Of course, such reasons for refusing to say what's true are not confined to causation by absences. "Counterfactual analysis of causation?—Yeah, yeah, my birth is a cause of my death!" said the scoffer. His birth is indeed a cause of his death; but it's understandable that we seldom want to say so. The counterfactual dependence of his death on his birth is just too obvious to be worth mentioning.

(In case you're tempted to agree with the scoffer, consider this comparison of cases. In actuality there are no gods, or anyway none who pay any heed to the lives of mere mortals. You are born, and after a while you die. In the unactualized comparison case, the gods take a keen interest in human affairs. It has been foretold that the event of your death, if it occurs, will somehow have a momentous impact on the heavenly balance of power. It will advance the cause of Hermes, it will be a catastrophe for Apollo. Therefore Apollo orders one of his underlings, well ahead of time, to see to it that this disastrous event never occurs. The underling isn't sure that just changing the time and manner of your death would suffice to avert the catastrophe; and so decides to prevent your death altogether by preventing your birth. But the underling bungles the job: you are born, you die, and it's just as catastrophic for Apollo as had been foretold. When the hapless underling is had up on charges of negligence, surely it would be entirely appropriate for Apollo to complain that your birth caused your death. And if it's appropriate to say, presumably it must be true. But now we may suppose that, so far as earthly affairs go, actuality and our unactualized comparison case are alike in every detail. After all, the underling didn't manage to do anything. We may also suppose that, so far as earthly affairs go, the two cases are subject to exactly the same laws of nature. So, if you agree with the scoffer that your birth didn't cause your death in actuality, you must think that idle heavenly differences can make a difference to what causes what here below! That is hard to believe. To be sure, we earlier dismissed the thesis of the intrinsic character of causation as an overhasty generalization. But here, all we need is that earthly causal relations supervene on the intrinsic and nomological character of all things earthly.)

As I mentioned previously, Jaegwon Kim has drawn our attention to several causes of noncausal counterfactual dependence. I said in reply that counterfactual dependence is causal when it is dependence between entirely distinct events, neither identical nor overlapping; and that events (or at least, those of them that are causal relata) must be predominantly intrinsic (see Kim 1973b and my 1986d). Xanthippe's becoming a widow is a particular having of an extrinsic property; so it is not an event at all (or anyway, it is not a causal relatum), unless it is taken to be identical to, rather than distinct from, the event of Socrates' death.

When we say that absences as well as events can be causes and effects, do Kim's problems reappear? I think not. First, it is hard to see how an absence could be essentially a having of an extrinsic property. Second, it is safe to say that absences and genuine events are always distinct from one another. And third, we can say when two absences are distinct from one another: namely, when the corresponding negative existential propositions are logically independent.

It doesn't make sense for two distinct absences to differ slightly in detail. When we have an absence, there's nothing (relevant) there at all, and that's that. So when an absence is caused, we would expect a pattern of influence that exhibits funneling to an unusual degree. We can imagine a device that works in an extraordinarily precise all-or-nothing fashion; or a Neuroscientist, or some other marvelous being, able to exert extraordinarily precise and complete control; or we can just imagine a perfectly ordinary case of prevention. If we then follow that with the funneling that comes from the presence of a preempted backup, we may well end up with a mismatch between patterns of influence in which transitivity of influence fails. Small wonder, then, that cases of *preemptive prevention*—preemptive causing of an absence—and preemptive double prevention have appeared along with the Black–Red examples in the debate over transitivity of causation. I say again that at worst we have causation without direct influence. I trace a chain; I take the ancestral; I say that when a preempted preventer causes an absence which in turn causes some further event or absence, then the preempted preventer is a cause of that further event or absence.

Part of what makes preemptive prevention hard, however, is doubt about whether the absence really does cause anything further. Here is an example, due to Michael McDermott.[32] The fielder catches the ball; he causes its absence just beyond his hand. But a little further along its path there is a wall—a high, broad, thick, sturdy wall. Further along still is a window. Does the fielder cause the window to remain unbroken? Does he thereby cause the owner of the window to remain cheerful?

We are ambivalent. We can think: Yes—the fielder and the wall between them prevented the window from being broken; but the wall had nothing to do with it, since the ball never reached the wall; so it must have been the fielder. Or instead we can think: No—the wall kept the window safe regardless of what the fielder did or didn't do.

A treatment of the case ought to respect our ambivalence. Rather than endorsing the "Yes" or the "No," it ought to show how we are within our linguistic rights in giving either answer. The indeterminacy of our naive judgments is best explained by invoking some indeterminacy in our analysis. We are in a position to do this.

We have C, the catch. We have D, the absence of the ball from the place just beyond the fielder's hand. We have E, the absence of the impact of the ball on the window, or the nonbreaking of the window, or the continued good cheer of the owner. Certainly we have a pattern of influence of C on D. Whether we have influence of D on E is doubtful. There are alterations of D in which not only is the ball present beyond the fielder's hand, but also it is on a trajectory that would take it over the high wall and down again, or it is moving with energy enough to break through the wall, and so on. Some of these alterations of D would indeed have led to alterations of E. But are they relevant, "not-too-distant," alterations? We may be in a mood to think so, or we may be in a mood to think not. If we are in a mood to think them relevant, we should conclude that D causes E, and by transitivity C also causes E. That is the mood we are in when we are swayed by the thought that the fielder and the wall between them prevented the window from breaking. Whereas if we are in a mood to think them not relevant, we should conclude that neither D nor C causes E, and so the question of transitivity from C to D to E does not arise. That is the mood we are in when we are swayed by the thought that the window was safe regardless. But if anyone says that D causes E but C doesn't, and concludes that transitivity fails, he is not stably in one mood or the other.

The Yale shadow puzzle is similar. Two opaque objects are between the sun and the ground, in such a way that either one without the other would cast exactly the same shadow. (There might be more than two; and they might even be many slices of a single thick object.) The upper one is illuminated and stops the sunlight; the lower one is unilluminated. Does the upper one cast a shadow on the ground? We can think: Yes—between them, the two cast a shadow, but the lower one stops no light because no light ever reaches it, so the upper one must have done the job. Or we can think: No—thanks to the lower one, the ground would have been shadowed regardless of whether the upper one was there or not.[33] Again our ambivalence ought to be respected. We can explain it as before. Consider the absence of light just beyond the upper object; some far-fetched alterations of this absence would result in light getting through or around the second object, but we may well be of two minds about whether those alterations are too distant from actuality to be considered.

Yet another example of preemptive prevention comes from Ned Hall. The bomber is protected by two escort fighters, piloted respectively by Billy and Hillary. When the enemy interceptor arrives, Billy shoots it down; but had Billy failed, Hillary would have succeeded. In either case, the shooting down of the interceptor prevents the shooting down of the bomber, which, had it happened, would have prevented the subsequent bombing of the target (Hall, "Two Concepts of Causation," chapter 9 in this volume). What Hall says about this case parallels the thoughts that favored saying that the fielder prevented the window from breaking, or that the upper object cast the shadow on the ground: "If Billy's action was a cause of the bombing ... where Hillary was absent, then so too in this second case, which merely adds an alternative that plays no active role." Hall's view is defensible, provided he is in a mood not to ignore those far-fetched alterations in which the interceptor succeeds in evading both Billy and Hillary. But if so, then it is misleading (though literally true) for him to deny, as he does, that the bombing depends on Billy's action. Ignoring the far-fetched alterations, it's false that without Billy's action the bombing would have occurred anyway; what's true is that it might or might not have occurred. Saying that it would have occurred is equally defensible—but that calls for a different mood, one in which those far-fetched alterations *are* ignored.

Notes

1. See, *inter alia*, D. M. Armstrong, "Going through the Open Door Again," in this volume.

2. Or perhaps I feel a pressure on my own body; and perhaps it is analytic that a pressure involves a force, and that a force is *inter alia* something apt for causing (or preventing) motion. Then it seems that I'm causally acquainted, if not with causation itself, at least with something conceptually linked to causation. See Armstrong, "The Open Door," this volume; and his (1962), p. 23, and (1997), pp. 211–216.

3. The Canberra plan is derived, on one side, from Carnap's ideas about analyticity in a theoretical language; and on the other side, from one version of functionalism about mental states. See *inter alia* Carnap (1963), pp. 958–966; my (1966); and Armstrong (1968). The Canberra plan has been applied to causation in Tooley (1987), and in Menzies (1996). I discuss Menzies's treatment in "Void and Object," in this volume, saying that at best Menzies's approach will succeed in defining one central kind of causation.

4. We could subsume the perceptual acquaintance strategy under the Canberra plan. We could take the job description that specifies the role occupied by causation to consist almost entirely of platitudes about how we are perceptually acquainted with causation.

5. *An Enquiry Concerning Human Understanding*, section VII.

6. For discussion of the problem, see *inter alia* Menzies (1989a); Woodward (1990); and Schaffer (2000a). Schaffer's version of the problem resists some of the strategies that might solve other versions.

7. Two points of terminology. Some say "overdetermination" to cover all sorts of redundancy; I limit it to the symmetrical cases. Some say "preemption" to cover only those asymmetrical cases that do involve cutting; I apply it to all asymmetrical cases.

8. For my former view, see the treatment of preemption in my (1986b), pp. 193–212. For a recent claim that all preemption involves cutting, see Ramachandran (1997a), p. 273: "... in all genuine causes of causal pre-emption, ... the pre-empted processes do not run their full course.... All genuine causes, on the other hand, *do* seem to run their full course; indeed, they presumably count as genuine precisely because they do."

9. This example, and the discovery of trumping, are due to Jonathan Schaffer. See his "Trumping Preemption," in this volume. The case of the soldiers is due to Bas van Fraassen.

10. See my (1986b), pp. 205–207. For a similar proposal, see Menzies (1996) and (1999).

11. Here I am pretty much following Paul (1998a).

12. Hall (1994); Hall, "Two Concepts of Causation," chapter 9 in this volume.

13. For a misguided conflation of causation at a distance with action at a distance, and consequent dismissal of causation at a distance as far-fetched, see my (1986b), p. 202.

14. Perhaps action at a distance is "production" at a distance, where production is one of the varieties of causation distinguished by Ned Hall in "Two Concepts of Causation." Or perhaps it is "process-linkage" at a distance, where process linkage is explained as in Schaffer (2001).

15. It is a problem that is seldom noted. However, see Bennett (1988), passim.

16. "Actually" is right, strictly speaking, only if the causal connection in question is set in the actual world. More generally, E depends causally on C in world W iff C and E occur in W and it's true in W that without C, E would not have occurred or would have occurred later than it did in W. But we need not speak so strictly.

17. For advocacy of just such an "asymmetry fact," see Bennett (1987); for reconsideration and rejection of it, see Bennett (1988), pp. 69–72.

18. Here I've adopted a suggestion made by D. H. Rice at the Oxford Philosophical Society in 1984: "If C_1 and C_2 are redundant causes of E, and E would have occurred more or less just as it did if C_2 had not occurred, but would not have occurred more or less just as it did if C_1 had not occurred, then C_1 is a cause simpliciter of E and C_2 is not."

19. Lewis (1986b), pp. 198–199. Here I am indebted to Ken Kress.

20. See Bennett (1987), pp. 369–370. (Bennett's point here is independent of his defense of a hastener-delayer asymmetry elsewhere in that article.)

21. Salmon abandoned his mark transmission account of causal processes after Nancy Cartwright and Philip Kitcher convinced him that it would need to be formulated in terms of counterfactuals; see Salmon (1994).

22. However, some cases of causation by double prevention do exhibit a many–many pattern of influence. Suppose a whole squadron of bombers, with fighter escort, are on their way to destroy an extended target by carpet-bombing; a squadron of interceptors arrives to attack the bombers. In the ensuing dogfight, some of the interceptors are shot down. The remaining interceptors shoot down some of the bombers. The remaining bombers proceed to their assigned targets. Which parts of the target area get hit depends on which bombers get through. Thus various alterations of the dogfight would lead to various alterations of the destruction of the target area.

23. Unless you alter Billy's throw so much that his rock arrives first, making Billy the preempting cause. In a context in which we're comparing Billy's throw and Suzy's, such alterations should be set aside as "too distant." I hope that the vagueness of the analysis at this point matches the vagueness of the analysandum, and so need not be regretted.

24. Here I am indebted to Ned Hall.

25. See my (1973b), pp. 4–19, on counterfactuals as variably strict conditionals.

26. But we couldn't have had one of those alterations of D; because it would have to have been produced by a prior brain state that would have led the Neuroscientist to intervene.—True, but so what? We can still entertain them as counterfactual suppositions, and they can still constitute part of the pattern of influence from D to E.

27. In the case of the deadly double dose, an inclination to accept the counterexample may have a fourth source as well. Hall says that half of the double dose will cure Billy's nonfatal illness. So when we are told (truly, I take it) that Monday's dose causes Billy to survive, we're apt to hear a hint that it does so by curing his nonfatal illness. We too easily mistake the falsity of what's hinted for the falsity of what's actually said.

28. Compare Lombard (1990), p. 197.

29. Where an absence of spacetime itself is, there is nothing whatever there at all, relevant or otherwise. See my "Void and Object," chapter 10 in this volume, on voids as absences of spacetime, and on obstacles to the reification of absences.

30. *Pace* Bennett (1988) and Mellor (1995), pp. 156–162. Both Bennett and Mellor are willing to say that one fact causes another, where a fact either is or corresponds to a true proposition. Mellor does indeed deny that the two facts stand in a causal relation, where by "relation" he means a genuine universal existing in the world. (I deny that too.) But I am unappeased: even if causation is a "relation" only in some lightweight, unserious sense, still it shouldn't be said to relate propositions.

31. Helen Beebee, in "Causing and Nothingness," chapter 11 in this volume, states just this dilemma, but chooses the wrong horn of it.

32. The example comes from McDermott (1995a). It is further discussed in Collins, "Preemptive Prevention," chapter 4 in this volume. The suggestion that our wavering intuitions are governed by how far-fetched we find the possibility of the ball getting past the wall comes from Collins; but I have transplanted it from Collins's theory of causation as would-be dependence to my theory of causation as influence.

33. The puzzle was much discussed at Yale *circa* 1968; see Todes and Daniels (1975). It reappears in Sorensen (1999).

4 Preemptive Prevention

John Collins

As the ball flew toward us I leapt to my left to catch it. But it was you, reacting more rapidly than I, who caught the ball just in front of the point at which my hand was poised. Fortunate for us that you took the catch. The ball was headed on a course that, unimpeded, would have taken it through the glass window of a nearby building. Your catch prevented the window from being broken.

Or did it? Had you not made the catch, I would have caught the ball instead. My leaping to catch the ball made your catch redundant. Given my presence, the ball was never going to hit the window.

The example is a variant of one discussed by Michael McDermott. McDermott writes:

Suppose I reach out and catch a passing cricket ball. The next thing along in the ball's direction of motion was a solid brick wall. Beyond that was a window. Did my action prevent the ball hitting the window? (Did it cause the ball to *not* hit the window?) Nearly everyone's initial intuition is, "No, because it wouldn't have hit the window irrespective of whether you had acted or not." To this I say, "If the wall had not been there, and I had not acted, the ball would have hit the window. So between us—me and the wall—we prevented the ball from hitting the window. *Which one* of us prevented the ball from hitting the window—me or the wall (or both together)?" And nearly everyone then retracts his initial intuition and says, "Well, it must have been your action that did it—the wall clearly contributed nothing." (McDermott 1995a, p. 525)

These two cases, mine and McDermott's, are certainly very similar. And what McDermott says about his example seems to me to be absolutely the right thing to say about mine. When the redundancy of your catch is raised, when it is pointed out that, given my presence, the window was never in any real danger of being broken, I reply (with McDermott) as follows. If neither of us had reached for the ball, then the ball would have hit the window. So between us—you and me—we prevented the ball from hitting the window. Which one of us prevented the ball from hitting the window—you or I (or both of us together)? Well, clearly it must have been you, for it was you and not I who took the catch. I contributed nothing.

Preemptive prevention is puzzling. My responses to these two cases differ, despite the fact that they share the same basic structure. I am happier to agree with what McDermott says about my version of the example than I am to concur with that

Originally published in a special issue of the *Journal of Philosophy* (April 2000). Minor revisions have been made for consistency.

same account of his own version of the story. When I stand between your catch and the window, I am happy to say that you prevented the window from breaking. It is far less clear to me that that is the right thing to say when it is not just me but a solid brick wall that stands as the second line of defense. When it comes to McDermott's version of the story, I find myself wanting to say the following things. (1) You prevented the ball from hitting the wall. (2) The wall would have prevented the ball from breaking the window. (3) Your catch prevented the wall from preventing the ball from breaking the window. (4) Likewise, the presence of the wall prevented your catch from preventing the ball from breaking the window. I am very reluctant to say, in this case, that your catch prevented the ball from breaking the window. Given that the wall was there, the window was never in any danger of being broken. The presence of the wall really does seem to make your catch irrelevant. At least, that is how it seems to me.

Most, but not all, of the people I have asked shared the sense of ambivalence I experience when contemplating these two cases. Many, but not all, of them agreed with my judgments about the two examples. I think that these two cases of preemptive prevention pose a genuine puzzle. But perhaps those not convinced that the presence of the wall makes the catch irrelevant might be persuaded by an even more extreme variation on the same theme. Consider a third version of the preemptive prevention story. There is only one potential fielder this time, no brick wall, and no window. Suppose that at the moment you take the catch, the instantaneous velocity of the ball is a vector directed at a point one hundred million miles from the Earth at which Halley's comet will be located during its next but one swing through the solar system. Suppose that the magnitude of the instantaneous velocity is exactly right for a collision between the ball and the comet at that distant point at that future date (on the supposition that is, that the Earth and its gravitational field are absent). Did your catch prevent the ball from hitting Halley's comet? No.

1   Counterfactual Dependence

Nonoccurrences of events, as well as occurrences, may act as causes and may be produced as effects. Prevention is a matter of causing the nonoccurrence of an event. To prevent the window from being broken is to cause the nonoccurrence of a window-breaking.

There are two ways we might proceed here. We might extend our ontology to include events of nonoccurrence, or we might continue simply to speak of the nonoccurrence of events. The first approach leads to some difficulties in specifying when two events of nonoccurrence are one and the same event. The second approach requires us to admit that causal relata may be other than events. Since I am dubious about the ontological status of events of nonoccurrence, I propose to proceed as follows.

To any possible event e there corresponds the proposition E that the event e occurs. If e is any possible event, then the propositions E and $\sim E$ will both be referred to as *propositions of occurrence*. Note that I am using the term in such a way as to include among the propositions of occurrence what might instead have been called propositions of nonoccurrence; no problem, as long as you understand what I mean. Whenever C and E are propositions of occurrence, E would be true if C were true, and E would not have been true had C not been true, we say that E is *counterfactually dependent* on C. A sequence of true propositions of occurrence is said to be a *chain of counterfactual dependence* when each proposition in the sequence is counterfactually dependent on the proposition that precedes it. According to the *simple counterfactual analysis of causation*, a *causal chain* is just a chain of counterfactual dependence. One event (or absence) is a *cause* of another event (or absence) if and only if the proposition of occurrence for the former is linked to the proposition of occurrence for the latter by some causal chain. (See Lewis 1973a.)

Suppose that C, D, and E are true propositions of occurrence. We have *redundant causation* just in case: (i) E would not have been true had neither C nor D been true; (ii) E would still have been true if exactly one of the propositions C and D had been true and the other false. In the particular case where E is a proposition stating that a particular possible event did not occur, we have a case of redundant prevention.

Preemption is a special kind of redundancy. Following Lewis, let us mark the distinction in the following way. Suppose that events c and d are redundant causes or preventers of e. If it is clear, intuitively, that one of the two events c and d caused or prevented e while the other waited in reserve, then we shall speak of *preemption*. Those situations, on the other hand, in which c and d have an equal claim to having caused or prevented e, will be referred to as cases of *overdetermination*. The distinction is a vague one to be sure, yet there are clear cases of preemptive causation and prevention. The example with which the essay began is one such case.

2 Quasi-dependence

The phenomenon of preemption stands in the way of a simple counterfactual analysis of causation. When it became clear that not all cases of preemption could be handled by the simple counterfactual analysis, Lewis introduced the notion of *quasi-dependence*. The idea was that whether or not a process is causal ought to depend only on the intrinsic nature of the process itself, and on the laws of nature. If a duplicate of some process is located in the same world, or in a world with the same laws of nature, call it an *isonomic duplicate*. Lewis's suggestion was that any isonomic duplicate of a causal process is a causal process. Call an isonomic duplicate of a counterfactually dependent chain a *quasi-dependent chain*. Then, according to the *quasi-dependence analysis* of causation, a *causal chain* is either a chain of counterfactual dependence or a quasi-dependent chain. (See Lewis 1986b, pp. 193–212.)

But the quasi-dependence strategy doesn't work either. There are clear counterexamples to the claim that every isonomic duplicate of a causal process is a causal process, that is, to the claim that causation is an intrinsic matter. One kind of counterexample involves cases of *causation by double prevention*: A cause produces an effect by preventing an event, which, had it not been prevented, would have prevented the effect (for details of the examples see McDermott 1995a and Hall 2000). But another kind of counterexample is provided by the phenomenon of preemptive prevention. Your catch prevents the window from breaking when it preempts my catch, but not when it merely prevents a collision with a brick wall from preventing the window breaking. Yet the only difference between these two cases has to do with features extrinsic to the simple process involving your catch. The process that includes the ball's flight, your catch, and the window's not breaking is causal in the case where my hand was poised behind yours to take the catch, but it is *not* causal in the case where a brick wall is there instead of me. (If you don't agree with me about this pair of examples, consider the Halley's comet case instead.) We are assigning a different causal status to processes that are isonomic duplicates. So whether or not a process is causal is not a matter intrinsic to it.

3 Dependence Prevention

Your catch prevented the window from breaking and also prevented me from catching the ball when I leapt. But my leap did some preventing as well. It was my leap that prevented the window's not breaking from being counterfactually dependent on your catch. My leap was a *dependence preventer*. I think that the reason we say your catch prevented the window from breaking, despite the absence of counterfactual dependence, is that it was *only* my happening to leap when I did that prevented the not-breaking from depending on the catch. Sometimes, when *e* is not counterfactually dependent on *c*, we count *c* as a cause of *e* when there would be dependence were it not for some dependence preventer.

Of course this is not always so. We might recast the definition of redundancy as follows: *c* and *d* redundantly cause *e* if and only if (i) *c* prevents *e* from being counterfactually dependent on *d*; and (ii) *d* prevents *e* from being counterfactually dependent on *c*. The redundant causes feature symmetrically in this definition. This symmetry creates a problem. For just as my leap prevented the not-breaking from depending on your catch, so did your catch prevent the not-breaking from depending on my leap. In cases of preemption not only does the preempted backup prevent the effect from depending on the preempting cause; the preempting cause also prevents the effect from depending on the preempted backup. Yet we judge the causal roles of preempter and preempted differently.

Might we account for this by distinguishing varieties of dependence prevention? I once hoped so. For there are two ways of preventing counterfactual dependence, and in many cases the distinction between these two kinds of dependence prevention matches the contours of our causal judgments. Consider some actual chain of counterfactually dependent events. The first way in which this chain of counterfactual dependence might have been prevented is if something had prevented one or more events in the chain from occurring. If you don't have a chain of actually occurring events, then you don't have a counterfactually dependent chain of actually occurring events. But an actual chain of events might have been prevented from being a chain of counterfactual dependence without any event in that chain itself being prevented. The second way of preventing dependence leaves the chain of events fixed and simply removes the counterfactual dependence. Call an event that prevents dependence in this second way a *pure dependence preventer*.

We may use this distinction to break the symmetry in our example of preemptive prevention. My leap and your catch were both dependence preventers, but only my leap was a *pure* dependence preventer. My action prevented the window's not breaking from being counterfactually dependent upon your reaching out to catch the ball, and it did so without preventing any occurrence (or nonoccurrence) in the sequence initiated by your reaching out. Your catch also prevented the window's not breaking from being counterfactually dependent upon my leap, but it did so only by preventing the occurrence of a key event in the chain that would otherwise have followed from my action. In particular: your catch prevented me from catching the ball. This suggests that:

c is a cause of *e* iff there is a chain of counterfactual dependence linking *c* to *e*, or there would be such a chain were it not for some pure dependence preventer.

This needs adjustment. To simplify things in the preceding paragraphs I wrote as though all of our causal relata—all of the elements of our causal chains—had to be actually occurring events. But as we have already noted, nonoccurrences can also cause and be caused. A more accurate expression of the above idea would be couched in terms of propositions of occurrence. Thus:

A *causal chain* is a chain of true propositions of occurrence that is a chain of counterfactual dependence or *would be* were it not for the truth of some proposition of occurrence.

Then finally we might say that one event *c* (or the absence of the event *c*) is a cause of another event *e* (or the absence of *e*) if and only if there is a causal chain linking the proposition that *c* occurs (or doesn't occur) with the proposition that *e* occurs (or doesn't occur). Think of this as the *would-be dependence* analysis of causation.[1]

The would-be dependence analysis handles well many of the hard cases of preemption that plagued the quasi-dependence theory. It has another nice feature as well. It allows a solution to our puzzle about preemptive prevention. And the solution it allows is an attractive one, for it not only enables us to distinguish cases like mine from McDermott's; it also explains our feeling of ambivalence about such examples.

I say that the difference between McDermott's example and mine is this: the counterfactual assumption of the absence of the pure dependence preventer in his story is *more far-fetched* than the corresponding assumption of absence in mine. It does not require much of a stretch to suppose that I simply get my timing slightly wrong, so that when I leap, I do so at not quite the right moment to be ready to take the catch. It is more far-fetched, on the other hand, to suppose that the brick wall be absent, or that the ball would miraculously pass straight though it.

So let us adjust the would-be dependence analysis accordingly:

A *causal chain* is a chain of true propositions of occurrence that is a chain of counterfactual dependence or *would be* were some true proposition of occurrence false *in some not too far-fetched way*.

This analysis is vague, since it is a vague matter which alternatives to actuality should count as being "too far-fetched" to be taken into account. But this vagueness is a strength of the analysis, for it properly matches the vagueness of the analysandum. Ambivalent intuitions about examples like McDermott's stem from uncertainty about which suppositions count as being too far-fetched. In the right frame of mind I might be persuaded to suppose away a solid brick wall. Some competent speakers are happy to do so, McDermott among them. But fetch mere possibility from far enough, and none will acquiesce in supposing the dependence preventer absent. The Earth, its atmosphere, and its gravitational field prevent the ball's non-collision with Halley's comet from depending on your catch. Far-fetched indeed the supposition that you catch the ball in the Earth's absence.

4   Trumping and Influence

But not every chain that would be dependent were it not for some pure dependence preventer is a causal chain. That is one of the lessons to be learned from Jonathan Schaffer's discovery of *trumping preemption* (Schaffer 2000b). So trumping preemption is bad news not only for the quasi-dependence theory, but for the would-be dependence account as well. I now think of the latter as the *would-have-been* theory; I no longer defend it.

In one of Schaffer's examples the laws of magic are such that what happens at midnight is determined by the first spell cast the previous day. At noon Merlin casts the first spell of the day: a spell to turn the prince into a frog. At six that evening Morgana casts the second (and last) spell of the day: a spell to turn the prince into a frog. At midnight the prince turns into a frog. The transfiguration is caused by Merlin and not Morgana, yet it would be dependent on Morgana's spell were it not for Merlin's trumping preemption, and Merlin's preempting spell is a *pure* dependence preventer if we allow that magical spells act without causal intermediaries.

It is tempting to dismiss such fantastic examples. More realistic cases have been offered, and of these it might be claimed that they owe what plausibility they have to a confusion of causes with norms—the only sense in which a major's order clearly *trumps* a sergeant's order rather than preempting it in some other way is a normative sense. But I think it would be a mistake to ignore the possibility of trumping preemption on such grounds. We cannot rule out *a priori* the possibility that some actual cases of preemption work that way. So trumping preemption must be dealt with. I shall stick to discussing the fanciful examples here, since they are the cases in which (by stipulation) the causal structure of the situation is most clear.

David Lewis has responded to the examples of trumping preemption by giving up on the idea of providing a counterfactual analysis of *c is a cause of e*. The new account provides in its place a counterfactual theory of *causal influence*. The idea is, roughly, this. Our original notion of the counterfactual dependence of one event on another was a notion of whether–whether dependence; *e* is dependent on *c* in this sense just in case whether or not *e* occurs depends on whether or not *c* occurs. But there are further varieties of dependence. Lewis's suggestion is that we think of degree of causal influence as being a matter of the degree to which *whether, when,* and *how* one thing happens depends on whether, when, and how something else happens (Lewis 2000). Thus the asymmetry in the Merlin–Morgana example is revealed by the fact that Merlin, but not Morgana, has a causal influence on what happens at midnight. Had Merlin cast a different spell at noon, something different would have happened at midnight, but what happened at midnight was in no way dependent on whether, when, or how Morgana acted later.

This new theory of causal influence amounts to a change of topic. Lewis is not offering a new answer to the old question: "what is it for this event to be a cause of that event?" He is rather, offering an answer to a quite new question: "what is it for this event to have a causal influence on that event?" Certainly one event can have a causal influence on another without being among its causes. An example is provided by the story of the "Poison and the Pudding" (Lewis 1986b, pp. 198–199). If a poison kills its victim more slowly and painfully when taken on a full stomach, then the victim's eating pudding before he drinks the poisoned potion has a causal influence on his death, since the time and manner of the death depend counterfactually on the eating of the pudding. Yet the eating of the pudding is not a cause of his death.

The relation of cause and effect does not reduce in any obvious way to degree of causal influence. Dependence of the whether–whether kind appears to play a special role in our judgments of what is a cause of what. As it stands, the new theory lacks the resources to identify an event's causes from among those things that merely had some causal influence on it.

Furthermore, as Jacob Rosen has pointed out to me, there are cases of trumping preemption that appear to be counterexamples to the necessity of Lewis's account of causal influence (Rosen, personal communication, November 1999). Changing Schaffer's story slightly, let us suppose that the laws of magic distinguish the powers of a wizard from those of a witch. As a wizard, Merlin's options are very limited indeed. There is only one spell he may cast (standard prince-to-frog) and only one time of day he may cast it (noon). No such limitations apply to Morgana. Let the rest of the story remain the same. The prince's transfiguration is now in no way dependent on whether, or when, or how Merlin acts. So according to Lewis's account, Merlin's spell has no causal influence on what happens at midnight. Yet I would claim, with Rosen, that it is still Merlin's spell, and not Morgana's, that causes the prince to turn into a frog.

5   Masking and Finkish Trumping

Time now to turn our attention to another failed counterfactual analysis. To say that a glass window is fragile, to say, that is, that the window is disposed to shatter when struck, would seem to be equivalent to saying that if the window were struck, it would shatter. However, as C. B. Martin noticed long ago, this simple counterfactual analysis of dispositions is false. For dispositions, like other properties, may be gained or lost, and the conditions under which a disposition would be lost might be exactly the disposition's conditions of manifestation. Call such dispositions *finkish* (Martin 1994).[2]

Further problems for the simple counterfactual analysis are presented by dispositions that *mask* other dispositions (see Johnston 1993). To say that I mean *addition* when I use the word "plus" is to ascribe certain dispositions to me; for example, the disposition to give the sum of two numbers x and y when asked "What is x plus y?" But of course it is not true for all values of x and y that were I asked "What is x plus y?" I would respond by giving their sum. That is because the disposition that constitutes my meaning addition by "plus" is masked by various other dispositions of mine: my disposition to make mistakes, my disposition to decline to answer annoying questions, my disposition to get old and die....

I say: a masked disposition may fail to manifest itself even though it remains present and its conditions of manifestation are satisfied. Some disagree. For example, David Lewis writes:

... the first problem we face in analysing any particular dispositional concept ... is the problem of specifying the stimulus and the response correctly.

We might offhand define a poison as a substance that is disposed to cause death if ingested. But that is rough: the specifications both of the response and the stimulus stand in need of various corrections. To take just one of the latter corrections: we should really say "if ingested without its antidote." (Lewis 1999, pp. 144–145)

Lewis may well be right about this particular case; it is probably false to say that the disposition of a poison to kill is masked by its antidote. But I deny the general claim that Lewis's example is intended to support. For to accept that claim would be to rob ourselves of one of the most crucial conceptual resources provided by the notion of a disposition. Some of our most important dispositional concepts are concepts of dispositions that are components of other dispositions. These component dispositions may have conditions of manifestation that fail to correspond to the antecedent of any appropriate counterfactual conditional. That is how, for example, we make sense of the dispositions of belief, desire, and meaning as component dispositions of an agent's total behavioral disposition (Collins 1999). And that is how we may reply to a Kripkensteinian skepticism about the notion of meaning (Kripke 1982). Kripke's rejection of a dispositional solution to the skeptical paradox presupposes the counterfactual analysis of dispositions.

David Lewis has offered a reformed counterfactual analysis of dispositions (Lewis 1999). The reformed theory relies on the thesis that a disposition must be absent whenever the conditions for manifestation are satisfied and yet the manifestation fails to occur. But if masking works the way I claim it does, that thesis is false.

Prior, Pargetter, and Jackson argue that every disposition must have a causal basis (Prior, Pargetter, and Jackson 1982). Lewis agrees with them. A *causal basis* for the window's disposition to shatter when struck is said to be some intrinsic property of the window that would cause it to shatter were it struck. But if this counterfactual analysis of the notion of a causal basis is correct, then examples of *finkish trumping* establish that not every disposition has a causal basis. Consider an example that involves preemption or *mimicking* rather than masking. Suppose that the window is fragile, but that a playful sorcerer watches and waits, determined that if ever the window is struck he will, quick as a wink, cast a spell to shatter the window. Suppose that the spell would work not by changing any of the intrinsic properties of the window, nor by cutting any causal chain initiated by the striking and any intrinsic property of the window, but simply by the trumping preemption of whatever ordinary causal process would lead an unenchanted duplicate of the window to shatter when struck. Then the window would shatter were it struck, but its shattering would not be caused by any intrinsic property. So, if the counterfactual analysis of the notion of a causal basis is correct, the window has the disposition to shatter when struck, but this disposition has no causal basis.

According to a (partially) reformed counterfactual analysis of what it is for the window to be fragile:

The window is disposed to shatter when struck if and only if the window has an intrinsic property B such that, if the window were struck and yet retained B, then the striking and the window's having property B would jointly cause the window to shatter. (Lewis 1999, pp. 148–149)[3]

If this is correct, then the window in the finkish trumping example is *not* disposed to shatter when struck, despite the fact that it is an isonomic duplicate of a window that is so disposed. Defenders of the reformed counterfactual analysis must deny that dispositions are an intrinsic matter.

6   Conclusion

When one event prevents a second from preventing a third, this may be either causation by double prevention, or a case of preemptive prevention. Cases of preemptive prevention deserve to be added to the standard set of hard cases against which theories of causation are tested. The puzzle about preemptive prevention with which this paper began reveals a new and interesting element of vagueness in our concept of cause. I believe that this puzzle is best resolved by thinking in terms of dependence prevention. When the occurrence of one event would have been dependent on another were it not for some dependence preventer, we are often inclined to take this as cause and effect, but provided only that it is not too far-fetched to suppose the dependence preventer absent. Our ambivalent reactions to these cases are due to the vagueness of "too far-fetched."

The possibility of trumping preemption stands in the way of turning this would-be dependence analysis into a general account of causation. And trumping cases, if admitted, also lead to new problems for the counterfactual analysis of dispositions. Discussions of causation and dispositions have, to a great extent, developed independently of one another in the philosophical literature. It is time to bring these two debates together, and time to consider alternatives to the counterfactual theory in both cases. Our concepts of disposition, cause, and counterfactual dependence are closely linked, and of these three the notion of a disposition appears to be most basic. I favor reversing the order of analysis and developing a dispositional account of both causation and the counterfactual conditional. But this is not the occasion to tell that story.

Acknowledgments

Earlier versions of this paper were read to the Princeton Philosophy Colloquium on March 28, 1997 and to my Fall 1999 Metaphysics Seminar at Columbia. Thanks are due to those audiences, and in particular to Cian Dorr, Ned Hall, David Lewis, Cei Maslen, Laurie Paul, Jacob Rosen, and Jonathan Schaffer.

Notes

1. The material in this section was developed independently in late 1996 and presented in an earlier version of this paper read to the Princeton Philosophy Colloquium in March 1997. In discussion following that paper Cian Dorr drew my attention to a version of the "would-be dependence" analysis presented in Ganeri, Noordhof, and Ramachandran (1996) and (1998).

2. It should be noted that Martin first came up with the idea of finkish dispositions in 1957.

3. I am simplifying matters by omitting two features of Lewis's final proposal, but those features are not relevant to the point being made here.

5 Advertisement for a Sketch of an Outline of a Prototheory of Causation

Stephen Yablo

1 Plato's Distinction

A couple of thousand years before Hume made the remark that inspired the counterfactual theory of causation, Plato said something that bears on the principal problems for that theory. The idea will seem at first utterly familiar and of no possible help to anyone, so please bear with me. What Plato said, or had Socrates say, is that a distinction needs to be drawn between *the cause* and *that without which the cause would not be a cause* (*Phaedo*, 98e).

This sounds like the distinction between causes and enabling conditions: conditions that don't produce the effect themselves but create a context in which something else can do so; conditions in whose absence the something else would not have been effective. And, indeed, that is what Plato seems to have had in mind. Crito offers Socrates a chance to escape from prison. Socrates refuses and sends Crito on his way. The cause of his refusal is his judgment that one should abide by the decision of a legally constituted court. But it is facts about Socrates' body that allow the judgment to be efficacious: "if he had not had this apparatus of bones and sinews and the rest, he could not follow up on his judgment, but it remains true that it is his judgment on the question that really determines whether he will sit or run" (Taylor 1956, pp. 200–201).

Socrates' bones and sinews are factors such that if you imagine them away, the cause (Socrates' judgment) ceases to be *enough* for the effect. Are there conditions such that the cause ceases to be *required* for the effect, if you imagine them away? There seem to be. Consider an example of Hartry Field's.

BOMB: Billy puts a bomb under Suzy's chair; later, Suzy notices the bomb and flees the room; later still, Suzy has a medical checkup (it was already arranged) and receives from her doctor a glowing report.

Field intends this as a counterexample to transitivity, and so it is. The bomb is a cause of the fleeing is a cause of the glowing report; the bomb is not a cause of the glowing report. But it is also an example of Plato's distinction. Were it not for the bomb's presence, the glowing report would not have hinged on Suzy's leaving the room. The bomb does not help Suzy's leaving to suffice for the glowing report; rather it makes Suzy's action important, required, indispensable.

Apparently there are two kinds of factors "without which the cause would not be a cause." On the one hand we have *enablers*: facts G such that $(Oc \ \& \ \neg G) \mathrel{\vcenter{\hbox{$\scriptscriptstyle\square$}}}\!\!\!\to \neg Oe$. On the other we have what might be called *ennoblers*: facts G such that $(\neg Oc \ \& \ G) \mathrel{\vcenter{\hbox{$\scriptscriptstyle\square$}}}\!\!\!\to$

$\neg Oe$. Enablers make a dynamic contribution. They help to bring the effect about. What an ennobler contributes is just a raising of status. Suzy's removing herself from the room is elevated from something that just happens to something that *had* to happen, if Suzy was later going to be healthy.

Plato thinks that factors "without which the cause would not be a cause" are one thing, causes another. He presumably, then, would say that enablers and ennoblers are not to be regarded as causes.

About enablers, at least, it is not clear we should go along with him. If G is an enabler, then it is a fact in whose absence the effect would not have occurred. And, although there is some dispute about this, most say that that is good enough for being a cause. Enablers are full-fledged causes; it is just that they are pragmatically counterindicated in some way. Plato's distinction in its cause/enabler form can easily be rejected. Let's suppose to keep things simple that it is rejected.

Consider now ennoblers. An ennobler contributes by closing off potential routes to e, that is, all the routes not running through c. This if anything *hurts* e's chances. So there is no question of confusing an ennobler with a cause. Plato's distinction in its (unintended) cause/ennobler form is real and important. That a potential cause is disarmed may be a factor in the manner of e's occurrence, but it is not a factor in its occurring as such.

2 Preemptive Causes

The counterfactual theory as handed down from Hume says that "if the first did not, then the second had not been." For this to be plausible, we need to add that the first and second both occur, that the first is distinct from the second, and so on. But let us imagine that all of that is somehow taken care of, because our concerns lie elsewhere. Let the "simple" counterfactual theory be just what Hume says:

(CF1) c causes e iff e depends on c, that is, $\neg O(c) \mathrel{\square\!\!\rightarrow} \neg O(e)$

The simple theory cannot be right, because it ignores the possibility of backup causes that would spring into action if the real cause failed. This is what Lewis used to call the asymmetric overdetermination problem, and now calls preemption. An example is

DEFLECT: Hit and Miss both roll bowling balls down the lane. Hit's heavier ball deflects Miss's lighter ball en route to the pin. Hit's throw caused the pin to fall. But there is no dependence since if it had not occurred, the effect would still have happened due to a chain of events initiated by Miss's throw. (Yablo 1986, p. 143)

The problem here is obvious enough that one should probably date the counterfactual *theory*, as opposed to the immediately withdrawn counterfactual *hunch*, to the moment when it was first clearly addressed, in Lewis's 1973 paper "Causation."

Here is what Lewis says. Notice something about the chain of events initiated by Miss's throw. The Miss-chain was cut off before the Hit-chain had a chance to reach the pin. It is true that the effect does not depend on the earlier part of Hit's chain. It does, however, depend on the part occurring later, after Miss's chain is dead and buried. And the part after the cutoff point depends in turn on Hit's throw. So the effect depends on something that depends on Hit's throw—which suggests that instead of (CF1) our analysis should be

(CF2) c causes e iff there are d_i such that $\neg O(c) \mathbin{\Box\!\!\rightarrow} \neg O(d_1) \ \& \ \dots \ \& \ \neg O(d_n) \mathbin{\Box\!\!\rightarrow}$ $\neg O(e)$

What (CF2) says is that causation need not be direct; it can be indirect, involving dependency chains. If the ancestral of a relation R is written R^*, it says that causation is dependence*.

The diagnosis implicit in (CF2) is that preemption arises because we had forgotten about causal chains. I want to suggest an alternative "Platonic" diagnosis. Preemption happens because to take away a cause c is, sometimes, to take away more. It is to take away the reason it *is* a cause. It is to take away factors that, although not themselves causal, contribute to c's causal status by putting e in need of c. e can hardly be expected to follow c out of existence, if the reasons for its depending on c disappear first.

So, look again at DEFLECT. Quoting a former self: "if in fact Miss's ball never reaches the pin, then that is an important part of the circumstances. Relative to circumstances including the fact that Miss's ball never makes it, what Hit did was necessary for the pin's toppling. If in those circumstances Hit hadn't rolled his ball down the alley, the pin would have remained standing" (Yablo 1986, p. 159). That Miss's ball never touches the pin is a fact that puts the effect in need of Hit's throw. It is a fact "in virtue of which Hit's throw is a cause." The trouble is that it is a fact put in place by the throw itself, hence one that finkishly disappears when the relation is counterfactually tested.

3   Holding Fixed

The diagnosis suggests a repair. If preemption is a matter of something finkishly giving way, the obvious thought is: Don't *let* it give way; hold the grounds of the causal connection fixed. The test of causation in these cases is not whether e fails if c does, but whether e fails if c fails *with the right things held fixed*.

By "dependence modulo G" I will mean dependence with G held fixed. This event depends modulo G on that one iff had that one failed to occur in G-type circumstances, this one would have failed to occur as well. Letting "$\rightarrowtail_G$" stand for dependence modulo G, the suggestion is that

(CF3) c causes e iff: for some appropriate G, $\neg O(c) \rightarrowtail_G \neg O(e)$.

Actually, of course, this is only an analysis-schema. An analysis would require a clear, non-causation-presupposing statement of what makes for an appropriate G.

What does make for an appropriate G? Certainly G should ennoble c. But all we have said about ennoblers is that they are conditions G such that e depends holding-G-fixed on c. As you might guess, and as will be discussed below, this purely formal requirement can be met by logical trickery almost whatever c and e may be.

Thus where the standard counterfactual theory undergenerates—the events that depend on c (or depend* on c) are not all the events it causes—the present theory has, or is in danger of having, the opposite problem. It may well be that e depends on each of its causes modulo a suitably chosen G. But this is true also of events that do not cause e.

4   Triviality/Polarity

There are actually two worries here, one building on the other. The first is a worry about trivialization: Everything depends on everything modulo a silly enough G. This is illustrated by

JUMP: Suppose that e is Bob Beamon's jumping 29'2 1/2" at the 1968 Olympics in Mexico City. And let c be the burning out of a meteor many light years away. It is not hard to find facts modulo which the jump depends on the burnout. First choose an event on which the jump depends pure and simple—say, Beamon's tying his shoes. Holding it fixed that *the tying occurs only if the burnout does*, without the burnout Beamon does not make the jump.

Unless some sort of restriction is put on admissible Gs, the requirement of dependence modulo G is a trivial one satisfied by any pair of events you like. One could stipulate that G should not be too cockamamie or too ad hoc or too cooked up for the occasion. But that is hopeless. It is not just that "too ad hoc" is so vague. Suppose that a standard of naturalness is somehow agreed on. No matter how high the standard is set, there will be G-dependence without causation.

Consider again BOMB. Certainly the doctor's glowing report does not depend simpliciter on Billy's planting the bomb. But it does depend on it modulo the fact that *Suzy's chair explodes*. Holding the explosion fixed, Suzy would not have been healthy unless she had moved away, which she would not have had she not noticed the bomb, which would not have been there to notice had it not been put there by Billy. It seems on the face of it insane to credit Suzy's good health to the bomb; she is healthy despite the bomb, not because of it. And yet her health depends on the bomb modulo a natural fact. Call that the *polarity* problem.

5 Stockholm Syndrome

Preemptive causes make themselves indispensable. They create the conditions given which the effect would not have occurred without them. But there is more than one way of doing that. The *normal* way is to produce the effect yourself, thereby preventing other would-be causes from doing the job instead. The effect needs c modulo the fact G that other avenues to the effect are closed off.

But if you look at our basic condition—the condition of dependence modulo G—you can see that it supports an almost opposite scenario. E was going to happen anyway, when c comes along to threaten it: to put its existence in jeopardy. Of course, putting the effect in jeopardy is not all c does, or it would not even resemble a cause. It also rescues e from the jeopardy. C threatens e with one hand, and saves it with the other. The effect needs c to counter the threat G that c itself has launched.

Should e be grateful to c for blocking with one hand a threat it launches with the other? Of course not. There is a word for that kind of inappropriate gratitude. You might remember it if I quote from a Web site on the topic: "In the summer of 1973, four hostages were taken in a botched bank robbery at Kreditbanken in Stockholm, Sweden. At the end of their captivity, six days later, they actively resisted rescue. They refused to testify against their captors, raised money for their legal defense, and according to some reports one of the hostages eventually became engaged to one of her jailed captors." Stockholm Syndrome is the gratitude hostages feel toward captors who help them with problems brought on by the captivity. To give the present sort of c causal credit would be the metaphysical equivalent of Stockholm Syndrome.

It is important to be clear about what is being rejected here. There is nothing wrong with gratitude for actions taken against a threat that has already been launched: not even if the action is taken by the one who launched it. If your kidnapper takes pity on you and gets you a Mars bar, there is no requirement of flinging it back in his face. But suppose your kidnapper says, "I appreciate that you are grateful to me for various particular acts of mercy. But still I am hurt. Where is the thanks I get for the action that occasioned these mercies, that is, the kidnapping?" That remark you *should* fling back in his face. I draw the following moral:

Dependence modulo G does not make for causation if (i) G is a threat to e that, although (ii) countered by c, was also (iii) launched by c.

With this in mind, let's go back to the BOMB example. There is nothing wrong with thanking the bomb for tipping you off to its presence, given that it has already been planted. But what we are talking about here is gratitude toward the planting itself. BOMB, then, is an example of Stockholm Syndrome. What may be less obvious is that JUMP is an example as well.

That there will be no shoe-tying unless the meteor burns out makes e vulnerable from a new and unexpected direction; events that would cancel the burnout are now being put in a position to cancel the jump too. (That's (i).) There would been no such fact as *shoe-tying only if burnout*, had the meteor not in fact burned out. (That's (iii).) It is the burnout, finally, that stops this fact from carrying out its threat against the effect. (That's (ii).)

6 Artificial Needs

If e depends on c holding G fixed, let us say that G *puts e in need of c*. Why is this not enough for causation? The answer is that some needs are trumped up or artificial. This shows up in the fact that among e's *other* needs are some that would, but for c, have been *all* its needs. Or, to look at it from the point of view of the fallback scenario—the closest scenario where c does not occur—c is able to meet a need only by making the effect needier than it had to be, indeed, needier than it *would* have been had c failed to occur.

Say that e is Beamon's big jump, and c is the burning out of that meteor. What are the effect's needs in the fallback scenario? What would the jump have depended on had the meteor not burned out? It would have depended on Beamon's tying his shoes; on various earlier jumps whereby he won a place in the finals; on Mexico's bid for the 1968 Olympics; and so on. *Bringing in the burnout does not diminish these needs one iota.* Everything that had to happen before, still has to happen with the meteor burning out. This is why the burnout's role is artificial. It is strictly additional to events that meet the effect's needs all by themselves in its absence.

Now let's try to make this a teeny bit precise. History let's suppose has a branching time structure. There is the trajectory actually taken through logical space, and the various branchings-off corresponding to other ways things could have developed. One branch in particular corresponds to the way things would have developed if c had not occurred. By the *fallback scenario* let's mean what happens after the branching-off point on that alternative branch. By the *actual scenario* let's mean what actually *does* happen after the branching-off point. The effect's fallback needs are the events it depends on in the fallback scenario, that is, the events it would have depended on, had c not occurred.[1] Recalling our subscripting conventions from above, this can be written

$$\text{FAN} = \{x \mid \neg Ox \mathbin{\square\!\!\rightarrow}_F \neg Oe\},$$

where "F" is short for "$\neg Oc$."[2] The effect's actual needs (for a given choice of G) are the events it depends on modulo G in the actual scenario. This can be written

$$\text{GAN} = \{x \mid \neg Ox \mathbin{\square\!\!\rightarrow}_G \neg Oe\}.[3]$$

The need for c is artificial iff GAN covers FAN with c to spare; or, taking the perspective of the fallback scenario, FAN is identical to a subset of GAN not including c. (I will write this $\text{FAN} = \text{GAN}^-$.) The point either way is that c speaks to a need that is piled arbitrarily on top of what would, in c's absence, have been all the needs.

7 Counterparts

Imagine that Beamon as a child was initially attracted to chess rather than long jump. He was waiting to sign up for chess club when someone threw a rock at him. It was because of the rock incident that he wound up in track. And now here is the interesting part: the rock came from the burnt-out meteor. If not for the burnout, it would not have been *that* rock-throwing the effect depended on but a related one (in which the bully hurled a different rock). Since the rock-throwing that e would have needed is a different event from the one it does need, it would seem that GAN does not cover FAN at all, let alone with c to spare.

I answer that different *event* does not have to mean different *need*. One event can meet the same need as another, as that need manifests itself in their respective scenarios.[4] Artificiality is still a matter of the effect's actual needs subsuming its fallback needs, so long as we understand this in the following way. Suppose that x is an event needed in the fallback scenario; one finds in GAN, not perhaps that very event, but *an* event meeting the same need (henceforth, a counterpart of x). This complicates things a little, but not much. Where earlier we required FAN to be identical to a subset of GAN not including c, now we ask only that it coincide with such a subset, where sets coincide iff their members are counterparts.[5] (I will write this $\text{FAN} \approx \text{GAN}^-$.)

When do events speak in their respective scenarios to the same need? The idea is this. Needs that e would have had in c's absence can be paired off with actual needs in ways that preserve salient features of the case: energy expended, distance traveled, time taken, place in the larger structure of needs. One wants to preserve as many of these features as possible, while finding matches for the largest number of needs. One asks: How much of the fallback structure is embeddable in the actual one? What is the maximal isomorphic embedding? Events speak to the same need if they are linked by this embedding.

8   De facto Dependence

It is not enough for causation that a G can be found that puts e in need of c. Causes must meet *real* needs, and the need met by c might be trumped up or artificial. A fact G makes the need for c artificial iff it assigns other needs that would, but for c, have been all of e's needs.

An issue I have finessed until now is how the first G—the one that puts e in need of c—lines up with the second one—the one that makes the need artificial. Suppose we say of the second G that it "enfeebles" c, as we said of the first that it ennobles it. Does it suffice for causation that an ennobler G exists that is not *itself* an enfeebler?

No, for there is almost always a G like that, namely, the material biconditional *e occurs* $\leftrightarrow$ *c occurs*. That this ennobles c should be clear. That it does not enfeeble c can be seen as follows. (1) GAN is limited to events x on which c counterfactually depends. (If $\neg Ox \mathbin{\Box\!\!\rightarrow} Oc$,[6] then $(Oc \leftrightarrow Oe) \mathbin{\Box\!\!\rightarrow} (\neg Ox \mathbin{\Box\!\!\rightarrow} Oc)$; so by the export-import law, $(\neg Ox \,\&\, (Oc \leftrightarrow Oe)) \mathbin{\Box\!\!\rightarrow} Oc$; so $(\neg Ox \,\&\, (Oc \leftrightarrow Oe)) \mathbin{\Box\!\!\rightarrow} Oe$ iff $(\neg Ox \,\&\, (Oc \leftrightarrow Oe) \,\&\, Oc) \mathbin{\Box\!\!\rightarrow} Oe$; so $(\neg Ox \,\&\, (Oc \leftrightarrow Oe)) \mathbin{\Box\!\!\rightarrow} Oe$; so x is not in GAN.) (2) FAN is almost certainly *not* limited to events on which c counterfactually depends. That c fails to depend on x has no tendency at all to suggest that e would not have depended on x in c's absence. (1) and (2) make it unlikely that GAN includes FAN, or hence that G enfeebles c.

Where does this leave us? It is not enough for causation that an ennobler G can be found that is not itself an enfeebler. It is, I suggest, enough that an ennobler can be found such that *no* comparably natural enfeeblers exist. And so I propose a definition

(DD)   One event *de facto depends* on another iff some G putting the first in need of the second is more natural than any H that makes the need artificial,

and I make the following claim

(CF3) c is a *cause* of e iff e de facto depends on c.

It is understood that c and e both occur, that they are suitably distinct, and that various unnamed other conditions are met; I have in mind the same sorts of extra conditions as the counterfactual theorist uses. Sometimes (CF3) will be written (DF) to emphasize that it relies on a new type of dependence, albeit one defined in terms of counterfactual dependence.

You might have expected me to say that c is a cause iff e either depends counter-factually on c or, failing that, de facto depends on it. That formulation is fine but it is equivalent to what I did say, for de facto dependence has ordinary counterfactual dependence as a special case. If e counterfactually depends on c, then it depends on c modulo the null condition. The null condition is our ennobler, and what needs to be shown is that there are no comparably natural enfeeblers. But there cannot be enfeeblers at all, for enfeeblers presuppose fallback needs—events that e depends on in c's absence—and e does not even occur in c's absence.

9   Triviality and Polarity

One worry we had is that even if c and e are completely unrelated, still e is put in need of c by the fact that k occurs only if c occurs, where k is an event on which the effect counterfactually depends.

I say that although this is true, the victory is short-lived, because the very fact of unrelatedness means that it will be easy to find an H making the need artificial. Usually we can let H be the null condition. That is, e counterfactually depends out-right (holding nothing fixed) on events that would have been enough in c's absence. This is just what we would expect if c has, causally speaking, nothing to do with e. Beamon's jump depends on all the same things if the burnout occurs as it would have depended on absent the burnout.

The need for c is artificial iff it is over and above what would, but for c, have been all the needs. An equivalent and perhaps clearer way of putting it is that c must either *meet* a fallback need—which it does if for some f in FAN, c meets the same need as f—or *cancel* one—which it does if for some f in FAN, no actual event meets the same need as f. The need for c is artificial iff c fails to address any fallback needs, meaning that it neither meets any fallback needs nor cancels any.

I take it as given that Billy's planting of the bomb does not meet any fallback needs. The question is whether it cancels any. Suppose that Suzy needs to stay hydrated, or she becomes very sick. She has set her Palm Pilot to remind her at noon to act on this need. The fallback scenario has her sitting quietly in her chair at noon. She has a drink of water, water being the one hydrous stuff available in the room. The actual scenario has Suzy catching her breath on the sidewalk when her Palm

Pilot beeps. She eats some Italian ice, that being the one hydrous stuff available on the sidewalk. Any isomorphism worth its salt is going to associate these two events. The drinking and eating are counterparts; they speak to the same need. One imagines that the same can be done for all of the effect's fallback needs. Anything the glowing report needed absent the bomb, it still needs. The reason Billy's action is not a cause is that it fails to address any fallback needs.

Suppose that I am wrong about that. Suppose the effect's fallback needs are *not* all preserved into the actual situation; or suppose they are all preserved but one maps to the planting of the bomb. Then, I claim, the planting starts to look like a cause.

Case 1: There is an f in FAN such that Billy's action meets the same need as f.

Suzy needs exercise or she becomes very sick. She has set her Palm Pilot to remind her to exercise at 11:45. As things turn out, she doesn't hear the beeping because she has just spotted a bomb under her chair. Running from the bomb gives her the needed exercise and so saves her health. If that is how it goes, then Billy's planting the bomb meets the same need as would have been met by Suzy's setting her Palm Pilot. And now we are inclined to reason as follows. Billy's planting the bomb meets the need for an exercise-reminder; the need was not artificial because it would have been there bomb or not; so there is no objection to treating what Billy did as a cause.

Case 2: There is an f in FAN such that no actual event meets the same need as f.

Billy's planting the bomb does not in fact meet the same need as Suzy's setting her Palm Pilot. The Palm Pilot, if she had heard it, would have led Suzy to do push-ups, thus exercising her muscles. The bomb leads her instead to run, thus exercising her heart and lungs. These are entirely different forms of exercise. Either one of them would have stopped Suzy from getting sick, but the similarity ends there. Now we are inclined to reason as follows. The effect originally had need of *muscle* exercise, that being the only kind of exercise possible in the room. It is *relieved* of that need by Billy's planting of the bomb; for Suzy now runs, thus exercising her heart and lungs. So there is no objection to treating what Billy did as a cause. (Analogy: You have a flat tire and need a jack to get back on the road. I can help you either by meeting that need, or by relieving you of it. I do the first if I provide you a jack. I do the second if I bend over and lift the car myself.)

10   Preemption

I say that effects really do depend on their preemptive causes. There is no counter-factual dependence, because the causality rests on a fact G; and had c not occurred, that fact would not have obtained. But we can restore the dependence by holding G fixed. I don't know how to argue for this except by going through a bunch of examples.

Recall DEFLECT. Certainly the effect is put in need of Hit's throw by the fact G that Miss's ball never gets close to the pin. It might be thought, though, that the need was artificial.

The effect's fallback needs are (let's say) for Miss's throw, her ball's rolling down the aisle, and her ball's hitting the pin. These needs would seem to recur in the actual situation as needs for Hit's throw, his ball's rolling down the aisle, his ball's hitting the pin. If that is how things line up, then Hit's throw meets the same need as was met in the fallback scenario by Miss's throw; and so the need it meets is not artificial.

Suppose on the other hand that the fallback needs are held *not* to recur in the actual situation. Then artificiality is averted through the canceling of needs rather than the meeting of them. These are intuitive considerations but they suggest that a fact that makes the need for Hit's throw artificial will not be easy to find. I do not doubt that you could construct one by brute force, but a brute force H will not be as natural as our existing G, the fact that Miss's ball never gets close.

A tradition has arisen of treating early and late preemption as very different affairs. But this is for theoretical reasons to do with Lewis's ancestral maneuver, which works for early preemption but not late; intuitively the two sorts of preemption seem much on a par. The de facto theory agrees with intuition here. Consider

DIRECT: Hit and Miss both roll balls down the lane. The balls do not come into contact. Hit's ball knocks the pin into the gutter. A moment later, Miss's ball reaches the spot where the pin formerly stood.

Once again, it is part of the circumstances that Miss's ball never gets close to the pin. That no other ball gets close puts the effect in need of Hit's throw. It is true that some H might expose the need as artificial. But such an H would have to be constructed by brute force. There is no more reason to expect a natural enfeebler in this case than in the previous one.[7]

11   Overdetermination

Overdetermination occurs when an effect e depends on two events taken together without depending on either taken alone; and (what distinguishes it from preemption) neither can lay claim to being more of a cause than the other. Consider

TOGETHER: Knock and Smack roll their balls at the same time; the balls hit the pin together and it falls over; either ball alone would have been enough.

It is not hard to find suitable Gs. The effect depends on Knock's throw, holding fixed the fact G_k that Smack's ball does not hit the pin unaccompanied, that is, unless another ball also hits. And it depends on Smack's throw, holding fixed the fact G_s that Knock's ball does not hit the pin unaccompanied.

It is not hard to find suitable Hs either; indeed we have already found them. G_k makes the need for Smack's throw artificial, and G_s does the same for Knock's. To see why, suppose that Knock had not thrown. The effect would have depended on Smack's throw, the forward motion of his ball, and the like. These events are still needed in the actual situation, if we hold fixed the fact G_s that Knock's ball does not hit alone.

Assuming that these are the most natural cause-makers and -breakers to be had, does the de facto theory call Knock's throw (e.g.) a cause? Is the effect put in need of it by a fact more natural than any fact making the need artificial?

That depends. One reading of "more natural" is *strictly* more natural. If that is what is meant, then neither throw is a cause; each prima facie connection is broken by a fact exactly as natural as the one that established it. But the phrase could also be taken weakly, to mean "at least as natural as." If, as claimed, the makers and breakers are the same, then the weak reading makes both throws out to be causes. True, each occurs under conditions given which the effect takes no notice of it; but then each also occurs under conditions no less natural given which the effect needs it. Ties go to the runner on the weak reading, so we have two bona fide causes. Our uncertainty about overdeterminers reflects indecision about what to mean by "more." (This is intended less as an explanation of the uncertainty than a rational reconstruction of it.)

12 Asymmetry

Suppose that c affects not whether e occurs but only when it occurs. Could that be enough to make c a cause? An example is given by Jonathan Bennett.

RAINDELAY: "There was heavy rain in April and electrical storms in the following two months; and in June the lightning took hold and started a forest fire. If it hadn't been for the heavy rain in April, the forest would have caught fire in May" (Bennett 1987, p. 373).

Bennett says that "no theory should persuade us that delaying a forest's burning for a month (or indeed a minute) is causing a forest fire...." And then he points out something interesting. "Although you cannot cause a fire by delaying something's burning, you can cause a fire by hastening something's burning" (ibid.). So, consider

LIGHTNING: There are no rains in April. The fire happens in May owing to May lightning, rather than in June owing to the lightning that strikes then. The lightning is a cause of the fire even though the fire would still have occurred without it. That the time of occurrence would have been later rather than earlier seems to make all the difference.

Bennett's examples raise two problems for standard counterfactual accounts. One is that they cannot explain the *asymmetry*, that is, why hasteners seem more like causes than delayers. Also, though, they have trouble explaining *why there should be causation here at all*. I assume with Bennett that hasteners bring it about that the very same event occurs earlier than it would have. If in fact the fire would still have occurred without the lightning, how can the lightning be regarded as a cause?

The form of that question ought to seem pretty familiar. It is the standard preemption question: How can c be a cause, when the effect would have occurred without it thanks to c' waiting in the wings? The answer is the same as always: It is a cause because the effect depends on it modulo a certain fairly natural fact, and nothing that natural exposes the dependence as fraudulent. It is a part of the circumstances that *the woods do not catch fire in June (or later)*. Holding that fixed, without the May lightning there would not have been a fire. The May lightning causes the fire because the fire depends on it, holding fixed that May is its last opportunity.

But there is an obvious objection. The effect also fails to occur *before* a certain time, and this would seem to obliterate the intended asymmetry. Holding fixed the lack of a fire before June, if not for April's rain there would not have been a fire at all. June was the window of possibility, and it was the rain that kept the forest going until that window opened.

The difference between rain and lightning is not that the first meets no need; rather, it has to do with the kind of need involved. Suppose the rain had not fallen, so that the forest burned in May. Then the things that were done to preserve it from May until June would not have been required. (The loggers wouldn't have had to go on strike, the rangers wouldn't have had to apply the flame retardant, and so on.) That the rain introduces new needs would not be a problem if it addressed some old ones. But it doesn't. The things that would have been needed for the May fire, had the rain not fallen, continue to be needed as conditions of the June fire. (A landslide late in April threatens to bury the forest under rubble; the June fire needs it to change course just as much as the May fire would have.)

Now we see why the rain makes a bad cause. It piles on new needs without canceling any old ones. The lightning, by contrast, cancels a whole month of old needs. The pattern here is typical of the genre. Just by their definition, hasteners are liable to speak to fallback needs; they reduce the time period over which the effect is in jeopardy and so cancel any needs pertaining to the period that is chopped off. Just by their definition, delayers often bring about a situation in which the effect needs more than it would have had the delaying event not occurred. The effect is in jeopardy for longer and has needs pertaining to the extra time. This is why hasteners tend to be causes and delayers tend not to be.

13   The Hastener Theory

I have treated hastening as a special case of preemption. One might try the reverse, assimilating preempters to hasteners (Paul 1998b). A cause is an event in whose absence e would not have occurred, or at any rate would not have occurred as early as it did. If we count never occurring as the limiting case of delay, then the claim is that causes are hasteners, that is, events in whose absence the effect would have been delayed. One problem for this view is that hasteners are not always causes. Here is an example due to Hugh Rice (1999, p. 160):

REFLEXES: Slow Joe and Quick-Draw McGraw are shooting at Billy the Kid. Joe fires first, but since his gun fires slower-moving bullets, it is not too late for McGraw (if he fires) to cause the death. And so it happens. "McGraw (blest ... with super fast reflexes) was aware of Joe's firing and as a result (wishing to have the glory of killing Billy for himself) fired a little earlier than he would otherwise have done.... It seems that McGraw's firing was a cause of e, but that Joe's firing was not" (ibid.). Both shots hasten the death. So both count on the hastener theory as causes. Intuitively, however, it is McGraw's shot that kills Billy.

What does the de facto theory say about this? It is not hard to find a G modulo which the death depends on McGraw's shot. As the situation in fact develops, Joe's bullet never comes into contact with Billy (it passes untouched through the hole left by McGraw's bullet). Holding that fixed, Billy's death would not have occurred were it not for McGraw. This same G also enfeebles Joe's shot. Had Joe not fired, Billy's death would have depended on McGraw's shot, the motion of his bullet, and so on. Those are its fallback needs. The death's actual needs are the events on which it depends holding fixed that Joe's bullet never made contact. Prima facie it would seem that the death's fallback needs are all preserved into the actual scenario: Anything the effect depended on absent Joe's shot, it continues to depend on given that Joe's bullet doesn't hit anything.

I said that hasteners tend to reduce needs pertaining to the time period over which the effect is no longer in jeopardy. That assumes, however, that the counterpart relation puts a lot of emphasis on temporal as opposed to other factors. Oftentimes other factors will seem just as important, or more important. Suppose that by kicking a bowling ball already en route to the pin, I get it to arrive more quickly. Ordinarily my kick would count as a cause. This time, though, the main threat to the ball's forward motion is from equally spaced gates that open and shut according to a complicated pattern. The effect occurs only if the ball makes it through each of the gates. Then we might feel that the effect's needs are better conceptualized in terms of number of gates than number of seconds. To the extent that kicking the ball leaves its chances with the gates unchanged, the "need" it meets comes to seem artificial. Certainly the kick seems like less of a cause when it is stipulated that the obstacles are distributed spatially rather than temporally.

I said that delayers often bring about a situation in which the effect needs strictly more than it would have, had the delaying event not occurred. The effect is in jeopardy for longer and has needs pertaining to the extra time. But again, this is only a trend, not a strict rule. Sometimes by putting an effect off for a bit we can cut down on other, more important needs. Consider a variant of REFLEXES: McGraw is standing further from Billy than Slow Joe. When Joe sees that McGraw has fired, he fires his slower bullet on a trajectory that has it deflecting McGraw's bullet off to the side before reaching Billy. Joe's firing makes the effect happen later than it would have, but it is still a cause. Counterparthood is judged in respect not of time but of dependency relations; Joe's firing meets the need that McGraw's would have met, or, on an alternative accounting, it cancels it. It is Joe's shot that kills Billy, despite the fact that Billy lives a little longer because of it.

14   Trumping Preemption

A second recent response to the preemption problem focuses on events causally intermediate between c and e. It exploits the fact that, in all the usual cases, e would have depended on events other than those actual intermediaries had c failed to occur (Ganeri, Noordhof, and Ramachandran 1998). A third focuses on the manner in which the effect occurs, if caused by something other than c. There is nothing in the nature of preemption, though, that requires intermediate events, or that the effect's characteristics should vary according to its cause.

SPELL: Imagine that it is a law of magic that the first spell cast on a given day [matches] the enchantment that midnight. Suppose that at noon Merlin casts a spell (the first that day) to turn the prince into a frog, that at 6:00 P.M. Morgana casts a spell (the only other that day) to turn the prince into a frog, and that at midnight the prince becomes a frog. Clearly, Merlin's spell … is a cause of the prince's becoming a frog and Morgana's is not, because the laws say that the first spells are the consequential ones. Nevertheless, there is no counterfactual dependence of the prince's becoming a frog on Merlin's spell, because Morgana's spell is a dependency-breaking backup. Further, there is neither a failure of intermediary events along the Morgana process (we may dramatize this by stipulating that spells work directly, without any intermediaries), nor any would-be difference in time or manner of the effect absent Merlin's spell.… Thus nothing remains by which extent [counterfactual accounts of causation] might distinguish Merlin's spell from Morgana's in causal status.   (Schaffer, "Trumping Preemption," chapter 2 in this volume, p. 59)

What does our sketch of a prototheory say about this case? First, we should look for a G such that the effect depends modulo G on Merlin's spell. How about the fact that no one casts a spell before Merlin does? Holding that fixed, there would have been no transformation had Merlin not cast his spell. Perhaps a no less natural H can be found that enfeebles Merlin's spell; I have not been able to think of one. It is perhaps enough to show that, unlike the other approaches mentioned, the de facto dependence account is not at an absolute loss here.

15   Switching

A switch is an event that changes the route taken to the effect. It may not be obvious how switching so described goes beyond standard preemption, but consider an example.

YANK: A trolley is bearing down on a stalled automobile. The car lies 110 yards ahead on the track—or rather tracks, for just ahead the track splits into two 100-yard subtracks that reconverge ten yards short of the car. Which subtrack the trolley takes is controlled by the position of a switch. With the switch in its present position, the trolley will reach the car via subtrack U (for unoccupied). But Suzy gives the switch a yank so that the trolley is diverted to subtrack O (for occupied). It takes subtrack O to the reconvergence point and then crashes into the car.

Certainly the crash does not counterfactually depend on the yank; had Suzy left the switch alone, the trolley would have taken subtrack U to the car, and the crash would have occurred as ever. Thus the simple counterfactual theory (CF1) does not classify the yank as a cause. The ancestralized theory (CF2) sees things differently;

the effect depends on events that depend on the yank—the trolley's regaining the main line from track O, for instance—so what Suzy did was a cause. (The verdict does not change if track O was mined; Suzy was hoping to get the trolley blown up, and would have succeeded had not the bomb squad arrived.)

What does the de facto theory say? There is no trouble finding a G such that the crash depends modulo G on the yank. Holding fixed that subtrack U is untraveled, had the switch not been pulled there would have been no way forward; the trolley would, let's assume, have derailed. The worry is that some comparably natural H makes the need artificial. And, indeed, the null fact makes it artificial. Here in the actual scenario, the effect has need of 100 one-yard motions down track O. Had the yank not occurred, its needs would have been for 100 one-yard motions down track U. Because the yank lies apart from what might as well have been all the effect's needs, the de facto theory does not call it a cause.

The de facto theory lets the yank be a cause iff it either *meets* a fallback need or *cancels* one. As the case was first stated, it does neither, but suppose we tweak it a little. Suppose that O is shorter, or that U was disconnected when Suzy pulled the switch. Then there are needs the effect would have had that the yank does away with, and so the role it plays is not entirely artificial. Alternatively, suppose the switch operates not by rearranging the tracks, but by physically grabbing hold of the train and forcing it away from U and down O. Then the yank does meet a fallback need, the one that would in its absence have been met by the train's continued momentum. The door is thus open to the yank's being classified as a cause.

This is a good a place to acknowledge that although *technically*, everything that e would have depended on counts as a fallback need,[8] *in practice* not all such needs are taken equally seriously. Suppose that track U has been disconnected for years, and heroic efforts are required to fix it. That it makes those efforts unnecessary earns the yank causal credit. But what if the track is constantly reversing itself; it is part of U's design to connect when it senses an approaching trolley and disconnect when the trolley is safely past. Then the need that gets canceled may be considered too slight to protect the yank from charges of artificiality. I have no criterion to offer of when a fallback need is sufficiently serious that c can escape artificiality by canceling it. But two relevant questions are these: were the effect to fail, what are the chances of its failing for lack of x? And how counterfactually remote are the scenarios where x is the culprit? A fallback need may not count for much if it is the last thing one would think of as the reason why e would fail.

Some have said that an event that makes "minor" changes in the process leading to e is not its cause, whereas an event that makes "major" changes is one. Our theory agrees, if "minor" changes are changes whereby all the same needs have to be met.

Consider in this connection an example of Ned Hall's, in "Causation and the Price of Transitivity" (chapter 7 in this volume, p. 191):

THE KISS: One day, [Billy and Suzy] meet for coffee. Instead of greeting Billy with her usual formal handshake, however, Suzy embraces him and kisses him passionately, confessing that she is in love with him. Billy is thrilled—for he has long been secretly in love with Suzy, as well. Much later, as he is giddily walking home, he whistles a certain tune. What would have happened had she not kissed him? Well, they would have had their usual pleasant coffee together, and afterward Billy would have taken care of various errands, and it just so happens that in one of the stores he would have visited, he would have heard that very tune, and it would have stuck in his head, and consequently he would have whistled it on his way home.... But even though there is the failure of counterfactual dependence typical of switching cases (if Suzy hadn't kissed Billy, he still would have whistled), there is of course no question whatsoever that as things stand, the kiss is among the causes of the whistling.

That seems right: The kiss is among the causes of the whistling. But the example is not really typical of switching cases, or at least, it is missing features present in "pure" cases like YANK. The effect's fallback needs (its needs absent the kiss) are heavily weighted toward the period after Billy leaves the coffee shop. They include, for instance, Billy's deciding to drop into that particular store, the store's staying open until he arrives, the playing of that particular tune, and so on. It is because Suzy's kiss relieves the effect of this heavy burden of late-afternoon needs that we are ready to accept it as a cause.

Notes

1. If it seems odd to think of events as needs, remember that "need" can mean thing that is needed. ("The dogsled was piled high with our winter needs.") Needs in the ordinary sense do not exist in our system. Their work is done by events considered under a soon to be introduced counterpart relation, the relation of meeting-the-same-need-as.

2. According to the export-import law for counterfactuals, $A \mathbin{\square\!\!\rightarrow} (B \mathbin{\square\!\!\rightarrow} C)$ is equivalent to $(A \ \& \ B) \mathbin{\square\!\!\rightarrow} C$. This implies that $(\neg Ox \ \& \ \neg Oc) \mathbin{\square\!\!\rightarrow} \neg Oe$, the membership condition for FAN, is equivalent to $\neg Oc \mathbin{\square\!\!\rightarrow} (\neg Ox \mathbin{\square\!\!\rightarrow} \neg Oe)$, which says that e would have depended on x had c not occurred. I assume that the law is close enough to correct for our purposes, or at least that the indicated consequence is close enough to correct.

3. FAN and GAN are to be understood as limited to events occurring *after* the point at which the actual world and the nearest c-less world begin to diverge.

4. Also, *same event* does not have to mean *same need*. An event that meets one need here might meet another there, or it might meet no need at all.

5. I will be taking counterparthood to be symmetric and one–one. But there might be reasons for relaxing these requirements. Take first symmetry. There might be an x in FAN whose closest actual correspondent meets, not the same need as x, but a "bigger" need: one with the need met by x as a part. This closest actual correspondent ought to qualify as a counterpart of x. So, the argument goes, counterparts should be events meeting *at least* the same need, which makes counterparthood asymmetric. There is a similar worry

about the one–one requirement. It might take a pair of events to meet the need x meets all by itself in the fallback scenario; or vice versa. I propose to ignore these complexities.

6. I get from $\neg(\neg Ox \mathbin{\square\!\!\rightarrow} \neg Oc)$ to $\neg Ox \mathbin{\square\!\!\rightarrow} Oc$ by conditional excluded middle (CEM). CEM is generally controversial, but it seems in the present context harmless; we are not trying to show that $Oc \leftrightarrow Oe$ is *bound* to ennoble c without enfeebling it, but just that this is the likely outcome.

7. What if we change the example so that Miss's ball *does* hit the pin, after it has been knocked down? Then G should be this: Miss's ball never gets close to the pin when it is in an upright position, i.e., when it is in a condition to be toppled. Holding fixed that Miss's ball never approaches the pin at any *relevant* time, it remains the case that without Hit's throw, the pin would not have been knocked over.

8. Remember that attention is limited to events occurring *after* the "branch-point": the point at which the nearest c-less world begins to depart from actuality.

6 Difference-making in Context

Peter Menzies

1 Introduction

Several approaches to the conceptual analysis of causation are guided by the idea that a cause is something that makes a difference to its effects. These approaches seek to elucidate the concept of causation by explicating the concept of a difference-maker in terms of better-understood concepts. There is no better example of such an approach than David Lewis's analysis of causation, in which he seeks to explain the concept of a difference-maker in counterfactual terms. Lewis introduced his counterfactual theory of causation with these words: "We think of a cause as something that makes a difference, and the difference it makes must be a difference from what would have happened without it. Had it been absent, its effects—some of them, at least, and usually all—would have been absent as well" (Lewis 1986a, pp. 160–161). According to Lewis, a cause c makes a difference to an effect e in the sense that if the cause c had not occurred, the effect e would not have occurred either. As we shall see in section 2, Lewis's theory says there is more to the concept of causation than this counterfactual condition.

Lewis is on the right track, I think, in saying that we think of a cause as something that makes a difference and that this thought is best explicated in terms of counterfactual concepts. However, I shall argue that the particular way in which Lewis spells out the concept of a cause as difference-maker is unsatisfactory. Lewis's articulation of this concept is distorted by a specific metaphysical assumption: specifically, that causation is an absolute relation, specifiable independently of any contextual factors.

The distortion induced by this assumption is reflected in the undiscriminating manner in which his theory generates countless causes for any given effect. However, commonsense judgment is much more discriminating about causes than is Lewis's theory. Accordingly, I claim that Lewis's analysis faces *the problem of profligate causes*, and I outline some specific problem cases in section 3. In the following section I argue that Lewis's most recent formulation of his counterfactual analysis (Lewis 2000) faces the same problem of profligate causes, and I also argue that an initially promising solution to the problem that appeals to pragmatics does not succeed.

The key to solving the problem of profligate causation, I argue, is to give up the metaphysical assumption that causation is an absolute relation, specifiable independently of context. In sections 5 and 6 I attempt to analyze the concept of a cause as a difference-maker in a way that integrates a certain contextual parameter into the relevant truth conditions. The analysis employs counterfactual concepts, but ones that are sensitive to context. I use this account in section 7 to explain the problem cases of profligate causation, cited in section 3.

I need to note two restrictions that I intend to impose on my discussion. The first restriction is that I shall consider only cases of deterministic causation. I shall ignore cases of probabilistic causation, not because they do not exist, but because they do not raise any special issues in connection with the problem of profligate causes.

The second restriction is that I shall consider only cases of nonredundant causation. Any counterfactual rendering of the idea of a cause as a difference-maker must address some tricky questions in dealing with redundant causation—both symmetrical cases involving overdetermination by two or more genuine causes and asymmetrical cases involving preemption by two or more potential causes only one of which is genuine. Such examples raise serious questions about the viability of purely counterfactual analyses of causation: They *seem* to show that a cause need not make a counterfactual difference to its effect owing to the presence of alternative causes waiting in the wings. It would take us a long way from our present concerns to determine whether these examples really show this.[1]

My aim in this essay is quite limited. I intend merely to explicate the idea of one condition's making a difference to another. I shall claim that the condition expressing this idea is a necessary, though not sufficient, condition for causation. To bring the necessary condition up to sufficiency further concepts have to be added: Specifically, I would argue, the concept of a process linking cause with effect. How such a concept is to be added to the difference-making condition, and whether the condition, so supplemented, is adequate to deal with cases of redundant as well as nonredundant causation, are questions to be pursued on another occasion. For my immediate purposes, it will suffice to have a necessary condition for causation, with which to rule out the profligate causes generated by Lewis's theory.

2 Lewis's 1973 Theory of Causation

Lewis has presented two counterfactual theories of causation: the original (1973a) theory and a later (2000) refinement of the theory.[2] In this section I shall discuss his conceptual analysis of causation in the context of the earlier (1973a) version of the theory, deferring consideration of the later version of the theory until section 4.

The way Lewis frames his conceptual analysis is influenced by a number of metaphysical assumptions about the causal relation. One of these assumptions, which I will not contest here, is that causation relates dated, localized events (Lewis 1986a, pp. 241–269). He means to include events, in the ordinary sense, that involve changes: explosions, battles, conversations, falls, deaths, and so on. But he also means to include events in a broader sense that do not involve changes: a moving object's continuing to move, the retention of a trace, the presence of copper in a sample, and so on.

Another metaphysical assumption Lewis makes about causation is that it is an absolute relation—absolute in the particular sense that it is not relative to any contextual parameter and so does not vary in nature from one context to another. It is this assumption that I wish to contest here. The assumption is not an explicit feature of his analysis, but is rather a consequence of the way he defines the central concept of causal dependence:

(1)   Where c and e are distinct actual events, e *causally depends* on c if and only if e counterfactually depends on c: That is, (i) if c were to occur, e would occur; and (ii) if c were not to occur, e would not occur.

Lewis actually works with a simpler definition than this. He imposes a centering principle on the similarity relation governing counterfactuals to the effect that no world is as similar to the actual world as the actual world is to itself. This principle implies that the counterfactual above, "If c were to occur, e would occur," is automatically true in virtue of the fact that c and e are actual events. So his simpler working definition is:

(2)   Where c and e are distinct actual events, e *causally depends* on c if and only if e would not occur if c were not to occur.

The absolute character of causal dependence does not follow from this definition alone. It is possible, after all, to argue that the counterfactual constructions that define causal dependence are to be understood in a context-dependent way. This move is far from implausible in view of the notorious sensitivity of counterfactual constructions to contextual factors. But, in fact, Lewis argues that the counterfactuals that define causal dependence are to be read as nonbacktracking counterfactuals; and he specifies the similarity relation that governs them in terms of a unique, context-invariant set of weights and priorities for comparing respects of similarity (Lewis 1979a). The absolute, invariant character of the concept of causal dependence stems ultimately from the absolute, invariant character of the similarity relation for non-backtracking counterfactuals.

A final metaphysical assumption that Lewis makes about causation is that it is a transitive relation. Causal dependence, as defined in terms of counterfactual dependence, is not transitive. To ensure the transitivity of causation, Lewis defines causation in terms of the ancestral of causal dependence:

(3)   Where c and e are distinct actual events, c *is a cause* of e if and only if there is a chain of stepwise causal dependences between c and e.

By defining causation in terms of the ancestral of causal dependence, Lewis is also able to deal with some examples of preemption—the so-called examples of early preemption. (See Lewis 1986a, pp. 193–212.) Though I believe this assumption is false and can be shown to be unnecessary for the treatment of preemption examples, I shall not dispute it here.

My present target, to repeat, is the second assumption, to the effect that causation is an absolute relation; or more precisely, the assumption that the truth conditions for causal claims can be specified without reference to any contextual factors. Lewis acknowledges that our causal talk is often selective, focusing on some salient causes while backgrounding other less salient causes. However, this selectivity is to be explained by pragmatic principles of conversational exchange, which leave the objective truth conditions of causal claims untouched.

On Lewis's view, the causal history of an event is a vast, complicated relational structure: the relata in the structure are events and the relation that structures them is causal dependence. Out of this vast structure, the human mind may focus selectively on some part and call it *the* cause of the given event. Indeed, different minds pursuing different inquiries may focus on different parts of this structure. But the "principles of invidious selection," as Lewis calls them, by which fragments of a causal history are selected for attention, operate on an already fully determinate causal history. The principles of selection are independent of the relational structure itself. In this connection he writes:

The multiplicity of causes and the complexity of causal histories are obscured when we speak, as we sometimes do, of *the* cause of something. That suggests that there is only one.... If someone says that the bald tyre was the cause of the crash, another says that the driver's drunkenness was the cause, and still another says that the cause was the bad upbringing that made him reckless, I do not think that any of them disagree with me when I say that the causal history includes all three. They disagree only about which part of the causal history is most salient for the purposes of some particular enquiry. They may be looking for the most remarkable part, the most remediable or blameworthy part, the least obvious of the discoverable parts.... Some parts will be salient in some contexts, others in others. Some will not be salient in any likely context, but they belong to the causal history all the same: the availability of petrol, the birth of the driver's paternal grandmother, the building of the fatal road, the position and velocity of the car a split second before the impact. (Lewis 1986a, pp. 215–216)

3 The Problem of Profligate Causation

How satisfactorily does this theory capture the idea of a cause as a difference-maker? A fair answer would have to be: "Not very well" or "Well enough, but only with a lot of auxiliary assumptions about pragmatics." The main problem I wish to highlight here is the profligate manner in which the theory generates causes for any given effect. Below I list a number of examples that illustrate this defect of the theory. They are familiar examples for the most part, but it is useful to have a catalog of them before us.

According to Lewis's theory, any event but for which the effect would not have occurred is one of its causes. But, as is widely recognized, this generates some absurd results.

Example 1, The Lung Cancer   A person develops lung cancer as a result of years of smoking. It is true that if he had not smoked he would not have developed cancer. It is also true that he would not have developed lung cancer if he had not possessed lungs, or even if he had not been born. But it is absurd to think his possession of lungs or even his birth caused his lung cancer.

Common sense draws a crucial distinction between causes and background conditions. It ranks the person's possession of lungs and his birth as background conditions, so disqualifying them from being difference-makers for the effect. Several philosophers of causation have stressed the importance of this commonsense distinction in connection with the view of causes as difference-makers. J. L. Mackie, for example, says that what we call a cause is "what makes the difference in relation to some assumed background or causal field" (1974, p. 35).[3]

Perhaps the most extensive and penetrating investigation of the distinction between causes and conditions is that of H. L. A. Hart and A. M. Honoré in their seminal work *Causation in the Law* (1985). They argue that the distinction is relative to context in two ways. One form of relativity might be called *relativity to the context of occurrence*.[4] They contrast our causal judgments about the following situations.

Example 2, The Presence of Oxygen   If a building is destroyed by fire, it may be true that the fire would not have taken hold but for the oxygen in the air, the presence of combustible material, and the dryness of the building. But these are mere *conditions* of the fire. On the other hand, if a fire breaks out in a laboratory or in a factory, where special precautions are taken to exclude oxygen during the experiment or manufacturing process, it would not be absurd to cite the presence of oxygen as a *cause* of the fire. In both situations it may be true that the fire would not have occurred if oxygen had not been present. (Modified from Hart and Honoré 1985, pp. 35–36.)

The second form of context-relativity might be called *relativity to the context of inquiry*. With this form, rather than two situations eliciting different judgments about causes and conditions, as in the example above, it is one and the same situation that elicits different judgments depending on the type of inquiry being undertaken. Here are some of Hart and Honoré's examples.

Example 3, The Famine and the Ulcerated Stomach   The cause of a great famine in
India may be identified by an Indian peasant as the drought, but the World Food
Authority may identify the Indian government's failure to build up reserves as the
cause and the drought as a mere condition. Someone who prepares meals for a
person suffering from an ulcerated condition of the stomach might identify eating
parsnips as the cause of his indigestion, but a doctor might identify the ulcerated
condition of the stomach as the cause and the meal as a mere condition. (Modified
from Hart and Honoré 1985, pp. 35–36.)

Lewis's theory is insensitive to the different context-relative ways in which common sense draws the distinction between causes and conditions. His theory treats
mere conditions as causes because they are factors without which the effect would
not have taken place.[5]

Hart and Honoré argue convincingly, in my view, that the suggestions made by
various philosophers for drawing the commonsense distinction between causes and
conditions are unsatisfactory. They reject J. S. Mill's suggestion that the distinction is
the epistemically based distinction between causal factors revealed by investigation
and causal factors known before investigation. They point out that we would count a
dropped cigarette as the cause of a fire even when we learn from science, what we
may not have initially known, that the presence of oxygen is among the conditions
required for its occurrence. Hart and Honoré also reject R. G. Collingwood's suggestion that the distinction is the practically based distinction between factors controllable by the investigator and factors not so controllable. They argue that the
discovery of the cause of cancer would still be the discovery of the cause, even if it
were useless for the cure of the disease; and that drought is the cause of the failure of
crops and so of famine, and lightning the cause of a fire even for those who can do
nothing to prevent them (Hart and Honoré 1985, pp. 34–37).

Hart and Honoré also argue that it is wrong to identify the conditions as the
ordinary course of nature unaffected by human intervention. They observe that the
commonsense distinction is often an artifact of human habit, custom, or convention.
Because nature can be harmful unless we intervene, we have developed customary
techniques, procedures, and routines to counteract such harm. These become a second "nature." For example, the effect of a drought is regularly neutralized by government precautions in conserving water; disease is neutralized by inoculation; rain
by the use of umbrellas. When such procedures are established, the cause of some
harm is often identified as an omission or failure on the part of some agent to carry
out the neutralizing procedures, as the example of the famine illustrates (Hart and
Honoré 1985, pp. 37–38).

The fact that omissions, absences, and failures are recognized as causes and effects
poses a prima facie difficulty for Lewis's theory, which requires causation to link

events. Lewis concedes that an absence is a bogus kind of entity that cannot be counted as an event. Nonetheless, in partial solution to this difficulty, he argues that the proposition that an absence occurs is not bogus; and since such propositions can enter into counterfactual dependences, we can talk in a derivative way about causation by absences.

Lewis's extension of causal relata to include absences exacerbates the problems already noted. With the inclusion of absences as possible causes of a given effect, the blurring of the distinction between causes and conditions by Lewis's theory generates even more counterintuitive results. The next examples are illustrative of the difficulties Lewis's theory encounters with absences and other nonoccurrences.

Example 4, The Absence of Nerve Gas   I am writing this essay at my computer. If, however, there were nerve gas in the air, or I were attacked with flamethrowers, or struck by a meteor shower, I would not be writing the essay. But it is counterintuitive to say that the absence of nerve gas, flamethrower attack, and meteor strike are causes of my writing the essay.

Example 5, The Multiple Omissions   A healthy plant requires regular watering during sweltering hot weather. A gardener whose job it is to water the plant fails to do so and the plant dies. But for the gardener's omission, the plant would not have died. On the other hand, if anyone else had watered the plant, it would not have died. But it seems to absurd to say that the omission of everyone else to water the plant was a cause of its death.

Common sense draws a distinction between these negative occurrences, ranking some of them as causes and others as mere conditions. In the first example, it rates all the absences as conditions, but in the second example it distinguishes the gardener's omission from the other omissions, making it a cause. In contrast, Lewis's theory treats all these nonoccurrences equally as causes.

In summary, the examples cited in this section all point to the counterintuitive causal judgments licensed by Lewis's theory. They illustrate that his theory, or at least its truth-conditional component, is too profligate in its attribution of causes because it does not respect the context-relative way in which common sense distinguishes between causes and conditions.

4   A Possible Defense in Terms of Contrastive Explanation

We have so far been considering the original (1973a) version of Lewis's counterfactual theory. Does the more recent (2000) version of the theory fare any better with these problematic examples?

The more recent version of the theory also employs a counterfactual rendering of the idea that a cause makes a difference to its effect. But the counterfactuals it employs do not simply state dependences of *whether* one event occurs on *whether* another event occurs. The counterfactuals state dependences of *whether*, *when*, and *how* one event occurs on *whether*, *when*, and *how* another event occurs. A key idea in the formulation of these counterfactuals is that of an *alteration of an event*. This is an actualized or unactualized event that occurs at a slightly different time or in a slightly different manner from the given event. An alteration is, by definition, a very fragile event that could not occur at a different time or in a different manner without being a different event. Lewis stipulates that one alteration of an event is the very fragile version that actually occurs.

The central notion of the new version of the theory is that of influence:

(4) If c and e are distinct events, c *influences* e if and only if there is a substantial range $c_1, c_2, \ldots$ of different not-too-distant alterations of c (including the actual alteration of c) and there is a range $e_1, e_2, \ldots$ of alterations of e, at least some of which differ, such that if c_1 had occurred, e_1 would have occurred, and if c_2 had occurred, e_2 would have occurred, and so on.

Where one event influences another, there is a pattern of counterfactual dependence of whether, when, and how on whether, when, and how. As before, the notion of causation is defined as an ancestral relation.

(5) c *causes* e if and only if there is a chain of stepwise influence from c to e.

This theory is designed to handle cases of redundant causation. For example, consider a standard case of late preemption. Billy and Suzy throw rocks at a bottle. Suzy throws first so that her rock arrives first and shatters the bottle. However, without Suzy's throw, Billy's throw would certainly have shattered the glass. Suzy's throw is the preempting cause of the shattered bottle, Billy's throw the preempted potential cause. The revamped theory explains why we take Suzy's throw, and not Billy's throw, to be the cause of the shattering of the bottle. If we take an alteration in which Suzy's throw is slightly different—her rock is lighter or she throws sooner—(while holding Billy's throw fixed), we find that the shattering is different too. But if we make the same alterations to Billy's throw (while holding Suzy's fixed), we find that the shattering is unchanged (Lewis 2000, p. 191).

The important question for our purposes is whether this new version of the theory helps to deal with any of the problematic examples above. I cannot see that it does. The theory might try to explain the distinction between causes and conditions by showing that effects are sensitive to alterations in causes in a way that they are not sensitive to alterations in conditions. But this does not seem to be the case. In the lung cancer example, for instance, altering the man's possession of lungs will change the way his lung cancer develops as surely as altering his habits of smoking. Effects are sensitive to alterations in conditions as much as to alterations in causes. So the theory does not do anything to explain the distinction between causes and conditions.

Indeed, Lewis concedes as much himself. He says that the new version of the theory, as much as the old version, appears to generate too many causes. Any presence or absence linked by a pattern of influence, or a chain of such patterns, will count as a cause, although this seems to go against how we think and speak of causes. However, he offers a defense of his theory in terms of Grice's (1975) pragmatic theory of conversational implicature. It is literally true that any presence or absence linked to an event in the way distinguished by his theory is a cause of that event, but it is not always conversationally appropriate to mention it as a cause. He writes: "There are ever so many reasons why it might be inappropriate to say something true. It might be irrelevant to the conversation, it might convey a false hint, it might be known already to all concerned ..." (this volume, p. 101).

Lewis belongs to a long tradition of philosophers who have tried to isolate objective truth conditions for causal statements from pragmatic considerations of context. J. S. Mill famously claimed that the only objective sense of cause is that of the total cause of some effect. He dismissed the context-dependent way in which we ordinarily talk of some partial conditions as causes and others as conditions.[6] Of course, Lewis's position is slightly more subtle than Mill's. Whereas Mill dismissed our ordinary talk as unsystematic and muddled, Lewis gestures at the outlines of a possible explanation in the form of Grice's maxims of conversational exchange.

However, Lewis provides scant detail of the way Grice's maxims are meant to apply to particular examples. Which maxims are relevant? How are they to be employed? There is, moreover, a question whether Grice's principles are especially well suited to explaining the specific causal judgments in question. Grice's maxims of conversation are very general principles of rationality applied to information exchange. Yet the principles that lie behind our judgments about the examples of the last section seem to be particular to causal judgments. As general principles of rational information exchange, Grice's maxims miss out on these particular causation-specific principles.

What are these causation-specific principles? Several philosophers investigating the pragmatics of causal explanation have stressed the importance of using contrastive why-questions to analyze the interest-relativity of causal explanation. (See, in particular, Garfinkel 1981 and van Fraassen 1980, chapter 5.) They have argued that seeing causal explanations as answers to contrastive why-questions affords a way of understanding how context filters out from the vast causal history of an event those causes that are salient for certain explanatory concerns. For example, an enormous range of causal factors can be cited in explanation of a particular eclipse of the moon. Nonetheless, we can restrict attention to certain kinds of causal factors by seeking explanations of specific contrasts: why did the eclipse occur rather than not occur? Why was it partial rather than complete? Why did it last two hours rather than some other interval of time? Different contexts can be seen as implicitly requesting explanations of these different contrasts. This work on contrastive explanation suggests a strategy for explaining our causal judgments about the examples of the last section: Preserve Lewis's counterfactual analysis of causation, but add to it an account of contrastive explanation that can explain the context-sensitivity of ordinary causal discourse.[7]

There are several accounts of contrastive explanation available. Which should we use? Lewis has developed one account, which, as it happens, is tailormade for our purposes, though it must be noted that Lewis himself does not envisage the applications to which we shall put it. He writes in his paper "Causal Explanation":

One way to indicate what sort of explanatory information is wanted is through the use of contrastive why-questions. Sometimes there is an explicit "rather than...." Then what is wanted is information about the causal history of the explanandum event, not including information that would also have applied to the causal histories of alternative events, of the sorts indicated, if one of them had taken place instead. In other words, information is requested about the difference between the actualised causal history of the explanandum and the unactualised causal histories of its unactualised alternatives. Why did I visit Melbourne in 1979, rather than Oxford or Uppsala or Wellington? Because Monash invited me. That is part of the causal history of my visiting Melbourne; and if I had gone to one of the other places instead, presumably that would not have been part of the causal history of my going there. It would have been wrong to answer: Because I like going to places with good friends, good philosophy, cool weather, and plenty of trains. That liking is also part of the causal history of my visiting Melbourne, but it would equally have been part of the causal history of my visiting any of the other places, had I done so.   (Lewis 1986a, pp. 229–230)

On this account, we explain why an event e rather than an event e^* occurred by giving information about the actual causal history of e that differentiates it from the counterfactual causal history of e^*.

Can the strategy of conjoining this account with the counterfactual analysis help to explain our intuitive judgments about the examples of section 3? Let us be clear about what the strategy is in the first place. It involves two auxiliary assumptions. The first is the assumption that every ordinary causal statement can be seen as a response to an implicit contrastive why-question. The second is the assumption that our ordinary talk about causes is to be explained in terms of the way contrastive

why-questions selectively filter out from the objective causes, delivered by the counterfactual analysis, those relevant in particular contexts.

Let us consider how well this strategy works by seeing how it applies to the examples of section 3. It must be said that it works surprisingly well with some of them.
For example, it explains reasonably well why we do not consider it appropriate to
say about the lung cancer example that the man's birth and his possession of lungs
were causes of his lung cancer. It is natural to assume that such causal statements
would be attempts to answer the why-question "Why did the man get lung cancer
rather than not?" However, the man's birth and possession of lungs fail to be objective causes that are present in the actual causal history of his lung cancer but absent
from the counterfactual causal history of his not getting lung cancer. If the man had
not developed lung cancer, it would still plausibly be part of his causal history that he
was born and possessed lungs.

The strategy also provides a convincing explanation of the relativity of our causal
judgments about causes and conditions to the context of inquiry. For instance, in the
ulcerated stomach example, the meal-preparer and the doctor make different judgments about causes and conditions because they address different contrastive why-
questions. The meal-preparer is addressing the question "Why did the person get
indigestion on *this occasion* rather than some other?" The person's ulcerated stomach
is a condition that is present in both the actual history and the counterfactual histories and so is disqualified from counting as a factor that differentiates between
them. On the other hand, the doctor is addressing the question "Why does *this person*
rather than other people get indigestion?" Here what the person ate is a factor common to his causal history and the causal histories of other people, while his ulcerated
stomach condition is a factor that differentiates them.

Without doubt, these explanations of our commonsense judgments have a ring of
plausibility to them. Nonetheless, I think they cannot be the complete story, as the
principles they rely on have some major gaps or inadequacies.

First, Lewis's account of contrastive explanation relies on backtracking counterfactuals. We have to be able to work out whether some objective cause would be
present or absent from the history that would have had to occur if some alternative
to the actual effect had occurred. But the principles that guide the reasoning behind
such backtracking counterfactuals have not been formulated. For example, to get the
right results in the lung cancer example we have to infer that that the person would
have been born and possessed lungs even if he had not developed lung cancer. And
to get the correct answer in the absence of nerve gas example we have to infer that
if I were not writing at my computer, it would not be because nerve gas had been
intruded into my office, or because I had been attacked by flamethrowers, or been

struck by a meteor. But why are these inferences alone reasonable? Backtracking reasoning, unguided by any principles or unconstrained in any way, could equally well lead to the opposite conclusions. Clearly, this strategy, if it is to give the correct verdicts about the examples, must articulate some fairly detailed principles regarding the appropriate kind of backtracking reasoning. Until these principles have been articulated, the strategy is incomplete.

Second, one of the central assumptions of the strategy—that every causal statement must be understood in the context of an implicit contrastive why-question—is too strong. This assumption may hold for some cases, but it is dubious whether it holds for all. This becomes clear if we allow, as I think we should, for cases of probabilistic causation, in which the cause brings about the effect but does so with a chance of less than one. It may be true, for instance, that bombarding a radioactive particle causes it to decay, but the bombardment is not something that differentiates the actual causal history leading to decay from the counterfactual history leading to nondecay. The atom may fail to decay in the counterfactual history not because the atom is not bombarded, but because the bombardment does not, as a matter of pure chance, lead to decay.

Third, Lewis's account of contrastive explanation does not capture an important feature of contrastive explanations. This point is clearer where contrasts between compatible alternatives, rather than incompatible alternatives, are being explained. An example of a contrast between compatible alternatives is Carl Hempel's (1965) much discussed example of syphilis and paresis. Paresis is a late developmental stage of the disease syphilis, but, as it happens, few people with syphilis contract paresis. Nonetheless, we can still explain why Jones, rather than Smith, contracted paresis by saying that only Jones had syphilis. But this cannot be the right explanation on Lewis's account: syphilis does not differentiate between the actual case in which Jones gets paresis and the counterfactual history in which Smith gets paresis, since the only way in which Smith could get paresis is by first developing syphilis. Such examples highlight a feature of contrastive explanations not captured in Lewis's account. Sometimes the correct contrastive explanation compares actual with actual, rather than actual with counterfactual. In the example under consideration, it cites an actual feature that differentiates Smith and Jones—a feature present in Jones's case but absent from Smith's case.

Finally, and most important, the two-part strategy is unsatisfactory from an explanatory point of view. It unnecessarily duplicates the use of the idea of a cause as something that makes a difference: first in the analysis of "objective cause" as something that makes a counterfactual difference; and then again in the contrastive explanation account of the "context-sensitive cause" as something that differentiates actual from counterfactual histories. These uses of the idea are clearly independent; neither is derived from the other. Yet it would surely be a surprising fact, requiring elaborate explanation, if our framework for conceptualizing causation used in two different but crucial ways the very same idea of difference-making. It would be much more likely that our conceptual framework was developed on the basis of a single fundamental application of this idea.

For these reasons, then, the two-part strategy is not as promising as it first appeared. What is required is a unitary account of causes as difference-makers that explains the success of this strategy while avoiding its failures. In my view, if we are to develop such an account, we must draw a distinction between two kinds of theories of the context-sensitivity of causal discourse. *Add-on context-sensitive theories*, like Lewis's, apply pragmatic principles such as Grice's maxims or principles about contrastive explanation to independently determined truth conditions. In contrast, *integrated context-sensitive theories* make the context-sensitivity intrinsic to the truth conditions of causal claims by making the truth conditions relative to certain contextual parameters. I shall recommend adopting an integrated rather an add-on account of causal claims.[8]

5   Causal Models

As we have seen, Lewis's view that causation relates events is confounded by the fact that common sense also allows absences and omissions as causes and effects. The difficulty shows that we need to be inclusive about the relata of causation. To be as inclusive as possible, I shall talk of *factors* as causes and effects. Factors are meant to include anything that common sense dignifies as causes and effects—events, states of affairs, absences, omissions, and other nonoccurrences.[9] I shall reserve the uppercase variables C, D, E, and so on for factors.

Any theory of causes as difference-makers must make a connection with Mill's method of difference for detecting causes and testing causal claims. A crucial part of the method is a *difference observation* between a positive instance in which some effect E is present and a negative instance in which E is absent. If some condition C is present in the positive instance and absent in the negative instance, it is, at least, part of what makes the difference to E. Mackie (1974, pp. 71–72) points out that there are two forms the classical difference observation can take. One form is the before-and-after experiment in which some change C is introduced, either naturally or by deliberate human action, into an otherwise apparently static situation. The state of affairs just after the introduction is the positive instance and the state of affairs just before it is the negative instance. If the introduction is followed, without any further intervention, by some change C, then we reason that C is part of what made the difference to E. The other form the classical difference observation can take is the standard controlled experiment, where what happens in the experimental case is compared with what happens in a deliberately controlled case that is made to match the experimental case in all ways thought likely to be relevant other than C, whose effects are under investigation.

Mackie points out that different conceptual analyses of causes as difference-makers are modeled on the two forms of the classical difference observation. For example, C. J. Ducasse's (1968) theory of causation is clearly modeled on the before-and-after observation. It states that the cause of a particular change E is the particular change C that alone occurred in the close environment of E immediately before it. However, I agree with Mackie that this analysis is inadequate as an account of causation, as it fails to distinguish between causal and noncausal sequences of events. Consider Mackie's pair of contrasting sequences (1974, p. 29). In one sequence, a chestnut is stationary on a flat stone. A person swings a hammer down so that it strikes the chestnut directly from above and the chestnut is flattened. In the other sequence, a chestnut is stationary on a hot sheet of iron. A person swings a hammer down so that it strikes the chestnut directly from above. At the instant the hammer touches it, the chestnut explodes with a loud pop and its fragments are scattered around. Couched as it is in terms of actual changes, Ducasse's theory is hard pressed to deliver the correct verdict that the hammer blow is a cause in the first sequence but not in the second.

Mackie argues that these examples show that the relevant contrast in the difference observation is not the before-and-after contrast, but the experimental-and-control contrast (1974, chapter 2). We judge that the hammer blow is the cause of the effect in the first sequence because if we were to intervene in the course of events to prevent the hammer from striking the chestnut, the flattening would not occur; and we judge that the hammer blow is not the cause of the effect in the second sequence because if we were to intervene to prevent the hammer striking the chestnut, the explosion would still occur. Mackie argues that the conceptual analysis based on the experimental-and-control form of the difference observation must appeal to modal notions, in particular to conditionals. More specifically, he argues that the conceptual analysis of cause as difference-maker must appeal to two conditionals, one factual and the other counterfactual:

(6)   Where C and E are distinct factors, C makes a difference to E if and only if E would occur if C were to occur and E would not occur if C were not to occur.

This analysis captures the idea involved in the experimental-and-control contrast precisely because one conditional represents what happens in the experimental case and the other what happens in the control case.

I find much of what Mackie says about the experimental-and-control contrast idea to be illuminating. However, his discussion of this idea is marred by confusions about the conditionals that are supposed to capture this contrast. Especially confusing is his metalinguistic account of conditionals, according to which they do not have truth conditions. Nonetheless, I am going to take, as a starting point for my discussion, Mackie's claim that the experimental-and-control form of the difference observation is the relevant analogical basis for a conceptual analysis of difference-making. I shall also take, as a starting point for my discussion, the thesis that this contrast can be spelled out in terms of a pair of conditionals, one representing what happens in the experimental case and the other representing what happens in the control case. (Unfortunately, we shall have to wait until the next section to see the full justification for these assumptions.) However, I shall reject Mackie's confusing account of conditionals, in favor of a more orthodox truth-conditional account in terms of possible worlds. Under such an account, the central idea of difference-making can be spelled out in the following schematic terms.

(7)   Where C and E are distinct factors, C *makes a difference* to E if and only if every most similar C-world is an E-world and every most similar $\sim C$-world is a $\sim E$-world.

This formulation neatly captures the idea of a cause as a difference-maker: Where two relevantly similar possible worlds differ with respect to C they also differ with respect to E, and vice versa. A condition that just happens to covary with another in their actual instances will not modally covary in the way required to count as making the difference.

I should state at the outset that, while using the standard possible worlds framework for understanding conditionals, I understand the possible worlds in a slightly unconventional way. The possible worlds I shall employ are miniworlds rather than alternative large-scale universes: they are alternative courses of development of typically small-scale systems. They are best understood as being similar to the trajectories in the state space posited by a scientific theory to describe the behavior of systems of a certain kind. A theory may seek to describe the behavior of a certain kind of system in terms of a set of state variables $\{S_1, \ldots, S_n\}$. The accompanying state space will be an n-dimensional space and the trajectories in this space will be temporally ordered sequences of states in this space. So while I use the traditional term "possible world," it should always be kept in mind that I understand it typically in the "miniworld" sense, where the miniworlds are analogous to trajectories in a state space for a typically small-scale system of a certain kind.

The all-important question to be answered about the possible worlds formulation of the difference-making idea is: which worlds count as relevantly similar to the actual world? As we have seen, Lewis thinks that, for each causal claim about an event that makes a difference to another, the corresponding counterfactuals are to be read in terms of a unique kind of similarity relation. In this respect, my position differs from Lewis's, in that I think that the relevant similarity relations are context dependent, with causal statements in different contexts requiring different similarity relations. Causal statements must be understood, I shall argue, as relative to a certain contextual parameter; and depending on the way the parameter is set, an appropriate kind of similarity is determined for a given causal statement.

The contextual parameter in question reflects the fact that our causal thinking is steeped in abstraction. It is a platitude—but one worth repeating—that the world is exceedingly complex in its causal structure. Within any spatiotemporal region, there are many levels of causation, and within each level many cross-cutting and intersecting causal processes. To determine the structure of these processes, we are necessarily forced, by the finitude of our minds, to focus selectively on some aspects of what is going on and to ignore others or place them in the background. The causal schemas by which we interpret the world are irremediably permeated by abstractions that enable this selective focusing. There seem to be several forms of abstraction that underlie our causal thinking.

One form of abstraction underlying our thinking about the causal structures of a concrete situation involves the identification within the situation of *a particular set of objects as forming a system of a certain kind*. A particular system may consist of a great many objects or very few, of very large objects or very small ones. Astronomers and cosmologists investigate vast systems—solar systems, galaxies, or the whole cosmos. The systems investigated by biologists and economists—economies, markets, species, populations, and so on—are smaller, but still large by human standards. On the other hand, the systems investigated by particle physicists are small by any standard. It is not always easy to determine which objects belong to a particular system. This is not just because of our epistemic limitations, but because the spatiotemporal boundaries of the system are indeterminate. How many astronomical bodies are in the Milky Way galaxy? How many organisms belong to a population of marsh frogs? It is difficult to answer these questions because the spatiotemporal boundaries of these systems are not perfectly determinate. Nonetheless, the indeterminate localization of systems does not stop scientists from conceptualizing causal structures in terms of them.

The form of conceptual abstraction under consideration involves not just the identification of a particular set of objects, but the identification of this set of objects as constituting *a system of a certain kind*. But what is a system? A simple answer to this question is that a particular system is a set of objects that have certain properties and relations. But not any old properties and relations are relevant to the identification of a system. For example, a set of astronomical bodies can be individuated as a particular planetary system by way of each astronomical body's relation to other bodies in the system, but not by way of their relations to objects outside the system; a particular population of marsh frogs may be individuated in terms of the frogs' relational property of living in a particular marsh, but not in terms of extraneous relational properties involving far-distant objects. In short, a system is a set of constituent objects that is *internally organized* in a distinctive fashion; and the properties and relations that configure the objects into a system must be *intrinsic* to the set of constituent objects.

The concept of intrinsic properties and relations has been much discussed. However, the significant concept under consideration here is not the concept of properties and relations that are intrinsic *tout court*, but those that are intrinsic to a set of objects. It will suffice for our purposes to explain the intuitive idea behind these concepts, rather than to present a full analysis of them, which turns out to be slightly tricky. Modifying an idea of Jaegwon Kim's (1982) concerning the simple concepts, I shall say that:

(8)   A property F is *extrinsic to a set of objects* if and only if, necessarily, one of its members has F only if some contingent object wholly distinct from the set exists.

For example, the extrinsic properties of a set of astronomical bodies would include being observed by some human and being a certain distance from the Earth (assuming the Earth is not in the set).[10]

The concept of a property intrinsic to a set of objects is defined in converse fashion:

(9)   A property F is *intrinsic to a set of objects* if and only if, possibly, one of its members has F although no contingent object wholly distinct from the set exists.

For example, the intrinsic properties of a set of astronomical bodies would include the mass and shape of the individual astronomical bodies. But the intrinsic properties of the set need not be all intrinsic properties simpliciter. For example, the property of being gravitationally attracted to another body that is also a member of the set is an intrinsic property of the set, though it is not an intrinsic property simpliciter.[11]

There are, literally, uncountably many particular systems, but very few of them are of any interest to us. For the most part, we are interested in the *kinds of systems* that evolve in lawful ways. For example, certain systems of astronomical bodies and certain systems of biological organisms have intrinsic properties and relations that change over time in regular ways described by certain laws. Identifying a kind of system involves identifying the intrinsic properties and relations that are shared by particular systems and that conform to certain laws. The state variables employed in a scientific theory correspond to the intrinsic properties and relations that constitute a kind of system. In Newtonian mechanics, for instance, the state variables used to describe the behavior of mechanical bodies are the properties of mass, position, and momentum. The following definition captures these ideas:

(10)   *A kind of system K* is a set of particular systems sharing the same intrinsic properties and relations (state variables) whose evolution over time conforms to certain laws.

By definition, the state variables that determine a given kind of system are intrinsic properties and relations of the particular systems belonging to the kind. More generally, a kind of system supervenes on a set of intrinsic properties and relations in the sense that any two particular systems with the same intrinsic properties and relations must both belong, or both fail to belong, to a given kind of system.

I have said that a certain contextual parameter determines the similarity relation relevant to working out whether some condition makes a difference to another in a given concrete situation. I propose that one element of this contextual parameter is a kind of system. It is, I claim, an automatic and inevitable feature of the way in which we conceptualize the causal relations of a concrete situation that we see the concrete situation as an instance of a certain kind of system.

The other element in the similarity-determining contextual parameter is the set of laws governing the kind of system under consideration. This element of the contextual parameter reflects a further type of abstraction involved in our causal thinking, for almost invariably the laws governing the kinds of system of interest to us are ceteris paribus laws. Such laws state that the relevant systems evolve along certain trajectories provided nothing interferes. For example, the law of gravity in Newtonian mechanics states that, *provided there is no other interfering force*, the force exerted by one object on another varies directly as the product of their masses and inversely as the square of the distance between them. The law of natural selection states that, *provided there is no force besides that of selection at work*, if organisms possessing a heritable trait *F* are fitter than organisms with an alternative heritable trait F', then the proportion of organisms in the population having F will increase. Geoffrey Joseph (1980) suggests that such laws would be better called ceteris absentibus laws, as they usually describe the evolution of the relevant systems under the assumption that all interfering factors or forces are *absent*. Such an assumption is, often enough, an idealization, because most kinds of systems are subject to interfering influences in addition to the causal influences described by their relevant laws.

Idealization is central to our causal thinking, as is evident from the ubiquity of ceteris paribus laws. Still, many philosophers have thought that ceteris paribus laws are disreputable in some way. For example, it is sometimes objected that ceteris paribus laws are vacuous because the ceteris paribus condition cannot be specified nontrivially. (See, for instance, Fodor 1991.) The law that ceteris paribus all Fs are Gs, the objection runs, is really just the vacuous law that all Fs, unless they are not Gs, are Gs. This objection has no cogency at all, in my view. The law of gravity that tells us how, in the absence of other causal influences, gravity exerts a force on objects is far from trivial. It makes a substantive claim about the world because the concept of an interfering causal influence can be explicated informatively. Without being overly precise, we can explicate the concept in the following terms:

(11)   A factor I is *an interfering factor* in the evolution of a system of kind K in conformity with the laws L if and only if:

(i) I instantiates an intrinsic property or relation in a particular system of kind K;

(ii) I is caused by some factor instantiating a property or relation extrinsic to the system of kind K; and

(iii) the laws governing the causation of I by the extrinsic factor are distinct from the laws L.

Condition (i) simply states that the interfering factor is an intrinsic feature of the system in question. But condition (ii) says that this factor must have a causal source extrinsic to the system. Condition (iii) says that the causation of the factor can be explained independently of the laws governing the system in question. The paradigm example of an interfering factor is the result of an intervention by a human agent in the workings of the system. For example, the gravitational force of the Earth on a simple pendulum can be counteracted by a simple human intervention in the swing of the pendulum. While human interventions are not the only kinds of interfering factors, they form the analogical basis for our thinking about interfering forces. They constitute the most familiar type of situation in which an external force, operating according to its own distinctive laws, can intervene or intrude into the workings of a system.

Given this explication, we can see that the hypothesis that the ceteris paribus laws of Newtonian mechanics hold true of some system, say, the system of planets orbiting around the Sun, involves a substantial claim about the world. The hypothesis commits one not only to making certain predictions about the orbits of the planets, but also to explaining prediction failures in terms of the external interfering forces whose causal explanation is, in some sense, independent of the system and laws under consideration. Ceteris paribus laws are, to use the words of Pietroski and Rey (1995), like "checks" written on the banks of independent explanations, their substance and warrant deriving from the substance and warrant of those explanations. It may be questionable on some occasions whether the check can be cashed, but that hardly demonstrates the general inadequacy of the institution of bank checks.

Another common objection to ceteris paribus laws is that, even if ceteris paribus clauses can be specified nontrivially, they cannot be specified determinately. (See, for instance, Schiffer 1991.) This is because it is impossible to specify in advance all the interfering factors whose absence is required to enable a given system to evolve in accordance with given laws. Without doubt, there is truth in this claim. But it is a mistake to think this somehow impugns the determinacy of a ceteris paribus law. It is a mistake to say that the statement "There is only one person in the room"—alternatively "There is one person in the room and no one else"—has no determinate sense because one cannot specify in advance every person whose absence is required to verify the negative existential. This mistake rests on a confusion about what the determinacy of negative existentials requires. The objection to the determinacy of ceteris paribus laws rests on exactly the same confusion.

To capture the fact that our causal thinking is permeated by the two kinds of abstraction identified above, I shall say our causal judgments about a concrete situation must be understood as relative to a *causal model* of the situation. I represent a causal model of a situation as an ordered pair $\langle K, L \rangle$, where the first element K is the kind of system in terms of which we conceptualize the situation, and the second element L is the set of laws, typically ceteris paribus laws, governing the evolution over time of that kind of system. In using the term "causal model," I hope to highlight the continuity between commonsense causal thinking and the causal theorizing of the natural and social sciences. Several philosophers of science—notably, Nancy Cartwright (1983, 1999), Ronald Giere (1988), Fred Suppe (1979, 1989), and Bas van Fraassen (1980, 1989)—have emphasized that theorizing in these sciences often proceeds by way of idealized causal models in which ceteris paribus laws play a central, indispensable role. I would claim that these features of scientific practice have their roots in everyday causal reasoning.

No doubt the claim that causal judgments about a concrete situation are to be understood as relative to a causal model of the situation will strike many as confused and erroneous. So let me try to forestall some misunderstandings of this claim.

First, I am *not* claiming that causation is mind-dependent in some idealist sense. I am simply explicating the scientific commonplace that the causal structure of any particular situation can be modeled in several ways. I interpret this commonplace as meaning that a given situation can be viewed as instantiating different kinds of systems obeying different laws. In the analysis to follow, the claim that the difference-making relation is relative to a causal model $M = \langle K, L \rangle$ should be understood in terms of a conditional construction of the following form: *if* the given situation instantiates a kind of system K governed by laws L, *then* C makes a difference to E if and only if ..., where what replaces the dots will state a perfectly objective condition about the world. If the given situation satisfies the antecedent of this conditional, it is a completely mind-independent matter whether some factor in the situation makes a difference to another.

Second, I am *not* endorsing a crude relativism to the effect that any causal model of a situation is as good as any other, or more specifically, any kind of system is just as natural as any other for determining causal relations. There are natural kinds, in my view, but it is the job of metaphysics and science rather than conceptual analysis to investigate what they are. However these investigations turn out, a plausible metaphysics is likely to allow that any particular spatiotemporal region instantiates several kinds of systems. Perhaps an extremely austere physicalism committed to the existence of a unified field theory would assert that every situation is to be modeled in terms of a unique physical kind of system subject to the unified field equations. However, any less austere metaphysics is likely to conclude that several, perhaps imperfectly natural kinds of systems may be instantiated in a given spatiotemporal region. In this case, a conceptual analysis should be able to make sense of the alternative causal judgments about these different kinds of systems.

Finally, I am *not* saying that a causal model must be specified in terms of known kinds of systems and known laws. My discussion has been influenced by philosophers of science who argue that scientific theories are best understood as abstract models. Of practical necessity, they discuss known scientific theories in terms of known kinds of systems and known laws. But I do not wish to confine causal models to what is actually known. Common sense and scientific practice accept a realism according to which we may be ignorant of the intrinsic properties and relations that constitute a kind of system, and we may yet have to discover all the laws governing a kind of system. Indeed, our causal judgments may presuppose a causal model that can be specified imperfectly only in terms of an incompletely known kind of system and set of laws. But the analysis to follow can proceed satisfactorily in terms of an *objectified* causal model along these lines: if the given concrete situation is an instance of this imperfectly known kind K obeying the imperfectly known laws L, then a difference making claim is true if and only if....

6   The Similarity Relation and Difference-making

How exactly are causal judgments about a concrete situation relative to a causal model? The relativity of causal judgments to a model consists, I shall argue, in the fact that the model determines the respects of similarity used in evaluating whether a putative cause makes a difference to an effect. I will try to explain the way a model determines these respects of similarity in several stages.

Let us suppose that we are considering the structure of causal relations in a particular system of kind K in a certain interval of time (t_o-t_n). The following definition captures the way in which a causal model determines the fundamental respects of similarity that are relevant to determining whether one condition makes a difference to another.

(12)   *A model $\langle K, L \rangle$ of an actual system of kind K generates a sphere of normal worlds* that consists of all and only worlds w such that:

(i) w contains a counterpart to the actual system and this counterpart has exactly the same K-determining intrinsic properties and relations as the actual system at time t_o;

(ii) w does not contain any interfering factors (with respect to the kind K and laws L) during the interval (t_o-t_n);

(iii) w evolves in accordance with the laws L during the interval (t_o-t_n).

For each sphere of normal worlds, there is a conjunctive proposition that is true of all and only the worlds in the sphere. I shall label this conjunctive proposition F_M, and, taking over terminology reintroduced by Mackie (1974, p. 35) say that it specifies a *field of normal conditions* (generated by the model M).

Each of the worlds in the sphere of normal worlds generated by the model M exemplifies a course of evolution that is *normal*, in a certain sense, for a system of the kind K evolving in accordance with the laws L.[12] The conditions imposed on the these worlds represent *default* settings of the variables—the initial conditions, the laws, and the absence of interferers—that can influence the way the system evolves through time. If we are investigating the causal relations in a system of a certain kind, as it evolves through a given interval of time, it is reasonable to assume that the initial conditions of the system are the kind-determining intrinsic properties and relations that the system possesses at the beginning of the interval; that the system evolves in accordance with the laws governing the kind of system in question; and that none of the factors that can interfere with the lawful evolution of the system is present. These are default settings in the sense that the assumption that they obtain constitutes a reasonable starting point for our causal investigations, an assumption that we relinquish only when forced to do so. This is not to say that we are always aware of what these default settings are. As mentioned above, there is no reason to think that we will always have complete knowledge of all the initial conditions of a given system, or all the laws governing systems of that kind, or all the possible interferers that can hinder the given system's lawful evolution. Nonetheless, we move from the assumption that the actual system will evolve in accordance with these default settings, whatever their precise details, only when we have good reason to think it must deviate from them.

The normal worlds generated by a model are those that form the background to any consideration of whether some factor makes a difference to another. These normal worlds may hold fixed, as part of the field of conditions, intrinsic properties and relations of the system that are causally relevant to the effects displayed by the system. A special case is that in which the system does not contain any such causally relevant factors. In Newtonian mechanics, a system subject to no forces at all is such a special case. The zero-force law of Newtonian mechanics—the first law of motion—tells us that such a system will remain at rest or travel at a constant velocity. Similarly, a special case in population genetics is a population subject to no evolutionary forces. The evolution of gene frequencies in such a population is described by the zero-force Hardy–Weinberg law. In contrast to these special cases, the typical case is one in which the initial conditions of the system already entail that the system is subject to certain forces. The very description of a Newtonian system consisting of two particles with certain masses and a certain distance apart will entail that it is subject to gravitational forces. And the very description of a population whose members have certain properties entailing differential fitnesses will ensure that the population is subject to the force of natural selection.[13] Even when a system already possesses an array of causal forces, it makes sense to ask about the causal significance of additional causal forces. The condition for difference-making provides us with a test of the causal significance of these extra factors.

The sphere of normal worlds generated by a model is tied, in some sense, to the actual world. Worlds earn their membership in the sphere by virtue of their resemblance to the way the actual system under consideration would evolve in conformity with actual laws. Nonetheless, it is important to note that the actual world need not itself belong to the sphere of normal worlds, for these worlds represent how the actual system would evolve in conformity with the laws *in the absence of any interferers*. In many cases, therefore, these worlds are ideal ones. The actual world, as we know, may be far from ideal in that the evolution of the actual system may be subject to many interfering forces. The presence of any interfering factor disqualifies the actual world from belonging to the sphere of normal worlds. It follows from this that the centering principle that Lewis (1973b, pp. 26–31) imposes on the similarity relation for counterfactuals fails to hold here, both in its strong and its weak forms. Its strong form states that there is no world as similar to the actual world as the actual world itself, so disallowing ties for most similar world. Its weak form, which allows for ties for most similar world, states that there is no world more similar to the actual world than the actual world itself. That the actual world need not belong to the sphere of normal worlds generated by a model means we must abandon the centering principle in both its forms.

So far, we have attended to the question of which worlds count as the normal worlds generated by a model. But definition (7) of a difference-making factor C requires a specification of the most similar C-worlds and the most similar $\sim C$-worlds. It is best to spell out the definition of the most-similar C-worlds by considering subcases.

One subcase we need not consider is that in which both the conditions C and $\sim C$ are consistent with the field of conditions F_M. This case cannot arise because it is self-contradictory. For both C and $\sim C$ to hold consistently with the field of conditions, C would have to hold in some of the normal worlds and $\sim C$ would have to hold in other normal worlds. But since the laws governing these worlds are deterministic, these worlds would have to differ either with respect to their initial conditions, or with respect to the presence of interfering factors. In either case, the worlds could not satisfy all the conditions (12(i)–(iii)) required for membership in the sphere of normal worlds.

The first subcase we need to consider—I shall call it subcase I—is the case in which the field of conditions F_M implies the putative difference-making factor C. In this kind of case, the initial conditions of the system and the laws, in the absence of interfering factors, imply that the factor C holds in the system. As an illustration, consider a slight modification of Mackie's example: A specially designed machine swings a hammer so that it strikes a chestnut directly from above. Suppose we are considering whether the hammer's striking the chestnut (C) makes a difference to the flattening of the chestnut (E), where the hammer strike is an outcome of the lawful evolution of the relevant system from its initial conditions.

In this kind of case, it is simple to specify which worlds are to count as the most similar C-worlds. They are simply the C-worlds that belong to the sphere of normal worlds, that is, those C-worlds that hold fixed the field of conditions F_M. A complication arises, however, when it comes to specifying which worlds are to count as the most similar $\sim C$-worlds. Clearly, $\sim C$ is not consistent with F_M, and so the normal worlds included in F_M are not eligible to be the most similar $\sim C$-worlds.

To work out which are the most similar $\sim C$-worlds in these circumstances, we need to specify the worlds that differ from the normal worlds no more than is necessary to allow for the realization of $\sim C$. In other words, we must find the minimal revision of the field of conditions F_M that is consistent with $\sim C$. There are three elements that determine F_M: the initial conditions of the system, the laws governing the system, and the absence of interfering factors. We can get a set of most similar $\sim C$-worlds by systematically revising each of these elements to allow for the realization of the counterfactual $\sim C$. And each of the resulting revisions counts, in some sense, as a minimal $\sim C$-inducing revision of F_M. Indeed, each of these revisions generates a similarity relation that corresponds to a certain style of counterfactual reasoning.

For example, we could revise the field of conditions F_M to allow for $\sim C$ by revising the laws that govern the system in question while holding fixed the initial conditions and the absence of interferers. Evidently, this kind of revision is required to entertain counterlegals such as "If force were given by mass times velocity, then. . . ." However, this kind of revision is not relevant in the present context, in which we are treating counterfactual antecedents that concern particular matters of fact. Another possibility, more relevant in the present context, is to revise F_M by altering the initial conditions while holding fixed the laws and the absence of interferers. This type of revision corresponds to the style of counterfactual reasoning by which we infer how the past conditions must have been different in order for some counterfactual antecedent to be true. This kind of backtracking reasoning lies behind a counterfactual such as "If the hammer had not struck the chestnut, then the operating machine would have had a malfunction of some kind." However, the one thing we know from counterfactual analyses of causation is that the required similarity relation must not allow for backtracking reasoning of this kind, on pain of generating countless instances of spurious causation.[14]

The only option left is to revise F_M by allowing for the presence of an interfering factor that would realize the counterfactual antecedent $\sim C$, while holding fixed the initial conditions and laws of the system. In other words, the most similar $\sim C$-worlds are like the worlds stipulated in (12) above, in that they preserve the initial conditions of the actual system (condition (i)) and the laws governing the system (condition (iii)), but they differ from these worlds in that they allow for an interfering factor that realizes the counterfactual antecedent $\sim C$ (*not* condition (ii)). As discussed above, the paradigm of such an interfering factor is an external human intervention in a system. In small-scale systems open to human manipulation, the kind of interference that would realize a counterfactual antecedent is to be understood in terms of a human intervention.

For example, in the modified Mackie example, the most similar worlds that make it true that the hammer does not strike the chestnut are easily imagined: they are simply worlds in which the relevant machine runs on from its initial conditions in conformity with the relevant laws, but at some point a human agent intervenes to prevent the hammer from striking the chestnut. With large-scale systems not open to human manipulation, the interference that realizes the counterfactual antecedent can be understood in terms of a miracle that interrupts the lawful evolution of the system.[15] But even here, I would argue, the analogy with human intervention guides the way we think in these cases about the miraculous realization of the counter-factual antecedents.

It is useful at this point to be able to specify which worlds are to count as the most similar C-worlds for any antecedent C, whether or not it is entailed by the field of conditions F_M. To be able to do this, we need an ordering of spheres of worlds in terms of their similarity to the normal worlds in F_M. (Compare Lewis 1973b, pp. 13–16.) If the ordering is to carry information about similarity to the normal worlds, it must satisfy certain conditions.

(13)   Let $\{S_0, \ldots, S_n\}$ be an ordered set of spheres of worlds. This set is *centered* on the sphere of normal worlds S_0 ($= F_M$) if and only if S_0 is included in every other sphere. The set is *nested* if and only if for any spheres S_i and S_j in the set, either S_i is included in S_j or S_j is included in S_i.

When the ordered set of spheres is centered and nested in this sense, it can convey information about the similarity of worlds to the normal worlds. A particular sphere around the sphere of normal worlds will contain just those worlds that resemble the normal worlds to a certain degree. The different spheres will correspond to different degrees of similarity to the normal worlds. The smaller the sphere, the more similar to the normal worlds will be a world falling within it. In other words, if one world falls within a sphere and another world lies outside that sphere, the first world will resemble the normal worlds more closely than the second.

This purely formal specification of the ordering of spheres answers some questions of logic. However, if it is to be applied to particular examples, it must be made more specific with a detailed description of the respects of similarity to the normal worlds that receive significant weighting in the interpretation of conditionals. A complete description of these weightings would require an extensive discussion. However, it will suffice for our treatment of the particular examples of this essay to note one important principle that seems to govern our intuitive judgments about this matter.

(14)   *Weightings of similarity principle*: In determining the respects of similarity to the normal worlds generated by a model M, it is of first importance to preserve the initial conditions and the laws of the relevant kind of system; and it is of second importance to preserve the absence of interfering factors.

One obvious implication of this principle is that it allows us to read certain counterfactuals in the characteristic nonbacktracking manner. It permits a counterfactual antecedent to be realized in a world by an external intervention in the relevant system if the laws and initial conditions of the system are preserved in that world. The principle has another implication that will be relevant to our discussion. We obviously entertain counterfactuals whose antecedents concern changes in the initial conditions of a system. It is perfectly intelligible to say about the modified Mackie example, for instance, "If the initial conditions of the hammer-striking machine had been different, then the situation would have evolved differently." But the principle at hand tells us that we have to go farther out from the normal worlds to find worlds that permit this counterfactual antecedent than we have to go to find worlds that permit the counterfactual antecedent of "If the machine's hammer had not struck the chestnut, it would not have been flattened." Both antecedents can be realized in a world that permits an external intervention in the system. But a world that realizes the first antecedent will, of necessity, involve a change in the initial conditions of the system, whereas a world that realizes the second antecedent will not. The weightings principle implies that the first world must be less similar to the normal worlds than the second world.

With this ordering in hand, we can define the most similar C-worlds in a perfectly general way that covers the case in which C is entailed by the field of conditions F_M and the case in which it is not entailed.

(15)   The *most similar C-worlds* generated by a model M are the C-worlds that belong to the smallest C-permitting sphere in the ordering of spheres governed by the weightings principle.

This is perfectly general also in that it covers not just subcase I, in which C is implied by the field of conditions F_M, but also the yet-to-be-considered subcase II, in which it is $\sim C$ rather than C that is implied by F_M. In this second subcase, the most similar $\sim C$-worlds are simply the $\sim C$-worlds belonging to the sphere of normal worlds. However, to find the most similar C-worlds in this subcase, we have to go out from the sphere of normal worlds to find worlds that allow for the realization of C by intervention or miracle.

We are finally in a position to explicate the idea of one factor making a difference to another in a way that acknowledges the relativity to models.

(16)   *C makes a difference to E* in an actual situation relative to the model M of the situation if and only if every most similar C-world generated by the model is an E-world and every most similar $\sim C$-world generated by the model is a $\sim E$-world.

Of course, these truth conditions bear an unsurprising resemblance to the standard truth conditions for counterfactuals. If the truth conditions for counterfactuals are relativized in a way to match those given above, then the condition can be reformulated to yield the following one:

(17)   *C makes a difference to E* in an actual situation relative to the model M if and only if $C \mathrel{\square\!\!\rightarrow}_M E$ and $\sim C \mathrel{\square\!\!\rightarrow}_M \sim E$.

Here the subscript M on the counterfactual operator signifies that the operator is defined with respect to the ordering of spheres generated by the model M.

This counterfactual construction is similar to the notion of counterfactual dependence that plays the central role in Lewis's counterfactual analysis. Indeed, it will be useful to be able to take over this terminology. But the way I will use the term is different from the way Lewis uses it in two respects. First, the counterfactuals that define counterfactual dependence do not, for the reasons given above, conform to the centering principle that Lewis imposes on counterfactuals. On the other hand, I believe that they conform to the limit assumption to the effect that there is a smallest sphere of antecedent-permitting worlds for any entertainable antecedent. Lewis considers this an optional principle for counterfactuals. But, in fact, it applies automatically to the counterfactuals I have defined, since it follows from the way in which a model generates an ordering of spheres of worlds centered on the normal worlds.

The other way in which the present definition of counterfactual dependence differs from Lewis's is the obvious one bearing on the relativity to a model. The notion of counterfactual dependence, as I will use it, inherits the relativity to a model of the counterfactuals that define it. The truth conditions of counterfactuals in my theory are defined over the most similar antecedent-worlds generated by a model. Lewis's notion involves no such relativity, for he assumes that there is only one kind of system to consider—the whole universe—and so his worlds are maximal worlds. He also assumes that worlds are governed by exceptionless laws without ceteris paribus conditions, and so he makes no use of the notion of an interferer in a system, which

I believe is required to explain the content of ceteris paribus conditions. There are further differences between the accounts, but they follow from these.

Let me conclude this section by connecting up our recent discussion with the earlier discussion of the idea that motivates analyses of causation in terms of making a difference. As we have seen, Mackie argues for a conceptual analysis of a cause as "what makes the difference in relation to some assumed background or causal field." This idea is best understood, he argues, in terms of the experimental-and-control contrast, rather than the before-and-after contrast. The former contrast can be captured by a pair of conditionals, with one conditional corresponding to the experimental case and the other conditional corresponding to the control case.

We can now see how to make sense of Mackie's claims. Let us suppose that a conditional is an "experimental" conditional if we do not have to leave the sphere of normal worlds to find the most similar antecedent-worlds. In other words, the antecedent would be realized by allowing the system in question to evolve lawfully without interference. On the other hand, let us suppose that a conditional is a "control" conditional if we do have to leave the sphere of normal worlds to find the most similar antecedent-worlds. Or, in other words, the antecedent would be realized only by an intervention in the lawful evolution of the system in question from its initial conditions. Given this terminology, we can see that one of the conditionals that define the difference-making condition (17) will be an "experimental" conditional and the other a "control" conditional.

It is important to realize, though, that the two conditionals in (17) do not always line up in the same way with the experimental and control cases. It depends on whether we are considering subcase I or subcase II. In subcase I, the "experimental" conditional is $C \mathbin{\square\!\!\rightarrow}_M E$ and the "control" conditional is $\sim\!C \mathbin{\square\!\!\rightarrow}_M \sim\!E$. An example in which both these conditionals are true is represented in figure 6.1. In this figure, the concentric circles represent the spheres of worlds, with the smallest sphere F_M representing the sphere of normal worlds generated by a model M. The symbol "@" denotes the actual world.

In subcase II, $C \mathbin{\square\!\!\rightarrow}_M E$ is the "control" conditional and $\sim\!C \mathbin{\square\!\!\rightarrow}_M \sim\!E$ the "experimental" conditional. An example in which both these conditionals are true is represented in figure 6.2. (Notice that in both subcases $C \mathbin{\square\!\!\rightarrow}_M E$ is a factual conditional in the sense that C and E both actually hold, while $\sim\!C \mathbin{\square\!\!\rightarrow}_M \sim\!E$ is a genuine counterfactual conditional since $\sim\!C$ and $\sim\!E$ actually fail to hold. Hence, the experimental–control dichotomy crosscuts the factual–counterfactual dichotomy.)

Finally, I wish to make a connection with another classic discussion of causation. In their work on causation in the law, Hart and Honoré claim that the concept of

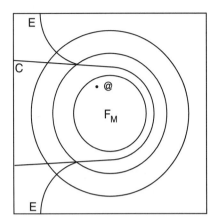

Figure 6.1

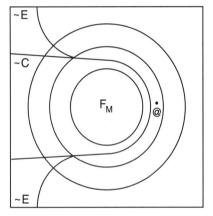

Figure 6.2

a cause as making a difference has its home in a certain paradigm situation. They write:

Human action in the simple cases, where we produce some desired effect by the manipulation of an object in our environment, is an interference in the natural course of events which *makes a difference* in the way these develop. In an almost literal sense, such an interference by human action is an intervention or intrusion of one kind of thing upon a distinct kind of thing. Common experience teaches us that, left to themselves, the things we manipulate, since they have a "nature" or characteristic way of behaving, would persist in states or exhibit changes different from those which we have learnt to bring about in them by our manipulation. The notion, that a cause is essentially something which interferes with or intervenes in the course of events which would normally take place, is central to the commonsense concept of cause, and at least as essential as the notions of invariable or constant sequence so much stressed by Mill and Hume. Analogies with the interference by human beings with the natural course of events in part control, even in cases where there is literally no human intervention, what is identified as the cause of some occurrence; the cause, though not a literal intervention, is a *difference* to the normal course which accounts for the difference in the outcome.   (Hart and Honoré 1985, p. 29)

Again it is possible to see the point of Hart and Honoré's remarks in the light of the framework developed above. They are, in effect, considering, as a paradigm case, the kind of causal situation that falls under subcase II. The normal course of events for a system of some kind, free from any external interference, makes $\sim E$ true. If it turns out that E actually holds, then an explanation is required in terms of some factor that makes a difference to this normal course of events. It will be some factor C such that both the "experimental" conditional $\sim C \mathrel{\Box\!\!\to}_M \sim E$ and the "control" conditional $C \mathrel{\Box\!\!\to}_M E$ are true. By the definition of these conditionals, C will count as an interfering factor in the normal course of development of the system, the kind of interfering factor that is paradigmatically exemplified by an external intervention in the system by an agent. My only reservation about the quotation from Hart and Honoré is that it focuses attention on just one of the two important subcases of the idea of making a difference, ignoring the important subcase I.

7   The Phenomena Explained

Let us return to the various puzzle cases that were cited as problems for Lewis's account of difference-making in section 3. As we saw in that section, Lewis's account blurs the commonsense distinction between causes and conditions. Let us see whether the present account of difference-making can explain this distinction.

Most philosophical discussions of the distinction between causes and conditions take it for granted that the distinction is best elucidated in a specific explanatory setting. (See, for example, Hart and Honoré 1985, pp. 32–44; and Mackie 1974, pp. 34–37.) The setting is one in which some unexpected factor E stands in need of explanation, specifically in terms of something that differentiates it from the normal situation in which $\sim E$ obtains. This assumption makes sense in terms of the present framework. It simply amounts to the supposition that the causes–conditions distinction is best understood in terms of examples falling under subcase II. In examples of this kind, the field of normal conditions F_M generated by a model entails $\sim E$, so that when E unexpectedly obtains, it requires explanation in terms of a difference-making factor. Let us proceed on the assumption of this explanatory setting, though always keeping in mind that this is just one of two possible subcases.

It is interesting to note in this connection a certain abstract implication of the logic of difference-making. It follows from the description of the assumed explanatory setting as exemplifying subcase II that the factor identified as making the difference to E must be identified as an interfering factor in the system. The logic of the situation implies that the factor C that makes the difference to E cannot intersect with the field of normal conditions F_M, so that the smallest C-permitting sphere of worlds includes worlds in which C is realized by way of an external interference or intervention in the system. (Figure 6.2 represents the situation of the explanatory setting.) This implication explains the way in which commonsense and scientific explanations of abnormal occurrences in systems often describe the difference-making factor as an interferer or intervention in the system. Such factors are seen as intrusions into the system that account for the deviation from the normal course of events.[16]

In terms of the explanatory setting we are assuming, it is easy to identify the conditions for a causal judgment made relative to a model M. They are simply the conditions that belong to the field of normal conditions F_M. Typically speaking, they will be conditions relating to the initial state of the system in question, conditions relating to the absence of interferers, and any conditions that follow from these and the laws governing the system. Notice that these conditions are not restricted to ones obtaining contemporaneously with the difference-making factor. To modify an example from Hart and Honoré (1985, p. 39): if lightning starts a fire in the grass, and shortly after, a normal gentle breeze gets up and the fire spreads to a forest, then the lightning caused the forest fire and the breeze was a mere condition of it. Even though the breeze was subsequent to the lightning, it can be identified as a condition so long as it arises lawfully from the initial conditions of the relevant system and is not an interference in the system.

It follows from this identification of the conditions that no condition can be cited as a difference-maker for the unexpected or abnormal event E in the explanatory setting under consideration. A difference-maker C must be an actually obtaining factor such that all the most-similar C-worlds are E-worlds and all the most-similar $\sim C$-worlds are $\sim E$-worlds. Figure 6.2, which illustrates this explanatory setting, shows that no actual condition entailed by F_M can meet this requirement. In particular, any actual condition X entailed by F_M will be such that all the most similar X-worlds are $\sim E$ worlds, contrary to what is required. Consequently, the identification of a condition as an actual factor entailed by F_M implies that conditions cannot be difference-making causes. This is exactly as it should be.

Let us make the discussion concrete by reconsidering the cases cited in section 3, starting with the lung cancer case (example 1). The essential step in treating this example is the identification of the causal model that guides our intuitions about it. It is natural to specify the relevant model here as involving a person living according to the laws of normal healthy functioning. If the person gets lung cancer, then it is reasonable to look for some factor that makes the difference to this effect with respect to the normal worlds generated by this model—some factor such as his smoking, for instance. Yet, even when the model is specified in these broad terms, we can see that the field of normal conditions generated by this model will hold fixed, as initial conditions, the fact that the person has been born and has lungs. Hence, these conditions cannot be cited as a difference-making factors.

The situation is represented diagrammatically in figure 6.3. The field of normal conditions F_M generated by the relevant model M entails that the person in question does not get lung cancer (LC). However, as things actually turn out, the person develops lung cancer, so that an explanation is required in terms of a difference-maker. The figure shows that person's smoking (S) is such a difference-maker, since

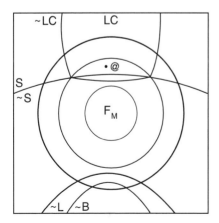

Figure 6.3

both of the conditionals $S \mathrel{\square\!\!\rightarrow}_M LC$ and $\sim\!S \mathrel{\square\!\!\rightarrow}_M \sim\!LC$ are true. However, the figure also shows that the person's birth (B) and his possession of lungs (L) are mere conditions in this example, as they are entailed by the field of normal conditions. As such, they cannot qualify as difference-makers for the person's lung cancer. (In particular, it turns out that the "wrong" conditionals $B \mathrel{\square\!\!\rightarrow}_M \sim\!LC$ and $L \mathrel{\square\!\!\rightarrow}_M \sim\!LC$ hold, so that B and L cannot be make the appropriate counterfactual difference to LC.) The figure also shows that there are outer spheres of worlds, quite dissimilar to the normal worlds of F_M, that permit the absence of these conditions. In these outer spheres, it is true that $\sim\!B \mathrel{\square\!\!\rightarrow}_M \sim\!LC$ and $\sim\!L \mathrel{\square\!\!\rightarrow}_M \sim\!LC$, as one would expect to be the case.

Of course, the causal claims about the person can be interpreted in terms of a different causal model. By changing the example, we can make a different causal model more salient. Consider an example given by Lewis, in which we are to suppose that there are gods who take a keen interest in human affairs:

It has been foretold that the event of your death, if it occurs, will somehow have a momentous impact on the heavenly balance of power. It will advance the cause of Hermes, it will be a catastrophe for Apollo. Therefore Apollo orders one of his underlings, well ahead of time, to see to it that this disastrous event never occurs. The underling isn't sure that just changing the time and manner of your death would suffice to avert the catastrophe; and so decides to prevent your death altogether by preventing your birth. But the underling bungles the job: You are born, you die, and it's just as catastrophic for Apollo as had been foretold. When the hapless underling is had up for charges of negligence, surely it would be entirely appropriate for Apollo to complain that your birth caused your death.   (Lewis, "Causation as Influence," chap. 3 of this volume, p. 101)

It would, indeed, be appropriate for Apollo to make this causal claim. But notice how the causal model has changed, with a different kind of system and different laws of functioning involved. Indeed, this example is better seen as exemplifying subcase I rather than II, as the field of normal conditions F_M generated by the relevant model entails the factor to be explained, namely, that you will die (D). This is represented diagrammatically in figure 6.4. Nonetheless, your birth (B) does make a difference to your death in view of the fact that Apollo's underling could have intervened in the system (I) to prevent your birth and so your death. Here the two counterfactuals required for your birth to be a difference-maker for your death, that is, $B \mathrel{\square\!\!\rightarrow}_M D$ and $\sim\!B \mathrel{\square\!\!\rightarrow}_M \sim\!D$, both hold true with respect to the sphere of normal worlds generated by the relevant model. But it does require a radical change of causal model to get this result.

The present framework provides a ready explanation of the two forms of contextual relativity underlying the commonsense causes–conditions distinction. It is easy

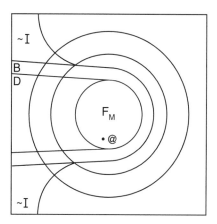

Figure 6.4

to see how the explanation should work for the presence of oxygen case (example 2). Here our readiness to rank the presence of oxygen as a condition in one situation and a cause in another simply reflects the fact that the two situations involve different kinds of systems with different initial conditions. In the first situation, in which a fire takes hold of a building, the presence of oxygen is an initial condition, held fixed in the field of normal conditions, whereas in the second situation, in which oxygen is excluded from a delicate experimental or manufactory setup, it is not an initial condition, and so it is eligible to be a difference-maker for the effect.

The explanation of the relativity of the causes–conditions distinction to the context of inquiry is equally straightforward. In the ulcerated stomach case (example 3), the causal claims made by the different inquirers are explained by the fact that they are employing different models. For example, the person who prepares meals for the patient implicitly employs a model that focuses on the person with the ulcerated stomach as a fixed initial condition. On the other hand, the doctor tacitly employs a model that focuses on the person as a normally functioning human without ulcerated stomach as a fixed initial condition. These inquirers both seek factors that make a difference to the patient's indigestion, but they do so with respect to the different spheres of normal worlds generated by their different models.

Another virtue of the present framework is that it allows us to discriminate between absences as causes and absences as mere conditions. In allowing absences and other nonoccurrences as causes, we need not open the floodgate to a host of spurious causes. For instance, the natural causal model for interpreting the multiple omissions case (example 5) ranks the gardener's omission as the cause of the plant's death,

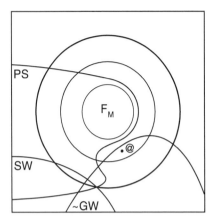

Figure 6.5

while backgrounding other people's omissions as mere conditions. This causal model is one that takes, as its system for investigation, a healthy plant functioning under a regime of regular watering by the gardener. Accordingly, this example can be seen to exemplify subcase II, in which the field of normal conditions F_M entails that the gardener waters the plant (GW) and the plant survives (PS). The situation is represented in figure 6.5. When the plant fails to survive, an explanation in terms of a difference-maker is required. The gardener's actual omission can act as such a difference-maker, since the two appropriate counterfactuals hold true, $GW \mathrel{\square\!\!\rightarrow_M} PS$ and $\sim GW \mathrel{\square\!\!\rightarrow_M} \sim PS$. (Notice that in this case what explains the abnormal occurrence of the plant's death is actually a nonoccurrence. It seems that common sense sometimes regards a nonoccurrence as an interfering factor that perturbs the normal course of development of some kinds of systems.) However, the omission by everyone else $(\sim SW)$ to water the plant is disqualified from acting as a difference-maker, as this omission is held fixed in the field of normal conditions. (However, an outer sphere allows it to be the case that someone else waters the plant and in this outer sphere it holds true that $SW \mathrel{\square\!\!\rightarrow_M} PS$.)

A similar explanation can be given of our causal judgments about the absence of nerve gas case (example 4), when it is interpreted as exemplifying subcase II. As a matter of fact, this is a rather strained interpretation, as one has to imagine a field of normal conditions generated by an appropriate model that entails that I am not writing at my computer. However, if we do imagine this, then given that I am so writing, it is reasonable to ask for some explanation in terms of a difference-maker.

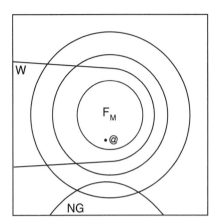

Figure 6.6

But this difference-maker cannot be supplied by the absence of nerve gas, the absence of flamethrower attack, or absence of meteor strike—for these absences are held fixed in the field of normal conditions, in view of the fact that the intrusion of nerve gas, or flamethrower attack, or meteor strike would count as an interference in the system.

It is much easier to understand this example as exemplifying subcase I; that is, the field of normal conditions generated by the relevant model entails the actually obtaining factor—my writing at my computer. However, a striking fact emerges when one construes the example in this way. The various absences mentioned above can each count as a difference-maker for my writing. For instance, the intrusion of nerve gas into the situation in which I am writing at my computer is naturally regarded as an interference, whose absence should be held fixed in the field of normal conditions. However, the rules for a model's generating spheres of worlds (in particular, the weightings principle) permit the presence of the nerve gas in an outer sphere of worlds. The consequence of this is that the two counterfactuals required for the absence of nerve gas ($\sim NG$) to count as a difference-maker for my writing (W) can both hold. Figure 6.6 represents the situation in which the two counterfactuals $NG \mathbin{\square\!\!\rightarrow}_M \sim W$ and $\sim NG \mathbin{\square\!\!\rightarrow}_M W$ hold. The same line of reasoning shows that the absence of any factor that could be regarded as an interferer can, in the right circumstances, act as a difference-maker for my writing at my computer, when the example is construed as exemplifying subcase I rather than II. I conjecture that it is not absurd to judge in these circumstances that a *sustaining cause* of my writing at my computer is the collective absence of all interfering factors, including the absence of nerve gas, the absence of flamethrower attack, and the absence of meteor strike.

In the discussion above, I have argued that the commonsense distinction between causes and conditions makes sense only relative to a field of normal conditions generated by a causal model. Given such a model, the conditions of some effect can be explained as those factors belonging to the field, and the causes as those factors that make the difference to the effect relative to this field. It is worth comparing this characterization of the distinction with an alternative one that has become popular. On this alternative characterization, the distinction is an entirely pragmatic one to be cashed out in terms of contrastive explanation. We have already seen the outlines of this kind of approach in section 4. The main idea is that commonplace causal judgments are implicit answers to contrastive why-questions of the form "Why does E_1, rather than $E_2, \ldots, E_n$, obtain?" where the members of the contrast class $\{E_1, \ldots, E_n\}$ may or may not be mutually compatible. On this approach, a cause is an actual "objective cause" that differentiates E_1 from the other members of the contrast class; and the conditions are those factors that are common to all possible situations that could realize a member of the contrast class. This approach also makes the distinction a context-sensitive one because different contexts may contrast E_1 with different sets of alternatives, so affecting which factors count as causes and conditions.

There are, to be sure, similarities between these characterizations of the causes–conditions distinction. One obvious similarity is that they both characterize the distinction in terms of a contextually generated space of possibilities. In the present framework, it is the space of normal worlds generated by a model; in the alternative framework, it is the space of contrasting alternatives. Still, there are, in my view, some serious shortcomings to this alternative characterization, some of which have been touched on earlier.

One of these is that the characterization must operate with an independently motivated notion of an "objective cause." The factor that differentiates E_1 from the other members of the contrast class cannot be a causally irrelevant factor: it must be an "objective cause" present in the E_1 situation, but not in the others. But this requires an explication of what an "objective cause" is. The explication cannot, on pain of unnecessary duplication, appeal to the idea of a difference-maker. Another shortcoming of the characterization is that it leaves radically underspecified what conditions are common to the realizations of the different members of the contrast class. A specification of these commonalities requires a description of a similarity relation between the possible situations realizing the various members of the contrast class. It is totally unclear what this similarity relation involves. Lewis attempts, as we have seen, to specify a similarity relation by appeal to backtracking reasoning, but this attempt fails to deliver determinate verdicts in many cases.

For these reasons, I believe, the alternative characterization of the causes–conditions distinction in terms of contrastive explanation cannot bear the explanatory weight that many have placed on it. Why then, it may be asked, does the account of the phenomena in terms of contrastive explanation, sketched in section 4, work as well as it does? There are several reasons, I would suggest. First, the treatment of causal judgments as answers to contrastive why-questions puts the emphasis in the right place, namely, on the context-relativity of these judgments. Second, the specification of the contrast class, embodied in a contrastive why-question, carries information about the kind of system that is being investigated and its laws of normal functioning. In other words, we can read off from a class of contrasting alternatives information about the real contextual determinant of our causal judgments—the underlying causal model. But the contrast class is, at best, an indirect source of this information.

So, I oppose the popular strategy of explaining the commonsense view of causes as difference-makers pragmatically in terms of contrastive explanation. Rather, I recommend the reverse procedure of explaining contrastive explanation in terms of the present independently motivated account of difference-making. Let me outline in broad detail how such an explanation should work. Suppose the contrastive why-question "Why does E_1, rather than $E_2, \ldots, E_n$, obtain?" has been posed, where the members of this contrast class are all actual or possible factors of systems of kind K operating according to laws L. Then, a satisfactory answer to this question should cite some actual factor C that makes a difference to E_1 relative to the model $M = \langle K, L \rangle$. Where the members of the contrast class are *incompatible* outcomes in the same system, it follows from the definition of C as a difference-maker for E_1 that we have an automatic explanation why none of the alternative possible outcomes could have occurred. Similarly, where the members of the contrast class are *compatible* outcomes of different systems of kind K, it follows from the definition of C as a difference-maker for E_1 that we have an automatic explanation why none of the alternative outcomes actually occurred (for, given that these have the same initial conditions and conform to the same laws, these systems would have to have E_1 if they had the factor C).

This account of contrastive explanation overcomes the difficulties facing Lewis's account that we encountered in section 4. For example, it does not leave indeterminate what the various members of the contrast class have in common. It specifies these commonalities precisely in terms of the field of normal conditions generated by the relevant causal model. Again, it handles the examples such as Hempel's, where a contrastive explanation is required of two compatible alternatives. We explain why Jones, rather than Smith, got paresis, by citing the difference-making factor of syphilis that actually applies to Jones, but not to Smith. Most important, this account does not involve an unnecessary duplication of the idea of a difference-maker. It follows from the definition of difference-making that, if we have factor C that makes a difference to E_1, then we have a contrastive explanation of why E_1 rather than $E_2, \ldots, E_n$ occurred. This factor does its work of differentiating the contrasting alternatives precisely because it is, by hypothesis, a difference-maker for E_1.

8 Conclusion

One of the aims of this essay has been to explore the conception of a cause as "what makes the difference in relation to some assumed background or causal field" (Mackie 1974, p. 71). I have tried to explicate this conception by giving an account of difference-making in terms of context-sensitive counterfactuals. This account explains the way in which we distinguish causes from background conditions in terms of the way in which an implicit contextual parameter of a causal model generates a similarity ordering among possible worlds. It is important to elucidate this dimension of context-sensitivity in our causal judgments not only to get the conceptual analysis of causation right, but also to avoid philosophical puzzles that arise from conceptions of causation that are too simplistic. For example, the puzzle in the philosophy of mind about mental causation—the puzzle of how mental states can play a role in the causation of behavior independent of the role played by the physical states on which they supervene—arises because philosophers overlook the way in which causal models implicitly guide our judgments about causation, or so I argue (in Menzies 2002).

Notes

1. I have considered some of the problems faced by the counterfactual approach to causation in connection with preemption cases in Menzies (1996). There I argue that cases of preemption show that a purely counterfactual analysis of causation will not work: at some point we must make an appeal to a concept of causation as an intrinsic relation or process in order to deal with them. (See also Menzies 1999.) I show how to marry counterfactual intuitions about causation with intuitions about intrinsic processes by way of a Ramsey–Carnap–Lewis treatment of causation as a theoretical relation. On this treatment, a counterfactual dependence is a defeasible marker of causation: when the appropriate conditions are satisfied, it picks out the process that counts as the causal relation. Such a treatment of causation as a theoretical relation obviously can be framed around the counterfactual explication of the idea of a cause as a difference-maker recommended in this chapter.

2. Actually, Lewis has presented three theories of causation, the third being the "quasi-dependence" theory that he tentatively sketched in postscript E to the paper "Causation" (Lewis 1986b).

3. Mackie credits the term 'field of causal conditions' to his teacher John Anderson, who used it to resolve difficulties in Mill's account of causation in Anderson (1938).

4. I take the terms for the different kinds of context relativity from Gorovitz (1965).

5. It might be argued that these examples demonstrate only that the construction "c is *the* cause of e" is context sensitive; and that the counterfactual theory is best understood as an account of the context-insensitive construction "c is *a* cause of e." Thus it might be argued that even the World Food Authority would admit that the drought was *a* cause of the famine and that the doctor would allow that eating parsnips was *a* cause of the indigestion. While this defense on the basis of common usage seems faintly acceptable with some examples, it fails in other cases. Even with a liberal understanding of the words, it seems a stretch to say that a person's birth and possession of lungs were among the causes of his lung cancer. It seems that even the expression "a cause" displays some degree of context sensitivity. For discussion and elaboration of this point see Unger (1977).

6. Mill wrote: "Nothing can better show the absence of any scientific ground for the distinction between the cause of a phenomenon and its conditions, than the capricious way in which we select from among the conditions that which we choose to denominate the cause." See Mill (1961), p. 214.

7. The clearest exponent of this strategy of adding on a theory of contrastive explanation to a theory of "objective causation" is Peter Lipton: see his (1990) and (1991), chapters 3–5. Lipton does not, however, endorse Lewis's counterfactual theory as the right theory of "objective causation." Others who have emphasized the importance of contrastive explanation for understanding ordinary causal discourse include Gorovitz (1965), Mackie (1974), Dretske (1973), Woodward (1984), and Hitchcock (1996b).

8. It is worth observing that the idea of an integrated account of context-sensitivity is not altogether foreign to Lewis's style of counterfactual theory. In the revamped (2000) version of the theory, context enters the theory in an important but inconspicuous way. The notion of a not-too-distant alteration of the cause introduces an important contextual element into the truth conditions of causal statements. A not-too-distant alteration of the cause is an alteration that is relevantly similar to the cause by the standards determined by the context. The approach I shall advocate is similar in building context-sensitivity into the truth conditions, but it will draw on contextually determined standards of similarity for counterfactuals rather than events.

9. I develop a fuller account of factors in Menzies (1989b), though that paper uses the term "situations" rather than "factors."

10. A problem infects these definitions that is parallel to the problem Lewis pointed out for Kim's definition of the simple concepts. Modifying some concepts Lewis introduced, let us say that a system S is *accompanied* if and only if it coexists with some contingent object wholly distinct from it, and *lonely* if and only if it does not so coexist. The definitions I have presented amount to saying that the extrinsic properties of a system are those implied by the accompaniment of the system and the intrinsic properties of a system are those compatible with its loneliness. The problem is that loneliness of a system is intuitively an extrinsic property of the system (since it can differ between duplicates of the system), but it counts as an intrinsic property by the definition (since it is compatible with itself). One possible remedy to this problem may be to adapt to our purposes the refinement of Kim's original idea to be found in Langton and Lewis (1998). This refinement is supposed to circumvent the defect Lewis detected in Kim's original idea.

11. The concepts of relations that are extrinsic or intrinsic to a set of objects can be defined in a similar manner. A relation R is *extrinsic* to a set of objects if and only if, necessarily, the relation holds between two members of the set only if some other contingent object wholly distinct from the set exists. Conversely, a relation R is *intrinsic* to the set if and only if, possibly, the relation holds between two constituents of the system although no contingent object wholly distinct from the set exists.

12. In using the terms "sphere of *normal* worlds" and "field of *normal* conditions," I am not invoking the ordinary notion of "normal." Rather, the given definitions stipulate the intended sense in which I use the terms, though I hope this sense bears some relation to the ordinary notion of "normal."

13. For an illuminating discussion of the role of zero-force laws, such as the first law of motion and the Hardy–Weinberg law, in default assumptions about the evolution of systems, see Elliott Sober's discussion (1984, chap. 1).

14. See, for example, Lewis's discussion of the perils of allowing backtracking counterfactuals in the counterfactual analysis of causation in his postscripts to "Counterfactual Dependence and Time's Arrow" and "Causation" in his (1986a).

15. For an account of the similarity relation for nonbacktracking counterfactuals that appeals to the miraculous realization of antecedents, see Lewis (1979a).

16. For discussions of episodes in the history of science that highlight the significance of causes as intrusions in the normal course of events, see Toulmin (1961), chapters 3–4; and Sober (1980).

7 Causation and the Price of Transitivity

Ned Hall

1 Introduction and Preliminaries

That causation is, necessarily, a *transitive* relation on events seems to many a bedrock datum, one of the few indisputable a priori insights we have into the workings of the concept. Of course, state this *Transitivity* thesis so boldly and it will likely come *under* dispute; one can reasonably worry that the appearance of a priori insight glosses over a lack of cleverness on our part. Might not some ingenious counterexample to *Transitivity* lurk nearby, waiting for a philosopher acute enough to spot it?

"Yes," comes the recent reply. In the last several years a number of philosophers, myself included, have exhibited examples that appear to undermine *Transitivity* (although, as we'll see, the target of my own examples was, and remains, quite different). I'll review a representative sample in the next section. First I need to sketch the main argument of the paper, and take care of some preliminaries.

I claim that the examples do have something to teach us about the metaphysics of causation, but that it is emphatically *not* that *Transitivity* fails. Close inspection reveals that they pose no threat to that thesis. But they—or rather, certain of them, constructed with sufficient care—*do* show that *Transitivity* conflicts with the following thesis:

Dependence Necessarily, when wholly distinct events *c* and *e* occur, and *e* counterfactually depends on *c* (read: if *c* hadn't happened, *e* wouldn't have), then *c* is thereby a *cause* of *e*.

Dependence should not be confused with the transparently false claim that counterfactual dependence is necessary for causation; it is rather the claim that such dependence is sufficient—at least, when the events in question are wholly distinct, so that the relation of dependence does not hold merely in virtue of their mereological or logical relationships.[1] Nor is *Dependence* the claim that causation can be given a counterfactual analysis, though most (if not all) counterfactual analyses endorse it. One might hold that no analysis of causation is possible, and yet endorse *Dependence*. Or again, one might hold that it is *counterfactuals* that demand an analysis in terms of *causation*, and yet maintain *Dependence*. What's more, *Dependence* surely has a great deal of intuitive plausibility, at least when we are careful to read the counterfactual in a suitable "nonbacktracking" sense, one that rules out such judgments as

Originally published in a special issue of the *Journal of Philosophy* (April 2000). Minor revisions have been made for consistency.

that if c had not occurred, then it would have to have been the case that those *earlier* events that were causally sufficient for it did not occur.[2] Given the plausibility of *Dependence*, its conflict with *Transitivity* is all the more striking.

In the end, I'll suggest that were we forced to choose, we should reject *Dependence* in favor of *Transitivity*. But I'll also suggest that we *aren't* forced to choose, since we can perfectly well recognize different *kinds* of causal relation in which events can stand, so that an obvious resolution of the conflict between *Dependence* and *Transitivity* presents itself: The kind of causal relation characterized by the first thesis is not the same as—indeed, fundamentally differs from—the kind of causal relation characterized by the second. Still, a manifest asymmetry distinguishes these causal relations, in that the kind of causal relation for which *Transitivity* holds is clearly the more central of the two. So the price of transitivity—a price well worth paying—is to give up on the claim that there is any *deep* connection between counterfactual dependence and (the central kind of) causation.

Here is the plan for getting to these conclusions: First I'll run through some of the alleged counterexamples to *Transitivity*, and highlight their apparent common structure (sec. 2); examples with this structure I call "short-circuits." An immediate problem will emerge for my claim that *Dependence* is the culprit, and not *Transitivity*; for while that claim neatly deflects *some* of the counterexamples (call these the "Easy" ones), it does not help deflect the others (call these the "Hard" ones). But the Easy and Hard cases share the "short-circuit" structure, and what's worse, it seems that it is *in virtue* of this structure that they are (or at least appear to be) counterexamples to *Transitivity*. So targeting *Dependence* seems quite mistaken.[3]

Not so, but it takes some work to see why. I start by sharpening the challenge the Hard cases pose to *Transitivity* by distinguishing three *different* problems for that thesis, arguing that they aren't deep problems, and observing that their solutions help not at all in dealing with the Hard cases, at least if those cases are formulated carefully enough (sec. 3). The main argument follows: In section 4 I'll introduce a kind of causal structure that I call a "switch," in which one event c interacts with a causal process in such a way as to redirect the causal route by which that process brings about a given event e. This structure differs in obvious ways from the apparent common structure of the alleged counterexamples. It also might seem to pose trouble of its own for *Transitivity*, for reasons that I explain. I'll argue that the trouble is illusory, and that a number of considerations tell in favor of counting c a cause of e, when c is a switch with respect to e. That argument sets the stage for section 5, where I revisit the alleged counterexamples to *Transitivity*, and show that what distinguishes the Easy cases from the Hard ones is exactly that the Hard ones, in addition to possessing the short-circuit structure, *also* possess a (much less noticeable) *switching* structure. So the intuitive verdict—that they provide us with cases in which *c* is a cause of *d*, and *d* of *e*, but *not c* of *e*—is mistaken: *c* is a cause of *e*, in virtue of being a *switch* with respect to *e*. Since the Easy cases do not exhibit the switching structure, no such maneuver helps neutralize their threat to *Transitivity*. But the original, obvious option—treat them as counterexamples only to *Dependence*— remains available, and should be taken.

I close, in section 6, by highlighting two different lessons we learn from the examples. The first is metaphysical: What the Easy cases show us is that *Transitivity* and *Dependence* conflict. Of course, that verdict leaves it open which one must go; I'll sketch a number of reasons to hold onto *Transitivity* at the cost of *Dependence*. The second is methodological: Briefly, the Hard cases remind us that the business of mining for intuitions about causation is risky. It is all too easy to mistake fool's gold for the real thing, and one must therefore be careful to subject one's hypothetical cases to careful analysis before trying to buy fancy conclusions with them. The Easy cases stand up under such analysis; the Hard cases don't.

2   The Counterexamples and Their Apparent Common Structure

Here is an example from Michael McDermott (1995a): A man plans to detonate a bomb. The day before, his dog bites off his right forefinger, so when he goes to press the button he uses his left forefinger instead. Since he is right-handed—and so would have used his right forefinger—the dogbite causes his pressing of the button with his left forefinger. This event in turn causes the subsequent explosion. But, intuitively, the dogbite does not cause the explosion.

Here is another example, adapted from one devised by Hartry Field: An assassin plants a bomb under my desk (philosophy is a dangerous business, you know). I find it, and safely remove it. His planting the bomb causes my finding it, which in turn causes my continued survival. But, intuitively, his planting it does not cause my continued survival.

Next, one from Igal Kvart (1991b): A man's finger is severed in a factory accident. He is rushed to the hospital, where an expert surgeon reattaches the finger, doing such a splendid job that a year later, it functions as well as if the accident had never happened. The accident causes the surgery, which in turn causes the finger to be in a healthy state a year later. But, intuitively, the accident does not cause the finger to be in a healthy state a year later.

Finally, a refreshingly nonviolent example of my own: Billy and Suzy are friends. Suzy is mischievous, and Billy is forever trying to keep her out of trouble. Billy sees Suzy about to throw a water balloon at her neighbor's dog. He runs to try to stop her, but trips over a tree root and so fails. Suzy, totally oblivious to him, throws the water balloon at the dog. It yelps. She gets in trouble. Billy's running toward Suzy causes him to trip, which in turn causes the dog to yelp (by *Dependence*: If he hadn't tripped, he would have stopped her from throwing and so the dog wouldn't have yelped). But, intuitively, his running toward her does not cause the dog's yelp.

This last example is an Easy case—Easy because it is so obvious how to respond to it in a way that safeguards *Transitivity*. After all, the only sense in which Billy's trip "causes" the dog's yelp is that it prevents something—Billy continuing to run toward Suzy, reaching her in time to stop her from throwing the balloon, and so on—which, had it happened, would have prevented the yelp. But no *causal process* connects the trip to the yelp (and not because the connection is an example of magical "action-at-a-distance"). So we are well within our rights to deny that, in this and similar cases of "double-prevention," the sort of dependence the yelp has on the trip is *causal* dependence—and if so, the example poses no threat to *Transitivity*. Or, more cautiously, we might allow that the trip is, in *some* sense, a cause of the yelp— but that it is not this rather nonstandard sense of "cause" we have in mind when we assert *Transitivity*, but rather the ordinary, garden-variety sense.[4] Still, no threat to *Transitivity*. The casualty, rather, is *Dependence*: It is either false, or must be taken to be true only of a sort of nonstandard, second-class kind of causation.

But this response falls limp when it comes to the three other cases. Take Kvart's, for example: It's not merely that the healthy state of the finger counterfactually depends on the surgery; no, a perfectly ordinary causal process also connects the two. Likewise, a perfectly ordinary causal process connects the accident to the surgery. So how can we blame *Dependence*, and not *Transitivity*, for the counterintuitive result? Worse, it might seem that I've misdiagnosed my own Easy case. For observe that all four examples have the following salient causal structure in common: An event c occurs, beginning (or combining with other events to begin) some process that threatens to prevent some later event e from occurring (call this process "Threat"). But, as a sort of side-effect, c also causes some event d that *counteracts* the threat (call this event "Savior"). So c is a cause of Savior, and Savior—by virtue of counteracting Threat—is a cause of e. But—or so it seems to many philosophers— c is not thereby a cause of e, and so *Transitivity* fails. That diagnosis seems to apply equally to all four examples. So shouldn't we favor it over a diagnosis that only fits the last of the examples?

No. The correct picture is a more complicated one, according to which the last example deserves exactly the diagnosis I gave it, and the first three "Hard" cases deserve a quite different diagnosis. And the reason is that the Hard cases have a quite different causal structure from the last, Easy case.

Bringing out this different structure will take some care. As a preliminary, I will contrast the foregoing alleged counterexamples to *Transitivity* with three very different kinds of counterexample. We will see that these other counterexamples are relatively benign—in that they leave ample room for a mildly qualified version of *Transitivity*—but that they are also quite unlike the apparently more virulent strain exhibited above.

3   Contrast Class: Benign Counterexamples to *Transitivity*

Take any event *e*—for example, my recent pressing of the letter "*t*" on my keyboard. Begin to trace its causes. Its immediate causes are relatively few, and near to hand: some signals in neurons in my brain, arm, and hand, the prior presence of that bit of the keyboard, and so on. As we trace back further, though, the causes become more numerous, scattered, and miscellaneous: They will likely include my birth, as well as the births of all those who were instrumental in the design and manufacture of this keyboard; if so, the number of more remotely ancestral births that count as causes of my simple act of typing becomes truly staggering. And we haven't even considered those parts of *e*'s causal history that concern more than its merely human aspect. Go back far enough, and it may be that *every* event (or at least: every event that takes place at that stage of *e*'s backward light cone) is a cause of *e*.

One might balk at calling all such events *causes* of *e*. Surely they are not as *much* causes of *e* as are its most proximate causes. Fair enough. The simplest way to accommodate this intuition is to say that causation comes in degrees, so that the more proximate a cause is to a given effect, the greater the degree to which it is a cause of that effect. Perhaps, then, what happens as we travel backward down *e*'s causal history is that the degree of causal influence of the events we find gradually diminishes; perhaps it eventually diminishes to the point where we must say that we no longer have causes of *e* at all. Such a picture of causation is harmless enough, though it raises the question of how to measure the attenuation of causal influence along a causal chain. Assuming that question settled, the needed modification to *Transitivity* is obvious. Ideally, it will have the following form: When *c* is a cause of *d* to degree *x*, and *d* is a cause of *e* to degree *y*, then *c* is a cause of *e* to degree $f(x, y)$—where the function f returns values lower than, but close to, the lesser of *x* and *y*. Assuming some low threshold value α such that for $\beta < \alpha$, "is a cause of *e* to degree β" no longer implies "is a cause of *e*," *Transitivity* will still hold for choices of *c*, *d*, and *e* where the values *x* and *y* lie well above the threshold. Or so we can hope the story would go.

At any rate, this issue, however interesting, has no bearing on our topic, as the examples discussed in the last section purported to exhibit failures of transitivity at *early* (backwardly speaking) stages of an event's causal history—too early to pin the blame on the sort of gradual attenuation of causal influence under discussion here.

Two other kinds of counterexample to *Transitivity* focus on the possibility of disconnect between the parts of d that c causes and the parts of d that cause e. It might be that c counts as a cause of d by virtue of causing one part of d, but that d counts as a cause of e by virtue of the causal action of a different part. If so, it need not follow that c is a cause of e.

What distinguishes the two kinds of counterexample is the notion of part at issue. Begin with the ordinary, mereological notion. A dance performance, for example, has as distinct parts the performances of each dancer. Let d be such a performance, and suppose that it has parts d_1 and d_2, consisting of the performances of Billy and Suzy, respectively. Among the causes of d_1 is, let us suppose, Billy's joining the dance troupe several months earlier. And among the effects of d_2 is, let us suppose, the appearance of a favorable review in the next morning's paper (for Suzy is the star of the show). We might count Billy's joining as a cause of the dance, in virtue of its role in causing one part of the dance (namely, Billy's). And we might count the dance as a cause of the favorable review, in virtue of the effect of one part of it (Suzy's brilliant performance). But we would not—or at least, not *thereby*—count Billy's joining as a cause of the favorable review. (E.g., suppose he's a lousy dancer.) If so, we need to modify *Transitivity* once again, presumably by introducing a distinction between primary and derivative senses of "cause," so that (for example) it is only in the derivative sense that Billy's joining the dance troupe is a cause of the performance, and the performance of the favorable review, whereas it is only in the primary sense that causation is transitive. Again, interesting but irrelevant, for none of our counterexamples takes advantage of this loophole.

Finally, L. A. Paul has highlighted a third—and arguably much more significant—way in which *Transitivity* must be qualified. (See her "Aspect Causation," chapter 8 in this volume.) Put abstractly, we might have a situation in which c causes d to have a certain property or (to use Paul's terminology) *aspect A*, and d in turn causes e, in virtue of some *other* aspect B, but intuitively c is not a cause of e. Arguably, McDermott's "counterexample" provides a case in point: The dog-bite does not cause the button-pushing *per se*, but rather causes it to have a certain aspect—that is, causes it to be a *button-pushing with the left hand*. Moreover, the button-pushing causes the explosion, but simply in virtue of being a button-pushing; that it is a button-pushing *with the left hand* is causally irrelevant to the explosion. Paul argues that in cases like this, *Transitivity*—properly construed—simply doesn't apply: In order for it to apply, we must not merely have a single intermediate *event* to serve as a link between *c* and *e*, but must have a single intermediate event-cum-aspect.

I think that is a very important point, and I highly recommend Paul's expert treatment of it. But observe that there is no hope of applying it uniformly to cases with the short-circuiting structure. Consider for example Kvart's case: We cannot single out some aspect of the surgery, and argue that (i) the injury causes the surgery to have that aspect, but (ii) it is only in virtue of some *other* aspect that the surgery causes the finger to be healthy. Or again, a simple modification of McDermott's example renders it immune to Paul's treatment: Suppose that after the dog-bite, the man does not push the button himself but orders an underling to do so. The relevant intuitions do not change: the dog-bite causes the order, and the order causes the explosion, but the dog-bite does not cause the explosion. The only way I can see to apply Paul's observations is by way of a rather strained insistence that there is one event—call it a "making the button be depressed"—which the dog-bite causes to have the aspect "being an order," and which otherwise would have had the aspect "being a button-pushing." That resolution is unattractive enough to warrant the search for an alternative. So while I certainly think that Paul's observation is very useful in a wide range of cases—indeed, I'll put it to use myself, in the next section— I don't think it provides the means for an adequate response to the challenge raised by the Hard cases. In fact, I think the right response has a quite different shape: *Transitivity does* apply to those cases, and yields the *correct* conclusion—intuition notwithstanding—that *c* is a cause of *e*. The next section provides the crucial underpinnings for this response.

4   Switches

A distinctive relationship that an event *c* can bear to an event *e* is that of helping to determine the causal route by which *e* is produced. In such cases, I call *c* a "switch" with respect to *e*. Here is an example.

The Engineer   An engineer is standing by a switch in the railroad tracks. A train approaches in the distance. She flips the switch, so that the train travels down the right-hand track, instead of the left. Since the tracks reconverge up ahead, the train arrives at its destination all the same; let us further suppose that the time and manner of its arrival are exactly as they would have been, had she not flipped the switch.

Let *c* be the engineer's action and *e* the train's arrival. Pick an event *d* that is part of the train's journey down the right-hand track. Clearly, *c* is a cause of *d* and *d* of *e*; but is *c* a cause of *e*? Is her flipping the switch a cause of the train's arrival? Yes, it is, though the opposing reaction surely tempts. "After all," goes this reaction, "isn't it clear that the switching event makes no difference to *whether* the train arrives, but merely determines the *route* by which it arrives?"

To some extent we can accommodate this reaction: Yes, of course the switching makes no difference to the arrival, in the sense that had it not occurred, the train would have arrived all the same. And yes, of course the switching helps determine the causal route to the arrival. But it goes too far to conclude that the switching is not itself among the causes of the arrival. A number of considerations reinforces this conclusion; since the issue is crucial to the proper diagnosis of the Hard cases, it will pay to review these considerations with some care.

The Explanation Test   Ask for a complete explanation of the train's arrival—"How did it get there? What processes led to its arrival?"—and a complete answer must include the switching event. But, plausibly, this complete answer will simply consist in a description of the arrival's *causal history*.

The Subtraction Test   Remember that the train travels down the right-hand track. Certain rather boring events extraneous to this causal process are the persistence through time of the various bits of left-hand track; these are events that would have combined with the presence of the train to cause its arrival, had it traveled down the left-hand track. Suppose some of these events away; that is, *subtract* them (you needn't go so far as to replace them by pure void; air and dirt will do). Subtract enough of them, in fact, that the left-hand track ends up having a sizable gap in it. Plausibly, this subtraction should not alter the facts about the arrival's causes, since the events subtracted are quite separate from and extrinsic to the events that constitute the causal processes leading up to the arrival.[5] But in the altered situation, the engineer's action quite obviously helps bring about the train's arrival; after all, she steers the train onto the only track that will get it to its destination. So, given that subtracting extraneous events should not alter the causal history of the arrival, we should also say that in the original case her switching is part of this causal history.

More generally, when a switch alters the causal pathway of some process M, there will typically be other processes that M *would* have interacted with to bring about the effect e, but that—thanks to the switch—it does not interact with. Since the events that go into these other processes are, as things stand, causally idle features of the environment, it seems plausible that we ought to be able to remove them from the environment without altering the causal status of the switch c with respect to the effect e. But in the scenarios where they are absent, it becomes perfectly clear that c is a cause of e.

The Variation Test   The example had a little intuition-pump built into it, given that we stipulated that if the engineer had not thrown the switch the train would have arrived at *exactly* the same time and in *exactly* the same manner. Suppose we had told the story slightly differently, so that if the engineer had not thrown the switch, the time and/or manner of the arrival would have been different—say, the train would have arrived an hour later. This alteration reverses, I think, the intuitive verdict (such as it was) that the switching is not a cause of the arrival. But that verdict should not be so sensitive to the details of the case—which in turn suggests that the no-difference-whatsoever intuition-pump was misleading us.

Paul's Observation   If the details of the train's counterfactual journey down the left-hand track are sufficiently similar to the details of its actual journey down the right-hand track—and it's certainly natural to interpret the story as if this were true—then the right thing to say might be that, at a suitably abstract (i.e., nondetailed) level of description, the two journeys consist of exactly the same events. To borrow Paul's terminology, what the switching does is make it the case that these events have certain *aspects*: Specifically, the switching makes it the case that they are travelings-down-the-right-hand-track rather than travelings-down-the-left-hand-track. On such an analysis, no two-step chain of the right sort connects the switching to the arrival, and so *Transitivity* simply does not apply. Perhaps our tendency to think of the actual and counterfactual journeys as really the *same* journey, differently realized, lies behind whatever reluctance we might feel to calling the switching a cause of the arrival.

As a test, hold the details of the arrival fixed, but alter the extraneous events so drastically that the *way* the train gets to its destination, in the counterfactual situation in which it travels down the left-hand track, is *completely different* from the way it in fact gets to its destination: It stops after a short while, gets taken apart, shipped piecemeal to a point near its destination, reassembled, and all this in such a way as to guarantee that nothing distinguishes its counterfactual from its actual arrival. Then Paul's observation doesn't apply, since there is no event that can happen as a traveling-down-the-right-hand-track, *and* as a shipping-of-disconnected-parts. But, by the same token, there is much less temptation to deny that the switching is a cause of the arrival.

Salience   Notice, first, that among the (highly nonsalient) causes of the train's arrival is the presence of a certain section S of the track down which the train travels, during the time that the train is in fact *on* S. And among the causes of the presence of S at this time is the presence of S a day earlier. So we should say: Among the causes of the arrival is the presence of S a day earlier. That's certainly odd, but it's odd in the familiar way that writers on causation have grown accustomed to: Whatever the exact nature of the causal concept we are trying to analyze, it surely picks out a very *permissive* relation, one that doesn't distinguish between events that we would normally single out as causes and events we would normally ignore because their causal relationship to the effect in question is too boring or obvious to be worth mentioning, or is easily hidden from view as part of the "background conditions." The presence of *S* a day earlier is like that.

But the relationship that the switching event bears to the arrival is just like the relationship that the earlier presence of *S* bears to the arrival: The relationship that the switching event bears to the setting of the switch as the train passes over it is just like the relationship that the earlier presence of *S* bears to the later presence of *S*, and the relationship the setting of the switch as the train passes over it bears to the arrival is just like the relationship the later presence of *S* bears to the arrival.

Switching *per se* Is Not Causing   The last paragraph helps bring out something rather important, which is that the switching bears two *distinct* causal relationships to the arrival. The first is the highly nonsalient one just outlined: The switching event causes the setting of the switch, which interacts with the passing train in the same way as the mere presence of a piece of track interacts with the passing train, etc. The second is the narratively more vivid relation: The engineer's action makes a difference to the causal route by which the arrival happens. But it is only in virtue of the *first* relation that the switching is a cause of the arrival. To see this, consider how the two relations can come apart, as in the following example: Billy and Suzy are about to throw rocks at a bottle. Suzy, the quicker of the two, is winding up when suddenly her muscle cramps, stopping her from throwing. So Billy's rock gets there first. Had there been no cramp, Suzy's rock would have struck the bottle before Billy's, breaking it—in which case Billy's rock would have struck only empty air. Either way, the bottle breaks; what the cramp does is to determine the causal route to the breaking (i.e., whether it happens via Suzy's throw, or via Billy's). But the cramp is manifestly not a cause of the breaking. What this shows is that switching *per se* is not causing; that is, it does not *follow* from the fact that an event *c* determines the causal route to an event *e* that *c* is among *e*'s causes.

But recall that the *kind* of switch I am focusing on—a kind of which the engineer's action is an instance—is an event *c* that *interacts* with a causal process in such a way as to redirect the causal route by which *that very process* brings about a given event *e*. I claim that in cases of this kind of switching—call them cases of "interactive switching"—*c* is a cause of *e*. But that will be so in virtue of *c*'s interaction with the causal process that results in *e*, and not merely because *c* is a switch with respect to *e*.

And this fact, in turn, helps account for our reluctance (such as it is) to count the switching as a cause of the arrival: We naturally focus on the narratively most salient relationship that the first event bears to the second—namely, that of helping to determine the causal route—and, recognizing that *this* relationship does not suffice for causation, conclude that there is none to be had.

An obvious test of this hypothesis is to construct a case where the *causal* role is the vivid one, and the switching role is not. Here is such a case:

The Kiss Billy and Suzy have grown up. One day, they meet for coffee. Instead of greeting Billy with her usual formal handshake, however, Suzy embraces him and kisses him passionately, confessing that she is in love with him. Billy is thrilled—for he has long been secretly in love with Suzy, as well. Much later, as he is giddily walking home, he whistles a certain tune. What would have happened had she not kissed him? Well, they would have had their usual pleasant coffee together, and afterward Billy would have taken care of various errands, and it just so happens that in one of the stores he would have visited, he would have heard that very tune, and it would have stuck in his head, and consequently he would have whistled it on his way home, and just to give the case the right "shape" let us stipulate that matters are rigged in such a way that the time and manner of the whistling would not have differed at all. So the kiss is an event that interacts with a certain process—call this process "Billy's day"—in such a way as to redirect the causal route by which that process bring about a certain effect (the whistling). But even though there is the failure of counterfactual dependence typical of switching cases (if Suzy hadn't kissed Billy, he still would have whistled), there is of course no question whatsoever that as things stand, the kiss is among the causes of the whistling.

Those who still balk at calling the engineer's action a cause of the train's arrival should answer the following question: What is the relevant difference between that case and this one? None, so far as I can see—that is, none relevant to the question whether the switching event c is a cause of the effect e. But there are clear and significant differences relevant to an explanation of why our intuitions about The Engineer are less firm and settled than our intuitions about The Kiss. For in The Engineer, it is the switching role of the engineer's action that stands out, and not her causal contribution to the arrival; and switching *per se* is not causing. But in The Kiss, the switching role is quite obscured—in fact, in telling the story one must forcibly draw attention to it—whereas the causal contribution of Suzy's kiss couldn't be more obvious.

To wrap up: The points canvased in this section (i) provide us with ample *positive* reason to count interactive switches as causes; and (ii) provide us with several plausible explanations of the source of any contrary intuitions. I conclude that the price of accepting interactive switches as causes is quite small, certainly small enough to be worth paying. Especially so since, as we're about to see, doing so provides us the means to disarm the Hard counterexamples to *Transitivity*.

5 Two Kinds of Short-circuits

Recall the apparent common structure of the counterexamples, common to both Easy and Hard cases: One event c helps to initiate a Threat, which, if not stopped, will prevent e from occurring. But c also causes a Savior event that in turn counteracts Threat. So c causes Savior, and Savior—by counteracting Threat—causes e. But c does not thereby cause e. Or so the stories go.

Now, however, we are in a position to see that there are two very different ways in which Threat might be counteracted. I'll bring them out by means of examples, building on the case discussed in the last section.

Drunken Bad Guys   The Bad Guys want to stop the Good Guys' train from getting to its destination. Knowing that the switch is currently set to send the train down the left-hand track, the Bad Guy Leader sends a demolition team to blow up a section of that track. En route to its mission, the team stops in a pub. One pint leads to another, and hours later the team members have all passed out. The Good Guys, completely oblivious to what has been going on, send the train down the left-hand track. It arrives at its destination.

Clever Good Guys   The Bad Guys want to stop the train from getting to its destination. Knowing that the switch is currently set to send the train down the left-hand track, the Bad Guy Leader sends a demolition team to blow up a section of that track. This time, it's a crack team, not so easily distracted. However, the Good Guys have gotten wind of the Bad Guys' plans, and send word to the engineer to flip the switch. She does so. The Bad Guy demolition team blows up a section of the left-hand track, but to no avail: Thanks to the engineer's action, the train travels down the right-hand track. It arrives at its destination.

Let c be the Bad Guy Leader's sending the team on its mission. Let e be the train's arrival. Let d_1 be the event, in Drunken Bad Guys, of the team's stopping in the pub. Let d_2 be the event, in Clever Good Guys, of the engineer's flipping the switch. Events d_1 and d_2 are, in each case, the Savior events. (Of course we could have chosen other events to play this role; nothing hinges on the particular choice made.) Clearly, c, in each case, causes them. But it turns out to be entirely too quick to assume that they have the same causal status with respect to e, for there is a world of difference between the *ways* that each event counteracts Threat.

In Drunken Bad Guys, what the Savior event does is to *cut short* the Threat process. Notice, furthermore, that the way that Threat is cut short requires *no causal connection whatsoever* between the Savior event (the team's stopping in the pub) and the final effect (the train's arrival). The intuition that c—the Bad Guy Leader's sending out the team—is not a cause of e—the train's arrival—is quite correct; but that fact poses no threat to *Transitivity*, for the intermediate event d_1 is likewise not a cause of e. *Dependence* may say otherwise—but so much the worse for that thesis.

The way the Threat is counteracted in Clever Good Guys, by contrast, is *entirely different*. The engineer's flipping of the switch does not cut short Threat at all; on the contrary, that process goes to completion, resulting in the destruction of a portion of the left-hand track. Rather, what the Savior event does is to *switch* the causal process leading to the train's arrival from a pathway that is *vulnerable* to Threat to one which is *immune* to Threat. Quite obviously, such a method for counteracting Threat must involve a switch, of the sort examined in the last section. Therefore, given the conclusions of that section, this way of counteracting Threat *necessarily* establishes a causal connection between the Savior event and the final effect (assuming, as I will throughout this discussion, that the switch is an interactive switch).

What of the event c, the Bad Guy Leader's sending out the team? That too, in Clever Good Guys, is a cause of the arrival, by virtue of being a cause of the engineer's flipping the switch. But isn't that counterintuitive? Counterintuitive enough that we should reject the tacit appeal to *Transitivity* made in the foregoing "by virtue of" clause? Well, yes, it's counterintuitive—but there is excellent reason to think that intuition is being misled, here. For what intuition naturally focuses upon is the narratively most vivid role that c plays in the story. And this is exactly the same "short-circuiting" role that c plays in Drunken Bad Guys: It initiates a Threat to e, and also causes that Threat to be counteracted. Intuition is perfectly right to insist that no event c can be a cause of an event e *merely* by virtue of (i) doing something that threatens to prevent e; and (ii) doing something that counteracts that very threat. Indeed, that is the lesson of Drunken Bad Guys, for in that story the *only* causal relationship c has to e is that of threatening to prevent e and simultaneously causing that threat to be counteracted. Intuition stridently objects to calling c a cause of e, in that case; and what's more, no argument can be found to persuade her to change her mind. So she should be heeded.

But in Clever Good Guys, such an argument *is* available. For what we naturally *fail* to notice—given the narrative prominence of the short-circuiting role—is that c bears *another* causal relation to e: namely, c begins a process that ultimately interacts with the processes leading up to *e* in such a way as to alter the causal route they follow to *e*. All the reasons for counting switches as causes apply here with equal force. So we must patiently explain to intuition that she is being distracted by irrelevant details of the case, and should reverse her verdict.

One way to see that these details—specifically, the fact that *c* is a short-circuit with respect to *e*—really *are* irrelevant is to compare Clever Good Guys to the following case:

Mischievous Bad Guys   This time, the Bad Guy Leader has no intention of stopping the train from getting to its destination. But he knows the Good Guys are paranoid, and likes to play tricks on them. Just for fun, he sends out the demolition team—not with orders to blow up the left-hand track, but with orders to go down to the pub and enjoy themselves. Still, he knows full well that once the Good Guy Spies have reported that the team has been sent out, the Good Guys will panic and order the engineer to flip the switch. Sure enough, they do. The engineer flips the switch. The train travels down the right-hand track. It arrives at its destination.

There is no short-circuit here, because there is no Threat to be counteracted. So in that sense, Mischievous Bad Guys differs dramatically from Clever Good Guys. But in the *important* sense, the two cases are exactly the same: The *relevant* relationship the Bad Guy Leader's action bears to the arrival differs not at all. What's more, there is no question (not, at least, once we absorb the lessons of the last section) that in Mischievous Bad Guys, the Leader's action is a cause of the arrival—a verdict we should therefore carry over to Clever Good Guys. The fact that in this latter case, the Leader's action is also a short-circuit with respect to the arrival matters not one whit; rather, it serves merely as a distraction, making the case difficult to judge, and off-hand intuitions about it quite suspect.

This diagnosis neatly extends to the Hard cases introduced in section 2. Consider Kvart's (I'll leave the others as an exercise). Does the injury cause the finger to be healthy? Intuitively no, but on inspection yes: For the accident that befalls the man redirects a certain process (namely, the process consisting, roughly, of him and his movements) onto a causal pathway different from the one it would have followed, and in fact both pathways (actual and counterfactual) issue in the same result (a healthy finger). So the accident is a switch with respect to the healthy finger. Observe, furthermore, how easily we can apply the various considerations canvased in the last section to reinforce this conclusion. I'll consider just the variation test: Alter events in the environment sufficiently to make it the case that if the accident had not occurred, the finger's state of health would have been *worse* (say, because the man would have suffered some other, much more serious accident). Then we would not hesitate to count the accident as one of the causes of the finger's later state of health.[6] Again, what this test brings out is the (somewhat hidden) *switching* structure of the example; that it has the short-circuiting structure as well is merely a distraction.

Here, then, is the point we have come to: (i) When *c* is a switch with respect to *e* (of the interactive kind), then *c* is a cause of *e*, although for various reasons this fact may not be immediately obvious. (ii) What distinguishes the Hard cases from the Easy cases is exactly that, whereas both exhibit events *c* and *e* such that *c* is a short-circuit with respect to *e*, in Hard cases it is also true that *c* is a switch with respect to *e*. (iii) When we render the intuitive verdict about Hard cases that *c* is not a cause of *e*, we wrongly focus solely on the fact that *c* is a short-circuit with respect to *e*. Observing (correctly enough) that *c* is not *thereby* a cause of *e*, we wrongly conclude that it is not a cause of *e*, *simpliciter*. But *c* is also a switch with respect to *e*, so that conclusion is mistaken. The mistake is natural enough, though, given that the short-circuiting role is by far the more vivid one. (iv) Since, however, no such diagnosis is available for the Easy cases, the intuitive verdict that, in such cases, *c* is not a cause of *e* stands. But in such cases we can always find an intermediate event *d* such that *c* is clearly a cause of *d*, and *e* counterfactually depends on *d*, but does so in the odd double-preventing kind of way. Hence such cases exhibit an intractable conflict between *Dependence* and *Transitivity*. (v) Since, in such cases, there are independent grounds for doubting that *d* is a cause of *e* (most notably: no causal process connects them), the appropriate response is to deny *Dependence*.

Points (iv) and (v) deserve more discussion; I'll reserve discussion of (v) for the next section. Now, given that I have been at such pains to find grounds for resisting the intuitive verdict about the Hard cases, one might reasonably wonder whether, with enough ingenuity, we might find similar grounds for resisting the intuitive verdict about the Easy cases. I say *no*: The intuitive verdict about those cases is correct, and that is why they have something useful to teach us about causation (namely, that counterfactual dependence does not suffice for it). While I cannot hope to establish this claim conclusively, I can at least show that not one of the strategies that helped us with the Hard cases helps in the slightest with the Easy cases. Let's review them, using Drunken Bad Guys as our canonical example of an Easy case:

The Explanation Test   Does the fact that the Bad Guy Leader sent out the demolition team help explain the train's arrival? Of course not. The closest this fact can get to appearing in an explanation of the arrival is to appear in a very specific sort of explanation-*request*: Namely, we can ask, "Why did the train arrive at its destination, *given that* the Bad Guy Leader sent out a demolition team to stop it from doing so?" The obvious and correct reply is to cite the relevant double-preventer: The demolition team got side-tracked by the pub; this event prevented it from doing something (blow up the track) which in turn would have prevented the train's arrival.

Keeping in mind that the "given that" clause might well be tacitly assumed in the context of the explanation-request, it seems plausible that double-preventers of the sort exhibited by this example can be explanatory *only* relative to this specific sort of explanation-request. But in the context of such a request, it would be silly to add the content of the "given that" clause as an *extra* bit of explanatory information. No: On the assumption that the "given that" clause cites a genuine threat (which we can take to be a presupposition of the why-question), the question is answered *completely* by citing those events that counteracted the threat, and explaining how they did so.

The Subtraction Test   Intuitively, the Bad Guy Leader doesn't help cause the train's arrival by sending out the demolition team. Can we reverse this intuitive verdict by "subtracting" events from the environment of the processes that issue in the arrival? At the very least, can a selective subtraction make it the case that the arrival counterfactually depends on the Leader's action? Well, let's review the events that are available for "subtraction." On the one hand, there are the events that make up the train's journey down the tracks, and the rather less noticeable events that consist in the persistence of the appropriate bits of track. No doubt there are other even less noticeable events that contribute to the arrival: the presence of sufficient oxygen to allow the train's engines to burn fuel, and so on. We needn't canvass them all, for it's clear that the most that can happen if we subtract some of *these* events is that the arrival won't happen. And that is, of course, not a situation in which (i) the arrival happens; and (ii) its occurrence counterfactually depends on the Leader's action.

Where else to look? Well, there are the events that make up the *rest* of the story: the Leader's action itself, the team's journey, the drunken revelry in the pub, and so on. Subtract some of these, and the most that will happen is that we get a situation in which the team *succeeds* in stopping the train (e.g., if we remove the pub itself). No help there, either. So the example fails the subtraction test.

The Variation Test   It likewise fails this test. Remember that the object here is to selectively *alter* events so that the *manner* of the arrival at least depends on the Leader's action. Keeping in mind the different sorts of events that are available, it becomes clear at once that the only effect such alterations could possibly have is to make the Leader's action *prevent* the arrival (e.g., alter the potency of the beer in the pub sufficiently so that the team doesn't become drunk, and therefore continues on its mission). So the example fails the variation test, as well.

It was clear all along that it was *bound* to fail both the subtraction test and the variation test. For what those tests bring out, when they succeed, is that (i) there is an alternative causal pathway to the given effect e; (ii) the effect of the alleged cause c is to switch the processes leading to e away from this alternative and onto a different path; and therefore (iii) altering the character of the path not chosen—either in an extreme way (the subtraction test), or in a modest way (the variation test)—will yield a situation in which e, or the manner of e's occurrence, *does* depend on c. In this new situation, if c had not happened, then the processes aimed at e would have followed the alternative (and now altered) causal pathway, and therefore either would have missed their mark (the subtraction test), or would have produced e in a slightly different manner (the variation test). But in the Drunken Bad Guys case—as, indeed, in all Easy cases—the alleged "cause" simply does not act as a switch. So of course the subtraction and variation tests fail, for such cases.

Paul's Observation   Could it be that *Transitivity* simply doesn't apply, because for any candidate intermediate event d, we will find that while in a *loose* sense, c (the Leader's action) causes d and d causes e (the train's arrival), strictly speaking what happens is that c causes d to have a certain aspect, but it is only in virtue of some *other* aspect that d causes e? Let's find out, by taking our intermediate d to be the team's decision to stop in the pub. Now, *Dependence* (and common sense) yields the verdict that the Leader's action is a cause of d; likewise, *Dependence* (but not, this time, common sense) yields the verdict that d is a cause of the arrival. But as far as I can tell, "aspect" intuitions are silent: It is not that we can fix on some *way* that d happens, and say with confidence that what the Leader's action *really* does is to cause d to happen in this way; likewise for the relationship d bears to e. So this strategy is not available: The defender of *Dependence* cannot say (not on these grounds, anyway) that *Transitivity* does not apply, and so the Easy cases exhibit no conflict between that thesis and *Dependence*.

Salience   Return to the case of The Engineer. In that case, it can be agreed on all sides that the engineer's action causes an event—the setting of the switch as the train passes over it—that *interacts* with the processes that lead to the arrival; the question was whether this interaction is of the right sort to qualify the engineer's action as one of the arrival's *causes*. And we were able to answer that question in the affirmative by observing that the setting of the switch bears the same sort of relationship to the arrival as other events that clearly *are* causes of the arrival, albeit highly nonsalient ones (e.g., the presence of the bits of track that the train passes over). But if we try to apply this strategy to the case at hand, arguing that the Bad Guy Leader's action is simply a highly nonsalient cause of the arrival, we cannot even get it off the ground—for the Leader's action causes no event that interacts *at all* with the processes that lead up to the arrival, let alone interacts with them in the right sort of way.

To put the point rather mildly, we appear to have run out of options for defending the claim that the Leader's action is too a cause of the arrival, and intuition be damned. I conclude that we should side with intuition in this, as in all other Easy cases. The conflict between *Dependence* and *Transitivity* is unavoidable.

6   Metaphysical and Methodological Lessons

Which to give up? Pose the question abstractly, and it may be hard to decide. But the details of the examples that exhibit the conflict in fact make the question easy: For what is so striking about those examples is that the intermediate event d "causes" the effect e *only* in the sense that it prevents something which would have prevented e. Thus, Billy's trip stops him from preventing Suzy's throw; the demolition team's decision to stop in the pub winds up preventing them from blowing up the track, which would in turn have prevented the train's arrival; and so forth. No *causal process* connects d with e; d does not interact with other events to help *bring about e*; and so on. Of all of the characteristics we expect from the causal relationship, the only one exhibited by the relationship between d and e is that e counterfactually depends on d. And even that characteristic is entirely optional, as witness standard cases of preemption, in which one event causes a second, even though an alternative, preempted process would have brought about the second, had the first not done so. The striking conflict with *Transitivity* thus confirms a suspicion that should have been there from outset: namely, that double-prevention is not causation. If we had *independent* reason to think that *Transitivity* fails, then we might hold on to *Dependence*, even in the face of the examples. But once the Hard cases have been defused, we have no such independent reason.

We *do* have independent reasons to doubt *Dependence*, on the other hand—reasons that go beyond (or, perhaps, simply properly articulate) the doubts about that thesis that naturally arise when we focus on cases of double-prevention. For example, *Dependence* can be shown to conflict both with a prohibition on action-at-a-distance, and with the claim that the causal structure of a process is determined by its intrinsic, noncausal character, together with the laws that govern it. But since that story is long—and I have told it elsewhere (in "Two Concepts of Causation," this volume)—I won't go into detail here. Given our focus on *Transitivity*, however, it is appropriate to point out two new sorts of trouble that arise if we extend *Dependence* in a natural way to cover cases of prevention, and of causation by omission. More exactly, suppose we endorse the following theses:

(1)   Event c causes the omission of an event of type E if it is the case that c occurs, no event of type E occurs, and if c had not occurred, an event of type E would have occurred.

(2)   The omission of an event of type C causes event e if it is the case that no event of type C occurs, e occurs, and if an event of type C had occurred, then e would not have occurred.

Thus, (1) is a natural application of *Dependence* to causation *of* omission, and (2) is a natural application of *Dependence* to causation *by* omission.

Then, if *Transitivity* holds, we get wonderful results, as in the following three cases:

Preemptive Strike   One day, Suzy suddenly and viciously attacks Billy—so viciously that he is quite incapacitated, as a result. Asked to explain herself, she states that she was merely preventing him from attacking her. "But," her interrogators exclaim, "you know full well that he had no intention of attacking you—the two of you were *friends*!" "Yes," she replies, "he had no intention of attacking me *then*. But he certainly does *now*—so it's a good thing I incapacitated him."

Unfortunately, the combination of *Dependence* (extended as in (1)) and *Transitivity* endorses this reasoning: For her attack causes his subsequent incapacitation; and, were he not incapacitated, he *would* attack her, whereby his incapacitation causes his failure to attack her. By *Transitivity*, her attack did indeed cause him to fail to attack her.

No Cure   Billy is sick, and needs a certain drug to cure his disease. But cure requires two doses, whereas only one is available. (Suppose further that one, by itself, has no effect on the disease.) In a gesture of futility, Dr. Jones gives Billy the one dose on Monday. On Tuesday, Dr. Smith comes in, intending to do the same thing, but of course failing to. Billy remains sick. What's worse, Dr. Jones gets *blamed* for Billy's continued ill health, on the following grounds: By giving Billy the dose on Monday, he caused Dr. Smith's *failure* to give Billy the dose on Tuesday (for if Jones hadn't given the dose, Smith would have). But Smith's failure to give the dose on Tuesday in turn caused Billy to remain ill, since if Smith had given Billy the dose, then—with one dose already in his system—Billy would have been cured. By *Transitivity*, Jones made Billy remain sick.

Collision Avoidance   The engineer flips the switch, sending the train down the right-hand track; recall that the tracks reconverge up ahead. She promptly puts in for merit pay, on the grounds that she has prevented a collision. After all, she causes the absence of a train on the left-hand track (for if she hadn't flipped the switch, the train would have been there), which in turn causes there to be no collision (for if there had been a train on the left-hand track, there would have been a collision at the point of reconvergence). So her action caused the omission of a collision.

Now, it is certainly true that in all of these cases, there is a great temptation to deny the relevant counterfactuals. For example, we all surely want to insist that if there had been a train on the left-hand track, that would have been because the engineer did *not* flip the switch, and so there (still) would have been no collision. But however sensible such "backtracking" reasoning is, it is simply not available to the loyal defender of *Dependence*, since that thesis requires a scrupulously nonbacktracking reading of the counterfactual. So the loyal defender must, on pain of denying *Transitivity*, embrace these remarkable results. All the more reason to shift allegiance elsewhere.

Moreover, the cost of denying *Dependence* should not be overestimated. We certainly need not abandon the truism that where there is counterfactual dependence between distinct events, there is *typically* causation. Nor, I think, need we deny that such dependence is a *kind* of causal relation—so long as we are clear that it is not the kind of causal relation we have in mind when we think of processes, interaction, and *Transitivity*. For obvious reasons, we might call this latter kind of causal relation *production*; our thesis should then be that production and counterfactual dependence are *both* causal relations, but that only production obeys *Transitivity*.[7] To this claim we should add that counterfactual dependence is not the *central* kind of causal relation. As evidence, observe that there is a clear asymmetry in our intuitive reactions to cases of counterfactual dependence without production, on the one hand, and cases of production without counterfactual dependence, on the other. As an example of the latter, suppose Billy and Suzy both throw perfectly aimed rocks at a window. Suzy's gets there first, breaking it. Intuition unhesitatingly picks out her throw, and not Billy's, as a cause of the breaking. But when we have a case of dependence without production—as in Drunken Bad Guys, for example—intuition is more equivocal; it makes sense, for example, to ask whether, by entering the pub, the demolition team *really* helps cause the train's arrival. Why such a question makes sense is perfectly clear: By stressing the word "really" (or functional equivalents such as "strictly speaking," etc.), one invokes a context where the *central* kind of causation is salient; and entering the pub is *not* a cause of the arrival, in this sense.

Let us now turn from the metaphysical to the methodological: What lessons does our discussion have to teach us about how we ought to conduct a philosophical investigation of causation? Very simply put, the lesson is this: *Treat intuitions about cases with care.* It will not do simply to construct hypothetical cases, consult our offhand intuitions about them, and without further ado use the results to draw sweeping (or less-than-sweeping, for that matter) conclusions about the nature of causation. For such an approach offers no insight into the *source* of our intuitions, and understanding *that* is crucial if we are to know what, if anything, these intuitions have to teach us. To gain such insight, there is no substitute for close inspection of the cases—close enough that we can be confident that we have adequately discerned their salient structure.

Ignoring this point can lead to either of two opposing errors, both of which are to be found in the literature. The first consists in excessive gullibility, a willingness to take intuitions about cases at face value, without interrogating their credentials. Thus McDermott, when discussing his dog-bite case as well as others, fails to conduct anything like a detailed analysis of his cases, and instead rests content with reporting the results of various informal polls (of "naive subjects," no less) about them—as if these results could establish anything more than the unsurprising result that most of us find it counterintuitive to count the dog-bite as a cause of the explosion. Of course that's counterintuitive, and of course such counterintuitive results count as *prima facie* reason to doubt *Transitivity*—but *prima facie* reasons can wither upon scrutiny, and these ones do. McDermott, unfortunately, seems not to see the need for such scrutiny.

Lewis, in his discussion of this issue, makes a rather more interesting mistake. Notice first the way he characterizes the alleged counterexamples to *Transitivity* ("Causation as Influence," chapter 3 in this volume, p. 96):

The alleged counterexamples have a common structure, as follows. Imagine a conflict between Black and Red. (It may be a conflict between human adversaries, or between nations, or between gods striving for one or another outcome, or just between those forces of nature that conduce to one outcome versus those that conduce to another.) Black makes a move which, if not countered, would have advanced his cause. Red responds with an effective countermove, which gives Red the victory. Black's move causes Red's countermove, Red's countermove causes Red's victory. But does Black's move cause Red's victory? Sometimes it seems not.

Now, one can argue about whether Lewis has adequately captured the common structure of the counterexamples. (What is Red's countermove in Drunken Bad Guys? Putting a pub in the path of the team?) Never mind: What is important to notice is that Lewis completely overlooks the crucial distinction between counterexamples that do and counterexamples that don't involve switches. And this leads him to a curious and quite fallacious dissolution of them. After running through various of the examples—*including* ones that involve no switches—he writes (p. 98):

In all these cases, there are two causal paths the world could follow, both leading to victory for Red. Black's thwarted attempt to prevent Red's victory is the switch that steers the world onto one path rather than the other. That is to say, it is because of Black's move that Red's victory is caused one way rather than the other. That means, I submit, that in each of these cases, Black's move does indeed cause Red's victory. Transitivity succeeds.

Patently, this argument applies only to those cases—my "Hard" cases—that involve a switch. By contrast, it's a confusion to think that in Drunken Bad Guys, for example, the Leader's decision to send out the team causes the train's arrival to come about one way rather than another: no, the processes leading up to the arrival are *exactly* as they would have been, had the Leader not made the decision.[8] Moral: If you're going to start the job of analyzing cases, then finish it.

Have *I* finished it? Yes, as far as I can tell. That is, on careful reflection I can't discern any *further* structure to the various examples that matters, or that distinguishes some of them from others. But of course such a conclusion is by its nature tentative. Supposing it correct, we can now measure the price of *Transitivity*, at least in the current market. Put the point this way: We knew all along that counterfactual dependence is not transitive; that is what we learn in our first course on the semantics of this conditional. And that should have at least raised the suspicion that there was something overly optimistic in the view that counterfactual dependence bears a deep connection to causation, in the way that the *Dependence* thesis brings out. The price of *Transitivity* is that we must finally face up to this suspicion, recognize that it was well founded—and therefore look elsewhere for the tools with which to analyze our central concept of causation.

Notes

1. For valuable discussion of this point, see Lewis (1986d).

2. See for example Lewis (1973a).

3. Autobiographical note: It was precisely because of this problem for my thesis that *Transitivity* conflicts with *Dependence* that I became interested in these counterexamples in the first place. For it had seemed clear enough to me that there were cases—my Easy cases—that exhibited this conflict; but then I found in the literature other cases, posed not as counterexamples to *Dependence* but as counterexamples to *Transitivity*, and I did not see how my thesis bore on them. Had I simply misdiagnosed my own cases, construing them as trouble for *Dependence* when in fact that principle was quite irrelevant, and they were—like their cousins in the literature—counterexamples to *Transitivity*, pure and simple? No, I hadn't. But it took me a while to see why not.

4. This is the response I favor. For reasons, together with much more detailed discussion of other "double-prevention" cases, see my "Two Concepts of Causation" (chap. 9 in this volume). For discussion of related issues, see my (2002a) and (2002b).

5. For detailed discussion and defense of the "intrinsicness" thesis being relied on here, see my (2002b).

6. A slightly different consideration pointed out to me by Tim Maudlin also applies: Alter the surgery enough so that the finger ends up in a much better state of health than it would have, without the accident. Here, too, we would not hesitate to count the accident as a cause of the finger's state of health. The relevant methodological point still applies: Prima facie, the correct judgments about the causal status of the accident should not be so sensitive to these fine details.

7. Certain other principles of interest distinguish the two varieties of causation as well; see my "Two Concepts of Causation," chapter 9 in this volume.

8. Perhaps Lewis thinks that the difference consists in this: Given the Leader's decision, the train's arrival is caused in part by the demolition team's stopping in the pub; without that decision, the arrival would not have this event as one of its causes. But the intuition that Lewis is leaning on, as applied to this case, is that the Leader's decision "is the switch that steers the world onto one path rather than the other." That intuition is obviously out of place, in this example: We do not have here a choice between two different "paths." Then again, perhaps Lewis means to be appealing to a much stronger principle to the effect that if c, d, and e are such that (i) d is a cause of e; and (ii) if c had not occurred, d would not have been a cause of e; then it follows that (iii) c is also a cause of e. But that principle is not available to him. To see why, ring a small change on the Drunken Bad Guys case. This time, the Leader sends the team out without telling them their mission; they are simply ordered to go to a certain point, and wait for written instructions to arrive. In fact, they never make it to the rendezvous, thanks to the pub. But if they hadn't stopped in the pub, they would have reached the rendezvous, shortly thereafter received instructions to blow up the track, etc. Then let c be the sending of the instructions to the rendezvous, d be the team's stopping in the pub, and e be the train's arrival. Lewis wants to endorse *Dependence*, so he will say that d is a cause of e (without, presumably, drawing a distinction between this kind of causation and the ordinary kind). But everyone must agree that if c had not occurred—if no instructions had been sent—then d would not have been a cause of e; for in such a circumstance, the team simply poses no threat whatsoever to the train's arrival. So by the principle under consideration, c is a cause of e: The sending of the instructions helps cause the train to arrive. Which, of course, is silly.

8 Aspect Causation

L. A. Paul

While skiing, Suzy falls and breaks her right wrist. The next day, she writes a phi-losophy paper. Her right wrist is broken, so she writes her paper using her left hand. (Assume, as seems plausible, that she isn't dexterous enough to write it any other way, e.g., with her right foot.) She writes the paper, sends it off to a journal, and it is subsequently published. Is Suzy's accident a cause of the publication of the paper?[1]

Of course not. Below, I will show that none of the major contenders for a theory of events coupled with a theory of causation succeeds against examples like that of Suzy's accident, and that the reason for this derives from an underlying tension between our beliefs about events and our goals for theories of causation. I will then argue that property instances should be taken, in the first instance, as the causal relata, and propose an analysis of causation that I call *aspect causation*.

Aspect causation combines elements of regularity theories and David Lewis's new influence theory of causation[2] with property instances. Combining lawful entailment with influence handles problems involving redundant causation for regularity and counterfactual based theories. Changing the causal relata to property instances re-solves transitivity problems and allows us to develop an account of events without holding our theory of causation hostage to our theory of event individuation.

1 Event Causation: Problems

First, we need some background and terminology: actual events can be defined ac-cording to a continuum from *fine grained* to *coarse grained*. Speaking loosely, the less fine grained a theory of individuation specifies events to be, the fewer events the theory implies. There is a parallel continuum from *fragile* to *robust* for the individu-ation of events with respect to modal contexts, needed for counterfactual theories of causation. The less fragile the event, the weaker the requirements events in other possible worlds must meet to be numerically the same as the event that actually occurred.

One of two approaches is usually used to analyze causation: a regularity approach or a counterfactual approach. Roughly, versions of regularity or covering-law anal-yses for events state that an event c causes an event e iff the occurrence of c, together with the right conditions and right regularities or laws, is sufficient for the occurrence of e. It is a consequence that causation is transitive: If c is a cause of d, and d is a

Originally published in a special issue of the *Journal of Philosophy* (April 2000). Minor revisions have been made for consistency.

cause of e, then c is a cause of e. Counterfactual analyses in their simplest form hold that for any two actual, distinct events c and e, e depends causally on c iff e depends counterfactually on c, that is, had c not occurred then e would not have occurred. Causation is usually distinguished from causal dependence in order to ensure transitivity: c is a cause of e iff there is a chain of causal dependencies running from c to e. Both accounts require transitivity to avoid important counterexamples,[3] and both require an acceptable theory of eventhood in order to provide an acceptable (reductive) analysis of causation. In order to provide an underpinning for analyses of causation based on events as causal relata, several characterizations of the identity conditions for events have been put forward.

Fragile Events   Under a fragility view, one must hold that when I pick up my cup of coffee, had I picked up the coffee a millisecond later, had the coffee swirled in a slightly different fashion, or had it been a fraction of a degree hotter, the event of my picking up the coffee cup would—necessarily—have been a different event. Since anything that brings about a new event counts as a cause of it, the view gives us a plethora of spurious causes. If an explosion on the sun makes the summer day on which I drink my coffee a fraction of a degree hotter, thus keeping my coffee ever so slightly warmer than it would have been had the explosion not occurred, that explosion counts as a cause of my drinking my coffee.

   If events are fragile, then Suzy's skiing accident is among the causes of her writing her paper with her left hand, and her writing of the paper is a cause of it being published. For fragility theorists, writing the paper with her left hand is necessarily a different event than writing the paper in some other way. So the skiing accident is a cause of the event that actually occurred: the event e of the paper's-being-written-with-the-left-hand, since the skiing accident is part of a sufficient condition for e, and if the skiing accident had not occurred, e would not have occurred. Given that the skiing accident occurred, if the writing of the paper occurs at all, it occurs with the left hand, since after the accident she can't write it any other way. Under a counterfactual analysis that ensures transitivity and treats events as fragile, if the event of the writing of the paper with the left hand had not occurred, then the publication would not have occurred. Such a fragility theorist is committed to the view that Suzy's skiing accident is a cause of her paper's being published.

   The implausibility of such conclusions increases with every link in the causal chain, and confronts advocates of fragility with a multitude of counterintuitive cases. Perhaps the fragile event theorist can provide some sort of an account that can make one-step cases such as the sun's explosion causing my drinking of my coffee seem less counterintuitive. But the implausibility of holding, for example, that the skiing accident is among the causes of Suzy publishing her paper, and the ease with which such two-step (or multi-step) examples can be constructed shows us that explaining one-step cases is not good enough.

Fine-grained Events   Using fine-grained events as part of a theory of causation gives us many of the same undesirable results as the use of fragile events, coupled with a need to accept an implausible ontology. Jaegwon Kim's view is perhaps the most well known: he combines a regularity approach with a very fine-grained theory of events. For Kim, events are identified by their constitutive triples, which comprise an individual, a property exemplified by that individual, and the time when the property is exemplified. Although an event may exemplify many properties, it is the constitutive triple that, in a sense, defines the event.[4] For Kim, we have two numerically different events when they differ in their constitutive triples: That is, when they differ in their constitutive individuals, properties, or times.

When cat C. Louise sneezes loudly, according to Kim at least two events occur in that region of spacetime: C. Louise's sneezing and C. Louise's sneezing loudly. Moreover, when she sneezes, she sneezes in the kitchen, on a summer morning while dislodging a flea; so we also have the simultaneously occurring events of a sneezing on a summer morning, a sneezing in the kitchen, and a sneezing while dislodging a flea. We can continue our modification of the constitutive property indefinitely, so we have an infinite number of events occurring in the region of C. Louise's sneezing. For Kim, these events are all different but not necessarily distinct: In some sense (although he does not develop the notion), he thinks the many events that occur when C. Louise sneezes are all "included" in her sneezing.[5] The claim is supposed to be similar to the claim that C. Louise is made up of many different C. Louises, one for each hair or molecule that C. Louise might lose but still remain C. Louise. C. Louise is made up of many spatiotemporal parts, and many of these parts are less maximal than all of C. Louise, but these proper parts are enough to count as C. Louise themselves.

But the attempt to run an analogy between included events and spatiotemporal parts fails.[6] The difference between events that are qualitatively richer than other events (such as the difference between a sneezing in the kitchen, and a sneezing at 10 A.M.) is not purely analogous to the difference between spatiotemporal parts. If Kim were claiming that the event of C. Louise's sneezing in the kitchen and sneezing at 10 A.M. occupied slightly different spatiotemporal regions, then we could see how one event could overlap another, and how part of one event could include part of another event. But both of these events are said to occupy the very same spatiotemporal region. The only way to make sense of the "parts" analogy is to take some events as logical parts of other events, giving logical overlap, not spatiotemporal overlap. But then the idea that these are different *events* (which are supposed to be particulars, or things that occupy regions of spacetime) rather than just different *properties* is still just as counterintuitive.

For Kim, when Suzy writes her paper with her left hand, multiple events occur: Suzy's writing of her paper, Suzy's writing of her paper with her left hand, and so on. All of the occurrent events that "include" Suzy's writing of her paper with her left hand (such as Suzy's writing her paper with her left hand by writing on a keyboard, Suzy's writing her paper with her left hand by pecking with one finger on a keyboard, and so on, if this was how Suzy actually wrote her paper) are effects of the accident. And all of these effects are among the causes of the publication of the paper, for they all "include" Suzy's writing of the paper, and so they are sufficient under the laws to cause the publication of the paper.

David Lewis argues for a counterfactual approach combined with fine-grained events, and denies that events must be fragile.[7] For Lewis, actual events have both strong and weak essences, so that when an event that is C. Louise's sneezing loudly occurs, a second event (with a weaker essence) *also* occurs—C. Louise's sneezing. Events, as under Kim's view, are greatly multiplied.

For Lewis, the skiing accident is among the causes of the event of Suzy's writing her paper that is essentially a writing of her paper and is essentially with her left hand, as well as a cause of all the other events that occurred essentially with the left hand (i.e., Suzy's writing of the paper that is essentially a writing of the paper and essentially with the left hand, but only accidentally a writing using a keyboard, etc.). If the accident had not occurred, none of these events, as essentially specified, would have occurred. And (holding that the appropriate closest possible world in which we evaluate whether or not the publication of the paper occurs is a world in which no event that is essentially Suzy's writing of her paper occurs) each of the events that involve Suzy's writing of her paper that is essentially a writing of her paper, which includes many events caused by the accident, is a cause of the publication of the paper. So Lewis must also accept the conclusion that the skiing accident is a cause of the publication.

The problems for the Kimian and Lewisian views highlight a side effect of their multiplication of entities: many unexpected instances of what we might call a kind of redundant causation. For Kim, each event that includes Suzy's writing of her paper causes the event that has as its constitutive property the publication of the paper. (Of course, there are many other publications of the paper caused at the same time as the one we are focusing on, but we'll ignore those events for simplicity's sake.) For Lewis, each event that involves Suzy's writing of her paper essentially causes a version of a publication of her paper that is essentially a publication. Multiplying events in either the Kimian or the Lewisian way gives counterintuitive results in examples like that of the accident, results in a new and implausible kind of redundant causation, and, as I shall argue below, is not necessary. The point is not that the size of the ontology of events is unacceptable, but rather that fine-grained theories of events cannot be motivated by the claim that they improve the results given by their companion theories of causation.[8]

Coarse-grained Events Donald Davidson holds that the correct theory of causation involves a regularity approach, and that events are individuated by the regions of spacetime they occupy.[9] This view has the happy consequence that C. Louise's sneezing is the same event as the event of her sneezing loudly, and the event of her sneezing in the kitchen, and so on. Such a view takes events to be coarse grained.

Defenders of coarse-grained events seem to have a natural solution to cases like the skiing accident causing the publication. They can hold that Suzy's writing the paper with her left hand and Suzy's writing the paper are one and the same event, and use this claim to break the link between the skiing accident and the writing of the paper. A natural way to justify the claim would be to point out that that the actual writing of the paper and the actual writing of the paper with the left hand occupy the same spatiotemporal region.

Those who hold a version of the regularity analysis could argue that the skiing accident is not a part of a sufficient condition for the writing of the paper, so it is not a cause of it. Counterfactual theorists could adopt a moderately robust view of events together with the coarse-grained approach and argue that the writing of the paper would have been the very same event even if it had been written with the right hand, so if the skiing accident had not occurred, the writing of the paper would still have occurred. With either approach, since Suzy's skiing accident was not a cause of the existence of the paper, it was not a cause of her publishing the paper.

Something about this seems right—it seems to capture part of what we mean when we deny that the accident was a cause of the publication of the paper. But it can't be quite right, because the response can be used to generate problems. For suppose there was more to tell about the case of the skiing accident. Suzy's left hand, unused to writing, begins to cramp severely after finishing the paper. She visits a doctor, and spends large amounts of money on prescription drugs in order to dull the pain. It seems right to say that the writing of the paper with Suzy's left hand is among the causes of the pain in her left hand, and her visit to the doctor and expenditure of large amounts of money on prescription drugs is caused by the pain. Moreover, it seems right to say that the skiing accident to Suzy's right hand is among the causes of her writing the paper with her left hand and so a cause of the pain in her left hand.

But if we are coarse-grained theorists, we have already decided in order to resolve earlier problems that the event of Suzy's writing the paper is the same event as her writing the paper with her left hand, and that the skiing accident did not cause the event of the writing of the paper. But if the skiing accident did not cause the event of the writing of the paper when we determine what caused the publication, then neither did it cause the event of the writing of the paper when we determine what caused the costly prescription. The link in the causal chain between the skiing accident and the writing of the paper has already been—by stipulation—broken. But we *do* want to say that the skiing accident was a cause of the cramping hand and the costly pre-scription, and moreover, we want to say this because we think that the accident, by causing the writing of the paper to occur in a particular way—it was a writing with the *left* hand—was a cause of the subsequent cramping of the left hand (and thus of the costly prescription).

So we shouldn't try to preserve causal intuitions by breaking the link between the skiing accident and the writing of the paper. Further, common sense would have it that the writing of the paper (however it was written) is a cause of the publication of the paper, so it's not a good idea for the coarse-grained theorist to try to deny the second link in the chain. I suspect that the problem is perfectly general: For any theory of events that individuates coarsely (i.e., for theories that do not individuate events as finely as can be with respect to properties), we can design puzzles like the one with the cramping hand.[10]

This leaves advocates of event causation in a predicament, since whatever standard of individuation for events they impose, there exist clear problem cases. Distinguish-ing between events coarsely respects many of our causal judgments and common-sense views about individuation. But by holding that some changes (no matter how minor) in events do not result in a different event, we lose needed flexibility when just such a minor change affects the causal story that we want to tell. On the other hand, theories of events that are as fine grained as can be build every detail of the event into the causal story that we tell. Such precise specification gives us many cases of spurious causation—unless we reject the transitivity of event causation—which is a steep price to pay for those of us who value our commonsense views about causation.

2 Property Instances

But there is a clear, intuitive solution to the case of the accident. To see it, set aside the idea that events are the only kinds of causes and effects, and think in terms of property instances with respect to events or individuals. With this in mind, consider our example. It seems right to say that because Suzy's accident involved Suzy's right hand being broken, it caused the writing of the paper to be a writing with the left hand. But the left-handedness of the writing had nothing to do with the paper's being accepted for publication: As I've told the story, all that caused the paper to be accepted for publication was that the paper was written in the first place, that (presumably) it was a good paper, and so on. So the accident's property of being an accident to Suzy's right hand did not cause the paper to have the property of being accepted for publication, but merely to have the property of being written with the left hand. This becomes clear when we think of causes and effects as instances of properties rather than as events. It's not that the case shows us causation isn't transitive, but rather that this is a case where the question of transitivity does not arise, since the property caused by the accident and the property that causes the publication are not the same property. Transitivity just doesn't apply.

The follow-up example, where the skiing accident is a cause of the cramping in my left hand, does involve transitivity: The skiing accident's property of being an accident to Suzy's right hand caused the writing of the paper to be a writing with the left hand, and the writing of the paper being a writing with the left hand caused the left hand to cramp. This solution conforms to our intuitive understanding of what happened, and as a result generates the correct answer. Examples like these give us a strong reason to accept the view that property instances rather than events simpliciter are the causal relata. We get further flexibility by allowing the property instances to involve individuals as well as events.

There is a related reason to take property instances as the causal relata. As the example of Suzy's accident helps to bring out, there is an essential tension between the goal of developing an adequate, acceptable theory of event individuation and the goal of developing an adequate theory of causation. It is not uncommon to adopt an extremely fine grained or fragile theory of events in order to get better results for one's theory of event causation (this is what usually motivates advocates of fine-grained views), but the example of the accident shows us that such maneuvers bring trouble elsewhere.

By separating the two accounts, we can be free to develop our best theory of event individuation (and our best theory of individuation for individuals) apart from our theory of the causal relata and the causal relation. Even if the Suzy examples don't convince, the history of problems developing an acceptable theory of events as a companion to a theory of causation, together with the lack of parsimony (both of causal claims and events) of views like Kim's and Lewis's, should be enough to motivate a switch to property instances.

There is one issue that needs immediate explication: how does my view that the causal relata are property instances differ from Kim's theory of events as property exemplifications? The obvious difference between the views is that my account shows us how to keep transitivity while explaining cases like Suzy's accident. But the root of the difference is less obvious: It is based on the fact that Kim's account requires that causation relate events, defined using constitutive triples, not property exemplifications simpliciter.

To see how this is important, recall that Kim's theory of events is metaphysically substantial: The property instances referred to by the triples *really are* events. It is *not* the view that we should define the causal relata and then call whatever we end up with "events." Because it is a definition of events, not just any property that can be exemplified counts as an event: Properties that modify other properties are not themselves events—presumably because modifiers are even less acceptable, intuitively, as real events than other properties are.

For Kim, our example of the property of being performed with the left hand would not count as an event itself but rather (as it should) as a modifier of the property of being a writing of a paper. It is hard to see a way to make sense of the idea that the property of being performed with the left hand could count as any sort of event. Kim handles modifiers by combining the modifier with an appropriate constitutive property to create a new constitutive property, which in turn defines a new event. So for Kim, the property of being performed with the left hand is not an event in its own right: The writing of the paper counts as an event, and the writing of the paper with the left hand is another event. In this way, Kim hopes to be able to make room for the ways in which we seem to want to take account of the importance of properties, including modifiers, in cases of causation, yet retain the idea that causation is a relation between events. Unfortunately, by creating new events for properties that are merely modifiers, Kim opens the door to counterexamples like that of Suzy's accident.

Kim could revise his view and claim that instead of creating a new event that is the writing of the paper with the left hand, we say instead that the event of the writing of the paper (defined by the triple of Suzy, the property of being a writing of a paper, and the time at which the writing occurred) has the property of being performed with the left hand.[11] But while this seems sensible, it won't help Kim, since in order to get the right result in the case of Suzy's accident, it is the *property* of the event, being performed with the left hand, that has to count as an effect (and as a cause, with respect to the cramping). Since Kim holds that causation is a relation between *events*, the modifying property of being performed with the left hand can't be a cause or effect unless it somehow counts as an event in its own right.

By switching to property instances as causes and effects we sidestep the problems that Kim, Lewis, Davidson and others with related views face when developing theories about causation. Of course, we must still rely on an adequate theory of property individuation, but any of these theories of events and event causation must rely on a theory of properties as well. Removing a problematic level of analysis and solving difficult problems with transitivity should be sufficient motivation to make the switch.

I will use "aspect" to refer to a property instance: an aspect is a particular's (a particular event or individual) having a property. Aspects are things that correspond one to one with thing-property pairs such that the property is had by the thing; so aspects are in an important sense part of the spatiotemporal world. Defined as such, aspects correspond to tropes (if there are any tropes), but the definition of "property" is intended to be flexible: Whether property instances involve exemplifications of universals, sets of particulars, states of affairs or tropes I need not say nor choose between.[12] A few more details: Aspects involving conjunctive properties can be causes or effects iff each conjunct is. The properties instanced must be suitably natural, so aspects that involve gruesome or disjunctive properties are not eligible to serve as causes or effects. The question of how extrinsic properties can be and still be paired with particulars to serve as causal relata needs further investigation.[13]

Taking aspects as the causal relata does not exclude events as causes and effects, for it may be that when an aspect causes another aspect or group of aspects, the aspect or aspects that are caused are sufficient to imply or constitute an event. In some cases, if an aspect causes enough properties to be instantiated, or perhaps enough essential properties to be instantiated, we may say that the aspect causes an event in virtue of causing the particular to have those properties.[14] If aspect c causes Billy to have the property of dying in a particular way at a particular time, this aspect might be sufficient for the instantiation of an event, namely, the death of Billy. If so, then aspect c is a cause of the event of the death of Billy, in virtue of being a cause of aspects sufficient to constitute the event. Depending on your standards for particulars, the aspects sufficient to constitute a particular may be many or few, common or rare. The power of the aspects account is that it will deliver the right causal judgment consistent with the standard of particulars adopted.

Counterfactual and regularity accounts based on aspects could rely on appropriate versions of the following definitions:

1. Counterfactual dependence of aspects: For any two distinct, actual events or individuals c and e, and logically distinct properties p and q: aspect e_q (e's having q) is counterfactually dependent on aspect c_p (c's having p) iff, had c occurred (existed) without p, then e would not have occurred (existed) with q. (I do not specify whether c without p is c or is numerically different from c.)[15]

2. Lawful entailment of aspects: For any two distinct, actual events or individuals *c* and *e*, and any two logically distinct properties *p* and *q*, aspect c_p (*c*'s having *p*) lawfully entails aspect e_q (*e*'s having *q*) iff *c*'s exemplification of *p* is subsumed by the antecedent of the right law or laws that entail a consequent subsuming *e*'s exemplification of *q*. This is a souped-up kind of sufficiency, one that excludes properties had by particulars not linked to the effect via a law of nature from being counted as part of a lawfully sufficient condition for an effect.[16]

Under a regularity account where lawful entailment implies causation, being a breaking of the right hand is a cause of the left-handedness of the writing. But it is the paper's property of being a good paper (rather than the property of being written with the left hand) that lawfully entails the paper's being published, so the accident's being a breaking of the right hand is not a cause of the publication.

Under a counterfactual analysis where dependence implies causation, the left-handedness of the writing depends on the breaking of the right hand. However, the publication of the paper does not depend on the left-handedness of the writing: It depends on the property of being a good paper. Our transitivity puzzle is dissolved.

3   Reductive Analysis: Problems

Although the simple versions of the counterfactual and regularity accounts can be used to solve the transitivity puzzles we have been discussing, they cannot serve as theories of causation. Recent work on causation shows that problems with preemption—where potential causes *c* and *b* both occur, and each in the absence of the other can cause the effect *e*, yet it is intuitively clear that *c* is a cause of *e* and *b* is not—require a more sophisticated treatment of the causal relation.

Two kinds of preemption are responsible for the worst of the problems: *late preemption* and *trumping*. In cases of late preemption, the central issue involves the fact that the preempted cause *b* would have caused the very same effect *e*, but slightly later than the preempting cause *c* caused it. In these cases, the preempted causal chain is prevented by the occurrence of the effect itself, before the preempted cause can cause it.

C. Louise crouches, aiming for an unfortunate fly. Possum also crouches, aiming for the same fly. C. Louise pounces, and catches the fly. She then eats it. Possum, though agile, is heavier than C. Louise and so pounces more slowly, and the fly is eaten by the time he arrives. If C. Louise hadn't eaten the fly, Possum would have eaten it in the very same way, but just a few moments later. Counterfactual and regularity theories of event causation seem to have serious problems with examples like these: The (event that is the robust) catching of the fly does not depend counter-factually on C. Louise's crouching, and conversely, both C. Louise's crouching and Possum's crouching seem to be lawfully sufficient for the catching.

I have argued elsewhere that effects in cases of late preemption *do* depend on their causes, for when the effect occurs depends on whether the preempting cause oc-curred, but when the effect occurs does not depend on whether the preempted cause occurs.[17] We can make a similar claim in terms of lawful entailment: The preempt-ing cause, but not the preempted cause, lawfully entails the effect's occurring when it did.

Trumping examples give a new twist to the problem. In these examples, preempted cause *b* would have caused the very same effect *e*, but for the fact that a law specifies that if *c* occurs, *c* causes *e* and *b* does not. In these cases, *b* could have brought about the effect at the very same time, and with the very same properties, as *c* did.[18]

C. Louise crouches, aiming for another fly. Possum also crouches, aiming for the same fly. C. Louise jumps. Possum, who has been practicing, jumps a moment later, but his (newly acquired) agility makes him able to catch the fly at the same time as C. Louise. Unfortunately for Possum, there is a little-known law that states that flies, when pounced on by multiple cats, are captured by the cat who jumps first. Since C. Louise jumps before Possum, she gets the fly. If C. Louise hadn't jumped, Possum would have captured the fly in the very same way and at the very same time. C. Louise's pounce, albeit through no intrinsic feline merit, trumps Possum's.

Trumping cases where the effect would have occurred at the very same time and in the very same way if it had been caused by the preempted cause are of concern only if we want our analysis to be able to handle action at a distance.[19] It seems to me that trumping is simply a new variant of early preemption, and cases not involv-ing action at a distance can be solved using stepwise dependence.[20] Nevertheless, the cases are quite interesting and I prefer an analysis that can handle them to one that cannot.

Unsurprisingly, counterfactual and regularity theories have problems with trump-ing: The catching of the fly does not depend on C. Louise's crouching, and con-versely, C. Louise's crouching and Possum's crouching each lawfully entail the catching. Since there is no difference in when or whether the effect occurs if the pre-empting cause does not occur, the solution for late preemption cannot be straight-forwardly applied to trumping cases.

Lewis sees that restricting dependence to when or whether an effect occurs if the cause occurs is too limiting[21] and proposes that we define causation in terms of a pattern of dependencies between events. The relevant events are *alterations* of the events for which the causal relation is being evaluated. These alterations are either the actual c and e ("actual" refers to the world of the example), or very fragile versions of, or alternatives to, c and e. The alterations are used to help us represent different ways c and e could have occurred (or different ways events that are very much like c and e could have occurred).

Under Lewis's account, an event c influences an event e iff there is a substantial range $c_1, c_2, c_3 \ldots$ and $e_1, e_2, e_3 \ldots$ of not-too-distant alterations of c and e such that if c_1 had occurred, then e_1 would have occurred, and if c_2 had occurred, e_2 would have occurred, and so on. In this way we check to see if whether, when, and how e occurs depends on whether, when, and how c occurs. If there is a sufficiently large range of direct dependencies between alterations of e and c, then c influences e, and so c causes e. To preserve transitivity, as in the original counterfactual analysis, Lewis takes the ancestral: c causes e iff there is a chain of stepwise influence from c to e.

The new analysis handles preemption problems elegantly: The preempting cause, if changed, would have caused changes in the effect. If C. Louise had batted the fly instead of catching it, or if she had caught the fly differently, the effect at the end of the corresponding causal chain would have been different: a batting instead of a catching, or a catching that occurred with more or less enthusiasm. Not so for Possum: Whether he'd bat or how he'd catch would make no difference to the effect.

But the approach has two serious defects. First, the weakening of the dependence requirement to include more ways in which the effect can depend on the cause allows spurious causation. In the preemption cases, it seems right that if Possum had pounced earlier or (in the late preemption case) with more agility, the effect would have occurred earlier or in a different way. But if the effect depends on Possum's acts, then by the analysis above Possum's act counts as a cause. This is clearly an undesirable consequence.

Lewis recognizes this problem and attempts to minimize it by arguing that in most cases alterations in C. Louise's act make more of a difference than changes in Possum's act, and further that alterations in Possum's act, in the context of comparing this act to C. Louise's, are much more distant than alterations of C. Louise's act. Differences in degree or distance correspond to differences in influence and justify calling C. Louise's act, but not Possum's, the cause. Lewis argues further that if it turned out after taking degree and distance into account that there was not much difference between the influence of Possum's act and C. Louise's act, we would be justified in calling Possum's a cause as well.

The view is defensible with respect to cases of trumping where both potential causes could bring about the very same effect. But in cases of late preemption we are not justified in calling Possum's preempted act a cause no matter how much influence he has. The fact remains that Possum's act does not lawfully entail the catching of the fly when it actually occurred, and intuitively, lawful entailment is a necessary condition for causation. (Or at least it is for worlds like our own.) The problem with influence can be put more generally: Consider two events a and b that we would normally take to be causally unrelated. Take a to be my body temperature and b to be the white pages of the manuscript strewn across my desk. If my body temperature were altered so that I radiated sufficient heat, the white paper would turn brown and curl at the edges. But surely the temperature of my body is not a cause of the whiteness of the paper: It does not lawfully entail the whiteness. Influence alone is not sufficient for causation.

The second problem with the account involves transitivity. To preserve transitivity (and to help solve some particularly worrying cases of early preemption), Lewis takes the ancestral of the influence relation to be causation. However, this move commits him to counterintuitive results with respect to a flock of (supposed) counterexamples to transitivity.[22]

Many of the cases have the same general form: Some series of events (call this event pathway A), initiated by event a, starts to occur. If all the threatened events of A occurred, the series would culminate in the causing of event c. However, before the series of events that make up event pathway A have all occurred, event b causes event c via a different chain of events (call this event pathway B) connected to but different from A. For example, a train rushes toward Jesse James, who is tied to the tracks. If the train continues on its track, it will run over and kill James (event pathway A). A few minutes before the train runs over Jesse, his brother Frank flips a switch that causes the train to veer left onto a different track (event pathway B). Unluckily for Jesse, this track converges to the original track just before the spot where he is tied, and the train runs him over anyway. We assume that the train's diversion to the left-hand track did not delay the train or change the event of Jesse's death in any way. (We might assume that the original track meandered a bit before converging with the left track, so that each track was exactly the same length.)

Now, intuitively, we want to deny that Frank's flipping of the switch was a cause of the train running over and killing James. But under the influence account—as under accounts of event causation generally—we cannot. The event of Frank flipping the switch influences the event of the train's being on the left hand track and the event of the train's being on the left hand track influences the convergence at the point just before it ran over Jesse, since there are alterations of the event of the train being on the left-hand track just before it converges (namely, the alteration where the event is completely excised from history) that would result in the convergence not occurring. Since the event of the train's running on the track through the convergence point toward Jesse influences his death, the event of the flipping of the switch is a cause of Jesse's death.

The case is related to our skiing accident case above, and Lewis's new account fails to handle it for the same reason that his earlier account fails it: A reliance on events as the causal relata allows too much information into the causal claim, and when this extra information is combined with transitivity, spurious causal results are easy to generate.[23]

4   Aspect Causation

Both lawful entailment and influence go some way toward capturing the content of the causal relation. So why not combine the two? For it is because of a lack of lawful entailment that the influence account errs in counting certain events as causes, and it is because *a* influences effect *e* and *b* does not in cases where *a* trumps *b* that a regularity account errs in counting *b* as a cause. Each analysis alone is too permissive, but combined they can give us a simple, strong, and elegant analysis of causation. In the first part of this paper, I argued that property instances, not events, are causes and effects: Problems with transitivity help to make this clear. Accordingly, I propose the following analysis of causation, based on the definitions (1) and (2) given in section 2 and Lewis's definition of influence given in section 3:

Aspect Causation: For any two aspects c_p and e_q:

(i) if c_p lawfully entails e_q, and

(ii) if c_p influences e_q,

then e_q is directly caused by c_p. Taking the ancestral of direct causation in order to give us causation, c_p is a cause of e_q iff e_q is directly caused by c_p or there is a chain of direct causation running from c_p to e_q.

The idea is this: Take any aspect c_p that lawfully entails an effect e_q; for each such aspect c_p, check to see that the effect exhibits dependence on the cause by checking for an appropriate pattern of dependence of aspects on aspects. Let alterations $p_1, p_2, \ldots$, and $q_1, q_2, \ldots$ of property instances p and q be property instances that might be similar to but numerically different from p or q, and check to see if c_{p1} had occurred, then e_{q1} would have occurred, and so on.[24] If and only if the appropriate pattern of dependence exists, c_p is a cause of e_q. By including influence in my account, I allow for a certain amount of vagueness, but for far less than in the original influence theory. The account tightens up the influence theory in two major ways: It prevents anything from counting as a cause if it does not lawfully entail the effect, and it prevents illicit information from being included in causal claims by taking aspects rather than events (in the first instance) as the causal relata. It seems correct to say that both influence and lawful entailment capture part of the nature of causation, and my hope is that the two combined suffice for a simple and strong analysis of the (deterministic) causal relation in the actual world.[25]

By requiring causes to lawfully entail their effects, we eliminate the major problems with spurious causation that Lewis faced. In our example of late preemption, C. Louise's having the property of pouncing in some particular way at some particular time counts as a cause of the fly's having the property of being caught in a particular way at a particular time. The properties of C. Louise's act, being a pouncing in such and such a way and at such and such a time lawfully entail the fly's having the property of being caught when and how it actually was, and if the properties of C. Louise's act, being a crouching in such and such a way and at such and such a time, were changed, the fly would not have been caught when and how it actually was. We can even say that since the properties of C. Louise's act caused the catching of the fly in a particular way at a particular time, the event of the fly's being caught was caused simpliciter.

But properties of Possum's act, being a pouncing with such and such a momentum and starting at such and such a time, do not lawfully entail the effect as it actually occurred. (Possum could not have pounced the way he did, when he did, and brought about the effect when it occurred the way it did.) Alterations of properties of his act that would affect the time of the fly-catching and thus give spurious dependence are not relevant to our evaluation of the situation, since these properties were what entailed his arriving too late in the first place. Likewise, my body's having a temperature of (about) 98.6°F does not lawfully entail the color of the paper on my desk, and so it cannot be counted as a cause no matter what the overall pattern of dependence looks like.

For those who resist analyses involving counterfactuals for fear of unwanted vagueness, my account should help to calm those worries as well. These worries can arise when determining the truth values of counterfactuals, for the selection function might specify more than one closest possible world, allowing conflicting truth values for the relevant counterfactuals. Unless we adopt a selection function that specifies only one closest world, ties in some cases are possible, and restricting causation to cases where there are no ties is ad hoc.[26] If we merely emend a counterfactual-based account of causation to say that a pattern of counterfactual dependence under some precisification of the similarity relation is sufficient for causation, then our counterfactual constraint is too permissive, allowing causation whenever there is vagueness. On the other hand, requiring dependence under all precisifications is clearly too restrictive, preventing causation whenever there is vagueness.

But if we require lawful entailment for causation, then we can rely on the more permissive version of counterfactual dependence, yet eliminate most of the vagueness worries. Although we might have not have a pattern of dependence under all pre-cisifications, intuitively, if we have dependence under one or more precisification of the similarity relation together with lawful entailment in the actual world we can say there is causation without being unduly permissive. There are additional benefits to combining lawful entailment with dependence, for lawful entailment brings in natu-ral restrictions with respect to disjunctive, overly gruesome, and logically necessary properties.[27] Including counterfactuals (and restrictions on backtracking counter-factuals) with an account of lawful sufficiency, on the other hand, helps us address problems for regularity accounts with distinguishing causes from effects and effects of a common cause.[28]

The second major change is the use of aspects rather than events simpliciter as causes and effects. Return to our case of late preemption with C. Louise and Possum. It seems right to say that Possum's mass lawfully entails some of the properties of C. Louise's eating of the fly (those properties caused by the minute gravitational forces his mass exerts on C. Louise and the fly), and that if Possum's mass were changed these properties would also change. So Possum's mass counts as a cause of some of the properties of the eating. Is this a problem for our account?[29]

I think rather that it is an advantage. In some contexts we might need to ask about what caused these minute gravitational effects, and then we would need to be able to cite Possum's mass as among the causes. Note that, unlike Lewis, I need *not* hold that Possum's mass is a cause of the eating of the fly; rather, his mass is merely among the causes of the minute gravitational effects. Lewis simply denies that we should attend to these negligible differences: But in a context where we need to ex-plain these differences such a denial is inexplicable. We need aspects to have an ade-quately precise account of the causal story.

Turning from the problems with simple spurious causation to those with transi-tivity, moving to aspects solves the so-called transitivity problem where the flipping of the switch has to count as a cause of Jesse's death. When we eliminate the extra, unwanted information brought in by the events, we see that transitivity is not the culprit: Events as the causal relata are responsible for the unwanted consequences.

As the story was told, when the switch is flipped, the only property (or properties) it causes are the train's being on the left-hand track, and any other properties to do solely with the train's being on the left (e.g., the train's having the property of passing the scenery on the left more closely than if it had traveled on the right). The flipping lawfully entails the train's traveling on the left, and the flipping of the switch influ-ences the traveling on the left. The other properties of the train's travel (which are relevant to Jesse's death) while it travels on the left are caused by properties of the train's prior motion, mass, and so on, not by the flipping of the switch: The flipping does not lawfully entail them, and they are not influenced by the flipping. (If the flipping had occurred differently or not at all, all of these properties would have occurred just as they did in the original story.)

Because the only (relevant) effect of the flipping is the train's traveling on the left, the flipping does not cause any of the properties of Jesse's death. The train's merely having the property of traveling on the left does not lawfully entail the death of James. Nor does the property of traveling on the left influence properties of James's death, since even if the train had traveled on the right, James's death would not have been affected.[30]

Note that, under the aspects account, if we were to tell the train story differently, the account would reflect the right changes in the results. Telling the story *very* differently might muddle our intuitions enough to make it unclear whether the flipping should count as a cause of properties of the death. In such a case, an answer either way, or no clear answer at all, is acceptable. Telling the story *slightly* differently, so that the train is somehow slowed or changed by taking the left track and the death happens later or is more violent than if the train had taken the right track, makes the flipping of the switch count among the causes of those properties (e.g., the time or manner of death)—just as it should.[31]

5   Conclusion

By recognizing that property instances are the causal relata, we can conform to common sense; we can develop, unimpeded, the account of the individuation of events (and individuals) that best conforms to our antecedent beliefs; and we can allow our causal relata to be at least as fine grained as facts.

By combining this view with lawful entailment and influence, we arrive at a well-developed theory of property causation (perhaps most useful in the context of current discussions of mental causation), we solve many of the most pressing problems with extant analyses of causation, and we have an account of causation that fits well with actual scientific practice. By this last claim, I mean that when doing science, we identify the potential causes eligible to bring about an effect (those that lawfully entail the effect), and then alter the potential causes and observe the effect for changes. When doing metaphysics rather than empirical science, we evaluate close possible worlds to see if alterations of the potential cause (one that lawfully entails the effect) result in alterations of the effect. If we have the right sort of dependence, we have causation. If not, not. The account I propose is modeled after the ways we rely on to learn about causation in experimental contexts, so it is no surprise that it does such a good job of handling cases where we have clear causal intuitions and a full description of the situation. We thus clear away a number of problems that have hampered the development of the analysis of the causal relation.

Acknowledgments

I received helpful comments from many, but I am especially indebted to Ned Hall, Chris Hitchcock, David Lewis, Jonathan Schaffer, Stephen Yablo, and an audience at the 1998 Australasian Association for Philosophy.

Notes

1. The example is modeled on a nice example used in Michael McDermott (1995a). McDermott uses his example to create trouble for a particular kind of counterfactual account that takes events to be coarse grained but does not discuss its broader implications.

2. Lewis (2000).

3. See David Lewis (1973a) and (1986b).

4. Kim (1973a) and (1993), pp. 33–52.

5. Kim (1993), pp. 45–46.

6. Bennett (1988), p. 83.

7. Lewis (1986d).

8. Stephen Yablo's work goes a great way toward handling many of the problems I discuss in this paper, but also relies on extremely strong essentialist claims and the ontology these claims imply. I prefer a more parsimonious account (if one can be had). Yablo develops his account in his (1992a, 1992b, 2000).

9. Davidson (1969, 1970) originally tried to individuate events by their causes and effects, but such a strategy requires a prior analysis of causation. Quine (1985) argued that the strategy didn't succeed, and Davidson (1985) agreed. After writing this paper, I learned that Douglas Ehring (1997) and Daniel Hausman (1998) raise similar transitivity worries for Davidson.

10. There is one more move that the coarse grained theorist might try: Following Davidson (1967), he might say that "The accident caused the publication of the paper" is true, but not causally explanatory. In other words, the claim would be that, strictly speaking, the accident caused the publication even though our singular causal statement doesn't mention any causally relevant properties of the accident as part of the description it gives of the cause (the accident). This seems as though it would allow the coarse-grained theorist to accept the first link of the causal chain (as well as subsequent links). But this response is inadequate, for the skeptic can return with the point that no matter *how* the accident is described, the event of the accident has *no* properties that are causally relevant to the effect (the publication). Davidson's argument requires that the event that counts as the cause have *some* properties under *some* description that are causally relevant to the effect, even if these are unobvious (e.g., such as the properties of Suzy's birth that are causally relevant to Suzy's writing her paper).

11. Kim (1993), pp. 44–45.

12. Williams (1953) and Campbell (1990) suggest that tropes should be the causal relata. Douglas Ehring (1997) argues for "persisting tropes" as causal relata, and Hausman (1998) argues that tropes aid causal explanation.

13. For the purpose of using aspects as part of a theory of causation, I leave the controversial question of how we define particulars aside by stipulating that the aspects don't have to be part of the structure we take to *be* the particular. Just as C. Louise's sneezing isn't part of the structure that is C. Louise (and unlike the way C. Louise's left front paw is part of the structure that is C. Louise), the aspects that are the causal relata need not be the structure we take to define them.

14. D. H. Mellor (1995, chap. 12) has a very nice discussion of (what he calls) the difference between causing and affecting particulars.

15. In my account of dependence, I am assuming a standard ordering relation on closeness of worlds based on Lewis's similarity ordering, in which propositions about property instances are eligible to be included among the relevant conditions for the evaluation of counterfactuals.

16. Viz., Kim's (1973a) account of subsumption. My account requires an adequate specification of the causal laws and the properties they refer to, but does not require allegiance to a particular theory of laws: one could rely on the Dretske–Armstrong–Tooley view of nomic necessity, some sort of primitiveness claim, or the Mill–Ramsey–Lewis view that the right regularities are those that belong to the set that does the best job of systematizing and organizing physical information. The definition might change slightly depending on the theory of properties adopted: For simplicity, I've written the definition here for aspects taken as tropes.

17. Paul (1998b).

18. Schaffer (2000b).

19. I do not claim that there can be no such thing as causation by action at a distance. Rather, once we eliminate the need for chains of events in our cases of causation, our intuitions change enough to motivate a change in the conditions necessary for causation: Causation by action at a distance is different enough from ordinary causation to need an analysis of its own. (So cases that combine "ordinary" causation with causation by action at a distance will require a combined analysis, and it's no surprise if cases involving action at a distance are not handled by an analysis for contiguous causation.) I suspect that the analysis of causation by action at a distance will be a version of the lawful entailment analysis for aspects. Hall, "Two Concepts of Causation," chapter 9 in this volume, argues that causation by action at a distance is a kind of causation that differs from the "ordinary" kind, and he develops an analysis based on minimally sufficient sets. Similarly, there are problems for causation by omission.

20. See Lewis's (1973a) and (1986b) discussions of early and late preemption, and his stepwise solution to early preemption. In these papers Lewis lumps cases involving action at a distance in with late preemption (where the effect is delayed): I think this is a miscategorization.

21. Lewis (2000).

22. Ibid. Lewis refers to these cases as "Black-Red examples." Also see Hall (2000) for some particularly ingenious cases. There are more variations of these kinds of cases than I can deal with here, including well-known probabilistic versions. The earliest discussions of the (deterministic) cases that I've found are in van Inwagen (1987), Rowe (1993), and Fischer and Ravizza (1993b).

23. Lewis's influence account also fails to handle the skiing example: The skiing accident influences the writing of the paper and the writing of the paper influences the publication.

24. Following Lewis's account of alterations of events, I take no rigid stand on much we can alter a property for our account of influence: It is a matter of degree and context. I also leave vague how we decide which alterations are closer to the original p and which are more remote.

25. I hope, with Lewis, that a suitably modified version will be able to handle indeterministic causation.

26. Adopting Stalnaker's (1980) account would allow us to select only one closest world. This does not solve our problem but merely shifts the worry, since depending on the selection function we adopt we could get different values for the counterfactual. In other words, truth or falsity of the counterfactual would be relative to the selection function. On Stalnaker's account we can supervaluate, so a counterfactual conditional is true (false) iff it is true (false) for every selection function, but the conditional is undefined in the case of vagueness.

27. For those who find influence unacceptable or who are not concerned about trumping cases, I advocate a view that combines simple counterfactual dependence and lawful entailment (versions of (1) and (2) in sec. 2) together with aspects.

28. Lewis (1973a) shows how counterfactual based accounts can address these problems.

29. Lewis discusses this problem in Lewis (2000), as does Jonathan Schaffer in Schaffer (2001).

30. Here I am relying on *traveling on the right* as the relevant property alteration to evaluate influence.

31. My solution in this section helps to resolve problems with explaining why Frank is not morally responsible for the death of James because he flipped the switch: Merely flipping the switch didn't make him causally responsible for the death, so neither did it make him morally responsible.

9 Two Concepts of Causation

Ned Hall

1 Introduction

Causation, understood as a relation between events, comes in at least two basic and fundamentally different varieties. One of these, which I call "dependence," is simply that: counterfactual dependence between wholly distinct events. In this sense, event c is a cause of (distinct) event e just in case e depends on c; that is, just in case, had c not occurred, e would not have occurred. The second variety is rather more difficult to characterize, but we evoke it when we say of an event c that it helps to *generate* or *bring about* or *produce* another event e, and for that reason I call it "production." Here I will articulate, defend, and begin to explore the consequences of this distinction between dependence and production. A synopsis:

After taking care of some preliminaries (sec. 2), I will argue for the distinction in a slightly devious manner, by starting with a broad-strokes critique of counterfactual analyses of causation (sec. 3). The reason for this approach is plain: Since I end up endorsing the simplest kind of counterfactual analysis—albeit only as an analysis of *one* kind of event-causation—it makes sense to pay some attention to the prospects for this and kindred analyses, and to examine why there is no hope of turning them into analyses of a *univocal* concept of event-causation. Specifically, my critique will aim to show that the best attempts to shore up counterfactual analyses in the face of well-known and stubborn counterexamples (involving certain kinds of overdetermination) rely on three general theses about causation:

Transitivity: If event c is a cause of d, and d is a cause of e, then c is a cause of e.

Locality: Causes are connected to their effects via spatiotemporally continuous sequences of causal intermediates.

Intrinsicness: The causal structure of a process is determined by its intrinsic, noncausal character (together with the laws).

These theses—particularly the second and third—will require more discussion and elaboration, which will come in due time. For now, contrast them with the thesis that lies at the heart of all counterfactual analyses of causation:

Dependence: Counterfactual dependence between wholly distinct events is sufficient for causation.

The simplest counterfactual analysis adds that dependence is *necessary* for causation. As a *general* analysis of causation, it fails for well-known reasons, which we will review shortly. Consequently, very few counterfactual analysts endorse this necessary condition (but see David Coady's "Preempting Preemption," chapter 13 in this volume). But to my knowledge, all endorse the sufficient condition codified in the thesis of *Dependence*. Indeed, it is probably safe to say that *Dependence* is the cornerstone of every counterfactual analysis.

What is the trouble? Simply this: A hitherto ignored class of examples involving what I call "double-prevention" reveals deep and intractable tensions between the theses of *Transitivity*, *Locality*, and *Intrinsicness*, on the one hand, and *Dependence*, on the other (sec. 4).

In section 5, I'll add to my case by arguing that exactly parallel tensions divide the first three theses from the thesis of

Omissions: Omissions—failures of events to occur—can both cause and be caused.

This thesis will also need further elaboration and discussion.

One immediate result is that counterfactual analyses are doomed to failure (unless, as I think, they are understood to be targeted narrowly at just one *kind* of event-causation): for they *need* the first three theses if they are to cope with the well-known counterexamples involving overdetermination, but they *cannot abide* these theses if they are to cope with the counterexamples involving double-prevention (or, for that matter, if they admit omissions as causes and effects).

Although important, this result is eclipsed by a more significant lesson that I will develop in section 6. For the five theses I have mentioned are, I claim, all *true*. Given the deep and intractable tensions between them, that can only be because they characterize *distinct concepts of causation*. Events can stand in one kind of causal relation—dependence—for the explication of which the counterfactual analysis is perfectly suited (and for which omissions can be perfectly suitable relata). And they can stand in an entirely different kind of causal relation—production—which requires an entirely different kind of analysis (and for which omissions are *not* suitable relata). *Dependence* and *Omissions* are true of the first of these causal relations; *Transitivity*, *Locality*, and *Intrinsicness* are true of the second. I'll close section 6 by defending this claim against some of the most obvious objections.

How are production and dependence to be analyzed? Dependence, I think, is easy; it is counterfactual dependence, nothing more nor less (with, perhaps, the proviso that counterfactual dependence itself can come in different varieties; see sec. 7 for brief discussion). Production is trickier, and in section 7 I'll offer a speculative proposal about its analysis, confined to the special case of deterministic laws that permit no action at a temporal distance or backward causation. But I'll say at once that I

am much more confident of the propriety of the distinction than I am of this particular gloss on the "production" half of it.

I'll close, in section 8, by suggesting some ways in which the distinction between
production and dependence might be put to work, and by highlighting what I think
are the most important bits of unfinished business.

2 Preliminaries, and a Brief Methodological Sermon

There are, in the literature, more than a dozen versions of a counterfactual analysis
of causation that I am aware of. To attack them all, in detail, would require (to
borrow an apt term from Tim Maudlin) a kind of philosophical "trench warfare"
that only deeply committed partisans could find engaging. I'll confess to a taste for
trench warfare, but I won't indulge it here. Instead, I will follow a different strategy, focusing my critique on the simplest counterfactual analysis, according to which
causation is counterfactual dependence between wholly distinct events. It will be far
more illuminating to explore the most basic problems for this analysis—along with
the clearest and most plausible strategies for confronting them—than it would be
to wind through the convolutions built into the multitude of more sophisticated
variants.

In order to develop this critique as constructively as possible, we must avoid various methodological pitfalls. For that reason, it will be important to characterize, if
only in a rough way, the causal relation that is the target of the counterfactual analysis. I take the analysis to concern the concept of causation as a transitive, egalitarian
relation between localized, datable events. Let's look at the parts of this characterization in turn.

Begin with the relata. In understanding them to be *events*, I am taking sides on
an issue that has seen much recent controversy.[1] I grant that there may be senses in
which nonevents—facts, properties, maybe even things—can cause and be caused;
certainly we speak of event *types* as doing so, as when we say that lightning causes
fires. All the same, I assume that there is a clear and central sense of "cause"—the
one at issue here—in which causes and effects are always events. (In sec. 6, I'll qualify this assumption slightly, suggesting that dependence, at least, can admit more
kinds of relata.)

I will, furthermore, follow common practice by stretching ordinary usage of the
term "event" to cover such things as, for example, the presence, at the appropriate
time, of the oxygen and dry timber that combine with the lightning bolt to produce
the forest fire. I will also take it for granted that we can adequately discern when

two events fail to be *wholly distinct*—that is, when they stand in some sort of logical or mereological relationship that renders them unsuited to stand in *causal* relationships—and that we can tell when a description is too disjunctive or extrinsic to succeed in picking out an event. Without such assumptions, it is far too easy to make a hash of the simple analysis, and the analyses that build on it, by way of alleged counterexamples to the claim that counterfactual dependence is sufficient for causation.[2]

Of course, I do not at all mean to suggest that it is an easy matter to provide an adequate philosophical account of events that meets these criteria. I certainly won't try to provide any such account here. What I *will* do is avoid choosing examples where any of the controversies surrounding the nature of events makes a difference.[3]

Turn next to the characterization of the relation. Transitivity is straightforward enough: If event *a* is a cause of event *b*, and *b* a cause of *c*, then *a* is thereby a cause of *c*. What I mean by "egalitarian" can best be made clear by contrast with our usual practice. When delineating the causes of some given event, we typically make what are, from the present perspective, invidious distinctions, ignoring perfectly good causes because they are not sufficiently salient. We say that the *lightning bolt* caused the forest fire, failing to mention the contribution of the oxygen in the air, or the presence of a sufficient quantity of flammable material. But in the egalitarian sense of "cause," a complete inventory of the fire's causes must include the presence of oxygen and of dry wood. (Note that transitivity helps make for an egalitarian relation: Events causally remote from a given event will typically not be *salient*—but will still be among its causes, for all that.)

Now for a brief methodological sermon: If you want to make trouble for an analysis of causation—but want to do so on the cheap—then it's convenient to ignore the egalitarian character of the *analysandum*. Get your audience to do the same, and you can proceed to elicit judgments that will appear to undermine the analysis, but which are in fact irrelevant to it. Suppose that my favorite analysis counts the big bang as among the causes of today's snowfall (a likely result, given transitivity). How easy it is to refute me, by observing that if asked what *caused* the snowfall (better still: what was *the* cause of it), we would never cite the big bang! Of course, the right response to this "refutation" is obvious: It conflates the transitive, egalitarian sense of "cause" with a much more restrictive sense (no doubt greatly infected with pragmatics) that places heavy weight on salience.

A simple mistake, it would seem. But the same sort of mistake shows up, in more subtle forms, in examples drawn from the literature. It will be helpful to work through a few illustrative cases—ones that show, incidentally, how even first-rate authors can sometimes go astray.

First, Bennett (1987, pp. 222–223; italics in the original), who is here concerned with Lombard's thesis that an event's time is essential to it:

Take a case where this is true:

There was heavy rain in April and electrical storms in the following two months; and in June the lightning took hold and started a forest fire. *If it hadn't been for the heavy rain in April, the forest would have caught fire in May.*

Add Lombard's thesis to that, and you get

If the April rain hadn't occurred the forest fire wouldn't have occurred.

Interpret that in terms of the counterfactual analysis and you get

The April rains caused the forest fire.

That is unacceptable. A good enough theory of events and of causation might give us reason to accept some things that seem intuitively to be false, but no theory should persuade us that delaying a forest's burning for a month (or indeed for a minute) is causing a forest fire.

Lombard agrees that Bennett's result "is unacceptable. It is a bit of good common sense that heavy rains can put out fires, they don't start them; it *is* false to say that the rains caused the fire" (Lombard 1990, p. 197; italics in the original).

Lombard discusses a second example that shows that the essentiality of an event's time is not at issue (ibid., pp. 197–198):

Suppose that Jones lives in a very dangerous neighborhood, and that one evening Smith attempts to stab him to death. Jones is saved because of the action of Brown who frightens Smith off. However, a year later, Jones is shot to death by the persistent Smith. So, if Brown's action had not occurred, Jones's death due to the shooting would not have occurred, since he would have died of stab wounds a year earlier. But, I find it intuitively quite unacceptable to suppose that Brown's action was a cause of Jones's dying as a result of gunshot a year later.

Finally, Lewis discusses a similar example (Lewis 1986d, p. 250):

It is one thing to postpone an event, another to cancel it. A cause without which it would have occurred later, or sooner, is not a cause without which it would not have occurred at all. Who would dare be a doctor, if the hypothesis under consideration [that an event's time is essential to it] were right? You might manage to keep your patient alive until 4:12, when otherwise he would have died at 4:08. You would then have caused his death. For his death was, in fact, his death at 4:12. If that time is essential, his death is an event that would not have occurred had he died at 4:08, as he would have done without your action. That will not do.

If these examples are meant to provide rock-solid "data" on which the counter-factual analysis (and perhaps others) founders, then they uniformly fail—for in each case, we can find *independently plausible* premises that entail the allegedly unacceptable consequences. Of course that doesn't show that the consequences are *true*. But it *does* show that we make a serious methodological mistake if we treat those of our intuitions that run counter to them as nonnegotiable "data."

First we must disentangle irrelevant but confusing issues. It is probably right that an event's time is not in every case essential to it; but (*pace* Lewis) that doesn't help in any of the three cases. This is more or less obvious in the first two cases (the June fire is not the same as the fire that would have happened in May; the death by shooting is not the same as the death by stabbing that would have happened a year earlier). So consider Lewis's case. Supposedly, it "will not do" to assert that the doctor's action is among the causes of the patient's death. But what does this have to do with the proximity of the actual time of death to the time at which the patient would have died? Suppose you manage to keep your patient alive until June of 2004, when otherwise he would have died in June of 2003. Would you then have caused his death, since without your action the death he in fact died would not have occurred? It is no less (and no more) unacceptable to say "yes" in this case than it is to say "yes" in Lewis's case. But if, following Lewis, we conclude that the actual death is the same as the death that would have occurred a year earlier, then we are taking the denial of the essentiality of times to a ridiculous extreme. Such a denial, however warranted, does not give the counterfactual analyst the means to respond effectively even to Lewis's problem.

The analyst can, however, draw on our brief methodological sermon to point to two sorts of judgments about causation that the three examples implicitly trade on— but illegitimately, since these judgments concern types of causation that are not at issue. We can all agree that "heavy rains can put out fires, they don't start them," just as we can agree that smoking causes lung cancer, but regular exercise doesn't. So what? The intuitions called on here do not concern the concept of causation as a transitive, egalitarian relation between events, but rather some other concept of causation as an inegalitarian relation between event-*types*. (Never mind that *starting* a fire is not the only way to be one of its causes!) Similarly, we can all agree that it is the *lightning* that causes the forest fire, and nothing else—including the heavy rains. Again, so what? Here we seem to have in mind a restricted, inegalitarian concept of event-causation according to which events that are to count as causes must be particularly salient in some respect; but judgments involving *this* concept matter not at all to the counterfactual analysis, since it concerns the weaker and more inclusive transitive, egalitarian concept.

Unfortunately, Bennett, Lombard, and Lewis have all muddied the question of whether the counterfactual analysis is adequate by choosing examples where intuitions of the two types just discussed are particularly strong and *seemingly* salient: It's not the *rainfall* that causes the June fire, but rather the lightning; moreover, it's just "good common sense" that heavy rains don't cause fires![4] Of course, while recognizing these points you might still judge these cases to have some intuitive force as counterexamples. Fair enough; they do. But a more careful examination shows how hasty it would be to take any such intuitions as decisive. I'll make the case against Bennett, after which it will be clear enough how to proceed against Lombard and Lewis that we can leave those cases aside.

The idea is to find an event intermediate between the cause and its alleged effect that is *clearly* a cause of the second, and at least plausibly an effect of the first. So observe that among the causes of the June fire is not just the lightning but also the very presence of the forest, filled with flammable material. The presence of the forest in the hours before the lightning strikes is itself an event, or perhaps a collection of events. This event is a cause of the June fire (albeit not a salient cause). What are *its* causes? A typical counterfactual analysis will claim that one of its causes is the April rainfall, since without the rainfall the forest would have been destroyed in May. But we can argue for the plausibility of this claim independently, by noting that the following judgments seem, intuitively, to be correct: It is in part *because of* the April rains that the forest is present in June; any complete *causal explanation* of the forest's presence must cite the role of the April rains in preventing its destruction; the April rains are at least in part *responsible for* the presence of the forest in June.[5]

One could deny the truth of these judgments, or deny that they show that the April rainfall is a cause of the forest's presence in June, or deny that causation is transitive in the way that is needed to complete the inference to the claim that the April rainfall is among the causes of the June forest fire. But unless one can find some grounds for supporting such denials—grounds independent of the mere intuitive implausibility of the claim in question—then this implausibility will fail to provide a particularly compelling reason for giving up the counterfactual analysis. (Exactly parallel points apply to the other two examples.) Happily, I think the conclusions drawn in section 6 clear up what is going on in the rainfall case (and the other cases), precisely by showing that counterfactual analyses utterly fail to capture one important sense of "cause"—production—and that in this sense the April rains are *not* among the causes of the June fire. But it will take some work to get there, and along the way we must not be distracted by the temptations of such bogus "refutations" as those we have just examined. Intuitions about cases must be heeded, to be sure. But not blindly.

Onward. It will help to have a means of representing simple causal structures; accordingly, I will adopt the "neuron" diagrams used by Lewis (1986b).

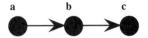

Figure 9.1

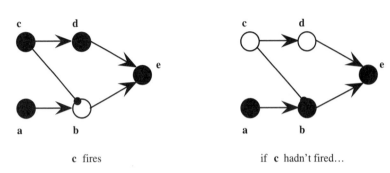

Figure 9.2

The diagram in figure 9.1 depicts a pattern of neuron firings. Dark circles represent firing neurons, while arrows represent stimulatory connections between neurons. The order of events is left to right: In figure 9.1 neuron *a* fires, sending a stimulatory signal to neuron *b*, causing it to fire; *b*'s firing in turn sends a stimulatory signal to neuron *c*, causing it to fire. We will also need a way to represent *prevention* of one event by another. So let us add inhibitory connections to the neuron diagrams, represented by a line ending in a solid dot, as shown in figure 9.2. In the left-hand diagram, neurons *a* and *c* fire simultaneously; *c*'s firing causes *d* to fire, which in turn causes *e* to fire. However, thanks to the inhibitory signal from *c*, *a*'s firing does *not* cause *b* to fire; *b*'s failure to fire is represented by leaving its circle unshaded. The right-hand diagram shows what would have happened if *c* had not fired.

Calling these diagrams "neuron diagrams" is merely picturesque; what is important about them is that they can provide, in a readily digestible form, partial representations of many causal structures.

3   The Simple Counterfactual Analysis, and Two Kinds of Overdetermination

3.1   The Simple Analysis

Both for simplicity and to avoid needless controversies, I will focus only on the counterfactual analysis as it applies to worlds with *deterministic* laws that permit neither backwards causation nor action at a temporal distance (although the lessons of the paper apply much more generally, as far as I can see). I will also leave aside cases, if such there be, where a cause is simultaneous with one of its effects.

Here and throughout I will denote events by lower-case italicized letters "a," "b," "c," and so forth; the proposition that an event e occurs by "Oe"; and the counterfactual or subjunctive conditional by "$\square\!\!\rightarrow$" (read: "were it the case that ... then it would be the case that ...").[6] The simple analysis is as follows:

Event c is a cause of event e iff

(i) c and e are wholly distinct events;

(ii) Oc, Oe, and $\neg Oc \,\square\!\!\rightarrow \neg Oe$ are all true.

An immediate problem arises, whose solution requires the counterfactual conditional to be understood in a rather specific way. In figure 9.1, it is certainly correct to say that if a hadn't fired, c wouldn't have; but it may also be correct to say that if c hadn't fired, a wouldn't have. (If you don't like the sound of that, try the happier locution: If c hadn't fired, it would have to have been that a didn't fire.) If so, the analysis wrongly says that c is a cause of a. (Note the harmless but convenient ambiguity: Letters sometimes refer to events, sometimes to neurons.)

Two responses seem possible. We could augment the analysis by adding some third condition to guarantee the asymmetry of causation (for example: causes must precede their effects). Or we could deny the truth of the offending counterfactual, appealing to an account of the conditional that secured the falsehood of all such "backtrackers" (to use Lewis's apt term: see his 1979a). Swain (1978), for example, opts for the first alternative, Lewis (1979a and 1986a) (and most other counterfactual analysts) for the second.[7]

The first response doesn't work, partly for reasons that have been well explored and that I won't rehearse in detail here (e.g., merely adding the requirement that causes precede their effects won't help if, say, c and e are joint effects of some event a, with c occurring before e; for we could still reason that if c hadn't happened, it would have to have been that a didn't happen, and therefore that e didn't happen). A different, often unnoticed reason for rejecting the first response deserves some discussion, however: The problem is that this response implicitly supposes that backtrackers threaten only the *sufficiency* of the above analysis. If that were true, it would make sense to add further conditions, so as to make the analysis less liberal. But backtrackers also undermine its *necessity*, as figure 9.2 shows.

In figure 9.2, d is, clearly, a cause of e. But if, in evaluating counterfactuals with the antecedent "d does not occur," we proceed by making minimal alterations to the past events that led to d, then we will reach a counterfactual situation in which c

does not occur, but *a* still does—that is, a counterfactual situation in which *e* occurs. That is, if we allow as true the backtracker $\neg Od \;\square\!\!\rightarrow\; \neg Oc$, then the right-hand diagram *also* describes what would have happened if *d* hadn't fired, and so the conditional $\neg Od \;\square\!\!\rightarrow\; \neg Oe$ is false. Then how can it be that *d* turns out to be a cause of *e*? Adding *extra* conditions to (i) and (ii) provides no answer.[8] (Nor will it help to liberalize the analysis in the standard way, by taking causation to be the *ancestral* of counterfactual dependence. For the problem that threatens the connection between *e* and *d* will equally threaten the connection between *e* and any event that mediates between *d* and *e*.)

In short, reading the counterfactual in a backtracking manner destroys the dependence of *e* on *d*. That's not only trouble for the simple analysis: It's just wrong, since it manifestly *is* the case that if *d* hadn't fired, *e* wouldn't have. Or, more cautiously, there manifestly *is* an acceptable reading of the counterfactual conditional according to which this is true. I will henceforth take it for granted that both the simple analysis and its more elaborate kin employ such a "nonbacktracking" reading of the conditional.

It is not obvious how to provide a general semantics for the counterfactual that will secure this reading. Fortunately, for the purposes of this paper we need only come up with a rule for evaluating counterfactuals of the form $\neg Oc \;\square\!\!\rightarrow\; \neg Oe$, where *c* and *e* both occur, and *c* precedes *e*. Following Maudlin (2000), I suggest the following: Letting *t* be the time of occurrence of the given event *c*, we evaluate the conditional $\neg Oc \;\square\!\!\rightarrow\; \neg Oe$ by altering the state of the world at *t* just enough to make the antecedent true, evolving that state forward in time in accordance with the (actual) laws, and seeing whether the consequent comes out true.[9] So, in figure 9.2, if *d* hadn't fired, circumstances contemporaneous with its firing such as the nonfiring of *b* would have been unchanged, and so *e* would not have fired.

3.2   Early Preemption

The simple analysis may appear quite able to stave off challenges to its *sufficiency*. But obvious problems beset its claim to necessity. Consider a case of ordinary preemption, as in figure 9.2. The firing of *e* is overdetermined by the simultaneous firings of *a* and *c*. But not in a way that leaves us at all uncertain as to what causes what: Without question, *c* (and not *a*) is a cause of *e*, even though if *c* hadn't occurred, *e* would have occurred anyway, thanks to an alternative process, beginning with *a*, that *c* preempts.

There is an obvious strategy for handling this kind of case. First, we liberalize our analysis, by taking causation to be the *ancestral* of counterfactual dependence: *c* is a cause of *e* iff there are events $d_1, \ldots, d_n$ such that d_1 counterfactually depends on *c*, d_2

depends on $d_1, \ldots,$ and e depends on d_n. Next, we look for an event d (or sequence of events) intermediate between the preventing cause c and the effect e, such that e depends on d and likewise d on c. The strategy works handily in the case before us (provided, once again, that we are careful *not* to interpret the counterfactual in a "backtracking" sense, according to which, had d not fired, it would have to have been the case that c didn't fire, and so b would have fired, and so e would still have fired).

Observe how natural this embellishment to the simple analysis is—and observe that it gives a central role to the *Transitivity* thesis.

3.3 Late Preemption

Other, quite ordinary cases of overdetermination require a different treatment. Consider a case of so-called late preemption, as in figure 9.3. Neurons a and c fire simultaneously, so that e fires at the same time as b; the inhibitory signal from e therefore prevents d from firing. If c hadn't fired, e still would have; for in that case d would not have been prevented from firing and so would have stimulated e to fire. Likewise for *every* event in the causal chain leading from c to e: If that event had not occurred, e would nevertheless have fired. So the strategy of finding suitable intermediates breaks down; for it to succeed, e would have to depend on at least *one* event in the chain leading back to c, and it does not.

Here is another example, with a slightly different structure; it illustrates how absolutely mundane these cases are. Suzy and Billy, expert rock-throwers, are engaged in a competition to see who can shatter a target bottle first. They both pick up rocks and throw them at the bottle, but Suzy throws hers a split second before Billy. Consequently Suzy's rock gets there first, shattering the bottle. Since both throws are perfectly accurate, Billy's would have shattered the bottle if Suzy's had not occurred, so the shattering is overdetermined.

Suzy's throw is a cause of the shattering, but Billy's is not. Indeed, every one of the events that constitute the trajectory of Suzy's rock on its way to the bottle is a cause of the shattering. But the shattering depends on none of these events, since had any of them not occurred the bottle would have shattered anyway, thanks to Billy's expert throw. So the transitivity strategy fails.

Three alternative strategies for dealing with this kind of case suggest themselves. The first rests on the observation that Suzy's throw makes a difference to the time and manner of the shattering, whereas Billy's does not. The second rests on the observation that Suzy's throw is connected to the shattering by a spatiotemporally continuous chain of causal intermediates, whereas Billy's is not. And the third rests on the observation that there is a sequence of events connecting Suzy's throw to the

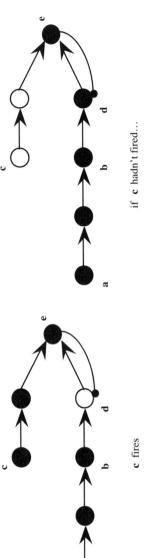

if **c** hadn't fired...

c fires

Figure 9.3

shattering that has the right sort of *intrinsic* character to count as a causal sequence, whereas no such sequence connects Billy's throw to the shattering. Let us consider these strategies in turn.

There are various ways to implement the first strategy. For example, we could deny that the effect that does the preventing is numerically the same as the effect that would have occurred via the alternative process. (E.g., in figure 9.3, the firing of e that *would have* occurred, had c not fired, is not the same event as the firing that *actually* occurs.) If so, then our two examples *do* exhibit the needed pattern of counterfactual dependence, since the effect that actually occurred would not have occurred without its cause (although a very similar event would have occurred in its place). Alternatively, we could remain silent about the individuation of events, and simply employ a slightly different counterfactual in the analysis—say, by counting c a cause of e if and only if, had c not occurred, e would not have occurred at the time it *actually* did (Paul 1998b). Lewis ("Causation as Influence," chapter 3 in this volume) argues that we should count c a cause of e if there is a suitable pattern of counterfactual dependence between various different ways c or something like it might have occurred and correspondingly different ways in which e or something like it might have occurred. (Lewis proposes taking causation itself to be the ancestral of this relation.)

These approaches are uniformly nonstarters. Never mind the well-known problems (e.g., that noncauses can easily make a difference to the time and manner of an event's occurrence—a gust of wind that alters the course of Suzy's rock ever so slightly, for example). What seems to have gone unnoticed is that it is not at all essential to examples of late preemption that the genuine cause make *any* difference to the time or manner of the effect. As Steve Yablo pointed out to me, it's easy enough to construct cases in which c is clearly a cause of e, but in which neither c nor any event causally intermediate between it and e makes the slightest difference to the way e occurs. Yablo observes that we can simply alter the story of Billy and Suzy. This time, Billy throws a Smart Rock, equipped with an onboard computer, exquisitely designed sensors, a lightning-fast propulsion system—and instructions to make sure that the bottle shatters in exactly the way it does, at exactly the time it does. In fact, the Smart Rock doesn't need to intervene, since Suzy's throw is just right. But had it been any different—indeed, had her rock's trajectory differed in the slightest, at any point—the Smart Rock would have swooped in to make sure the job was done properly. Sure, the example is bizarre. But not in a way that matters in the slightest to the evaluation of the causal status of Suzy's throw: Smart Rock notwithstanding, her throw is *still* a cause of the shattering—even though neither it nor any event that mediates between it and the shattering makes a difference to the time or manner of that shattering.

I won't consider these approaches further. It will be far more instructive for us to focus on the two alternative strategies.

Suzy's throw is spatiotemporally connected to the shattering in the right way, but Billy's is not. So perhaps we should add the *Locality* thesis as a constraint on the analysis: Causes have to be connected to their effects via spatiotemporally continuous sequences of causal intermediates. Now, on the face of it this is a step in entirely the *wrong* direction, since it makes the *analysans* more stringent. But if we simultaneously liberalize the analysis in other respects, this strategy might work. For example, we might say that c is a cause of e just in case there is a spatiotemporally continuous sequence of events connecting c with e and a (possibly empty) set S of events contemporaneous with c such that each later event in the sequence (including e) depends on each earlier event—or at least *would have*, had the events in S not occurred. That will distinguish Suzy's throw as a cause, and Billy's as a noncause.

Of course, since action at a distance is surely *possible*, and so *Locality* at best a highly interesting contingent truth, this amended counterfactual analysis lacks generality. But it is patently general enough to be of value. At any rate, it is not so important for our purposes whether this strategy, or some variant, can handle all cases of late preemption. What is important is that it is a plausible and natural strategy to pursue—and it gives a central role to the *Locality* thesis.

Lewis has proposed a third, different strategy. He begins with the intuition that the causal structure of a process is intrinsic to it (given the laws). As he puts it (1986b, p. 205):

Suppose we have processes—courses of events, which may or may not be causally connected—going on in two distinct spatiotemporal regions, regions of the same or of different possible worlds. Disregarding the surroundings of the two regions, and disregarding any irrelevant events that may be occurring in either region without being part of the process in question, what goes on in the two regions is exactly alike. Suppose further that the laws of nature that govern the two regions are exactly the same. Then can it be that we have a causal process in one of the regions but not the other? It seems not. Intuitively, whether the process going on in a region is causal depends only on the intrinsic character of the process itself, and on the relevant laws. The surroundings, and even other events in the region, are irrelevant.

In cases of late preemption, the process connecting cause to effect does not exhibit the right pattern of dependence—but only because of accidental features of its surroundings. The process that begins with Suzy's throw and ends with a shattered bottle does not exhibit the right pattern of dependence (thanks to Billy's throw), but it is intrinsically just like other possible processes that do (namely, processes taking place in surroundings that lack Billy, or a counterpart of him). Lewis suggests, in effect, that *for that reason* Suzy's throw should count as a cause.

Clearly, Lewis is trying to parlay something like the *Intrinsicness* thesis into an amended counterfactual analysis, one adequate to handle cases of late preemption. Now, I think there are serious problems with the details of Lewis's own approach (spelled out in the passage following that just quoted), but since that way lies trench warfare, I won't go into them. I do, however, want to take issue with his statement of the *Intrinsicness* thesis, which is too vague to be of real use. What, after all, is a "process" or "course of events"? If it is just any old sequence of events, then what he says is obviously false: We might have a sequence consisting of the lighting of a fuse, and an explosion—but whether the one is a cause of the other is not determined by the intrinsic character of this two-event "process," since it obviously matters whether *this* fuse was connected to *that* exploding bomb.

I will simply give what I think is the right statement of the *Intrinsicness* thesis, one that eschews undefined talk of "processes."[10] Suppose an event e occurs at some time t'. Then consider the structure of events that consists of e, together with all of its causes back to some arbitrary earlier time t. That structure has a certain intrinsic character, determined by the way the constituent events happen, together with their spatiotemporal relations to one another. It also has a certain causal character: In particular, each of the constituent events is a cause of e (except e itself, of course). Then the *Intrinsicness* thesis states that any possible structure of events that exists in a world with the same laws, and that has the same intrinsic character as our given structure, *also* duplicates this aspect of its causal character—that is, each duplicate of one of e's causes is itself a cause of the e-duplicate.[11]

Three observations: First, "same intrinsic character" can be read in a very strict sense, according to which the two structures of events must be *perfect* duplicates. Read this way, I think the *Intrinsicness* thesis is close to incontrovertible. But it can also be read in a less strict sense, according to which the two structures must be, in some sense, sufficiently *similar* in their intrinsic characters. Read this way, the thesis is stronger but still highly plausible. Consider again the case of Billy and Suzy, and compare the situation in which Billy throws his rock with the situation in which he doesn't. Clearly, there is a strong intuition that the causal features of the sequence of events beginning with Suzy's throw and ending in the shattering should be the *same* in each case, precisely *because* Billy's throw is extrinsic to this sequence. But it is too much to hope for that the corresponding sequences, in each situation, be *perfect* duplicates; after all, the gravitational effects of Billy's rock, in the situation where he throws, will make minute differences to the exact trajectory of Suzy's rock, and so on. So if it is the *Intrinsicness* thesis that gives voice to our conviction that, from the standpoint of Suzy's throw, the two situations must be treated alike, then we should read the "same intrinsic character" clause in that thesis in the less stringent way.

Doing so quite obviously leaves us with the burden of explaining what near-but-not-quite-perfect duplication of intrinsic character consists in. I won't try to unload that burden here. It will emerge that for my *main* purposes, that doesn't matter, since in order to use the *Intrinsicness* thesis to argue that dependence and production are two distinct kinds of causation, I can read "same intrinsic character" in the more stringent sense. (Alas, we will also see that my own preferred *analysis* of production will require the less stringent reading. For extensive discussion of these and other issues involving *Intrinsicness*, see my 2002b.)

The second observation to make about the *Intrinsicness* thesis is that it is somewhat limited in scope: it does not apply, in general, to situations in which there is causation at a temporal distance, or to situations in which there is backward causation. Roughly, the problem is that the relevant structure of events must be *complete* in a certain respect, consisting in a complete set of joint causes of the given effect *e*, together with all those events that mediate between these causes and *e*. I won't go into the reasons why it must exhibit this kind of completeness (but see my 2002b). But consider a case where the effect takes place at one o'clock, and we have collected together all of its causes that occur at noon, as well as those that occur between noon and one. If there is action at a temporal distance, then some of the other causes with which the noon causes combine to bring about the effect might have occurred *before* noon, in which case our structure won't be sufficiently complete. If there is backward causation, then some of the events that mediate between the noon causes and the effect might occur *outside* the given interval, in which case our structure won't be sufficiently complete. Either way, there is trouble. It is partly in order to finesse this trouble that I have limited my focus by ignoring both backward causation and causation at a temporal distance.

The third observation to make about the *Intrinsicness* thesis is that we must assume—on pain of rendering the thesis trivially false—that the structure of events against which we compare a given structure includes no *omissions*. Let the structure S consist of *e*, together with all of its causes back to some arbitrary earlier time t. And let the structure S' simply consist of S, together with some arbitrary omission that "occurs" at some point in the relevant interval. Plausibly, this omission will contribute nothing to the intrinsic character of S'—for it simply consists in the *failure* of some type of genuine event to occur. So S' will perfectly match S. If we apply the *Intrinsicness* thesis uncritically, we immediately get the absurd result that the added omission—whatever it is—counts as a cause of *e*. Now, it was already fairly clear that whatever the guiding intuition is behind the *Intrinsicness* thesis, it does not concern omissions. This result confirms the suspicion. So the final clause of the *Intrinsicness* thesis should read: "... any possible structure of *genuine* events (not including any omissions) that exists in a world with the same laws, and that has the same intrinsic character as our given structure, *also* duplicates...." (It doesn't follow that *S*—the structure picked out as consisting of *e*, together with all of its causes back to some earlier time *t*—must include no omissions. We'll take up the question of whether it can in sec. 5, below.)

Perhaps the counterfactual analyst can use the *Intrinsicness* thesis to handle the problem of Billy and Suzy. After all, in the alternative circumstances in which Billy's throw is absent, it seems correct to say that the causal history of the shattering (back to the time of Suzy's throw) consists exactly of those events on which it depends. What's more, this structure matches a structure that takes place in the actual circumstances, where Billy's throw confounds the counterfactual relations; Suzy's throw, being a part of this structure, will therefore count as a cause of the shattering, thanks to the *Intrinsicness* thesis. To be sure, this is no more than a suggestion of a revised analysis. But again, what is important is that it is a plausible and natural suggestion to pursue—and it gives a central role to the *Intrinsicness* thesis.

4   Double Prevention

And now for something completely different: a kind of example that spells trouble for the *sufficiency* of the simple analysis, by showing that the cornerstone thesis of *Dependence* runs headlong into conflict with each of *Transitivity*, *Locality*, and *Intrinsicness*.

4.1   Example

Suzy and Billy have grown up, just in time to get involved in World War III. Suzy is piloting a bomber on a mission to blow up an enemy target, and Billy is piloting a fighter as her lone escort. Along comes an enemy fighter plane, piloted by Enemy. Sharp-eyed Billy spots Enemy, zooms in, pulls the trigger, and Enemy's plane goes down in flames. Suzy's mission is undisturbed, and the bombing takes place as planned. If Billy hadn't pulled the trigger, Enemy would have eluded him and shot down Suzy, and the bombing would not have happened.

This is a case of what I call "double prevention": one event (Billy's pulling the trigger) prevents another (Enemy's shooting down Suzy), which had it occurred would have prevented yet another (the bombing). The salient causal structure is depicted in figure 9.4. Neurons *a*, *b*, and *c* all fire simultaneously. The firing of *c*

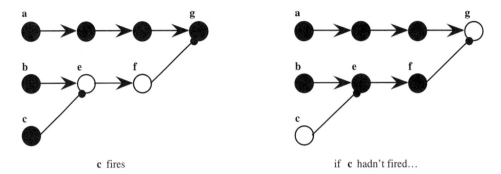

c fires   if c hadn't fired...

Figure 9.4

prevents *e* from firing; if *e* had fired, it would have caused *f* to fire, which in turn would have prevented *g* from firing. Thus, if *c* had not fired, *g* would not have. So *c* is a cause of *g*: Billy's pulling the trigger is a cause of the bombing.

This consequence of the counterfactual analysis might seem natural enough. After all, wouldn't we give Billy part of the credit for the success of the mission? Isn't Billy's action part of the explanation for that success? And so on. On the other hand, it might seem quite unnatural—for the scuffle between Billy and Enemy takes place, let us suppose, hundreds of miles away from Suzy, in such a way that not only is she completely oblivious to it, but it has absolutely no effect on her whatsoever. Here she is, in one region, flying her plane on the way to her bombing mission. Here Billy and Enemy are, in an entirely separate region, acting out their fateful drama. Intuitively, it seems entirely unexceptionable to claim that the events in the second region have no causal connection to the events in the first—for isn't it plain that no *physical* connection unites them?

So far, it might seem that we have a stalemate: two contrary intuitions about the case, with no way to decide between them. (Indeed, my informal polling suggests that intuitive judgments vary quite a lot.) Not so: Both the judgment that we have a case of causation here, and the thesis of *Dependence* that endorses this judgment, run into trouble with each of the theses of *Locality*, *Intrinsicness*, and *Transitivity*.

4.2 Problems with Locality

We all know what action at a distance is: We have a case of it if we have a cause, at least one of whose effects is not connected to it via any spatiotemporally continuous causal chain.[12] I take it that action at a distance is possible, but that its manifestation in a world is nevertheless a highly nontrivial fact about that world. Yet if Billy's action counts as a cause of the bombing, then the quite ordinary and mundane relationship it bears to the bombing also counts as a case of action at a distance. Worse: It counts as a case of action at a *temporal* distance—something that one might reasonably argue is *not* possible, and at any rate something for which one will search the history of physics in vain for precedent. Is *this* all it takes to achieve such nonlocality? (And to think that philosophers have been fussing over Bell's inequalities!) If so, we would be hard pressed to describe laws that *didn't* permit action at a (temporal) distance. For example, even the classical laws that describe perfectly elastic collisions would have to be judged nonlocal, since they permit situations in which one collision prevents a second, which, had it happened, would have prevented a third—so that we have dependence of the third collision on the first, but no connecting sequence of causal intermediates. In short, it appears that while *Dependence* doesn't *quite* contradict *Locality*, it renders it satisfiable only by the most trivial laws (e.g., laws that say that nothing ever changes). That's wrong: The distinction between laws that do and laws that don't permit action at a distance is interesting; to assimilate it to the all-but-vacuous distinction between laws that do and laws that don't permit double prevention is a mistake.

A remarkably frequent but entirely unsatisfactory response is the following: Billy's action *is* connected to the bombing via a spatiotemporally continuous causal chain—it's just that this chain consists, in part, of *omissions* (namely, the various failures of Enemy to do what he would have done, had Billy not fired). Now, it's not just that such reliance on causation by omission is desperate on its face. It's that even if we grant that these omissions exist and are located where the events omitted would have occurred (a nontrivial supposition: right now I am at home, and hence fail to be in my office; is this omission located there or here?), it doesn't help. For there is no reason to believe that the region of spacetime these omissions occupy intersects the region of spacetime that Suzy and her bomber *actually* occupy; to hold otherwise is just to mistake *this* region with the region she *would have* occupied, had Billy not fired. We can agree that had Billy not fired, then the Enemy-region would have intersected the Suzy-region; but if, say, Suzy would have swerved under those circumstances, then it's just false to suppose that this counterfactual Enemy-region (= the *actual* omission-of-Enemy-region) intersects the *actual* Suzy-region.

Of course, the debate can take various twists and turns from here: There are further stratagems one might resort to in an effort to interpolate a sequence of omissions between Billy and the bombing; alternatively, one might deny that causation without a connecting sequence of causal intermediates really *is* sufficient for action at a distance. It won't profit us to pursue these twists and turns (but see my 2000b); suffice it to say that the stratagems fail, and the prospects for a replacement for the sufficient condition seem hopeless.

4.3   Problems with Intrinsicness

Let's first recall what the *Intrinsicness* thesis says, in its careful formulation: Suppose an event *e* occurs at some time t'. Consider the structure of events *S* that consists of *e*, together with all of its causes back to some arbitrary earlier time *t*. Then any possible structure of events that exists in a world with the same laws, and that has the same intrinsic character as *S*, *also* has the same causal character, at least with respect to the causal generation of *e*.

For the purposes of this section, we can read "has the same intrinsic character as" as "perfectly duplicates"—we won't need to compare structures of events that exhibit near-but-not-quite-perfect match of intrinsic character.

Now for some more detail. When Billy shot him down, Enemy was waiting for his home base—hundreds of miles away—to radio him instructions. At that moment, Enemy had no particular intention of going after Suzy; he was just minding his own business. Still, if Billy hadn't pulled the trigger, then Enemy would have eluded him, and moments later would have received instructions to shoot down the nearest suitable target (Suzy, as it happens). He would then have done so. But Billy does shoot him down, so he never receives the instructions. In fact, the home base doesn't even bother to send them, since it has been monitoring Enemy's transmissions and knows that he has been shot down.

Focus on the causal history of the bombing, back to the time of Billy's action. There is, of course, the process consisting of Suzy flying her plane, and so on (and, less conspicuously, the process consisting in the persistence of the target). If *Dependence* is true, then the causal history must also include Billy's action and its immediate effects: the bullets flying out of his gun, their impact with Enemy's fuselage, the subsequent explosion. (Perhaps we should also throw in some omissions: the failure of Enemy to do what he would have done, had he somehow eluded Billy. It makes no difference, since their contribution to the *intrinsic character* of the resulting causal history is nil.) Let this structure of events be *S*.

Two problems now emerge. In the first place, the intrinsic character of *S* fails to determine, together with the laws, that there are no *other* factors that would (i) stop Enemy, if Billy somehow failed to; (ii) do so in a way that would reverse the intuitive verdict (such as it is) that Billy's action is a cause of the bombing. Suppose, for instance, that we change the example by adding a bomb under Enemy's seat, which would have gone off seconds after the time at which Billy fired. And suppose that within this changed example, we can find a duplicate of *S*—in which case the specification of the intrinsic character of *S* must leave out the presence of the bomb. That shows (what was, perhaps, apparent already) that the dependence of the bombing on Billy's action is a fact *extrinsic* to *S*. If we decide that in this changed example, Billy's action is *not* a cause of the bombing (since, thanks to the bomb under Enemy's seat, he in fact poses no threat to Suzy), then we must either give up the *Intrinsicness* thesis, or grant that the causal history of the bombing (back to the time of Billy's action) wasn't described completely by *S*. Neither option is attractive. Let us call this the problem of the *extrinsic absence of disabling factors* (disabling in the sense that if they were present, there would be no dependence of the bombing on Billy's action).

Much more serious is the problem of the extrinsic *presence* of *enabling* factors (enabling in the sense that if they were absent, there would be no dependence of the bombing on Billy's action). For consider a third case, exactly like the first except in the following critical respect: The home base has no intentions of sending Enemy orders to shoot anyone down. In fact, if Billy hadn't pulled the trigger, then the instructions from the home base would have been for Enemy to return immediately. So Enemy poses no threat whatsoever to Suzy. Hence Billy's action is *not* a cause of the bombing. Yet the structure of events *S* is duplicated *exactly* in this scenario. So if the *Intrinsicness* thesis is right, then that causal history *S* must not in fact have been *complete*; we must have mistakenly excluded some events for which the third scenario contains no duplicates. Presumably, these events will be the ones that constitute the monitoring of Enemy by his home base, together with the intentions of his superiors to order him to shoot down the nearest appropriate target.

But now we are forced to say that these events count as *causes* of the bombing. That is ridiculous. It is not that they have *no* connection to the bombing, it's just that their connection is much more oblique: All we can say is that if they hadn't happened, then the bombing would not have depended on Billy's action. And notice, finally, that it is exactly the inclusion of Billy's action as part of the causal history *S* that is the culprit: Once we include it, we must also include (on pain of denying *Intrinsicness*) all those events whose occurrence is required to secure the counterfactual dependence of the bombing on this action.

To see this problem more vividly, compare the events depicted in figures 9.5 and 9.6. Here, f is a stubborn neuron, needing two stimulatory signals in order to fire. Neuron h, in figure 9.5, fires shortly after the time at which neurons a, b, and c all fire (so I have abused the usual left-to-right conventions slightly). In the left-hand diagram of figure 9.5, g depends on c, but in figure 9.6 it does not; indeed, it would be quite ridiculous to claim, about the left-hand diagram of figure 9.6, that c was in *any* sense a cause of g.

But now consider the causal history of g, in the left-hand diagram of figure 9.5, and suppose that—in keeping with *Dependence*—we count c as part of this causal history. Then it would seem that this causal history is duplicated *exactly* in the left-hand diagram of figure 9.6—in which case either *Intrinsicness* is false, or c in

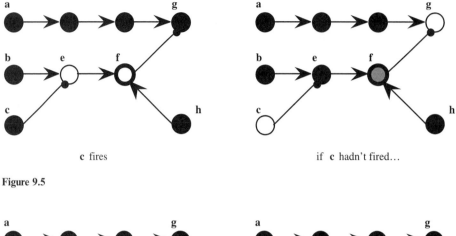

Figure 9.5

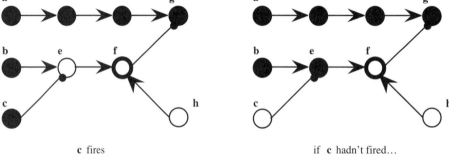

Figure 9.6

figure 9.6 is, after all, a cause of *g*. The only way out of this dilemma is to deny *Dependence*—or else to insist, against all good sense, that the causal history of *g*, in figure 9.5, *also* includes the firing of *h* (which is not duplicated in figure 9.6). But of course it does not: In figure 9.5, the firing of *h* is necessary, in order for *g* to depend on *c*; but that does not make it one of *g*'s causes.

4.4 Problems with Transitivity

A more striking problem appears when we focus on the transitivity of causation. I begin by adding yet more detail to the example.

Early in the morning on the day of the bombing, Enemy's alarm clock goes off. A good thing, too: If it hadn't, he never would have woken up in time to go on his patrolling mission. Indeed, if his alarm clock hadn't gone off, Enemy would have been nowhere near the scene at which he was shot down. It follows that if Enemy's alarm

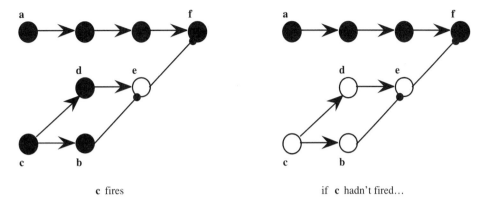

c fires   if c hadn't fired...

Figure 9.7

clock hadn't gone off, then Billy would not have pulled the trigger. But it is also true that if Billy hadn't pulled the trigger, then the bombing would never have taken place. By transitivity, this ringing is one of the causes of the bombing.

Figure 9.7 helps to reinforce the absurdity of this conclusion. Neuron e can never fire. If c does not fire, then e won't get stimulated by d, whereas if c *does* fire, then the stimulation from d will be blocked by the inhibitory signal from b. So e poses no threat whatsoever to the firing of f. The little four-neuron network that culminates in e is, from the standpoint of f, totally inert.

Clearly, c's firing cannot be a cause of f's firing. At most, we might character-ize c's firing as something which *threatens to prevent* f's firing, by way of the *c-d-e* connection—with the threat blocked by the *c-b-e* connection. Yet if both *Depen-dence* and *Transitivity* are correct, then c's firing *is* a cause of f's firing. For if c hadn't fired, then b would not have fired. Likewise, if b had not fired, then f would not have fired (recall here that backtracking is forbidden: We cannot say that if b had not fired, then it would have been that c didn't fire, and so f would have fired all the same). Since f depends on b, and b depends on c, it follows from *Depen-dence* and *Transitivity* that c's firing is a cause of f's firing. That consequence is unacceptable.

Certain examples with this structure border on the comic. Billy spies Suzy about to throw a rock at a window. He rushes to stop her, knowing that as usual he's going to take the blame for her act of vandalism. Unfortunately for him, he trips over a tree-root, and Suzy, quite oblivious to his presence, goes ahead and breaks the win-dow. If he hadn't tripped, he would have stopped her—so the breaking depends on the tripping. But if he hadn't *set out* to stop her, he wouldn't have tripped—so, by the combination of *Transitivity* and *Dependence*, he has helped cause the breaking after all, merely by setting out to stop it! That conclusion is, of course, just silly.[13]

Conclusion: If the thesis of *Dependence* is true, then each of *Locality*, *Intrinsicness*, and *Transitivity* is false. More precisely, if *Dependence* is true at a world, and the events in that world exhibit a causal structure rich enough to provide even one case of double prevention like each of the ones we have been examining, then each of *Locality*, *Intrinsicness*, and *Transitivity* is false at that world. In the next section, we'll see that an exactly parallel conclusion can be drawn with respect to the thesis that omissions can be causes and effects.

5   Omissions

The thesis of *Omissions* brings in its wake a number of difficult questions of ontology: Does it imply a commitment to a peculiar kind of "event" whose occurrence conditions essentially involve the *failure* of some ordinary type of event to occur? Does it make sense to speak of "the failure of *c* to occur," where "*c*" is supposed to refer to some ordinary event? (For perhaps such singular reference to nonactual events is impossible; alternatively, perhaps it is possible, but the circumstances in which we want to cite some omission as a cause or effect typically underdetermine which ordinary event is "omitted.") Do omissions have locations in space and time? If so, what determines these locations? (Recall the remarks in sec. 4.2: Right now I am at home and hence fail to be in my office; is this omission located there or here?) And so on. I am simply going to gloss over all of these issues and assume that a counterfactual supposition of the form "omission *o* does not occur" is equivalent to the supposition that some ordinary event of a given type *C does* occur (at, perhaps, a specific place and time)—where the type in question will be fixed, somehow, by the specification of *o* (or perhaps by context, or perhaps by both). At any rate, however justified complaints about the ontological status of omissions might be, they are emphatically not what is at issue, as we're about to see.

In what follows, I'll make the case that examples of causation *by* omission routinely violate each of *Locality* and *Intrinsicness*. The techniques I employ can be adapted so straightforwardly to make the same points about prevention (i.e., causation *of* omission) that we can safely leave those cases aside. Displaying the conflict between *Omissions* and *Transitivity* will require a case in which we treat an omission as an effect of one event and as a cause of another.

Finally, I am also going to gloss over the remarkably tricky question of when, exactly, we *have* a case of causation by or of omission—a question to which the thesis of *Omissions* only gives the vague answer, "sometimes." For example, is it enough to have causation of e by the failure of an event of type C to occur for e to counter-factually depend on this omission? Or must further constraints be satisfied? If not—if dependence is all that is required—we get such unwelcome results as that my act of typing has among its causes a quite astonishing multitude of omissions: the failure of a meteorite to strike our house moments ago, the failure of the President to walk in and interrupt me, and so on. If, on the other hand, we insist that mere dependence is not enough for causation by omission, then we face the unenviable task of trying to characterize the further constraints. I'm going to sidestep these issues by picking cases that are uncontroversial examples of causation by omission—uncontroversial, that is, on the assumption that there are *any* such cases.

5.1 Problems with Locality
We can draw on the story of Suzy, Billy, and Enemy to show that, even if we waive worries about whether omissions have determinate locations, *Locality* fails for typical cases of causation by omission. Focus on a time t at which Enemy would have been approaching Suzy to shoot her down, had he not been shot down himself. Had Enemy not been absent, Suzy's mission would have failed; so the bombing depends on, as we might put it, the omission of Enemy's attack. More than this: The omission of Enemy's attack is among the *causes* of the bombing—at least, if there is to be causation by omission *at all*, this case should certainly be an example. But once again, it appears that the connection between this omission and the bombing must also qualify as a case of action at a distance, for no spatiotemporally continuous sequence of causal intermediates connects the two events. As before, the problem is not with finding a suitable location for the omission; it is rather that nothing guarantees that the sequence of omissions that proceeds from it (Enemy's failure to approach, pull the trigger, etc.) will intersect Suzy's *actual* flight. We can grant that the region of spacetime in which these omissions "take place" intersects the region she *would have* occupied, had Enemy not been absent. But to suppose that this region is the same as the region she *actually* occupies is to commit the same mistake as before.

5.2 Problems with Intrinsicness
Whatever omissions are, they are notably lacking in intrinsic character. We already saw that for this reason, the *Intrinsicness* thesis needed to be phrased rather carefully: When we have picked out an event e and a structure of events S comprising e and all causes of e back to some earlier time, it is to be understood that any structure against which we compare S is composed solely of *genuine* events, not omissions. (On the other hand, no harm comes of letting S include omissions, at least on the assumption that they contribute nothing to its intrinsic character.) Still, it is for all that consistent

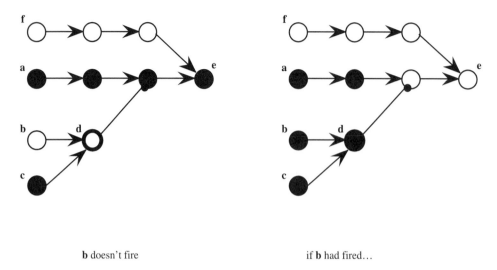

<table>
<tr><td align="center">**b** doesn't fire</td><td align="center">if **b** had fired…</td></tr>
</table>

Figure 9.8

to hold that *Intrinsicness* applies to causation by omission, as follows: Suppose that *e* occurs at time t', and that *S* consists of *e* and all causes of *e* back to some earlier time *t*. Suppose further that we count the omission *o* as one of *e*'s causes, and that *o* "occurs" (in whatever sense is appropriate for omissions) in the interval between *t* and t'. Then if structure S' intrinsically matches *S*, there must be some omission o' "corresponding" to *o* that causes the event e' in S' that corresponds to *e* in *S* (never mind that o' is not *part* of S'). In short, we might think that causation of an event by omission supervenes on the intrinsic character of that event's "positive" causal history.

This conjecture is false. To show why, I'll argue that both of the problems we saw in section 4.3—the problem of the extrinsic lack of disabling factors and the problem of the extrinsic presence of enabling factors—recur in this context. A simple neuron diagram will serve to illustrate each. In figure 9.8, *d* is a dull neuron that needs two stimulatory signals in order to fire. Thus, *d* fails to fire even though stimulated by *c*; still, since *c* fires, *e*'s firing depends on the *failure* of *b* to fire (at, say, time *t*, which we will take to be the time of *a*'s firing). Note finally that if *b* had fired and *f* had as well (at *t*), then *e* would have fired all the same.

Let us suppose, in keeping with the *Omissions* thesis, that the failure of *b* to fire at *t* is among the causes of *e*'s firing. Let *S* consist of *e*, together with all of its (positive) causes back to time *t*. Then if *Intrinsicness* applies to causation by omission in the way we have suggested, any nomologically possible structure that duplicates *S* will

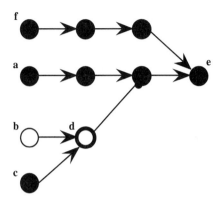

Figure 9.9

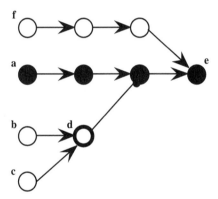

Figure 9.10

exhibit the same causal relationships: In particular, there will be an omission that "duplicates" b's failure to fire and that will be a cause of the event that duplicates e's firing. Shown in figure 9.9 is one such possible structure, embedded in slightly different surroundings. And another is shown in figure 9.10, again in different surroundings.

The problem is that in each case, b's failure to fire is no longer a cause of e's firing, *contra* the requirements of our conjecture about how *Intrinsicness* covers causation by omission. In figure 9.9, the firing of f renders b's failure to fire quite irrelevant to whether e fires, showing that when b's failure to fire *is* a cause of e's firing, this is owing in part to the extrinsic absence of disabling factors. Likewise, in figure 9.10, c's failure to fire renders the behavior of b irrelevant, showing that when b's failure to fire is a cause of *e*'s firing, this is owing in part to the extrinsic presence of enabling factors. So the leading idea behind the *Intrinsicness* thesis—that it is the intrinsic character of some event's causal history that (together with the laws) makes it the case that this *is* its causal history—comes directly into conflict with the *Omissions* thesis.

5.3   Problems with Transitivity

As before, more striking problems emerge when we combine the theses of *Omissions* and *Transitivity*. To see how easy it is to concoct an absurdity from these two ingredients, consider the following variant on our story: This time, Enemy's superiors on the ground had no intention of going after Suzy—until, that is, Billy shoots Enemy down. Outraged by this unprovoked act of aggression, they send out an all-points-bulletin, instructing any available fighter to go after Suzy (a much more valuable target than Billy). Alas, Enemy was the only fighter in the area. Had he somehow been present at the time of the broadcast, he would have received it and promptly targeted and shot down Suzy; his *absence* is thereby a cause of the bombing. But, of course, his absence is itself caused by Billy's action. So by *Transitivity*, we get the result that Billy's action is a cause of the bombing. Lest the details of the case be distracting, let's be clear: *All Billy does is to provoke a threat to the bombing*; luckily for him, the very action that provokes the threat also manages to counteract it. Note the similarity to our earlier "counterexample" to *Transitivity*: Enemy's action (taking off in the morning) both causes a threat to the bombing (by putting Enemy within striking range of Suzy) and counteracts that threat (by likewise putting Enemy within Billy's striking range).

Conclusion: If the thesis of *Omissions* is true, then each of *Locality*, *Intrinsicness*, and *Transitivity* is false. More precisely, if *Omissions* is true at a world, and the events in that world exhibit a causal structure rich enough to provide cases of the kinds we have just considered, then each of *Locality*, *Intrinsicness*, and *Transitivity* is false at that world.

6   Diagnosis: Two Concepts of Causation

Here are two opposed reactions one might have to the discussion so far:

Counterfactual dependence is *not* causation. In the first place, it's not (as everyone recognizes) necessary for causation. In the second place, the best attempts to tart it up in such a way as to yield a full-blown analysis of causation rely on the three theses of *Locality*, *Intrinsicness*, and *Transitivity*—and the lesson of double prevention (a lesson also supported by considering the causal status of omissions) is that these theses *contradict* the claim that dependence is sufficient for causation. The theses are too important; this latter claim must be given up. But give up *Dependence*, and you've torn the heart out of counterfactual analyses of causation.

Nonsense; counterfactual dependence *is too* causation. Here we have two wholly distinct events; moreover, if the first had not happened, then the second would not have happened. So we can say—notice how smoothly the words glide off the tongue —that it is in part *because* the first happened that the second happened, that the first event is partly *responsible for* the second event, that the occurrence of the first event helps to *explain why* the second event happened, and so on. Nor do we reverse these verdicts when we discover that the dependence arises by way of double prevention; that seems quite irrelevant. All of these locutions are *causal* locutions, and their appropriateness can, quite clearly, be justified by the claim that the second event depends counterfactually on the first event. So how could this relation fail to be causal? To be sure, it's another question whether we can use it to construct a full-blown analysis of causation, but at the very least we have the result that counterfactual dependence (between wholly distinct events) is *sufficient* for causation—which is just to say that *Dependence* is true.

The claims of both of the foregoing paragraphs are correct, but not by making a contradiction true: Rather, what is meant by "causation" in each case is *different*. Counterfactual dependence is causation in one sense: But in *that* sense of "cause," *Transitivity*, *Locality*, and *Intrinsicness* are all false. Still, they are not false *simpliciter*; for there is a *different* concept of causation—the one I call "production"—that renders them true. Thus, what we have in the standard cases of overdetermination we reviewed in section 3 are not merely counterexamples to some hopeless attempt at an analysis of causation, but cases that reveal one way the concepts of dependence and production can come apart: These cases uniformly exhibit production without dependence. What we have in the cases of double prevention and causation by omission we examined in sections 4 and 5 are not merely more nails in the coffin of the counterfactual analysis, but cases that reveal the other way the two causal concepts can come apart: These cases uniformly exhibit dependence without production. Similarly, we can now diagnose the intuitions Bennett is pumping in his April rains/June forest fire case. For while there is a sense in which the rains *do* cause the fire—the fire clearly depends on the rains—there is an equally good sense in which they don't— the rains do not help to produce the fire. That is because (surprise!) we have here a case of double prevention: The rains prevent an event (fire in May) that, had it occurred, would have prevented the June fires (by destroying the flammable material).

The principal virtues of my claim are thus clear: It allows us to maintain each of the five theses. It provides us with a natural and compelling diagnosis of the most important problem cases for analyses of causation. And it should come as no surprise that the distinction between production and dependence has gone unnoticed, for *typically* the two relations coincide (more exactly, I think, production typically coincides with the ancestral of dependence; more on this in sec. 7.4, below).

An additional virtue of the position, perhaps less obvious than the foregoing ones, concerns the ontological status of omissions. Those who endorse the *Omissions* thesis might worry that they are thereby committed to the existence of a special sort of event—as if the truth of "the failure of an event of type C to occur caused e to occur" required the existence of something that answered to the description, "failure of an event of type C to occur." But if the only sense in which omissions can cause and be caused is that they can enter into relations of counterfactual dependence, then this worry is quite misplaced. For talk of causation by and of omissions turns out to be nothing more than a way of talking about claims of the form, "if an event of type C had occurred, then ..." and "if ..., then an event of type C would have occurred." Manifestly, neither locution carries an ontological commitment to a strange sort of "negative" event. So, if I am right, anxieties about whether we can find a place for omissions in the causal order rest on a basic confusion about what it means to attribute causal status to omissions.

This observation connects to a broader point, which is that dependence, understood as a relation *between events*, is unduly restrictive. Quite generally there can be counterfactual dependence between *facts* (true propositions), where these can be "positive," "negative," "disjunctive," or whatever—and where only rarely can we shoehorn the facts so related into the form, "such-and-such an event occurred." When we can—when we can say that the fact that e occurred depends on the fact that c occurred—then we can go ahead and call this a kind of event-causation. But to see it as anything but a special case of a causal relation with a much broader domain would be, I think, a mistake.[14]

We can bring my thesis into still sharper focus by considering some of the more obvious objections to it. It seems wise to begin by directly confronting what many will see as the most damning objection—which is simply that it posits *two* concepts of event-causation. This might strike some as an extravagantly high price to pay: After all, when possible we should be conservative, and conservatism argues for taking our concept of event-causation to be univocal. At the very least, shouldn't we view the bifurcation of our concept of event-causation as a serious cost of my proposal?

No, we should not—and not because we shouldn't be conservative. It's rather that this objection mistakes a perfectly sensible *methodological maxim* with a *reason to believe*. The methodological maxim goes: When trying to come up with an analysis of a concept, start out by operating under the assumption that the concept is univocal. I think that's sound. But it doesn't at all follow that it is somehow *antecedently more probable* that the concept in question is univocal—let alone *so* probable that any analysis that says otherwise pays a "high price." In the face of the right sorts of reasons to prefer a nonunivocal analysis, we should give up our operative assumption—and we shouldn't expect those reasons to have to carry an extra-heavy burden of proof because of the "intrinsic plausibility" of the hypothesis of univocality.

To think otherwise manifests a basic confusion. It's rather as if I had lost my keys somewhere in this room; I have no idea where. They might be over there, where it's dark and a lot of debris obscures things; or they might be over here, where it's sunny and uncluttered. It makes exceedingly good sense for me to start by looking in the sunny and uncluttered part of the room—to *act as if* I believed my keys were there. But that is not because I *do* believe they are there, or even because I consider it more likely than the alternative (as if the hypothesis that life is easy has some intrinsic plausibility to it!). It's rather that if my keys *are* in the uncluttered area, then I will soon find them—and if they are not, I will quickly find that out as well.

In the same way, when we go to analyze some concept of philosophical interest, it makes exceedingly good sense to start by looking for a univocal analysis. For even if we are wrong, and some hidden ambiguity lurks in our ordinary applications of the concept, the very problems we will encounter in trying to come up with a univocal analysis will (if we are careful and attentive) be diagnostic of this ambiguity. (The critique of the counterfactual analysis carried out in secs. 3–5 was partly designed to be a case in point.) But it is foolishness to mistake this advice for a reason to *believe* that the concept is univocal. Indeed, if I consider the hypothesis that our concept of event-causation is univocal, I see no reason whatsoever to judge it to be highly probable, antecedently to any investigation. And *after* sufficient investigation—in particular, after basic principles governing our application of "cause" have been shown to come into conflict—I think its plausibility is just about nil.

A more subtle objection is the following: What I have really shown is not that there are two *concepts* of causation, but rather that there are two *kinds* of causation, two different ways in which one event can be a cause of another. That may well be right; certainly, I was happy to begin this paper by announcing that event-causation comes in two "varieties." I do not know how to judge the matter, because I am not sufficiently clear on what underlies this distinction between concepts and kinds. Compare a nice example borrowed from Tim Maudlin: There are at least three different ways of being a mother. We might call them "DNA-mother," "womb-mother," and "nurturing mother." Does that mean we have three different concepts of mother—an ambiguity largely unnoticed only because those we call "mothers" are typically all three? I don't know. At any rate, in the case at hand it doesn't matter in the slightest. I am quite content to agree that I have (merely) shown that there are two kinds of causation—as long as those who insist on this rendering of my thesis agree that the two kinds answer to very different criteria and consequently require very different analyses. That claim alone is enough to show how unwise it would be, when attempting to provide a philosophical account of event-causation, merely to forge blindly ahead, trying to come up with an analysis that can successfully run the gauntlet of known problem cases. If I am right, any such *single* analysis is doomed to failure.

A third, more congenial objection begins by granting the distinction between production and dependence, but denying that dependence deserves to be counted a kind of causation at all. Now, I think there is *something* right about this objection, in that production does seem, in some sense, to be the more "central" causal notion. As evidence, consider that when presented with a paradigm case of production without dependence—as in, say, the story of Suzy, Billy, and the broken bottle—we unhesitatingly classify the producer as a cause; whereas when presented with a paradigm case of dependence without production—as in, say, the story of Suzy, Billy, and Enemy—our intuitions (well, those of some of us, anyway) about whether a genuine causal relation is manifested are shakier. Fair enough. But I think it goes too far to deny that counterfactual dependence between wholly distinct events is not a kind of *causal* relation. Partly this is because dependence plays the appropriate sort of roles in, for example, explanation and decision. (See sec. 8, below, for more discussion of this point.) And partly it is because I do not see how to accommodate causation of and by omissions (as we should) as a species of production; counterfactual dependence seems the only appropriate causal relation for such "negative events" to stand in.

This last point brings up a fourth possible objection, which is that in claiming that there are two kinds of causation, each characterized by a different subset of the five theses, I have overstepped my bounds. After all, even if the arguments of sections 4 and 5 succeed, all they establish is, roughly, (i) that *Dependence* contradicts each of *Locality*, *Intrinsicness*, and *Transitivity*; and (ii) that *Omissions* likewise contradicts each of *Locality*, *Intrinsicness*, and *Transitivity*. It obviously doesn't follow that *Dependence* and *Omissions* should be bundled together and taken to characterize one kind of causation, nor that *Locality*, *Intrinsicness*, and *Transitivity* should be bundled together and taken to characterize another. Perhaps the ambiguity in our ordinary causal talk is more multifarious and messy than this claim allows.

Dead right. And even though I think that further investigation could unearth more positive reasons for dividing the five theses into the two groups I have chosen, I do not have such reasons to offer here. For what it's worth, I do have a strong hunch that, as noted above, there couldn't *be* anything more to causation of and by omissions than counterfactual dependence; hence the pairing of *Omissions* with *Dependence*. And in the next section I'll propose an analysis of production that gives central roles to both *Intrinsicness* and *Transitivity*, as well as to a slightly weakened version of *Locality*. But that's hardly enough to warrant conviction. Rather, what's wanted are more probing arguments as to why our ordinary notion of event-causation should fracture cleanly along the lines I have drawn. Lacking such arguments, I will fall back on the methodological maxim discussed above: Given that we can no longer take it as a working hypothesis that the concept of causation is univocal, let us nevertheless adopt the most conservative working hypothesis available to us. Since we have yet to find any reason to think that *Dependence* conflicts with *Omissions*, or that conceptual tensions threaten the happy union of *Locality*, *Intrinsicness*, and *Transitivity*, let us assume—again, as a working hypothesis—that the first two theses characterize one causal notion, the last three another.

And let us now consider how the two causal notions are to be analyzed.

7   The Two Concepts Analyzed

Part of the task—analyzing dependence—is easy: It is simply counterfactual dependence between distinct events. More cautiously, we might want to admit another kind of counterfactual dependence as well. Perhaps counterfactual *covariation*—manifested when the time and manner of one event's occurrence systematically counterfactually depend on the time and manner of another's—should count as a kind of causation as well, to be classified as a close relative of dependence. (It's clearly possible to have dependence without covariation, as in typical cases of double prevention; Schaffer ["Trumping Preemption," chapter 2 in this volume] provides compelling examples of covariation without dependence, as well.) No matter; given that these counterfactual locutions are themselves well understood, our work here is basically already done for us. (But see sec. 8.2 for some tentative reservations.)

Production is harder. In this section I will put forth my own proposal—speculative, and, as we'll see, somewhat limited in scope—for a reductive analysis of this relation. I will set it out in two parts. The first, less speculative part outlines a certain strategy for developing an analysis, which I call the "blueprint strategy." The second, more speculative part describes my (currently) preferred way of implementing this strategy.

7.1   The Blueprint Strategy

Suppose we have an analysis that succeeds—when circumstances are nice—in singling out a portion of the causal history of some target event *e*, where this is understood to be the history of *e*'s *producers*. (When circumstances are not nice, let the analysis fall silent.) It might be a simple counterfactual analysis: When circumstances are nice (when there is no double prevention, overdetermination, etc.), the causal history of *e* back to some earlier time *t* consists of all those events occurring in that interval on which *e* depends. Or it might be a Mackie-style analysis: The causal history consists of all those events (again, occurring in that interval) that are necessary parts of some sufficient condition for *e*. Or it might be some other kind of analysis. Then—provided we can say with enough precision what it takes for circumstances to be "nice"—we can use the *Intrinsicness* and *Transitivity* theses to extend the reach of this analysis, as follows:

First, suppose we examine some events *c* and *e*, and find that our analysis is silent as to whether *c* is a cause of *e*. Still, we find that *c* and *e* belong to a structure of events *S* such that (i) *S* intrinsically matches some *other* structure of events *S'* (occurring in a world with the same laws as the world of *S*); and (ii) our analysis counts *S'* as a segment of the causal history of *e'* (where *e'* is the event in *S'* that corresponds to *e* in *S*). That is, our analysis counts *S'* as a *rich enough set of causes of e' for the Intrinsicness thesis to apply*. It follows that *S* has the same causal structure as *S'* (at least, with respect to the target event *e*), and hence that *c* is a cause of *e*.

For convenience, let us say that when the conjunction of our analysis with the *Intrinsicness* thesis counts *c* as a cause of *e*, *c* is a "proximate cause" of *e*. Then, second, we parlay proximate causation into causation *simpliciter* by means of the *Transitivity* thesis: Causation is simply the ancestral of proximate causation. In short, we use our original analysis to find a set of *blueprints* for causal structures, which we can then use to map out (if we are lucky) the causal structure of *any* set of events, in *any* circumstances, by means of the *Intrinsicness* and *Transitivity* theses.

This strategy has the virtue of factoring the analysis of production into two parts: the analysis that produces the "blueprints," and the extension of any such analysis into a full analysis of production by means of the *Intrinsicness* and *Transitivity* theses. Still, two potential difficulties deserve mention. First, recall that the *Intrinsicness* thesis as I've stated it presupposes that there is neither action at a temporal distance nor backward causation—so without a more general statement of the *Intrinsicness* thesis, the full analysis of production will necessarily be limited in scope. Second, recall that for the purposes to which I put the *Intrinsicness* thesis above (to reveal conflicts with *Dependence* and *Omissions*), the "same intrinsic character" clause in that thesis could be understood in a relatively clear and uncontroversial sense, namely as requiring that the two structures of events in question be *perfect duplicates*. That is, to make trouble for *Dependence* and *Omissions* we only needed to assume, roughly, that two event-structures that *perfectly* match one another in intrinsic respects likewise match in causal respects. But the blueprint strategy affords us no such luxury.

To see why, consider our old standby example of Billy, Suzy, and the broken bottle. Suppose that our unadorned analysis (whatever it turns out to be) falls silent about whether Suzy's throw is a cause of the breaking—and this, thanks to the confounding presence of Billy's throw. And suppose that the counterfactual situation in which Billy's throw is absent is one whose causal structure our analysis succeeds in capturing—in particular, the counterpart to Suzy's throw, in that situation, is counted a cause of the counterpart to the breaking. Victory!—for surely we can say that when Billy's throw is present, Suzy's still counts as a cause, because it belongs to a structure of events (the throw, the flight of the rock, etc.) that matches an appropriate "blueprint" structure—namely, the structure found in the counterfactual situation where Billy's throw is absent. Don't we have here a vindication of the blueprint strategy?

Yes, but only if the notion of "matching" is more liberal and, regrettably, vague than the restrictive, relatively precise notion of *perfect* match. For the two sequences of events—the one beginning with Suzy's throw, in the case where Billy also throws, and the one beginning with her throw, in the case where he doesn't—will *not* match perfectly: For example, tiny gravitational effects from Billy's rock will guarantee that the trajectories of Suzy's rock, in each case, are not *quite* the same. So we are left with the unfinished business of saying what imperfect match consists in, and of specifying how imperfect it can be, consistent with the requirements of the blueprint strategy. While I do not think these difficulties undermine the blueprint strategy, I won't try to resolve them here. (But see my 2002b for a detailed proposal.)

7.2   Implementing the Strategy (First Pass)

Now for my own story about what makes for "nice" circumstances, and how an analysis should proceed under the assumption that they obtain. As usual, I will assume determinism, but I will also assume that there is no action at a temporal distance, nor backward causation (not merely because I wish to slot the following analysis into the blueprint strategy, but also because I do not yet know how to make the analysis itself work, without these assumptions). First, some terminology.

Suppose that at time t, the members of some set S of events all occur, and that e occurs at some later time t'. I will say that S is *sufficient* for e just in case the fact that e occurs follows from

(i) the laws, together with

(ii) the premise that all the members of S occur at t, together with

(iii) the premise that no other events occur at t.

The entailment here is metaphysical, not narrowly logical. I will say that S is *minimally sufficient* for e just in case S is sufficient for e, but no proper subset of S is. (We might want to add a premise to the effect that relevant background conditions obtain. I prefer to treat any such conditions as "encoded" as members of S.) Do not be distracted by the fact that in typical situations, (iii) will be *false* (though (i) and (ii) will of course be true); that is quite irrelevant to the purposes to which we will put the notions of sufficiency and minimal sufficiency.

Finally, the quantifier in (iii) must be understood as ranging over only *genuine* events, and not omissions, else this premise is inconsistent. Suppose, for example, that our set S does *not* include a kiss at a certain location l; the "no other events occur" requirement will therefore entail that no kiss occurs at t at l. Then consider the omission o, which consists in the *failure* of a kiss to take place at t at l, and suppose that o is also not a member of S. To require, in addition, that this "event" not occur, is just to require that a kiss *does* take place at t at l. Quite obviously, we can't add that requirement consistently.

It is a more or less obvious consequence of the foregoing restriction that omissions cannot be producers. With modest assumptions about the laws, we can also prove that no omission can be produced—that is, there is no omission o and event c such that c helps to produce o. For in order for some omission to be produced, there must be at least one example of an omission o and a set of events S such that S is minimally sufficient for o. Now for the assumption: The laws of evolution are such that the unique state of the world in which *nothing at all* happens—no event occurs— remains unchanged, evolving always into itself. If the laws are like this, then S cannot possibly be minimally sufficient for o, simply because a proper subset of S— namely, the empty set—will be sufficient for o.

Roughly, we can say that where the members of S occur at t, S is sufficient for later event e just in case, had only the events in S occurred at t, e would still have occurred; S is minimally sufficient if the same is not true for any proper subset of S. (Since I have employed a counterfactual locution here, one might want to call the resulting analysis a counterfactual analysis. Call it what you will—just don't confuse it with those analyses that take *Dependence* as their starting point.)

It seems that the problems that confound the usual attempts to analyze causation all have to do with stuff going on in the environment of the genuine causal process, stuff that ruins what would otherwise be the neat nomological relationships between

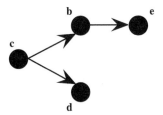

Figure 9.11

the constituents of that process and the given effect. An attractive and simple idea is that *if*, at a time, there is a unique minimally sufficient set for our target effect *e*, then such environmental "noise" must be absent—so that circumstances are "nice"—and we can take it that *this unique minimally sufficient set contains all and only the producers of e that occur at that time*. If so, then one way of implementing the blueprint strategy becomes obvious: Suppose that *e* occurs at *t'*, and that *t* is an earlier time such that at each time between *t* and *t'*, there is a unique minimally sufficient set for *e*; then the segment of *e*'s causal history back to time *t* consists of all and only the events in these sets.

It will turn out that this simple idea won't work without a significant adjustment. But first some good news.

One embarrassment for a Mackie-style analysis is the so-called problem of common effects (figure 9.11): *d* and *e* are both effects of *c*; hence from the fact that *d* occurs (at *t*, say), together with the laws, together with an appropriate specification of the circumstances, it follows that *e* occurs (at *t'*, say). (The reasoning is something like the following: Given the circumstances, *d* could occur only if *c* caused it; but in that case *e* must have occurred as well.)

Our provisional analysis has no such problem, since *d* cannot be part of a minimally sufficient set for *e*. To see why, let us first simplify matters by folding a specification of the background conditions (i.e., the existence of and connections between the various neurons) into the definition of sufficiency (nothing will hinge on this). Then there are, at the relevant time *t*, only two events occurring: *d* and *b*. The set $\{b\}$ is of course sufficient for *e* (hence minimally sufficient, since it contains but one member), since it follows from the claim that *b* alone occurs at time *t*, together with the laws, together with the description of the neuron network, that *e* occurs. Put more simply, had *b* alone occurred at time *t*, *e* would (still) have occurred. But the set $\{d\}$ is *not* sufficient for *e*, since, clearly, in a circumstance in which *d* alone fires, *e* does not fire. So $\{b\}$ is the unique minimally sufficient set for *e*. So *b* is a (producing) cause of *e*.

Objection: It is nomologically impossible for *b* to occur alone—for if it occurs, then *c* must have fired, and so *d* must fire as well.

The best reply is to insist that once we get clear on what the relevant dynamical laws are, we will see that they do allow as a possibility an instantaneous state of the world in which the four neurons are connected as shown, but *b* alone is firing. (The idea is that, in general, dynamical laws place only relatively weak constraints on which instantaneous states are possible.) Since that reply requires too long a digression to develop here, let me fall back on a simpler one: If the objection has any force, then it spells just as much trouble for the notion that there is a coherent nonbacktracking reading of the counterfactual conditional. For consider the conditional "if *d* had not fired, *e* would have fired anyway." True, yes? But if true, it is true only on a nonbacktracking reading. And that reading requires us to make sense of a possibility in which (i) at the relevant time, the instantaneous state of the world is one in which the four neurons are connected as shown, but *b* alone is firing; (ii) the actual dynamical laws govern the evolution of that state from the given time onward. That is exactly the possibility that my account requires.

So our analysis does not count *d* as a cause of *e*. Nor will it, when we add in the *Intrinsicness* and *Transitivity* theses: For *d* cannot inherit causal status from any blueprint; in order to do so the blueprint would have to contain a copy of *d*, a copy of *e*, and other events contemporaneous with the *d*-duplicate and with which it formed a minimally sufficient set. These other events, moreover, would have to be duplicated in the events of figure 9.11. In short, the duplicate would have to be the result of *subtracting* events from figure 9.11 in such a way that *d* remained, and belonged to a minimally sufficient set for *e*. But there is manifestly no way to perform such a subtraction. And it is equally clear that no *sequence* of blueprints can connect up *d* with *e*.

Next, consider ordinary preemption (see fig. 9.2). At the time of occurrence of *a* and *c*, there are two minimally sufficient sets for *e*: {*c*} and {*a*}. (For ease of exposition, here and in the rest of this section I'll suppress mention of those events whose occurrence consists in the presence of the relevant stimulatory and inhibitory connections.) So circumstances are not "nice." Still, there is no problem with getting *c* to come out as a cause of *e*, for there is an obvious blueprint contained within the circumstances that would have occurred, if *a* had not fired. But no such blueprint connecting *a* with *e* can be found in the circumstances that would have obtained, had *c* not fired; for in those circumstances, the causal history of *e* will include the firing of *b*, and so there will be no "match" between this causal history and any part of the actual structure of events.

Next, late preemption: Happily, such cases receive exactly the same diagnosis as the case of ordinary preemption, and so need no special treatment.

Finally, double-prevention (see fig. 9.4). Observe first that there is, at the time of occurrence of a, b, and c, a unique minimally sufficient set for g, namely, $\{a\}$. So if c is to qualify as a cause of g, we must find a blueprint, or sequence of blueprints, that will connect up c with g. But that is evidently impossible. For such a blueprint would have to describe a causal history for g that is different from the one that actually obtains; otherwise, this causal history would contain a duplicate of a, in which case the duplicate of c could not be part of a minimally sufficient set for the duplicate of g. But it is apparent that there is no sequence of events connecting c with g that could serve as such an alternate causal history.

7.3   Implementing the Strategy (Final Pass)

So far, so good. Unfortunately, two difficulties scotch the key idea that when there is a unique minimally sufficient set for e at a time, then its elements are all and only the producers of e (at that time).

First, there are producers that belong to no minimally sufficient set (figure 9.12). In the diagram, a and c are clearly the producers of e; yet the unique minimally sufficient set for e contains just c. (Remember that e, here, is a stubborn neuron, requiring two stimulatory signals to fire.)

Second, there are nonproducers that belong to unique minimally sufficient sets (figure 9.13). In the diagram, a is clearly not a producer of e; yet it is included in $\{a, c\}$, the unique minimally sufficient set for e. (Notice that this is a special case of

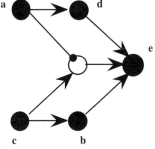
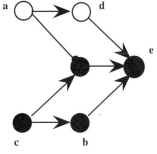
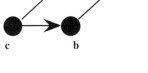

a fires   if **a** hadn't fired…

Figure 9.12

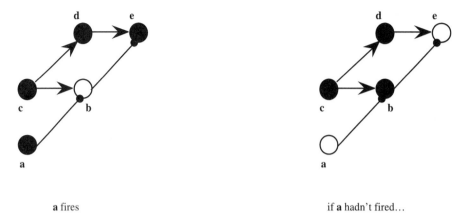

a fires   if a hadn't fired…

Figure 9.13

double prevention, one that eludes the treatment we gave of the standard sort of case exhibited by figure 9.4.)

I suggest these problems arise because we have overlooked an important constraint on the internal structure of causal histories. Suppose that e occurs at time t_2, and that we have identified the set of its producers at both time t_0 (call this set S_0) and time t_1 (call this set S_1) $(t_0 < t_1 < t_2)$. Then it had better be the case that when we trace the causal histories of the elements of S_1 back to t_0,

(i) we find no events *outside* of S_0—for otherwise transitivity of production would have been violated; and

(ii) we *do* find all the events *inside* S_0—for otherwise we would have to say that one of these events helped produce e, but not by way of any of the t_1-intermediates.

Return to the diagrams. In figure 9.12, our analysis tells us (among other things) that d is a producer of e and that a is a producer of d—but fails to deliver the consequence that a is a producer of e. That is an example of a failure to meet constraint (i). In figure 9.13, our analysis identifies d as the sole intermediate producer of e, and identifies c as *its* only producer—thus misdescribing a as a producer of e that somehow fails to act by way of any intermediates. That is an example of a failure to meet constraint (ii).

The way to fix these problem is to make our "nice circumstances" analysis still more restrictive, by building into it the two foregoing constraints. We begin as before, by supposing that e occurs at t', and that t is an earlier time such that at each time between t and t', there is a unique minimally sufficient set for e. But now we add the requirement that whenever t_0 and t_1 are two such times $(t_0 < t_1)$ and S_0 and S_1 the corresponding minimally sufficient sets, then

(i) for each element of S_1, there is at t_0 a unique minimally sufficient set for it; and

(ii) the union of these minimally sufficient sets is S_0.

This added requirement gives expression to the idea that when we, as it were, identify the producers of e *directly*, by appeal to their nomological relationship to e, we must get the same result as when we identify them by "tracing back" through intermediate producers.

We're now in a position to state the analysis of production:

Given some event e occurring at time t' and given some earlier time t, we will say that e has a *pure causal history* back to time t just in case there is, at every time between t and t', a unique minimally sufficient set for e, and the collection of these sets meets the two foregoing constraints. We will call the structure consisting of the members of these sets the "pure causal history" of e, back to time t.

We will say that c is a *proximate cause* of e just in case c and e belong to some structure of events S for which there is at least one nomologically possible structure S' such that (i) S' intrinsically matches S; and (ii) S' consists of an e-duplicate, together with a pure causal history of this e-duplicate back to some earlier time. (In easy cases, S will itself be the needed duplicate structure.)

Production, finally, is defined as the ancestral of proximate causation.

I do not mean to pretend for an instant that the analysis I have offered stands in no need of detailed elaboration or defense. Of course it does. But that task can be left for another occasion, since my aim here is quite modest: I mean only to make it at least somewhat plausible that a reductive analysis of production can be had— thereby blocking the objection that once we distinguish production and dependence and relegate counterfactual analyses to the role of explicating only the latter concept, then we will be stuck with "production" as an unanalyzable causal primitive. That would indeed be unfortunate. But I think there is little reason for such a pessimistic assessment.

7.4   The Coincidence of Production and Dependence

Let me close this section by considering more closely why production and dependence so often coincide. First, suppose that c, which occurs at t, is a producer of e. In *typical* cases—that is, if the environment does not conspire in such a way as to ruin the ordinarily neat nomological relationships between c and e—c will belong to a unique minimally sufficient set for e. Let S be this set. Other events occur at t; let us collect these together into the set T. Then consider what happens in a counterfactual situation where c does not occur (keeping in mind that there may be more than one such situation): (i) The other events in S occur. (ii) The events in T occur. (iii) Possibly, in place of c, some other event c' occurs.[15]

Let $S' = S - \{c\}$. Then—modulo a small assumption—$S' \cup T$ cannot be sufficient for e. For suppose it is. Then given (the small assumption) that not every subset of $S' \cup T$ that is sufficient for e contains a proper subset that is also sufficient for e (given, that is, that the sufficient subsets of $S' \cup T$ are not infinitely nested), $S' \cup T$ will contain a minimally sufficient set for e. But then S will not be the unique such minimally sufficient set, contra the hypothesis.

So it will not follow from the premise that all the events in $S' \cup T$ occur, together with the premise that no other events occur, together with the laws, that e occurs. And that means that in a counterfactual situation in which c does not occur, *and in which no event takes its place*, e does not occur. That is one way it could turn out that e depends counterfactually on c.

More likely, though, some event c' *will* take the place of c. Furthermore, if this event conspires in the right way with the other events in $S' \cup T$, then e will occur all the same. Suppose, for example, that in the actual situation, Suzy throws a rock, breaking a window. Billy is absent this time, so we can assume that her throw is part of a unique minimally sufficient set for the breaking. But suppose further that if she hadn't thrown, her hand would (or simply *might*) have fallen by her side, brushing against a switch, flipping it and thereby activating a catapult that would have hurled a brick at the window, breaking it. Then that is a situation in which the counterfactual alternative to c (or: one of the alternatives) conspires with other events to bring about e. But notice that it takes some work to rig an example so that it has this feature; *typically*, when c is part of a unique minimally sufficient set for e, it will be the case that if c hadn't occurred, then whatever event replaced it would *not* so conspire—which is to say that it will be the case that e depends on c.

Finally, even in the case of Suzy, the rock, and the stand-by catapult, we will have *stepwise* dependence of the window's breaking on her throw: Picking an event d that forms part of the rock's flight, we will have dependence of the breaking on d and of d on the throw. We could tinker further to destroy one of these dependencies, but of course that is not enough: We would need to tinker enough to block *every* two-step chain of dependencies—and every three-step chain, and every four-step chain, and so on. It is possible to do this—even while guaranteeing the existence, at each stage, of a unique minimally sufficient set for the window's breaking—but only at the cost of making the example even more atypical.[16] And that shows that if I am right about the correct analysis of the central kind of causation, then it is no great surprise that the simple idea that causation should be understood as the ancestral of counterfactual dependence worked as well as it did.

8 Applications, Open Questions, and Unfinished Business

8.1 Applications

In the last three decades or so, causation seems to have become something of a philosophical workhorse: philosophers have offered causal accounts of knowledge, perception, mental content, action, explanation, persistence through time, and decision making, to name a few. It won't be possible to discuss any of these topics in detail, but I will focus briefly on the latter three as a way of beginning to explore the broader consequences of the distinction between dependence and production.

Before doing so, however, let us just observe that even the most cursory inspection of the philosophical roles causation plays vindicates one of the three central arguments for the distinction, which is that *Transitivity* and *Dependence* conflict. Recall one of the examples used to display the conflict: Billy spies Suzy, and runs toward her in an effort to stop her from throwing a rock at a window; en route he trips, and as a consequence doesn't reach her in time to stop her. The window breaks. If Billy hadn't tripped, the window would not have broken (because he would have stopped Suzy). If Billy hadn't run toward Suzy, he wouldn't have tripped. Suppose we conclude, via a confused appeal to *Dependence* and *Transitivity*, that Billy's running toward Suzy was one of the causes of the window's breaking. Still, we will have to admit that for a "cause" that is so proximate to its "effect," it is quite strange: It is not something we would cite as part of an explanation of the breaking, we would not hold Billy at all responsible for the breaking on account of having helped to "cause" it in this way, and so on. In short, consider any of the typical roles that causation plays in other arenas, and you will find that the sort of relation Billy's action bears to the breaking quite obviously plays none of those roles. That should add to the conviction (if such addition were needed) that this relation is not one of causation.

That is not to say that we cannot describe this relation in causal terms, since of course we can: Billy does something that both (i) initiates a process that threatens to interrupt the window-breaking process, and (ii) causes an event that interrupts this potential interrupter. So the relation of Billy's action to the window-breaking has a perfectly definite causal structure. But that does not make it a kind of causation.

If we look more closely at some "causally infused" concepts, I think we can find more direct manifestation of the difference between production and dependence, even in the kind of brief and selective treatment I am about to offer.

Begin with persistence. On one well-known view, what it is for an object to persist from time t_1 to time t_2 is for it to have temporal parts at t_1, t_2, and the intervening times such that earlier ones are appropriately connected to later ones. What I want to focus on is not the controversial ontology of temporal parts, but the nature of the connection—which, on typical formulations, has got to be partly *causal*. The question is: Could the causal relation involved in this connection be one of mere dependence, without production?

Good test cases are not easy to come by, mainly because we already know that for an enduring object of any complexity, the causal component of the connection between its earlier and later stages has to be understood as much more restrictive than *either* dependence or production, and the restrictions are not easy to spell out.[17]

Let's strive for as simple a case as possible—say, one involving the persistence through time of an electron (assuming for the moment a naive conception of the electron as a classical point-particle). Suppose we have two electron-stages, located at t_1 and t_2 ($t_1 < t_2$). Plausibly, it is a necessary condition for the stages to be stages of the same persisting electron that the first be a cause of the second. But I think this necessary condition cannot possibly be met if the second merely *depends* on the first. Suppose, for example, that the presence of the first results in the prevention of something that would itself have prevented the presence of the second. If we know that that is the *only* causal connection that obtains between the two stages, then we know enough to conclude that they cannot be stages of one and the same electron. On the other hand, if we know that the first stage helps to produce the second stage, then while we may not yet know enough to conclude that they belong to the same electron, it does *not* matter whether we learn that the second stage fails to depend on the first (as it might, because of some backup process that would have led to an electron in the same place at the same time).

Thus, while the matter certainly merits further investigation, we can conclude that with respect to persistence through time of a simple object like an electron, production is the important causal notion (or at least: one of the basic ingredients in this causal notion), whereas dependence is irrelevant. Persistence of more complex objects seems unlikely to differ in this respect.

Consider next an arena in which the relative importance of the two kinds of causation is reversed: causal decision theory. When you face a range of options, and causal decision theory says (very roughly) that the rationally preferable one is the one most likely to have as a causal consequence the best (by your lights) outcome, the notion of "causal consequence" at work is clearly that of dependence, and not production. Or rather, it is a natural generalization of dependence, where we allow that more than just *events* can be suitable relata: facts, say, or states of affairs.

Our standard stories of double prevention already illustrate the irrelevance of production to decision making. There is, we can suppose, nothing whatsoever that Billy can do to help *produce* the bombing, but that doesn't matter in the slightest: Whether there is a bombing clearly *depends* on the action he takes, and it is his beliefs about this dependence and its detailed structure that will guide his decisions, insofar as he is rational.

Here is another kind of example that makes vivid the irrelevance of mere production (once you see the trick you can generate endless variations): You want your team to win; that is the only thing in the world that matters to you. You know that if you do nothing—just stay where you are, sitting on the sidelines—your fellow teammates will, with certainty, achieve victory. On the other hand, if you insist on playing, the team will probably lose (you are not, alas, very good). Still, if you play and the team manages to *win*, then your own actions will have helped to produce that win (you have your good days, and with luck this might be one of them). If what matters in decision is what your different courses of action would be likely to *produce*, then you should play—for only then does your action have a chance of helping to produce something desirable. That you should clearly *not* play helps show that the productive upshot of your actions is not what matters. (Don't say: "But if you sit on the sidelines, then you help produce the victory by not playing." That is to confuse the kind of causation that omissions can enter into with production, and we have already seen ample reason why such confusion should be avoided.)

There is a needed qualification that by now might be obvious. For there is an obvious way that production *can* matter, quite a lot, to decision: namely, if the outcomes to which the agent attaches value are themselves partly characterized in terms of what produces what. To modify our example, suppose that what matters to you is not that your team win, per se, but that you *help bring about* your team's victory. If so, then it will be perfectly rational (though selfish) for you to insist on playing. Again, if something awful is going to happen no matter what you do, it may yet matter quite a lot to you whether it happens partly as the productive upshot of your behavior.

So production can matter to decision, after all. But seen as an objection to my thesis this is just an equivocation, since that thesis concerns the kind of causal relation that connects action to outcome, and not the taxonomy of outcomes themselves. Even when you choose to avoid a certain course of action because it would result in *your* having helped produce the evil deed, the sense of "because" is clearly that of dependence: What matters is how the possible outcomes (evil deed you helped produce vs. evil deed in which you had no hand) *depend* on your action.

Let us finally consider an arena—causal explanation—in which *both* production and dependence play a role; what we'll find is that these roles are interestingly different.

Recall, once more, the story of Billy's failed attempt to stop Suzy from breaking the window. In seeking an explanation of the window's shattering, we might, on the one hand, ask what *brought that event about*, what *led up to it*. To questions of this sort, it would be strange, to put it mildly, to cite Billy's trip; rather, what's wanted is information about the *producers* of the shattering. On the other hand, we can ask why the shattering occurred, *given that* Billy started running toward Suzy. When we ask a question of this form—"Why did *e* occur, given that *c* occurred"?—we are obviously presupposing that *c* set in motion some process or processes that would have prevented *e*, had circumstances been different—and so we want to know about events whose occurrence *kept* circumstances from being different. (Sometimes we make the presupposition quite explicit: "Why did the window break, given that Billy set out to stop Suzy?") With respect to our story, the obviously correct answer is that Billy tripped (or that he wasn't watching where he was going, or that he's clumsy and so prone to tripping, etc.). It *won't* do to cite an arbitrary producer or *e*, unless it also happens to play the role of stopping *c*'s occurrence from preventing *e*'s. Try it: "Why did the window shatter, given that Billy started running toward Suzy (with the intention of stopping her)?" "Because Suzy threw a rock at the window." Highly misleading, to say the least.

The catch-all explanation-request that philosophers often focus on—"Why did the window break?"—obscures the difference between these two more refined ways of requesting an explanation. Indeed, in the right contexts, the question "Why did the window break?" might be appropriately answered either by "Billy tripped" or by "Suzy threw." That shows that both dependence and production have causal-explanatory roles to play. But it doesn't show—indeed it hides the fact—that these roles exhibit interesting and striking differences. There is, after all, a world of difference between asking, of some event, what led up to it, and asking why it occurred, given that something else was poised to prevent it—never mind that each question could, in the right context, be conveyed by "Why did it happen?"

That concludes my necessarily brief discussion of the implications that the distinction between production and dependence might have for other areas of philosophy. I hope it has been detailed enough to make further such inquiry seem worthwhile. I will close now with a brief look at a few ways in which the picture of causation that

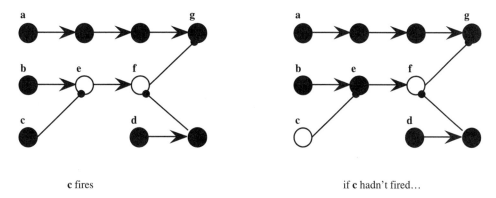

c fires   if c hadn't fired...

Figure 9.14

emerges from the foregoing treatment turns out to be more complicated than one might have thought.

8.2 Unfinished Business

First, there are certain kinds of cases that we have some inclination to call cases of causation, but that also elude classification in terms of production or dependence. Here is an example, a slight variation on the story of Billy, Suzy, and Enemy: This time, there is a second fighter plane escorting Suzy. Billy shoots down Enemy exactly as before, but if he hadn't, the second escort would have. Figure 9.14 captures the salient causal structure.

It is no longer true that if Billy hadn't pulled the trigger, then the bombing wouldn't have happened. In figure 9.14, it is no longer true that if c hadn't fired, then g wouldn't have. Nevertheless, given that Billy's action is partly responsible for the success of the bombing in the first case, where the second escort was absent, then surely there is some inclination to grant him such responsibility in this second case, which merely adds an alternative that plays no active role. In the diagram, the superfluous preventive chain from d should not, it seems, change c's status as a kind of cause of g.

Notice that our judgment that Billy is partly responsible for the success of the bombing is quite sensitive to the nature of the backup preventer. For example, suppose that Suzy is protected not by a second escort, but by a Shield of Invulnerability that encloses her bomber, making it impervious to all attacks. We have the same relations of counterfactual dependence: If Billy had not fired, the bombing would still have been a success, but if Billy had not fired and the Shield had not been present, the bombing would not have been a success, and so on. But only with great strain can we get ourselves to say that, in this case, Billy is partly responsible for the success of the bombing.

The issue here is really exactly the same as one that has received some discussion in the literature, concerning the nature of prevention and how best to analyze it. Thus, McDermott (1995a) asks us to consider a case in which a catcher catches a ball flying toward a window; the window, however, is protected by a high, thick brick wall, and so of course would not have broken even if the catcher had missed her catch. Does the catcher prevent the window from being broken? It seems not. But if we replace the wall with a second catcher—one who would have caught the ball if the first catcher had missed—then judgments tend to be reversed. All I have done with the case of Billy, Suzy, and the backup escort is to insert such a case of "preempted prevention" into the story. In short, the tricky problem of how to understand the exact nature of preempted prevention generates, as a kind of side effect, a problem for how to understand certain kinds of double prevention (namely, where the first preventer has a preempted backup). (For an insightful treatment of the problem of preempted prevention, see Collins 2000, reprinted as chapter 4 in this volume.)

Here is one possible explanation for what is going on in these cases:[18] When we judge that Billy is partly responsible for the success of the bombing, that is because we are treating the bombing as counterfactually dependent on his action—not, admittedly, on the ordinary way of understanding the counterfactual, but on a slightly different way that holds fixed slightly different facts about the scenario. That is, in the actual scenario the backup escort does not, let us suppose, fire on Enemy. If we hold *that* fact fixed when evaluating the counterfactual, then we get the result that if Billy had not fired, then (holding fixed the fact that the backup escort does not fire) the bombing would not have succeeded. Moreover, this reading of the counterfactual seems permissible (although not obligatory). On the other hand, a parallel reading of the counterfactual in the version of the story where Suzy is protected by a Shield of Invulnerability seems strained: What extra fact is to be held fixed? Presumably, we have to hold fixed the fact that the Shield does not repel Enemy's missiles—but it is not at all clear how to construct (without overly gratuitous deviations from actuality) a counterfactual situation in which this is the case, but Billy does not fire.

I am not at all sure about the prospects for this proposal, and hence I take it that solving the problem of preempted prevention is a piece of unfinished business that affects my account of causation, by way of complicating the "dependence" half of it.

A different issue arises from cases that look like production until they are examined up close. I will consider just one such case, and then tentatively offer a lesson I think we should draw from it. The boxed neuron in the diagram in figure 9.15 func-

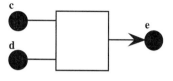

AND gate

Figure 9.15

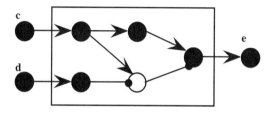

AND gate, close-up

Figure 9.16

tions as an "AND" gate: When and only when "input" neurons c and d both fire, it fires, causing e to fire. A paradigm case of the production of one event by two other events, it would seem. But is it? Note that I did not tell you *what it was* for the boxed neuron to fire, what such firing *consists in*. Figure 9.16 offers a closer look at the inner workings of the box. Here it appears that d is not a producer after all. We could leave the matter there, with the fairly obvious observation that our judgments about the causal structure of this setup are, of course, going to be defeasible, given further information about the detailed workings of the setup. But I think a different and somewhat more interesting lesson is called for. Notice first that it would be inapt to say that d is not a producer of the *firing of the box*; it is rather that *within* the chain of events that constitutes the firing of the box, the incoming signal from d plays the role of double-preventer. It does not, for example, help produce the firing of the rightmost minineuron inside the box.

Now, that observation might seem to be of little import. For example, it doesn't seem to bear at all on the question of what the relationship between the firing of d and the firing of e is. Is that production or dependence? But in fact I think the observation is relevant. For I think it is correct to say that when c and d both fire, the firing of d helps produce the firing of the "AND" neuron, but I also think it is correct to say that the firing of d does not help to produce the firing of the right-most constituent neuron in the box. So far that leaves us some room to maneuver with respect to the firing of e: We could, for example, adopt the view that if d helps produce *any* event that is itself a producer of e, then by transitivity d helps produce the firing of e. Then d comes out as a producer of e, since it helps produce the firing of the "AND" neuron, which in turns helps produce the firing of e. Alternatively, we could adopt a much more stringent standard, and say roughly that in order for d to be a producer of e, *every* event causally intermediate between the two must be produced by d and producer of e. Since the firing of the right-most neuron in the box is such a causally intermediate event—and since d does not help produce it—d will not come out as a producer of e.

What I think we should say is that depending on context, either answer can be correct. More specifically, I think that causal judgments are tacitly relative to the level of description we adopt when giving an account of the relevant chain of events (and that this choice of level of description will be a feature of the context in which we are making our causal judgments). In giving an account of the events in figure 9.15, for example, we can adopt a level of description that includes such categories as "firing of the 'AND' neuron"; that is, we will provide some such description as "neurons c and d both fire, each sending a stimulatory signal to the boxed neuron, which then fires, emitting a stimulatory signal that reaches e, which then fires." Alternatively, we can adopt a level of description that speaks not of the firing of the "AND" neuron, but rather of the various firings of the neurons within it and of the stimulatory and inhibitory connections between them. Relative to the first choice of level of description, d comes out as a producer of e; relative to the second, it does not.[19]

Obviously, another major piece of unfinished business is to spell out the relevant notion of "levels of description," and to explain exactly how such levels find their way into the contexts in which we make our causal judgments. Here I'll content myself with responding to one objection. Some may view this introduction of context-sensitivity into the account as a cost; but as far as I can see such an attitude manifests the same confusion we saw earlier of a sound methodological precept with an unsound a priori conviction about the workings of our causal concepts. Just as it makes good methodological sense to begin an investigation of our concept of causation with the working hypothesis that it is univocal, so too it makes good sense to adopt as an initial working hypothesis the view that it is not context sensitive. But there's no sense whatsoever in maintaining such hypotheses when our investigations have revealed complexities too serious for them to accommodate. If I am right, the view we are pushed to is that our thinking about causation recognizes two basic and fundamentally different varieties of causal relation, and that which relation is in play in any given situation is—or least can—depend on contextually specified features of how we are conceptualizing that situation. That this is a view that quite obviously needs detailed argument and defense should make it seem unattractive only to those with an excessive devotion to the curious notion that philosophical life should be easy.

Notes

1. See for example Mellor (1997) and Bennett (1988), as well as Mellor, "For Facts as Causes and Effects," chapter 12 in this volume.

2. See Kim (1973b); see also the discussion in Collins, Hall, and Paul, "Counterfactuals and Causation: History, Problems, and Prospects" (chapter 1 in this volume) and Lewis, "Causation as Influence" (chapter 3 in this volume).

3. For excellent discussions of the issues involved in providing a full-blown philosophical account of events, see Lewis (1986c) and Bennett (1988).

4. Notice also that Bennett and Lewis both use the locution "*A* causes *B*" rather than the weaker "*A* is *a* cause of *B*"—thus illegitimately suggesting that a particularly *salient* causal connection is being asserted. That won't do; after all, doesn't it also sound wrong to say, e.g., that the forest's presence caused the fire? But it doesn't sound so bad to say that it was *a* cause of, or *among* the causes of, the fire.

5. Notice that the distracting intuitions evoked by Bennett's example are silent here: There is no "good bit of common sense" analogous to Lombard's observation that "heavy rains ... don't start [fires]"; furthermore, no event stands out as a particularly salient cause of the forest's presence (although in the right context, the April rains just might).

6. For standard treatments of the counterfactual, see, e.g., Stalnaker (1968), Lewis (1973a), and Lewis (1973b). Whether these standard treatments are adequate to the needs of the counterfactual analysis is a question we will take up shortly.

7. Note that Lewis's account of the counterfactual conditional does not rule out backtrackers in principle, but only when the world exhibits an appropriate sort of (contingent) global asymmetry; in this way he hopes to leave room for the possibility of backward causation.

8. Swain (1978, see especially pp. 13–14) has overlooked this point. He considers a case with exactly the structure of that described by figure 9.2, yet fails to notice that his views on counterfactuals deny him the resources needed to secure the link between *c* and *e*.

9. The usual caveats apply: There might be more than one such minimal alteration to the state at *t*, or there might be an infinite sequence of minimal alterations, each more minimal than its predecessor. Either way, the proper fix is to take the conditional to be true just in case there is some alteration *A* such that the consequent comes out true for every choice of alteration *A'* that is at least as minimal as *A*. Note also that we would need to amend this rule, if we wanted our analysis to accommodate backward causation and action at a temporal distance.

10. But see Hall (2002b) for detailed argument and discussion.

11. The word "structure" is intentionally ambiguous: We could take the structure to be the mereological fusion of all the events, or we could take it to be a set-theoretic construction out of them (most simply, just the set of them). It doesn't matter, as long as we're clear on what duplication of event-structures amounts to.

12. For various reasons, not worth the long digression their spelling out would require, I do not think we can add an "only if" to the "if" to get "iff." See my (2002b) for discussion.

13. There are, in the literature, various other apparent counterexamples to *Transitivity* that cannot be handled merely by denying *Dependence* (see, e.g., McDermott 1995a). But on my view they are only apparent; see my "Causation and the Price of Transitivity" (chapter 7 in this volume) for detailed discussion.

14. I do not think that *whenever* we have counterfactual dependence between two facts, the statement asserting this dependence should be construed as causal. It depends on why the dependence holds. For example, "If it hadn't been that P, it wouldn't have been that Q" could be true because Q entails P, in which case we shouldn't view this sentence as expressing a *causal* truth. Alas, I don't think we can hope to circumscribe the *causal* dependence claims merely by demanding that the facts in question be logically independent; for what of counternomics, such as "If gravity had obeyed an inverse-cube law, then the motion of the planets would not have obeyed Kepler's laws"? While it seems intuitively clear when we have a relation of dependence that holds for the right sorts of reasons to count as causal and when we don't, I will leave the project of elucidating these reasons for another occasion.

15. Consider, for example, Suzy's throw, in the simple situation where Billy's doesn't also throw: Had this throw not occurred, it is not that *nothing* would have happened in its place; rather, her arm would have (say) simply remained at her side. That's an event, even if not one ordinarily so called.

16. For example, imagine that there is some exquisitely sensitive alarm system, which will be triggered if the rock deviates at all from its actual path; triggering it in turn initiates some other process that will break the window. It is possible to set up such an example so that at each moment t of the rock's flight, there is a unique minimally sufficient set for the breaking (a set that will include the part of the flight that is occurring at t); but plausibly the breaking will depend on not one of the events making up the flight. It's worth contrasting this sort of failure of dependence with the more usual cases of preemption: In those cases, there is in addition to the process that brings about the effect some other, rival process that somehow gets cut off. Here, by contrast, there *is* no such rival process; there only *would* be, if the events in the main process were different. We might therefore call these cases of overdetermination by a "preempted" merely *potential* alternative. They pose special problems for counterfactual analyses, since many of the strategies for dealing with cases of overdetermination by preempted *actual* alternatives fail to apply.

17. You step into the machine, and as a consequence (i) your body dissolves, and (ii) the machine transmits a signal to a second, distant machine. It receives the signal and as a consequence produces a body that is an exact replica of yours, as it was when you stepped into the first machine. Is it you? Even those of us who believe that teletransportation is possible can't say "yes" without knowing more of the causal details. For example, it might be that the second machine had been ready for a long time to produce a body—one that just by chance happened to be exactly like yours—and that the signal from the first machine merely acted as a catalyst. Then the two person-stages are stages of different people, even though the first is a cause, in both senses, of the second.

18. Inspired by a proposal of Steve Yablo's (personal communication).

19. Although I will not pursue the matter here, it is worth noting that it is quite easy to accommodate this relativity to level of description within the analysis of production offered in section 7.

10 Void and Object

David Lewis

1 The Deadly Void

The void is deadly. If you were cast into a void, it would cause you to die in just a few minutes. It would suck the air from your lungs. It would boil your blood. It would drain the warmth from your body. And it would inflate enclosures in your body until they burst.[1]

What I've said is literally true, yet it may be misleading. When the void sucks away the air, it does not exert an attractive force on the air. It is not like a magnet sucking up iron filings. Rather, the air molecules collide and exert repulsive forces on one another; these forces constitute a pressure that, if unresisted, causes the air to expand and disperse; the void exerts no force to resist the pressure; and that is why the air departs from the lungs.

Likewise, when the void boils the blood, there is no flow of energy from the void into the blood. It isn't like a stove boiling a kettle of water. The blood is already warm enough to boil, if its vapor pressure is unresisted; the void exerts no counterpressure; and so the boiling goes unprevented.

Likewise, when the void drains your warmth, what happens is that your thermal energy, left to itself, tends to dissipate; and the void provides no influx of energy to replace the departing heat.

And when the void inflates enclosures, again what happens is that the enclosed fluids exert pressure and the void exerts no counterpressure. So nothing prevents the outward pressure from doing damage.

In short, you are kept alive by forces and flows of energy that come from the objects that surround you. If, instead of objects, you were surrounded by a void, these life-sustaining forces and flows would cease. Without them, you would soon die. That is how the void causes death. It is deadly not because it exerts forces and supplies energy, but because it doesn't.

2 Void and Vacuum

The deadly effects of a void would be just like those of a commonplace vacuum. Nevertheless, I distinguish the two. The more we learn about the vacuum, the more we find out that it is full of causally active objects: force fields, photons, and "virtual" particles. Spacetime itself, if curved, can serve as a repository of energy. And perhaps that is not the end. The void, on the other hand, is entirely empty. Thus, if there is a vacuum within these four walls, there may be quite a lot of objects between the walls that are capable of exerting forces and supplying energy. Whereas if there is a void within these walls, then (even though the walls are some distance apart) there is nothing at all between the walls. What?—Not even any spacetime? Not even any flat, causally inert spacetime?—No, not even any spacetime. Nothing at all.

The void is what we *used* to think the vacuum was. It is what the vacuum is according to a relational theory of spacetime, according to which particles are surrounded by nothing at all, and are separated not in virtue of substantival spacetime between them but rather by direct external distance relations from one particle to another.

Whether or not any such relational theory is true, I take it to be, in some good sense, a genuine possibility for the world. Nothing rules it out a priori. It is a "broadly logical" or "conceptual" possibility. But conceptual possibility is governed by a combinatorial principle that says that we can generate new possibilities by patching together (copies of) parts of other possibilities.[2] So if a relationist world is possible, and a world full of substantival spacetime is likewise possible, then by patching together parts of these two worlds, we get a world that consists of substantival spacetime interrupted by occasional voids. The walls and the spacetime within them are distinct existences; ergo it is possible for either one to exist without the other. If the walls exist without the spacetime (and without any other objects between the walls) then there is a void between the walls.

A void is conceptually possible. But probably it is impossible in another sense: It violates the laws of nature. Nothing you or nature can do will make a void, but only a vacuum. Our horrific counterfactuals about what would happen if you were cast into a void are contrary not only to fact but to law.

Yet they are none the worse for that. It is no mistake to conflate the deadly void and the deadly vacuum in our counterfactual reasoning, because the difference between the two makes very little difference to the lethal effects. If you were cast into the vacuum of outer space, high-energy photons would be the least of your problems. It is the absences that would do you in. And when it comes to absences, the void is like the vacuum, only more so. Therefore, although presumably we may not entertain the supposition that you are cast into a void under laws that are exactly those of the actual world, we know very well which features of actuality to hold fixed in supposing there to be a void.

3   Menzies on Causation as Intrinsic

Peter Menzies has identified a source of dissatisfaction with our most popular approaches to the analysis of causation.[3] We would prefer, he says, to think of the causal relation as an *intrinsic relation* between cause and effect: a relation that is instantiated by a pair of events just in virtue of the (natural) properties and relations of that pair itself, and so supervenes just on the (natural) properties and relations of the pair; a relation that is independent of the (natural) properties and relations of all things that are entirely distinct from that pair; and hence a relation that would be instantiated equally by any other pair of events that shared exactly those (natural) properties and relations. It would be instantiated equally by any such duplicate pair regardless of whether the duplicate pair was actual or merely possible; regardless of whether the duplicate pair was all alone in its universe or whether it was accompanied by contingent objects distinct from itself; and regardless of what pattern was constituted by the accompanying objects, if there were any.[4]

Two events c and e stand in a relation of constant conjunction iff, throughout the universe, there are many events of the same kind as c, and every one of them is accompanied by an event of the same kind as e. An analysis that identifies causation with constant conjunction is subject to many difficulties and admits of many improvements, but one difficulty remains: constant conjunction is not an intrinsic relation, and neither is any of its improved descendants.

Two events c and e stand in a relation of counterfactual dependence iff, if c had not occurred, e would not have occurred either.[5] A counterfactual analysis of causation is again in need of improvement. We need to consider a pattern of counterfactuals that goes well beyond the simple counterfactual dependence of e on c.[6] Whatever this pattern may be, it obtains in virtue of whatever makes single counterfactuals true or false. And in this, a large part is played by the laws of nature. (That is so even when we entertain counterlegal suppositions. We may have to bend the laws, but we do not give them away altogether.) And laws, whatever else they may be, are at least exceptionless regularities throughout the universe (or some large part of the universe). So counterfactual dependence is not an intrinsic relation, and neither is any of its improved descendants.

If we thought that causation ought to be analyzed as an intrinsic relation between events, then constant-conjunction analyses and counterfactual analyses would both be in trouble. The trouble would go deep. It would persist no matter how well we succeeded in the game of counterexamples and improvements.

4   Menzies on Causal Functionalism

What sort of analysis of causation would portray the causal relation as intrinsic? Menzies offers a plausible recipe: he applies the "Canberra plan" to causation.[7] We start with a platitudinous folk theory of the causal relation. This theory says that the causal relation does so-and-so and such-and-such. Thereby it specifies a functional role that the causal relation is said to occupy. We stipulate that the causal relation is the relation, if there is one, that does in fact occupy the specified role.

(At least, that is the ideal case. But if there is no unique relation that perfectly occupies the role, we might resort to semantic satisficing. We might grant that an imperfect occupant of the role is an imperfect, but good enough, deserver of the name "causal relation," if it comes near enough and there is no better candidate to be had. Or if several candidates were tied for best, so that they deserved the name equally, we might grant them equal claim by treating the name as ambiguous or indeterminate in reference.)[8]

Menzies lists three "crucial platitudes." First, the causal relation is a relation between wholly distinct events. Second, it is a relation that is intrinsic to the event-pairs that instantiate it. Third, it is typically, though perhaps not invariably, associated with a probabilistic version of counterfactual dependence. In most cases in which it relates an event c to an event e, though perhaps not in a minority of atypical cases, the actual objective single-case probability of event e is substantially higher than it would have been if c had not occurred. (For instance, in the most extreme case, the actual probability of e is exactly 1, without even an infinitesimal chance of not-e; whereas without c, the probability of e would have been exactly 0, without even an infinitesimal chance of e, so that e would definitely not have occurred.)

By building the intrinsic character of the causal relation into the definitive functional role as a crucial platitude, Menzies makes sure that the occupant of the role, if there is one (and if it is a perfect occupant) must be an intrinsic relation. Does this strategy satisfy Menzies's desideratum?

Not entirely. In this case, as in others, the functionalist strategy creates an ambiguity. We have the functional role; we have the relation that is the actual occupant of that role. But presumably it is a contingent matter what relation occupies the role. In a different possible world, perhaps with different laws of nature, some different relation may occupy the role. Now let c and e be two events that both occur in some possible world w. Shall we say that c causes e iff c stands to e in the relation that occupies the role in actuality? Or iff c stands to e in the relation that occupies the role in world w? If we make the former decision, then indeed (at least if the actual occupation of the role is perfect) causation is an intrinsic relation. But if we make the latter decision, then causation—by which I mean the relation such that, for any events c and e in any world w, c bears it to e in w iff c causes e in w—will be a disjunctive affair. It will not be the same as any of the various role-occupants in the various worlds.[9] So even if all these role-occupants are intrinsic relations, it will not follow that causation itself is an intrinsic relation.

The folk well might have left this subtle ambiguity unresolved. Indeed, they might never have noticed it. After all, they are mostly interested in causation as it takes place here in our actual world (or in worlds similar enough to ours that they could be expected to have the same role-occupant). What mostly matters is that the actual occupant of the role is an intrinsic relation. So I think that if Menzies's strategy is otherwise successful, then it satisfies his intuitive desideratum quite well enough. But we cannot say unequivocally that he has *analyzed* causation as an intrinsic relation.

5   Causal Functionalism and the Void

Menzies's strategy is not otherwise successful. What purports to be a general analysis of causation turns out to apply only to one kind of causation. Causation by the void, and causation by absences more generally, have no place in Menzies's account. Omission is omitted.

Menzies's topic is the causal relation. A relation requires relata. The void affords no causal relata: There's nothing there at all, so there's nothing for events to happen to, so the void is devoid of events. And even if we allow causal relata to belong to other categories, still there would be none of them in the void—because there's nothing at all in the void. A vacuum, or an almost-void that still contains flat, inert spacetime, is almost as bad. It has parts; and it may contain events in some tolerant sense of that word. But it contains nothing that could plausibly be said to bear a causal relation to the death of a victim. The victim dies, as I said before, not because of what *is* there, but because of what *isn't*. Indeed, whenever any effect is caused by an absence of anything, we have the problem of the missing relatum. (And likewise whenever anything causes an absence.) A void, being the absence of any objects at all, is just the most extreme case of an absence.

Faced with the problem of the missing relatum, we have four possible lines of response.

(1) We could deny, in the face of compelling examples to the contrary, that absences ever cause anything. We could deny, for instance, that the void is deadly. (Likewise, we could deny that anything ever causes an absence. In other words, we could deny that there is any such thing as prevention.) Simply to state this response is to complete the reductio against it.

(2) We could reify absences nonreductively. A void, so we might say, is a sui generis entity, but it is none the worse for that. It is eligible to serve as a causal relatum. It springs up automatically and necessarily whenever, and only whenever, all else goes away; it is conceptually impossible not to have a void between the walls and not to have anything else there either. So much the worse, says the reifier, for the

combinatorial principle, which claims that existential statements about distinct things are independent.[10]

(3) We could reify absences reductively. We could identify absences with comparatively uncontroversial objects that, as others would say, are somehow associated with those absences. For instance, we could identify a hole with the hole-lining that, as we'd normally say, immediately surrounds the hole. (Strange to say, some holes are made of cheese and some of limestone! Strange to say, no holes are exactly where we would have thought they were!) Or we could identify an absence with a bit of unoccupied spacetime, if we were not such uncompromising combinatorialists as to countenance an absence of spacetime itself. One way or another, we can cook up ersatz absences to serve as relata of the causal relation—though surely they will seem to be the wrong relata, since we don't really think of these ersatz absences as having the same effects (or causes) as the absences they stand in for.[11] We might, for instance, imitate the identification of holes and hole-linings on a grander scale. Take the most inclusive void of all; and take the mereological fusion of all objects of whatever kind. On the principle of identifying hole with hole-lining, and void with surrounding objects, we might identify this greatest void with the greatest object.[12]

(4) The best response is to concede that a void is nothing at all, and that a lesser absence is nothing relevant at all and therefore cannot furnish causal relata. Yet absences can be causes and effects. So I insist, *contra* Menzies, that causation cannot always be the bearing of a causal relation. No theory of the causal relation, neither Menzies's theory nor any other, can be the whole story of causation.

The intrinsic character of causation is not our present problem. I do indeed fear that the intrinsic character of causation is more a hasty generalization than an a priori desideratum.[13] But even if we struck the intrinsic character of causation off our list of folk platitudes, we'd still be trying to characterize the causal relation, so we'd still be in trouble. *Any* relation needs relata, whether it is intrinsic or not. So the problem of missing relata hits any relational analysis of causation.[14]

But does any analysis escape the problem of missing relata?—Yes; a counterfactual analysis escapes. We do not have to reify the void in order to ask what would have happened if the void had not been there. The void causes death to one who is cast into it because if, instead, he had been surrounded by suitable objects, he would not have died. (Here we must assume that if the victim had not been surrounded by the void, he would instead have been surrounded by the life-sustaining objects that normally surround us—not by liquid nitrogen, or clouds of nerve gas, or a hail of bullets.) Likewise for lesser absences. If the cause is an absence, then to suppose away the cause counterfactually is not to attend to some remarkable entity and suppose that it does *not* exist. Rather, we need only suppose that some *un*remarkable entity *does* exist. Absences are spooky things, and we'd do best not to take them seriously. But absences of absences are no problem.

Note well that in defending a counterfactual analysis, I am not claiming that all causation consists in a relation of counterfactual dependence between (distinct) events. That theory would not escape the problem of missing relata. A relation of counterfactual dependence is still a relation, a relation still needs relata, and absences still fail to provide the needed relata. The counterfactual analysis escapes the problem because, when the relata go missing, it can do without any causal relation at all.

6 Menzies's Analysis Retargeted

So far, I have been arguing that Menzies is not entirely right. But in fact I think that a large part of what he says is right, can be separated from the parts that are wrong, and can be accepted even by one who favors a counterfactual analysis. That will be our business for the rest of this essay. Menzies has not given us a fully general analysis of causation, but he has given us something. I think he has given us the right analysis of the wrong analysandum. Let us introduce a name for that which Menzies's functionalist analysis succeeds in analyzing. Let us call it *biff*. That word enjoys some unofficial currency among those who conceive of causation much as Menzies does; so let it be our word for the kind of causation that fits their conception, even if we accept as we should that this is not the only kind of causation.

A theory built around Menzies's three "crucial platitudes" specifies a functional role for a relation: an intrinsic relation between distinct events that is typically, but perhaps not invariably, associated with a probabilistic version of counterfactual dependence. *Biff* is defined to be the occupant of this functional role, if such there be. There is the actual occupant of the biff-role, unless we are badly wrong about the ways of our world. Other possible worlds, some of them, might have different relations occupying the biff-role. In case of imperfect or nonunique occupation of the biff-role, we might resort to semantic satisficing in the ways already considered.

What sort of relation might biff be? We can echo much of what Menzies says, overlooking that he says it not about biff but about causation.[15] Biff—the actual occupant—might, or it might not, be some relation well known to physics. It might, for instance, be force. (More precisely, it might be the relation of exerting a force upon.) Or, taking up David Fair's suggestion about the actual nature of causation,[16] it might be a relation of transfer of energy or momentum. It might be a Humean-supervenient relation. Or it might be a relation posited by some anti-Humean metaphysic of nomological necessity.[17] It might be a perfectly natural relation, or it might be more or less disjunctive. Myself, I'd like to think that the actual occupant of the biff-role is Humean-supervenient, physical, and at least fairly natural; but nothing else I shall say here is premised on that hope.

Biff might have been one of the relations posited by bygone physical theories that have turned out to be false in our actual world, but are true in various other worlds. Some worlds obey Aristotelian dynamics; the occupant of the biff-role in such a world might be a kind of "force," if we may call it that, which is proportional to velocity rather than acceleration. Or the occupant of the biff-role might have been a relation of transfer of impetus, where impetus is rather like inertia except that it fades away spontaneously, like the heat in a red-hot poker.[18] Or biff might have been some otherworldly physical relation unlike anything that has ever crossed our minds.

Or biff might have been something even stranger. Consider a possible world where occasionalism is true: God is a third party to every causal relationship between events in nature. Then the best available candidate to occupy the biff-role would be an imperfect occupant of the role and an imperfect deserver of the name. It would be a relation between events that did not require accompaniment by anything else in nature but did require accompaniment by God; so it would not be, strictly speaking, an intrinsic relation. Yet we could reasonably judge that this imperfect candidate deserved the name quite well enough.

7   Varieties of Causation

Causation by absence is not an instance of biff. Nevertheless it can be described in terms of biff. If you were cast into the deadly void, the absences that would kill you would be absences of biff; because, if instead you were surrounded by suitable objects, events involving those objects would stand in the biff-relation to the events that would constitute your continuing life. Equivalently: Events involving those objects would prevent the event of your death by standing in the biff-relation to events incompatible with it.

Beginning with biff itself, we can define several varieties of causation.

(1)   Event c directly causes event e iff c stands to e in the relation that occupies the biff-role. For short: iff c biffs e.

(2)   The absence of any event of kind C directly causes event e iff, had there been an event c of kind C, c would or might have biffed some event d incompatible with event e.

(3)   Event c directly causes the absence of any event of kind E iff c biffs some event d incompatible with any event of kind E.

(4)   The absence of any event of kind C directly causes the absence of any event of kind E iff, had there been an event c of kind C, c would or might have biffed some event e of kind E.[19]

But there are also cases of *in*direct causation: An event (or absence) c causes an event (or absence) that then causes another event (or absence) e. Or c may cause both an event and an absence, which then jointly cause e. Or there may be a chain with three steps, or four, or any number. Cases of indirect causation need not reduce to direct causation. Take, for example, a case of causation by double prevention: Event c causes the absence of any event of kind D, which absence in turn causes event e.[20] It does not follow, and it may be false, that c biffs e. Even if biff itself is intrinsic, the causal relation of c to e in cases of double prevention is sometimes extrinsic.[21]

So the functional analysis of biff affords a basis for defining many varieties of causation. All the varieties there could possibly be? We have no assurance of that. Maybe some possible worlds have no occupant at all of the biff-role, not even an imperfect occupant; and maybe in some such worlds the actual occupant of the biff-role also is nowhere to be found. And when we depart counterfactually from such a biffless world, taking care to avoid gratuitous differences from our starting point, presumably the counterfactual situations we reach will be equally biffless. Yet might there not be some sort of causation in a biffless world? Maybe all the causal relations of events in such a world are thoroughly extrinsic, far more so than in the case of the occasionalist world we imagined before. The "intuition" of the intrinsic character of causation may indeed be right for one basic variety of causation in the actual world, but it is by no means given a priori.

8   Ambiguity? Disjunction?

What shall we conclude from this proliferation of different varieties of causation? Has it turned out that we have not one concept of causation but many, so that many different analyses are required to capture the many different senses of the word "cause"? Or is it rather that our one concept of causation is a radically disjunctive concept, so that a correct analysis must consist in a long list of alternative cases? We're in trouble either way.

If causation in a biffless world is possible, that is a problem equally for both hypotheses. On the many-concepts hypothesis, the problem is that one concept of causation (at least) will never be reached by our chain of definitions starting with the functional definition of biff. On the disjunctive-concept hypothesis, the problem is that one disjunct (at least) will never be reached. To complete an inventory of senses, or to complete the disjunctive analysis of the single sense, it seems that we must find some different starting point.

Another problem for the many-concept hypothesis is that it requires distinctions in our thinking that sometimes we do not make, need not make, and are in no position to make. If one event directly causes another, for instance, that is causation in one sense; whereas if one event causes another indirectly, in a case of double prevention (or in some still more indirect case) that is causation in a different sense. But when we neither know nor care whether the causation we have in mind is direct or indirect, what concept of causation are we employing then?

(Example: The frightened passenger pulls the cord, knowing that this will cause the train to stop. Being moderately well informed, he knows that pulling the cord opens a valve connecting a reservoir to the outside air. The changed pressure in the reservoir changes the balance of forces on the brake shoes, thereby applying the brakes and stopping the train. But the passenger doesn't know whether this train is fitted with air brakes or vacuum brakes. If air brakes, then the air in the reservoir is normally above atmospheric pressure; so opening the valve lowers the pressure and removes a force, and so the stopping of the train is a case of double prevention. If vacuum brakes, then the air in the reservoir is normally below atmospheric pressure; so opening the valve raises the pressure and applies a force, and so the stopping of the train is a case of direct causation. But so long as he can cause the train to stop, it's all the same to the passenger what kind of causation it is.)

The disjunctive-concept hypothesis now seems better. But it faces an urgent, if not absolutely compulsory, question. Why do we disjoin exactly these disjuncts? Why is the disjunction of just this long list of alternatives anything more than a miscellaneous gerrymander? What makes it a natural kind?

It is as if we came upon some people who had a peculiar taxonomy for birds. They group together a kind that includes swans, but not ducks or geese; eagles and hawks, but not vultures; magpies and crows, but not ravens or currawongs or mudlarks, and indeed no other birds at all. We would be entitled to ask why just these birds are included, and it would not be good enough just to say that all classes are equally classes, and that these people happen to have picked out this class.

The many-concepts hypothesis and the disjunctive-concept hypothesis are both unsatisfactory. Yet if we analyze causation by starting with the functional analysis of biff, and going on to define other varieties of causation one by one in terms of biff, that is the choice we come to.

9   Conclusion

I think we are aiming our answers at the wrong question. Menzies went wrong when he took the functional definition of biff to be the whole of a conceptual analysis of causation. We still go wrong if we take it to be even a first step toward conceptual analysis. We should look elsewhere for a conceptual analysis. And we should look elsewhere for a question to which the invocation of biff affords a satisfactory answer.

What is causation? As a matter of analytic necessity, across all possible worlds, what is the unified necessary and sufficient condition for causation?—It is somehow a matter of counterfactual dependence of events (or absences) on other events (or absences).

What is causation? As a matter of contingent fact, what is the feature of this world, and of other possible worlds sufficiently like it, on which the truth values of causal ascriptions supervene?—It is biff: the pattern of relatedness of events to one another by the relation that is the actual occupant of the biff-role. Biff is literally the basic kind of causation, in this world anyway: the basis on which other varieties of causation supervene.

Two different answers to two different questions. They are not in competition. I conjecture that both are right.

If biff is offered not as conceptual analysis but as a basis for supervenience, then it matters little if the varieties of causation, when described in terms of biff, are many and diverse. Unifying the miscellany is a job for conceptual analysis. And if biff is offered as a supervenience basis for causation as it takes place here in our world, then the possibility that some other variety of causation takes place in biffless worlds remote from actuality is no cause for alarm.

Let me say more fully what I have in mind. Doubtless all will agree that the visual qualities of dot-matrix pictures—say, the quality of looking cluttered—supervene on the arrangement of light and dark pixels, at least if we restrict our attention to black and white pictures with maximum contrast. This means that no two possible pictures, at least no two that both fall within our restricted class, differ in their visual qualities without also differing in their arrangement of pixels. If one looks cluttered and the other doesn't, they cannot be alike pixel for pixel. Likewise, the thesis under consideration says that no two possible worlds, or at least no two that fall within a certain restricted class, differ in respect of the truth values of causal ascriptions without also differing in their biff-relations. At least one biff-related pair of events in one world must fail to correspond to any biff-related pair in the other world, and that is what makes the causal difference.

The narrower is the restricted class of worlds within which all causation is said to supervene on biff, the weaker and safer and less interesting our thesis will be. How shall we strike the balance between safety and interest? Since we are especially interested in causation as it takes place in our actual world, the actual world had better fall within the restricted class. But our supervenience thesis, if restricted to one single world, would be utterly trivial; and besides, our interest extends at least to worlds that only narrowly escape being actual. I propose that the restricted class should consist of exactly those worlds that satisfy two conditions. (1) They are worlds where the relation that occupies the biff-role is the same relation that occupies that role in actuality. And (2) they are worlds where the laws of nature are the same as the actual laws of nature.

Condition (2) is not motivated just by caution. Remember our starting point: when the void, or some lesser absence, causes an effect, that is because of the absence of what it takes to prevent that effect (nothing counteracts the vapor pressure that would cause warm blood to boil, and so on). At any rate, that is how causation by absences works under the actual laws of nature, or so we think. But might it not be otherwise under different laws? Suppose there were a fundamental law that said that a certain spell would turn a prince into a frog iff that prince was within a mile of the edge of a void. Under such a law, a void could cause a transmogrification in a way that had nothing to do with absence of biff. There could be such a law—why not? But it is irrelevant to capturing our opinions about how causation works in actuality. So we unabashedly bar the monster: We stipulate that a world with such a law falls outside the range to which our actuality-centered supervenience thesis is meant to apply. And for good measure, but perhaps with needless caution, we likewise stipulate that all worlds that depart from the laws of actuality fall outside the range.

It is because our supervenience thesis is restricted, and because the restriction makes reference to actuality, that our thesis is contingent. Had we started from some different possible world, and restricted according to the same two conditions, we would have restricted the thesis to a different class of worlds. The thesis restricted to worlds that satisfy our conditions relative to this world may be true, but the thesis restricted to worlds that satisfy the same conditions relative to some other world may be false. Or, if we are unlucky, vice versa.

We saw how causation by absences, at least as it takes place in our actual world, could be defined piecemeal using various counterfactuals about biff. So if all causation is to supervene on biff, these counterfactuals about biff must supervene on biff. That is plausible enough. For when we depart counterfactually from a given world, we make no gratuitous changes. Except insofar as the supposition we are making requires differences, the character of the given world carries over into the counterfactual situation. In particular, the laws governing biff tend to carry over.[22] Return, one last time, to the victim cast into the void (or into something as much like a void as the actual laws allow). If instead he were surrounded by suitable objects, those objects would conform to the laws that actually govern biff. If not, that would be a gratuitous difference between the counterfactual situation and the actual world.

Notes

1. Here I follow the lead of Martin (1996): "it seems that the void has ... terrible causal powers" (p. 62). Martin later says that voids are "causally *relevant* but not causally *operative*" (p. 64), but I do not know what he means by this.

2. On combinatorial principles see my (1986e), pp. 86–92; and Armstrong (1989).

3. Menzies (1996) and (1999). Menzies might better have suggested not that causation is an intrinsic relation, but rather that being a causal chain is an intrinsic property. For present purposes, we may leave this correction unmentioned.

4. Here I have combined definitions of intrinsic relations taken from my (1983b), n. 16; and from Langton and Lewis (1998). These definitions differ, but can be expected to pick out the same class of relations.

5. See my (1973a) and (1986b).

6. See my "Causation as Influence," chapter 3 in this volume.

7. Menzies (1996). The Canberra plan is modeled on analytic functionalism in the philosophy of mind, and on Carnap's proposal for defining analyticity in a theoretical language. See Carnap (1963).

8. See Bedard (1993).

9. It will be what I called a "diagonalized sense" in my (1970).

10. Casati and Varzi (1994) defend nonreductive reification of holes: Holes are immaterial bodies that depend for their existence on the arrangement of matter. Martin, in his (1996), is probably best classed as a nonreductive reifier, despite his emphatic warnings that absences are not things. (His conflicting suggestion that they are "localized states of the universe" would seem to be retracted by his denial that they are natural properties of things [p. 58]. The universe would seem to be a thing, states would seem to be properties, and properties of local emptiness would seem to be not unnatural.)

11. Lewis and Lewis (1970) is, for the most part, a dialogue between a reductive and a nonreductive reifier. Neither one notices the option of paraphrasing hole-statements in terms of quantification over ersatz holes without also claiming that holes are identical to ersatz holes. Frank Jackson calls attention to that option in his (1977), p. 132.

12. Or, since the greatest object has the property of totality—of being all there is—we might identify the greatest void with the having by that object of the property of totality. This ersatz void is as wrong as it can be in its effects (and causes): It causes what objects cause, not what the void unassisted by objects causes. And it is as wrong as it can be in its location, being exactly where the void isn't. It violates a combinatorial principle, since it cannot possibly coexist with any extra object. For that very reason it is of doubtful ontological status, being a having of a merely extrinsic property.

   D. M. Armstrong uses havings of totality as truthmakers for negative existential statements, *inter alia* in his (1997), chapter 13. But he never asks these totality states of affairs to serve as ersatz absences.

13. See "Causation as Influence," chapter 3 in this volume.

14. How about an analysis in terms of a relation between propositions, where, in the case of causation by or of an absence, one of the related propositions is a negative existential?—Not problematic; but not what I'd call a relational analysis of causation. We don't want to say that a cause- or effect-describing proposition is *itself* the cause or effect.

15. Menzies (1999).

16. Fair (1979).

17. It might for instance be the relation of instantiating a law, where a law is taken to be at once a state of affairs involving universals and a universal in its own right. See Heathcote and Armstrong (1991).

18. See Butterfield (1957), pp. 8–13.

19. The definitions of cases (2)–(4) resemble, but differ from, the definitions given in Fair (1979), p. 247, and also the somewhat different definitions given in the final section of Dowe (1999). Note that these counterfactual definitions are not the same as the counterfactuals about events and absences that would appear in a counterfactual analysis of causation.

20. See Ned Hall, "Two Concepts of Causation," chapter 9 in this volume; and McDermott (1995a).

21. As is noted in McDermott (1995a) in connection with his example of Nixon, Haig, and Joe Blow's breakfast. See also the billiard-ball example in "Causation as Influence," p. 84 of this volume.

22. Unless violating a law yields the least departure overall. See Lewis (1979a).

11 Causing and Nothingness

Helen Beebee

1 Introduction

According to the way we normally speak about the world, absences can be causes. We might say, for instance, that Jones's failure to close the fire doors was a cause of the raging fire that destroyed the building, or that Smith's failure to water her office plants was a cause of their death, or that lack of rain was a cause of the bush fire. So it seems that an adequate theory of causation is going to have to rule that there is such a thing as causation by absence.

I don't believe there is any such thing as causation by absence. In this essay I'm going to try to defend that claim against the objection just raised, partly by arguing that there are features of commonsense assertions and denials of causation by absence to which *no* theory of the metaphysics of causation ought to be doing justice, and partly by making a positive claim about the role absences play in our explanatory practices, a claim that, I think, allows me to rebut the objection that the repudiation of causation by absence flies in the face of too much of our commonsense understanding of causation to be taken seriously.

The reason I deny that there's any such thing as causation by absence is that I want to uphold the view that causation is a relation between events. To be rather more picturesque, I subscribe to what Helen Steward has recently dubbed the "network model of causation": The complete causal history of the universe can be represented by a sort of vast and mind-bogglingly complex "neuron diagram" of the kind commonly found in discussions of David Lewis, where the nodes represent events and the arrows between them represent causal relations.[1] Or, to put it another way, the causal history of any event is, as Lewis puts it, "a relational structure" (1986c, p. 216).

I think it's fair to say that the network model is the dominant model of causation in contemporary metaphysics—largely owing to the influence of Lewis and Davidson.[2] The network model lies behind most of the theories of causation currently on offer; it also lies behind a vast amount of the literature on the philosophy of mind.

If there *is* causation by absence, then the network model can't be right—or at least, it can't be right assuming there are no such things as negative events. And I assume in what follows that there are no negative events—which is to say, more or less, there are no events whose essence is the absence of a property or particular. If Jones's failure to close the fire door is not an event, and if this failure was a cause of the fire, then the full causal history of the fire is not exhausted by the network of events and causal relations between them, for there will be no event of Jones's failure, and hence no causal relation between his failure and the fire. The network model cannot accommodate the fact—if it is a fact—that Jones's failure caused the fire, and hence cannot be the whole causal truth about reality.

How should we solve the problem? One solution—the one I favor—is to hang onto the network model of causation and deny that there is any causation by absence. On this view, Smith's failure to water her office plants was not a cause of their death. This seems to be a deeply unpopular solution—and surprisingly so, given the prevalence of the network model in contemporary metaphysics. Here's what Lewis has to say about it in "Void and Object" (chapter 10, this volume): "We could deny, in the face of compelling evidence to the contrary, that absences ever cause anything. We could deny, for instance, that the void is deadly.... Simply to state this response is to complete the *reductio* against it."[3]

The other obvious solution is to hang onto causation by absence and scrap the network model. This is the solution for which Hugh Mellor has long been arguing,[4] and has been suggested more recently by Lewis in "Void and Object." According to Mellor's view, causation is not a relation—or at least, the most basic kind of causation is not relational. Rather, causal facts have the form "*E* because *C*," where *C* and *E* are facts and "because" is a sentential connective. Since facts are not particulars, on Mellor's view causation is not a relation. And since facts can be facts about absences, causation by absence causes no special problems on his view. In much the same vein, Lewis proposes that causation be analyzed in terms of counterfactual dependence not between events, but between propositions—propositions that need not assert that some event or other occurs.

A third solution—one that is suggested but not condoned by Lewis in "Void and Object"—is to take the relational kind of causation as the most basic kind of causation, and define causation by absence in terms of relational causation.[5] According to this kind of solution, the network model captures all the *basic* causal facts, but there are other causal facts whose obtaining supervenes on the actual pattern of causal relations together with some extra counterfactuals.

I shall call the first view the *relationist* view, since it upholds the thesis that causation is a relation between events. I call the other two views *nonrelationist* views, since they both uphold the thesis that causation is not always a relation. The central claim of this essay is that, if our aim is to do as much justice as possible to commonsense intuitions about causation by absence, then it doesn't much matter whether we uphold relationism or nonrelationism.

This might seem like a surprising claim, since relationism, unlike nonrelationism, is forced to deny a whole host of causal claims that common sense holds true. As I said at the beginning, undoubtedly many of us think that Jones's failure to close the fire doors was a cause of the fire, or that the lack of rain was a cause of the bush fire, and so on. Fair point: The relationist view really does deny all of that. But this is to tell only half the story. For common sense also makes a lot of *negative* causal claims about absences. Take Brown, who lives on the other side of the city and has no connection whatever with either Smith or Jones. Commonsense intuition has it, I think, that neither Brown's failure to close the fire doors nor his failure to water Smith's plants were causes of the fire or of the plants' death. The relationist view, of course, gets these cases right: Brown's omissions are not causes, because *no* absences—and therefore no omissions—are. But nonrelationism gets these negative causal judgments wrong. According to the relationist, the commonsense claim that Jones's omission caused the fire is false; according to the nonrelationist, the commonsense claim that *Brown's* omission did *not* cause the fire is false.

So when it comes to doing justice to commonsense intuitions about causation by absence, neither view fares very well. Luckily, I don't think this matters very much. Briefly, the reason it doesn't much matter is this. As I'll argue in sections 2 and 3, commonsense intuitions about which absences are causes and which aren't are highly dependent on judgments that it would be highly implausible to suppose correspond to any real worldly difference at the level of the metaphysics of causation. For instance, sometimes common sense judges the *moral* status of an absence to be relevant to its causal status. But no philosopher working within the tradition I'm concerned with here thinks that the *truth* conditions for causal claims contain a moral element. It follows that whatever we think about whether or not causation is a relation, we're going to have to concede that common sense is just wrong when it takes, say, moral differences to determine causal differences. There is no genuine causal difference between those cases that common sense judges to be cases of causation by absence and those that it judges *not* to be cases of causation by absence. Hence both the relationist and the nonrelationist must agree, and with good reason, that commonsense judgments about causation by absence are often mistaken—though of course they disagree about *which* commonsense judgments are mistaken.

In sections 4 and 5, I show how absences can figure in causal explanations even though they do not cause anything. So although it is false to say that Smith's failure to water her office plants caused their death, it is nevertheless true to say that the plants died because Smith failed to water them. Here I appeal to Lewis's analysis of causal explanation, according to which to explain an event is to provide information about its causal history: information that need not be restricted merely to citing the event's causes. I claim that common sense judges some absences to be causes because it fails to distinguish between causation and causal explanation, and (in section 6) that the sorts of distinctions discussed in sections 2 and 3 that ground commonsense assertions and denials of causation by absence are best seen as distinctions between explanatorily salient and nonsalient absences. The moral is that commonsense intuitions about causation by absence are no more damaging to the relationist than they are to the nonrelationist; hence, those intuitions provide no good reason for abandoning the network model of causation.

2   Causation by Absence and Common Sense

In what follows, I'm going to assume that absences that are causes—if there are any—are at least necessary conditions of their effects. I dare say this is a false assumption: Maybe (again, if there is any causation by absence at all) there are cases where, had the absent event occurred, the effect in question would still have had some chance of coming about. I ignore this possibility for the sake of simplicity.

With the assumption that absences are at least necessary conditions of what they cause in place, we might try the following definition of causation by absence:

(I)   The nonoccurrence of an event of type A caused event b if and only if, had an A-type event occurred, b would not have occurred.

This definition is different from both Lewis's and Dowe's,[6] and may well be inadequate for reasons other than the one discussed below. However, since both Lewis's and Dowe's definitions can easily be seen to fall prey to the objection too, it will make things easier if we make do with the simpler definition (I).

Not surprisingly, (I) gets the right answer in cases that common sense judges to be genuine cases of causation by absence. Here are some examples.[7] Flora normally gratuitously waters her neighbor's orchids. But she stops watering them, and they die. Common sense judges that Flora's omission was a cause of the orchids' death, since had she watered them, as she usually does, the orchids would not have died. Second example: Z's dog is bitten by an insect, contracting an eye disease as a result, which Z ignores. The dog loses its sight. Intuitively, Z's negligence caused the dog's blindness; and again, the definition gets this right: Had Z not ignored the eye disease, the dog would not have lost its sight. Third example: An old tree decays and falls to the ground, crushing some rare wild flowers. The park ranger failed to inspect the tree, thereby making himself a cause of the flowers' death. Again, (I) gets this right: Had the park ranger inspected the tree (and thus had it carefully removed rather than allowing it to fall), the flowers would have survived. Fourth example: A geranium survives the London winter because there is no frost. Intuitively the absence of frost was a cause of its survival; and, once again, this judgment is in accordance with (I).

So far so good. The trouble is that our definition is too inclusive: It renders all sorts of absences as causes that common sense does not *recognize* as causes. Commonsense intuition identifies Flora's failure to water the orchids as a cause of their death, but not the failure of the other neighbors, and certainly not the failure of people on the other side of the world who neither know nor care about the orchids— even though it's perfectly true of each of them that had they watered the orchids, they would not have died. Similarly, while common sense judges the dog owner's or the park ranger's omission to be a cause of the dog's blindness or the crushing of the flowers, it does not judge the omissions of others as causes of those events, even though the relevant counterfactuals are true too. And similarly for the geranium example: We would ordinarily judge that the absence of a hungry geranium-eating koala was no part of the causal history of the geranium's survival, even though had such a koala been present the geranium would not have survived.

Why is this? What grounds common sense's discrimination between absences that are and are not causes of an event? Hart and Honoré, in their book *Causation in the Law*—a classic text for those interested in commonsense causal judgments—claim that what makes us single out one omission as a cause but not another is *abnormality*. We regard Flora's failure to water her neighbor's orchids as a cause of their death because Flora's failure is abnormal: She normally *does* water them. On the other hand, there is nothing abnormal in the failure of the other neighbors, or of other people in other countries, to water the orchids; hence, those failures are not causes of the orchids' death.[8]

The abnormality criterion seems to work for the orchid case, and it seems plausible to suppose that it also works for cases like the geranium case: cases that are not omissions by human agents. The absence of frost in winter in London is quite unusual, and hence according to Hart and Honoré's criterion may count as a cause of the geranium's survival. The absence of hungry geranium-eating koalas, on the other hand, is perfectly normal, and hence does not qualify as a cause of the geranium's survival.

Stapleton claims, however—and I think she's right—that there are many cases in which the abnormality criterion fails to explain our commonsense causal judgments. In the case of Z's dog, for instance, she says that we would regard Z's conduct as a cause "because against the backdrop of Z's ownership of the dog we expect Z to have acted, not because of expectations generated by past conduct but for moral reasons" (1994, p. 122). And in the park ranger case, she says, we single out the park ranger and nobody else because she, and nobody else, has a legal duty to inspect the tree. The point here is that we take these causal judgments to be correct even if the relevant omissions are not in any way abnormal: The judgments stand even if Z is generally very bad at looking after his dog, or if it is the park ranger's first day on the job.

Stapleton also claims that whether an omission is to count as a cause can depend on epistemic features. Suppose, for instance, that a certain drug in fact has harmful side effects, but that this risk is unforeseeable: We could not reasonably expect the drug manufacturer to have known about it. In such a case, she says, we should not say "it was the defendant-manufacturer's failure to warn of the unforeseeable risk which caused the injury—clearly a silly idea which no common sense version of causation could accommodate" (ibid., p. 124). On the other hand, if the manufacturer *did* know of the risk, or if we could reasonably have expected them to have found out about the risk, then we *would* say that their failure to warn consumers of the risk was a cause of the side effects.

So it seems that common sense singles out an absence as a cause when, and only when, it stands out in some way—either from what normally happens, or from some norm the absence of which (generally an omission) counts as a violation. The norm might be moral, legal, or epistemic, as Stapleton's examples illustrate; but other sorts of norm may well play a similar role. Owen's failure to get to the ball after Beckham's cross into the penalty area counts as a cause of England's defeat, but Seaman's failure to do so does not—even though, had Seaman (the goalkeeper) somehow managed to get to the ball, he would undoubtedly have scored and England would have won. Why? Because Owen is an attacker and Seaman is the goalkeeper; it's an attacker's job, and not the goalkeeper's, to score goals from crosses into the penalty area.

What all this points toward is a definition of causation by absence that goes something like this:

(II)   The absence of an *A*-type event caused *b* if and only if

(i) *b* counterfactually depends on the absence: Had an *A*-type event occurred, *b* would not have occurred; and

(ii) the absence of an *A*-type event is *either* abnormal *or* violates some moral, legal, epistemic, or other norm.

This definition, I think, does justice to as many commonsense causal judgments about absences as anyone could wish for. The trouble is that although it works *qua* linguistic analysis of the ordinary *concept* of causation by absence, it doesn't look like the sort of analysis we ought to be giving of the *metaphysics* of causation by absence.

Take the violation-of-norms part of the definition. If we take the definition to give the *truth conditions* of causation by absence claims, then causal facts about absences depend in part on normative facts: facts about whether a moral or epistemic or other norm has been violated. But nobody within the tradition of the metaphysics of causation that I'm concerned with here thinks that causal facts depend on human-dependent norms.

Even if taking causal facts to depend on normative facts weren't in itself such a bad thing, it would in any case make the truth of causal claims turn out to be a relative matter. For instance, you and I might differ in our epistemic standards, so that I count the side effects of a drug as foreseeable and you don't; hence I count the drug manufacturer's failure to warn consumers as a cause of their side effects but you do not. Either there is some absolute epistemic standard that marks out what someone can reasonably be expected to foresee—which seems wildly implausible—or the causal status of the failure is relative to different standards.

A similar point applies to the abnormality part of the definition. For one thing, how often something has to happen in order to count as "normal"—and hence for its absence to count as abnormal—is always going to be rather fluid. And for another, the same absence might count as normal relative to one kind of regularity and abnormal relative to another. Suppose, for instance, that Flora is in the habit of doing gratuitous repetitive favors for her neighbors, like watering their gardens or washing their cars, but that she invariably stops doing them after a month or so. Now is Flora's failure to water her neighbor's orchids after thirty days of watering them normal or abnormal? There doesn't seem to be any principled way of answering that question, so it looks as though the causal status of her omission is simply indeterminate.

It follows that if we want facts about causation to be reasonably determinate and not relative to extraneous facts about whether a putative cause happens to count as abnormal, immoral, illegal, or whatever, then any account of the metaphysics of causation by absence is going to have to be pretty revisionary: No adequate account of what in the world makes causal claims about absences true or false is going to be able to condone all, or even most, of the verdicts given by commonsense usage.

3   A Way Out for the Nonrelationist?

The definition (II) of causation by absence I proposed in the previous section had two conditions on when the absence of an A-type event is to count as a cause of b: the counterfactual condition—had an A-type event occurred, b would not have occurred—and the condition that the absence be either abnormal or the violation of some norm. I claimed that no respectable theory of the truth conditions of causal claims ought to respect the second of these conditions; which leaves us with the first, counterfactual condition, that is, with (I). As we've already seen, an analysis of causation by absence that consisted solely in this condition would be far too inclusive. It would render all of us causally responsible for indefinitely many events happening right now, all over the world—and doubtless beyond. One of the causes of Maite's drinking her coffee in Mexico City just now was my failure to shoot her before she had a chance to put the kettle on. One of the causes of your reading these words right now is the absence of a lion from the room. And so on.

But, in principle at least, the nonrelationist who thinks there really is such a thing as causation by absence is not required to think that there's *that* much causation by absence, for she might be able to invent a more restrictive definition that will do a lot better than what we've got so far. That is to say, maybe our original definition (I) can be supplemented by some other clause that rules out the spurious cases of causation by absence like the one I just gave, without ruling out the allegedly nonspurious cases we want to keep, but which doesn't appeal to normative features of absences.

Well, on behalf of my nonrelationist opponent, I generously offer the following definition. It's the best I can do—but not, as we'll see, good enough:

(III)   The absence of an *A*-type event caused *b* if and only if:

(i) if an *A*-type event *had* occurred, *b* would not have occurred; and

(ii) an *A*-type event occurs at a world that is *reasonably close* to the actual world.

The definition discounts vast numbers of absences from being causes on the grounds that worlds where the absent event occurs are very distant worlds. For instance, my failure to shoot Maite no longer counts as a cause of her drinking her coffee because, I'm happy to say, a world where I *do* shoot her is a very distant world indeed.

One might even go so far as to claim that the definition gets *all* the cases right (though I'll argue in a moment that it doesn't). We might try to claim, for instance, that what makes Flora's failure to water her neighbor's orchids a cause of their death but not the failure of her other neighbors is not, as we first thought, the fact that Flora's failure, unlike those of the other neighbors, is abnormal; rather, the difference is that Flora is more strongly disposed to water the orchids than are her neighbors—as evidenced by the differences in her and their past behavior. So a world where Flora waters the orchids is closer to our own than is a world when another neighbor does so. *Z*'s failure to attend to his dog's eye infection, as opposed to our failure, counts as a cause of its blindness because *Z* was in a position to do something about it and we were not: Hence a world where *Z* takes his dog to the vet is reasonably close to our own, and one where one of us takes the dog to the vet is not.

The thought here, then, is that abnormality and violation of norms are not part of the *truth* conditions of causation by absence claims. Rather, those considerations inform our judgments about how reasonable it is—that is to say, epistemically reasonable—to expect the absent event to happen; and thus how reasonable it is to suppose that the event in question happens at a reasonably nearby world. For example, we generally assume that dog owners are disposed to behave in a way conducive to the welfare of their pets, whereas people in general are not particularly disposed to go out of their way to behave in a way conducive to the welfare of other people's pets. And we can construe this assumption as an assumption about closeness of worlds: If Z is strongly disposed to keep a close eye on his dog's welfare and I am not, then a world where Z manifests this strong disposition and takes the dog to the vet is plausibly closer than a world where I, who have no disposition whatever to do so, take Z's dog to the vet for him. Hence Z's omission is a cause of the dog's blindness but mine is not.

Things seem to be looking up for the nonrelationist; but unfortunately I don't think the situation is as rosy as I've made it look. I have two objections to the suggested definition. First, I think that commonsense intuition would still discriminate between, say, Z's omission and mine even if we knew perfectly well that Z is a terrible pet owner and consistently fails to look after his dog properly. Even if we think that Z has no disposition whatever to take the dog to the vet, and hence that a world where he does so is just as distant as a world where someone else does it for him, we still think of Z's omission and nobody else's as a cause of the dog's blindness.

Similarly, we still judge a drug company's failure to warn consumers of foreseeable side effects as a cause of their illness even if we know that the company is extremely disreputable and rarely bothers to carry out the proper tests. I take it that common sense simply doesn't endorse the view that if you're negligent enough—if your disposition to behave in accordance with norms is weak enough—your negligence literally won't have any effects.

These observations support my initial claim that the norms are doing the work by themselves, as it were, rather than merely informing our judgments about closeness of worlds. Still, I'm basing this conclusion on some disputable claims about commonsense intuition that you may not share, so this isn't a decisive objection.

The second objection, I think, is more telling: I can see no sensible way of specifying what "reasonably close" amounts to. It's one thing to judge *relative* similarity of worlds—to judge that, say, a world where Flora waters her neighbor's orchids is closer than any world where someone else waters them. But it's quite another thing to try and impose a *metric* on this ordering, so that any A-world within a certain distance from the actual world is close enough for the absence of A to count as a cause, whereas any A-world outside that distance is too far away for the absence of A to count as a cause.

Even if there *were* a way of specifying what "reasonably close" amounts to, there are two further problems. One is that any choice of maximum distance is going to be entirely arbitrary; and the question of which absences are causes and which are not ought not to be decided by a piece of arbitrary stipulation. The other problem is that whereas relative similarity of worlds might explain why one absence and not another counts as a cause in any particular case—Z's taking his dog to the vet happens in a close enough world, say, but not my taking it—I see no reason to suppose that the same standards will apply across all cases. What counts as close enough for causation in one case might not count as close enough for causation in another.

All of these problems for the proposed definition (III), I think, have the same source: There just *isn't* any objective feature that some absences have and others lack in virtue of which some absences are causes and others are not. So *any* definition of causation by absence that seeks to provide a principled distinction between absences that are and are not causes is bound to fail: No such definition will succeed in carving nature at its joints. If this is right, then the nonrelationist is going to have to concede that there just *is* no principled reason to regard Flora's failure to water the orchids as a cause of their death but not to regard my failure to shoot Maite as a cause of her coffee-drinking. And this, I suggest, hardly puts nonrelationism ahead of relationism when it comes to doing justice to commonsense intuitions.

In fact, there is another possible way out of the problem for the nonrelationist, and that is to deny that the alleged distinction in our commonsense talk and thought between absences that are and are not causes really exists. I have been claiming that, according to commonsense intuition, Flora's failure to water her neighbor's orchids was a cause of their death, but the failure of other people—people who neither know nor care about the orchids—was not. But one might object that this is not really the position endorsed by common sense. Rather, in ordinary circumstances we fail to identify the failures of other people as causes of the orchids' death, in the sense that it does not occur to us to mention those failures' part in the causal history of the death of the orchids (since in ordinary conversational circumstances it would be inappropriate for us to do so). But to fail to mention that those other failures are causes is not to hold that they are *not* causes.

No doubt there is some truth in this suggestion. Perhaps, if asked directly whether the failures of other people to water the orchids was a cause of their death, at least some people would say yes—presumably because they would appreciate the similarity between Flora's failure, which they do count as a cause, and the failures of those other people.

I see no reason to suppose, however, that the point generalizes. The number of possible events, or combinations of events, that are such that, had they occurred, the orchids would not have died, is absolutely enormous. The plants would have survived, for example, if Flora's neighbor had installed a sprinkler system that then got activated accidentally while she was away, or if her roof had started leaking at a point just above the orchids during a rainstorm, or if a cow had somehow entered her house and flicked a nearby glass of water onto the orchids with its tail, or—. I do not think that most people would happily accept that the failure of each of these events to occur was equally a cause of the orchids' death. Of course, this is an empirical claim about what people are ordinarily inclined to judge. But I have not come across any evidence to suggest that the claim is false.

4   Causation and Causal Explanation

I shall return to the commonsense distinction between absences that are and are not causes in section 6. In this section and the next, however, I set this issue aside in order to focus on another distinction: the distinction between causation and causal explanation. In this section I defend the view that not all causal explanations are reports of causation: The explanans of a causal explanation need not stand to the explanandum as cause to effect. And in section 5 I defend the view that causal explanations that involve facts about absences can be seen as explanations of just this kind: We do not need absences as causes in order for facts about absences to be the explananta of causal explanations.

In "Causal Relations" (1967), Davidson argues for a distinction between causation and causal explanation by concentrating on the logical form of causal statements. He argues, using a version of the "Slingshot" example, that causation is a relation between events rather than facts—in other words, that the canonical form of causal statements is "*c* caused *e*," where *c* and *e* are events and *caused* is a two-place relation, rather than "*E* because *C*," where *C* and *E* are facts and "because" is a sentential connective. Davidson reserves the "*E* because *C*" locution for causal explanation. For Davidson, then, no causal explanations are themselves causal claims, since they simply do not have the right logical form.

In opposition to Davidson, Mellor has long maintained that *all* causal explanations are in fact causal claims. For Mellor, facts are the most basic kind of causal relata, and the canonical form of causal statements is "*E* because *C*."[9] According to Mellor, causation *sometimes* also relates events—but only sometimes. When it's true that the match lit because I struck it, it's also true that the striking caused the lighting; but when it's true that, say, Kim has no children because she used contraception, there is no corresponding true statement of the form "*c* caused *e*."[10]

If absences are to figure in causal explanations without doing any causing, there must be a distinction between causation and causal explanation: Some causal explanations cannot be reports of causation. But this latter claim needs to be defended against the following objection: How, one might ask, can a causal explanation be genuinely *causal* if the explanans doesn't stand to the explanandum as cause to effect? Or, as Mellor puts it, "how can facts explain other facts causally without causing them?" (1995, p. 130). Well, here I want to appeal to Lewis's theory of explanation. For Lewis, "to explain an event is to provide some information about its causal history" (1986b, p. 217); and the causal history of an event, he says, is "a relational structure" (ibid., p. 216). Not surprisingly, then, Lewis's account of explanation is tailor-made to fit the network model of causation. For present purposes, the most important feature of Lewis's account of explanation is that it does *not* amount to the view that every explanation involves picking out a cause (or some causes) of an event; the way in which causal facts enter into an explanation can be more complex than that. One can give information about an event's causal history in all sorts of other ways—by saying, for instance, that certain events or kinds of event do *not* figure in its causal history, or by saying that an event of such-and-such *kind* occurred, rather than that some *particular* event occurred. The moral here, then, is that something can be the explanans of a causal explanation without itself being a cause of the event cited in the explanandum.

For example, suppose that Lee Harvey Oswald really did shoot JFK. Then the following three sentences are all true:

(1)   Oswald's shot caused JFK's death.

(2)   JFK died because Oswald shot him.

(3)   JFK died because somebody shot him.

On Mellor's view, all three are *causal* truths. On Lewis's view (as expressed in Lewis 1973a, 1986b,c), only the first is, strictly speaking, a causal truth; the second and third are causal explanations rather than reports of causation. It's pretty obvious what makes (2) a *causal* explanation: Each of the explanans and the explanandum asserts that a particular event (Oswald's shot and JFK's death respectively) occurred, and those two events are in fact causally related. The case of (3) is a little more complicated: Here, the explanans does not assert that a *particular* event occurred, for there is no event essentially describable as *someone's* shooting JFK. Such an event would be disjunctive: It would be the event of Lee Harvey Oswald's shooting or the man on the grassy knoll's shooting or Jackie Kennedy's shooting or ... and so on. And there is no more such an event than there is an event of my-birthday-party-or-your-morning-bath.[11] Rather, the explanans of (3) asserts that there was some event or other that was a shooting of JFK by someone. Hence the explanans of (3) does not stand to the explanandum as cause to effect. Nonetheless, (3) still counts as a true causal explanation because, although it doesn't tell us *which* event caused JFK's death, it tells us something about the death's causal history, namely, that it included a shooting by someone.

The notion of providing information about an event's causal history is further expanded by Jackson and Pettit's account of program and process explanations.[12] This account is designed to show how multiply realizable properties (like functional and dispositional properties) can figure in true causal explanations without being "causally efficacious." For example, suppose that to be fragile is to be disposed to break when dropped, and that a glass is dropped and duly breaks. We recognize that it is the glass's molecular structure that causes it to break, and not its fragility; but we do not want to conclude that the fragility cannot figure in a worthwhile *explanation* of why it broke. (Likewise, we do not want the view that mental states are functional states to preclude the possibility of explaining, say, actions in terms of beliefs and desires.)

Jackson and Pettit's solution to the problem is to distinguish between "process" and "program" explanation. "Process" explanation is explanation in terms of actual underlying physical processes: an explanation of why the glass broke in terms of molecular structure, say, or an explanation of why I went to the shop in terms of my neural processes. Program explanations, on the other hand, tell us not what the actual underlying processes were, but rather that those processes satisfy a particular functional or dispositional or higher-order description. The presence of fragility "programs for" the presence of a causally efficacious molecular property. Although it is the actually present causally efficacious property, and not the programming property, that figures in the causal history of the breakage, the program explanation still tells us something *about* that causal history—namely, that it involves *some efficacious property or other* for which fragility programs.

As Jackson and Pettit say:

The process story tells us about how the history actually went: say that such and such particular decaying atoms were responsible for the radiation. A program account tells us about how that history might have been ... telling us for example that in any relevantly similar situation, as in the original situation itself, the fact that some atoms are decaying means that there will be a property realized—that involving the decay of such and such particular atoms—which is sufficient in the circumstances to produce radiation. In the actual world it was this, that and the other atom which decayed and led to the radiation but in possible worlds where their place is taken by other atoms, the radiation still occurs.[13]

If we adopt Lewis's analysis of causal explanation, then, we can distinguish between causation and causal explanation and still be able to say why causal explanations count as *causal* explanations; for such explanations can give information about the causal history of the event to be explained even though the explanans does not stand to the explanandum as cause to effect.

5   How Can Causally Inert Absences Explain Anything?

In the last section, I defended the view that facts can causally explain without being *causes* of what they explain. In this section, I argue that facts about absences, omissions, and failures do just that. The "because" locution is—or at least sometimes is—an explanatory locution; moreover, as we have seen, "because" claims can be true—can reveal information about causal history—without the explanans standing to the explanandum as cause to effect. So we can repudiate the claim that absences can be causes and perfectly well grant that there are true causal explanations whose explananta concern absences.

First, though, a point about the logical form of causation by absence claims. Much of the time in our everyday talk, we speak as if absences, omissions, and failures are *things*. We say that the void is deadly just as we would say that the Chrysler Building is very tall: The sentence has the same subject-predicate form, and we count it as true, even though there could be no *object* in the world picked out by the definite description "the void." Similarly, we say that Flora's failure to water the orchids caused their death just as we might, in different circumstances, say that Flora's throwing them on the fire, or cutting them up, caused their death. Our everyday causation-by-absence claims often have the logical form of a relational sentence—and we count them as true—even though one of the singular terms flanking the relation does not refer to anything. Absences, omissions, and failures get assimilated to the familiar ontological category of events even though they are *not* events.

So what? Well, suppose for a moment that there really is causation by absence, as the nonrelationist claims. Even so, one ought to think that expressing causation by absence facts using the "*c* caused *e*" locution is at best highly misleading. For such sentences have a relational form, yet whatever it is that makes them true, it is not the obtaining of any relation. The discussion in section 4 suggests an obvious paraphrase of causation-by-absence claims into the "because" locution: A more ontologically perspicuous way of saying that Flora's failure to water the orchids caused their death is to say that the orchids died—or that their death occurred—because Flora failed to water them.

The relationist, on the other hand, cannot claim that "the orchids died because Flora failed to water them" is a paraphrase of "Flora's failure caused the orchids' death," for, although we can perhaps paraphrase away the relational form of the latter sentence, we cannot paraphrase away the fact that it is a *causal* claim; and according to the relationist, absences do not *cause* anything. So if we want—as I want—to hold that the sentence "the orchids died because Flora failed to water them" is explanatory but *not* causal, it cannot be a paraphrase of the relational sentence.

Still, I agree with the nonrelationist (as I have portrayed her) on this much: We would do better to use the "because" locution than the "caused" locution when we are talking about absences. The nonrelationist should think so because the "because" locution is less misleading, whereas I think so because the "because" locution will allow us to say something true, whereas the "caused" locution will not.

I say that common sense is just mistaken when it asserts that an absence or an omission *caused* some event. It's not an especially bad mistake. Often we move between the "*E* because *C*" and "*c* caused *e*" locutions without going wrong: It doesn't much matter whether I say "the match lit because I struck it" or instead "my striking the match caused it to light"; or whether I say "the crash occurred because there was an avalanche" or instead "the avalanche caused the crash." Often causal explanations go hand in hand with causal relations between events. Often, but not always. When I say "Flora's failure to water the plants caused their death" instead of "the death occurred because Flora failed to water them," I say something false instead of something true. It's not surprising, nor a matter for particular concern, that we make this error in our everyday talk; no serious harm is done. But I see no reason why, from a philosophical perspective, we should not rule the move out of order.

It remains to be shown, of course, that "because" claims involving absences really can give information about the causal history of the event to be explained without the absence being a *cause* of that event. What sort of information does such an explanation give us about the event whose occurrence we want to explain? Well, when I say that the orchids' death occurred because Flora failed to water them, you learn something minimal about the death's causal history: that it did not include an event of Flora's watering the orchids. But you also learn something about the causal structure of nearby worlds where Flora *didn't* fail to water the orchids—namely, that the causal processes that ensued at those worlds did not cause (or perhaps might not have caused) the orchids' death. And if you doubted the veracity of my explanation, I could fill in more details about how the causal history of the world would have gone had Flora watered the plants: Water would have been taken up by the roots, sustained the cell structure, and so on. None of this, of course, is information about what causal processes there were in the *actual* world; it is information about what causal processes there are in the closest world(s) where the actually absent event occurs. As with program explanation, the information provided about causal history is *modal* information; and it is information that is explanatorily relevant to the orchids' death.

Similarly for Lewis's void. Suppose that as punishment for her negligence, Flora's neighbor casts her into the deadly void. Flora's blood boils, the air is sucked from her lungs, and so on. If, as I claim, there is no causation by absence, then the void causes none of these unfortunate events. Strictly speaking, the void is not deadly—if deadliness is the capacity to cause death. But Flora's death is not thereby rendered uncaused: There are plenty of positive events going on in her body that *do* cause her death. Nor, on the account offered here, is the void explanatorily irrelevant to Flora's death. It's perfectly true to say that Flora's blood boiled because there were no forces present—forces that ordinarily keep us alive—to stop it. When we cite the void in our explanation of Flora's death, we describe how Flora's causal history *would* have gone had she *not* been cast into the void. We do not say what *actually* caused her death; rather we point out that the sorts of events that would have caused her to remain alive did not occur.

I see no reason, then, why explanations invoking facts about absences should not be seen as genuine causal explanations, even though absences do not cause anything. Of course, I have not shown that this relationist account of the role of absences in causal explanations is any better than a nonrelationist account like Mellor's, according to which facts about absences causally explain in virtue of their being causes. I merely hope to have shown that the relationist about causation is not committed to denying that absences have a legitimate role to play in our explanatory talk.

6 Commonsense Judgments and the Pragmatics of Explanation

It's time to return to the issues discussed in the first three sections of the essay. There I argued that commonsense assertions and denials of causation by absence depend on considerations—normative features, for example—that have no place in an account of the metaphysics of causation. Since, from the perspective of metaphysics, we can draw no relevant distinction between, for example, Flora's failure to water the plants and your failure to do so, or between Z's failure to attend to his dog's eye infection and Z's neighbor's cousin's best friend's failure to do so, the defender of causation by absence must concede that there is much more causation by absence about than we ordinarily think there is. The denier of causation by absence, on the other hand, must concede that there is much *less* causation by absence than we ordinarily think there is: There is none at all, in fact.

As a denier of causation by absence, what do I say about the commonsense distinction between "Flora's failure to water the orchids caused their death" (true) and "your failure to water the orchids caused their death" (false)? I say, of course, that both are false. But the corresponding *explanatory* claims ("the orchids died because Flora failed to water them"; "the orchids died because *you* failed to water them") are both true. However, they do not, in most contexts, count as equally *adequate* explanations. When we explain why the orchids died, we must, if our explanation is to count as adequate as well as true, be sensitive to why the explanation was requested in the first place. In the context where my interlocutor is requesting information that is relevant to the issue of whom to *blame* for the death of the orchids, it would be highly misleading of me to say that they died because you didn't water them. The *truth* of my utterance doesn't depend on the moral question of who is to blame; but the *adequacy* of my explanation does, in this context, so depend. Similarly, it's true to say that I attended the seminar because I wasn't attacked by a hungry polar bear; it's just *very* hard to imagine a context within which someone who asked me why I attended would be satisfied with that explanation.

Like the distinction between events and absences, the distinction between a true explanation—a true "because" statement—and an adequate explanation is one that common sense has a tendency to ignore. If you judge that the orchids died because Flora didn't water them but not because you didn't water them yourself, or that I attended the seminar because I didn't have anything better to do and *not* because I was not attacked by a hungry polar bear, you mistake lack of explanatory salience for falsity.

Of course, the believer in causation by absence can tell the same story. I do not claim that my account is any more plausible than that of someone who thinks there *is* causation by absence; I merely hope to have persuaded you that it is no *less* plausible, and hence that it is no objection to the network model of causation that it entails that there is no causation by absence.

The causal history of the world is a mass of causal processes: Events linked by a vast and complex web of causal relations. In order that the causal history of the world should look the way it does look, rather than some other way, there must have been no *extra* events impinging on it—for those extra events would have had effects that would have changed the causal history of the world in various ways. If Godzilla had impinged upon the causal history of the world, that causal history would have gone very differently. We might even, if circumstances demanded it, want to explain happenings in the world by citing Godzilla's absence (though it's hard to imagine that we should ever want to do so). But I see no need to think of Godzilla's lack of impingement as a kind of causation.

Notes

1. See Steward (1997), chapter 7.

2. See for instance Lewis (1973a, 1986b), and Davidson (1967).

3. Lewis, chapter 10 in this volume, p. 281.

4. See Mellor (1987) and (1995, chapter 11). Steward (1997) also believes that the network model should be abandoned.

5. See Lewis, chapter 10 in this volume, pp. 284–285. Another proposal along similar lines can be found in Dowe (1999).

6. See Lewis, chapter 10 in this volume, p. 284 and Dowe (1999).

7. The first three examples are taken from Stapleton (1994), chapter 6, section 2.

8. See Hart and Honoré (1985), p. 38.

9. Of course, "relata" isn't really the right word, since Mellor agrees with Davidson that "because" does not pick out a causal relation.

10. See Mellor (1995), pp. 162–165.

11. See Lewis (1986d), p. 267.

12. See, for example, Jackson and Pettit (1990).

13. Jackson and Pettit (1990), p. 117.

12 For Facts as Causes and Effects

D. H. Mellor

1 Introduction

Philosophers of causation, including those who deny that there is any, need to say what they take it to be; just as atheists need to say what they disbelieve in. So, to avoid begging the question for or against gods or causation, we must start not with the debatable extensions but with the intensions of these concepts. That is, we must say what we think the existence of gods or of causation entails. Only then can we say whether and where they exist and what follows from that. In short, to reverse an overrated adage, we must start not with the use—the unreflective application—of these terms by believers but with the point of that use, that is, with their meaning.

But while semantics may have to have the first word here, it can hardly have the last, at least not in the case of causation. Only if what we must mean is demonstrably necessary or impossible, as in the case of gods it might be, can that fact settle the question. With causation, the question is more complex, since different people have taken "causation" to mean too many vague, contentious, and conflicting things, not all of which we can have.[1] We must therefore be prepared to find that whatever in the world, if anything, deserves to be called "causation" fails to live up to some of our ideas of it. Take the pre-Humean idea that we can know a priori what causes what. Now that we know that we cannot know this (with trivial exceptions, like "the cause of e, if any, causes e"), most of us have dropped the idea rather than conclude that there is no causation.

Similarly with other erstwhile connotations of causation, such as determinism. By this I mean the idea that the presence and/or absence of causes somehow compels that of their effects: in other words, that causes must in some strong sense be sufficient and/or necessary for what they cause. This idea too has been challenged, by convincing cases of seemingly indeterministic causation ranging from medicine (people's smoking causing them to get cancer) to microphysics (the triggering of atomic explosions). But what makes these cases convincing, that is, what makes us want to keep them in causation's extension, is that they do meet other connotations of causation. For despite the indeterminism, these apparent causes still precede, explain, give grounds for predicting, and provide means to, their apparent effects (Mellor 1995, chs. 5–7). That is why we want to call them causes.

In short, the conflict of determinism with causation's apparent extension arises because it is not required by other, more important connotations. However, it is at least consistent with them, unlike the transitivity that Lewis (1973a, in 1986a, p. 167) and others have foisted on causation, by making it the ancestral of an otherwise credible but nontransitive relation R. This contradicts most of causation's other connotations, as such notorious causal chains as those from losing a nail to losing a kingdom (e.g., Lowe 1980), or from a butterfly wing's flapping to a tornado (Stewart 1989, p. 141), show. For while each member of such chains explains, gives grounds for predicting, and is a means to the next one, their first and last members stand in none of these relations, which is why no one really thinks the first causes the last. So here too, but with far less excuse, a failure to fit causation's apparent extension arises from forgetting its principal connotations, that is, what we think follows from saying that one thing causes another. Still, at least in this case the question is simple—should we identify causation with the nontransitive R or its trivially transitive ancestral?—even if the answer usually given is wrong.

Determinism is of course a harder and tastier nut to crack than transitivity, being related in more complex and interesting ways to causation's other connotations. Here, however, having tried to crack it in my (1995), I merely note that cracking such nuts takes more than semantics, that is, more than specifying a relation and calling it "causation." We must also see if a real relation exists that both meets enough of the specification to count as causation and has a credible extension, that is, links most if not all of what we take to be causes and effects.[2] And to do that we need not only a semantics but a metaphysics, and in particular an ontology, to tell us first what relations there are that might serve our turn, and then how much of our turn they can serve.

It is of course no news that theories of causation need an ontology as well as a semantics, Davidson's well-known theory being an obvious case in point. For on the one hand in his (1967) he argues on semantic grounds that causation must relate particulars, in the sense of entities that first-order quantifiers range over, of the kinds that he calls "events."[3] And on the other he argues independently in his (1969) that there must be particulars of these kinds, as well as of the less contentious kinds exemplified by people, plants, and planets.

That Davidson's semantics for causation needs an ontology that includes events is obvious, since without them he would have far too few particulars to provide all singular causes and effects. Suppose, for example, you do something because you decide to. Then if there are events, your decision (one particular) can cause your action (another particular). But if there are not, and the only relevant particular is you, the causation here must link not particulars but facts, namely the fact of your deciding to do something and the fact of your doing it. To yield an extensionally credible theory of causation, Davidson's semantics needs events.

Similarly for those who argue, as I do (1995, chs. 9–11), that most causes and effects are facts. We need a credible ontology of facts, defensible against among other things the so-called slingshot arguments of Davidson (1967) and others, which purport to show that if causation links any facts it links them all, which we know it does not do. Here too, having argued the matter in my (1995), I shall simply assume that these and other objections to facts can be met, and that neither facts nor events can be ruled out independently of the theories of causation that invoke them. How, then, are we to decide between these theories?

The answer, as in boxing and science, is that what cannot be settled by a knockout must be settled on points. What matters is which theory of causation does best overall, when rated not only for its semantics and ontology but also, and mainly, for how well it explains its subject matter, namely the connotations and apparent extension of causation. That is the question here, as it is for other philosophical theories, and as it is for scientific ones; and here, as there, the eventual answer may well alter some of our initial semantic and ontological assumptions.

Compare, for example, an imaginary history of scientific theories of fish, that is, theories of—to start with—middle-sized self-propelled organisms living under water. Theories of fish can of course not alter this ontology or semantics too much, on pain of changing the subject: No theory of galaxies will ever be a theory of fish. Even so, our current theory of fish has changed our initial piscatory assumptions quite a lot. On it, many self-propelled underwater organisms are not fish: Some because they are not animals; others, like whales, because they are mammals, that is, they work differently and hence are only "fools' fish."[4]

Similarly, I say, with philosophical theories, including theories of causation. Some apparent cases of causation (such as the phenomena of nonlocality in quantum physics) may, like whales, need excluding on theoretical grounds from what we end up calling causation. New distinctions, such as that between causing and affecting (see sec. 6), may also need drawing in our theory, just as shellfish may need distinguishing from other underwater animals.

This view of scientific theories is familiar enough in the philosophy of science. But it may still need selling to some philosophers of philosophy, for whom semantic analysis remains the be-all and end-all of the subject. I should say therefore that denying that this is what distinguishes philosophy from science is not to try and reduce the former to the latter. On the contrary, it is to try and restore to philosophy the serious ontological theorizing that an unwarranted subservience to science and semantics has inhibited for too long, and which is only now reviving as metaphysicians shake off their scientific and semantic shackles.

2   Facts and Particulars

How, then, do facts and particulars compare as singular causes and effects? Particulars may indeed have a semantic head start: Even to me "the spark caused the fire" sounds more natural, or at least more causal, than "there was a fire because there was a spark." But that of course is not the end of the matter. It certainly does not rule out causal truths of the form

(1) E because C,

where "C" and "E" are sentences and "because" is a sentential connective, as opposed to

(2) c causes e,

where c and e are particulars and "causes" is a two-place predicate. (1) may still, as I shall argue, win on points. But how?

   First, to give (1) a chance, we must exclude its noncausal instances, such as those used to give noncausal explanations. This we can do by fiat, by restricting it to instances that are equivalent to "the fact that C causes the fact that E." This restriction begs no relevant questions, because it relies only on the uncontentious assumption that "E because C" entails "C" and "E," just as "c causes e" entails the existence of c and e. For then, on the weak reading of "fact" given by the principle that, for all sentences, statements or propositions "P,"

(3)   "P" is true iff it is a fact that P,

it follows that the facts that C and that E exist iff "C" and "E" are true. And this being so, we can simplify what follows by reading "C" and "E" not only as sentences but also as shorthand for "the fact that C" and "the fact that E," a usage in which we can then rewrite (1) as

(1′) C causes E,

where C and E are facts in the weak sense given by (3). It is in this sense that (1′) and hence (1) represent causes and effects as facts, just as (2) represents them as particulars.

   The contentious assumptions here are not semantic but ontological. Do the facts that (1) and (1′) require, and the particulars that (2) requires, really exist? More precisely, do most if not all of the facts and particulars entailed by seemingly true instances of (1), (1′), and (2) exist?[5] This is not an easy or uncontentious thing to show. Some philosophers, for example, still reject the Davidsonian events needed for my doing something because I decide to (an instance of (1)) to yield an instance of (2), namely "my decision causes my action." Here, however, if only to keep (2) in the race, I shall take for granted the existence of the particular events, such as decisions, actions, sparks, and fires, that true instances of (2) need.

What of the facts that true instances of (1) and (1′) need? To these there are several objections, notably the slingshot mentioned above, an argument whose validity means we can reject it only by rejecting one of its assumptions. These assumptions are that we cannot falsify a true "E because C" by replacing either

(i)   "C" or "E" with a logical equivalent, or

(ii) a term referring to a particular with a coreferring term,

that is, with another term referring to the same particular. Of these two assumptions the one I reject is the transparency assumption, (ii). I reject it because it implies, for example, that if "Tony Blair is the Prime Minister because he won the election" is true, so is "Tony Blair is Tony Blair because he won the election," which is absurd. For if Tony Blair *is* the Prime Minister, "Tony Blair" and "the Prime Minister" refer to the same person. So for "Tony Blair is Tony Blair because he won the election" to fail to follow, as it must, (ii) must fail in this case, no doubt because the fact that Tony Blair is Tony Blair differs from the fact that he is Prime Minister.

But what makes these facts differ? What, in general, individuates the facts that I say are causes or effects? My answer is the one that Davidson gave for events in his (1969), namely that any events d and d' are identical iff they have all the same causes and effects, that is, iff replacing "d" by "d'" in any "c causes d" or "d causes e" would never change its truth value. Similarly, I say in my (1995, ch. 9.3), for facts that are causes or effects. Any such facts D and D' are identical iff they have all the same causes and effects, that is, if replacing the sentence "D" by "D'" in any causal "D because C" or "E because D" would never change its truth value.[6]

From this the falsity of (ii) follows at once. For as Tony Blair's being Tony Blair does *not* have all the same causes and effects as his being the Prime Minister, "Tony Blair is the Prime Minister because he won the election" can be, as it is, opaque, that is, *not* transparent. So some instances of "E because C" are opaque.[7] But then why should they not be?

3   The Relata of Causation

The stock answer to this question relies on the seemingly innocuous assumption that causation is a *relation*. It relies on this assumption because, for any (e.g., two-term) relation R, we must be able to say transparently that it relates any entities a and b. For if what R relates are a and b themselves—as opposed to aspects of or facts about them—then to say so we must need only to refer to a and b and say that R relates *them*: *How* we refer to a and b must be irrelevant to the truth of what we say. This is why any simple relational statement of the form "aRb" must be transparent for a and b. Yet, as we have just seen, some instances of "E because C" are opaque. Does this not show that causation does not relate facts, and hence that causes and effects are not facts but particulars?

No; but to see why not we must first look not at (1) but at (1′), "C causes E." This *is* transparent for the *facts* C and E: Replacing the referring term "C" or "E" in (1′) by any other term for the same fact will never change its truth value. That follows at once from my causal criterion of identity for facts. For if replacing "C" by "C'" (or "E" by "E'") did change the truth value of "C causes E," that criterion would automatically make C and C' (or E and E') different facts, so that "C" and "C'" (or "E" and "E'") would *not* refer to the same fact. But then this change in the truth value of "C causes E" would not show it to be opaque.

All that the opacity in some "E because C" shows is that, *within* a true *sentence* "C" or "E," substituting coreferring terms for a *particular* may make that sentence correspond to a different fact: as replacing "the Prime Minister" by "Tony Blair" does in "Tony Blair is the Prime Minister." But as this induces no opacity in sentences of the form "C causes E," it does not show that causation cannot relate facts.

Nor of course have we shown that causation cannot relate particulars: As causal relata, both facts and particulars are still in the ring. But facts still seem to win on points. For if there can be a fire because there is a spark, there can also *fail* to be a fire because there is *no* spark. Similarly, if I can act because I decide to, I can also *fail* to act because I do *not* decide to. In other words, just as "E because C" can be true if "E" and "C" are true, so "$\sim E$ because $\sim C$" can be true if "E" and "C" are false. This poses no problem for facts, because the weak sense of "fact" given by our principle (3) allows there to be negative facts.

For particulars, however, these cases do pose a problem. What particulars does causation relate when there *not* being a spark causes there *not* to be a fire? They cannot be negative ones—a *non*spark and a *non*fire—as there are demonstrably no such entities. For suppose there is a *long* spark and a *hot* fire: This entails that there is a spark and a fire, since something that is both a spark and long must be a spark, just as something that is both a fire and hot must be a fire. In short, these entailments are, as Davidson (1969) says, just cases of conjunctions entailing their conjuncts. But with negative particulars, the entailments go the other way: If there is *no* spark, it follows that there is no long spark, and no short one either. But this cannot be because a nonspark exists and is both long and short, since nothing can be that; any more than a nonfire can be (as it would have to be) both hot and cold, to make its existence entail (as it would have to) that of both a hot nonfire and a cold nonfire.

How, then, without negative particulars, can causation relate particulars when the cause or effect is that there is *no* particular of some kind—a spark, a fire, a decision, an action? Here advocates of particular causes and effects face a dilemma, since they must either deny that there is causation in these cases or find some positive particulars for causation to relate. But the former restricts causation's extension too much, by ruling out too many obvious cases; and the latter is often made impossible by the lack of suitable particulars. For positive particulars in most of these cases are clearly either irrelevant (one need not decide not to act in order not to decide to act), inscrutable (what particulars does the nonexistence of sparks and fires entail that can make the former cause the latter?) or nonexistent, as in what Lewis (following Martin 1996) starts his second paper in this volume by calling "the deadly void," that "would cause you to die in just a few minutes. It would suck the air from your lungs. It would boil your blood...." Yet in all these cases, most of which lack any particular that is obviously capable of being the cause or effect, there is always an obviously capable fact: namely, the fact that there is *no* particular of a suitable kind.

4 Negative Causes

Semantically, then, facts in my weak sense can provide causes and effects in far more apparent cases of causation than particulars can, because they can be negative. But semantics, I have argued, is not enough: we also need a credible ontology, which we shall now see that negative facts may not provide. So as King Lear says to his silent daughter Cordelia: "How? Nothing can come of nothing. Speak again." And so, being more willing than Cordelia to heave my heart into my mouth, I shall.

There is of course an innocuous reading of Lear's maxim, namely that only actual causes can have actual effects. This I accommodated in section 2 by requiring "*C* causes *E*" to entail the existence of the facts *C* and *E*. However, this reading is not strong enough to make the present point, since in my weak sense of "fact" all it means is that "*E* because *C*" entails "*C*" and "*E*." But when, as here, "*C*" or "*E*" is a negative existential sentence, all this means is that *no* particular satisfies some description. That is the kind of absence that many philosophers find it hard to credit with any efficacy.

Yet why should absences not have effects? Perhaps it is because causes need to come in kinds to enable laws of nature to fix the kinds of effects they have: making forces cause accelerations, sparks fires, decisions actions, and so on. But then how can nothing, being of no specific kind, have specific kinds of effects? The answer is of course that absences can come in as many kinds as presences can. A lack of force causes a lack of acceleration; an absence of sparks causes an absence of fire; indecision causes inaction; and so on. These are all well-defined kinds of absence, with well-defined kinds of effects; and the presence of nothing is merely the conjunction of all such absences. Why then should we deny that absences in general, and a void in particular, can have effects of specific kinds?

I can think of three sources of this denial. First, there is the contingency of most and perhaps all causation, which may make the efficacy of even negative causes contingent on the existence of something else. That I grant: but then this "something else" may also be a negative fact, as when the absence of one force will cause an object not to accelerate only in the absence of other forces. So although some negative facts will certainly lack their normal effects in Lewis's void, it does not follow that they will have *no* effects, still less that the void itself will have none.

Next, there is the idea of causal efficacy as an intrinsic property of causes, in some sense of "intrinsic" that would stop absences having such properties. But what can this sense be? It cannot be the usual one, of failing to entail the existence of other things. For in that sense the absence of a force, a spark, or a decision is as intrinsic as its presence; and so therefore may its efficacy be. And yet in this sense, of course, efficacy can *never* be intrinsic, since being a cause always means having, that is, entailing the existence of, a distinct effect. So either way negative causes are no worse off than positive ones.

This is why few if any philosophers now think that having effects is a *property* of causes, as opposed to the *relation* between causes and effects discussed in section 3. That relation may indeed depend on its relata having—or, if its relata are facts, containing—the properties that make them instantiate the laws that fix the kinds of effects that given kinds of causes have; and I agree with most philosophers that causation does depend in this way on laws and hence on the properties of causes. But as laws can and often do include negations—as in the law that bodies acted on by *no* forces will *not* accelerate—this still gives us no reason to deny that negative facts can be causes or effects.

What does give us a reason to deny this is the very idea of causation as a relation in the sense of note 2, the reason being that real relations need real relata, which negative facts cannot be. Let us see why not. The objection here is not that the opacity of "*E* because *C*" stops it reporting a relation, since it does not, as we saw in section 2: "*C* causes *E*" is as transparent for *C* and *E* as "*c* causes *e*" is for *c* and *e*. The real objection to negative causes and effects is, as I hinted at the start of this section, not semantic but ontological.

To see the objection, let us look again at the principle I used in section 2 to generate all the facts I needed to supply my factual causes and effects, namely that for *all* "*P*," including negative existential ones,

(3)   "*P*" is true iff it is a fact that *P*.

Together with the uncontentious principle that, for all "*P*,"

"*P*" is true iff *P*,

(3) entails that, for all *P*,

P iff it is a fact that *P*.

This reading of "fact" thus makes it trivially true that, for example,

murder is wrong iff it is a fact that murder is wrong;
Jim will probably win tonight iff it is a fact that Jim will probably win tonight; and
quarks have spin iff it is a fact that quarks have spin.

Yet it cannot follow from this that, for murder to be wrong, Jim to probably win tonight, and quarks to have spin, the world must contain objective values, probabilities, future-tensed facts, and theoretical entities. Theories of value, probability, time, and the nature of scientific theory that deny this are not so easily refuted.

The sense of "fact" given by (3) is thus far too weak to show that causation relates facts, since (3) does not tell us what in the world, if anything, by *making* "*P*" true, makes *P* a fact in this weak sense.[8] So in particular, (3) does not show that a negative existential "*P*" is made true by the existence of something which a causal (or any other) relation could link to anything else. And indeed it is obvious that it is not, since by definition what makes any such "*P*" true is that *no* particular of some kind exists. But then facts can no more supply all the relata that causation seems to need than particulars can: Negative facts cannot have effects by being related to them. So what *does* causation relate?

5   Nonrelational Causation

To answer this question we need to apply Ramsey's "heuristic maxim," that in such stalemates "the truth lies not in one of the two disputed views but in some third possibility which has not yet been thought of, which we can only discover by rejecting something assumed as obvious by both the disputants" (Ramsey 1925, pp. 11–12). Here the assumption I propose to reject is that *causation is a relation*. It is not, and the idea that it is—like the idea that it is transitive—is a mere formal prejudice, unwarranted by any of its substantive connotations.

To see this, we must note first that, for causation to be a relation, statements of it, like

(1′) C causes E, and

(2) c causes e,

must do more than meet the semantic criteria for relational statements by

(a)   entailing C and E, and c and e, and

(b)   being transparent for them;

they must also be made true by a relation holding between C and E or c and e. It is this ontological assumption that I say the lack of relata in many apparent cases of causation should make us reject, to prevent an implausible restriction on causation's extension.

To show how this can work, I start with my innocuous reading of King Lear's maxim that nothing can come of nothing, namely that only actual causes can have actual effects. This, as we saw in section 2, requires "E because C" to entail "C" and "E," and hence the facts C and E, and "c causes e" to entail c and e. So for C and c to be causes, and for E and e to be effects, these entities must exist, whether or not they are the relata of any relation. Of course if causation does relate C and E, or c and e, this will indeed entail that the entities it relates exist. But if they must exist in any case to satisfy Lear's maxim, that entailment is superfluous. In other words, the fact that causes and effects meet the merely semantic existential criterion (a) is no reason to think that causation really *is* a relation, since they must meet this criterion anyway.

Nor should we be impressed by the fact that causes and effects meet the transparency criterion (b). For as we saw in section 2, the transparency for C and E of "C causes E," and for c and e of "c causes e," will follow from a causal criterion of identity for C and E, and for c and e, whether causation is a relation or not.

If these criteria are neutral, others, notably criteria for what factual properties and relations there are, imply that causation is *not* a relation.[9] Take Shoemaker's (1980) criterion, that the factual properties that exist are those that combine to fix the causal powers of particulars—as when having the properties of being steel and of being sharp-edged combine to give a knife the power to cut. By that criterion causation itself will obviously not be a property in this world or any other. Nor will causation meet my (1997) criterion, that the factual properties and relations that exist are those that occur in laws of nature, since in my view no such law includes causation itself as a property or relation.

Nor do substantive theories of what makes "*C* causes *E*" or "*c* causes *e*" true support the idea of causation as a relation, as we shall now see. There are of course many such theories, but for present purposes we may divide all the serious ones into just two kinds: those that require causes and effects to instantiate laws of nature, and those that require causation to imply something about an effect's prospects without its cause. Let us take these in turn.

Some theories make laws, and hence general causation (such as smoking causing cancer), a relation between the properties and relations involved (Armstrong 1983). But this, even if true (which I doubt), does not make the singular causation that concerns us relational. For suppose it is a law that all *F*s are, in certain circumstances, followed by *G*s.[10] How does this help to make (the fact that there is) an *F* cause (there to be) a *G*? The answer, on almost any view, is that it does so by making a certain non-truth-functional conditional true (or assertible),[11] namely that, in any relevant circumstances, if there *were* an *F*, it *would* be followed by a *G*. But as this conditional entails neither its antecedent nor its consequent, it does not entail that any such particulars exist. So whatever makes it true need not—and clearly does not —entail the existence of the *F* and the *G* (or of the facts that there is an *F* and is a *G*) that are thereby shown to be cause and effect. In short, far from law-based theories of causation requiring it to be a relation, they imply that it is not.

Similarly for theories that invoke an effect's prospects without its cause: These too require causation only to entail conditionals, for example, that if in the circumstances there were *no F*, there would also be no *G*.[12] But as this does not entail the *falsity* of either its antecedent or its consequent, its truthmaker also need not—and again clearly does not—entail the existence of either the cause or the effect, and so cannot be a relation between them.

So far so good for the idea that causes and effects need not be relata and can therefore include negative facts. But not yet good enough, for even if causation itself is not a relation, it may still require causes and effects to be related in space and time. It may, for example, require that causes precede their effects, be contiguous to any immediate effects, and be linked to others by dense sequences of intermediate causes and effects. Does this not require causes and effects to be the relata, if not of causal then at least of temporal and spatial relations, which we have seen that negative facts cannot be?

To see why it does not require this, consider first the temporal analogue of (1), namely "*E after C*," as in "there was a fire after there was a spark," "I did it after I decided to do it," and so on. There are also spatial analogues, as in "there was a fire above where there was a spark" and "I did it where I decided to do it." In short, spatial and temporal relations can relate facts as easily as particulars. But then what about negative facts: How can the nonexistence of a spark or a fire, or my *not* deciding or *not* doing something, be the relata of such relations?

The answer is that they need not be. For all these negative facts have locations, just as positive ones do: There is always a time and place at which there is no spark, fire, decision, action, and so on. So even if these are negative facts about things or events, they are positive facts about times and places. But then whatever spacetime relations causation entails need not relate these causes and effects but only their spatiotemporal locations.[13] Causes and effects themselves need not be relata at all.

6 Particular Causes and Effects

By denying that causation is a relation, and thus enabling negative facts to be causes and effects, we can match causation's apparent extension far better than any theory that limits causes and effects to particulars. But on the other hand, we need not limit causes and effects to facts. For since our causes and effects need not be truthmaking facts, they need not be facts at all. As well as the nontruthmaking facts C and E entailed by true instances of "E because C," our causes and effects can include all the particulars referred to in true instances of "c causes e."

But then, since many truths of these forms come in pairs that clearly stand or fall together—as "I acted because I decided to" does with "my decision caused my action"—we must ask which comes first: the factual causes and effects or the particular ones? In my (1995, ch. 11.3), I show how facts can come first, by instances of "E because C" entailing all true instances of "c causes e," as follows: c causes e only if, in a suitably restricted region of spacetime, for some F and G,

(i)   there is a G because there is an F,

(ii) c is the F, and

(iii) e is the G.[14]

This is what makes facts the primary singular causes and effects, since what makes particulars causes or effects is that facts about them are, not that a causal relation holds between them.

Can the derivation also go the other way, from particulars to facts? Yes, but only up to a point, and then only by making particulars too fact-like. Take Lewis's (1973a) analysis of "c causes e," using conditionals like "if c did not occur (i.e., exist), e would not." This does yield some instances of "E because C," but only of the form "*e* exists because *c* does," which fits far too few cases, and not only because it cannot cope with negative causes and effects. It also cannot cope with the many cases in which *c* does not *cause e*, but only *affects* it, by causing an *e* to be *G* that would exist even if it were not G:[15] as when an injection affects a dentist's drilling of a tooth, by making it painless, without causing it, that is, without causing there to be a drilling. Similarly, different facts about *c* may affect *e* in different ways, as when an unwelcome content "*P*" of my speech (*c*) causes you (*e*) to believe "*P*" while its quiet tone causes you to react calmly to that news.

All these cases yield natural instances of "*e* is *G* because *c* is *F*," true for some *F* and *G* and false for others. It is far harder to fit them into the Procrustean form of "*e* exists because *c* does." That requires distinguishing the event of a drilling from the event of its being painless, the event of my saying something from the event of my saying it quietly, and so on. But this multiplies particulars beyond all necessity and sense, destroying in particular Davidson's (1969) obviously correct explanation, endorsed in section 3 above, of why, for example, a painless drilling must be a drilling and a quiet speech a speech. The plain fact is that these so-called events are not particulars at all but facts: the fact that there is a drilling, and the fact that it is painless; that I say something, and that I say it quietly; and so on. To call these entities "events" just to preserve the claim that causation relates particulars is to evacuate that claim of almost all its content: a sure sign in philosophy, as in science, of a degenerating research program.

7   The Positive Facts of Causation

I conclude that causation is not only not a relation, but that most causes and effects are not particulars but facts, in the nontruthmaking sense of "fact" given by the principle that "*P*" is true iff it is a fact that *P*. But how then is causation embodied? What must our world contain, besides whatever is needed to make "*C*" and "*E*" true, to make "*E* because *C*" true?

We saw in section 5 that most if not all theories make causation entail one or two conditionals, about an effect's prospects with and without its cause. For "*E* because *C*" we may for present purposes write these conditionals as "$C \mathbin{\square\!\!\rightarrow} E$" and "$\sim\!C \mathbin{\square\!\!\rightarrow} \sim\!E$," where "$\mathbin{\square\!\!\rightarrow}$" is a connective that we may assume has something like Lewis's (1973b) possible-world semantics. This is of course contentious, but that does not matter here. Whatever their semantics, as these conditionals are contingent, and incomplete truth-functions of "*C*" and "*E*," at least one of them will need something in this world besides *C* and *E* to make it true. And whatever that is will be what embodies causation. All the other apparent consequences of *C*'s causing *E* are either also causal (if causation is dense) or spatiotemporal (C's preceding or being contiguous to E) or not ontological at all: for example, that C explains E, gives grounds for predicting E, and provides a means to E. It is the truthmakers for conditionals like "$C \mapsto E$" and "$\sim C \mapsto \sim E$" that add causation to a world of spatiotemporally ordered facts.

And what those truthmakers are we already know from section 5. They are particulars having those properties discussed in my (1997) or Shoemaker (1980), namely those that make particulars instantiate laws, or combine to give particulars their causal powers. In either case, the way they do this is by being truthmakers for conditionals: as when any thing of mass m, if acted on by any net force f, would accelerate in the direction of f at f/m.[16] And similarly for temperatures, pressures, the strengths of fields across spacetime, and so on. It is particular things, events, and spacetime points having properties like these that are the positive facts that embody the world's causation. Hence the causal limitations of the void. The problem is not that a void cannot contain causes and effects: It can, since its negative facts can make just as good causes and effects as positive facts. The problem is that it lacks the positive facts, the instances of properties, that such negative facts need in order to *make* them causes and effects. It is our properties, not the void's, that make it deadly to us.

Notes

1. By "causation" here I mean singular causation, as in Fred's smoking causing him to get cancer, rather than general causation, as in smoking's causing cancer.

2. By "real relations" (hereafter "relations") I mean the relational counterparts of what Lewis (1983b) calls "natural" properties, and I and Alex Oliver (1997) just call "properties": namely, those that entail an objective resemblance between the particulars that share them. Relations then are simply properties of ordered pairs, triples, etc. of particulars, i.e., respects in which the ordered n-tuples that share them objectively resemble each other. Whether these properties and relations are universals, resemblance classes of particulars or tropes, or something else again, is immaterial for present purposes.

3. For clarity I too shall only use "events" to mean certain kinds of particulars. The common habit of calling causes and effects "events," whatever they may be, only causes confusion when, as here, we are trying to say what causes and effects are.

4. Compare: "Animals with the appearance of cats but reptilic internal structure ... would not be cats; but 'fools' cats'" (Kripke 1972, p. 321).

5. I.e., exist in the past, present, or future of the actual world. In what follows, those who think that only the present exists should read my "exists" as "did, do, or will exist," whereas those who think that other possible worlds exist should read it as "is actual."

6. Note that these criteria, being only of actual and not of counterfactual identity, do not require events or facts that have causes or effects to have them necessarily. Just because d and d' or D and D' are identical iff they have all the same *actual* causes and effects, it does not follow that the very same d (i.e., d') or D (i.e., D') *could* not have had any different causes and effects, and often it clearly could.

7. "C" and "E" need not state identities, or be necessary truths, for "E because C" to be opaque, as many cases of mental causation show. For example, seeing Jim win his race may cause you to believe that he

does so without causing you to believe that the youngest runner (which he is) does so. For other opaque instances of "*E* because *C*," see my (1995, ch. 12.4–5).

8. By a truthmaker for "*P*" I mean something whose existence entails "*P*": see, e.g., Restall (1996). Disputes about which "*P*" needs truthmakers need not concern us here, except that I take it for granted that if "*P*" does, "∼*P*" does not, since all it takes to make "∼*P*" true is that the truthmaker for "*P*" does not exist. (This distinction is not syntactic or semantic: However "*P*" and its negation may be represented in thought or language, I take the positive one—"*P*"—to be the one that has a truthmaker.) This is why I deny that negative existential instances of "*C*" and "*E*" in "*E* because *C*" have truthmakers that could be the relata of a causal relation.

9. By "factual properties and relations" I mean nonevaluative and nonidentity ones whose instances are not provable a priori, as opposed to such apparent properties and relations as being *good*, *better than*, or *identical to Fred*, and such properties and relations of numbers as being *prime* or *less than*. If causation is a relation at all, it is certainly factual.

10. By "*F*s" and "*G*s" I mean particulars satisfying the predicates "*F*" and "*G*," whether or not *F* or *G* is a property by my or Shoemaker's criteria. In particular, to cover indeterministic laws, "*G*" may mean having a certain chance of satisfying another predicate "*H*."

11. This is just to cater for those who think these conditionals lack truth values; it makes no odds to the ensuing argument.

12. Or, in indeterministic cases, that the chance of a *G* would be such-and-such, e.g., less than it would have been with an *F*; again, it makes no odds to the argument.

13. For more details, see my (1998), chs. 8.6 and 10.4.

14. (i)–(iii) are necessary, not sufficient, since they only entail that *c* causes or *affects* e: causing it if being *G* is essential to *e*, affecting it if not. See my (1995), ch. 12.

15. See note 14.

16. Provided *f* does not alter *m*, a proviso needed to enable so-called finkish properties to provide truthmakers for conditionals: See Lewis (1997) and Mellor (2000).

13 Preempting Preemption

David Coady

1   The Naive Counterfactual Analysis of Causation

Since David Lewis first published "Causation" it has been generally assumed that the most straightforward counterfactual analysis of causation (henceforth, "the naive analysis") cannot succeed, because of a class of counterexamples that, following Lewis's nomenclature, have come to be called cases of *preemption*. Consequently, there has been a debate about how to respond to this alleged fact.[1] I argue that this debate is premature, since the naive analysis has not been refuted or been shown to conflict with any compelling intuitions.

The naive analysis, which is widely believed to be refuted by the existence, or possible existence, of cases of preemption, claims that a singular causal proposition of the form "*c* caused *e*" (where *c* and *e* are distinct events) is true iff a counterfactual of the form "If *c* had not occurred, then *e* would not have occurred" is true.[2]

Restricting the scope of the analysis to distinct events is necessary, if we are to exclude certain noncausal relations. Although there is no standard definition of "distinctness" in the literature, it seems clear that it is at least partly a mereological notion: Two events are not distinct, if they have a common part. For example, it is probably true that without World War I, none of the battles of that war would have occurred, but this does not, I think, mean that World War I caused those battles.

Counterfactual dependence can also be due to a logical rather than a causal (or mereological) relation between events. It seems to be the case, for example, that when one slams a door, one also closes it: Without the closing, the slamming would not occur. This does not mean, however, that the closing causes the slamming (see Kim 1973b, p. 571). Although there seems to be some sense in which these events are not distinct, it is not obvious what that sense is. We could say that "they" are identical and therefore not distinct, but this seems hard to reconcile with the intuition that they may differ causally.[3] We could say that they have a common part, but it is not clear that we are entitled to do so.[4] It remains an important task to articulate a satisfactory sense of "distinctness"; the standard objections to the naive analysis, however, have nothing to do with this difficulty.

While there is widespread agreement that the naive counterfactual analysis is a nonstarter, defenders of some kind of counterfactual analysis (as well as those who reject the counterfactual approach altogether) are divided among themselves over whether the naive analysis fails in both directions, that is, the truth of a causal proposition is neither necessary nor sufficient for the truth of its *corresponding* counterfactual, or just one direction, that is, the truth of a causal proposition is sufficient, but not necessary, for the truth of its corresponding counterfactual.

Maudlin and Horwich are members of the former group. Their views about counterfactuals entail that there are circumstances in which it would be correct to say that if c had not occurred, neither would e, but wrong to say that c caused e, even though c and e are distinct events.[5] This could be the case if c is an effect of e rather than a cause of it (Horwich 1989, pp. 169–170; Maudlin 1994, pp. 128–129). Maudlin argues that it could also be the case if c and e are effects of a common cause (1994, p. 129).[6] The issue is not strictly whether *backtracking* or *effects-of-a-common-cause* counterfactuals can be true. It would not be credible to suppose that they are never true (or at least assertible). Rather, the issue is whether they are true in the same sense as *causal* counterfactuals are.[7]

Defending the naive analysis does not necessarily mean defending Lewis's position that causal counterfactuals are *standard*, whereas the others are *nonstandard*; it would be enough to establish that the causal ones are different from the other two, and that this difference can be explicated without appeal to causal notions. Although I believe this can be done, it is beyond the scope of the current essay, in which my ambition is restricted to persuading you that the analysis does not fail in the other direction.

David Lewis and many of those influenced by his work agree with me that the right kind of counterfactual proposition entails its corresponding causal proposition, but they claim that there are realistic thought experiments about *redundant causation* that show that the entailment doesn't go in the other direction. Without exception, the extensive philosophical literature that has been generated from Lewis's discussion of these cases accepts his claim that they provide counterexamples to the naive analysis. I disagree.

Lewis defines redundant causation in "Postscript E" of "Causation":

Suppose we have two events c_1 and c_2, and another event e distinct from both of them; and in actuality all three occur; and if either one of c_1 and c_2 had occurred without the other, then also e would have occurred; but if neither c_1 nor c_2 had occurred, then e would not have occurred. Then I shall say that c_1 and c_2 are *redundant causes* of e.   (Lewis 1986a, p. 193)[8]

As a defender of the naive counterfactual analysis, I must either deny that there are redundant causes, or deny that redundant causes are ever genuine causes. I will do the latter; that is, I will insist that in circumstances like those described by Lewis, neither c_1 nor c_2 causes e, since e does not depend counterfactually on either of them. I do, however, count the combination of c_1 and c_2 as a cause of e.[9]

The Lewiseans will have no problem with this approach for some cases. Lewis claims there are two kinds of redundant causation; preemption and *symmetrical overdetermination*.[10] In a case of symmetrical overdetermination, c_1 and c_2 have an equal claim to being causes of e. In such cases it may be unclear whether we should say that c_1 and c_2 are each causes of e or that neither is, but it is at least clear that there is no reason to say that one is whereas the other is not. Because it is unclear what to say about such cases, Lewis correctly considers them to be poor test cases for analyses of causation. This is not true of cases of preemption, however:

> In a case of preemption, the redundant causes are not on a par. It seems clear that one of them, the *preempting cause*, does the causing; while the other, the *preempted alternative*, waits in reserve. The alternative is not a cause; though it could and would have been one, if it had not been preempted.   (Lewis 1986a, p. 199)

A preempting cause, then, is an event that is both a genuine cause, and a redundant cause, of another event—a possibility that is inconsistent with the naive analyis.

There are cases in which it does seem clear that a redundant cause is a genuine cause, but I believe this appearance is illusory and can be explained away. I will argue that each apparent case of preemption should be redescribed in one of two ways, with the correct way depending on context. In some contexts, I will argue, the alleged preemption is in fact symmetrical overdetermination, in which case neither of the redundant causes is a genuine cause. In other contexts, the alleged preempting cause is in fact a straightforward (i.e., nonredundant) cause.

The context-dependence of some examples results from an ambiguity about the identity of "the effect" (i.e., the "e" of the analysis). In other examples, it results from an ambiguity about the identity of "the cause" (i.e., the "c" of the analysis).

2   Ambiguity about the Identity of "the Effect"

Lewis has recently offered the following example of what he calls "commonplace preemption": "Billy and Suzy throw rocks at a bottle. Suzy throws first or maybe she throws harder. Her rock arrives first. The bottle shatters. Billy's rock passes innocuously through the place where the bottle has just been" (Lewis 2000, p. 184).[11] Allegedly this is a counterexample to the naive analysis, because the bottle shattering is caused by Suzy's throw, despite not being counterfactually dependent on it.

2.1   A Common Suggestion
Lewis anticipates one objection to this description of the example, namely that the shattering that would have occurred without Suzy's throw would have been a

different event from the one that did occur (Lewis 2000, p. 185; see also Lewis 1986a, p. 197).[12] This may seem plausible, since the counterfactual shattering clearly would have occurred differently from the actual one; specifically, the counterfactual shattering would have occurred later than the actual shattering.

2.2   The Standard Reply

Lewis responds to this suggestion by saying that it presupposes extremely stringent criteria for the transworld identity of events: In the terminology popularized by Lewis, it takes events to be modally *fragile*. An event is fragile, in this sense, if, or to the extent that, it could not have occurred differently.[13] Lewis offers two arguments against extreme fragility. First, it seems evident that we can engage in counterfactual suppositions in which an actual event occurs very differently; so, it seems, we ordinarily suppose that events are reasonably robust.[14] Second, when combined with counterfactual analyses of causation, extreme fragility would imply the falsehood that events are caused by anything that even slightly affects them.[15] Common sense seems clear that there is a distinction between affecting an event and causing it, and supposing events to be too modally fragile would rob us of this distinction.

2.3   A New Suggestion

I think the appropriate response to both of these arguments is to concede that not all events are fragile and, specifically, that there is an event that is a legitimate candidate for being called "the shattering" that is sufficiently robust that, had Suzy not thrown, it would still have occurred. I think there is another event, however, that is an equally legitimate candidate for being called "the shattering," which is sufficiently fragile that it would not have occurred without Suzy's throw. The fragile shattering is caused by Suzy's throw, and is counterfactually dependent on it. The robust shattering is not caused by Suzy's throw, and is not counterfactually dependent on it: Rather, the robust shattering is caused by the combination of Suzy's and Billy's throws, and is counterfactually dependent on this combination. On neither interpretation do we have a counterexample to the naive counterfactual analysis of causation.[16]

Objection 1: There is obviously only one shattering in this example.

Reply: Lewis's own arguments against extreme fragility suggest that there are both fragile and robust shatterings. Furthermore, a plurality of shatterings is not really a problem, if we can also defend a sense in which there is only one. I will do so.

Although it is true, as Lewis points out in his first argument against extreme fragility, that we can make counterfactual suppositions according to which an actually occurring event would have occurred at a quite different time, or in a quite different manner, we can also often (and perhaps always) make a qualitatively identical sup-position according to which it would have been a different event that occurs at that time and in that manner. Lewis gives the following example of this phenomenon:

> You can say: the performance should have been postponed until the singer was over his laryngitis; then it would have been better. You can just as well say, and mean nothing differ-ent: the performance should have been cancelled, and another, which would have been better, scheduled to replace it. There's no right answer to the question how fragile the performance is. (Lewis 1986a, p. 197)

Or rather, there is more than one right answer, because there is a fragile perfor-mance, which could not have occurred very differently, and there is a robust perfor-mance, which could. Both are permissible referents of "the performance."

These performances are logically related; the fragile performance *implies* the ro-bust performance.[17] Elsewhere, Lewis has explicitly argued that some events imply other events, and that a natural language description may refer to the implying event in some contexts, and to the implied event in others (Lewis 1986d, p. 255). I will follow Michael McDermott in calling this position "the profligate theory of events" (McDermott 1995a, pp. 531–532).[18] Lewis's argument for it can be understood as a natural development of his second argument against extreme fragility.[19] That argu-ment invited us to draw conclusions about the fragility of events from our considered beliefs about what caused them. As Lewis recognizes, however, our considered causal beliefs about what we are inclined pretheoretically to call a single event may vary, depending, as he puts it, on how fragile we *take* the event to be (Lewis 1986a, p. 197; 2000, p. 186).[20] Sometimes, this will depend on how detailed the expression used to denote the event is.[21] Sometimes the same natural language expression can be used to refer, in different contexts, to either fragile or robust *versions* of the event.[22]

In either case, so long as we are committed to the idea that causation is a relation between events, we need events that imply other events, in order to accommodate the kind of fine-grained causal judgments we actually make. Without them we would not be able to distinguish the question "What caused the bottle to shatter?" from the question "What caused it to shatter at the particular time it did?"[23] Surely these are different questions; surely an adequate theory of causation should be able to distin-guish them.

An adequate theory of causation, in this respect, is like an adequate theory of probability, and, for a closely related reason, standard probability theory is also committed to what seems pretheoretically to be too many events. I throw a single die, for example, and get a two; I also get an even number. To speak of "the outcome" of this probability experiment (without specifying a sample space) is to speak ambigu-ously.[24] One may be referring to the relatively fragile *event* of getting a two, or the relatively robust one of getting an even number, even though we are strongly inclined to say that *these* are the same event. If the profligate theory of events is committed to invidious double-counting, so is standard probability theory.

It may be replied that this shows only that standard probability theory is wrong to treat probabilities as attributes of events, and that a great deal of philosophical literature is equally wrong to treat causation as a relation between events. In fact, it is partly our ability to understand causal propositions of differing degrees and kinds of specificity that has led some philosophers to deny that causation, at least in its most fundamental sense, is a relation between events.[25] It has been suggested that it is instead a relation between aspects of events, or between events-in-contrast-to-alternatives, or between facts (see respectively Paul 2000; Hitchcock 1996b; Bennett 1988).

I suggest that we should say instead that what is, in one sense, a single event, may, in another sense, be many; there is one for each of the shifting judgments about *its* causes that we want to make.[26] It is a familiar kind of paradox: "Fred's house taken as including the garage, and taken as not including the garage, have equal claim to be his house. The claim had better be good enough, else he has no house. So Fred has two houses. No!" (Lewis 1999, p. 180).[27] In fact, Lewis allows that there is *some* sense in which Fred has two houses, but he also recognizes the need to articulate a sense in which he has just one. To do this he borrows van Fraassen's strategy for dealing with unmade semantic decisions: We may say a statement is *super-true* iff it is true on all interpretations; it is *super-false* iff it is false on all interpretations; it has a *super-truth-value-gap* iff it is true on some interpretations and false on others (van Fraassen, 1966).

Super-truth occupies the role in a less than fully interpreted language that truth simpliciter occupies in a fully interpreted language: It is that at which honest speakers aim. So we are entitled to say that Fred has only one house, because it is super-true that Fred has only one house, that is, it is true on each interpretation of "house." Similarly, I can agree with common sense that there is only one bottle shattering, since it is super-true, that is, true on each interpretation of "the shattering," that there is only one of them.

Even if you are unconvinced by van Fraassen's approach, I do not see any reason to suppose that the profligate theory of events gives us any problems we didn't already have. A new example of an old problem is not a new problem.

Objection 2: This position does not do justice to the intuition that Suzy's throw caused the shattering.

Reply: I think it does, because not only does it grant that there is a sense in which this intuition is accurate, it is also consistent with the position that anyone who asserts that Suzy's throw caused the shattering is asserting something true. In defense of this claim I can do no better than quote Lewis on a closely related issue:

There is a rule of accommodation: what you say makes itself true, if at all possible, by creating a context that selects the relevant features so as to make it true. Say that France is hexagonal, and you thereby set the standards of precision low, and you speak the truth; say that France is not hexagonal ... and you set the standards high, and again you speak the truth. In parallel fashion, I suggest that those philosophers who preach that origins are essential are absolutely right—in the context of their own preaching. They make themselves right: their preaching constitutes a context in which *de re* modality is governed by a way of representing ... that requires match of origins.   (Lewis 1986e, pp. 251–252)

In parallel fashion, I suggest that the philosophers who say that Suzy's throw caused the shattering are right—in the context created by what they say. Thus I think I do justice to this intuition, despite there being a sense in which it is mistaken.

My position requires there to be contexts in which Suzy's throw would not count as a cause of the shattering. This seems to be true of contexts in which we have no detailed interest in when the bottle shatters. I submit that in such contexts we should deny that Suzy's throw caused it, since it would have occurred anyway.

Objection 3: Suppose Billy's throw had some slight influence on the time or manner of the shattering, thus causing a very fragile shattering. My account would then imply, contrary to intuition, that there is a sense in which Billy's throw is a cause of the shattering.

Reply: I do not think this is a problem. There is no danger of losing the obvious causal asymmetry between Billy's throw and Suzy's throw. Both may both be causes of the shattering according to very stringent standards of fragility; neither will be causes according to very robust standards of fragility; but according to ordinary standards of fragility, Suzy's throw will be a cause and Billy's will not. I think this does justice to the intuition that Billy's throw is, and Suzy's throw is not, a cause of the shattering *simpliciter*.

Objection 4: It is not an essential feature of this example that there be any time difference between the shattering that occurred with Suzy's throw and the shattering that would have occurred without Suzy's throw. Suppose, for example, that if not for Suzy's throw, Billy would have thrown harder or earlier than he actually does, in which case the bottle would have shattered at the same time it actually did.[28]

Reply: Just as we can distinguish the question "What causes the bottle to shatter?" from the question "What causes the bottle to shatter at the particular time it does?" we can also distinguish both these questions from the question "What causes the bottle to shatter in the particular way it does?" I submit that we can defend the intuition that Suzy's throw causes the bottle shattering in these circumstances, if

"Suzy's throw" is a correct answer to the third question, even if it is not a correct answer to the first two.

Objection 5: Suppose the bottle was valuable, and that later in the day its owner was disappointed to discover that it had shattered. The intuition that Suzy's throw caused the disappointment is, if not as strong as the intuition that it caused the shattering, then almost as strong. There is no need, however, to suppose that there was any difference (temporal or otherwise) between the disappointment that occurred with Suzy's throw and the one that would have occurred without it.

Reply: I think there are two reasonable responses to this challenge. The first tries to respect the intuition that Suzy's throw is, and Billy's throw is not, a cause of the disappointment. The second tries to explain the intuition away. Which response is best will depend on context.

To respect the intuition that Suzy's, but not Billy's, throw is a cause of the disappointment, I must identify the actual disappointment with the one that would have occurred without Billy's throw, but not with the one that would have occurred without Suzy's throw. I can justify doing so by appealing to the fact that the former pair of events (actual disappointment, disappointment without Billy's throw) have a common history that the latter pair (actual disappointment, disappointment without Suzy's throw) lack.

Many Lewiseans will reject this approach because of the extrinsic identity conditions of the postulated disappointment. Lewis and Maudlin have argued that such *extrinsic* events should be treated with suspicion, because they appear to stand in relations of noncausal counterfactual dependence (Lewis 1986d, pp. 263–264; Maudlin 1994, p. 128). If Oedipus had not killed Laius, Jocasta would not have been widowed; but does that mean that the killing caused the widowing? "We do not want to waste our time on such *scheinprobleme* as exactly when Jocasta became a widow (instantaneously in some preferred reference frame? When she intersects the light cone of the murder?) ... If this is superluminal causation, it is not the sort to be of any concern" (Maudlin 1994, p. 128). Maudlin suggests that the way to avoid such *scheinprobleme* is to restrict the analysis of causation to "local physical events." We need not be persuaded by this reasoning. We could instead say that the killing does not cause the widowing because they are not distinct events, rather than because the latter is not local.

Suppose you remain suspicious of extrinsic events, or are convinced that the disappointment that appears to be caused by Suzy's throw is not one of them. Another approach to this kind of example is suggested by Lewis himself in a passage in which he considers whether it is plausible to eliminate redundant causation altogether by taking events to be extremely fragile (i.e., the common suggestion). He rejects one possible objection:

Suppose we did follow this strategy wherever we could. Wouldn't we still have residual cases of redundancy, in which it makes *absolutely* no difference to the effect whether both of the redundant causes occur or only one? Maybe so; but probably those residual cases would be mere possibilities, far-fetched and contrary to the ways of this world. Then we could happily leave them as spoils to the victor. For we could plausibly suggest that commonsense is misled: its habits of thought are formed by a world where every little thing that happens spreads its little traces far and wide, and nothing that happens thereafter is quite the same as it would have been after a different past.   (Lewis 1986a, pp. 197–198)

If this were right, then we could assume that the absence of Suzy's throw would have made some difference to the shattering, even though no such difference is explicitly mentioned in the story.

If Suzy's throw were to make no difference at all to the shattering, I think we are entitled to dismiss any inclination we have to think of it as still being a cause as mistaken, this mistake being the product of a persistent (though in this case erroneous) assumption that the shattering would have occurred somewhat differently, if not for it.

3   Ambiguity about the Identity of "the Cause"

The strategy I have outlined so far will not be applicable to every putative example of preemption in which it appears that the absence of the so-called preempting cause would have made little or no difference to the time or manner of the effect. Lewis attributes the following example of *trumping* preemption to van Fraassen:

The Sergeant and the Major are shouting orders at the soldiers. The soldiers know that in case of conflict, they must obey the superior officer. But, as it happens, there is no conflict. Sergeant and Major simultaneously shout "Advance!"; the soldiers hear them both; the soldiers advance. Their advancing is redundantly caused: if the Sergeant had shouted "Advance!" and the Major had been silent, or if the Major had shouted "Advance!" and the Sergeant had been silent, the soldiers would still have advanced. But the redundancy is asymmetrical: since the soldiers obey the superior officer, they advance because the Major orders them to, not because the Sergeant does. The Major preempts the Sergeant in causing them to advance.   (Lewis 2000, p. 183)[29]

Rather than appealing to the fragility of "the effect" to respect the intuition that the Major's order is, and the Sergeant's order is not, a cause, I will appeal to the fragility of "the cause," that is, the fragility of the Major's order.

The profligate theory of events allows us to distinguish two orders shouted by the Major; the more robust one is essentially an order, but only accidentally an order-to-advance (it would still have occurred had the Major shouted a different order); the more fragile one is essentially an order-to-advance. The robust one is not a cause of the soldiers' advance, since to suppose it not to have occurred is to suppose that the Major shouted no order at all, in which case the Sergeant's order would have been effective.

But, I claim, the fragile version of the Major's order does cause the soldiers' advance: If the fragile version of the Major's order had not occurred, the soldiers would not have advanced. This seems to follow from familiar possible worlds semantics for counterfactuals, according to which counterfactuals are true iff the *nearest* possible worlds in which the antecedent is true are also worlds in which the consequent is true. The nearest worlds in which the Major's fragile order does not occur are not worlds in which he shouts no order, but worlds in which he shouts a different order. In such worlds the soldiers would not have advanced, since they would still have obeyed the Major. This gives us a sense in which the Major's order caused the soldiers' advance. By contrast, even an extremely fragile version of the Sergeant's order did not cause the soldiers' advance, since that advance would have been unchanged (or close enough) by him either shouting a different order or none at all.

Yet again my position is inspired by Lewis himself. He once argued that a robust version of a greeting, but not a fragile version of the same greeting, may cause a reply, because the nearest worlds in which the fragile one does not occur are worlds in which the robust one still does (Lewis 1986d, p. 255).[30] Lewis no longer seems to accept this kind of reasoning. He now claims that to suppose a cause not to have occurred is to suppose it to be "completely and cleanly excised from history, leaving behind no fragment or approximation of itself" (Lewis 2000, p. 190). The naive analysis will have difficulty reconciling Lewis's new position with the intuition, which I mentioned earlier, that the closing of a door may prevent someone from entering a room whereas the slamming of the door (which implies the closing) does not. Lewis's earlier position and mine accommodate the variability of our considered judgments about the effects of what seems pretheoretically to be a single event.[31]

Objection 1: Worlds in which the Major shouts no order will, all else being equal, be closer to the world of this example than worlds in which he shouts a different order. This is because the closest worlds in which the Major shouts no order are, like the world of the example, worlds in which the soldiers advance; whereas the closest worlds in which the Major shouts a different order will, unlike the world of the example, be worlds in which the soldiers do not advance.

Reply: The objection assumes, and I agree, that closeness is something like similarity. Similarity, after the time of the antecedent, however, should play little or no role in our calculations. Otherwise we would have to say that if Nixon had pressed the button, nuclear war would have been avoided (see Lewis 1986a, pp. 43–48). I am inclined to agree with Jonathan Bennett that similarity at the time of the antecedent is the only relevant similarity (Bennett 1984, pp. 72–74). Surely, all else being equal, a world in which the Major shouts just about any order is, at that time, more like a world in which he shouts an order to advance than to a world in which he shouts no order at all.

Objection 2: Suppose the Major very much wanted the soldiers to advance, but hesitated to order them to do so, because he does not like giving orders.[32] Arguably, in this situation, the nearest possible worlds in which a fragile version of his order does not occur are ones in which he gives no order, since it appears that the change required for there to be a different order would be greater than the change required for there to be no order.

Reply: In this situation the relevant version of the Major's order—the one that does the causing—would be not only essentially an order to advance, but also one that was essentially given by someone who does not like giving orders. If it had not occurred, a sufficiently fragile version of the soldiers' advance would not have occurred either.

4   Conclusion

Lewis recognizes that questions about the fragility of what seems pretheoretically to be a single event need not have a determinate answer. This feature of his thought has been largely ignored in the philosophical literature influenced by his work on causation.

One of the many places in which it plays a role is his discussion of what he calls "a class of cases distinguished by doubt as to whether they exhibit redundancy at all" (Lewis 1986a, p. 195). He asks us to suppose, for example, that neurons c_1 and c_2 are set up in such a way that, if fired, they will stimulate neuron e to fire, and that neuron e will fire more vigorously if it is stimulated by both neurons, than if it is stimulated by just one. In fact, both c_1 and c_2 fire, doubly stimulating e, which fires vigorously:

Is this vigorous firing of e a different event from the feeble firing that would have occurred if either one of c_1 and c_2 had fired alone? Then we have joint causation, in which the effect depends counterfactually on each of the causes, and there is no redundancy. Or is it that numerically the same firing would have occurred, despite a difference in manner, with single stimulation? (Lewis 1986a, p. 196)

Lewis's answer is that it "is hard to say." He adds that "the difficulty cannot be blamed on underdescription of the details" (ibid.). He does not blame the difficulty on our epistemic faculties either; we do not have to resign ourselves to not knowing whether this is a case of redundant causation. Rather, he suggests that "there may be no right answer" (ibid., 197). Perhaps a better way to put his point, however, is to say that there is no wrong answer. I think Lewis would agree with me, that we can say that this is a case of redundant causation or we can say that it is a case of joint causation without redundancy, preferably on different occasions, and either way we will be right. As Lewis has pointed out, by saying something the truth of which depends on context, we can often create a context that makes it true.

If I am right, putative cases of preemption are also cases distinguished by doubt as to whether they exhibit redundancy. In the example under consideration the indeterminacy is between symmetrical overdetermination and joint causation, whereas the relevant indeterminacy in putative cases of preemption is between symmetrical overdetermination and causation by the so-called preempting cause.[33]

It is a tribute to the profound influence of David Lewis's work on the study of metaphysics in general, and causation in particular, that there is such widespread acceptance of the position that the most straightforward counterfactual analysis of causation breaks down in cases of preemption. The real explanation, however, for what I have argued is a mistake, are the ways in which putative cases of preemption are represented—ways that make it natural to conflate different (though not distinct) events. I have tried to show how natural language can conflate logically related events. If I am right, the neuron diagrams popularized by Lewis do so as well.

I do not claim to have proven that my position is correct. If anyone continues to believe that one or more cases of preemption are genuine, that is, that they really do represent a situation in which an effect does not depend counterfactually on one of its causes, then I do not know how to convince them. But I hope I have at least undermined the popular notion that it is obvious that the naive counterfactual analysis of causation is refuted by cases in which a causal proposition is true, even though its corresponding counterfactual is not.

Acknowledgments

I thank Hartry Field, without whom this article would have been very different in time and manner (i.e., later and worse), and David Lewis, without whom not even a very robust version of it could have occurred at all.

Notes

1. Participants in this debate, other than Lewis, include Tim Maudlin, Paul Horwich, Jonathan Bennett, David Armstrong, Martin Bunzl, Douglas Ehring, Michael McDermott, Richard Miller, Murali Ramachandran, L. A. Paul, Paul Noordhof, Alex Byrne, Ned Hall, Jonathan Schaffer, Bruce LeCatt, William Goosens, Judea Pearl, and others. See the references for those who have published on this subject.

2. This is historically related to one of Hume's analyses of causation. The form of the analyzing counterfactual used by him, however, was "if the first object had not been, the second never had existed" (*An Enquiry Concerning Human Understanding*, section VII). I doubt that this difference is philosophically significant. The problems with his *regularity* analysis are another story about another body of literature. I think general causal propositions, like "Smoking causes lung cancer" may also be analyzed in counterfactual terms, but that too is another story about another body of literature.

3. Suppose the slamming, but not the closing, is caused by bad temper; and that the closing, but not the slamming, causes someone to be unable to enter. (See Goldman 1970, p. 3.)

4. In fact, it is an implication of Lewis's theory of events that the closing and the slamming may well have a common part, in virtue of the latter literally being a part of the former. Unfortunately Lewis's theory of events has ontological commitments (i.e., unactual entities) that many, myself included, do not accept. (See Lewis 1986d.)

5. Strictly speaking, Lewis (or at least a temporal part of him) would not disagree. He would claim, however, that such counterfactuals are true only on a nonstandard interpretation that is irrelevant to the analysis of causation. (See Lewis 1986c.)

6. I assume Horwich would agree.

7. For the sake of clarity I am interpreting "backtracking counterfactual" more narrowly than does Lewis, from whom I take the terminology. A backtracker, for me, is a counterfactual that asserts that if an event had not occurred, then neither would one of its causes; an effects-of-a-common-cause counterfactual is one that asserts that if one of a pair of events with a common cause had not occurred, then neither would the other; a causal counterfactual is one that asserts that if an event had not occurred, then neither would one of its effects.

8. Lewis takes this to be redundant causation in its simplest form. He passes over other kinds of redundant causation. One example of another alleged kind of redundant causation is "probabilistic redundant causation." I think of putative cases of this phenomenon as situations in which there is a certain probability of redundant causation *simpliciter*, rather than as situations exhibiting a special type of probabilistic redundant causation. This will not be relevant to my discussion.

9. The mode of composition could be mereological or set-theoretical.

10. It is convenient to think of preemption as *asymmetrical redundancy*, and to think of symmetrical overdetermination as *symmetrical redundancy*. My position is that all redundancy is symmetrical.

11. According to Lewis's original taxonomy of preemption, this would be *late* preemption, since the preempted process is cut off by the effect itself. Lewis no longer thinks that preemption requires the preempted process to be *cut* (whether by the effect or otherwise); it is clear, however, that most, if not all, realistic examples of it do involve cutting. This issue is not relevant to my approach.

12. Lewis calls this a "common suggestion" in "Causation." His response to it remains unchanged in "Causation as Influence."

13. I will say that an event is *robust* if, or to the extent that, it is not fragile. The distinction between fragility and robustness can also be drawn in terms of essences; a fragile event has a rich essence, whereas a robust event has an impoverished essence.

14. Of particular relevance to the example under consideration is our ability to engage in counterfactual suppositions in which an actually occurring event is delayed.

15. Lewis attributes this argument against extreme fragility to Ken Kress. It has been extremely popular. Peter Menzies has argued against extreme fragility by appealing to the undesirability of treating an

explosion at the center of the sun, which produces a neutron, which in turn passes through a person's body as she dies, as a cause of her death (Menzies 1989a, 649). Jonathan Bennett has cited in support of the same conclusion the unacceptability of supposing that Plato's wiping of Socrates' brow just before Socrates died was a cause of his death (Bennett 1988, p. 65).

16. It should become increasingly clear how my approach is intended to apply to other putative cases of preemption in the literature.

17. For the sake of simplicity, I interpret the concept of *implication between events* more broadly than does Lewis, from whom I take the terminology. I say that event *e* implies event *f* iff, the proposition that *e* occurs implies the proposition that *f* occurs; in other words, every possible world in which *e* occurs is a world in which *f* occurs. The difference between our concepts of implication between events is not relevant to my argument.

18. McDermott does not explicitly define profligacy, but I think my definition conforms closely to his usage. McDermott does not approve of profligacy. He claims that "Lewis seems to find the profligate theory of events an embarrassment." I do not believe this is true; but I do think that Lewis's discussion of preemption fails to do justice to its implications.

19. I endorse the following argument, whether or not it is Lewis's.

20. Lewis and I disagree, however, about the extent of this indeterminacy. He claims, for example, that Ned Kelly would have died a different death, if not for being hanged (Lewis 2000, p. 185). I think it all depends on context. One can imagine Kelly consoling himself for his premature death with the thought that it would have happened eventually anyway, thus taking his death to be extremely robust.

21. Kim's example of a slamming that is also a closing illustrates this phenomenon.

22. Lewis has argued that John's tension may cause a relatively fragile greeting that is essentially too loud, and not cause a relatively robust version of the same event that is only accidentally too loud. Furthermore, he suggests that the expression "John's 'Hello'" may refer to the fragile version in some contexts, and the robust one in others (Lewis 1986d, p. 255).

23. There do seem to be contexts in which they would be the same question. In particular, the former question could be an abbreviation of the latter. I think, however, that the distinction I'm speaking of is clear, and of a familiar kind.

24. Just as, on my account, to speak of "the bottle shattering," without contextual guidance, is to speak ambiguously.

25. Another reason is that unchanging states, as well as what we would ordinarily think of as events seem, at least sometimes, to cause and be caused. A third reason is that the failure of an event to occur can, at least sometimes, appear to cause and be caused. I think unchanges and omissions should both be treated as kinds of events, but that is yet another story about yet another body of literature.

26. There may also be some that we do not want to make for pragmatic reasons.

27. I use so many examples from Lewis's own work because I like them, but also because I want to persuade him that he should adopt my approach. So far I have been unsuccessful.

28. This has now become a case of *early* preemption, in which the preempted process is cut off by a branch process diverging from the process that connects the preempting cause with the effect. This contrasts with late preemption in which the preempted process is cut off by the effect itself. In this case the branch process would be the flow of information by which Billy becomes aware that Suzy will throw. This causes him to throw later or less forcefully than he otherwise would have.

29. Jonathan Schaffer is responsible for the term "trumping." Like Lewis, he has discussed this example as a possible case of it (Schaffer 2000b). This would qualify as a case of trumping, in Lewis's and Schaffer's sense, only if no cutting (early or late) takes place in it. The alleged possibility of this is not relevant to my approach. I think Schaffer's other putative example of trumping preemption should get similar treatment.

30. Jonathan Bennett seems to be reasoning in the same way when he says that, on the counterfactual analysis, an extremely fragile death of Socrates would not have caused Plato to grieve (Bennett 1988, p. 65).

31. This is similar to the way in which, as we have seen, the profligate theory of events, when combined with the naive analysis, accommodates the variability of our considered judgments about the causes of what seems pretheoretically to be a single event.

32. Hartry Field has pointed out this possibility to me.

33. There may also be a legitimate (if nonstandard) sense in which putative cases of preemption exhibit joint causation.

14 Causes, Contrasts, and the Nontransitivity of Causation

Cei Maslen

1 Introduction

Whether one event causes another depends on the contrast situation with which the alleged cause is compared. Occasionally this is made explicit. For example, a toothpaste company claims that regular brushing with their product will cause teeth to become up to two shades whiter than brushing with "another leading brand." Here, the comparison not only helps to specify a range of shades of white, but also to specify a contrast situation. Regular brushing with their product is not compared with, say, irregular brushing with their product or not brushing at all, but with regular brushing with another leading brand.

More often the contrast situation is not made explicit, but is clear from the context. Hence, in general, the truth and meaning of causal statements depend on the context in which they occur. In section 2, I give a more complete formulation of this claim, illustrate it with an example, and compare it with similar and superficially similar views. The theory is incomplete without a description of how contrast events are fixed by the context, which I supply in section 3. In section 4, I discuss the context-dependence of counterfactuals. Of course, a major motivation for the theory is the extent to which it can avoid obstacles that have defeated other theories of causation, problems such as the nontransitivity of causation, preemption, causation by absences, and causation under indeterminism. In section 5, I explain how a contrastive counterfactual account solves the first of these problems: analyzing the nontransitivity of causation.[1]

2 A Contrastive Counterfactual Account

Causal statements are systematically dependent on context.[2] The meaning and truth conditions of causal statements are dependent on contrast events that are seldom explicitly stated, but are fixed by conversational context and charity of interpretation. Occasionally confusion about contrast events leads to misunderstandings and indeterminacy of meaning and truth value. This may be expected when causal statements are taken out of context, for example, in some philosophical discussions.

This isn't to make causation a subjective matter. The causal structure of the world is an objective, mind-independent three-place relation in the world between causes, contrasts, and effects. (Compare this with discovering that motion is relative to frame of reference. This is not to discover that motion a subjective matter.)

It would perhaps be ideal to study the properties of causal statements (e.g., nontransitivity and context-dependence) without appealing to a specific formal analysis of our concept of causation. All formal analyses of causation are controversial, and complicated. The claims that causation is context dependent and that it is nontransitive are partly independent of any specific analysis. However, in practice it is impossible to have detailed discussions of these aspects without settling on one analysis. The few philosophers who discuss the context-dependence view can be classified into all the major schools of thought on causation. Hitchcock[3] incorporates it into a probability-raising account. Field[4] discusses probabilistic and nonprobabilistic versions of a regularity or law-based view. Holland[5] presents a counterfactual account. I support a counterfactual account also, and I concentrate on singular causal claims.

2.1 Account₁

For distinct events c, c^* and e, c is a cause of e relative to contrast event c^* iff c and e actually happened and if c had not happened, but contrast event c^* had happened instead, then e would not have happened.

This account takes events as the fundamental causal relata. Either Kim's or Lewis's definitions of events would serve this purpose.[6] My hope is that causal sentences with other kinds of relata (physical objects, processes, facts, properties, or event aspects) can be reexpressed in terms of event causation, but I will not argue for this claim here.[7] I discuss counterfactuals briefly in section 4 below. I think that our intuitive understanding of this grammatical form is strong, so I do not commit myself to an analysis here.[8]

The only restrictions I place on the contrast event is that it be compossible with the absence of the cause and distinct from the absence of the cause.[9] I also require that the cause, effect, and contrast event be distinct events.[10] This may seem hopelessly liberal. What is to stop someone from claiming that brushing my teeth this morning, in contrast to being hit by a meteorite, was a cause of my good humor, or that the price of eggs being low, in contrast to the open fire having a safety guard, was a cause of the child's burn? The inanity of these examples arises from inappropriate contrast events. Describing appropriateness of contrast is a difficult task, and I have little more to say about it at this stage than that events are usually contrasted with events that occur at a similar time, and that might have replaced them.[11]

Let's assume that any complex of events (the event that occurs just in case the constituent events occur) is itself an event. It will be useful to define a *contrast situation* as the complex of a contrast event and the event in which the absence of the cause consisted.[12] With this terminology, account₁ is:

Event c is a cause of event e relative to a contrast situation iff had the contrast situation happened, then e would not have happened.

There may also be explicit and implicit alternatives to the effect. For example, a friend's opinions were a cause of my renting the video *Annie Hall* rather than the video *Mighty Aphrodite*. Account$_1$ can be generalized in the following way to allow for contrasts to the effect and for a range of implicit contrasts. (However, I will mostly continue to work with the simpler account$_1$.)

2.2 Account$_2$

Event c, relative to contrast situations $\{c^*\}$, is a cause of event e, relative to contrast situations $\{e^*\}$, iff had any events from $\{c^*\}$ occurred, then an event from $\{e^*\}$ would have occurred.[13]

2.3 Illustrations

Here are two examples to illustrate the context-dependence of causation. First, suppose I have recipes for three cookies: hazelnut cookies, walnut cookies, and pecan cookies. I decide to make hazelnut cookies, and then I offer one to Stuart. Unfortunately Stuart has a nut allergy; he is allergic to all nuts. He eats the cookie and becomes ill. Was making the hazelnut cookies one of the causes of his illness?

Well, if I hadn't made the hazelnut cookies I would have made the pecan cookies, because I have only three cookie recipes and I have no walnuts in the house. So in one sense, making the hazelnut cookies was not a cause of his illness: Relative to making pecan cookies, making hazelnut cookies was not a cause of his illness. However, relative to the alternative of making no cookies at all, making the hazelnut cookies was a cause of his illness. Taken out of context, there is no correct answer to the question of whether making hazelnut cookies was a cause of Stuart's illness. Out of context, the only valid claims we can make are relative claims. However, the conversational context and unspoken assumptions can make some alternatives more salient than others. Our awareness that I have only nut cookie recipes makes the alternatives of baking pecan cookies and walnut cookies salient alternatives for us, and in the context of this paper the causal claim "making hazelnut cookies was a cause of his illness" is naturally interpreted as meaning "making hazelnut cookies, relative to making pecan cookies or walnut cookies, was a cause of his illness."

The second example, of an electric circuit, comes from Daniel Hausman, though he uses it for a different purpose:

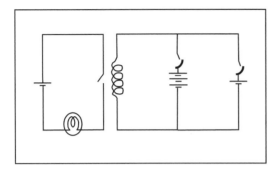

Figure 14.1

The "weak circuit" and the "strong circuit" power a solenoid switch, which closes the "bulb circuit." If only the weak circuit is closed, the current through the solenoid is 4 amperes. If only the strong circuit is closed, the current through the solenoid is 12 amperes. If both are closed, about 16 amperes flow through the solenoid. It takes 6 amperes to activate the solenoid switch, close the bulb circuit, and turn on the light bulb. Whether the weak circuit is closed or not affects how much current is flowing through the solenoid, but it has no influence on whether the light goes on.[14]

Suppose that on this occasion, I close both the strong and the weak circuit, a current of 16 amperes flows through the coil, the solenoid switch closes, and the bulb lights. Was the presence of a current of 16 amperes through the coil a cause of the bulb lighting? The answer to this question is relative to the contrast event.

16 amperes flowing through the coil, rather than 12 amperes flowing through the coil, was *not* a cause of the bulb's lighting.

16 amperes flowing through the coil, rather than 4 amperes flowing through the coil, was a cause of the bulb's lighting.

16 amperes flowing through the coil, rather than 0 amperes flowing through the coil, was a cause of the bulb's lighting.

The fact that there are cases like these, where the context-dependence is clear, gives excellent support to the context-dependence view.

2.4   Other Views
At this point, it will be helpful to compare account$_2$ with similar and superficially similar views.

I am not proposing a revisionary account of causation. The realization that causation is context dependent and that this can lead to misunderstandings might prompt us to propose a revisionary account of causation. We could suggest that in the future, to avoid misunderstandings in precise or important uses of causal claims, we should always state alternative events together with our causal claims. We could even follow Bertrand Russell in suggesting that we abandon the concept of causation altogether.[15] Instead we would use only precise counterfactuals with our assumptions spelled out. But the state of our causal concept does not warrant such an extreme reaction.

The context-dependence that I have described in the concept of "a cause" is additional to the generally accepted context-dependence of "the cause" or "the decisive cause." I am concerned here only with what it takes to be "a cause" or "one of the causes" of a given effect. The context-dependence of the concept of "the cause" is more obvious. It might be suspected that there is only one source of context dependence here and that is from the concept of "the cause." It could be argued that we confuse "a cause" with "the cause" when we read the examples, and this is why we find them convincing. However, this simply isn't borne out by our intuitions. We do have an additional contextual element here.

The context-dependence of causation is distinct from the widely accepted view that explanation is context dependent. Van Fraassen is the major defender of the latter view: "If, as I'm inclined to agree, counterfactual language is proper to explanation, we should conclude that explanation harbors a significant degree of context-dependence."[16] He argues that the context-dependence of explanation takes the form of determining both the salience of explanatory factors and also the contrast class. However, those who claim that explanation is dependent on context assume that causation is independent of context. For example, it seems to be implied by van Fraassen's claims that the propositions of the causal net are scientific propositions and "scientific propositions are not context-dependent in any essential way"[17] that causal statements are (essentially) independent of context. I disagree; both explanation and causation are context dependent.

Account$_2$ is similar in many ways to Lewis's recent "causation as influence" view and to event-feature views of causation, for example, Paul's "aspect causation" view. I do not have space to discuss all the similarities and differences here. However, note that all three views imply that causal statements are strongly context dependent. Lewis talks of "a substantial range of not-too-distant alterations" of the cause; what constitutes a *substantial* range and what constitute *not-too-distant* alterations of the cause presumably differ with context. Event-feature views require the context to determine event features from event nominalizations.

3   Contrast Events and Context

The context of a statement is the circumstances in which it occurs. The truth of a statement may depend on features of the context as well as on matters of fact. Dependence on matters of fact is contingency; dependence on features of context is context-dependence. Following the two-stage scheme of Stalnaker, we may say that an interpreted sentence together with a context determines a proposition, and a proposition together with a possible world determines a truth value.[18] Hence, which proposition is expressed by an interpreted sentence may depend on the context in which it occurs. A classic example of a context-dependent sentence is "I went to the store"; its interpretation depends on the identity of the speaker, owing to the indexical "I."[19]

In general, a large variety of contextual features may be required to interpret a sentence on a particular occasion, for example, "the intentions of the speaker, the knowledge, beliefs, expectations, or interests of the speaker and his audience, other speech acts that have been performed in the same context, the time of utterance, the effects of the utterance, the truth-value of the proposition expressed, the semantic relations between the proposition expressed and some others involved in some way."[20] Features of context such as speaker and time of utterance are almost always obvious and readily observable. The set of contrast events is a theoretical feature of context; hence, we owe a description of how contrast events connect with more obvious features of context. Otherwise, when disputes arise it might seem as though the metaphysician is magically summoning the set of contrast events or choosing the set to fit her case.

Suppose that the contrast event is what the speaker has in mind for replacing the cause. That is, it is what the speaker has in mind to be different in an imagined counterfactual situation where the cause is removed. Two objections to this immediately arise. Firstly, unphilosophical speakers may not have anything of the right sort in mind when uttering causal statements. When asked what they had in mind, many speakers may admit that they hadn't thought about it. However, usually these speakers have no problem responding with a contrast event when prompted. These responses give the intended interpretation of the original causal statement, in some sense of "intended." Second, as we are not mind readers, if the "have in mind" picture were the whole story then communication would be very haphazard.

The rest of the story is that which contrast set the speaker has in mind, if not communicated directly, may be clear to the audience by the previous course of the conversation, acknowledged assumptions, limitations, plans, and presuppositions. General pragmatic principles play a large part in this. The set of contrast events is what Lewis calls a "component of conversational score."[21] We have a tendency to interpret utterances generously or charitably, as true or probable, relevant, useful, and informative. The set of contrast events is fixed and developed through the course of the conversation. Sometimes the set is left unsettled or vague until a dispute arises. In a few cases this vagueness even leads to ambiguity in the causal statement.

Often there are physical limitations on the ways in which the cause could have been omitted. This gives us a "default" set of contrast events. Consider the following example. My opponent and I are both very competitive. We each would have been happy to win, but we are both unhappy when we reach a draw at chess.

Reaching a draw at chess was a cause of us both being unhappy.

Presuming that we finish the chess game, there are only two ways in which the event of reaching a draw could have been omitted: by my winning the game, or by my opponent winning the game. Hence, there are two natural interpretations of the causal statement: "Reaching a draw at chess, in contrast to my winning the game, was a cause of us both being unhappy"; and "Reaching a draw at chess, in contrast to your winning the game, was a cause of us both being unhappy."

Either of these alternative outcomes would have left one of us happy. Hence, reaching a draw can truly be called a cause of us both being unhappy. The natural set of contrasts here are the events in which the absence of the cause would have consisted. Given our assumption that we did actually finish the chess game, the absence could only have consisted in my winning the game, or my opponent's winning the game.

In some cases, there is only one probable way in which the cause would have been omitted, and this is the natural or default contrast. Suppose that my opponent is a much better chess player than I. If we hadn't reached a draw, he would almost certainly have won. Given our assumptions, the contrast situation here is naturally limited to one alternative. The following causal claim is probably true in that context.

Reaching a draw on the chess game was a cause of my opponent being unhappy.

The default contrast is always overruled by what the speaker has in mind or intends as the contrast. For instance, suppose I mistakenly believe that I am the better player. I could have in mind a contrast with the case in which I had won the game and deny the above causal claim. (If my opponent does not realize I have this mistaken belief, then this will probably lead to misunderstanding.) Even if I recognize that my opponent would have won the game if we hadn't drawn, I could make it clear that I'm contrasting with a wider set, and then deny the causal statement above. I could contrast with the set {playing the chess game and my winning, playing the chess game and his winning, not playing the chess game at all}.[22]

4   The Context-dependence of Counterfactuals

The counterfactual analysis of causation is one of the most popular approaches to analyzing causation. Hence, it is strange that counterfactuals are widely acknowledged to be context dependent, while causation is not widely acknowledged to be so.

The context-dependence of counterfactuals has been observed and discussed in most major works on counterfactuals.[23] Here are some classic examples exhibiting context-dependence:

If Caesar had been in command in Korea he would have used the atom bomb.

If Caesar had been in command in Korea he would have used catapults. (Example due to Quine 1960, p. 222)

If this were gold it would be malleable.

If this were gold then some gold things would not be malleable. (Example due to Chisholm 1955, p. 103)

If New York City were in Georgia then New York City would be in the South.

If New York City were in Georgia then Georgia would not be entirely in the South. (Example due to Goodman 1947, p. 121)

All of these counterfactuals are context dependent. Consider just the first pair. Each statement can be reasonably asserted in the same situation. (We presuppose that Caesar was ruthless, ambitious, and indifferent to higher authority.) Yet the first statement implies that the second statement is false. (We presuppose that it is possible that Caesar was in command in Korea and it is not possible that he uses both catapults and atom bombs.) The second statement cannot be both true and false, so it must express at least two different propositions depending on factors other than the background facts. It is context dependent.

Acknowledging the context-dependence of counterfactuals can help us to understand the context-dependence of causation. I do not wish to commit myself to one analysis of counterfactuals here. However, let me mention how two successful and sophisticated analyses of counterfactuals account for their context-dependence. One formulation of Lewis's analysis of counterfactuals is as follows: "A counterfactual 'If it were that A, then it would be that C' is (non-vacuously) true if and only if some (accessible) world where both A and C are true is more similar to our actual world, overall, than is any world where A is true but C is false."[24] On this account, the context-dependence of counterfactuals arises because our judgments of overall similarity of possible worlds depend on context. "The delineating parameter for the vagueness of counterfactuals is the comparative similarity relation itself: the system of spheres, comparative similarity system, selection function, or whatever other entity we use to carry information about the comparative similarity of worlds."[25]

The tacit premise view of counterfactuals is presented by Chisholm and also by Tichy.[26] On this view, a counterfactual is true iff its antecedent together with its tacit premises logically entail its consequent, and the tacit premises are true. The tacit premises are simply those assumptions that have been presupposed in the conversation or those that the speaker has in mind on the occasion of utterance. The context-dependence is obvious on this view.

It is interesting that Lewis observes in his original paper on causation that "The vagueness of similarity does infect causation, and no correct analysis can deny it."[27] His original theory already accounts for some context-dependence, admittedly in a subtle way.

5   The Nontransitivity of Causation

Is causation transitive? That is, is it true for all events a, b, and c that if a is a cause of b and b is a cause of c then a is a cause of c? Some causal chains are clearly transitive. Suppose that the lightning is a cause of the burning of the house, and the burning of the house is a cause of the roasting of the pig. (Suppose that the pig was trapped in the house.) Then surely the lightning is also a cause of the roasting of the pig. But is this true for all events a, b, and c?

In the past, the transitivity of causation was commonly assumed in the literature without argument.[28] But more recently a host of ingenious examples have been presented as counterexamples to the transitivity of causation.[29] Before discussing these examples, let's briefly consider one argument for the transitivity of causation.

The only argument that I have found in the literature for the claim that causation is transitive comes from Ned Hall. Hall argues that "rejecting transitivity seems intuitively wrong: it *certainly* goes against one of the ways in which we commonly justify causal claims. That is, we often claim that one event is a cause of another precisely *because* it causes an intermediate, which then causes another intermediate, ... which then causes the effect in question. Are we to believe that any such justification is fundamentally misguided?"[30]

That we do sometimes justify causal claims this way is an important consideration. I agree with Hall that it is common practice to refer to intermediates in a causal chain in justifying causal claims. This seems to apply across many different fields of application of the singular causal concept: history, science, law, and ethics. I don't think that this practice is fundamentally misguided, but it may be a rule of thumb that should be supplemented with restrictive guidelines. If we are to reject transitivity, we have a pressing need for a general rule for distinguishing the cases in which transitivity holds from the cases in which it fails, and an explanation of why transitivity sometimes fails. Hall agrees with me here. He issues a challenge: "Causation not transitive? Then explain under what circumstances we are right to follow our common practice of justifying the claim that *c* causes *e* by pointing to causal intermediates."[31] I take up this challenge in the next section after presenting the counterexamples.

The alleged counterexamples to transitivity are diverse; I will describe three difficult and representative cases: "bomb," "birthday," and "purple fire." The first comes from Field.[32] Suppose that I place a bomb outside your door and light the fuse. Fortunately your friend finds it and defuses it before it explodes. The following three statements seem to be true, and thus seem to show that causation is nontransitive.

(1a)   My placing the bomb outside the door is a cause of your friend's finding it.

(1b)   Your friend's finding the bomb is a cause of your survival.

(1c)   My placing the bomb outside the door is not a cause of your survival.

On a more cheerful note, suppose that I intend to buy you a birthday present, but when the time comes I forget. Fortunately, you remind me and I buy you a birthday present after all. The following three statements seem to be true, and thus seem to show that causation is nontransitive.

(2a)   My forgetting your birthday is a cause of your reminding me.

(2b)   Your reminding me is a cause of my buying you a birthday present.

(2c)   My forgetting your birthday is not a cause of my buying you a birthday present.

Finally, consider Ehring's purple fire example.[33] Davidson puts some potassium salts into a hot fire. Because potassium compounds give a purple flame when heated, the flame changes to a purple color but otherwise stays the same. Next, the heat of the fire causes some flammable material to ignite. Soon the whole place is ablaze, and Elvis, sleeping upstairs, dies of smoke inhalation. The following three statements seem to be true and again seem to show that causation is nontransitive.

(3a)   Davidson's putting potassium salts in the fireplace is a cause of the purple fire.

(3b)   The purple fire is a cause of Elvis's death.

(3c)   Davidson's putting potassium salts in the fireplace is not a cause of Elvis's death.

6   A Contrast Analysis of the Counterexamples

Transitivity is defined only for binary relations, but, on the context-dependence view, causation is not a binary relation. (It is either a three-place relation between a cause, a context, and an effect, or a four-place relation between a cause, two sets of contrast events, and an effect, depending on how you count it.) We will discuss a related property, the "variable-context transitivity" of the three-place causal relation. The three-place causal relation has variable-context transitivity just in case for all events e_1, e_2, e_3, and for all contexts c_1, c_2, c_3, if e_1 causes e_2 in context c_1, and e_2 causes e_3 in context c_2, then e_1 causes e_3 in context c_3. That is, the causal relation has variable-context transitivity just in case it appears transitive no matter how you change the context.

Let's analyze the bomb example. The example can be interpreted in many ways depending on the contrast events assumed in statements (1a), (1b), and (1c). Two natural contrasts with the cause in (1a) are the contrast with my placing nothing outside the door and the contrast with my carefully concealing the bomb outside the door. My placing the bomb outside the door, in contrast to my placing nothing outside the door, is a cause of your friend's finding the bomb, because if I had placed nothing outside the door your friend wouldn't have found the bomb. My placing the bomb outside the door, in contrast to my carefully concealing the bomb outside the door, is a cause of your friend's finding the bomb, because if I had carefully concealed the bomb outside the door your friend would not have found it (let us say).

Some interpretations of the example do not yield counterexamples to transitivity. Statement (4c) of the following is false: It seems plausible that my placing the bomb outside the door, in contrast to my carefully concealing the bomb outside the door, *is* a cause of your survival. So the following causal chain is transitive.

(4a)   My placing the bomb outside the door (vs. carefully concealing it) is a cause of your friend's finding it (vs. overlooking it).

(4b)   Your friend's finding the bomb (vs. overlooking it) is a cause of your survival (vs. death).

(4c)   My placing the bomb outside the door (vs. carefully concealing it) is not a cause of your survival (vs. death).

However, with other natural contrasts, we do have a nontransitive causal chain. For example, all three of the following statements seem true.

(5a)   My placing the bomb outside the door (vs. placing nothing outside the door) is a cause of your friend's finding the bomb (vs. finding nothing).

(5b)   Your friend's finding the bomb (vs. finding nothing) is a cause of your survival (vs. death).

(5c)   My placing the bomb outside the door (vs. placing nothing outside the door) is not a cause of your survival (vs. death).

We can develop a sufficient condition for a causal chain to be transitive from a special case of inference by transitivity of counterfactuals:

(T) $\varphi \mathbin{\Box\!\!\rightarrow} \chi$, $\chi \mathbin{\Box\!\!\rightarrow} \varphi$, $\varphi \mathbin{\Box\!\!\rightarrow} \psi$ $\therefore$ $\chi \mathbin{\Box\!\!\rightarrow} \psi$.[34]

Consider a general causal chain:

(6a) a, with contrast situation c_1 is a cause of b, with contrast situation d_1.

(6b) b, with contrast situation c_2, is a cause of e, with contrast situation d_2.

(6c) a, with contrast situation c_3, is a cause of e, with contrast situation d_3.

Suppose that (C1) $c_1 = c_3$, $d_1 = c_2$, and $d_2 = d_3$ (in other words, events a, b, and e have the same contrasts throughout) and that (C2) if c_2 had occurred then c_1 would have to have occurred (a backtracking counterfactual).[35] Given (T), and account$_2$, these conditions together, (C1) and (C2), are sufficient for a causal chain to be transitive.

This sufficient condition can help us to understand what is going on in example (5) to yield nontransitivity. Example (5) passes (C1), but fails (C2). It is not true that had your friend found nothing outside the door then I would have to have placed nothing outside the door. Had your friend found nothing outside the door, it might have been because I had carefully concealed the bomb so that she overlooked it. There is a sense in which the contrast situations in the example are incompatible with each other, and this incompatibility leads to nontransitivity.

Let's return briefly to the other counterexamples. Here is one natural interpretation of the birthday example:

(7a)   My forgetting your birthday (vs. my remembering your birthday) is a cause of your reminding me (vs. your forgetting to remind me, or our both forgetting your birthday).

(7b)   Your reminding me (vs. your forgetting to remind me, or our both forgetting your birthday) is a cause of my buying you a birthday present (vs. buying you nothing).

(7c)   My forgetting your birthday (vs. my remembering your birthday) is not a cause of my buying you a birthday present (vs. buying you nothing).

Notice that condition (C2) fails. It is not true that if you had forgotten to remind me about your birthday then I would have to have remembered by myself. If you had forgotten to remind me about your birthday then I might have forgotten too. Also, it is not true that if we had both forgotten your birthday then I would have to have remembered your birthday. On the contrary, if we had both forgotten your birthday then I would not have remembered your birthday.

Here is the example with some other contrast situations. Statement (8b) is false: If I had remembered your birthday by myself then I would have bought you something (let us say). So the example exhibits transitivity. Furthermore, conditions (C1) and (C2) are satisfied. The same events always have the same contrasts throughout, and if I had remembered your birthday by myself then I would have remembered your birthday.

(8a)   My forgetting your birthday (vs. my remembering your birthday) is a cause of your reminding me (vs. my remembering your birthday by myself).

(8b)   Your reminding me (vs. my remembering your birthday by myself) is a cause of my buying you a birthday present (vs. buying nothing).

(8c)   My forgetting your birthday (vs. my remembering your birthday) is not a cause of my buying you a birthday present (vs. buying nothing).

Finally, here is the purple fire example with some natural contrasts spelled out:

(9a)   Davidson's putting potassium salts in the fireplace (vs. Davidson's putting nothing in the fireplace) is a cause of the purple fire (vs. a yellow fire).

(9b)   The purple fire (vs. no fire) is a cause of Elvis's death (vs. Elvis's survival).

(9c)   Davidson's putting potassium salts in the fireplace (vs. Davidson's putting nothing in the fireplace) is not a cause of Elvis's death (vs. Elvis's survival).

This case is nontransitive because it fails both conditions (C1) and (C2). The event of the purple fire is contrasted with a yellow fire in (9a) but contrasted with no fire in (9b). Furthermore, it is not true that if there had been no fire then Davidson would have to have put nothing in the fireplace. If there had been no fire, he might have decided to put potassium salts in the fireplace anyway.

7   A Fine-grained Event Analysis of the Counterexamples

Hausman describes how allowing for fine-grained events enables us to explain examples of this sort without rejecting the transitivity of causation.[36] The example is not of the right form to be a counterexample to transitivity, because of the equivocation about which event is being referred to by the phrase "the purple fire." In terms of Kimian events, "the purple fire" could either designate the triple [the fire, being purple, time] or the triple [the fire, being a fire, time]. In terms of Lewisian events, the phrase could either designate a strong event, "the purple fire," which is essentially purple, or designate a weak event, "the fire," which is only accidentally purple. It is the strong event of the purple fire (or the triple [the purple fire, being purple, time]) that is caused by Davidson's action, and it is the weak event of the fire (or the triple [the purple fire, being a fire, time]) that is a cause of Elvis's death.

The fine-grained event analysis of the purple fire example is similar to the analysis in terms of implicit contrasts that I gave above. Whereas Hausman locates context-dependence in the reference of the phrase "the purple fire," I locate the context-dependence in the interpretation of the whole sentence, "Davidson's putting potassium salts in the fireplace is a cause of the purple fire." However, if the phrase "the purple fire vs. a yellow fire" designates a strong event of the purple fire and the phrase "the purple fire vs. no fire" designates a weak event of a purple fire, which they plausibly do, then it can be shown that the two analyses of this example are equivalent.

However, I do not see how the fine-grained event analysis can explain in a similar fashion the nontransitivity of the bomb example. Perhaps we can locate an equivocation in the event referred to by the phrase "your friend's finding the bomb" by looking at the contrast analysis of the example. Suppose that there are two different events referred to by the phrases "your friend's finding the bomb, in contrast to your friend's overlooking the bomb" and "your friend's finding the bomb, in contrast to there being no bomb and your friend finding nothing," and that the phrase "your friend's finding the bomb" could designate either event. Perhaps we could define event$_1$ as an event that occurs in worlds in which I place a bomb outside the door and your friend finds it, and that does not occur in worlds in which I place a bomb outside the door and your friend overlooks it or in worlds in which I do not place a bomb outside the door. And we could define event$_2$ as an event that occurs in worlds in which either I place a bomb outside your door and your friend finds it or I place a bomb outside your door and your friend overlooks it, and that does not occur in worlds in which I do not place a bomb outside the door. Then, after some work, we could show that the example involves an equivocation rather than a failure of transitivity.

But how could the phrase "your friend's finding the bomb" designate event$_2$? (Surely overlooking the bomb is not just another way of finding the bomb!) To analyze the example in this way we have to build conditions external to the event into the event identity conditions for the event. The contrast analysis of this example is more plausible.

Acknowledgments

Thanks to David Lewis, Ram Neta, and Nick White for helpful comments on drafts of this paper.

Notes

1. In my dissertation (Maslen 2000) I argue that the contrastive counterfactual account can also solve the problems of preemption, causation by absences, and causation under the indeterminism of modern physics.

2. This context-dependence is additional to any context-dependence arising from indexicals in the cause or effect phrases of the statement.

3. Hitchcock (1996a).

4. Fall 1997 seminar on causation at New York University.

5. Holland (1986).

6. Kim (1973a, p. 222) defines an event as a "concrete object (or n-tuple of objects) exemplifying a property (or n-adic relation) at a time." According to Lewis (1986d), for the purposes of causation an event may be defined as a predominantly intrinsic, nondisjunctive property of spacetime regions.

7. For a detailed discussion of the varieties of causal relata and one way of reducing causal sentences involving other relata to those involving Kim-style events see Menzies (1989b).

8. However, at the least a distinction between "backtracking" and "standard" counterfactuals must be drawn, in order to rule out spurious cases of backward causation. For example, see Lewis (1979a), p. 34. In normal conditions, backtracking counterfactuals are those "saying that the past would be different if the present were somehow different." It must be shown that backtracking counterfactuals can always be identified syntactically.

9. I do not discuss the status of absences in this essay. However, if, for example, the contrast event were itself the absence of the effect, the causal statement would clearly be trivially true.

10. See Lewis (1986d) for a sophisticated treatment of the distinctness of events. If cause and effect are not required to be distinct events, then this definition would mistakenly judge various relations of noncausal determination to be causation. Furthermore, it would entail that every event is self-caused. However, requiring cause and effect to be distinct events rules out self-causation by fiat—an unwelcome result. (Thank you to an anonymous referee for pointing this out.) Lewis neatly sidesteps this problem in his

original account, by requiring only events that are directly causally dependent to be distinct (see postscript F of Lewis 1986b). He thus allows for the logical possibility of the closed causal loops that appear in some time-travel stories. I cannot see how to expand account$_1$ to yield the same results without assuming transitivity.

However, notice that account$_1$ does not require cause and effect to be distinct; rather, account$_1$ is restricted to cases where cause and effect are distinct. It is simply silent about self-causation and other cases of causation between nondistinct events.

11. Lewis solves a similar problem in his (2000), where alterations play a similar role to that of contrast events in account$_2$. Lewis limits his account to not-too-distant alterations of the cause, where "an *alteration* of event E [is] . . . either a very fragile version of E or else a very fragile alternative event that is similar to E, but numerically different from E" (p. 188).

12. If the contrast event is itself the event in which the absence of the cause consisted, then the contrast situation is the same as the corresponding contrast event.

13. This claim is ambiguous. I mean: "Event c, relative to a set of contrast events $\{c^*\}$, is a cause of event e, relative to a set of contrast events $\{e^*\}$, iff for every c_i^* in $\{c^*\}$ there is an e_i^* in $\{e^*\}$ such that if c_i^* had happened then e_i^* would have happened." Often there is only one natural contrast to the cause c^*, and one natural contrast to the effect e^*. In that case account$_3$ simplifies to the following: "Event c, relative to contrast events c^*, is a cause of event e, relative to contrast event e^*, iff if c^* had happened then e^* would have happened."

14. Hausman (1992). A solenoid is a coil of wire and a solenoid switch is a relay; when current passes through the coil a magnetic field is induced in the coil, and the switch closes. There are also two manual switches in the circuit. A circuit like this is common in many household appliances, for example the three-way switch found on some standing lamps.

15. "The word 'cause' is so inextricably bound up with misleading associations as to make its complete extrusion from the philosophical vocabulary desirable." Instead we should talk of functional dependence, according to Russell (1953).

16. Van Fraassen (1980), p. 118.

17. Van Fraassen (1980). Van Fraassen then uses this to reject the counterfactual theory of causation on the grounds that counterfactuals are context dependent and causation is not.

18. Stalnaker (1972), p. 385. However, see Lewis (1980), for a discussion of how a one-level scheme differs only superficially from Stalnaker's two-level scheme, and for a broader construal of context-dependence encompassing contingency.

19. Note that there is further context-dependence in this sentence associated with the past tense of the sentence, the use of the definite article "the" and the use of the verb "went" (see Fillmore 1971). In total, the truth and meaning of the sentence depend on many features of the context including the identity of the speaker, the location of the speaker, the location of the audience, the time of utterance, and previous statements in the conversation.

20. Stalnaker (1972), p. 384.

21. Lewis (1979b).

22. Van Fraassen (1980), pp. 126–146, treats the question of how a contrast class is obtained from the context in the case of explanation and why-questions, and some of this also applies to the case of causation. This is very relevant to the discussion in this section. However, note that van Fraassen is analyzing explanation, not causation, and that his examples are of contrasts with the effect.

23. For example, Chisholm (1946), Goodman (1979), Lewis (1973b), and Stalnaker (1972).

24. Lewis (1979a), p. 41.

25. Lewis (1973b), p. 93.

26. Chisholm (1946); Tichy (1984).

27. Lewis (1986a), p. 163.

28. For example, Lewis (1986a), p. 167, simply asserts "[c]ausation must always be transitive," and proceeds to add this requirement to his analysis of causation. Further examples of those writing around the same time who simply assume the transitivity of singular causation are Ehring (1987), Rosenberg (1992), and Hitchcock (1995a).

29. As far as I can see, these date back to Jig-chuen Lee (1988), but similar examples have been presented independently, and it took some time for their existence to be widely recognized.

30. The passage quoted appeared in an earlier draft version of Hall's essay, chapter 9 in this volume.

31. Ibid.

32. In conversation.

33. Ehring (1987), p. 323. A version of this example and a discussion also occurs in Ehring (1997), p. 76.

34. See Lewis (1973b), p. 33.

35. If an analysis of backtracking counterfactuals is not available, the following condition is also sufficient for transitivity together with (C1): $(c_1 \& c_2) \mathrel{\Box\!\!\rightarrow} d_3$.

36. Hausman (1992). Also see Ehring (1997), p. 76. Ehring accounts for examples of this sort in a parallel way by employing an "event-feature" theory of causation.

15 Causation: Probabilistic and Counterfactual Analyses

Igal Kvart

In the bulk of this essay (sections 1–13) I offer a probabilistic analysis of token causation. The probabilities employed are chances. In the analysis of cause, the main task is identifying the right notion of probability increase; but causal relevance is a crucial, delicate, and widely overlooked ingredient in the analysis of causation (and of counterfactuals). In a chancy world, causal irrelevance is secured either through probabilistic irrelevance or through the presence of a so-called neutralizer, which essentially screens off C from A in a stable way and is such that A is not a cause of it. Despite appearances to the contrary, the account is not circular. The core diagnosis of early preemption, late preemption, double preemption, and overlapping cases is that the preempted cause is causally irrelevant to the effect (and thus is not a cause of it). The proper analysis of such cases consists in establishing this causal irrelevance by specifying the pertinent neutralizer.

Various workers in the field have in the past become convinced that a probabilistic analysis of cause is not viable and that other resources such as processes must be employed. The major problem that beset probabilistic analyses was the problem of causes that lower the probability of their effects. In the analysis of cause in section 1, I show how this difficulty can be overcome. Since the requisite notion of causal relevance is also analyzed probabilistically, one upshot of this essay is that probabilistic analysis of (token) causation has been abandoned prematurely.

In the remainder of the essay (sections 14–15) I derive a counterfactual analysis of cause from my account of counterfactuals and the thesis that cause amounts to some positive causal relevance. Although the account is extensionally adequate and (I hope) illuminating, it turns out to be circular. (This part may be read independently of the first part.)

1 Cause

I assume a chancy world, where the chance of C is conditional on some prior[1] world-state or history (and possibly other events), that is, having the form: $P(C|W_t)$, where W_t is the world history up to (or a world-state just prior to) t (t being earlier than the beginning of t_C, which is the interval to which C pertains).[2] It is crucial for the proper understanding of the account presented here, and in particular regarding particular examples, that the notion of probability employed throughout be construed as that of chance.

I have argued that, for A to be a token cause of C,[3] A must raise the chance of C **ex post facto**, that is, while taking into account the interval between A and C. Traditionally, probabilistic analyses of causation have had to face the difficulty of how to reconcile the intuitive idea that causes raise the probability of their effects with certain cases where causes seem to lower them. On the token level, this problem arises in particular when only the history of the world prior to the antecedent is taken into account.[4] Put in terms of chances, the natural way of expressing probability increase is:

$$P(C/A.W_A) > P(C/{\sim}A.W_A) \tag{1}$$

(called **ab initio probability increase**; in short: *aipi*). For instance, suppose I drop the chalk (A), and the chalk then falls on the floor (C) (absent any complications). A, intuitively, is a cause of C, and ab initio probability increase obtains.

However, in (1), only the history prior to A, that is, W_A, is taken into account. Ex post facto probability increase, on the other hand, must take into account the intermediate history as well—that between A and C. The condition for being a cause, then, is not ab initio probability increase, which is *not* sufficient for being a cause,[5] but rather a condition of ex post facto probability increase (and a particular form of it at that), which I shall spell out now.

Ex post facto probability increase can be illustrated in cases of ab initio probability decrease (i.e., (1) with "$<$" instead of "$>$"; in short: *aipd*). Ex post facto probability increase despite ab initio probability decrease requires that there be an actual intermediate event E that yields probability increase when held fixed, that is, when added to both sides of the ab initio probability decrease condition. Thus:

$$P(C/A.E.W_A) > P(C/{\sim}A.E.W_A). \tag{2}$$

Call an event such as E an **increaser**.[6] To illustrate:

Example 1 The Comeback Team had been weak for quite a while, with poor chances of improving during the next season. Consequently, there were very high odds of its losing. Nevertheless, x bet \$$Y$, a significant portion of her financial worth, on its winning (A). Later, but before the beginning of the games, the Comeback Team was acquired by a new wealthy owner, an event that had been quite unlikely earlier. The new owner then acquired a few first-rate players. Consequently, the team's performance was the best in the season (E), x won her bet, and C occurred: x improved her financial position.[7]

As of t_A, A yielded a probability decrease of C, that is, ab initio probability decrease. But given E, A yielded a higher chance of C.[8] Hence E is an increaser for A and C. And indeed, intuitively, A was surely a cause of C.

A note of caution: The term "increaser" should not lead one to think that an increaser increases the chance of C when added to the condition in $P(C/A.W_A)$. The import of an increaser E as such does *not* involve the characterization of the relation between a conditional probability once with E added to the condition and once without it. Rather, it's the relation of two conditional probabilities, *both with E* in the condition, one with A, the other with $\sim A$. For instance, consider a student x who took an exam:

A: x gave a bad answer to question b.

Yet:

E: x answered question d correctly.

C: x received a high grade.[9]

Of course A yields ab initio probability decrease for C. Yet E is not an increaser, since:

$$P(C/A.E.W_A) < P(C/\sim A.E.W_A).$$

So E does *not* raise the probability of C when held fixed in the condition on both sides of the ab initio probability decrease condition. Yet E raises the probability of C given A (and W_A) when considered *by itself*, that is:

$$P(C/A.E.W_A) > P(C/A.W_A).$$

Thus, E is not an increaser (for A and C).

However, ab initio probability increase for A and C need not yield that A is a cause of C, since there might be a **decreaser** for A and C, that is, an intermediate E fulfilling (2) with "<" instead of ">," which undermines the indication of ex post facto probability increase of the ab initio probability increase. Hence ab initio probability increase is not a sufficient condition for being a cause. That raising the probability is not a sufficient condition for being a cause, absent cutting of causal routes, has not been properly noticed in the literature.[10] Call an intermediate event that is either an increaser or a decreaser a **reverser**.

An analogous problem may plague the presence of an increaser: An increaser might have a further decreaser *for it*, that is, an intermediate event[11] F fulfilling

$$P(C/A.E.F.W_A) < P(C/\sim A.E.F.W_A).\tag{3}$$

Condition (3) undermines the indication of ex post facto probability increase yielded by the increaser E. The possibility of a decreaser for an increaser shows that the indication of ex post facto probability increase yielded by an increaser depends on the choice of that increaser, and that a choice of other intermediate events that are held fixed need not yield probability increase. For A to be a cause of C, it must have an increaser E *without* a further decreaser for it (such as F in (3)). Call such an increaser **stable** (or *strict*).[12] The probability increase indicated by a stable increaser is stable since it is not reversed when other intermediate events are taken into account.

In addition to being extensionally adequate, it is also intuitively plausible that the notion of cause is one of probability increase that is both ex post facto and stable. Compare the assertibility conditions of a causal claim from a retrospective perspective (from some sufficiently later time) without limitations of knowledge of facts or of chances. The role of an assertion of ab initio probability increase, when restricted to knowledge of facts that pertain up to t_A[13] (rather than the objective notion used above, which is relativized to W_A) is useful for prediction when one is at t_A and is concerned to assess whether A will bring about C—this is ab initio assessment. But the notion of A's raising the probability of C that is needed for the notion of A's being a cause of C must be robust enough so that the probability increase involved proves stable across the intermediate history. Stable ex post facto probability increase is thus the requisite constraint for the notion of cause.

For the sake of a uniform terminology, consider the case of ab initio probability increase a case of a **null** increaser[14] (as in the above example of the chalk that fell to the floor); similarly, consider the case of ab initio probability decrease a case of a *null* decreaser. A null increaser may be stable (i.e., if there is no decreaser). In such a case, its presence constitutes a sufficient condition for being a cause.[15]

In analogy to a stable increaser, we have the notion of a *stable decreaser*, namely, a decreaser for which there is no further increaser. The presence of a stable increaser yields *positive causal relevance*, and the presence of a stable decreaser yields *negative causal relevance*. The copresence of a stable increaser and a stable decreaser yields *mixed causal relevance*.

We saw that for A to be a cause of C there must be a strict increaser for A and C. We can thus reformulate this conclusion by stating that A's being a cause of C amounts to there being some positive causal relevance for A and C.[16]

2 Hitchcock's Randomizer and Doctor's Dispositions

Against probabilistic accounts of causation, and in favor of contrastive accounts, Hitchcock raised an example of the following kind:

A: the doctor prescribed to the patient *x* 100 ml of the medicine;

and indeed:[17]

C: the patient recovered.

Accordingly, the medicine was indeed helpful at the level of 100 ml. 200 ml would have been very likely to be much more effective.

Was *A* a cause of *C*? I say, intuitively, yes. Hitchcock says no, at least not without contrastive qualification. On his view, whether *A* comes out a cause of *C* on a probabilistic analysis depends on the doctor's dispositions. Assume, in variation 1, that the doctor above was disposed to prescribe 200 ml (he acted in fact contrary to his disposition). Variation 2 is just like variation 1 except that the doctor was disposed to prescribe 0 ml, yet here too he acted contrary to his own disposition. That is, in the two variations the doctor was on different dispositional curves between the values of 0 ml and 200 ml even though in fact he acted in the same way (prescribed 100 ml), and the patient recovered. Whether there is probability increase or decrease depends on the dispositional curve of the doctor in question and thus varies between the two variations, since the most likely event in the nonactual case, namely, given ~*A*, would be very different for different curves. But, Hitchcock says, the outcome of whether *A* was a cause of *C* must not depend on these dispositions. Hence probabilistic accounts fail and a contrastive account is called for, in which cause in analyzed as a three-term relation between *A*, *C*, and a contrastive alternative. In sum, Hitchcock correctly observes that the result of whether *A* was a cause of *C* must not come out differently in the two variations. But since, on his view, probabilistic accounts of causation yield just this result, he concludes that the fault lies with the notion of cause being construed as a two-place relation.

However, Hitchcock's reasoning relies on a simplistic conception of probabilistic causation. In view of the account of the last section, *A* here had a *mixed causal impact* on *C*: a positive causal impact in view of the doctor's not having avoided giving the patient this medicine (prominent in the case of the second variation), and a negative causal impact in view of his failing to give the patient the higher dose (prominent in the case of the first variation). Thus, consider:

E: the dosage that the patient took didn't exceed 100 ml

E is a strict increaser, since, given *E* and the fact that the doctor prescribed 100 ml (*A*), the probability of the patient's taking a 100 ml dosage is high, and thus the probability of *C* (the patient was cured) is higher than it is given *E* and ∼*A* (i.e., its not being the case that the doctor prescribed 100 ml).[18] On the other hand,

F: the dosage the patient took was not less than 100 ml

is a stable decreaser, since, given *F* and *A*, again, the probability that the patient took 100 ml is high, and thus the probability of *C* (the patient was cured) is lower than it is given *F* and ∼*A*. Hence in both variations there is a stable increaser and a stable decreaser, which is characteristic of mixed causal relevance cases. To be a cause, recall, is to have some positive causal relevance, and obviously there is some positive causal relevance in all mixed causal relevance cases, including the above. Hence, on the above analysis, *A* comes out a cause of *C* in both variations, as it should.

This is the outcome of the analysis regardless of the disposition of the doctor, and Hitchcock's main concern is to secure just such independence. The crucial point here, again, is to recognize the importance of stable reversers and to avoid construing probability increase in the simplistic form of ab initio probability increase. Once stable reversers are taken into account, the outcome of the above probabilistic account (regarding whether *A* was a cause of *C*) does not vary with the doctor's dispositions. This fits not only Hitchcock's intuitions but also his robustness principle, to the effect that whether *A* was a cause of *C* in the two variations ought to depend on the physiological condition of the patient and the chemical properties of the pill but be independent of the doctor's dispositions. Hitchcock considers a randomizer that determines a pattern of such dispositions, and he maintains that whether *A* was a cause of *C* should be independent of the randomizer's selected pattern of dispositions. Hitchcock's intuitions and principle are, therefore, respected on the above analysis. For Hitchcock, this example motivates favoring a contrastive account of cause in view of the inadequacy of the simplistic form of the probabilistic account of causation. But once an adequate probabilistic account is adopted, the counter-intuitive outcome is blocked, and Hitchcock's example no longer provides a motivation for ruling out the ordinary construal of causation as a two-place relation and opting, instead, for a contrastive conception.

A much briefer, and ultimately more satisfactory, response to Hitchcock is that *A'* is a cause of *C* on the analysis presented here:

A': the doctor prescribed the medicine to the patient.

There is ab initio probability increase of *A'* to *C*, with no reversers. Hence *A'* is a cause of *C* (given causal relevance). *A*, however, is an informational expansion of *A'*, and hence it is also a cause of C, in view of the principle of Cause Preservation under Informational Expansion.[19]

Yet there remains the issue of the causal impact of the aspect "at a dose of 100 ml" in A on C. The analysis of whether this aspect of A was a cause of C requires an analysis of aspect causation,[20] though its outcome would not change the conclusion that A was a cause of C.

3   Causal Relevance Neutralizers

The existence of a stable increaser is a necessary but not a sufficient condition for something's being a cause. Causal relevance (of A to C) is also a necessary condition for A's being a cause of C. So if A is not causally relevant to C, A is not a cause of C even if there is a stable increaser for A and C. This happens if there is, in addition to the stable increaser, an intermediate event that *neutralizes* the would-be causal relevance of A to C. So, the presence of a stable increaser does not suffice for causal relevance, and thus does not suffice for being a cause. Consider the following example:

Example 2 x was pursued by two enemies who wanted to kill him. They discovered that he was about to be at a particular meeting place in an area covered with heavy snow at a particular time. Enemy 1 arrived with his attack dog, discovered that there was a cave with a very small entrance right next to the meeting place, and hid there with his dog. Enemy 2, with his gun ready, found another place to hide, overlooking that meeting place. At the designated time, x arrived at the meeting place, and indeed:

A: enemy 1 released his dog at t_1.

However, owing to the heavy mass of snow that covered the slope above the entrance of the cave:

E: an avalanche completely sealed the entrance to the cave at $t_1 + dt$.

This happened right after the dog was released, and before it had a chance to charge forward. Both enemy 1 and his dog were thus trapped in the blocked cave. However, on observing the arrival of x:

B: enemy 2 shot at x

and indeed hit his mark:

C: x was injured.

Intuitively, A was not a cause of C, but B was. However, A had ab initio probability increase to C, that is:

$$P(C/A.W_A) > P(C/{\sim}A.W_A),$$

and no decreaser,[21] so A had a null stable increaser to C. But A was nonetheless not a cause of C, since A ended up being causally irrelevant to C.

For there to be causal relevance, there must be probabilistic relevance of A to C. A is **probabilistically relevant** to C if there is either an increaser or a decreaser for A and C. Increasers and decreasers may be null or not. The presence of a null increaser or a null decreaser for A and C is tantamount to:

$$P(C/A.W_A) \neq P(C/{\sim}A.W_A) \tag{4}$$

A non-null increaser or decreaser F for A and C yields:

$$P(C/A.F.W_A) \neq P(C/{\sim}A.F.W_A) \tag{5}$$

Call such an F a **differentiator** (for A and C). In the case of the ab initio inequality of (4), consider an empty intermediate event a *null differentiator* (for A and C). Thus, a null differentiator is either a null increaser or a null decreaser, and a differentiator (null or not) is either an increaser or a decreaser (null or not). Thus, A is probabilistically relevant to C just in case A makes a probabilistic difference to C, either directly (as in (4)) or via an intermediate event that is held fixed (as in (5)). A is therefore probabilistically relevant to C just in case there is a differentiator (null or not) for A and C.

The absence of a null differentiator amounts to (4) not holding, that is, to the presence of probabilistic equality:

Equiprobability: $P(C/A.W_A) = P(C/{\sim}A.W_A)$

Without probabilistic relevance there is no causal relevance; and yet A was probabilistically relevant to C in the last example. What accounts, then, for the causal irrelevance there? It was the presence of an intermediate event that *neutralized* the would-be causal relevance of A to C. In that example it was E. Call such an event a **causal relevance neutralizer**. So if A is probabilistically relevant to C, A is causally relevant to C just in case there is no causal relevance neutralizer for them. That is, if there is a causal relevance neutralizer for them, A is not causally relevant to C, despite probabilistic relevance. Our problem, then, is how to characterize causal relevance neutralizers. (We can call them for short just **neutralizers**.)

A would-be causal chain from A to C may be neutralized if it is cut off; but this is not the only way. Such a chain may be diverted or simply dissipate. Further, even if the would-be causal chain from A to C was cut off, the event that did the cutting need not secure that there was no causal relevance.[22] The role of securing that there was no causal relevance of A to C is that of a neutralizer.

4 Candidates for Causal Relevance Neutralizers

A neutralizer E, which secures causal irrelevance of A to C (despite probabilistic relevance), must *screen off A from C*; that is, it must fulfill:

$$P(C/A.E.W_A) = P(C/\sim A.E.W_A) \tag{6}$$

An event E satisfying (6) is a **screener** for A and C (or, alternatively, a *blocker* for them).[23] But a neutralizer for A and C must also screen A off from C in a *stable*, that is, unreversed way: There must not be any intermediate event F that undoes this screening-off. In other words, there must not be an intermediate[24] event F such that:

$$P(C/A.E.F.W_A) \neq P(C/\sim A.E.F.W_A) \tag{7}$$

As an illustration, consider example 3.

Example 3 Two pipes lead from a faucet to a pool. The faucet can be in only one of two positions. The faucet's being in any one of the two positions allows the water to flow exclusively through one pipe or exclusively through the other. I switched the faucet in the direction of the right-hand pipe (A). That pipe allowed for a much better water flow than the other pipe. And indeed, the pool filled up in due course (C). Hence there is ab initio probability increase for A and C (and thus there is a null differentiator for them). But after I switched the faucet, a stray bullet hit the right-hand pipe at a certain spot before the water reached it. Consequently, there was a large hole in the right-hand pipe, and both pipes became equal in terms of their water-flow conductivity (E). E is thus a screener for A and C.

The mere presence of a screener need not yield stable ex post facto probabilistic equality, since a screener may have a differentiator *for it*. If E is a screener, fulfilling (6), for which there is no F, fulfilling (7), then the probabilistic equality of (6) is indeed stable. Call such an event E that satisfies (6) for which there is no such F satisfying (7) a **stable screener** for A and C (or, alternatively, a *stable blocker*). A stable screener, then, yields a stable probabilistic equality. A neutralizer for A and C must be a stable screener.[25]

If E is a stable screener (for A and C), so would be conjunctive expansions of E.[26] To focus on the intrinsic features of neutralizers, we'll confine our attention to *lean* stable screeners, that is, stable screeners without extra information that plays no role in their being stable screeners.[27] Call lean stable screeners *candidates for causal relevance neutralizers* (or for short: **candidates for neutralizers**).

5 The Analysis of Neutralizers

So far we have specified what role a neutralizer is taken to play. But we must specify now what a neutralizer is. My thesis is the following:

Thesis: E is a neutralizer for A and C just in case E is a lean stable screener for A and C of which A is not a cause.

This thesis need not strike us as being intuitively compelling; but, I hold, it is correct[28] (although space doesn't allow to spell out the full motivation here).[29] It also threatens circularity, since it employs the notion of cause, but this threat of circularity will evaporate, as we will see below.

First, let us apply the above analysis to example 2 above, with the dog and the avalanche. Surely, intuitively, A (enemy 1 released his dog at t_1) ended up being causally irrelevant to C (x was injured), even though there is a null differentiator for A and C. Yet E (i.e., an avalanche completely blocked the entrance to the cave at $t_1 + dt$) was a stable screener for A and C, and intuitively A was not a cause of E (and indeed, in terms of our analysis, there was also no differentiator for A and E). Yet B (i.e., enemy 2 shot at x) has a null stable increaser for C, and thus there is a differentiator for them, and there is no causal relevance neutralizer. B, therefore, intuitively as well as by the above analysis, ended up being a cause of C, whereas A wasn't, since it ended up being causally irrelevant to C.

Now to the threat of circularity. Suppose that there is no differentiator for A and C (null or not). Then A is causally irrelevant to C, since probabilistic relevance is a necessary condition for causal relevance.

So suppose there is no equiprobability for A and C, or else there is equiprobability but there is a differentiator. Then A is probabilistically relevant to C, and so it is causally relevant to it unless there is a neutralizer for A and C.

So consider a candidate for neutralizer E_1 for A and C: a lean, stable screener for A and C. It now remains to be established whether A is a cause of E_1 in order to determine whether E_1 is a neutralizer for A and C. If there is no stable increaser for A and E_1, A is not a cause of E_1; E_1 is therefore a neutralizer for A and C, and A is causally irrelevant to C.

So suppose there is a stable increaser for A and E_1. Then A is causally relevant to, and a cause of, E_1 (and hence E_1 is not a candidate for a neutralizer for A and C) unless there is a neutralizer for A and E_1. So consider a candidate for neutralizer E_2

for A and E_1. If there is no stable increaser for A and E_2, A is not a cause of E_2; hence E_2 is a neutralizer for A and E_1; so A is causally irrelevant to E_1 and thus not a cause of it; hence E_1 is a neutralizer for A and C, and A is thus causally irrelevant to C.

Otherwise, if there is a stable increaser for A and E_2, we must look for a candidate neutralizer for A and E_2. And so on. This procedure may terminate if there is an E_n with no stable increaser for A and E_n; or else there may be an infinite regress.

If a chain of this sort terminates, it terminates in the establishment of some E_n as a neutralizer (for A and E_{n-1}); hence A is, in this case, causally irrelevant to C. Thus, if such a chain terminates, there is a conclusive positive result of causal irrelevance; call such an E_n an *endpoint* neutralizer. But what happens if no such chain terminates? Recall that this is a prima facie case of causal relevance of A to C, since there is a differentiator for them. Yet there is no neutralizer for A and C, since no such chain terminates. Hence there is no neutralizer to overrule the prima facie causal relevance of A to C. So A is therefore causally relevant to C.[30]

Thus, there may be infinite regress, but there is no circularity, since the infinite regress case is a case of causal relevance.

The above presentations of the analyses of cause and of causal relevance summarize the more detailed analyses, presented elsewhere with more detailed arguments for their adequacy.[31] The reader who needs to be further convinced by the adequacy of these analyses is advised to look at the more detailed presentations.[32]

6 Illustrating Causal Relevance through Infinite Regress

Consider *example 4*:

A: x fired at y at t_0.

C: y was shot at t_1.

A, in this case (which is a simple, straightforward case with no complications),[33] is intuitively a cause of C; hence it is causally relevant to C. Surely there is ab initio probability increase of A to C; hence there is a null differentiator. So in checking for causal relevance of A to C, by our analysis, we look for a neutralizer candidate for A and C. And indeed, consider:

E_1: x's bullet was at t_1 at point p_1 in midair, with momentum m_1, spin s_1, etc.

E_1 does screen off A from C and is in fact a lean, stable screener, and thus it is a neutralizer candidate. But intuitively, A is surely a cause of E_1. And indeed, there is ab initio probability increase of A and E_1, and hence there is a null stable increaser. So E_1 is not a neutralizer for A and C unless there is a neutralizer E_2 for A and E_1. And indeed, consider E_2, which is just like E_1 only with t_2, p_2, m_2, s_2, and so on instead of t_1, p_1, m_1, s_1, and so on. E_2 is a neutralizer candidate for A and E_1 just as E_1 was a neutralizer candidate for A and C. But again, A is intuitively a cause of E_2. And indeed, A has a null stable increaser to E_2. Hence E_2 is not a neutralizer for A and E_1 unless there is a neutralizer E_3 for A and E_2; and so on.

There is thus an infinite series of such E_is[34] where the corresponding t_is converge to some temporal point between A and C. That there is only infinite regress of this sort (i.e., there not being a suitable terminating chain) establishes that A is causally relevant to C, since it establishes that there is no neutralizer for A and C (in the presence of a differentiator).

7   Lewis's Two Bombs and the Newspaper

Consider the following example:[35]

A: terrorist 1 places a bomb on flight 13 at t_1.

B: terrorist 2 places a bomb on flight 17 at t_2.

Both bombs are unreliable. The bomb of terrorist 1 goes off, and:

C: the newspaper prints a headline at t_3: "Airline bomb disaster."

The bomb of terrorist 2 fails; thus:

E: no bomb went off on flight 17,

but the headline would have been just the same had it gone off (with or without the other bomb). The bomb on flight 17 raises the probability of the effect, yet it is not a cause of C. Clearly, A is intuitively a cause of C, and B is not.

Indeed, both A and B bear ab initio probability increase to C, with no reversers. The difference between them is that A is causally relevant to C but B is not. E is a stable screener for B and C,[36] and B is not a cause of E, since there is ab initio probability decrease of B to E and no reverser. So E is a neutralizer for B and C, and B comes out as causally irrelevant to C and thus not as a cause of it. (Hence B didn't cause C, since being a cause of C is a necessary condition for causing C.) On the other hand, there is no neutralizer for A and C; hence A is a cause of C. The outcome then is intuitively the right one, and the analysis yields it in a noncircular way.

8   Late Preemption

I will now illustrate the analysis by applying it to the case of late preemption[37] that posed a severe problem for Lewis's analysis of causation.

Suzy threw a stone at the window at t_1 (A_1), and Billy threw a stone at the window at t_2 (A_2).[38] Suzy's stone hit the window first (it doesn't matter which one of the two threw the stone first), and the window shattered at t_3 (C). Intuitively, A_1 was a cause of C, and A_2 was not.

However, both A_1 and A_2 yield ab initio probability increase for C, and neither has a reverser. A_2, however, should come out as causally irrelevant to C. And indeed, consider:

G: Billy's stone did not hit the window (until $t_3^- - \varepsilon$).

(t_3^- is the upper edge of the interval t_3.) G is a stable screener for A_2 and C, and there is ab initio probability decrease for A and G (and there is no increaser). Hence G is a neutralizer for A_2 and C, and so A_2 is causally relevant to C.

Another neutralizer for A_2 and C is:

E: Billy's stone was at $t_3^- - \varepsilon$ at a distance not smaller than d from the window, not traveling toward it at velocity greater than v.

(d and v are the actual distance and velocity of Billy's stone at $t_3^- - \varepsilon$.)

E is a screener for A_2 and C,[39] since, given E, B makes no difference to the window's shattering at t_3, and E is a stable increaser. A_2 is not a cause of E since A_2 doesn't increase the chance of E (and there is no stable increaser).[40] Hence E is a neutralizer for A_2 and C, and A_2 is not a cause of C. A_1, on the other hand, has no neutralizer for C, and so it is thus a cause of C.

By way of testing probabilistic accounts of cause (including the account above), Christopher Hitchcock offered a counterexample of late preemption that is structurally similar. In it, bullet 1 shattered a fragile vase by hitting it, though barely so, while bullet 2, shot at around the same time, missed the vase by an extremely tiny distance at the very same time. A (bullet 1 was emitted) was a cause of C (the vase shattered at t), but B (bullet 2 was emitted) was not. Yet, Hitchcock claims, B increased the probability of C all the way through.[41]

However, A comes out as a cause of C and B does not, since G^*, a counterpart of the above G, is a neutralizer for B and C (though not for A and C):

G^*: bullet 2 did not hit the vase (until $t^- - \varepsilon$).

G^* screens off B from C and lowers the chance of C (without an increaser). So G^* is a neutralizer for B and C, and B doesn't come out as a cause of C.

Yet E^*, a counterpart of the above E, is also a neutralizer for B and C (though not for A and C):

E^*: bullet 2 was at $t^- -\varepsilon$ at a distance not smaller than ds from the window, not traveling toward it at velocity greater than v.

(ds and v are the actual distance and velocity of bullet 2 at $t^- -\varepsilon$.)[42]

Again, E^* is a stable screener for B and C, and B is not a cause of E^* for the same considerations regarding E above. Hence E^* is a neutralizer for B and C, so B does not come out as a cause of C. There is ab initio probability increase for A and C, with no reverser and no neutralizer (including E^*); hence A comes out as a cause of C, which is the right result.[43]

9   Early Preemption

Consider *example 5*, a neuron-type case (of the sort introduced by Lewis). Suppose both neurons c_1 and c_2 fire. Neuron c_1 has a single, direct connection to neuron e. Neuron c_2 also has a single connection to e, but one that passes through neuron d. These connections transmit stimulatory signals. There is also a connection from c_1 to d that transmits an inhibitory signal. Assume that the inhibitory and stimulatory signals respectively yield high probability that the inhibited neuron does not fire and that the stimulated neuron fires.[44] Finally, assume that the inhibitory signal from neuron c_1 reaches neuron d before the stimulatory signal from neuron c_2. So:

A: neuron c_1 fired;

B: neuron c_2 fired;

C: neuron e fired;

D: neuron d didn't fire.

Intuitively, A, but not B, was a cause of C.[45] There is ab initio probability increase for A and C and for B and C, and there are no reversers. There is no neutralizer for A and C; but D is a lean stable screener for B and C, and B is not a cause of D (there is ab initio probability decrease for B and D, no reverser, and hence no stable increaser). So D is a neutralizer for B and C, and hence A is a cause of C whereas B is not.

One can further assume, without changing the significant features of the case, that the route from c_1 to e was sufficiently less conducive to e's firing than the route from c_2. In this case, A lowered the probability of C (ab initio), while still being a cause of it.

Lewis's way of handling early preemption relied on the presence of an intermediate event between A and C (later than D), in the form of an intermediate neuron on the path from c_1 to e, which allowed his counterfactual analysis to resort to stepwise causation, essentially relying on such an intermediate event. Note, however, that the above analysis of the example resorts to no such intermediate event. Although a suitable intermediate event need not involve an additional neuron,[46] Lewis's handling of the example requires the presence of some suitable intermediate events, whereas the above analysis does not. Thus, a fictional example that involves action at a distance or discrete time, with no intermediate events between A and C (at least after D), seems immune to Lewis's standard counterfactual treatment of early preemption, but not to the above analysis.

10   The Doctor and the Convict

The convict was executed at 11:00 P.M. as scheduled. He was, however, terminally ill and on the verge of dying at any moment.

A: the doctor made great efforts throughout the evening to keep him alive until 11:00 P.M.

C: the convict died at 11:00 P.M.[47]

A, a delayer, is intuitively a cause of C, even though A is not a cause of C_1:

C_1: the convict died that evening.

A has ab initio probability increase to C, since it raised the chance that the convict was alive until 11:00 P.M., and there is no neutralizer for A and C. Yet there is no ab initio probability increase for A and C_1: There is ab initio probability decrease, and there is no reverser, so A doesn't come out as a cause of C_1.[48]

11   Early Preemption with Different Time Specifications

Early preemption cases allow for variations that yield different results depending on how the temporal parameter is specified. Consider, for instance, the following example.

Example 6

A: Oswald fired at Kennedy at t_1.

C: Kennedy was hit at t_3.

(t_3 is instant-like.)

Contrary to the Warren commission, assume that there was a standby assassin x, highly proficient and well positioned. However, x didn't shoot, since Oswald did. Consider:

G: x didn't shoot at (t_3-T)

(for a suitably very short T).[49] Intuitively, G was not a cause of C: G does not have any positive causal impact on C. Indeed, there is ab initio probability decrease of G and C, and there is no reverser.[50]

Consider, on the other hand:

B: x came to the knoll.

Intuitively, B was not a cause of C.[51] G', however, is a stable screener for B and C:

G': x didn't shoot during $(t_3-T', t_3-\varepsilon)$

(for a suitably short T').[52] But B ended up not being a cause of G', since there is ab initio probability decrease for B and G', and there is no reverser. Hence G' is a neutralizer for B and C, and B comes out as causally irrelevant to C—the right result.

But now consider a candidate other than B and G:

D: x didn't shoot at t_2

(t_2 is considerably prior to t_1). Intuitively, the fact that x didn't shoot at t_2 made it feasible for Kennedy to be hit at t_3 (rather than at an earlier time), and thus was a cause of it. D is thus an omission that is a cause of C.[53]

On our analysis, there is ab initio probability increase of D and C, no reverser, and no neutralizer. (D is of course a cause of neutralizer candidates such as "there was no bullet at the air at $t_2 + dt$.")[54] Such outcomes reflect the use of narrow event individuation that provides for flexibility regarding the choice of the temporal parameter.[55]

12 Double Preemption

Consider *example 7* (due to Ned Hall):

A: Suzy set out on a bombing mission.

Yet:

D: an enemy interceptor was launched to abort Suzy's mission.

However, his own mission was aborted, since:

E: Billy's plane intercepted the enemy's interceptor.

Consequently, Suzy's mission was successful:

C: Suzy's bomb hit the target.

A and *E* were, intuitively, causes of *C*. Surely there is ab initio probability increase for *A* and *C* and for *E* and *C*, and no reversers. Moreover, there is no neutralizer for *A* and *C* and for *E* and *C*. In particular, *F*:

F: Suzy's bomb was launched as planned

is not a neutralizer for either event, since, although it is a lean stable screener for both vis-à-vis *C*, both *A* and *E* were intuitively causes of *F* (and indeed, there is ab initio probability increase, no reverser, and no neutralizer for both).

   D, however, was intuitively not a cause of *C*. It had ab initio probability decrease to *C* with no reverser and thus with no stable increaser. Thus, *D* surely had no positive causal relevance to *C*. Yet *D* was not purely negatively causally relevant to *C*, as one may think in view of the presence of a stable decreaser and the absence of any stable increaser. Rather, *D* was causally irrelevant to *C*. This is so because there was a neutralizer for *D* and *C*. It is not *E*, since *D* was a cause of *E* (there is a null stable increaser, and no neutralizer). But *F* is a lean stable screener for *D* and *C*, and *D* was not a cause of *F* (there is ab initio probability decrease with no reverser, and so with no stable increaser). Hence *D* ended up being causally irrelevant to *C*.

   This aspect of the case illustrates the following phenomenon. In general, a neutralizer *E* (for *A* and *C*) is causally relevant to *C*: if it secures the abortion of a would-be cause of *C*, it has negative causal relevance to *C*; if it secures the abortion of a would-be negative cause of *C* (a negative cause is an event which bears purely negative causal relevance to *C*), it has positive causal relevance to *C* (and thus is a cause of *C*). It fails to be either, and thus to be causally relevant to *C* as well, in case there is yet another neutralizer for it and *C*. That is, there may in general be a later neutralizer for *A* and *C*, which is also a neutralizer for the earlier neutralizer *E* and *C*, thus rendering the first neutralizer causally irrelevant to *C*.

13   Omissions

Example 8   1, 2, and 3 are billiard balls. 2 was hit (B), and in turn it hit 3 (C). In the meantime, x had an opportunity to hit 1 as it started its course in a certain direction d (during a brief interval T). x didn't hit 1 in that direction during T (A). $\sim A$ would yield a high chance of 1's colliding with 2 on its way, diverting it from its course and preventing 3 from being hit. Hence there is ab initio probability increase of A and C, and intuitively A (which is an omission) is a cause of C. Indeed, there is no reverser, and hence there is a null stable increaser.

There are stable screeners for A and C; yet A is a cause of them. For instance:

F: 2 is at s' at t'

(on its way to hit 3, after T and close to but before t_C; s' is outside the range of direction d for ball 1). There is ab initio probability increase of A and F; there are no reversers; hence there is a stable increaser, and, intuitively, A was a cause of F (there is no neutralizer—it is an infinite regress case).

Or, alternatively, consider:

E: 1 is stationary at s during T_1.

T_1 is a suitable, large enough interval before t_C;[56] s is where 1 was all along. There is ab initio probability increase of A and E, and there is no reverser; hence there is a stable increaser, and no neutralizer. Hence A comes out as a cause of C by the analysis, which is the right result. Omissions, on widespread intuitions, can be causes, and the above analysis allows for this phenomenon.

Concluding Remark about Type Causation   An account of token causation in terms of chances of the sort presented here would, if successful, open the way to analyzing type (generic) causation in terms of token causation. A main ingredient of type causation, I suggest, would be that type causation requires sufficient presence of token causes; that is, there should be enough[57] token events of the cause type that are token causes of token events of the effect type. (The notion of generic cause seems to allow for relativity to a reference class, e.g., a country, an era, or circumstances.)

So much for the probabilistic analysis of cause. We now move to a counterfactual analysis of cause (section 15).

14   Counterfactuals

Lewis offered a counterfactual analysis of causation for an indeterministic world in terms of chance-consequent counterfactuals, which I discussed elsewhere.[58,59] The probabilistic analysis of causation offered above was designed for an indeterministic world, with the probabilities being objective chances.[60] At the end of section 1 we saw that the informal thrust underlying this probabilistic analysis is that A is a cause of C iff A has some positive causal relevance to C. But the details of this probabilistic analysis need not concern us regarding the counterfactual analysis of cause in the next section.

The notion of some positive causal relevance stems from my analysis of counter-factuals,[61] some main points of which I will summarize here. I argued that the core counterfactuals of the form $\sim A > \sim C$ are counterfactuals with false, factual ante-cedents $\sim A$ compatible with their prior history W_A (called n-d counterfactuals, for natural divergence).[62] My analysis for these counterfactuals has been that the coun-terfactual is true iff the consequent is inferable on the basis of the antecedent and the so-called *implicit premises* (through the laws of nature).[63] The implicit premises for such counterfactuals consist of the following three sets: first, the history prior to A, that is, W_A. Second, the set of true statements describing events belonging to the *in-termediate course* (i.e., the actual course of events pertaining to the interval between t_A and t_C[64]) that are causally independent of A. Third, the set of true statements describing events belonging to the intermediate course to which A is purely nega-tively causally relevant.[65] (For an example illustrating this analysis, see the stock market example below, this section.)

As an example of purely negative causal relevance, consider: z struggled to prevent x from firing at y (A), though unsuccessfully—x shot y (E) nonetheless. The fact A that z struggled to prevent x from firing was purely negatively causally relevant to E—the fact that x shot y.

E is causally independent of A just in case A is causally irrelevant to E.[66] A has some positive causal relevance to E just in case A is causally relevant to E but not purely negatively causally relevant. The notions of causal relevance and purely neg-ative causal relevance, which are crucial to the above analysis of counterfactuals, thus provide for a definition of the notion of some positive causal relevance, which is, as I argued above, tantamount to the notion of cause. A has purely negative causal relevance to C just in case A is causally relevant to C but has no positive causal relevance to C. Thus, analyses of causal relevance and of some positive causal rele-vance, which have been provided in this paper, yield an analysis of purely negative causal relevance.

If A is causally irrelevant to E, A is not a cause of E.[67] According to the above conception of cause, if A is purely negatively causally relevant to E, then again A is not a cause of C. If A is causally relevant to E without being purely negatively caus-ally relevant to E, then A has some positive causal relevance to E and thus is a cause of E. Consequently, the above analysis of counterfactuals $\sim A > \sim C$[68] and of **semi-factuals** $\sim A > C$ (i.e., counterfactuals with true consequents) can be presented in terms of the notion of cause as follows:

$\sim A > \sim C$ (or $\sim A > C$) is true just in case $\sim C$ (or C) is inferable on the basis of $\sim A$, W_A and the set of true statements describing events in the intermediate course of which A is not a cause.

In view of the above, a counterfactual analysis of cause follows, as we shall see.[69] In *A Theory of Counterfactuals* I divided the set of semifactuals exclusively and exhaustively into three sets: First, **irrel-semifactuals**, that is, semifactuals $\sim A > C$ such that A is causally irrelevant to C. From the above analysis it follows that all such counterfactuals are true, since C is preserved among the implicit premises in virtue of its causal independence from A. Second, **pn-semifactuals** (*pn* for purely negative), which are the semifactuals $\sim A > C$ such that A has purely negative causal relevance to C.[70] All these semifactuals are also true, since C qualifies as an implicit premise. Third, the remaining set of semifactuals, called **cts** (for con-type-sems, abbreviating *counterfactual-type-semifactuals*), since they may be true or false, just like regular counterfactuals.

As another example of irrel-semifactual (as well as a further illustration of the above analysis), consider the following.[71] x contemplates selling certain stocks. After deliberating, x sells his stock (A) on Monday. On Tuesday morning, the stock market skyrockets (E). Consider someone saying on Tuesday evening: Had x not sold his stock, he would have been able to retire. On a plausible way of fleshing out this example, this counterfactual is intuitively true.[72] On the above inferential schema, the counterfactual is true only if event E—the stock market skyrockets on Tuesday morning—is retained among the true statements from which the counterfactual consequent is to be inferred (through the laws). And indeed, the actual A is causally irrelevant to E. $\sim A$ and its prior history W_A do not suffice to yield the consequent $\sim C$ (C—x is not able to retire) through the laws. A different intermediate history $W_{A,C}$ that does not include events such as E need not uphold this counterfactual.

As an example of a pn-semifactual, consider the above example of purely negative causal relevance where z struggled to prevent x from firing at y (A), though unsuccessfully. Had z not struggled to prevent x from firing at y, a fortiori x would have shot y. This semifactual is true. The fact A that z struggled to prevent x from firing at y was purely negatively causally relevant to E—the fact that x shot y. $\sim A > E$ here is thus a pn-semifactual and is therefore true.

15   The Counterfactual Analysis of Cause

We can now deduce a counterfactual analysis of cause from this analysis of counterfactuals and the above conception of cause. If $\sim A > C$ is an irrel-semifactual or a pn-
semifactual, then A is not a cause of C, since the requirement of some positive causal
relevance is violated. Now consider any other semifactual $\sim A > C$ (which, as such, is
a cts). A is causally relevant to C and without purely negative causal relevance to C.
Hence A has some positive causal relevance to C and thus is a cause of C.

This last conclusion covers *any* semifactual not belonging to the above two sets
(i.e., of irrel-semifactuals and pn-semifactuals) regardless of whether the semifactual
is true or false. Hence, if $\sim A > C$ is a cts, A is a cause of C. If $\sim A > C$ is a false
semifactual, then it's not an irrel-semifactual or a pn-semifactual (since the latter are
always true); so $\sim A > C$ is a cts and A is a cause of C. In particular, if the counterfactual $\sim A > \sim C$ is true, then the complementary semifactual $\sim A > C$ is false, and
hence A is a cause of C. The venerable intuition that if the counterfactual $\sim A > \sim C$
is true, then A is a cause of C, thus logically follows from the above analyses of
counterfactuals and the above conception of cause.

This completes the counterfactual analysis of cause. A is a cause of C[73] iff the
semifactual $\sim A > C$ is neither an irrel-semifactual nor a pn-semifactual.

We can summarize these findings by providing a breakdown of the conditions for
A's being a cause of C and for A's not being a cause of C in counterfactual terms of
the above sort, thereby providing a counterfactual analysis of cause. This summary
can be expressed by the chart in figure 15.1 (where "A c C" abbreviates "A is a cause
of C" and "sem" abbreviates "semifactual").

Hume considered the truth of $\sim A > \sim C$ as necessary and sufficient for A's being a
cause of C. In that Hume was wrong: The truth of $\sim A > \sim C$ is indeed a sufficient
condition (as shown above—Hume was right about that), but it falls considerably
short of being a necessary condition for A's being a cause of C. Lewis's analysis
required causation to be transitive.[74] However, transitivity cuts across the various
categories in the above analysis and, as I have argued elsewhere,[75] causation is not
transitive. In addition to the cases where the nonsemifactual counterfactual $\sim A >
\sim C$ is true, in which A is a cause of C, there are two other important types of cases,
characterizable counterfactually, where A is a cause of C as well: the set of cases
in which the counterfactual $\sim A > \sim C$ as well as the complementary semifactual
$\sim A > C$ are both false; and the set of cases with true cts. These three counterfactual
categories together constitute the scope of cases where A is a cause of C.[76]

Although it is extensionally adequate, this analysis of causation is circular, since
the above analysis of counterfactuals is based on the ingredients of the notion of

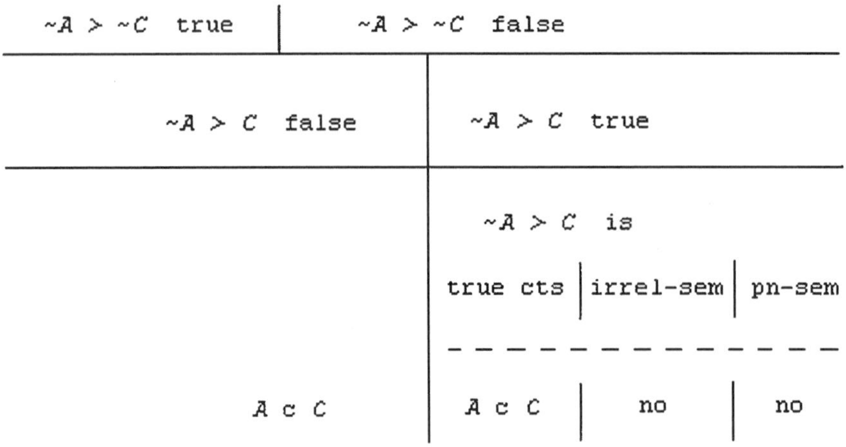

~A > ~C true	~A > ~C false		
~A > C false	~A > C true		
	~A > C is		
	true cts	irrel-sem	pn-sem
A c C	A c C	no	no

Figure 15.1

cause (i.e., if not on the notion of cause itself, then on the notions of causal relevance and purely negative causal relevance). An analysis of cause in terms of counterfactuals, which themselves are analyzed in terms of cause (or sufficiently closely related notions) is circular. I have argued at length that any adequate analysis of n-d counterfactuals must respect the constraint that all intermediate events causally independent of the negation of the antecedent, A (or such that A is purely negatively causally relevant to them), be preserved among the implicit premises.[77] Hence an adequate analysis of counterfactuals should be based on causal notions, and thus no noncircular counterfactual analysis of cause is feasible.

Acknowledgments

A much longer version of this essay was written in summer 1997. The account of the first 6 sections was presented as a series of two lectures in UNAM, Mexico City, in early August 1997, and I thank the audience, and particularly Dorothy Edgington, for their reaction. It was also presented in California State University at Sacramento and at the University of Washington in October 1997, and at the University of Miami in April 1998, and I thank the audience, particularly Marc Lange, Alan Goldman, and Risto Hilpinen, for their reactions. Section 2 was added in August 1998, after a discussion with Ned Hall. Sections 2 and 10 and were added in October 1998. Section 7 was added in the middle of March 1999. I also want to thank Alex Byrne and Christopher Hitchcock for discussions of some of these themes.

Notes

1. I assume a nonrelativistic framework. However, since in general the order of temporal priority is assumed here, this assumption can be construed as having the effect that the notion of cause is frame dependent.

2. I thus assume an indeterministic world.

3. In this essay I deal only with token causes and token causal relevance. I employ narrow event individuation, Kim-style (which is called for if token events are to have probabilities), appropriately extended. For further details, see my (2001b), note 21.

4. The problem arose both in cases of generic causation as well as in cases of token causation. Recourse to the purported transitivity of causation partly addresses this issue, but only regarding the necessary condition for being a cause, where transitivity might be taken to play a role. However, as various people have argued (myself included), causation is not transitive. For my arguments against transitivity, see my (1991b), pp. 125–160, section 5, where I argued that owing to diagonalization causal relevance is not transitive. But causal relevance is a necessary condition for being a cause, which gives rise to the nontransitivity of cause. And indeed, the notion of cause is vulnerable to diagonalization as the notion of causal relevance is. Cause is thus not transitive as well. For a different counterexample against the transitivity of causation, see my (1997), section 5, and my (2001a), section 1. Michael McDermott (1995a) offered the dog-bite counterexample, which, however, I argued, is unsuccessful (see my 2001a, section 1, and my forthcoming b, section 12). Other successful counterexamples against cause transitivity have been offered by Ned Hall and Hartry Field (see Lewis 2000, p. 194; Hall, chapters 7 and 9 in this volume).

The problem of causes that lower the probability of their effects, which has often been handled by recourse to transitivity, is here handled by the requirement of a stable increaser (see below). The corresponding problem of noncauses despite probability increase is handled on my account, in one kind of case, through the requirement of a stable increaser (and not just ab initio probability increase—see below), and in another kind of case, through the requirement of causal relevance, which involves another kind of intermediate events—neutralizers (see below). (Peter Menzies noted the failure of raising the probability of the effect as a sufficient condition for being a cause in view of causal chains that are cut off. See Menzies 1989a; see also my 1991a.)

5. For detailed arguments, see my (1991a), which shows that causal relevance depends strongly on the intermediate course. Cause of course requires causal relevance. See also my (1997), section 8.

6. For a detailed analysis of this notion of cause, understood in terms of ex post facto probability increase and employing the notion of an increaser, see my (1997), sections 6–12.

It is desirable to compare the advantages and disadvantages of the approach summarized here with alternative approaches, e.g., the counterfactual approach (for an indeterministic world, for instance à la Lewis) or with the process approach (e.g., à la Salmon or Dowe). Limitations of space for this essay preclude such a detailed comparison. In my (1997) I have undertaken a fairly detailed critical comparison, insofar as the notion of cause is concerned, to Lewis's (1986b), Salmon's, and Dowe's analyses (see sections 1, 2, 3, 4, 15, 16, 17). Suffice it to say, with respect to the process approach, that the process account of cause has a hard time handling instances of causation that are not processlike, such as cases of omissions, absences, preventions, and double preventions. Attempts to extend the approach by relying on counterfactuals (e.g., Dowe's 2000) to make it possible to address such cases, as well as Salmon's original resort to counterfactuals in characterizing causal processes (in Salmon 1984, chapter 7), lead to circularity when considered in terms of my analysis of counterfactuals in terms of causal ingredients (see my 1997) and undermine causation as a unified phenomenon once based both on processes as well as counterfactuals. Further, noncircular analyses of exactly what in general a process and in particular a causal process is are hard to come by. Salmon's (1984) attempt regarding causal processes relied on counterfactuals, and its extensional adequacy has been criticized (see, among others, my critique in my 1997, sections 3, 4, 15, 17, and further references there). Still further, attempts to define causal processes without reliance on counterfactuals, such as Dowe's, seem to be limited to processes characterized in physical terms and to be incapable of moving up to higher levels involving human actions and mental states, thereby limiting the applicability of the approach. (See also the discussion of Dowe's position in my 1997, notes 22, 31, 34.)

7. Assume that x's financial state at t_A can be summarized by Z. Strictly speaking, C should be read as: x's financial position was significantly better than Z.

8. This notion, strictly speaking, doesn't carry causal implications and is strictly probabilistic: All it means is that, when E is held fixed, the probability of C with A is higher than with $\sim A$.

9. Assume that x answered the questions in their alphabetical order.

10. Menzies noted such insufficiency in cases when causal routes are cut off (note 3 above).

11. In discussing intermediate events, I will consider only actual events.

12. I have used the notion of a strict increaser in my earlier writings, but the notion of a stable increaser seems more suitable.

13. t_A is the time interval to which A pertains.

14. Thus, one may consider an empty intermediate event as the null increaser in this case.

15. Given causal relevance (see below). I offered this account of stable increasers as a solution to the problem (for probabilistic accounts of causation) of causes that lower the probability of their effects, a well-known problem, as well to the problem of events that raise the probability of later events that are nonetheless not their effects, in my (1994). When I wrote that paper I was not yet entirely sure whether to commit myself fully to the thesis that a case with some positive causal impact, or a case with a stable (strict) increaser (given causal relevance), amounts to a case of causation, and I thus proceeded to use, instead, the stable increasers analysis as a stepping stone to the more complex notion of overall positive causal impact.

16. Given, of course, causal relevance—here and above regarding causal relevance. For more on mixed causal relevance, see my (2001a), section 3.

17. Hitchcock (1993) and (1996a). For an analogous example, see Hitchcock (1996b). I assume that the chances that the patient x would follow his doctor's orders were high (and x did indeed follow them). The way the patient recovered was as expected in both variations.

18. In the $\sim A$-case, it is plausible that there is a higher chance that the patient did not act on his disposition to fulfill his doctor's orders, and thus the chances that he did not take the medicine at all seems higher than in the A-case.

19. See my (2001a), note 54. The recourse to A' and to the principle of Cause Preservation under Informational Expansion might be indispensable if a radical enough version of the case is articulated. Notice, however, that here I do not address explanation. In particular, I do not address contrastive explanation. Regarding the first doctor, I do not address the issue of whether the patient recovered *because* the doctor prescribed 100 ml. I exclusively address the issue of whether the fact that he prescribed 100 ml was a cause of the fact that the patient recovered, and this, I submit, is true.

20. See my (forthcoming b).

21. I assume here that the avalanche didn't affect the chance that the second enemy hit x. If, contrary to this assumption, the avalanche decreased it, A may well have had purely negative causal relevance to C, yet still without having been a cause of C. For how purely negative causal relevance implies no cause, see my (1997), sections 6, 7 and 13; my (2001b), section 3; and my (2001a), section 4. For a more detailed account of this conception of causal relevance, see my (2001b).

22. For further details, see my (2003), sections 7 and 8. Here I abbreviate "a causal-relevance neutralizer" as "a neutralizer," rather than as "a crn," as I did in earlier writings.

23. I use these two terms interchangeably.

24. I.e., its occurrence time must be between A and C.

25. In general (as will be clear once we present the full analysis of a neutralizer), if there is one neutralizer, there are many. Various informational expansions of a neutralizer also fulfill the role of a neutralizer. In securing causal irrelevance, we need to secure the presence of just one event fulfilling the role of a neutralizer. If a certain event E in fact secures the neutralization of the causal relevance of A to C, but this is not revealed ab initio, that is, from our usual perspective of (the lower limit of) t_A, i.e., given W_A alone, then

some informational expansion of E secures it ab initio as well if the informational expansion adds further information that secures that various would-be causal threads were neutralized. Therefore, if causal irrelevance is attested to by an event E that in fact secures the neutralization of the would-be causal relevance of A to C, but is not a stable screener, it will also be attested to by a neutralizer, which is a stable screener (e.g., by some conjunctive expansion of E). Hence, without loss of generality, we can confine our attention in securing the condition for a neutralizer to stable screeners.

26. A conjunctive expansion of a stable screener E that yields a stable screener of it is an event $E.F$, for some intermediate F.

27. We need not be terribly precise here—see note 24: All we need is to characterize an event that secures the neutralization of would-be causal relevance. If there is one, there are many, and for establishing causal irrelevance it doesn't matter which one we pick. Hence we may characterize neutralizers in a way that brings out the fact that they serve that role and yet do not include ingredients that are immaterial to that role.

28. Exception: Causal relevance and the presence of a stable increaser are necessary, but not entirely sufficient, for an event's being a cause. It must further be ascertained, when checking for causes, that there is no purely negative causal relevance despite the presence of a stable increaser. This can happen if the route of the would-be positive causal relevance (indicated by a stable increaser) is neutralized by a *positive relevance neutralizer*. This case can be analyzed with the notions used here to analyze causal relevance, but I will not discuss it further. See my (forthcoming c). I ignore this complication below.

29. For a motivation for this thesis, see my (2001b), esp. section 5. Stable screeners can be exhaustive channelers (see there) or neutralizers. Exhaustive channelers typically are such that A is a cause of them (though not always, since causal relevance transitivity fails, as I have argued in my 1991b, section 5). Thus, a promising way of excluding exhaustive channelers from the array of stable screeners while retaining neutralizers is by requiring that A not be a cause of the stable screener.

30. One might say that the presence of an endpoint neutralizer is a *conclusive defeater* for the prima facie causal relevance presented by the presence of a differentiator.

31. For a more detailed presentation of the above analysis of cause, see my (1997), sections 6–12. For a more detailed presentation of the above analysis of causal relevance, see my (2001b).

32. See the references in the previous note.

33. Assume x had only one bullet.

34. In fact, many.

35. The following example was given by David Lewis in his (2000), as an example of probabilistic causation for which he has no analysis.

36. The outcome would have been different if the bomb on flight 17 had been discovered and the paper had printed the headline: "Airline bomb disaster; another bomb discovered." But in the story as specified above, the headline is as specified in C.

37. The classification and the terminology of early and late preemption are due to David Lewis.

38. The example is Ned Hall's. In the version of late preemption discussed here, the time of the effect, t_C (which is t_3) is a small interval covering just the time of the actual shattering. An analogous treatment applies when the temporal quantifier in C is construed as existential, with t_C specifying a reference time rather than an occurrence time, and thus with the effect being construed as nonfragile; see my (2003), section 9.

39. The distance d could not be traversed at velocity v within the time interval ε under the circumstances. To take an extra precaution to secure that E is a screener, one can add to E a clause to the effect that the circumstances surrounding the trajectory of Billy's stone during $(t_E, t_3^- - \varepsilon/10)$ were as could be expected as of t_2, given B. (Of course, if they were different, one might need to have a different clause regarding such facts, e.g., that there was no sudden intermediate thrust accelerating Billy's rock.) A requisite neutralizer need not stretch all the way to the upper end of the (t_2, t_3) interval, as is evidenced in ε in E. And indeed, since the temporal interval for E involved ε, the upper limit of t_E was earlier than that of t_C. Yet one may

opt for a neutralizer for A_2 and C that does not employ such an ε; but then one needs to heed the constraint on such neutralizers (applying when the upper limit of the occurrence time of the neutralizer coincides with that of C). See my (2003), sections 7, 8.

40. On a natural and plausible reading of the example, A_1 and A_2 are causally independent of each other. Surely the example is entirely different if one assumes that A_2 was a cause of A_1 (with A_2 being earlier). (Note: The two throws may be epiphenomena of a common cause. But such cases do not pose a problem for a chance analysis of cause such as the one presented above since whatever is indicated by the earlier A_i that might tempt you to think it increases the probability of A_j is already indicated by W_{A_i} [since the common cause is recorded there], and hence there is no ab initio probability increase.)

41. Christopher Hitchcock, "Do All and Only Causes Raise Probabilities of Effects?" (chapter 17 in this volume). t is a time interval consisting of the actual occurrence time of C.

42. Under the circumstances, the distance d could not be traversed at velocity v within the time interval ε. One may take here too an extra precaution of the sort suggested in note 38.

43. Again, on a natural and plausible reading of the example, A and B are causally independent of each other.

44. That is, given that no opposing signal arrived first. Later signals don't matter.

45. One can set the pertinent times to suit the example. One can assume that, without an inhibitory signal from c_1 to d, the signal from c_2 is likely to reach e before (or at least no later than) the signal from c_1.

46. It can be the passage of the stimulatory signal through an intermediate point.

47. A was in particular a cause of the timing of C, i.e., that it was at 11:00 P.M. that the convict died. This is a version of Lewis's Kelly example. A similar example is in Michael McDermott (1995a). I have used an example of a cause that is a delayer (though I didn't call it so) to a similar effect in the case of the wife and her husband's pills in my (1994), section IV. For an analysis of causes of timing and of delayers, see my (forthcoming b).

48. In this kind of case there may be a difference between adherents of narrow and broad event individuation. Adherents of broad individuation may feel ambiguous about whether the doctor's action was a cause of the murderer's death: in an obvious sense it was not, yet in another sense, it was a cause of the timing of the death (since it was a delayer). Narrow individuation, as used here, makes it possible to bring out the difference vis-à-vis the timing factor in an explicit and nonambiguous way. For further elaboration on the time-and-manner directedness of being a cause (which is also alluded to briefly in the next section) and the way it is brought out in the above probabilistic treatment, see my (forthcoming b).

49. I.e., take T that maximizes the chance of x's hitting Kennedy at t_3. I take it that, under a plausible construal of the example, ab initio probability decrease is built into the case. In a variation structured differently, in which G raises the chance of C, G may well be a cause of C.

50. G is causally relevant to C, since there is a differentiator and no neutralizer: Candidates such as "x's bullet is in his gun at t_3-t," for small enough t, are not neutralizers since, intuitively, G is a cause of them.

51. Assume that Oswald was not aware that B (and that x did not in fact make a difference to the efficacy of Oswald's firing in any other way).

52. I.e., take T' that allows for a nonnegligible probability of Kennedy's being shot at t_3 by x given that x shot at t_3-T'.

53. Thus, D is a delayer. In particular, D was a cause of the timing of C; see my (forthcoming b).

54. If one takes D', which is D but with an extended temporal interval T instead of an instant-like t_2, and similarly if one takes such an A' instead of A and such a C' instead of C, then, whether D' is a cause of C' depends on various features of the case, unspecified so far, that have to do with whether there is ab initio probability increase for D' and C' (such as: Who is a better shooter—x or Oswald? How much better? To what extent would a shot by one shooter spoil the chances of the other to aim well and be in a position to shoot?). That is, the example is then underspecified regarding the presence of a stable increaser.

55. E.g., as between fragile and nonfragile temporal specifications, as reflected in the difference between "at a temporal point" vs. "during" (where the latter is construed as an existential temporal quantifier). This

difference in turn reflects (especially in cases of nonomissions) the difference between occurrence times and reference times; see the previous note and the previous section. For an elaborate treatment of this flexibility, see my (forthcoming b).

56. It may overlap with T.

57. That is, more than a relatively low threshold. The threshold seems to be numeric rather than proportional, e.g., relative to the set of events that are tokens of the cause type, or relative to the set of events that are tokens of the cause type for which a token of the effect type is also present.

58. This section and the next, which offer a counterfactual analysis of cause, are quite condensed. For a more detailed and less condensed presentation, see my (2001a).

59. See my (1997), esp. sections 1, 2, 5, 15, and 16.

60. For my first attempt to analyze causal notions by chance conditions, see chapter 4 of my (1975), which became chapter 4 of my (1986) (currently available from Ridgeview). (But note endnote 22 in the *Errata* there.) The formal analysis of counterfactuals and, in particular, the version presented there of the chance analysis of related causal notions, appeared in my (1979). The analysis of causal relevance and of purely positive causal relevance presented in my (1986) was superseded by the accounts I have offered later (including the one in this essay).

61. Kvart (1986), especially chapter 2. For a summary of the analysis of n-d counterfactuals (see below), see also my (1992), and especially my (2001a), section 5. This analysis of counterfactuals is conducted under the assumption of indeterminism.

62. See my (1986), p. 29. What this terminology reflects is that alternative courses of events in which $\sim A$ is true are pertinent to this kind of counterfactuals only if they diverge from the actual course right before t_A. For present purposes, we can assume standard temporal order, i.e., that $t_A < t_C$.

63. Regarding inferability, see my (2001a), note 19.

64. All the way to the upper end of t_C.

65. This notion of causal independence was analyzed probabilistically in the first part of this essay (since causal independence is the converse relation of causal irrelevance). Purely negative causal relevance amounts to no positive causal relevance and some negative causal relevance. Some positive causal relevance and some negative causal relevance amount to the presence of a stable increaser and a stable decreaser, respectively, given causal relevance (but note the qualification in note 27).

66. In various discussions of mental causation, causal relevance is considered to be some variant of positive causal relevance. I take this to be a misnomer, and this is emphatically *not* the sense of causal relevance I employ here and elsewhere: negative causal relevance is also causal relevance.

67. This is true apart from any particular analysis. But it follows from the above conception of cause, since some positive causal relevance implies causal relevance.

68. Of the n-d type.

69. The analysis here is of A's being a cause of C, where A and C are true, factual statements.

70. See above, the end of section 1. Purely negative causal relevance amounts to causal relevance without positive causal relevance. In my (1986) I talked about pp-semifactuals, since I focused there on $\sim A$ rather than on A.

71. This example is a variant of example 8 in my (1986), chapter 2. For convenience, I allow A, B, E, etc. to vary through facts (states, events, etc.) as well as through the sentences that specify them.

72. I assume that the stock, which was of substantial value, was sold in a private transaction (which remained confidential at least until Tuesday evening) to an individual who, in turn, was not at all interested in further selling the stock and in fact did not sell it (at least until Tuesday evening). The sharp increase of x's stock investment would allow for his retirement. x's stock was invested in an index fund that reflects the overall performance of the stock market.

73. A and C are true; A is temporally prior to C.

74. In Lewis (1973a) and (1986b). Lewis needs transitivity to handle cases of early preemption. Lewis's analysis in his (2000) retains his adherence to cause transitivity. For a discussion of Lewis's theory in his (2000), see my (2001c).

75. See my (1997), section 5, and my (2001a), section 1. Other effective examples against cause transitivity were offered by Ned Hall (chapter 9 in this volume) and Hartry Field (unpublished).

76. For further details, see my (2000a), section 7 and 8.

77. See, in addition to the previous section, my (1986), ch. 2, sec. V, esp. V.6 and V.7 (pp. 38–40). This holds not just for n-d counterfactuals, but for l-p counterfactuals as well; ibid., ch. 9, sec. I.2 (pp. 236–237).

16 A Counterfactual Analysis of Indeterministic Causation

Murali Ramachandran

Attempts to analyze indeterministic causation in terms of counterfactual conditionals have generally met fairly persuasive refutations.[1] An account is developed in this essay that avoids many of the problems encountered so far. Section 1 outlines David Lewis's counterfactual approach and five problem-cases for his (1986a) probabilistic account of causation—these problems motivate the present project. In section 2, the idea of *background chance* leads to a notion of time-invariant *overall world chance*; the thesis that overall-world-chance-raising is sufficient for causation forms the basis of the new analysis. In section 3 a simple version that handles three of the five problems noted in section 1 is considered. Section 4 concerns the issue of transitivity; the idea of *accumulative chance-raising* is used to discriminate between causal and non-causal chance-raising chains. On the resulting account, causation is not transitive (but it is not *in*transitive either). Section 5 introduces the idea of *potential* chance-raisers as a means of handling cases of overdetermination by nonactual events. The account arrived at in section 5 is intended to work under the assumption that *no* event is determined. Section 6 proposes a simple modification in order to accommodate deterministic causation as well. Section 7 concludes the essay with a couple of caveats.

1   Lewis's Approach

1.1   Deterministic Causation

Lewis (1973a) analyzes deterministic causation in terms of *counterfactual dependence*, this in terms of *counterfactual conditionals*, and these in terms of *possible worlds* plus *degree of similarity* between these worlds and actuality. In short: For any actual, distinct events C and E, C *causes* E if

(1) E (counterfactually) depends on C, that is: *if*

(1a)   If C were to occur, then E would occur; and

(1b)   If C were not to occur, then E would not occur, that is: *if*

(1a*)   The nearest (i.e., most similar) C-worlds are E-worlds; and

(1b*)   The nearest not-C-worlds are not-E-worlds.

C *causes* E iff there is a series of events $[C, X_1, \ldots, X_n, E]$ such that each event in the chain depends on the former one. Here are some of the salient definitions and features of the account:

• The nearest *A*-world is a world that differs *just enough* from actuality so as to render *A* true. (So, (1) and (1*) are trivially true if *C* and *E* are actual events, for the nearest *C*-world will in that case be the actual world itself, which is also an *E*-world.)

• Dependence is *asymmetric*: If *A* depends on *B*, *B* cannot also depend on *A*. (This enables Lewis to resolve the problems of *effects, epiphenomena*, and simple cases of *preemptive causation*—see Lewis 1986a, pp. 170–172.)

• Causation is a relation between *events*; events are *particulars*—they have specific spatiotemporal locations; but it is important that where and when an event occurs are generally not *essential* to its occurrence: It might have occurred at a (slightly) different time and place.

• The analysis identifies what are "loosely speaking" causes; it does not identify "dominant" causes, or *the* cause.

• Singular (brute, one-off) causation is permitted: There may be causation without covering laws (or regularities).

• Causation at a distance is permitted: Causes and their effects need not be linked together by a series of spatiotemporally "contiguous" events.

• Simultaneous and backward causation is permitted: Causes need not precede their effects.

• The transitivity of causation is assumed: If *A* causes *B*, and *B* causes *C*, then *A* causes *C*.

1.2   Indeterministic Causation

The world is *indeterministic* if there are actual events that might have failed to occur without violation of any actual laws. A natural way of capturing this idea in terms of chance is to say that the world is indeterministic if there is at least one actual event, *E*, such that the chance of *E*'s occurring, given that its (actual) causes have occurred, is less than 1. Indeterminism denies the *sufficiency* of causes for their effects, not their (nearby) *necessity*; in other words, an event, *C*, may not *guarantee* the occurrence of an effect, *E*, but this is not to deny that if *C* had not occurred, then *E* would not have occurred. So, one may wonder why Lewis's original theory needs to be modified at all. The problem arises when *E* has a *background chance* of occurring, as in the following example:

The nucleus of an atom in a radioactive substance is bombarded by a subatomic particle (event *C*) and the atom decays (event *E*). Event *C* greatly increased the chance of event *E* occurring, *but E* had a nonzero background chance of occurring regardless; hence, if C had not occurred, *E might still have occurred*. (See Mellor 1995, pp. 52–53, for an informed outline.)

Lewis wants C to count as a cause of E in such cases, where E has a greater chance of occurring because of C's occurrence. So, he incorporates counterfactual chances into his account. The new account is given by the following definitions. For any distinct events C and E,

(*Df1*) C *raises the chance* of E iff the chance of E's occurring would be much higher if C were to occur than if C were not to occur.

(*Df2*) A series of events $[X_1, \ldots, X_n]$ forms a *chance-raising chain (CR-chain)* iff each event in the chain raises the chance of the subsequent one. (X_1 is then said to *chainwise-raise* the chance of X_n.)

(*Df3*) C *causes* E iff C chainwise-raises the chance of E.

Two features of the notion of chance at play here are significant. First, Lewis takes the chance of E's occurring, ch(E), to vary over time; so, for example, E's occurrence might have been very unlikely ten minutes ago, but quite likely two minutes ago. So, in the above definition of chance-raising, ch(E) is to be assessed immediately after the time of C's actual occurrence (t_{C+}). The second significant feature is that for any time t *after* the period over which E might have occurred, the chance *at* t of E's occurring is 1 if E did occur, or 0 if E failed to occur.

1.3   Problems for Lewis's Theory
I will outline five problems for Lewis's theory—these motivate the new account to be developed in this essay.

Problem 1. Nonoccurrence of (required) intermediary event (fig. 16.1)   Suppose C, A, B, and E are neurons linked by very reliable stimulatory axons (signified by the forward arrows). C and A fire, B fails to fire, and E fires spontaneously, unstimulated—(its background chance of occurring is fulfilled, as it were). Now, at time t_{C+}, just

C   A   B   E

Figure 16.1
Nonoccurrence of intermediary events.

after C's actual firing (event C^*), the chance of E's firing (E^*) is higher than it would have been *at that time* if C hadn't fired: Thus, C^* raises the chance of E^*. So, by Lewis's theory, C^* is a cause of E^*, which is plainly incorrect, since the C^*–E^* process was cut short.

Problem 2. "Timely" chance-raising is necessary   Suppose C raises the chance of E's occurring, but that E occurs spontaneously outside the range of C's influence; that is, E occurs *before* or *after C could have* caused it. But, by Lewis's theory C nevertheless comes out a cause of E. The simple solution to this problem we shall be adopting, roughly, is to make it a necessary condition of C's causing E that C chainwise-raises the chance, not just of E's occurring, but also of its occurring *when it did*.[2]

Problem 3. Chancy "backward" causation is precluded by the definition   Lewis thought it a virtue of his account of deterministic causation that it did not rule out the possibility of backward causation, that is, the possibility of an effect preceding its cause. However, the present theory rules out direct indeterministic backward causation, because it is not possible for an event, C, to be a chance-raiser of an earlier event, E, that had a chance of occurring regardless. Here's why: $ch(E)$ is to be assessed at time t_{C+}, immediately *after* C's occurrence; in the actual world (the nearest C-world), $ch(E)$ at t_{C+} will be 1, since E has already occurred by then; if C had not occurred, E might still have occurred when it did (by hypothesis), so $ch(E)$ at t_{C+} might still have been 1.

Problem 4. Causation is transitive by the definition   On Lewis's account causation is transitive by stipulation—for, if there is a CR-chain between A and B and between B and C, there will be one between A and C. But there appear to be counterexamples to transitivity. Here is a variation on Michael McDermott's (1995a) dog-bite example. Singh was due to detonate a bomb but is involved in an accident (event C) that prevents this. Patel detonates the bomb instead (event D) and the bomb duly explodes (event E). C raises the chance of D, and D raises the chance of E; thus, C causes D and D causes E; but it seems plainly wrong to hold that C (the accident) is a cause of E (the explosion). So, causation is not transitive.

However, this is not to say that causation is *in*transitive. Suppose Patel has a stiff drink (event F) after pressing the button to calm his nerves. C is a cause of D and D is a cause of F; and in this case, it seems right to say C is a cause of F. So, to solve the transitivity problem, we need a way to discriminate between the two sorts of cases.[3]

Problem 5. Overdetermination by nonactual events (fig. 16.2)   Take the diagram in figure 16.2 to be a neuron diagram as in figure 16.1. Suppose the CE-axon is un-

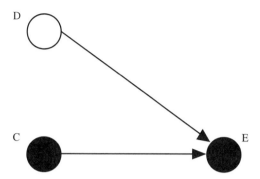

Figure 16.2
Overdetermination by nonactual event.

reliable and the DE-axon is very reliable; C fires (event C^*), D fails to fire (D^* fails to occur), and E fires (E^*). Clearly, C^* is a cause of E^*; but C^* does not raise the chance of E^*; indeed, if C had not fired, D might have fired, in which case the chance of E^* would have been *higher* than it actually is.

The account to be developed in this paper is intended to handle all of the above problems.[4]

2 Overall World Chance

In the decay example E was said to have a small, nonzero *background chance* ($= \beta$ say) of occurring. I take this to mean that there are nearby worlds with the same laws where C (the bombardment) does not occur and where E has chance β of occurring regardless of whether E does occur there or not. In the E-worlds among these worlds, it would seem quite proper to say that E occurred despite having only β chance of occurring. On this notion of chance, the chance at a time t of E's occurring is not 1 if E has already occurred by t; likewise, it is not 0 if t is after the time E might have occurred and E has failed to occur. The chance, in this sense, of E's occurring is *constant*: It is the chance E had of occurring *in the world in question*.

One may think of such chances as being determined by the laws of the world taking all the events of that world into account. If the laws of the world are deterministic, these chances will be 0 or 1; if the laws are not all deterministic, at least some of these chances will be between 0 and 1.

We should not think of chance in this sense as simply being the *background chance* of an event's occurring. The world considered in the decay example is a world in which both C and E occur. It would seem perfectly proper to say of this world that E had a much higher than β chance, $= \alpha$, say, of occurring. What chance it had of occurring does not become 1 after it occurs; it had α chance, period. And it would seem correct to say, since we are assuming indeterminism, that there is a nearby world where E had the same chance, α, of occurring, but simply failed to occur.

I shall call chance in this sense *overall world chance* (or simply *owchance*), and say that $owch(E)$ is α at w when the owchance of E's occurring in world w is α. I propose to analyze causation in terms of *owchance-raising*, defined as follows:

(*Df4*) For any distinct events C and E, C *raises* $owch(E)$ iff $owch(E)$ would be much higher if C were to occur than if C were not to occur.

One of the problems we noted for Lewis's theory was that an event C may raise $ch(E)$ without raising the chance of E's occurring *when it did*. The same presumably goes for owchance-raising. In such cases, it does not seem correct to count C a cause of E. So, our analysis needs to take the owchance of E's occurring *when it did* into account.

For any event E and time t, let "$owch(E, t)$" stand for the owchance of E's occurring *at time t*.[5] Where E is an actual event and t_E is the time of E's actual occurrence, $owch(E, t_E)$ is the owchance of E's occurring when it did.

(*Df5*) For any event C and actual event E, C raises $owch(E, t_E)$ iff $owch(E, t_E)$ would be much higher if C were to occur than if C were not to occur.

The core idea behind the new account of causation then is that raising both $owch(E)$ and $owch(E, t_E)$ is sufficient for being a cause of E.

3 Causation by Way of Owchance-raising: A Simple Analysis

In developing the theory, I shall make the simplifying assumption that *no* event is fully determined, that is, there is no event E such that $owch(E) = 1$ in the actual world.

The first point to note is that it is not *necessary* for causes to be owchance-raisers of their effects. For example, C will not raise the owchance of E if there is a crucial intermediary event D that does not counterfactually depend on C. Consider figure 16.3. In this scenario, neurons C, D, and E fire (events C^*, D^*, and E^*); suppose D has a small background chance of firing even if *un*stimulated. Now, if C^* had not occurred, D^* might have occurred spontaneously, in which case $owch(E^*)$ would be the same as, not lower than, its actual value. So C^* does not raise the owchance of

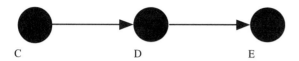

C   D   E

Figure 16.3
Nontransitivity of owchance-raising.

E^*. Yet, if other conditions are met—if, say, the events occur at appropriate times—we might well want to count C^* a cause of E^*. So, being an owchance-raiser is not necessary for causation.

This result compels us to accept that what are only "chainwise" owchance-raisers of an event may be causes of that event, which suggests the following simple analysis.

(*Df6*)   A series of events $[X_1, \ldots, X_n]$ forms an *owchance-raising chain* (an *owchain*) iff each event in the chain raises the owchance of the next event.

(*Df7*)   A series of actual events $[X_1, \ldots, X_n]$ forms a *temporal owchance-raising chain* (a *towchain*) iff each event in the chain raises the owchance of the next event's occurring when it did.

Analysis 1: For any actual, distinct events C and E, C *causes* E iff there is a series of actual events $[C, X_1, \ldots, X_n, E]$ that forms an owchain and a towchain.

The analysis resolves three of the problems for Lewis's theory mentioned in section 1.3.

Problem 1: No causation if the process is incomplete   Consider figure 16.1 again; because B fails to fire, there is no appropriate owchain between C^* and E^*. For example, owch(E^*) would not be lower than it is if A^* had not occurred: B^*'s failure to occur means that A^* had no influence on E^* in the first place.

Problem 2: Causation requires "timely" owchance-raising   This is explicit in the specification of the analysis.

Problem 3: Backward causation is not ruled out   The analysis does not preclude the possibility of an event C being a cause of an earlier event E. The analysis does not consider the chance *at a certain time* of E's occurring (the owchances in question are constant over time in any world). Of course, this does not *explain* how backward owchance-raising is possible or render it more plausible; but the important point is that, unlike Lewis's approach, this analysis allows that backward owchance-raising and hence backward causation are not explicitly ruled out by the very definition of causation.

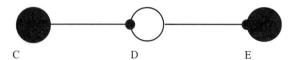

C   D   E

Figure 16.4
Inhibition of an inhibitor.

Another result of note is that *inhibitors of inhibitors* of an event E do not generally come out as causes of E.

In figure 16.4, C *lowers* the owchance of D (shown as a line ending in a dot) and of D's occurring when it did, and D fails to occur; D, had it occurred, would have lowered the owchance of E and of E's occurring when it did. If C had not occurred, D might still have failed to occur, in which case owch(E) and owch(E, t_E) would not be any lower. So, C does not come out a cause of E. This contrasts with the deterministic case, where preventers of preventers *do* come out as causes by Lewis's approach: If C had not occurred, D *would have* occurred and prevented E's occurrence; so, C comes out a cause of E because E straightforwardly depends on C.

Theorists are divided on the question of whether inhibitors of inhibitors are causes, and intuitions seem to vary from case to case; so, I do not think the above result presents a decisive point for or against the present account.[6] But the account must be rejected nevertheless—at any rate, modified—because it does not resolve the transitivity problem or the problem of overdetermination by nonactual events (problems 4 and 5 in sec. 1.3).

4   The Transitivity Problem and *Accumulative* Owchance-raising

Let us reconsider the transitivity problem. Our problem was that we wanted the accident to come out a cause of Patel's taking the stiff drink, but not a cause of the explosion, even though there are owchains linking the accident to both. But, as figure 16.5 reveals, there *is* a significant difference between the two chains. If *neither* the accident *nor* Patel's pressing of the button had occurred, then the owchance of the explosion's occurring *might not have* been lower than it is—for, Singh might have pressed the button instead (an event inhibited if not prevented by the accident). By contrast, if *neither* the accident *nor* Patel's pressing of the button had occurred, then the owchance of Patel taking the stiff drink *would have been* less than it is. This difference between the owchains suggests a simple modification to analysis 1 to cope with the transitivity problem.

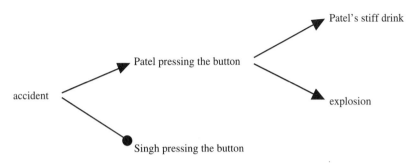

Figure 16.5
Failure of transitivity.

(*Df8*) An owchain of actual events, $[X_1, \ldots, X_n]$, is an *accumulative owchain* iff the owchance of any event in the chain would have been lower than it actually is if *none of the former events* in the chain had occurred. (X_1 is then an *accumulative owchance-raiser* of X_n.)

Analysis 2: For any distinct actual events C and E, C *causes* E iff there is a series of actual events $[C, X_1, \ldots, X_n, E]$ that forms a towchain and an accumulative owchain.[7]

In our example, the series of events [the accident, Patel pressing the button, the explosion] is an owchain but not an *accumulative* owchain; so, the accident does not come out a cause of the explosion. But, [the accident, Patel pressing the button, Patel taking the stiff drink] is an accumulative owchain, so we get the desired verdict that the accident is a cause of Patel's drinking the hard stuff. Let us turn our attention now to the remaining problem, that of overdetermination.

5   Overdetermination and *Potential* Owchance-raising

Consider figure 16.2 again. Intuitively, C^* causes E^*; but it fails come out as such by analysis 2, for if C^* had not occurred, then D^* might have occurred, in which case owch(E^*) and owch(E^*, t_{E^*}) would have been *higher* than they actually are. The key to resolving this problem lies in the fact that the actual values of owch(E^*) and owch(E^*, t_{E^*}) are higher than they would have been if *neither C^* nor D^* were to oc-cur. C^* raises these owchances *relative to the nonoccurrence of D^**; in other words, it *would have* raised them *but for the possible occurrence of D^**. The idea that causes need only raise owchances *relative to the nonoccurrence of other events* forms the basis of the successor to analysis 2.[8]

The following definitions, cousins of *Df4–Df8*, simply incorporate the idea of *relative owchance-raising* (*C* and *E* are distinct actual events and Σ is a [possibly empty] set of possible events):

(*Df4**)   *C* Σ-*raises* owch(*E*) iff *C* raises owch(*E*) *relative to the nonoccurrence of the events in* Σ; that is, iff owch(*E*) would be much higher if *C* were to occur without the events in Σ than if *neither C nor* the events in Σ were to occur.

(*Df5**)   *C* Σ-raises owch(*E*, t_E) iff *C* raises owch(*E*, t_E) relative to the nonoccurrence of the events in Σ.

(*Df6**)   A series of events $[X_1, \ldots, X_n]$ forms a Σ-*owchain* iff each event in the chain raises the owchance of the next event relative to the nonoccurrence of the events in Σ. (X_1–X_n are said to form a *potential owchain* if there is such a Σ.)

(*Df7**)   A series of actual events $[X_1, \ldots, X_n]$ forms a Σ-*towchain* iff each event in the chain raises the owchance of the next event's occurring when it did relative to the nonoccurrence of the events in Σ.

(*Df8**)   A Σ-owchain of events, $[X_1, \ldots, X_n]$, is an *accumulative* Σ-*owchain* iff the owchance of any event in the chain would have been lower than it actually is if none of the former events in the chain *nor any of the events in* Σ had occurred.

Now, causation is defined thus:

Analysis 3: For any distinct actual events *C* and *E*, *C causes E* iff there are (possibly empty) sets of possible events, Σ and Ω, and a series of actual events $[C, X_1, \ldots, X_n, E]$ that forms an accumulative Σ-owchain and an Ω-towchain.

(The definition allows that in some cases there may be no single set of events Σ such that the events in a causal process form both a Σ-owchain and a Σ-towchain. Of course, Σ and Ω will be one and the same set on many occasions.)

Simple result 1   If *C* Σ-raises owch(*E*) and *C* Ω-raises owch(*E*, t_E), where *C* and *E* are distinct actual events and Σ and Ω are sets of possible events, then *C* causes *E*.

Proof   Suppose the antecedent of the above conditional is met. Then, it follows trivially by definition that $[C, E]$ is a Σ-owchain and a Ω-towchain. Now, $[C, E]$ is an accumulative Σ-owchain if it is true that the chance of *E* would be lower than it actually is if none of the former events in the chain (i.e. *C*) nor any of the events in Σ were to occur. But this condition is already met if, as has been assumed, *C* and *E* are actual events and *C* Σ-raises owch(*E*). Hence, *C* comes out a cause of *E*.

Simple result 2 If C raises owch(E) and owch(E, t_E), where C and E are distinct actual events, then C causes E.

Proof Take $\Sigma = \Omega = \varnothing$, the empty set. Then C Σ-raises owch(E) and C Ω-raises owch(E, t_E). From simple result 1 we then get that C causes E.

Let us check whether we get the right verdict in our overdetermination example (figure 16.2). Let $\Sigma = \Omega = \{D^*\}$. C^* Σ-raises owch(E^*): As noted earlier, owch(E^*) would be higher if C^* were to occur without D^* than if neither C^* nor D^* were to occur. The same goes for C^*, which likewise Ω-raises owch(E^*, t_{E^*}). It now follows from simple result 1 that C is a cause of E, as required.

Analysis 3 handles all the problem-cases we have considered so far. But, the sigma-chance-raising approach, as we might call it, ushers in a fresh problem that calls for a qualification to the condition specified in the analysis.

Problem 6 Suppose a stone is thrown at a window (event A); someone in the building, unaware of event A, opens the window slightly (event C)—(imagine here a window that opens *outward* rather than *upward*). The stone hits the window, and the window shatters (event E); however, E would have occurred even if the window hadn't been opened: The stone would simply have struck and shattered it a bit later. Intuitively, C (the opening of the window) is *not* a cause of E (the window's shattering), but the present analysis delivers the opposite verdict.[9] Here's why:

Step 1 Let $\Sigma = \Omega =$ the set of possible but *nonactual* movements of the stone between the open-window position and the closed-window position that are *prevented* by the actual impact.

Step 2 C Σ-raises owch(E): owch(E) would be much higher if C were to occur without any of the events in Σ than it would be if neither C nor these events were to occur. If the window is not opened and none of the events in Σ occurs, then *the stone does not even reach the window*.

Step 3 C Ω-raises owch(E, t_E).—If the window is not opened and none of the events in Ω occurs, then there is (close to) zero chance of the window shattering *when it did*.

Step 4 By simple result 1, steps 2 and 3 dictate that C causes E, as claimed (but not as desired).

My strategy for tackling this problem rests on the following observations. There is a *possible* owchain from A (the stone-throwing) to E (the window shattering) that involves (a) the *actual* movements of the stone up until the impact with the open window and (b) certain *nonactual* events that are in Σ, namely, certain possible-but-unrealized movements of the stone between the open-window position and the closed-window position that were prevented from occurring by actual window-shattering. What is special about this possible owchain is that if *none of its actual events* were to occur, then C (the window-opening) *would not have been* a Σ-owch(E)-raiser at all. C's being a Σ-owch(E)-raiser *depends* on the occurrence of these events; if these events do not occur, the stone does not reach even the open-window position —hence, the owchance of the window shattering will be close to zero whether the window is open or closed.

So, I suggest that an event, C, should count as a cause of another event, E, if C and E meet the condition specified by analysis 3 *but only so long as they are not in a situation structurally similar to the above example.* Formally:

Analysis 4: For any distinct actual events C and E, C *causes* E iff

(1)   there are sets of possible events, Σ and Ω, and a series of actual events $[C, X_1, \ldots, X_n, E]$ that forms an accumulative Σ-owchain and an Ω-towchain; *and*

(2)   there is *no potential* owchain $[Y_1, \ldots, Y_j, Z_1, \ldots, Z_k, E]$ where (2_1)–(2_3) all hold:

(2_1)   the Y-events are actual;

(2_2) Z_1 is *non-actual* and in Σ; and

(2_3)   if none of the Y-events were to occur, then C might have occurred but would not have been a Σ-raiser of owch(E).

This is the final analysis I put forward for indeterministic causation. I believe it handles all the problem-cases that have been mentioned in this essay. So far, we have been working under the assumption of full-scale indeterminism, the view that *no* event is fully determined. The question arises: Can the proposed approach be developed so as to accommodate deterministic causation?

6   A Counterfactual Analysis of Causation (Deterministic or Not)

At present, the only problem I see emerging from the relaxing of the assumption of full-scale indeterminism is of the following sort.

Problem 7   Read figure 16.6 as a neuron diagram, and suppose that any neuron has zero chance of firing if unstimulated and a chance of 1 of firing if stimulated *without*

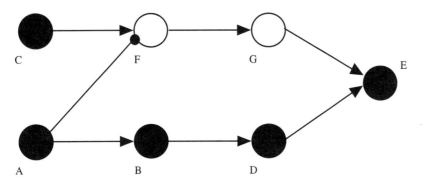

Figure 16.6
Deterministic preemption.

interference. In this case, A fires (A^* occurs) and prevents F from firing, thereby cutting the C–E process. Intuitively, A^* is a cause of E^*, but C^* is not. Analysis 4, however, delivers the verdict that both A^* and C^* are causes of E^*. Here's how C^* comes out a cause:

Step 1   Let $\Sigma = \Omega = \{A^*\}$.

Step 2 C Σ-raises owch(E^*): If C^* had occurred without A^*, F^* and G^* would have occurred, in which case owch(E^*) would have been 1; and if *neither C^* nor A^** had occurred, then E^* would have had zero owchance of occurring.

Step 3 C Ω-raises owch(E, t_E) (reasoning as above).

Step 4   Hence, by simple result 1 in section 5, C^* comes out a cause of E^*, as claimed (but not as desired).

By similar reasoning, letting $\Sigma = \Omega = \{G^*\}$, say, we get the correct verdict that A^* causes E^*. To resolve this problem, then, we must find a significant difference between any Σ (or Ω) set one may use to get C^* to come out a cause and any Σ (or Ω) set one may use to get A^* to come out a cause.

Here is such a difference. In the case of C^*, we can add a *nonactual* event to the given Σ set—call the resulting $\Sigma\#$—such that C^* does *not* $\Sigma\#$-raise owch(E^*). For example, we had $\Sigma = \{A^*\}$; add G^* to this, so $\Sigma\# = \{A^*, G^*\}$; now, if C^* were to occur without any of the events in $\Sigma\#$—namely, A^* and G^*—then E^* would have 0 owchance of occurring; hence, C^* does not $\Sigma\#$-raise owch(E^*).

By contrast, in the case of A^*, there is no nonactual event we can add to a corresponding Σ set to get a parallel result. The reason for this disparity between A^* and

C^* is simple: the A^*–E^* process is actually complete—every event in it actually occurs—whereas the C^*–E^* process is incomplete—it does involve nonactual events.

This suggests a simple solution to problem 7. All we need modify in the account we currently have are the Σ-owchance raising definitions, *Df4** and *Df5** in section 5; we simply replace them with:

(*Defn4†*) C Σ-*raises* owch(E) iff for any superset of Σ, $\Sigma\#$, containing just nonactual events in addition to the members of Σ, C raises owch(E) *relative to the nonoccurrence of the events in $\Sigma\#$.*

(*Defn5†*) C Σ-*raises* owch(E, t_E) iff for any superset of Σ, $\Sigma\#$, containing just nonactual events in addition to the members of Σ, C raises owch(E, t_E) *relative to the nonoccurrence of the events in $\Sigma\#$.*

These minor modifications are, I hazard, sufficient to handle the problems determinism throws up. We need not, the reader will be pleased to note, modify analysis 4's specifications at all.

One interesting result is that counterfactual dependence is no longer sufficient for causation. Consider the inhibitor-of-an-inhibitor from section 3 (figure 16.4) again. We noted that in the deterministic version of that problem, we have counterfactual dependence: E depends on C because it prevents a preventer, D, of E. By Lewis's accounts, C is therefore a cause of E. But not by our account. Let Σ be any set of events such that C Σ-raises owch(E)—(consider $\Sigma = \varnothing$, the empty set, for example); adding the nonactual event D to Σ will yield a set $\Sigma\#$ where C does not $\Sigma\#$-raise owch(E). For, owch(E) would be no higher if C were to occur without D than if neither C nor D occurred. This result is fortuitous, because it means that inhibitors of inhibitors are treated alike whether indeterminism is assumed or not.

7   Summing Up

The analysis we have arrived at is, so far as I know, the only counterfactual account on the market that promises to handle the problems mentioned in the essay. Of course, everything hinges on the coherence of *overall world chance*, or at any rate, on the existence of a suitable notion of *overall chance* that does not vary over time. The few remarks I have made in support will strike some readers as quite inadequate. It *may* turn out that no such notion is tenable, or, what I think is more likely, that the most feasible candidates are ones that do preclude the possibility of backward causation. But I hope to have at least shown how the mentioned problems may be resolved with a suitable, albeit pending, notion of time-invariant chance.

One problem I have left well alone: Schaffer's (2000b) problem of *trumping pre-emption*.[10] I cannot at present see how any counterfactual account will be able to handle all the varieties of trumping preemption. But I do not think one should reject the counterfactual approach on the basis of just this; if, overall, the approach sits better with our intuitive verdicts on the whole range of test-cases than do other approaches, one should perhaps question our intuitive verdicts in this special case.[11]

Acknowledgments

The earliest incarnation of this essay was presented at a workshop on *Chance and Cause* jointly organized by the University of Tasmania and the London School of Economics in September 1999. Other versions have been presented at the University of Sheffield, the University of Sussex, and the London School of Economics. I thank the audiences involved for the valuable discussions. Thanks in particular to Stephen Barker, Helen Beebee, Ron Chrisley, Cian Dorr, Phil Dowe, Jonardon Ganeri, Paul Noordhof, and David Papineau. Rob Charleston deserves special thanks for extensive comments on late drafts, as does Ned Hall for doing the diagrams for this essay.

Notes

1. Some examples: Lewis (1986b) has been refuted by Menzies (1989a); Menzies (1989a) has been rejected, if not refuted, by Menzies himself (1996); Noordhof (1998) persuades me that my *M*-set analysis (1997a, 1998)—which I claimed handled indeterministic causation without invoking chances at all—ignores indeterminism proper; and, to my mind at any rate, Noordhof's own (1999) account has decisive counterexamples (see my 2000; Noordhof 2000).

2. This problem is mentioned in Byrne and Hall (1998, p. 44, fn. 4), Paul (1998a), and Noordhof (1998). Lewis (2000) now takes it to be sufficient for C being a cause of E that E's time of occurrence chainwise depends on C; the trouble with this proposal is that *mere hasteners* and *delayers* of an event come out as causes of that event. I find this counterintuitive. The solution proposed here (*pace* Ramachandran 1998 and Noordhof 1999) does not have this consequence. See Paul (1998b) for an alternative line.

3. Paul (2000) despairs of finding a solution to this problem on the counterfactual approach and proposes a radically different account that, e.g., makes explicit appeal to laws and takes the causal relata to be features of events (*property instances*) rather than the events *simpliciter*. As we shall see, however, the problem can be resolved with counterfactuals alone.

4. For the record, Lewis (2000), his latest, "causation as influence" approach, is vulnerable to all of these problems, save the problem about "timely" chance-raising—but even here, the problem is avoided only at the cost of ushering in new problems (see note 2 above).

5. Some remarks on owch(E, t). First, owch(E, t) will typically vary with t: so, e.g., one might hold that E has a smaller owchance of occurring now than in 2 minutes time. Second, since we are taking events to be particulars, for any event E, there will be times t_1 and t_2 such that owch(E, t) = 0 for any time t before t_1 or after t_2—intuitively, t_1 and t_2 mark the time interval within which E might have occurred, or, rather, had a positive owchance of occurring. Third, for any time t, owch(E, t) will be less than owch(E)—unless t is the *only* time at which E has a positive owchance of occurring, in which case these chances will be the same. (I expect owch(E) can be defined in terms of owch(E, t), taking the latter to be a function of time; I

leave the formulation to the experts.) Finally, I have taken t to be an *instant* for the sake of simplicity; obviously, an event will have a *duration*, so it is wrong to talk of its occurring at a particular instant t. But, so far as I can see, no major difficulties arise if we take the "t" in "owch(E, t)" to stand for a particular *time interval* rather than an instant.

6. I am actually inclined towards the view that inhibitors of inhibitors are causes (see my 1998); but Hall (2000), for example, is inclined to the opposite view.

7. The reader may wish to test his or her grasp of the definitions by checking that this condition is trivially met if C raises owch(E) and owch(E, t_E).

8. This idea is used in the analysis of deterministic causation by Ganeri, Noordhof, and Ramachandran (1996), (1998) and is utilized for the indeterministic case by Noordhof (1999).

9. I initially presented this as a problem for Noordhof's (1999) account but owned that it might be an inescapable problem for the sigma-dependence approach generally (see my 2000, pp. 312–313, including fn. 4 on p. 313). The solution offered in this essay gets the approach off the hook.

10. Many of the articles in this collection discuss the problem, so I will not rehearse it.

11. For example, I have mild but persistent misgivings about the fact that the formulations of trumping preemption examples beg the question in favor of the covering-law model of causation. Maybe reductionist-minded counterfactual-theorists should just deny the coherence of the examples.

17 Do All and Only Causes Raise the Probabilities of Effects?

Christopher Hitchcock

1 Introduction

According to probabilistic theories of causation, causes raise the probabilities of their effects. Opponents of probabilistic theories of causation offer putative counterexamples. A moment's reflection should lead us to expect such counterexamples to be of two types: (1) causes that appear *not* to raise the probabilities of their effects; and (2) events that appear to raise the probabilities of other events, without causing those events. Almost all of the cases that have been discussed in the literature have been of the first sort; these can be effectively handled using resources that are already available. Counterexamples of the second sort, which have been largely ignored, still pose a threat. I will explore some options for avoiding these counterexamples, and more important, argue that they raise fundamental questions about the nature of indeterministic causation—questions that transcend issues about the correctness of any particular philosophical theory.

2 Probabilistic Causation

The motivation for a probabilistic theory of causation lies in the desire to have a theory that encompasses causal relationships that are inherently indeterministic or "chancy." The central idea behind probabilistic theories of causation is that causes raise the probabilities of their effects. Perhaps the simplest and most natural way to formulate this idea is in terms of conditional probability. C raises the probability of E, and hence C causes E, exactly if $P(E/C) > P(E/\sim C)$.

This proposal is subject to a well-known problem. Coughing raises the probability of lung cancer: Coughers are more likely to be smokers than are noncoughers, and since smokers are more likely to contract lung cancer than nonsmokers, coughers will also be more likely to contract lung cancer than noncoughers. Coughing does not, however, *cause* lung cancer—the correlation between coughing and lung cancer is *spurious*. Spurious correlations can give rise to counterexamples of both sorts described in the introductory section.

The standard solution to this problem is to require that causes raise the probabilities of their effects ceteris paribus. There are at least two well-developed approaches based on this idea. According to one (see, e.g., Cartwright 1979; Skyrms 1980; Humphreys 1989; Eells 1991), C causes E iff $P(E/C\&B) > P(E/\sim C\&B)$, for a variety of background conditions B. By conditioning on background conditions, we hold fixed the presence or absence of confounding factors.

Lewis (1986) analyzes the concept of ceteris paribus probability-raising differently. According to his theory, C causes E if the probability that E would occur in the actual world, at the time when C occurred, is higher than the probability that E would occur at the corresponding time in any of the closest possible worlds in which C does not occur.[1] In this theory single-case probabilities in different possible worlds, not conditional probabilities, are compared. For example, suppose that Barney smokes, coughs, and develops lung cancer. Barney's coughing is a cause of his lung cancer if he would have been less likely to contract lung cancer had he not coughed. But the relevant counterfactual is false: The closest possible world in which Barney does not cough is one in which he nonetheless smokes. In such a world, the probability of his developing lung cancer remains unchanged. In what follows, I will not distinguish between the different methods of articulating the basic probability-raising idea unless necessary.

My focus will be on what I call "actual causation": the relation that holds between two particular events when one does, in fact, cause the other. This is to be distinguished from the relation that holds when one event has (or is of a type that has) a *tendency* to cause another.[2] As we shall see, the most troubling sort of counterexample to probabilistic theories of causation threatens only theories of *actual* causation. Even if the counterexamples cannot be circumvented, probabilistic theories of causal tendencies remain attractive. Unlike some authors (e.g., Sober 1985; Eells 1991), I find it unpalatable that these are simply two independent causal relations: Surely whether one event did in fact cause another has a great deal to do with whether the one (was of a type that) had a tendency to cause the other (see Hitchcock 1995a for further discussion). This leaves us with good reason to continue pursuing probabilistic theories of causation even in the face of the difficulties discussed below.

3   Making It the Hard Way

Many authors have argued that there are examples in which a cause lowers the probability of its effect, even when one holds other factors fixed. Perhaps the most famous example, due originally to Deborah Rosen, is presented in Suppes (1970). (See also Salmon 1984, chapter 7.) A golfer lines up to drive her ball, but her swing is off and she badly slices the ball, sending it on a trajectory well to the right of the hole. Her slice decreases the probability that it will land in the cup for a hole-in-one. By chance, however, the ball bounces off a tree trunk at just the right angle to send it on a trajectory back toward the cup. As it happened, her slice did cause the ball to go into the cup, even though the slice lowered the probability of this outcome.

This sort of example has received considerable attention. I will present only the solution that I favor. Probabilistic theories of causation require that we compare the probability of the effect in the presence of the cause, and also in its absence. But a cause may be absent in many ways. For example, our golfing heroine might have hit the ball squarely, hooked the ball to her left, or barely nicked the ball (causing it to move hardly at all); her swing might have been so bad that she missed the ball completely, or she might have refrained from swinging. These are all ways in which she might not have sliced the ball. The intuition appealed to in the previous paragraph, that the slice lowered the probability that the ball would land in the cup, suggests that the relevant alternative is the one where she hits the ball squarely. But why should this be so? Perhaps the relevant alternative is the one in which the golfer refrains from swinging altogether; relative to such an alternative, the slice actually increases the probability of a hole-in-one. My view (developed in Hitchcock 1993, 1996a,b) is that there is no objectively correct alternative for purposes of probability comparison. Rather, causal claims are contrastive in nature; they are true or false relative to a specific alternative. Thus, the golfer's slice caused the hole-in-one, relative to the alternative in which she abstains from swinging, but not relative to the alternative in which she hits it squarely. In the latter case, we say that the ball landed in the cup *despite* the badly sliced shot.

There are a number of advantages to this approach. First, it avoids the need to select a privileged alternative from among the many alternatives to the candidate cause. Second, it can accommodate the seemingly incompatible judgments that "the golfer's slice caused the hole-in-one" and "the ball landed in the cup *despite* the badly sliced shot" are both true causal claims. We can accept both claims because we can hear them (perhaps with the help of a pragmatic rule of accommodation) as being made relative to different alternatives. Third, the relativity of causal claims to specific alternatives can account for a curious linguistic feature of causal claims. To borrow an example from Dretske (1977b), suppose that Susan has stolen a bicycle, resulting in her arrest. We might agree that Susan's *stealing* the bicycle caused her to be arrested, while denying that Susan's stealing *the bicycle* caused her to be arrested. The placement of stress in a causal claim can affect its truth value. According to the proposed view, the different placement of stress points to different alternatives. Susan's stealing the bicycle caused her to be arrested relative to alternatives in which she acquired a bicycle by some other means, but not relative to alternatives in which she stole some other item.

I conclude that putative counterexamples involving probability-lowering causes can be eliminated using a refinement to probabilistic theories of causation that is motivated on a number of independent grounds.

4   Three Scenarios

Peter Menzies (1989a, 1996) describes a case involving causal preemption in which a probability-raising event is not a cause. He takes such cases to be isolated and atypical:[3] "It is striking how a probabilistic theory of causation, appropriately formulated, follows the contours of our intuitive conception of causation with amazing accuracy—with the exception of the problem cases to do with pre-emption and over-determination" (Menzies 1996, p. 100).

In fact, however, preemption is in no way essential to Menzies's example. James Woodward (1990) describes a case with the following structure. Suppose that C_1 and C_2 both increase the probability of E, and would do so regardless of whether the other is present or not. On some particular occasion, C_1, C_2, and E occur. Although both C_1 and C_2 are potential causes of E, could it not be the case that in fact only C_2 causes E on this particular occasion? That is, couldn't this be one of those cases where C_1 fails to cause E, not because it is preempted, but simply because its operation is chancy? If so, then C_1 raises the probability of E without causing it.[4]

Woodward offers the following more specific example in a review of Humphreys (1989):

Scenario 1: Suppose we know ... that each of two different carcinogenic materials C_1 and C_2 [e.g., gyromitrin and diazonium metabolite] can cause [stomach tumors] in mice (E). Suppose also that the operation of each of these causes is non-deterministic but governed by a stable probability distribution: each increases the probability of cancer, although to some value strictly less than one. Suppose also that there is no evidence for any interaction effect between C_1 and C_2 when both are present. Now suppose that a particular mouse is exposed to ... C_1 and C_2 and develops cancer E. It follows on Humphreys' account that since both C_1 and C_2 increase the possibility of cancer, both cause or have causally contributed to cancer. But why should we believe this? How do we know that the cancer was not instead caused by C_1 alone or C_2 alone? We know that when ... C_1 occur[s] in isolation (without ... C_2) ..., it is perfectly possible for [it] to increase the probability ... of E and yet ... fail to cause ... E. Here probability increase is not sufficient for actual ... causation. How do we know that the envisioned case is not also one of these cases, in which C_1 fails to cause E ... and E is instead caused by C_2 [alone]? (Woodward 1994, p. 366; with minor changes in notation. Woodward notes that the example is originally due to Humphreys 1989, p. 15)

The potentially troublesome implication—that both carcinogens caused the stomach tumor—is not unique to Humphreys's theory, but it is shared by all of the probabilistic approaches to singular causation mentioned above. Note that the assumption of indeterminism is essential to the example. If, given the relevant background conditions, the presence of diazonium metabolite increases the probability of stomach tumor to 1, then the presence of gyromitrin cannot further raise the probability.

Is Woodward's scenario coherent? Could it be that only one of the carcinogens actually causes the stomach tumor? Consider two potential analogues.

Scenario 2   Maria and Lucinda are neighbors. Every week, each of them buys a one-dollar ticket for the state lottery, which pays one million dollars as the grand prize. Due to the diminishing marginal utility of money, Lucinda and Maria decide that they would each rather have two chances at half a million dollars than one chance at a million, and so they decide to pool their resources. Each of them buys a ticket as before, but under the agreement that the prize money will be shared if *either* of them wins. In fact, Maria's ticket wins, and the neighbors split the million-dollar prize.

Scenario 3   Desmond and James decide to do something similar. They walk to the store together, slap their dollars down simultaneously, and purchase two tickets, each registered in both names. In fact, one of those tickets wins, and the two men share a million dollars.

In each scenario, how might we address the question: whose dollar purchased the winning ticket? Although the two women shared the money as agreed, and although each ticket increased the chance that the prize would be won, there is still a fact of the matter as to *whose* dollar had been converted to one million: It was Maria's. In scenario 3, however, there is no such fact. Although only one of the *tickets* actually won, there is no fact of the matter about whose dollar had actually purchased this ticket.

Probabilistic theories of causation presuppose that indeterministic causation works on analogy with the third scenario. Various causes increase the probability of an effect by contributing to a "probability pool." Once the probability of the effect is determined, the dice are cast, and the event either occurs or it does not. The individual causes make no additional contribution to the outcome; they bring it about (or not) only via their contribution to the probability pool. David Lewis and Paul Humphreys both defend the analogy between scenario 1 and scenario 3. Humphreys (1989) discusses scenario 1 explicitly:

In the example at hand, the situation with both carcinogens present *is* different from the situation with only one—the chance is higher than with either alone because both chemicals have contributed to the value of that chance. And that is all there is. To think otherwise is to conceive of the example in terms of a deterministic image where the tumor was "entirely caused" by the first chemical and the second chemical was thereby irrelevant. But that is not the situation. The second chemical is not irrelevant on this (or any other) occasion for it contributes to the chance on this occasion, as does the first chemical, and after they have done this, *nothing else causal happens*. It is ... a matter of sheer chance whether the tumor occurs or not.   (pp. 36–37)

Lewis rejects an analogous counterexample: "[T]he objection presupposes that the case must be of one kind or the other: either E definitely *would* have occurred without C_2, or it definitely would not have occurred without C_2. But I reject the presupposition that there are two different ways the world could be, giving us one definite counterfactual or the other ..." (Lewis 1986, p. 180, with minor modifications in notation). Both writers articulate a picture of probabilistic causation in which causes bring about their effects only via their contributions to a probability pool.

At issue is not merely the correctness of the probabilistic approach to causation— although that is important in itself—but how we are to conceive of indeterministic causation in general. This has implications that extend beyond metaphysics into risk analysis and tort law. Suppose, for example, that a pregnant woman is exposed to a particular teratogen, which increases the probability that her child will possess a particular kind of birth defect (which may also occur in the absence of the teratogen). Assume, moreover, that these are objective probabilities and do not merely reflect our ignorance about background conditions. If the birth defect occurs, is there a residual issue of whether it was caused by the teratogen, and hence of whether the woman may be entitled to receive payment for damages? American tort law answers in the affirmative, but it is plausible that this answer is founded on a denial of the assumption that the underlying probabilities are objective and not merely epistemic. If the relationship between exposure to the teratogen and the formation of birth defects is indeterministic, however, current jurisprudence may be deeply misguided on this issue. This critique of existing tort law is carried out in some detail by Parascondola (1996), although he assumes without argument that scenario 1 assimilates to scenario 3.

Although the intuitions of the opposing camps are clear, the case seems inconclusive. In particular, our immediate reaction to scenario 1 is to request more information. By what mechanism do the tumors form? How was the mouse exposed to the carcinogens? Which molecules of which substance made contact with which tissue cells? Which cells are the tumorous ones? And so on. In the absence of such further information, we have no clear intuitions about whether this case assimilates to scenario 2 or scenario 3. It will thus be helpful to examine some further examples that elicit clearer intuitions.

5   Three More Scenarios

Consider three more examples in which two potential causes are present and an effect occurs.

Scenario 4   Suppose that a source emits polarized photons where the angle of polarization depends on the physical configuration of the source. The emitted photons then strike a polarizer that is aligned so that horizontally polarized photons are transmitted. Initially, the source is configured so as to emit vertically polarized photons; any such photon will be absorbed by the polarizer. Now suppose that Juan and Jennifer simultaneously push the source, each pushing it with a force sufficient to rotate the apparatus through 30°. The source emits a photon, which now has a probability of $\sin^2(60°) = 0.75$ of being transmitted by the polarizer, and the photon is in fact transmitted.

In this scenario, each push increased the probability that the photon would be transmitted. It seems clearly wrongheaded to ask whether the transmission was *really* due to Juan's push rather than Jennifer's push. Rather, this case seems to fit the model of probabilistic causality described by Humphreys and Lewis: Each push increased the probability of the effect (the transmission of the photon), and then it was simply a matter of chance. There are no causal facts of the matter extending beyond the probabilistic contribution made by each. This is a very simple case in which our intuitions are not clouded by tacit deterministic assumptions. If this case is typical of genuine indeterministic causation, then the sort of case envisaged by Woodward would indeed be incoherent.

Scenario 5 also supports this conclusion:

Scenario 5   A series of identical ropes are tied to a wall, and it is determined that when either Gene or Pat pulls on a rope as hard as possible for ten seconds, there is a fifty percent chance that the rope will break. When both pull on a rope for ten seconds, there is a seventy-five percent chance that it will break. On a given occasion, both pull and the rope does break. (Woodward, personal communication.)

Once again, our intuition is that it would be wrongheaded to say that on this occasion the breaking of the rope is due to the pull of Gene rather than Pat or vice versa. This example is less esoteric than the previous one, although we currently have no principled reason to think that in a scenario such as this, the probabilities would be irreducible and have this structure. This is a common problem in discussions of indeterministic causation: The only examples in which we have principled reasons for thinking that there are irreducible probabilities having a certain structure involve microphysics, where our normal causal intuitions begin to lose their moorings.

Scenario 6 spells trouble.

Scenario 6 Suppose that two gunmen are shooting at a Ming vase. Each one has a fifty percent chance of hitting the vase, and each one shoots independently, so the probability that the vase shatters is 0.75. (For simplicity, we will ignore the possibility that the vase might survive a bullet hit.) As it happens, the first gunman's shot hits the vase, but the second gunman misses.

In this example, the second gunman shot at the vase, his shooting increased the probability that the vase would shatter (from 0.5 to 0.75), and the vase did in fact shatter. Nonetheless, it seems clear that we should not say that the second gunman's shot *caused* the vase to shatter. So here we have an apparent counterexample to probabilistic theories of causation: The second shot increased the probability that the vase would shatter, but it did not cause the vase to shatter. This example has the same structure as Woodward's, but here it is *clear* that the effect is due to one of the probability-raising factors, and not to the other. The two gunshots do not simply contribute to the probability of the vase's shattering, after which "nothing else causal happens." Something else causal does happen: The bullet fired from the first gun strikes the vase, while the bullet from the second gun misses. Note that this example threatens only probabilistic accounts of *actual* causation. This example would not lead us to withdraw the causal tendency claim that shooting at vases causes them to shatter. Likewise, even if Woodward's intuitions about scenario 1 are correct, that would not lead us to deny that gyromitrin or diazonium metabolite tend to cause stomach tumors.

In the next three sections, I will discuss prospects for replying to this counterexample. The results will be seen to be inconclusive: although no line of response suffers a knockout blow, none is wholly persuasive, either. In particular, many of the responses to be considered must postulate further empirical facts, beyond those presented above. While we do not know for sure that those facts do not obtain, we readily judge that the second shooter did not cause the vase to shatter without asking whether such facts obtain. Moreover, the facts adduced are sufficiently esoteric that it is implausible that our judgment about this case tacitly presupposes them.

6 Causal Processes

The shattering of the vase can be traced back to the firing of the first shooter's gun via the bullet that was fired from his gun, whereas there is no analogous process connecting the second shooter to the target. It is natural to point to this asymmetry in judging that the firing of one of the guns, but not the other, was a cause of the vase's shattering.

Spatiotemporal causal processes, such as the speeding bullets of scenario 6, play a central role in Salmon's (1984) theory of causation (see also Dowe 1992; Salmon 1994). It is not clear, however, how the appeal to causal processes can resolve our problem. There *are* processes connecting the second shooter to the vase: photons and sound waves, for example. Intuitively, these are not processes of the right sort. Unfortunately, causal process theories such as Salmon's do not have the resources to formulate the distinction between causal processes "of the right sort" and those "of the wrong sort"; at the very least, such a distinction will presuppose something like the probabilistic theory of causation that is at issue. Thus, for example, if we try to get around this problem by saying that there must be a connecting process that transmits a sufficient quantity of energy to shatter the vase, we must then address the question of what constitutes a sufficient amount of energy. The answer to this question will almost certainly have to be formulated in terms of counterfactuals or ceteris paribus conditional probabilities.[5]

In any event, there are reasons that mitigate against requiring that causation always involve connection via continuous processes. Suppose that a gunman fires at a human target, but a secret service agent jumps in front of the gunman's bullet, allowing herself to be hit by it. The agent's brave action caused the target to remain alive, even though there are no processes connecting the agent and the target (except for irrelevant ones such as sound waves and photons).[6] A probabilistic theory of causation thus cannot be saved by adding the simple requirement that causes be connected to their effects by continuous processes.

7 Precise Specification of Events

Consider the following scenario:

Scenario 7 Barney smokes, and he also spends a lot of time in the sun. These two proclivities are not connected; for example, Barney is not forced to go outside in order to smoke. Barney's smoking increases the probability that he will get lung cancer. By increasing his probability of getting lung cancer, Barney's smoking increases the overall probability that he will suffer from some form of cancer, and analogously for his exposure to the sun. In fact, Barney develops skin cancer. A fortiori, Barney develops cancer of some form or other.

Since Barney's smoking increased the probability that he would develop cancer of some sort, and Barney did indeed develop cancer, probabilistic theories of causation would seem to rule that his smoking caused him to develop cancer. But this seems clearly wrong: Barney's cancer is *skin* cancer, not lung cancer, so it was not caused by his smoking. Although both smoking and sun exposure increased the probability that he would develop cancer, only Barney's exposure to the sun actually caused him to get cancer.

Few philosophers would be troubled by this prima facie counterexample to probabilistic theories of causation. Our first reaction is that such theories yield the wrong verdict only because we have described the effect—Barney's getting cancer—imprecisely. There is a more detailed level of description—Barney's contracting skin cancer—where probabilistic theories render the correct verdict: Barney's smoking did not raise the probability of skin cancer, and hence it did not cause Barney's skin cancer.

Let us formulate the general principle that seems to be at work here:

(*PSE*)   Suppose that on a particular occasion, events occur that instantiate types C and E. Even if, relative to the relevant background conditions, C raises the probability of E, if there are more precise specifications of the events in question, C' and E', such that C' does not raise the probability of E', then we should not say that C causes E.

How, precisely, one ought to formulate this principle of the precise specification of events will depend on one's theory of events—I will leave it to the reader to reformulate (PSE) in accord with her favorite theory of events.

Perhaps appeal to (PSE) will enable us to avoid the counterexample of the second shooter. Although the firing of the second shot increased the probability that the vase would shatter, there may exist a more precise specification of the outcome (say, involving the shattering into very small pieces of a certain region of the vase directly facing the first shooter) such that the second shot did not increase *its* probability.[7] But although (PSE) seems to provide a natural diagnosis of scenario 7, it does not seem to get at our reasons for saying that the first gunman's shot caused the vase to shatter, while the second gunman's shot did not. Moving from the description "Barney's cancer" to the more specific "Barney's skin cancer" seems wholly natural, whereas the move from "the vase's shattering" to the more detailed level of description seems ad hoc.

Moreover, the application of (PSE) in this case involves an empirical presupposition: that there is some level of description such that the second gunman's shot made *no difference whatsoever* to the probability that the vase would shatter in just that way. Perhaps the second gunman's shot did increase the probability, ever so slightly, that the vase would shatter *in precisely the manner that it did*. If so, (PSE) will be of no avail. If (PSE) succeeds at all, then, it will succeed because of empirical facts we have no (current) warrant for accepting, and which appear to play no role in our straightforward causal judgments about scenario 6.

8 Ebb and Flow in the Probability Pool

There is one regard in which scenarios 4 and 6 are significantly different. In scenario 4, both Juan and Jennifer push the polarizer, yielding a 0.75 probability that the photon will be transmitted. Nothing further happens to affect the probability of transmission once the position of the polarizer is set. This fits nicely with the probability pool conception of indeterministic causation: The two pushes determine the probability of transmission, and nothing else causal happens—transmission follows by sheer chance. Time is not literally discrete in this scenario, but it might as well be. It is implausible that scenario 6 works in this way: We do not imagine that the two guns fire, fixing the probability of shattering at 0.75 until the very moment of shattering. Rather, we imagine that the actual trajectory followed by the bullets depends on random gusts of wind, fluctuations of air pressure, or perhaps even on indeterministic fluctuations intrinsic to the bullets themselves. The initial 0.5 probability that each shot will hit the target is an average over all of these possibilities. As the bullets speed through the air, the probability that each one will hit the vase does not remain frozen at 0.5, but changes in response to indeterministic events that occur after the guns were fired. The probability pool does not remain calm, but rises and falls as probability flows in and out.

In cases such as that described in scenario 6, there may be a vast number of intermediate events whose chance occurrence will affect the probability of the outcome. Perhaps a probabilistic theory of causation that is sensitive to the ebb and flow of the probability of shattering after the two shots are fired could yield the right verdict about scenario 6. Such theories have been offered by Kvart (1997, inter alia), Menzies (1989a, but repudiated in 1996), and Eells (1991, chapter 6). I will not describe each of these theories in detail, but will rather focus on the features of the probability pool that they might exploit in dealing with the case of the two gunmen.

Suppose that there is some time *t* before the shattering of the vase, such that the trajectory of the bullet from second gun at *t* gives it no chance of hitting the vase: Although the bullet from the second gun emerged from the barrel with a probability of 0.5 of hitting the vase, by time t, random changes in the bullet's trajectory have put it on a path that will definitely steer clear of the vase. Then, the probability at t that the vase will shatter is exactly the same as it would have been had the second gunman never fired. Under this supposition, the accounts of Menzies (1989a) and Eells (1991) correctly rule that second gunman's shot did not cause the vase to shatter. I will not defend these claims in detail here, but will instead focus on a simpler proposal suggested by Hall (personal communication). Hall recommends a minor modification of Lewis's counterfactual theory of causation: Instead of requiring that causes raise the probability of their effects *at the time the cause occurs*, we must require that causes raise the probabilities of their effects *shortly before the time at which the effect occurs*. In the case at hand, the probability at time t that the vase will shatter would have been no different if the second gunman had never fired; hence Hall's proposal rules that the second gunman's shot is not a cause of the shattering.

Another possibility emerges if instead we focus on the trajectory of the *first* bullet. Suppose now that there is some time t at which the bullet fired from the first gun is determined to hit the vase. If we hold fixed the trajectory of this bullet at time t, then the firing of the second gun no longer makes a difference to the probability of shattering: The probability is 1 either way. This move is not ad hoc: The trajectory of the first bullet at time t is a cause of shattering, and so should (according to many probabilistic theories of causation) be held fixed when evaluating the probabilistic relevance of the second gunman's shot. If the trajectory of the first bullet at time t is held fixed, the second gunman's shot no longer raises the probability of shattering; hence, a sufficiently refined probabilistic theory of causation correctly rules that the second shot is not a cause of shattering.

While these approaches hold out some promise for handling the case of the second shooter, each of them requires assumptions about the probabilistic details that were not included in the original description of the scenario. If the probability that the first bullet will miss the vase or that the second bullet will hit remains positive right up until the time of shattering, the proposed resolutions will not succeed.[8] Although the probabilistic assumptions discussed above are not altogether implausible, our ignorance about such matters of probabilistic detail surely outstrips our ignorance of the causal relations in scenario 6. Our intuition that the first shot caused the shattering and the second did not does not depend on such probabilistic details. It is particularly troubling that the proposals discussed in sections 7 and 8 presuppose that certain probabilities take on values of 0 and 1. One of the motivations for developing probabilistic theories of causation was the thought that the world, for all we know, might be indeterministic. It might, for all we know, be *thoroughly* indeterministic; perhaps everything is possible, no matter how improbable. Surely we should want our probabilistic theories of causation to apply in such a world as well.

9 The Last Scenario

I present for consideration a final scenario.

Scenario 8 A box contains two carbon-14 atoms, and a very sensitive detector is placed near the box. The presence of each atom increases the probability that a decay event will be detected during some given time interval. In fact, a decay event is detected, and one of the atoms in the box is now a nitrogen atom.

Intuitively it seems that it was the presence of one atom (the one that is now a nitrogen atom), and not the other, that caused the detection event.[9] Yet in this scenario, *none* of the maneuvers canvased in sections 6 through 8 seems possible. Is this, at long last, a clean counterexample to probabilistic theories of causation?

We must proceed with caution here, for we are within the realm of the notorious measurement problem of quantum mechanics. There are many interpretations of what is going on in this example, no one of them universally accepted. As it turns out, those interpretations that lend themselves to the natural conclusion that it is the presence of one atom and not the other that caused the detection event tend not to be the ones that close the door on the various maneuvers described above. Suppose we understand the decay event in terms of a realist, or hidden-variable interpretation (such as that of Bohm 1952). In this case, one of the atoms decays at some time prior to the detection event, and a decay particle travels to the detector. There *is* a spatio-temporally contiguous process (the decay particle) connecting the atom to the detector, and there *is* a more detailed specification of the detection event available (one including hidden variables).

Suppose, by contrast, that we understand this scenario in terms of a more traditional Copenhagen-style interpretation. The atoms enter into superpositions of decayed and undecayed states, thus bringing about a certain probability that a measurement will reveal that a decay event has occurred. When the measurement is performed, the superposition collapses and a decay is in fact detected. On this picture, the detection of the decay particle is not a distinct event from the decay event itself. As an indeterministic result of that decay/detection event, one of the atoms is now a nitrogen atom. The decay of that atom is better thought of as a part of the measurement interaction than as a cause of it.

This is not an exhaustive partition of possible interpretations of scenario 8, of course; but it should suffice to convince us that this is the wrong place to look for a trouble-free counterexample to probabilistic theories of causation.

10   Conclusion

Note that our question is not one of epistemology—how do we know in cases like scenario 6 which potential cause is an actual cause? We do know—otherwise the counterexamples would have no force. In scenario 6, we know that the second gunshot did not cause the vase to shatter because the two events were not connected by an appropriate type of spatiotemporal process. In scenario 7, we know that Barney's smoking did not cause his cancer because Barney developed skin cancer, and that is not the sort of cancer that smoking causes. In scenario 8 (assuming some realistic interpretation of atomic decay), we know that the presence of one atom but not the other caused the detection event, because atoms cause detection events by decaying, and atoms that decay are transformed from an atom of one type to another. In each case, there is a *marker* that distinguishes the genuine cause from the spurious probability-raiser.[10] But as metaphysicians, we are interested in providing a general theory of causation. The markers described above are heterogeneous in nature: in scenario 6, the marker resides in events intermediate between the putative cause and its putative effect; in scenario 7, it is the nature of the effect itself that marks the actual cause; in scenario 8, a separate effect (the transformation of the decaying atom) marks the actual cause of the detection event. For a theory of causation to exploit these markers, something more must be said about what they have in common in virtue of which they are causal markers. It will not do to simply say that the actual cause is the one that is marked as such.

It might be tempting to conclude that probabilistic theories of actual causation must ultimately fail. But there are still reasons for resisting this conclusion. The success of probabilistic theories of causal tendencies, together with the presumed connection between causal tendencies and actual causation, should lead us to resist the conclusion that actual causation has nothing to do with probability-raising. Even if we accept the example of the two gunmen as a direct counterexample to probabilistic theories of actual causation, scenarios 4 and 5 suggest that there are cases in which the probability pool model articulated by Lewis and Humphreys is appropriate. It will still be necessary, then, to map out the boundaries of this form of indeterministic causation, where probabilistic theories of causation directly apply. The counterexample of the second shooter, therefore, is not offered as a call to abandon probabilistic theories of actual causation, but rather as a call for more work to be done. Whatever the result, our picture of causation in an indeterministic world can only come into sharper focus.

Acknowledgments

For helpful comments and suggestions, thanks go to Joseph Berkovitz, Phil Dowe, Ellery Eells, Dan Hausman, Paul Humphreys, Igal Kvart, Laurie Paul, Jon Schaffer, and Jim Woodward.

Notes

1. The condition described is only sufficient, according to Lewis. Since we will be primarily concerned with counterexamples to the sufficiency of probability-raising for causation, I will not present the more complex, weakened requirement that Lewis takes to be both necessary and sufficient.

2. Note, however, that not all of the probabilistic theories of causation mentioned above are intended by their authors as theories of actual causation.

3. Menzies does also mention problems due to "randomly occurring events" (1996, p. 100, n. 24), but he does not state clearly what sort of problems he has in mind.

4. Woodward notes that a similar counterexample is possible without the presence of C_2, if there is some probability that an event of type E will occur spontaneously.

5. For a more detailed critique of causal process theories of causation, see my (1995b).

6. A similar example is described in Otte (1986); see also my (1998) and Hall, "Two Concepts of Causation" (chapter 9 in this volume).

7. Note that this proposal differs slightly from a similar proposal rejected by Lewis (1986b, pp. 204–205). That proposal was to move to a more precise specification of events in order admit the existence of certain causal relations otherwise denied by the theory; (PSE) aims to reject the existence of causal relations otherwise admitted by the theory.

8. If the probabilities remain positive but approach zero in the limit as the actual time of shattering nears, then suitable reformulations of the proposals discussed above may succeed. I will not explore this possibility further here.

9. Schaffer (2000a) presents an example with a similar structure.

10. This line of thought has been pressed on me independently by Joseph Berkovitz and Jonathan Schaffer. See also Hausman (1998), section 13.2.

18 Causation, Counterfactuals, and the Third Factor

Tim Maudlin

In his classic paper "Causation" (1973a), David Lewis urged that regularity accounts of causation, having continually failed to resolve the counterexamples and problematic cases with which they were faced, be abandoned in favor of an alternative strategy: the analysis of causation in terms of counterfactuals. More than a quarter of a century later, the time has come to evaluate the health and prospects of Lewis's program in its turn.

No one would now deny that there is some deep conceptual connection between causation and counterfactuals. As Lewis points out, Hume himself (incorrectly) paraphrased one of his analyses of causation using a counterfactual locution (Hume 1902 [1748], sec. VII):

> ... or in other words, *where if the first had not been, the second had never existed.*

In honor of Hume, let us call the counterfactual "If *C* had not occurred, *E* would not have occurred," when both *C* and *E* did actually occur, the *Hume counterfactual.* When we think we know a cause of some event, we typically assent to the corresponding Hume counterfactual. Furthermore, our interest in causes often has a practical aspect: We want to know the causes of events so that we can either prevent or foster similar sorts of events at other times. Causal claims are therefore deeply implicated with the sorts of future subjunctives used in practical deliberation: If we should do *X* (which we might or might not, for all we now know) then the result would be *Y*. The future subjunctive is a close cousin to the counterfactual conditional, since accepting a future subjunctive commits one to accepting the corresponding Hume counterfactual in the event that the antecedent does not come about.

But Hume's dictum hardly survives a few minutes contemplation before counterexamples crowd into view. The sort of counterfactual dependency Hume cites is not necessary for causation: Perhaps the effect still would have occurred despite the absence of the cause since *another* cause would have stepped in to bring it about. The dependency is also not uncontroversially sufficient for causation. If John Kennedy had not been assassinated on November 22, 1963, he would have still been president in December 1963. But surely too, if Kennedy had still been president in December 1963, he would not have been assassinated in November of that year: When asked to consider the latter counterfactual we do not imagine Kennedy killed in November and resurrected in December. So the counterfactual dependencies go both ways and the causal arrow only one.

These sorts of problems have been thoroughly chewed over in the literature, and no detailed review of the strategies used to respond to them is needed here. The problem of backup (potential) causes can perhaps be solved by using counterfactual dependency to define direct causation and then taking the ancestral to define causation, or by making the effect *qua* effect very fragile in some way and arguing that the backup could not have produced it at exactly the right time or right place or with all of the right properties, or by appealing to a matching strategy, in which the cause that is operative when the backup is present is identified by matching it to an otherwise identical case where the backup is absent (and the Hume counterfactual holds). Attempts to fix the counterfactual analysis have become ever more subtle, and complicated, and convoluted (as perhaps some other essays in this volume will attest). I have neither the space not the desire to address them all individually.

I do not want to quarrel with these sorts of solutions in detail because I want to argue that the attempt to analyze causation in terms of counterfactuals of this sort is wrongheaded in a way that no amount of fine-tuning can fix. Causation is not to be analyzed in terms of counterfactual dependency at all, no matter how many equants and epicycles are appended to the original rough draft.[1]

If causation is not to be analyzed in terms of counterfactual dependency, how are we to explain the systematic connections between judgments about causes and judgments about counterfactuals? Such connections may be secured analytically if causation can be defined in terms of counterfactuals, but I am denying that this can be done. Connections would also obtain if counterfactuals could be reduced analytically to causal claims, but that is an even less appetizing project than the one we are rejecting. The only other possibility is that a third factor is involved, some *component* of the truth conditions of counterfactual claims that is also a component of the truth conditions of causal claims. This third factor would provide the analogue of a "common cause" explanation for the systematic connections between causal claims and counterfactuals: Neither underpins the other, but the third factor underpins them both.

The prospects for a "third factor" explanation obviously depend on the identification of the missing factor. I think it can be identified: What links causation and counterfactuals by figuring in the truth conditions for both is natural law. Laws play one role in determining which counterfactuals are true, and another role in securing causal connections. The "necessary connexion" that Hume sought at the heart of causation is nomic necessity.[2]

1   Knowledge of Causation without Knowledge of any Hume Counterfactual

Let us consider what one must know, in at least one case, in order to know what caused an event. Suppose you know that the laws that govern a world are the laws of

Newtonian mechanics. And suppose you also know that forces in this world are all extremely short range: forces exist only between particles that come within an angstrom of each other. And suppose particle P is at rest (in an inertial frame) at t_0 and moving at t_1, and that in the period between t_0 and t_1 only one particle, particle Q, came within an angstrom of P. Then, I claim, we know with complete certainty what caused P to start moving: It was the collision with Q.

Thus: Given that we know the laws and we know some very circumscribed set of particular facts, we know the cause of P's motion. But do we know what would have happened if Q had not collided with P (i.e., if Q had not approached within one angstrom of P)? We do not. Suppose, for example, that the vicinity of our particles is chock-a-block full of monitoring equipment, which tracks the exact trajectory of Q, and jammed with particle-launching devices loaded with particles just like Q and designed to launch these particles so as to collide with P just as Q did if Q should deviate in any way from its path. There are (for all I have told you) innumerable such devices, monitoring the path at arbitrarily close intervals, all prepared to step in should Q fail to collide with P. I hereby warn you of the presence of these contraptions, unspecified in number and construction, and ask you now whether we know what would have happened if Q had not collided with P.

We do not have enough information to evaluate this counterfactual, both because the *way* Q fails to collide has not been specified and because the exact construction and disposition of the monitoring devices has not been indicated. Perhaps for many sorts of deviation, some other particle, just like Q, would have collided with P at just the same time and in just the same way. Perhaps this is even true for *all* possible deviations, or all the sorts of deviation we would consider relevant. So perhaps we could be convinced that P would have moved at exactly the same time and in just the same way even if Q had not collided with it. Still, *none of this has anything at all to do with the fact that the collision with Q is what caused P to move.* The existence of the monitoring devices and potential backup particles is simply *irrelevant* to the claim that the collision with Q was the cause. In fact, once we know the laws we don't even *care* what would have happened if Q had not collided with P: Perhaps P would not have moved, or perhaps it would have because something else collided with it. The information we have (viz., the laws of nature in this world) allows us to identify the cause without knowing that *any* Hume counterfactual is true.

The counterfactual analyst can respond in several ways. One would be to insist that we know the causes in this case because we know that *some* Hume counterfactual is true, although (owing to the lack of information) we don't know which one. No matter how many backup systems there are, there must be some point on the trajectory of Q such that had it miraculously swerved at that point, P would not have moved since none of the backups would have had a chance to fire. But since I have not specified the number or location of the backups, how does one know this is true? What if there is an infinite sequence of backups, progressively faster and faster reacting, monitoring at ever closer and closer intervals?

Lewis (1986b) addresses this sort of criticism, claiming that we need not pay much heed to our intuitions about such recondite circumstances. Discussing exactly this sort of problem (as raised by William Goosens) and a case involving action at a distance, he responds: "I do not worry about either of these far-fetched cases. They both go against what we take to be the ways of this world; they violate the presuppositions of our habits of thought; it would be no surprise if our common-sense judgments about them went astray—spoils to the victor!" (1986b, p. 203). Lewis's strategy here deserves some comment. The rules of the game in this sort of analytic project are relatively clear: Any proposed analysis is tested against particular cases, usually imaginary, for which we have strong intuitions. The accuracy with which the judgments of the analysis match the deliverances of intuition then constitutes a measure of the adequacy of the analysis. Unfortunately, it is often the case that the question of *how* the intuitions are arrived at is left to the side: Getting the analysis to deliver up the right results, by hook or by crook, is all that matters, and this, in turn, encourages ever more baroque constructions. But if we care about intuitions at all, we ought to care about the underlying mechanism that generates them, and in this case it seems plausible that a simple *argument* accounts for our judgment, *an argument entirely unaffected by the existence of backup devices, no matter how numerous.* The case does differ from those of our actual experience, and in such a way that the envisioned situation will surely never occur. But the *way* that the example differs from more familiar ones *makes no difference whatsoever to the reasoning that allows us to identify the cause*: So long as none of the backup devices *fires*, their number and complexity is perfectly irrelevant. We have such strong intuitions about the case even though it is far-fetched because the respect in which it is far-fetched makes no difference to the method by which the cause is identified. The example shows that causes are not identified via the Hume counterfactual.

What one would like to say, of course, is that the following counterfactual it true: If Q had not collided with *P and none of the back-up devices had fired*, then *P* would not have moved. And this is correct. So we want to hold fixed, in evaluating the counterfactual, *the nonfiring of potential alternative causes*. But in order to know what to hold fixed, we already have to know quite a lot about the (actual and counterfactual) causal structure, since we have to identify the possible-but-not-actual-alternative-causes to hold fixed. But now the project looks pretty hopeless as a way of using counterfactuals to get a handle on causation: We already have to bring in causal judgments when determining which counterfactual to consider.

So if we do not know that the collision with Q caused P to move by knowing what would have happened if Q had not collided with P, how do we know it? The argument is quite simple and straightforward, but it is worth laying out. Since the laws of this world are by hypothesis those of Newtonian physics, we know that particle P, which is at rest at t_0, will remain at rest unless some force is put on it. And since the forces in this world are all short range, we know that no force will be put on P unless some particle approaches within one angstrom of it. And since P does start to move, we know that some particle did approach within one angstrom of it, which is why it started moving. And since Q was the *only* particle to approach closely enough, we know that it was the collision with Q that caused P to move. End of story.

There are some counterfactuals implicit in this reasoning. If *nothing* had put a force on P it would not have accelerated. That, of course, follows from Newton's first law of motion. And if we knew that if Q had not put a force on P *nothing else* would have, then we would have the Hume counterfactual. But we do not know this. So as it stands we can only infer: If Q had not collided with P, either P would not have started moving or something else would have collided with it. This is not the Hume counterfactual; hence the headaches for the counterfactual analysis.

Various sorts of sophistication of the original simple counterfactual analysis might succeed in getting the case right, once enough detail is given. For example, if Q had not collided with P, but some other particle had instead, then it does seem plausible that P would not have moved off in quite the same way as it did. This seems plausible even though we cannot begin to specify *how* P's motion would have differed. It also seems plausible that there is *some* moment in Q's trajectory late enough that, had Q miraculously disappeared, it would be too late for a backup to fire—even though we have no clue about *how late* that point must be. So maybe these sorts of analysis can get the right result. But the curious thing is that even if they do get the right result, *it is obviously not on the basis of that result that we judge Q to be the cause. Rather, it is because we already judge Q to be the cause that we think that, with enough detail, we would get the right result.* This is obvious since our judgment that Q is the cause is secure *even before the details are filled in.* And the advantage of the little argument rehearsed above is that it explains how we know that Q was the cause, given the laws of motion and the fact that only Q collided with P, without having to know any more details about the situation. So even if it does turn out that had Q not collided, P would have at least moved differently, that is irrelevant (given the laws) to identifying the cause.

Since it is facts about the laws that help us identify the cause in this case, and since laws are obviously deeply implicated in the evaluation of counterfactuals, I suggest that we stop trying to analyze causation directly in terms of counterfactuals and consider anew how laws play a role in determining causes. At one end of the spectrum we have seen how the laws of Newtonian mechanics can enable one to identify the cause in the example discussed above, even if one does not know any Hume counterfactual. Let us now look at an example from the other end of the spectrum.

2   Knowledge of Counterfactuals without Knowledge of Causes

If an analysis of causation in terms of counterfactuals were correct, then, unless the analysis itself contains some vague concepts, fixing determinate truth values for all counterfactuals should fix the truth values of all causal claims. Of course, in many circumstances counterfactuals themselves may not have classical truth values: The antecedent or consequent of the conditional may be too vague. But supposing that the truth values of all relevant counterfactuals are sharp, then one would suppose that an analysis of causation in terms of counterfactuals should render the causes sharp. But we can imagine situations in which all relevant counterfactuals are determinate but causal claims are not, because it is unclear exactly what the laws are. The example is rather artificial, but illustrative.

Recall the rules of John Conway's Game of Life. Life is played on a square grid, using discrete moments of time. At any moment, each square in the grid is either empty or occupied. At any given moment of time, whether a square is occupied or not depends on the how that square and the eight immediately adjacent squares were occupied at the previous moment. For example, if four or more of the adjacent squares are occupied at one instant then the given square will be empty at the next instant, and if one or none of the adjacent squares are occupied then at the next moment the square will be empty. Conway's rules cover all possibilities, so the state of the grid evolves deterministically through time.

Now imagine a world in which space and time are discrete, and in which space consists in a rectangular grid of points that persist through time. And imagine that there is only one sort of matter in this world, so that every discrete part of space is, at any moment, either empty or occupied by the matter. And imagine that the patterns of occupation evolve in definite deterministic patterns similar to those in Conway's game, but somewhat less orderly. As in Conway's game, one can predict with certainty whether a given point will be occupied or not at an instant if one knows only the previous pattern of occupation of that point and the eight adjacent points. But unlike Conway's game, the rules of evolution cannot be distilled into a few simple rules.

In principle, the rules of evolution must specify for each of the 512 possible patterns of occupation of a 3-by-3 grid whether the central square is or is not occupied at the next instant.[3] Imagine picking the rules in a random way: For each of the 512 possible input patterns, flip a coin. If the coin lands heads, the central square will be occupied the next instant, if tails it will be empty. One now has a complete set of rules that will determine how patterns evolve through time. Now imagine a physical world of infinite extent and with a completely variegated state of occupation whose evolution in time always conforms to these rules.

(It is a key point that we are now imagining a world whose evolution everywhere *conforms to* these rules, but we are reserving judgment about whether we ought to say that the evolution is *generated by* these rules.)

If we have chosen the rules randomly, then it is overwhelmingly likely that there will be patterns of occupation that differ only in a single location, but which both yield the same result. For example, suppose it turns out that both patterns A and B in figure 18.1 are always succeeded by the central square being occupied. The question I want to ask is this: In such a world, is the bit of matter in the bottom central location of pattern A a *cause* (or an essential part of a cause) of the central square being occupied the next instant or not?

In the course of this inquiry, I will take a few points to be uncontroversial. First, I take it that the sort of physical world I have described at least *could be* a world that follows laws of the evolution of the distribution of matter. On anything like the Mill–Ramsey–Lewis account of laws, I take it that if the world is extensive and variegated

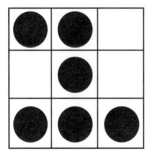

Pattern A   Pattern B

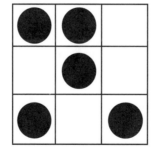

Figure 18.1

enough, then there *must be* laws: After all, of all possible distributions of matter throughout space and time, only a set of measure zero will conform to these rules through all time. It is therefore extremely informative to know that these rules are always obeyed. I further assume that having granted that the world is law governed, we grant that the truth values of all counterfactuals concerning the evolution of distributions of matter are determined. Since the rules are deterministic, we can use them to determine how any distribution of matter would have evolved, even if that distribution never actually occurs in the world we are imagining. So at the fundamental physical level, there is no dispute about counterfactuals: Given any complete pattern at a time, we know how it would have evolved had it been different in some precisely specified way.

My central claim is this: Even though there is no dispute, at the fundamental level, about counterfactuals, there can still be a dispute about causation, and further, this dispute about causation arises as a consequence of a parallel dispute about laws. The issue here is not how the case ought to be judged, or what our intuitions are about the case, or whether a particular theory gets the intuitions right. The issue is rather that unproblematic knowledge of all counterfactuals in this case does not seem to settle the question of causal structure, and furthermore, unproblematic knowledge of counterfactuals does not settle what the laws are in this same case. This again suggests that it is the laws, not the counterfactuals per se, that underwrite causal claims.

There are two lines of argument that can be addressed to the question of whether the bit of matter in the bottom central location of pattern A is a cause of the succeeding occupation or not. The first line makes straightforward appeal to the Hume counterfactual, and denies that the matter in that location is a cause. It is beyond dispute in this case that the Hume counterfactual is false: Even if the bottom central location had not been occupied (i.e., even if what was pattern A had been instead pattern B), still the central square in the succeeding instant would have been occupied. In this sense, it is beyond dispute that the presence or absence of matter in that location makes no difference to how the distribution of matter will evolve. Furthermore (this argument continues) although sometimes the Hume counterfactual can fail to be true for genuine causes and effects, that is only because causation is the ancestral of *direct* causation, and in direct causation the Hume counterfactual is always true. But since space and time are discrete here, and there are no intervening moments of time or intervening places in space, if there is any causation it must be direct causation. There is simply no place for there to be a chain of direct causes between pattern A and the succeeding occupation of the central square. So since there is no indirect causation (no room for it) and there is no direct causation (the Hume counterfactual is false) there is no causation at all linking the matter in the bottom

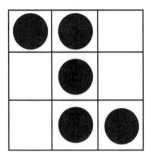
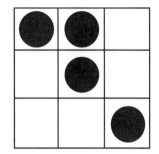

Pattern C   Pattern D

Figure 18.2

central location to the matter occupying the central square in the next instant. Hence the case against causation.

Now the case for causation. In arguing in favor of the matter in the bottom center being a cause, one would first point out that in general the laws of evolution in this world seem to link complete 3-by-3 patterns of occupation to the succeeding state of the central square. If the state of the central bottom location were *never* relevant to the evolution, then there would be little dispute about its causal efficaciousness. But suppose that patterns *C* and *D* in figure 18.2 are such that *C* is always followed by an occupied central square and *D* by an empty one. In this case, the Hume counter-factual holds, and the matter in the bottom central square of pattern *C* would be among the causes of the occupation of the central square in the next instant. The idea is that the complete set of 512 transition rules is so miscellaneous that there is no significantly *more* compact way to convey it than by specifying each of the 512 rules separately. It does not, for example, make things significantly simpler to try to bundle patterns *A* and *B* together into *one* rule (which refers to only the pattern of occupation of the eight locations other than the bottom central one) since one would have to indicate, either explicitly or implicitly, that in this case the state of the bottom central location need not be specified, although in other cases it must be.

So the advocate of causation argues as follows. The overall structure of the evolution in this world suggests that the laws of nature connect complete 3-by-3 patterns to the succeeding state of the central square. (After all, that is how *we* generated the rules: by flipping a coin anew for each of the 512 patterns.) Since there is no interesting generic pattern to the rules, the most *uniform* thing to do is to regard the fundamental laws of this world as all rules that take complete 3-by-3 patterns as input and give either an occupied or empty central square as output. From this point of view, it is just a *coincidence* that pattern A and pattern B, which differ only in the state of the bottom central square, both lead to occupied central squares. (After all, if we generate the rules by flipping a coin, it *is* just a coincidence that they do.) As far as the laws of nature are concerned, pattern A and pattern B have *nothing in common at all*; they are, as it were, each atomic and distinct. From this point of view, then, the state of the central bottom square is of vital importance, for it determines whether the transition falls under the law governing pattern A or the law governing pattern B, where these *laws* are regarded as fundamentally distinct. If an A pattern gives rise to an occupied central square, then although it is true that the square would still have been occupied had the bottom central location been empty, that would have been a case of an *alternative and distinct cause of the same effect*. The B pattern is a sort of backup mechanism, on this view, which would produce the same effect as the A pattern had the A pattern been different in a specified way. But whether the transition from the B pattern counts as *alternative mechanism* or as an instance of the *same* mechanism as the transition from the A pattern depends on what the laws are that govern the situation. Both transitions could be instances of the operation of the same law, or instances of two distinct laws, and our causal judgments depend on which we take to be the case.

We saw above that one route to save the counterfactual analysis was to add something to the antecedent: that all potential backup causes be held fixed as non-firing if in fact they did not fire. We saw that this spells trouble for trying to use the counterfactuals to analyze causation. Now we are seeing that what counts as an alternative or backup cause may depend on the nature of the laws governing the situation, so it is not puzzling that analyses that leave the laws aside will run into trouble.

I do not wish to adjudicate between the arguments pro and con the causal effectiveness of the bottom central location in this case; I rather simply want to acknowledge that there can be a dispute, a *reasonable* dispute, in a case like this where the counterfactuals are all beyond question. I do think, as a matter of fact, that the pro causation argument would eventually win out, if no interesting generic metarules could be found that simplified the presentation of the 512 different transitions. But even if one thinks that the con side would win, it is hard to deny that each side *has a point*, and that the point ultimately turns on how one is to conceive of the laws of nature in such a world.

We can easily imagine the 512 different transitions being such that they can be encapsulated by very simple rules, such as the Conway rules mentioned above. And we can imagine intermediate cases, where instead of giving all 512 transitions separately, one can give a few very complicated, generic rules. And we can imagine the case discussed above, where no interesting simple metarules exist. There is a slippery slope between these cases. I take it that on Lewis's account of laws, there will be points along this slope where it will be indeterminate what the laws are: points where there will be reasonable disagreement about whether the fewer complicated generic rules are *simpler overall* than the 512 separate transition rules. And where the laws are in dispute, it may turn out (as it does above) that the *causes* are in dispute, all while the truth values of the counterfactuals remain unquestioned.

So our pair of examples displays a nice symmetry. In the Newtonian case, we showed that we can know the causes without knowing any Hume counterfactuals if only we know the laws. And in our modified Game of Life, we have shown that we can know all the counterfactuals without being sure about the causes if there is a dispute about the laws. Between the two of them, they make a strong case for the idea that it is the laws rather than the counterfactuals that determine the causes.

3 The Role of Laws

If we are to explain the ubiquitous connections between causal claims and counterfactuals by appeal to the role of laws in the truth conditions of each, we must at least sketch how those truth conditions go. In the case of counterfactuals the basic story is extremely obvious and requires little comment. If I postulate that a world is governed by the laws of Newtonian mechanics, or the laws of the Game of Life, then certain conditionals are easy to evaluate: those that postulate a particular complete physical state at a given time as the antecedent and some other particular or generic physical state at a later time as the consequent. Given the state specified in the antecedent, the laws then generate all later states, and the sort of state specified by the consequent either occurs or does not. That is, one uses models of the laws as possible worlds and then employs the usual possible worlds semantics for the truth conditions of the conditional.

If the antecedent is not stated directly in the physical vocabulary, or is vague or generic, or is only a partial specification of the state of the world, then various sorts of filling in must be employed to yield a set of states that satisfy the antecedents, which then generate a set of models, and again things proceed in the usual way. There is much to be amplified in this sketch, and emendations needed for probabilistic laws, and so on, but the role of laws in the whole process is evident enough. Let us omit any more detail about counterfactuals, then, and turn to the much more interesting topic of causation.

I do not think that there is any *uniform* way that laws enter into the truth conditions for causal claims, as there is a fairly uniform way they enter into the truth conditions for counterfactuals. Rather, I think that laws of a very particular form, wonderfully illustrated by Newton's laws of motion, support a certain method of evaluating of causal claims, whereas a more generic and somewhat less intuitive use must be found for other sorts of laws. As we will see, the laws of the Life world lack all of the interesting characteristics of Newton's laws, so we will again use them for illustrative purposes.

Let's start, then, by returning to our colliding particles. Why are we so confident in identifying the collision with particle Q as the cause of particle P being set in motion? Recall the exact form of Newton's laws, the form that makes them so useful as aids for tracking causes in a case like this. The first law, the *law of inertia*, states that a body at rest will remain at rest and a body in motion will continue in motion at a uniform speed in a straight line, unless some force is put on it. The first law specifies *inertial motion*, that is, how the motion of an object will progress if nothing acts on it. The second law then specifies how the state of motion of an object will *change* if a force is put on it: It will change in the direction of the force, and proportionally to the force, and inversely proportionally to the mass of the object. Note that the second law is in a way parasitic on the first: The first specifies what is to count as a state of motion (uniform motion in a straight line), and the second how, and in what circumstances, the state changes.

The structure of Newton's laws is particularly suited to identifying causes. There is a sense, I think, in which the continuation of inertial motion in a Newtonian universe *is not caused*. If a body is at rest at one time, and nothing acts on it (i.e., no force acts on it), then it sounds odd to ask what causes it to remain at rest. It sounds odd to say that the body's own inertial mass causes it to remain at rest, since there is no force that the mass is resisting, and the inertial mass is just a measure of a body's resistance to force. And it sounds odd to say that the law of inertia itself causes the body to remain at rest, since it seems similar to a category mistake to ascribe causality to those very laws. Of course, the body remains at rest because no force acts and because the inertial state of motion of a body at rest is to remain at rest, but it certainly sounds odd to cite the absence of forces as a cause of remaining at rest.

Or at least, if there is any cause of a body at rest remaining at rest in a Newtonian universe it is a sort of *second-class* cause: The first-class Newtonian causes are forces (or the sources of forces), and what they cause, the first-class form of a Newtonian effect, is a change or deviation from an inertial state of motion. There is no doubt that for Newton, once the first law is in place, one can ask what causes the Earth to orbit the Sun (rather than travel at constant speed in a straight line), and that the cause in this case is the gravitational force produced on the Earth by the Sun. It is this sort of conceptual structure that allows us to so readily identify the cause of the motion in particle P above: Since the inertial state of P is for it to remain at rest, its change into a state of motion requires a cause, that is, a force, and the only force is provided by Q. Without the law of inertia, it would not be clear that the sudden onset of motion in P required any cause at all: Perhaps particles sometimes just spontaneously start moving. Or perhaps the inertial state of motion of a particle could be a jerky motion: The particle moves at a given velocity for a while, then stops for a while, then resumes at the same velocity, so the onset of motion in P is just the continuation of its natural state of motion.

Let us denominate laws *quasi-Newtonian* if they have this form: There are, on the one hand, *inertial* laws that describe how some entities behave when nothing acts on them, and then there are laws of *deviation* that specify in what conditions, and in what ways, the behavior will deviate from the inertial behavior. When one conceives of a situation as governed by quasi-Newtonian laws, then typically the primary notion of an effect will be the deviation of the behavior of an object from its inertial behavior, and the primary notion of a cause will be whatever sort of thing is mentioned in the laws of deviation.

Laws, of course, need not be quasi-Newtonian. At a fundamental level, the laws of the Game of Life are not. In that game, if a cell is occupied at one moment then it has no "natural" or "innate" tendency to remain occupied—or to become unoccupied—at the next moment. The patterns evolve in an orderly way, but the behavior of the overall pattern cannot be analyzed into, on the one hand, inertial states of the parts and, on the other, interactions that cause deviations from those states. There is no division of the rules of evolution into the inertial rules and the rules for change of inertial state.

That does not, of course, mean that the Life world is without causes. There are causes and effects, but the way we conceive of them, at the fundamental level, is quite different from the way we think of causes in a quasi-Newtonian setting. If a particular cell in the Life world (or, more obviously, the modified Life world) is occupied at a moment, then the cause of that is the complete 3-by-3 pattern of occupation centered on that cell the instant before, and similarly if a cell is empty. And the cause of that 3-by-3 pattern a moment before is the complete 5-by-5 pattern of occupation centered on that cell two moments before, and so on. As we go further back in time, the reach of the ancestral causes grows outward like a ziggurat, the Life-world analogue of the past light-cone of an event in a relativistic universe. At a fundamental level, the only proper causes in the Life world are these complete patterns at a time, which—in conjunction with the laws—generate the successive patterns that culminate in the given cell being occupied or empty at the given moment. (In the context of the discussion I am assuming that we agree that only a full 3-by-3 pattern is a cause of the succeeding state of the central square.)

This notion of causation will be available in any world governed by deterministic laws, whether quasi-Newtonian or not, and so the philosopher hankering after the most widely applicable concept of causation will likely be drawn to it. It is obviously an instance of the INUS concept of causation, for example. But I think that we fall back on this notion of causation only when circumstances demand it: Our natural desire is to think of the world in quasi-Newtonian terms, in terms of inertial behavior (or "natural" behavior) and deviations from inertial behavior: in terms of, to use a concept from mathematical physics, perturbation theory. Largely, this is because it is much easier to think in these terms, to make approximate predictions on the basis of scanty data, and so on. And often circumstances allow us to think in quasi-Newtonian terms even when the underlying laws are not quasi-Newtonian, or to think in macrolevel quasi-Newtonian terms quite different from the laws that obtain at the fundamental level. Indeed, the search for quasi-Newtonian laws does much to explain the aims of the special sciences.

4   Causation and Macrotaxonomy in the Special Sciences

I am a realist about laws: I think that there are laws, and that their existence is not a function of any human practices. I am also a primitivist about laws: I do not think that what laws there are is determined by any other, distinctly specifiable set of facts, and that in particular it is not determined by the total physical state of the universe. And I am a physicalist about laws: The only objective primitive laws I believe in are the laws of physics. Speaking picturesquely, all God did was to fix the laws and the initial state of the universe, and the rest of the state of the universe has evolved (either deterministically or stochastically) from that. Once the total physical state of the universe and the laws of physics are fixed, every other fact, such as may be, supervenes. In particular, having set the laws of physics and the physical state, God did not, and could not have, added any further laws of chemistry or biology or psychology or economics.

We do not, however, understand the vast majority of what we do understand by reflecting on the laws of physics. For example, there is much that I understand about how the computer I am now using works, and precious little of that derives from detailed knowledge of the physics of the machine. Rather, I understand its operation by thinking about it in terms of some *lawlike generalizations*, generalizations that resemble laws at least insofar as being regarded as supporting counterfactual claims and being confirmed by positive instances.

In this sense, it is a lawlike generalization about the computer that when it is turned on and the word processing program is running and there is document open, pressing a key on the keyboard will be followed by the corresponding letter appearing at the point where the cursor is, and the cursor will move over one space to the right (unless it is the end of a line, in which case it moves all the way to the left on the next line, unless it is at the bottom of the window, etc.). This generalization, which could be made more precise and extensive at the cost of much tedium, is taken to support counterfactuals: If I had hit the letter "*z*" on the keyboard instead of "*s*" just before the last colon, the word that would have appeared would have been "counterfactualz."

No doubt it is by means of such generalizations that we understand how to use the computer, predict how it will function, explain it to others, and so on. And no doubt this generalization, albeit lawlike in certain respects, is not in any metaphysically interesting sense a law. If I should hit a key and the corresponding letter did not appear, then it is not that any *law* would be broken: Rather, *the computer* would be broken (or misprogrammed, or crashed, etc.). And no doubt if the generalization is correct and the counterfactuals it implies are true, that is ultimately because of the *physical* structure of the machine operating in accord with the laws of physics. The lawlikeness of the macrogeneralizations, insofar as they are lawlike, is parasitic on the laws of physics in a way that the laws of physics are not parasitic on anything.

The point is that this is how the special sciences work: They seek to impose a taxonomy on the physical structure of the world (the concept "keyboard," for example, is not and cannot be reduced to the vocabulary of physics) in such a way that the objects as categorized by the taxonomy fairly reliably obey some lawlike generalizations that can be stated in terms of the taxonomy. Generalizations about how computers, or cumulus clouds, or volcanoes, or free markets behave are evidently of this sort.

Talk about "carving nature at the joints" is just shorthand for "finding a macro-taxonomy such that there are reasonably reliable and informative and extensive lawlike generalizations that can be stated in terms of the taxonomy," and the more reliable and informative and extensive, the closer we have come to the "joints." Again, I claim nothing particularly novel, or astounding, about this observation.

But if the foregoing analysis is correct, we are now in a position to add something new. We have already seen that certain forms of laws, namely, quasi-Newtonian laws, allow the identification of causes to be particularly simple and straightforward. So insofar as the special sciences seek to use causal locutions, it will be a *further* desideratum that the lawlike generalizations posited by the sciences be quasi-Newtonian. The special sciences, and plain common sense as well, will seek to carve up the physical world into parts that can, fairly reliably, be described as having inertial states (or inertial motions) that can be expected to obtain unless some specifiable sort of interference or interaction occurs. Or at least, those special sciences that manage to employ taxonomies with quasi-Newtonian lawlike generalizations can be expected to support particularly robust judgments about causes.

A few examples. We obviously understand computers in quasi-Newtonian terms: Depending on the program being run, there is an inertial state or inertial motion, and that motion can be expected to continue unless some input comes from the keyboard or mouse. The input is then an interfering factor, whose influence on the inertial state is specified by some "laws" (the program). We similarly understand much of human biology in quasi-Newtonian terms. The inertial state of a living body is, in our usual conception of things, to remain living: That is why coroners are supposed to find a "cause of death" to put on a death certificate. We all know, of course, that this macrogeneralization is only a consequence of the clever construction of the body and a lot of constant behind-the-scenes activity: By all rights, we should rather demand multiple "causes of life" for every day we survive. Nonetheless, the human body, in normal conditions, is sufficiently resilient that the expectation of survival from day to day is a reliable one, and the existence of the right sort of unusual circumstance immediately preceding death is typical. We do sometimes say that people just die of old age (which is obviously not a normal sort of cause) when no salient "cause of death" exists, and our acceptance of this locution illustrates our awareness that the quasi-Newtonian generalization "In the normal course of things (in the absence of 'forces') living human bodies remain alive" is not really a law at all.

Most critically for our present purposes, we typically think of the operation of *neurons* in quasi-Newtonian form: The inertial state of a neuron is not to fire, and it departs from that state only as a result of impinging "forces," namely, electrochemical signals coming from other neurons. These "forces" come in different strengths and can be either excitatory or inhibitory, and there is a lawlike formula that describes how the neuron will depart from its inertial state depending on the input to it. Of course, I do not mean to defend this conception as a bit of real neurophysiology, but that is how we lay people (and particularly we philosophers) tend to think of neurons. So conceived, it is often very easy to identify the cause of the firing of a neuron. If a neuron fires and only one excitatory impulse came into it, then that impulse was the cause of firing. End of story. Counterfactuals about what would have happened had that excitatory impulse not come in (whether, for example, some *other* impulse would have come in) are simply irrelevant. Details of the larger neural net in which these two are embedded are simply irrelevant. The only thing that would *not* be irrelevant would be the discovery that the quasi-Newtonian generalization is false, for example, because neurons sometimes spontaneously fire with no input.

The widespread use of Lewisian "neuron diagrams" in discussions of the nature of causation is, from this point of view, both a beautiful confirmation and a deep puzzle. We like neuron diagrams because our intuitions about what is causing what are strong and robust. Those who want to analyze causation in terms of counterfactuals think that the diagrams are useful as tests of counterfactual analyses: The trick is to find some condition *stated in terms of counterfactuals about firing patterns* that picks out all and only the causes. Those conditions then tend to get very complicated and quickly embroil one in issues like backtracking, miracles, intermediate states, and so on. But it is perfectly apparent that our strong and robust intuitions in this case are not generated by fancy considerations of counterfactuals at all: They are generated by the application of quasi-Newtonian *laws* to the situation, and the counterfactuals be damned. So the puzzle is why it has not been apparent that the very diagrams used to discuss counterfactual analyses have not been recognized as clear illustrations of the wrongheadedness of the counterfactual approach.

The great advantage of the special sciences *not* being fundamental is the latitude this provides for constructing macrotaxonomies well described by quasi-Newtonian generalizations. For example, one can try to secure the reliability of a quasi-Newtonian law of inertia by *demanding* that one find an interfering factor if the inertial state changes. In a case like finding the "cause of death" this can often be done. There is a lot of biological activity all the time, and even absences and lacks can count: One can die of starvation or suffocation. There is also latitude in carving the joints: One can shift boundaries so as to identify systems that obey more robust generalizations. This sort of boundary-shifting helps explain our causal intuitions in some cases that have been discussed in the literature.

Consider the following example by Michael McDermott:

Suppose I reach out and catch a passing cricket ball. The next thing along in the ball's direction of motion was a solid brick wall. Beyond that was a window. Did my action prevent the ball hitting the window? (Did it cause the ball *not* to hit the window?) Nearly everyone's initial intuition is, "No, because it wouldn't have hit the window irrespective of whether you had acted or not." To this I say, "If the wall had not been there, and I had not acted, the ball would have hit the window. So between us—me and the wall—we prevented the ball from hitting the window. *Which one* of us prevented the ball hitting the window—me or the wall (or both together)?" And nearly everyone then retracts his initial intuition and says, "Well, it must have been your action that did it—the wall clearly contributed nothing." (1995a, p. 525)

McDermott's argument is quite convincing, but a puzzle remains. Why was nearly everyone's *initial* reaction the "wrong" one? What were they thinking? Was it merely the falsehood of the Hume counterfactual, "If you had not caught the ball it would have hit the window," that makes people judge that catching the ball is not a cause of the ball failing to hit the window? Then why does one *not* make this error (or not so easily) when the first catcher is followed by a second, infallible catcher rather than a brick wall?[4] The Hume counterfactual also fails here (if you had not caught the ball, the second catcher would have, and it still would not have hit the window), but it seems clear in this case that you are the actual cause here, and the second catcher merely an unutilized backup. The pair of examples makes trouble for any counterfactual analysis, since the counterfactuals in each case are identical, substituting the second catcher for the wall. So if we judge causes by means of counterfactuals, our intuitions should swing the same way in both cases, but they don't.

Here is an account that makes sense of the data. In judging causes, we try to carve up the situation into systems that can be assigned inertial behavior (behavior that can be expected if nothing interferes) along with at least a partial specification of the sorts of things that can disturb the inertial behavior, analogous to the Newtonian forces that disturb inertial motion. Let us call the things that can disturb inertial behavior "threats": They are objects or events that have the power—if they interact in the right way—to deflect the system from its inertial trajectory. We then think about how the situation will evolve by expecting inertial behavior unless there is an interaction with a threat, in which case we see how the threat will change the behavior. A threat can itself be threatened: Its inertial trajectory might have it interacting with a target system, but that trajectory be deflected by something that interferes with *it*. This is what we mean by *neutralizing* a threat, or by *preventing* an event.

Now what counts as inertial behavior, and what counts as a threat, depends on how we carve the situation up into systems. If we consider a normal window on its own, its inertial behavior is to remain unbroken (something must cause it to shatter, but nothing causes it not to if nothing interferes with it). The sorts of thing that count as threats are objects with sufficient mass and hardness and (relative) speed: A hurled rock is a threat to a window but a lofted marshmallow is not. The cricket ball in the example is obviously a threat to break the window (although the case just deals with hitting the window, the same point holds). The cricket ball is furthermore in a state of motion such that its (Newtonian) inertial trajectory has it hit the window, so for the threat to be neutralized, something must act to deflect the ball. This is clearly the first catcher in both cases, and the presence of the wall or second catcher never comes into the analysis.

But let us now carve up the situation a bit differently. Let us call the window plus brick wall system a "protected window." The inertial state of the window in a protected window system is to remain unbroken, and indeed to remain *untouched*. To count as a threat to this state, an object must be able to *penetrate* (or otherwise *circumvent*) the wall, at least if it is approaching from the direction protected by the wall. Thought of this way, the cricket ball is *not* a threat to the inertial behavior of the window; only something like an artillery shell would be. So in the given situation, there are no threats to the window at all, and a fortiori there are no threats that are neutralized, and so no prevention: *Nothing* causes the protected window not to be hit since that is its inertial state and nothing with the power to disturb the inertial state threatened.

In sum, if we carve things up one way (window plus wall plus catcher plus ball) we get systems governed by quasi-Newtonian generalizations that yield the judgment that the catcher prevented the window being hit; if we carve them up another way (protected window plus catcher plus ball) we get systems governed by quasi-Newtonian generalizations that yield the judgment that the window was never threatened with being hit, so nothing had to prevent it. And the interesting thing is that *both systematizations, together with the corresponding quasi-Newtonian generalizations, yield the same counterfactuals.* So no counterfactual analysis of causation has the resources to account for the disparity of judgments: Carving up the world differently can give different (special science) *laws*, governing different *systems*, but it should not give different truth values to counterfactuals.

If this analysis is correct, McDermott has played something of a trick on his test subjects. Their original intuition that the catcher does not prevent the window being hit is perfectly correct, relative to conceptualizing the situation as containing a protected window. McDermott then asks a series of questions that essentially require that one reconceive the situation, carving it instead into a window, a ball, and a compound wall plus catcher system. So thought of, the ball is clearly a threat to the window, the threat needs to be neutralized (or deflected) to prevent the window being hit, and the wall plus catcher system does the deflecting. The last step is to give the credit to either the wall or the catcher or both, and here the catcher clearly wins. All of this is perfectly legitimate: It is just no *more* legitimate that lumping the window and wall together and judging that nothing prevented the hit.

The window plus two catchers example tends to confirm the analysis: Here the natural tendency would be to regard the two catchers as equally autonomous systems. It would be odd to carve up the situation so that the window plus second catcher is regarded as a single system (although one could tell stories that would promote this). So our intuitions go differently from the wall case, even though the corresponding counterfactuals are the same.

The only remaining question is why typical subjects would have the tendency to regard the situation as containing a protected window, rather than in terms of a regular window, a threatening ball, and a pair of potential neutralizers. Lots of hypotheses come to mind, and the only way to test them would be to try many more sorts of examples. Windows and walls are obviously more similar than catchers and walls, since windows and walls are inert bits of architecture. It is *simpler* to keep track of things using the "protected window" systematization, since there are fewer threats and hence fewer threats that need to be tracked. The "protected window" systematization also has the advantage of yielding (in this case, at least) causal judgments that agree with the Hume counterfactual: The catcher does not prevent the window from being hit, and the window would not have been hit even if the catcher had not acted. (The last two considerations are held in common with the "two catcher" case, where our intuitions go the other way, but in that case there is positive pressure to group the catchers together.)

A thought experiment recommends itself: Imagine various ways for the wall to metamorphose into a second catcher and track when one's causal intuitions flip. But that is a task for another paper.

Alternative taxonomies need not be at the same degree of resolution, as in the foregoing example. Ned Hall has argued ("Two Concepts of Causation," chap. 9, this vol.) that cases of double prevention (preventing an event that would have prevented another event) are typically not regarded as causation (in the sense of production). Jonathan Schaffer (2000c) has then pointed out that guns fire by double prevention, but one is not tempted to conclude that pulling the trigger of a gun is not a cause of the firing. But surely what guides out intuitions in this case are lawlike macrogeneralizations in quasi-Newtonian form. The "inertial law" for guns is just: A gun doesn't fire if nothing acts on it (e.g., pulls the trigger, jars it, etc.). *Anything* that regularly results in a gun firing (particularly pulling the trigger) counts as a cause that changes the inertial state, no matter how the trick is done at the microlevel. *This judgment is not reversed even if one decides that the right thing to say at the microlevel is that pulling the trigger does not produce the firing.* If different taxonomies can allow for different lawlike generalizations and hence different causal judgments, we have all the makings for interminable philosophical disputes, since causal judgments can be reversed simply by changing taxonomies, as McDermott's example illustrates.

5   Remote Causation

The foregoing account has been concerned with the analysis of what we may call *proximate* or *immediate* causation: Where a situation is conceptualized as governed by quasi-Newtonian laws, the laws will specify what counts as an inertial state and therefore what counts as a deviation from an inertial state (a first-class effect), and also what sorts of things or events (causes) bring about such deviations. The interfering factor is then the proximate cause of the deviation, as in the billiards example.

This analysis does not, however, solve the problem of *remote* causation. We commonly identify events or actions as causes that are not the proximate causes of their effects: The loss of the horseshoe nail ultimately causes the loss of the battle not directly but by a long chain of intermediates. The loss of the horseshoe nail is only the proximate cause of the loss of the horseshoe.

Prima facie, the use of quasi-Newtonian laws appears to be of some help in this regard. If the laws have the form of specifying inertial states and interfering factors, then any concrete situation can be represented by what we may call an *interaction diagram*, a graph depicting inertial motions of objects as straight lines and divergences from inertial motion as always due to the interaction with some interfering element. One might think, for example, of Feynman diagrams as examples of the form. Note that if all interactions are local, or by contact, then interaction diagrams will look like spacetime diagrams, and the lines will represent continuous processes in spacetime, but this is not essential to the form: if there is action-at-a-distance, then two lines can intersect on an interaction diagram even if the objects they represent never come near each other in spacetime.

Interaction diagrams supply one simple method for identifying remote causes: Trace the diagram backward from an event, and every node one comes to counts as a cause. But this method will not, in many cases, accord with our intuitions. Being in the interaction diagram for an event may well be a necessary condition for being a cause, but it is unlikely to be sufficient. Interaction diagrams will include events that we consider not to be causes (in the usual sense) but failed attempts at prevention, such as the futile course of chemotherapy that fails to stem the cancer. Interaction diagrams also stretch back indefinitely in time, to events too remote to be commonly considered causes. They are a bit more parsimonious than the entire back light-cone of an event, but not that much.

This sort of situation is, of course, the siren song for the analytic philosopher. Perhaps we can identify commonsense remote causes by use of an interaction diagram plus some further condition (the Hume counterfactual, for example). But the avalanche of counterexamples to the many theories of causation that have been floated ought to give us pause. Perhaps there is some reason that the analysis of remote causation has proved so difficult.

So let's step back a moment and ask what *purpose* there is to identifying remote causes in the sort of situation we are contemplating, that is, where we know the laws, the immediate causes of events, and the complete interaction diagram. What more could we want? What do we gain by trying to distinguish events that count as remote causes from others that are not?

One thing we might have is a practical concern for prediction and/or control. We might like to know how we could have prevented a certain event, or whether a similar event is likely to occur in future situations that are, in some specified respects, similar. But in that case, all we would really care about is the Hume counterfactual —and that, as we know by now, is neither sufficient nor necessary for causation. So what other aim might we have?

In some circumstances, we are interested in remote causes because we wish to assign *responsibility* for an event, for example, when offering praise, or assigning blame, or distributing rewards, or meting out punishments. In these circumstances, identifying a remote cause is often tantamount to establishing a responsible agent, and many of our intuitions about remote causes have been tutored by our standards of culpability. If this is correct, then we might make some progress by reflecting on such standards.

The game of basketball provides an example where rules for assigning credit as a remote cause have been made reasonably explicit. Consider this case: A pass is thrown down court. The center leaps and catches the ball, then passes it to Forward *A*, who dunks the ball. Forward *A* gets credit for the field goal, and the center gets an assist: He counts as a remote cause of the points being scored. Note that these attributions do not change even if it is also true that the pass was intended for Forward *B*, who was standing behind the center, and that had the center not touched the ball, Forward *B* would have caught the pass and scored, or would have passed it to *A*. Even if the Hume counterfactual does not hold for the center (even had he not caught the ball, the points would have been scored), the center counts, unproblematically, as a cause.

Now consider an apparently analogous case. John enters a car dealership, unsure whether he will buy a car. He is met by an Official Greeter, who directs him to Salesman *A*. Salesman *A* makes the pitch and convinces John to buy the car. Had the Greeter not intercepted him, John would have run into Salesman *B*, who also would have convinced him to buy the car (or who, perhaps, would have directed him to Salesman *A*). In this case, the Greeter can not, intuitively, claim credit for the sale: He did not even remotely cause John to buy the car. He was a cause of the cause, a cause of John's hearing Salesman *A*'s pitch (at least in the scenario where the alternative is a pitch from Salesman *B*), but we are not inclined to accept transitivity here.

Doubtless there are perfectly good reasons for the difference in practices for assigning credit in these cases: *Typically*, in a basketball game, had the assist not occurred points would not have been scored, so one wants to recognize and encourage those who give assists. But *typically*, in the sort of situation described in the car dealership, whether a sale is made does not depend on the actions of the Greeter. But what is typical does not affect the individual case: We can make the counterfactual structure of this *particular* pair of examples as analogous as we like (the schematic "neuron diagrams" for the scenarios can be made identical) without changing our views about who deserves credit and who does not. If so, then *no* generic account of remote causation couched in terms of interaction diagrams or counterfactual structure will always yield intuitively acceptable results: In different contexts, our intuitions will pick out different nodes on the same diagram as remote causes. In these cases, the definition of a remote cause is, as Hume would put it, "drawn from circumstances foreign to the cause," that is, from statistical features of other cases that are regarded as similar. As such, the standards violate the desideratum that causation be intrinsic to the particular relations between cause and effect.

If standards for identifying remote causes vary from context to context, and, in particular, if they depend on statistical generalities about *types* of situations rather than just on the particular details of a single situation, then the project of providing an "analysis" of remote causation is a hopeless task. We might usefully try to articulate the standards in use in some particular context, but no generic account in terms of interaction diagrams or counterfactual connections will accord with all of our strongly felt intuitions.

6   The Metaphysics of Causation

If the foregoing analysis is correct, then (1) what causes what depends on the laws that govern a situation; (2) judgments of causation are particularly easy if the laws have quasi-Newtonian form; (3) everyday judgments ("intuitions") about causation are based not on beliefs about the only completely objective laws there are (viz., physical laws) but rather more or less precise and reliable and accurate lawlike generalizations; (4) the same situation can be brought under different sets of such generalizations by being conceptualized differently, and those sets may yield different causal judgments even though they agree on all the relevant counterfactuals.

To what extent, then, is causation itself "objective" or "real"? At the level of everyday intuition, the freedom to differently conceptualize a situation implies that one's causal judgments may not be dictated by the complete physical situation per se. Further, the lawlike generalizations appropriate to the conceptualization can be criticized on objective grounds: They could be more or less accurate or clear or reliable. If, for example, windows sometimes spontaneously shatter (as a result of, say, quantum fluctuations), then the reasoning that the ball made it shatter because the ball was the only thing to hit it (and its inertial state is to remain unbroken unless something hits it) is no longer completely trustworthy, the less so the more often spontaneous shattering occurs. Lawlike generalizations are also supposed to support counterfactuals, but those counterfactuals must ultimately be underwritten by physical law, so a close examination of the physics of any individual situation could undercut the macrogeneralization applying to that case. The quest for greater scope, precision, and reliability of generalizations tends to force one to more precise microanalysis, ultimately ending in the laws of physics, which brook no exceptions at all.

If the laws of physics turn out to be quasi-Newtonian, then there could be a fairly rich objective causal structure at the fundamental level. But if, as seems more likely, the laws of physics are not quasi-Newtonian, then there may be little more to say about physical causation than that the entire back light-cone of an event (or even the entire antecedent state of the world in some preferred frame) is the cause of the event, that being the minimum information from which, together with the laws of physics, the event can be predicted. Quasi-Newtonian structure allows one to differentiate the "merely inertial" part of the causal history of an event from the divergences from inertial states that are paradigmatic effects, but without that structure it may be impossible to make a principled distinction within the complete nomically sufficient antecedent state. In that case, causation at the purely physical level would be rather uninteresting: If all one can say is that each event is caused by the state on its complete back light-cone, then there is little point in repeating it. None of this, of course, is of much interest to physics per se, which can get along quite well with just the laws and without any causal locutions.

There is much more that needs to be said about the role laws, or lawlike generalizations, play in the truth conditions of causal claims. The proposal I have made is more of a sketch than a theory, and it has all the resources of vagueness to help in addressing counterexamples and hard cases. Perhaps there is no adequate way to make the general picture precise. But the counterfactual approach to causation has had a good long run, and it has not provided simple and convincing responses to the problem cases it has faced. Perhaps it is time to try another approach.

Notes

1. Ned Hall has suggested that there are really two concepts of causation, one of which ("dependence") amounts to nothing more than the Hume counterfactual, whereas the other ("production") cannot be so

analyzed (cf. his "Two Concepts of Causation," chapter 9 in this volume). If one wishes, this essay can be read as an account of production, although I suspect that at least many cases of dependence can be covered using these methods.

2. Natural law can be employed in analyses of causation in many ways. One interesting, and distinct, approach is advocated by Schaffer (2001) in his PROPs analysis: Schaffer uses laws to identify the process that actually brought an event about.

3. If one imposes some natural symmetry constraints, such as 90° rotational symmetry, then there will be fewer than 512 distinct cases to deal with.

4. This example is discussed by John Collins in "Preemptive Prevention," chapter 4 in this volume.

19 Going through the Open Door Again: Counterfactual versus Singularist Theories of Causation

D. M. Armstrong

1 Introduction

This is a revised version of "The Open Door" (Armstrong 1999), a paper that criticized David Lewis's counterfactual theory of causation, arguing instead for a singularist theory. Things move quite fast in contemporary analytic philosophy, because workers on a particular topic are now much more likely to know each others' work and to communicate and influence each other. This is a great advance. Philosophical problems are so difficult to resolve that they seem beyond the compass of individuals working on their own. I've already found reason to try to rework a number of the things that I said in the original version.

2 Lewis's Theory

In a volume such as this, devoted to causation, we can summarize Lewis's theory rather quickly.[1] He is concerned with causation in particular cases, one token event bringing about another, rather than (true) causal generalizations. Causation is the ancestral of the relation of *causal dependence*, and causal dependence holds between events if and only if the counterfactual "if C had not occurred, then E would not have occurred" holds, with the counterfactual stipulated not to be a "backtracker." This counterfactual, Lewis asserts, is true if and only if there exists a possible world where c fails to occur and e fails to occur, a world that is closer in overall similarity to the actual world than any world in which c fails to occur but e does occur. Instructions are given for ranking different worlds in terms of overall resemblance. Holding previous history fixed, keeping the laws of nature as constant as possible, and minimizing the size of the miracles required to instantiate the antecedents of the counterfactuals are the most important ways of maximizing such resemblance.

Lewis's talk of possible worlds here is to a degree misleading. It is important to realize, as I did not originally realize, and I think many others have not realized, that these counterfactuals are supposed to hold solely in virtue of features of the world in which the causal relation holds. As I would put it, the *truthmaker* for causal truths is to be found solely in the world in which the relation holds. (I think this follows straight from the contingency of the causal relation, a contingency that Lewis does not doubt.) *In his theory of causation* the possible worlds enter as mere calculational devices. He has given me as an example the way that we might say with truth that a

Originally published in Preyer and Siebelt (2001). Minor revisions have been made for consistency.

person is a Montague rather than a Capulet, without being committed to the view that these families are actual. The fictional families are used as no more than a sort of calculational device.

An important doctrine that Lewis upholds is the thesis of Humean supervenience, the thesis that causes and laws supervene on the particular, local, matters of fact. But we should not let this encourage us to run his theory of causation together with his theory of law. His theory of law is neo-Humean, the Mill–Ramsey–Lewis view that laws are the most systematic and coherent subset of the regularities that the world contains. It is interesting to notice that given this theory of laws, including causal laws, but also given irreducibly singular causation, something close to Humean supervenience still holds: Causes have become particular, local, matters of fact.[2] It seems possible, also, to hold a Lewisian counterfactual theory of causality, together with a *non-Humean* theory of laws. For instance, one might hold that laws are contingent connections holding directly between universals. (If the connections are held to be necessary, that might be difficult to fit together with counterfactual causality.)

3 Neuron Diagrams and Singular Causation

Lewis has examined at length many types of situation that constitute prima facie objections to a counterfactual analysis, and I will shortly discuss three of these. But first a general remark. In the course of these discussions Lewis introduces his justly celebrated "neuron diagrams." These involve imaginary systems of neurons that are hooked up according to certain often quite complex causal patterns of firings and inhibitions of firing. They are then used to illustrate such situations as epiphenomenal events, preemptive causation, causal redundancy, and so on.

When we look at these diagrams, we can immediately see that they are possible causal patterns, in most cases empirically possible patterns (you could construct such a circuit). Counterfactual theories of causation (and, it may be added, regularity theories and probability-raising theories of causation) struggle with these diagrams. Wittgenstein spoke of an open door that we had only to see and go through to escape philosophical confusion. See Malcolm (1958), p. 44.[3] The solution that I recommend to the problems posed by the neuron diagrams is very simple. Where there is an arrow in a diagram showing that one neuron brings it about that another neuron fires, or is rendered incapable of firing, take it that here there is a genuine two-term relation of singular causation holding between cause and effect. Where there is no such arrow, deny that there is any such relation. This is the open door.

4   Negative Causes and Effects

There is a deep predisposition to think that where cause and effect are not contiguous in both space and time we can always trace an intermediate chain of causes that links the cause to its distant effect. It is true that we do admit cases of the following sort. An object is struck, but does not break. Later it is struck again, rather lightly, and unexpectedly breaks. We understand very well the suggestion that the object broke because the original striking caused a weakness that persisted and at least helped to cause the later breaking. This notion that objects can continue to bear effects would readily be admitted as a qualification of the doctrine of contiguity.

I will, however, record here, but not argue for the position, that I think that the persistence is still a case of causation. It is however, *immanent*, that is, "remaining within" causality, as opposed to *transeunt*, that is, interactive causality. (The terminology is due to W. E. Johnson 1924, ch. 9.) This is because I accept the doctrine of temporal parts for continuing objects and, further, think that the glue that holds the parts together has to be more than spatiotemporal continuity and a certain continuity of character. So, like Russell, I think of a continuing thing as a causal line, an information-preserving causal line. However, perhaps unlike Russell, I think of the line as a line of singular causes. If this is granted, the theory becomes much easier to defend.

Some think that this contiguity may break down in certain cases. It has been feared that gravitation would have to be taken as action at a distance. Now, however, gravitational waves are accepted. More recently, it has been wondered whether the puzzling EPR phenomenon may force the abandonment of "locality." But, prima facie, we do not expect causes to "jump gaps" in either space or time.

But what about preventions and omissions? We regularly speak of preventions as causes of what they prevent, "effects" that never occur. Omissions are things that are not done but that have positive effects. What is more, preventions and omissions seem susceptible to a Lewisian counterfactual analysis. The father grabs the child running down the drive, thus preventing the child from being hit by the car approaching in the road. If he had not acted thus, the child would have been run over. The grabbing is causal interaction in good standing. But there is no causal chain that leads from the grabbing to the "effect" of the child's not being run over. Or again, the father nods off and fails to grab the child. *As a result* the car hits the child. If he had not nodded off, he would have grabbed the child. Child and car interact, but no causal chain proceeds from the father. Preventions, something positive, bring about the absence of the thing prevented (often desirable). Omissions are absences that result in something positive happening (often undesirable). But how can absences have a place in a causal chain? Nothing will come of nothing.

Let us consider the great causal net of the world,[4] the total causal history of the world, the great neuron diagram as it were, where cause and effect are at every point positive realities (positive events, states of affairs, or whatever). What needs to be added to this causal net to give us the preventions and the omissions, the causal relations that involve absences? It seems that we need to add the laws of nature (taken ontologically, not as statements). They are needed as truthmakers for the counterfactual truths that are obviously involved in preventions and omissions. But given the causal net and its laws, we do not need *in addition* preventions and omissions. Preventions and omissions exist, of course. But they are not an ontological addition.

Lewis, it seems, should not deny the existence of the causal net in my sense of the phrase, the net that involves positive causation alone. (He would, of course, deny that it is a net involving genuine singular causal connections.) But since the laws for him are no more than the most systematic and pervasive regularities to be found in the world, this causal net is no more than the series of instantiations of these regularities, or if he admits fundamental noncausal laws, a subset of these instantiations of regularities. So causation involving prevention, omission, or absence is no ontological addition to his Humean world.

But what positive account are we to give of these negative effects and negative causes? I believe that Phil Dowe has shown us the way here. His first presentation of his view is to be found in section 6 of "Good Connections: Causation and Causal Processes" (Dowe 1999). The account is developed at much greater length in chapter 6 of his book *Physical Causation* (2000). Let us speak of the causation to be found in the causal net as *causal action*. (It has been spoken of as *biff*.) Dowe argues that when we have prevention, omission, and so on, then some causal action is always found. In prevention, for instance, the actual preventing is always causal action. Flipping a switch to turn a light off is causal action. We may call the current not reaching the bulb an "effect" of this action. But if we are thinking solely in terms of causal action, the only relevant effect is the positive happenings that break the connection of current and bulb.[5]

What has to be added is, fairly obviously, a counterfactual. In the present case, the counterfactual will perhaps be "if the switch had not been flipped, then the current would have continued to flow, and so kept bulb burning." But now follows the key feature in Dowe's account. These counterfactuals are not the familiar Lewis counterfactuals that have as their aim giving an account or analysis of causality. We may call them instead Dowe counterfactuals. Their special feature is that they make no attempt to *analyze* causality. Causality—causal *action*—appears as an *unanalyzed* notion in these counterfactuals. In the case of prevention, the counterfactuals give us in the consequent condition the *causal* consequences that would flow from the absence of the successful prevention.

These Dowe counterfactuals will have to have truthmakers, of course. Counterfactuals cannot hang on ontological air. A key part of the truthmaker will be the *relevant laws of causal action*, together presumably with the boundary conditions in which the prevention takes place. But I will not go into further detail. Dowe's latest discussion of the topic, in chapter 6 of his book, finds a great deal of complex detail to discuss in the various cases where the causality involved is not mere causal action. But it seems to me that he has succeeded in showing that, ontologically, negative causation is a sort of parasitic case. Henceforth, therefore, this essay is concerned with causal action, positive causality, alone.

But before leaving the topic I call attention to one important point that Dowe makes. Because causal action is left unanalyzed in his account of prevention and omission, his account of these phenomena is available, pretty well promiscuously, to other theories of causation. Regularity theories, probability-raising theories, counterfactual theories, singularist theories, "empirical" theories such as transference of energy or the conservation of certain quantities, can all avail themselves of Dowe's treatment of negative causation, and in particular the Dowe counterfactuals. (Counterfactual theories would plug in, say, Lewisian counterfactuals in giving, in terms of their lights, a deeper account of the Dowe counterfactuals.) The only exception is agency theories, since prevention, at least, is a means to an end, and the end may be something negative.

5 Probabilistic Causation

I will now consider Lewis's discussion of "chancy causation" in section B of the 1986 postscript to his 1973 paper "Causation," the sort of thing that we perhaps get in quantum phenomena. The following case gives him difficulty:

> ... c occurs, e has some chance x of occurring, and as it happens e does occur; if c had not occurred, e would still have had some chance y of occurring, but only a very slight chance since y would have been very much less than x. We cannot quite say that without the cause, the effect would not have occurred; but we can say that without the cause, the effect would have been very much less probable than it actually was.... I think we should say that e depends causally on c, and that c is a cause of e. (p. 176)

The obvious thing to say instead, it seems to me, is that e may or may not causally depend on c, and that c may or may not be the cause of e. Suppose, to take the case that seems to have the best chance of empirical instantiation, that besides c a potential cause c_1 is also present and that it is the latter that gives the smaller chance y of e occurring. It seems to be a perfectly objective question, when e occurs, whether it is c or c_1 that is the cause, although it is more likely to have been c. It might even be possible to settle the matter empirically. If the counterfactual theory cannot deliver this answer, that seems to be a weakness of that theory.

As he makes clear on page 180, Lewis would reject this reply. My style of answer is considered there. He points out that in the sort of case just considered, two different counterfactuals would compete in cases where c and c_1 were both present followed by the occurrence of e. In one case, where c is the cause, we have "if not c, then not e," but it is false that "if not c_1, then not e." But with c_1 as the cause, the truth values of these two conditionals are reversed. He says:

> But I reject the presupposition that there are two different ways the world could be, giving us one definite counterfactual or the other. That presupposition is a metaphysical burden quite out of proportion to its intuitive appeal; what is more its intuitive appeal can be explained away.
> The presupposition is that there is some hidden feature that may or may not be present in our actual world, and which if present would make true the [relevant] counterfactual. (1986b, pp. 180–181)

Lewis goes on at some length discussing candidates for the "hidden feature." But there is an obvious candidate, and not a mysterious one either if we are not blinded by the rhetoric of Hume and the Humeans. It is simply causation in the single case. Either c does this causing, or c_1 does. And some of us believe that we *observe* that this relation holds in particular favorable cases. If so, singular causation is not even hidden in every case.

A case that Lewis does not consider, but which brings out the strength of the singularist position here, is one where there are two possible probabilistic causes of just one effect, and the chance of each possible cause being the actual cause is equal. (Perhaps with a multiplication of the two chances giving the chance of an overdetermination.) Suppose that there are two bombardments of an atom, with the same chance of the atom emitting a particle, which the atom duly does.[6] Does there not seem to be an objective question, which of the two bombardments actually did the job?

Notice that we can very well have "probabilistic causation of a genuine chance event" (Lewis 1986b, p. 183) on this singularist view, although "probabilistic causation" is a rather unhappy and potentially misleading phrase. What we have rather, I suggest, is the probability, less than strictly 1, of causing occurring. This causing is the very same causing that we have with deterministic causing. Event c had a genuine chance of causing event e. Perhaps it did. The causing will then be ordinary singular causation. Event c_1 had a lesser chance of causing e. Perhaps c_1 was lucky—you can't lose them all, as the folk say—and c_1 was the event that caused e. Ordinary singular causing again. An open door, I suggest. It is a measure of the power of a singularist theory that it sweeps aside problems about chancy causation so easily.

I find that a little mnemonic is useful: not probabilistic causation but the probability of causing. In cases where an event c has a less than strictly 1 chance of causing e and does cause e then we can say that c "fires." If c fails to fire, there is no causation at all, though there was a chance of it.[7]

A final point. Lewis proposed his counterfactual theory as a conceptual analysis of causation. I have been arguing that a singularist theory is preferable as conceptual analysis, because it yields more intuitive results in difficult and disputed cases. (The elimination of negative causation is an add-on that seems to simplify the ontology of singular causation.) Lewis suggested to me that quantum physics may actually provide evidence against singularism. If so, as a scientific realist I ought to bow to the scientific evidence. I am not sure how to take this. It does not seem to me that singular probabilistic causation would be a "hidden variable" in the sense abjured in quantum theory. But I may be wrong here, or perhaps there are other strong reasons in quantum theory to reject singularist causation. I can certainly conceive giving up singularism under the weight of such evidence, but like St. Augustine, I say not now. But even if the theory had to be abandoned, I would still claim that it does best justice to our concept of causation.

6   Causation and Counterfactuals

Suppose it is true that event c causes event e. We know that, because of the possibility of a backup cause, it is false that it is *entailed* that if c had not occurred, then e would not have occurred. There also seems to be the bare possibility, pointed out to me by Michael Tooley, that, without c, e would have occurred without any cause at all. So what entailment can we find? It is not at all clear that we can do anything better than this: "c causes e" entails that: "if not-c, then, in the absence of a backup cause, or e coming to exist totally uncaused, then not-e."

It may well be, of course, both that a backup cause is absent, and that, likely enough, totally uncaused events never occur. If so, then the stronger "if not-c, then not-e" will be *true*. Because of this, it seems fair enough to say that the truth that c

causes *e supports* the proposition "if not-*c*, then not-*e*." But without the qualifying clauses, this support is not entailment.

It seems to me that this throws out an important challenge to those, such as Lewis, who hold that the counterfactual analysis of causation is conceptually true. The onus is on them to give us an entailment of "*c* causes *e*" that involves counterfactuals but makes no mention of causation. I have no proof that the onus cannot be discharged, but I do suspect that it cannot be.

7   Menzies on Singular Causation

But what is this causation that so many analytic philosophers find so mysterious? In what I think is a very important paper, "Probabilistic Causation and the Pre-emption Problem" (1996), Peter Menzies suggests that such causation is a "theoretical entity." Look at the difference a word or two makes! Lewis stigmatized singular causation as a "hidden feature," a phrase well calculated to arouse our Humean reflexes. He also says that it is "mysterious" (1986b, p. 182). But the phrase "theoretical entity" puts a new complexion on matters. And then Menzies goes on to suggest that we should avail ourselves here of the treatment of theoretical entities to be found in the work of—David Lewis. For some further development of Menzies's position, see his paper "Intrinsic versus Extrinsic Conceptions of Causation" (Menzies 1999).

Lewis's best-known application of his theory of theoretical entities is to our concepts of mental states. His idea is to collect the platitudes of folk psychology that concern the causal relations of mental states, sensory stimuli, and behavioral responses. Call these platitudes when confined to a particular sort of mental state, pain, say, the *causal role* of pain. Pain is a theoretical entity, namely, that entity that plays the causal role of pain. Here the notion of cause is treated as an undefined primitive. But, says Menzies, why not apply the same treatment to causation itself? Collect the platitudes of singular causation in the same sort of way. Causation is that intrinsic relation between singular events for which the causal platitudes hold.

In previous work on causality Menzies had emphasized not so much counterfactuals as the raising of probabilities: A cause raises the probability of its effect. It is known, however, that there are cases that pose great difficulty for theories of this type. But we know that a cause does *typically* raise the probability of its effect. Menzies therefore offers us the following Lewisian-style definition of the causal relation: It is *the intrinsic relation that typically holds between two distinct events when one increases the chance of the other event* (Menzies 1996, p. 101). The word "intrinsic" here is meant to capture the singularist insight. Menzies says, furthermore, that the notion of increase of chance is to be understood in the counterfactual manner found in Lewis's theory. So the counterfactuals that *typically* hold in the case where one event causes another, but which may fail in cases of late preemption and other sorts of unusual cases, can be part of the causal platitude.

All very fine, I think. For myself I would favor taking Menzies's "causal platitude" as fixing the reference of the singular causal relation rather than analyzing the concept. Menzies tells me that his treatment was meant as conceptual analysis, but he does not want to bar a retreat to reference-fixing. But I have three further points to make about Menzies's treatment, points to be developed in the succeeding sections. First, I think that we can supplement the epistemology involved in a quite important way. Second, I think that Menzies's platitude stands in need of some expansion. Third, and more speculatively, I have hopes that we can get behind the Menzies definition to a deeper, more ontologically revealing, account of the nature of singular causation.

8   The Epistemology of Singular Causation

I begin by noting that Lewis's causal role account of the mind makes the notion of the mental a theoretical one. I have great sympathy with this idea, though I might elsewhere niggle about details. But Lewis would not have denied that this theoretical entity is also one to which we have some observational access in the first-person case. We have introspective access to some of our own mental goings-on. We do not have introspective access to the intrinsic nature of these goings-on, certainly not if this intrinsic nature is as Lewis and I believe it is, namely, physical in nature and going on inside our heads. But we do have introspective access to our own mental goings-on, perhaps *as* goings-on that typically play a certain causal role.

This should embolden us to wonder whether we do not have observational access to singular causation, at least in certain favorable cases. There is in fact a good deal of evidence that opponents need to explain away.

(i)   Ordinary Language   Our ordinary language, as a number of philosophers have emphasized, constantly involves reference to the perception of causality in the singular case. This is a little obscured in the reporting of what we perceive, because we so often use verbs that make no explicit mention of the causality involved. G. E. M. Anscombe (1971, p. 8) offers what she calls "A small selection: *scrape, push, wet, carry, eat, burn, knock over, keep off, squash, make,* (e.g. noises, paper boats), *hurt.*" It would seem that all theories that deny the existence of singular causation must assert that such perceptual reports invariably involve (unselfconscious and immediate) inference. The contrast will be with the perception of shapes, color-surfaces, motions, smells, and so on. The contrast does not seem particularly plausible on the surface, but it must be made if there is no genuinely singular causation.

(ii) Two Salient Cases Two sorts of case that philosophers have advanced as involving noninferential perception of singular causation are our awareness of pressure on our own body, and our introspective awareness of the (successful) operation of our own will. I myself think that perception of pressure on our own body is the nearest there is to a knock-down case for noninferential perception of causality, though strangely enough there has been little discussion of it in the literature. (I incline to suspect the fell influence of the old representative or veil-of-perception theory of perception.) I first argued for this view in my (1962), though not then perceiving that it was incompatible with Humean theories of causation, and more recently in my (1997), section 14.6. An important defense of the same position is to be found in Evan Fales (1990), chapter 1. He points out, very interestingly, that the phenomenology of the perception of pressure matches the properties of a physical vector.

Many philosophers have pointed to the introspective awareness of the causality of the will. Fales gives names (see his ch. 1, n. 12). I suppose the case is more salient in the literature than that of pressure because few would dare to postulate a veil-of-perception intervening between oneself and one's own mental operations. Hume is aware of this objection to his position, and he argues against it in the appendix to the *Treatise* and later at length in the *Enquiry Concerning Human Understanding*, sections 52–53. But it is clear he had come to see that here, perhaps, was a place where the idea of causality might be derived from an impression, but that he had this realization only after he had given his own account of causation. The arguments he gives require attention, as one would expect, but they are not especially impressive. See the thorough and convincing examination of these arguments in Menzies (1998).

(iii) Experimental Work Finally, there is the experimental work of the psychologist A. Michotte of Louvain University (1963). He argues for a *visual* apprehension of causality, and in chapter 13 for a tactile-kinaesthetic awareness.[8] The visual case, I think, though quite strong, is not quite so convincing as the perception of pressure, or even awareness of the operation of our own will.

9   Some More Platitudes

It seems to me that Menzies has left out two things from his collection of platitudes that (in my view) "fix the reference" for the singular causal relation. The first is what we might call the "same cause, same effect" platitude. I mean by this that it is regularly true, even allowing that there are many apparent exceptions in ordinary experience, that from the same *sort* of cause the same sort of event, or at least roughly the same probability distribution of events, will follow. We might call it the regularity platitude, and we can see it as the truth that the regularity theory of causation grasps but misleadingly makes the whole truth about causation. Perhaps, however, addition of this platitude is implicit in Menzies (1996) section 5, where he follows up his Lewisian-style definition of causation by calling attention to: "... the powerful intuition that causal relations relate events in virtue of specific features of the events themselves, in particular the properties they exemplify" (1996, p. 105).

But the intuition as stated is not quite enough. We want the idea that not only does causation depend on the properties of the thing doing the causing, but also that from the same properties the same effects tend to flow.

A final platitude that I think we should include is linked with the agency or manipulative theory of causality.[9] Causes characteristically stand to their effects as *means*, or empirically possible *means* stand to their *ends*. We see, then, that regularity, counterfactual, probability-raising, and agency theories, though all should be rejected, each do contribute their important platitude to fixing the reference of the causal relation.

10 The Deeper Nature of Causation

Finally, we come a deeper, if more controversial suggestion, which I owe to Adrian Heathcote (Heathcote and Armstrong 1991), that an account of singular causation can be given as *the instantiation of a law*.

Laws link properties. In the simplest case, the instantiation of a certain property determines, or in the probabilistic case merely makes probable, that either that same particular or some related particular instantiates a certain property. That, surely, would *explain* the raising of the probability of the effect that is so regularly involved. (It would also explain the counterfactuals that we associate with causation, and why causes are means to ends.) A law (an entity in the world) provides the ground in nature for an inference. The cause is like the antecedent. If you know the singular cause and the law (which may be probabilistic only and/or may involve ceteris paribus conditions of operation) then, in general though not invariably, you can infer a raised probability of the presence of the effect.

Heathcote and I think of this *identity* thesis as an *empirical* identity claim.[10] It will not, however, be like the identification of the player of the mental causal role with brain processes. The latter is a *contingent* identity claim, because it does not tell us the purported *essence* of the mental. The brain processes are just those entities that happen to play the mental role. But our claim is that instantiation of law gives us the essence (or perhaps only part of the essence—explanation to come shortly) of singular causation. A better model than mind–brain identity will therefore be the identity of heat with molecular motion or water with H_2O molecules. It is a "Kripkean" necessity.

I now indicate briefly a consequence of combining the identification of singular causes with instantiations of a law (or laws) with my view, argued at length elsewhere,[11] that laws are relations of universals. Suppose that laws link properties; suppose that the ultimate properties, the properties that divide the world along its ultimate joints, are universals; suppose that the ultimate laws, at least, are linkages of universals. Such a linkage of universals will itself be a (complex) universal. It follows that each instantiation of a fundamental law will be the instantiation of a universal. But, famously, each instantiation of a universal is complete in itself, so the law will be present *completely* in each instantiation. Hence singular causation will be a completely intrinsic relation. The causal structure of a process will be determined solely by the intrinsic character of that process.

This result was unsought, but I think it is a welcome consequence of my theory of laws.[12] By contrast, any Hume-inspired theory of laws makes the lawlike nature of an instantiation of the law an *extrinsic* property of the instantiation.

But there is a problem that my view of singular causation faces. I said three paragraphs ago, in an aside, that instantiation of a law may be no more than *part* of the essence of singular causation. My reason was this. Not all laws are causal laws, or at least not all are obviously so. So it seems that all I am entitled to say is that singular causation is instantiation of *a certain sort of* law. My identification is therefore incomplete. And it would be a sad anticlimax to say that singular causation is instantiation of a causal law.

One satisfactory solution to this problem from my point of view would be that all the *fundamental* laws are, or can fairly be represented as being, causal laws. The notion of the causal net has already been introduced. What will need to be said is that the net exhausts reality and is causal through and through. The lines of the net proceed by immanent singular causation. Where lines intersect there is transeunt causation. It would be a natural corollary of this thesis that the fundamental laws are all causal.

A final word about the attractive "empirical" theories of Aronson, David Fair, and Phil Dowe. (Among these theories, I lean to Dowe's conserved quantity approach.) If the theory sketched above is on the right track, it would seem that these theories are really giving us theses about the most general laws that govern all physical action. The theories, I think, require the notion of singular causal connection to make them work, and so they cannot be the account of what that connection is.

Acknowledgments

A slightly earlier version of this paper was published in *Reality and Humean Supervenience: Essays on the Philosophy of David Lewis*, eds. Gerhard Preyer and Frank Siebelt, New York: Rowman and Littlefield, 2001, by kind permission of the editors of the present volume.

I am indebted for comments to Phil Dowe, Michael McDermott, and Peter Menzies. Particular thanks go to the late David Lewis.

Notes

1. Lewis's essay in this volume, "Causation as Influence," is not examined here. It is my impression, however, that the new points presented there do not change matters much from my point of view.

2. As Lewis pointed out to me, the definition he gives of Humean supervenience in his (1986a), pp. ix–x. explicitly restricts the fundamental external relations to the geometrical ones.

3. The full quotation runs: "A person caught in a philosophical confusion is like a man in a room who wants to get out but doesn't know how. He tries the window but it is too high. He tries the chimney but it is too narrow. And if he would only turn around, he would see that the door had been open all the time!" I am indebted to Nicholas Smith for tracing the reference. Like all of us, Wittgenstein failed to go through a few open doors himself.

4. The phrase "causal net" is inspired by C. B. Martin's "power net." See also his (1993), but without that striking phrase.

5. Lewis in his last years was keen to emphasize that even where we flip the switch to turn the light on, rather than off, there is still what he calls "prevention of prevention." The gap in the circuit when the switch is switched off prevents the current flowing to the bulb. Switching on "prevents this prevention." But notice that here there is nothing that is not causal action. This "prevention" enables the current to flow and light the bulb. To represent a situation of this sort in a neuron diagram, one would need a side chain coming in and affecting a particular neuron in the main chain in such a manner that the main chain was able to continue firing beyond that neuron.

6. For cases of this sort I am beholden to Michael Tooley. See my (1983), p. 133.

7. I may well have picked up this term "fires" from the writings of Nancy Cartwright, who tells me that she sometimes uses it in the same way. In her (1989), p. 108, she says that she is "trying to model a very special concept of probabilistic causality, a concept according to which the cause either contributes its entire influence or it does not contribute at all." That is my idea also, although it does not seem so special to me.

8. Menzies (1998) also cites Michotte and illuminatingly links his work with Fodor's modularity hypothesis.

9. See Gasking (1955) and (1996), and Mellor (1995), ch. 7.

10. Davidson (1995), replying to criticism from Elizabeth Anscombe, argues that it is possible to get from causes to laws by conceptual argument alone. I am inclined to think that this does not work, but if it does, then so much the better.

11. Most recently in my (1997), chs. 15 and 16.

12. In the case of a merely probabilistic law I contend that the law, as opposed to the antecedent condition of the law, is instantiated only in the positive cases, only where the law "fires."

References

Albert, David. 2000. *Time and Chance*. Cambridge, Mass.: Harvard University Press.

Anderson, John. 1938. "The Problem of Causality." *Australasian Journal of Philosophy and Psychology* 16: 127–142.

Anscombe, G. E. M. 1971. *Causality and Determination: An Inaugural Lecture*. Cambridge: Cambridge University Press.

Armstrong, D. M. 1962. *Bodily Sensations*. London: Routledge and Kegan Paul.

Armstrong, D. M. 1968. *A Materialist Theory of the Mind*. London: Routledge and Kegan Paul.

Armstrong, D. M. 1983. *What Is a Law of Nature?* New York: Cambridge University Press.

Armstrong, D. M. 1989. *A Combinatorial Theory of Possibility*. New York: Cambridge University Press.

Armstrong, D. M. 1997. *A World of States of Affairs*. New York: Cambridge University Press.

Armstrong, D. M. 1999. "The Open Door." In Sankey (1999): 175–185. A revised version, "Going through the Open Door Again: Counterfactual vs. Singularist Theories of Causation," appeared in Preyer and Siebelt (2001) and is reprinted in this volume.

Bacon, John, Keith Campbell, and Lloyd Reinhardt (eds.). 1993. *Ontology, Causality, and Mind: Essays in Honour of D. M. Armstrong*. New York: Cambridge University Press.

Barker, S. 1999. "Counterfactuals, Probabilistic Counterfactuals and Causation." *Mind* 108: 427–469.

Bedard, Katherine. 1993. "Partial Denotations of Theoretical Terms." *Noûs* 27: 499–511.

Bell, J. S. 1964. "On the Einstein–Podolsky–Rosen Paradox." *Physics* 1: 195–200.

Bennett, Jonathan. 1984. "Counterfactuals and Temporal Direction." *Philosophical Review* 93: 57–91.

Bennett, Jonathan. 1987. "Event Causation: the Counterfactual Analysis." *Philosophical Perspectives* 1: 367–386. Reprinted in Sosa and Tooley (1993): 217–233.

Bennett, Jonathan. 1988. *Events and Their Names*. Indianapolis, Ind.: Hackett.

Bogdan, R. J. (ed.). 1984. *D. M. Armstrong*. Boston: Reidel.

Bohm, D. 1952. "A Suggested Interpretation of Quantum Theory in Terms of 'Hidden Variables,'" Parts I and II. *Physical Review* 85: 166–193.

Bunzl, Martin. 1980. "Causal Preemption and Counterfactuals." *Philosophical Studies* 37: 115–124.

Butterfield, H. 1957. *The Origins of Modern Science, 1300–1800*, second edition. New York: Macmillan.

Byrne, Alex, and Ned Hall. 1998. "Against the PCA-analysis." *Analysis* 58: 38–44.

Campbell, Keith. 1990. *Abstract Particulars*. Oxford: Blackwell.

Carnap, Rudolf. 1963. "Replies and Systematic Expositions." In Schilpp (1963): 963–966.

Carroll, John. 1994. *Laws of Nature*. New York: Cambridge University Press.

Cartwright, Nancy. 1979. "Causal Laws and Effective Strategies." *Noûs* 13: 419–437.

Cartwright, Nancy. 1983. *How the Laws of Physics Lie*. Oxford: Clarendon Press.

Cartwright, Nancy. 1989. *Nature's Capacities and Their Measurement*. Oxford: Clarendon Press.

Cartwright, Nancy. 1999. *The Dappled World*. Oxford: Oxford University Press.

Casati, Roberto, and Achille Varzi. 1994. *Holes and Other Superficialities*. Cambridge, Mass.: MIT Press.

Chisholm, Roderick M. 1946. "The Contrary-to-Fact Conditional." *Mind* 55: 219–307.

Chisholm, Roderick M. 1955. "Law Statements and Counterfactual Inference." *Analysis* 15: 97–105.

Collins, John. 1999. "Indeterminacy and Intention." In Lewis Hahn (ed.), *The Philosophy of Donald Davidson*, The Library of Living Philosophers, volume 27, 501–528. Chicago, Ill.: Open Court.

Collins, John. 2000. "Preemptive Prevention." *Journal of Philosophy* 97: 223–234. Reprinted in this volume.

Davidson, Donald. 1967. "Causal Relations." *Journal of Philosophy* 64: 691–703. Reprinted in Davidson (1980): 149–162.

Davidson, Donald. 1969. "The Individuation of Events." In Nicholas Rescher (ed.), *Essays in Honor of Carl G. Hempel*, 216–234. Dordrecht: Reidel. Reprinted in Davidson (1980): 163–180.

Davidson, Donald. 1970. "Events as Particulars." *Noûs* 4: 25–32. Reprinted in Davidson (1980): 181–187.

Davidson, Donald. 1980. *Essays on Actions and Events*. New York: Oxford University Press.

Davidson, Donald. 1985. "Reply to Quine on Events." In Lepore and MacLaughlin (1985): 172–176.

Davidson, Donald. 1995. "Law and Cause." *Dialectica* 49: 263–279.

Davidson, Donald, and Gilbert Harman (eds.). 1972. *Semantics of Natural Language*. Dordrecht: Reidel.

Dowe, Phil. 1992. "Wesley Salmon's Process Theory of Causality and the Conserved Quantity Theory." *Philosophy of Science* 59: 195–216.

Dowe, Phil. 1996. "Backwards Causation and the Direction of Causal Processes." *Mind* 105: 227–248.

Dowe, Phil. 1999. "Good Connections: Causation and Causal Processes." In Sankey (1999): 247–263.

Dowe, Phil. 2000. *Physical Causation*. New York: Cambridge University Press.

Dretske, Fred. 1973. "Contrastive Statements." *The Philosophical Review* 82: 411–437.

Dretske, Fred. 1977a. "Laws of Nature." *Philosophy of Science* 64: 248–268.

Dretske, Fred. 1977b. "Referring to Events." *Midwest Studies in Philosophy* 2: 90–99.

Ducasse, C. J. 1926. "On the Nature and the Observability of the Causal Relation." *Journal of Philosophy* 23: 57–68.

Ducasse, C. J. 1968. *Truth, Knowledge, and Causation*. London: Routledge and Kegan Paul.

Earman, John. 1984. "Laws of Nature: The Empiricist Challenge." In Bogdan (1984): 191–223.

Edgington, D. 1995. "On Conditionals." *Mind* 104: 235–329.

Edgington, D. 1999. "Counterfactuals and the Importance of Hindsight." Unpublished paper, delivered at a London School of Economics workshop on Chance and Cause.

Eells, Ellery. 1991. *Probabilistic Causality*. Cambridge: Cambridge University Press.

Ehring, Douglas. 1987. "Causal Relata." *Synthese* 73: 319–328.

Ehring, Douglas. 1989. "Preemption and Probabilistic Counterfactual Theory." *Philosophical Studies* 56: 307–313.

Ehring, Douglas. 1990. "Preemption, Direct Causation, and Identity." *Synthese* 85: 55–70.

Ehring, Douglas. 1994. "Preemption and Eells on Token Causation." *Philosophical Studies* 74: 39–50.

Ehring, Douglas. 1997. *Causation and Persistence*. New York: Oxford University Press.

Elga, Adam. 2000. "Statistical Mechanics and the Asymmetry of Counterfactual Dependence." *Philosophy of Science* (suppl. vol. 68, PSA 2000): 313–324.

Fair, David. 1979. "Causation and the Flow of Energy." *Erkenntnis* 14: 219–250.

Fales, Evan. 1990. *Causation and Universals*. London: Routledge.

Fetzer, James H. (ed.). 1988. *Probability and Causality*. Boston: Reidel.

Fillmore, Charles. 1971. "How to Know Whether You're Coming or Going." In Karl Hyldgard-Jensen (ed.), *Linguistik*. 369–379. Frankfurt: Athenäum Verlag.

Fine, Kit. 1975. "Review of Lewis, *Counterfactuals*." *Mind* 84: 451–458.

Fischer, John Martin, and Mark Ravizza (eds.). 1993a. *Perspectives on Moral Responsibility*. Ithaca, NY: Cornell University Press.

Fischer, John Martin, and Mark Ravizza. 1993b. "Responsibility for Consequences." In Fischer and Ravizza (1993a): 322–347.

Fodor, J. 1991. "You Can Fool Some of the People All the Time, Other Things Being Equal: Hedged Laws and Psychological Explanation." *Mind* 100: 19–34.

Frankfurt, Harry. 1969. "Alternate Possibilities and Moral Responsibility." *Journal of Philosophy* 66: 829–839.

Ganeri, Jonardon, P. Noordhof, and M. Ramachandran. 1996. "Counterfactuals and Preemptive Causation." *Analysis* 56: 219–225.

Ganeri, Jonardon, P. Noordhof, and M. Ramachandran. 1998. "For a (Revised) PCA-analysis." *Analysis* 58: 45–47.

Garfinkel, A. 1981. *Forms of Explanation*. New Haven, Conn.: Yale University Press.

Gasking, Douglas. 1955. "Causation and Recipes." *Mind* 64: 479–487. Reprinted in Oakley and O'Neill (1996): 106–115.

Gasking, Douglas. 1996. "Hypotheticals, Recipes, and Causation." In Oakley and O'Neill (1996): 116–131.

Giere, R. 1988. *Explaining Science*. Chicago, Ill.: University of Chicago Press.

Goldman, Alvin. 1970. *A Theory of Human Action*. Englewood Cliffs, N.J.: Prentice-Hall.

Goodman, Nelson. 1947. "The Problem of Counterfactual Conditionals." *Journal of Philosophy* 44: 113–128. Reprinted in Goodman (1979).

Goodman, Nelson. 1979. *Fact, Fiction, and Forecast*. Cambridge, Mass.: Harvard University Press.

Goosens, William K. 1979. "Causal Chains and Counterfactuals." *Journal of Philosophy* 76: 489–495.

Gorovitz, S. 1965. "Causal Judgements and Causal Explanations." *Journal of Philosophy* 62: 695–711.

Grice, H. P. 1975. "Logic and Conversation." In P. Cole and J. L. Morgan (eds.), *Syntax and Semantics*, volume 3. New York: Academic Press.

Hall, Ned. 1994. "New Problems for an Analysis of Causation." Unpublished paper presented at the annual conference of the Australasian Association of Philosophy.

Hall, Ned. 2000. "Causation and the Price of Transitivity." *Journal of Philosophy* 97: 198–222. Reprinted in this volume.

Hall, Ned. 2002a. "Non-locality on the Cheap? A New Problem for Counterfactual Analyses of Causation." *Noûs* 36: 276–294.

Hall, Ned. 2002b. "The Intrinsic Character of Causation." In Dean Zimmerman (ed.), *Oxford Studies in Metaphysics*, volume 1. Oxford: Oxford University Press, 2002.

Harper, William L., and B. Skyrms (eds.). 1988. *Causation in Decision, Belief Change, and Statistics*. Boston: Kluwer.

Hart, H. L. A., and A. M. Honoré. 1985. *Causation in the Law*, second edition. Oxford: Clarendon Press.

Hausman, Daniel. 1992. "Thresholds, Transitivity, Overdetermination, and Events." *Analysis* 52: 159–163.

Hausman, Daniel. 1998. *Causal Asymmetries*. New York: Cambridge University Press.

Heathcote, Adrian, and D. M. Armstrong. 1991. "Causes and Laws." *Noûs* 25: 63–73.

Heinlein, Robert. 1951. *The Puppet Masters*. Garden City, N.Y.: Doubleday.

Hempel, C. 1965. *Aspects of Scientific Explanation*. New York: The Free Press.

Hitchcock, C. 1993. "A Generalized Probabilistic theory of Causal Relevance." *Synthese* 97: 335–364.

Hitchcock, C. 1995a. "The Mishap at Reichenbach Fall: Singular vs. General Causation." *Philosophical Studies* 78: 257–291.

Hitchcock, C. 1995b. "Discussion: Salmon on Explanatory Relevance." *Philosophy of Science* 62: 304–320.

Hitchcock, C. 1996a. "Farewell to Binary Causation." *Canadian Journal of Philosophy* 26: 267–282.

Hitchcock, C. 1996b. "The Role of Contrast in Causal and Explanatory Claims." *Synthese* 107: 395–419.

Hitchcock, C. 1998. "Causal Knowledge: That Great Guide of Human Life." *Communication and Cognition* 31: 271–296.

Holland, Paul. 1986. "Statistics and Causal Inference." *Journal of the American Statistical Association* 81: 945–960.

Horwich, Paul. 1989. *Asymmetries in Time*. Cambridge, Mass.: MIT Press.

Hume, David. 1888 (1739). *A Treatise of Human Nature*, ed. L. A. Selby-Bigge. Oxford: Clarendon Press.

Hume, David. 1902 (1748). *An Enquiry Concerning Human Understanding*, ed. L. A. Selby-Bigge. Oxford: Clarendon Press.

Humphreys, P. 1989. *The Chances of Explanation: Causal Explanations in the Social, Medical, and Physical Sciences*. Princeton, N.J.: Princeton University Press.

Jackson, Frank. 1977. *Perception: A Representative Theory*. Cambridge: Cambridge University Press.

Jackson, Frank, and Philip Pettit. 1990. "Program Explanation: A General Perspective." *Analysis* 50: 107–117.

Johnson, W. E. 1924. *Logic*, vol. 3. Cambridge: Cambridge University Press.

Johnston, M. 1993. "Objectivity Refigured: Pragmatism without Verificationism," Appendix 2: "Complexities in the Notion of a Disposition." In J. Haldane and C. Wright (eds.), *Reality, Representation, and Projection*, 119–121. New York: Oxford University Press.

Joseph, G. 1980. "The Many Sciences and the One World." *Journal of Philosophy* 77: 773–790.

Kim, Jaegwon. 1971. "Causes and Events: Mackie on Causation." *Journal of Philosophy* 68: 426–441.

Kim, Jaegwon. 1973a. "Causation, Nomic Subsumption, and the Concept of Event." *Journal of Philosophy* 70: 217–236.

Kim, Jaegwon. 1973b. "Causes and Counterfactuals." *Journal of Philosophy* 70: 570–572.

Kim, Jaegwon. 1980. "Events as Property Exemplifications." In M. Brand and D. Walton (eds.), *Action Theory*, 159–177. Dordrecht: Reidel. Reprinted in Kim (1993): 33–52.

Kim, Jaegwon. 1982. "Psychophysical Supervenience." *Philosophical Studies* 41: 51–70.

Kim, Jaegwon. 1993. *Supervenience and Mind: Selected Philosophical Essays*. New York: Cambridge University Press.

Knowles, Dudley (ed.). 1990. *Explanation and Its Limits*. Cambridge: Cambridge University Press.

Kripke, Saul. 1972. "Naming and Necessity." In Davidson and Harman (1972): 253–355.

Kripke, S. 1982. *Wittgenstein on Rules and Private Language*. Cambridge, Mass.: Harvard University Press.

Kvart, Igal. 1975. *Counterfactual Conditionals*. Ph.D. dissertation, University of Pittsburgh.

Kvart, Igal. 1979. "A Formal Semantics for Temporal Logic and Counterfactuals." *Logique et Analyse* 22: 35–62.

Kvart, Igal. 1986. *A Theory of Counterfactuals*. Indianapolis, Ind.: Hackett.

Kvart, Igal. 1991a. "Counterfactuals and Causal Relevance." *Pacific Philosophical Quarterly* 72: 314–337.

Kvart, Igal. 1991b. "Transitivity and Preemption of Causal Impact." *Philosophical Studies* 64: 125–160.

Kvart, Igal. 1992. "Counterfactuals." *Erkenntnis* 36: 1–41.

Kvart, Igal. 1994. "Overall Positive Causal Impact." *Canadian Journal of Philosophy* 26: 267–282.

Kvart, Igal. 1997. "Cause and Some Positive Causal Impact." In J. Tomberlin (ed.), *Philosophical Perspectives 11: Mind, Causation, and World*, 401–432. Atascadero, Calif.: Ridgeview.

Kvart, Igal. 2001a. "A Counterfactual Theory of Cause." *Synthese* 127: 389–427.

Kvart, Igal. 2001b. "Causal Relevance." In Bryson Brown (ed.), *New Studies in Exact Philosophy: Logic, Mathematics and Science*, 59–90. Oxford: Hermes Scientific Publications.

Kvart, Igal. 2001c. "Counterexamples to Lewis's 'Causation as Influence.'" *Australasian Journal of Philosophy* 79: 411–423.

Kvart, Igal. 2003. "Probabilistic Cause, Edge Conditions, Late Preemption and Discrete Cases." In Phil Dowe and Paul Noordhof (eds.), *Cause and Chance: Causation in an Indeterministic World.* London: Routledge.

Kvart, Igal. Forthcoming a. "Mental Causation and Probabilistic Causation." *Pacific Philosophical Quarterly.*

Kvart, Igal. Forthcoming b. "Cause: Time and Manner."

Kvart, Igal. Forthcoming c. "Partial Causal Neutralizers."

Langton, Rae, and David Lewis. 1998. "Defining 'Intrinsic.'" *Philosophy and Phenomenological Research* 58: 333–345. Reprinted in Lewis (1999): 116–132.

LeCatt, Bruce. 1982. "Censored Vision." *Australasian Journal of Philosophy* 60: 158–162.

Lee, Jig-chuen. 1988. "The Nontransitivity of Causation." *American Philosophical Quarterly* 25: 87–94.

LePore, Ernest, and Brian McLaughlin. 1985. *Actions and Events: Perspectives on the Philosophy of Donald Davidson.* New York: Blackwell.

Lewis, David. 1966. "An Argument for the Identity Theory." *Journal of Philosophy* 63: 17–25. Reprinted with additional material in Lewis (1983a): 99–107.

Lewis, David. 1970. "How to Define Theoretical Terms." *Journal of Philosophy* 67: 427–446. Reprinted in Lewis (1983a): 78–95.

Lewis, David. 1973a. "Causation." *Journal of Philosophy* 70: 556–567. Reprinted in Lewis (1986a): 159–172.

Lewis, David. 1973b. *Counterfactuals.* Cambridge: Harvard University Press.

Lewis, David. 1973c. "Counterfactuals and Comparative Possibility." *Journal of Philosophical Logic* 2: 418–446. Reprinted in Lewis (1986a): 3–31.

Lewis, David. 1979a. "Counterfactual Dependence and Time's Arrow." *Noûs* 13: 455–476. Reprinted with postscripts in Lewis (1986a): 32–66.

Lewis, David. 1979b. "Scorekeeping in a Language Game." *Journal of Philosophical Logic* 8: 339–359. Reprinted in Lewis (1983a): 233–249.

Lewis, David. 1980. "Index, Context, and Content." In Stig Kanger and Sven Öhman (eds.), *Philosophy and Grammar.* Dordrecht: Reidel. Reprinted in Lewis (1998): 21–44.

Lewis, David. 1983a. *Philosophical Papers*, volume I. Oxford: Oxford University Press.

Lewis, David. 1983b. "New Work for a Theory of Universals." *Australasian Journal of Philosophy* 61: 343–377. Reprinted in Lewis (1999): 8–55.

Lewis, David. 1986a. *Philosophical Papers*, volume II. Oxford: Oxford University Press.

Lewis, David. 1986b. "Postscripts to 'Causation.'" In Lewis (1986a): 172–213.

Lewis, David. 1986c. "Causal Explanation." In Lewis (1986a): 214–240.

Lewis, David. 1986d. "Events." In Lewis (1986a): 241–269.

Lewis, David. 1986e. *On the Plurality of Worlds.* Oxford: Blackwell.

Lewis, David. 1993. "Many, but Almost One." In Bacon, Campbell, and Reinhardt (1993): 23–38. Reprinted in Lewis (1999): 164–182.

Lewis, David. 1997. "Finkish Dispositions." *Philosophical Quarterly* 47: 143–158. Reprinted in Lewis (1999): 133–151.

Lewis, David. 1998. *Papers in Philosophical Logic.* Cambridge: Cambridge University Press.

Lewis, David. 1999. *Papers in Metaphysics and Epistemology.* Cambridge: Cambridge University Press.

Lewis, David. 2000. "Causation as Influence." *Journal of Philosophy* 97: 182–197. An expanded version of the paper appears in this volume.

Lewis, David, and Stephanie Lewis. 1970. "Holes." *Australasian Journal of Philosophy* 48: 206–212. Reprinted in Lewis (1983a): 3–9.

Lipton, P. 1990. "Contrastive Explanation." In D. Knowles (ed.), *Explanation and Its Limits*. Cambridge: Cambridge University Press, 1990.

Lipton, P. 1991. *Inference to the Best Explanation*. London: Routledge.

Lombard, Lawrence. 1986. *Events: A Metaphysical Study*. London: Routledge and Kegan Paul.

Lombard, Lawrence. 1990. "Causes, Enablers, and the Counterfactual Analysis." *Philosophical Studies* 59: 195–211.

Lowe, E. J. 1980. "For Want of a Nail." *Analysis* 40: 50–52.

Mackie, J. L. 1965. "Causes and Conditions." *American Philosophical Quarterly* 2: 245–264.

Mackie, J. L. 1974. *The Cement of the Universe*. Oxford: Clarendon Press.

Mackie, Penelope. 1992. "Causing, Delaying, and Hastening: Do Rains Cause Fires?" *Mind* 101: 483–500.

Malcolm, Norman. 1958. *Ludwig Wittgenstein: A Memoir*. New York: Oxford University Press.

Martin, C. B. 1993. "Power for Realists." In Bacon, Campbell, and Reinhardt (1993): 175–186.

Martin, C. B. 1994. "Dispositions and Conditionals." *Philosophical Quarterly* 44: 1–8.

Martin, C. B. 1996. "How It Is: Entities, Absences, and Voids." *Australasian Journal of Philosophy* 74: 57–65.

Maslen, Cei. 2000. *Causes, Effects, and Contrasts*. Princeton Ph.D. dissertation. Ann Arbor, Mich.: University Microfilms International.

Maudlin, Tim. 1994. *Quantum Non-locality and Relativity*. Oxford: Blackwell.

Maudlin, Tim. Forthcoming. "A Modest Proposal Concerning Laws, Counterfactuals, and Explanation."

McDermott, Michael. 1995a. "Redundant Causation." *British Journal for the Philosophy of Science* 46: 523–544.

McDermott, Michael. 1995b. "Lewis on Causal Dependence." *Australasian Journal of Philosophy* 73: 129–139.

McGrath, Sarah. 2002. "Causation by Omission." Chapter 2 of Sarah McGrath, *Causation in Metaphysics and Moral Theory*, Ph.D. dissertation, Massachusetts Institute of Technology.

Mellor, D. H. 1987. "The Singularly Affecting Facts of Causation." In P. Pettit, R. Sylvan, and J. Norman (eds.), *Metaphysics and Morality*. Oxford: Basil Blackwell.

Mellor, D. H. 1988. "On Raising the Chances of Effects." In Fetzer (1988): 229–240.

Mellor, D. H. 1995. *The Facts of Causation*. London: Routledge.

Mellor, D. H. 1997. "Properties and Predicates." In Mellor and Oliver (1997): 255–267.

Mellor, D. H. 1998. *Real Time II*. London: Routledge.

Mellor, D. H. 2000. "The Semantics and Ontology of Dispositions." *Mind* 109: 757–780.

Mellor, D. H., and A. Oliver (eds.). 1997. *Properties*. Oxford: Oxford University Press.

Menzies, Peter. 1989a. "Probabilistic Causation and Causal Processes: A Critique of Lewis." *Philosophy of Science* 56: 642–663.

Menzies, Peter. 1989b. "A Unified Theory of Causal Relata." *Australasian Journal of Philosophy* 67: 59–83.

Menzies, Peter. 1996. "Probabilistic Causation and the Pre-Emption Problem." *Mind* 105: 85–117.

Menzies, Peter. 1998. "How Justified Are the Humean Doubts about Intrinsic Causal Links?" *Communication and Cognition* 31: 339–364.

Menzies, Peter. 1999. "Intrinsic versus Extrinsic Conceptions of Causation." In Sankey (1999): 313–329.

Menzies, Peter. 2002. "The Causal Efficacy of Mental States." In J. Monnoyer (ed.), *The Structure of the World: The Renewal of Metaphysics in the Australian School*. Paris: Vrin.

Menzies, Peter, and Huw Price. 1993. "Causation as a Secondary Quality." *British Journal for the Philosophy of Science* 44: 187–205.

Mill, J. S. 1961. *A System of Logic*. London: Longmans.

Miller, Richard W. 1987. *Fact and Method: Explanation, Confirmation, and Reality in the Natural and the Social Sciences*. Princeton, N.J.: Princeton University Press.

Michotte, A. 1963. *The Perception of Causality*. Translated by T. R. Miles and Elaine Miles. London: Methuen.

Noordhof, P. 1998. "Problems for the M-set Analysis of Causation." *Mind* 107: 457–463.

Noordhof, P. 1999. "Probabilistic Causation, Preemption and Counterfactuals." *Mind* 108: 95–125.

Noordhof, P. 2000. "Ramachandran's Four Counterexamples." *Mind* 109: 315–324.

Oakley, I. T., and L. J. O'Neill. 1996. *Language, Logic, and Causation: Philosophical Writings of Douglas Gasking*. Melbourne: Melbourne University Press.

Otte, R. 1986. "Reichenbach, Causation, and Explanation." In A. Fine and P. Machamer (eds.), *PSA 1986*, volume 1, 59–65. East Lansing, Mich.: Philosophy of Science Association.

Parascondola, M. 1996. "Evidence and Association: Epistemic Confusion in Toxic Tort Law." In L. Darden (ed.), *PSA 1996, Part I. Philosophy of Science* 63: S168–S176.

Paul, L. A. 1998a. "Problems with Late Preemption." *Analysis* 58: 48–53.

Paul, L. A. 1998b. "Keeping Track of the Time: Emending the Counterfactual Analysis of Causation." *Analysis* 58: 191–198.

Paul, L. A. 2000. "Aspect Causation." *Journal of Philosophy* 97: 235–256. Reprinted in this volume.

Pearl, Judea. 2000. *Causality: Models, Reasoning, and Inference*. Cambridge: Cambridge University Press.

Pietroski, P., and G. Rey. 1995. "When Other Things Aren't Equal: Saving *Ceteris Paribus* Laws from Vacuity." *British Journal for the Philosophy of Science* 46: 81–110.

Preyer, Gerhard, and Frank Siebelt (eds.). 2001. *Reality and Humean Supervenience: Essays on the Philosophy of David Lewis*. New York: Rowman and Littlefield.

Price, Huw. 1994. "A Neglected Route to Realism about Quantum Mechanics." *Mind* 103: 303–336.

Prior, Elizabeth, Robert Pargetter, and Frank Jackson. 1982. "Three Theses about Dispositions." *American Philosophical Quarterly* 19: 251–253.

Quine, W. V. O. 1960. *Word and Object*. Cambridge, Mass.: MIT Press.

Quine, W. V. O. 1985. "Events and Reification." In LePore and McLaughlin (1985): 162–176.

Ramachandran, Murali. 1997a. "A Counterfactual Analysis of Causation." *Mind* 151: 263–277.

Ramachandran, Murali. 1997b. "Redundant Causation, Composite Events, and M-sets." *Acta Analytica* 16/17: 149–158.

Ramachandran, Murali. 1998. "The M-set Analysis of Causation: Objections and Responses." *Mind* 107: 465–471.

Ramachandran, Murali. 2000. "Noordhof on Probabilistic Causation." *Mind* 109: 309–313.

Ramsey, F. P. 1925. "Universals." In Ramsey (1990): 8–30.

Ramsey, F. P. 1990. *Philosophical Papers*. Ed. D. H. Mellor. Cambridge: Cambridge University Press.

Reichenbach, Hans. 1928. *Philosophie der Raum-Zeit-Lehre*. Berlin: Walter de Gruyter. English translation published as Reichenbach (1958).

Reichenbach, Hans. 1958. *The Philosophy of Space and Time*. New York: Dover.

Restall, G. 1996. "Truthmakers, Entailment, and Necessity." *Australasian Journal of Philosophy* 74: 331–340.

Rice, Hugh. 1999. "David Lewis's Awkward Cases of Redundant Causation." *Analysis* 59: 157–164.

Rosenberg, Alex. 1992. "Causation, Probability, and the Monarchy." *American Philosophical Quarterly* 29: 305–318.

Rowe, William L. 1993. "Causing and Being Responsible for What Is Inevitable." In Fischer and Ravizza (1993a): 310–321.

Russell, Bertrand. 1953. "On the Notion of Cause." In Russell, *Mysticism and Logic*. London: Penguin.

Salmon, W. C. 1984. *Scientific Explanation and the Causal Structure of the World*. Princeton, N.J.: Princeton University Press.

Salmon, Wesley. 1994. "Causality without Counterfactuals." *Philosophy of Science* 61: 297–312.

Sankey, Howard (ed). 1999. *Causation and Laws of Nature*. Dordrecht: Kluwer.

Schaffer, Jonathan. 2000a. "Overlappings: Probability-raising without Causation." *Australasian Journal of Philosophy* 78: 40–46.

Schaffer, Jonathan. 2000b. "Trumping Preemption." *Journal of Philosophy* 97: 165–181. Reprinted in this volume.

Schaffer, Jonathan. 2001. "Causes as Probability-raisers of Processes." *Journal of Philosophy* 98: 75–92.

Schiffer, S. 1991. "Ceteris Paribus Laws." *Mind* 100: 1–18.

Schilpp, P. A. (ed.). 1963. *The Philosophy of Rudolf Carnap*. La Salle, Ill.: Open Court.

Shoemaker, S. 1980. "Causality and Properties." In van Inwagen (1980): 109–135.

Shope, R. K. 1978. "The Conditional Fallacy in Contemporary Philosophy." *Journal of Philosophy* 75: 397–413.

Skyrms, B. 1980. *Causal Necessity: A Pragmatic Investigation of the Necessity of Laws*. New Haven, Conn.: Yale University Press.

Sober, E. 1980. "Evolution, Population Thinking, and Essentialism." *Philosophy of Science* 47: 350–383.

Sober, E. 1984. *The Nature of Selection*. Cambridge, Mass.: MIT Press.

Sober, E. 1985. "Two Concepts of Cause." In P. D. Asquith and P. Kitcher (eds.), *PSA 1984*, vol. II, 405–424. East Lansing, Mich.: Philosophy of Science Association.

Sorensen, Roy. 1999. "Seeing Intersecting Eclipses." *Journal of Philosophy* 96: 25–49.

Sosa, Ernest, and Michael Tooley (eds.). 1993. *Causation*. Oxford: Oxford University Press.

Stalnaker, Robert. 1968. "A Theory of Conditionals." In Nicholas Rescher (ed.), *Studies in Logical Theory*. Oxford: Blackwell.

Stalnaker, Robert. 1972. "Pragmatics." In Davidson and Harman (1972): 380–397.

Stalnaker, Robert. 1980. "A Defense of Conditional Excluded Middle." In William L. Harper, Robert Stalnaker, and Glenn Peirce (eds.), *Ifs: Conditionals, Belief, Decision, Chance, and Time*, 87–104. Dordrecht: Reidel.

Stapleton, J. 1994. *Product Liability*. London: Butterworths.

Steward, H. 1997. *The Ontology of Mind*. Oxford: Clarendon Press.

Stewart, I. 1989. *Does God Play Dice?* Oxford: Blackwell.

Suppe, F. 1979. "Introduction" to *The Structure of Scientific Theories*. Urbana, Ill.: University of Illinois Press.

Suppe, F. 1989. *The Semantic Conception of Theories and Scientific Realism*. Urbana, Ill.: University of Illinois Press.

Suppes, P. 1970. *A Probabilistic Theory of Causality*. Amsterdam: North-Holland.

Swain, Marshall. 1978. "A Counterfactual Analysis of Event Causation." *Philosophical Studies* 34: 1–19.

Taylor, A. E. 1956. *Plato: The Man and His Work*. Cleveland, Ohio: Meridian.

Tichý, Pavel. 1984. "Subjunctive Conditionals: Two Parameters vs. Three." *Philosophical Studies* 45: 147–179.

Todes, Samuel, and Charles Daniels. 1975. "Beyond the Doubt of a Shadow: A Phenomenological and Linguistic Analysis of Shadows." In D. Ihde and R. M. Zaner, (eds.), *Selected Studies in Phenomenology and Existential Philosophy*. The Hague: Nijhoff.

Tooley, Michael. 1987. *Causation: A Realist Approach*. New York: Oxford University Press.

Tooley, Michael. 1990. "Causation: Reductionism versus Realism." *Philosophy and Phenomenological Research* 50 (supplement): 215–236.

Toulmin, S. 1961. *Foresight and Understanding: An Inquiry into the Aims of Science*. Indianapolis, Ind.: Indiana University Press.

Unger, Peter. 1977. "The Uniqueness of Causation." *American Philosophical Quarterly* 14: 177–188.

van Fraassen, Bas. 1966. "Singular Terms, Truth-Value Gaps, and Free Logic." *Journal of Philosophy* 63: 481–495.

van Fraassen, Bas. 1980. *The Scientific Image*. Oxford: Clarendon Press.

van Fraassen, Bas. 1989. *Laws and Symmetry*. Oxford: Oxford University Press.

van Inwagen, Peter (ed.). 1980. *Time and Cause*. Dordrecht: Reidel.

van Inwagen, Peter. 1987. "Ability and Responsibility." *Philosophical Review* 87: 201–224.

White, Morton. 1965. *Foundations of Historical Knowledge*. New York: Harper and Row.

Williams, Donald. 1953. "On the Elements of Being." *Review of Metaphysics* 7: 3–18, 171–192.

Woodward, J. 1984. "A Theory of Singular Causal Explanation." *Erkenntnis* 21: 231–262.

Woodward, J. 1990. "Supervenience and Singular Causal Statements." In Knowles (1990): 215–216.

Woodward, J. 1994. "Review of Humphreys *The Chances of Explanation*." *British Journal for the Philosophy of Science* 45: 353–374.

Woodward, J. 2003. *Making Things Happen: A Theory of Causal Explanation*. Oxford: Oxford University Press.

Yablo, Steve. 1986. *Things*. Ph.D. dissertation, University of California–Berkeley. Ann Arbor, Mich.: University Microfilms International.

Yablo, Steve. 1992a. "Cause and Essence." *Synthese* 93: 403–449.

Yablo, Steve. 1992b. "Mental Causation." *Philosophical Review* 101: 245–280.

Yablo, Steve. 2000. "The Seven Habits of Highly Effective Thinkers." In Bernard Elevitch (ed.), *Proceedings of the Twentieth World Congress of Philosophy*, volume IX: *Philosophy of Mind and Philosophy of Psychology*. Charlottesville, Virginia: Philosophy Documentation Center.

General Index

Absences. *See also* Facts, negative; Void
and abnormality criterion, 295
of absences, 283
as background conditions, 173–175
and biff, 284–285, 288, 448–449
cannot be causes, 25, 34–36, 49, 53, 281, 291–308
and causal explanation, 291, 293–294, 301, 304–306
and two concepts of causation, 253
as causes and effects, 99–102, 108–109, 112, 248–249, 341
as causes and effects on Lewis's original analysis, 19, 24–25, 144–145, 447
common sense and causation by, 294–297, 300, 306–307
and intrinsic character of causation, 240–241, 244, 248–252
location of, 243, 248–249
moral norms and the causal status of, 293, 296–299, 306
and the nature of causal relata, 48–49, 77, 100, 151, 281–282, 314
and neuron diagrams, 232
and nonrelational view of causation, 100, 283, 292, 298–300, 304
ontological status of, 49, 100, 145, 248, 254, 281–283, 304, 448
and probabilistic causation, 376
and production, 226, 256, 260
spurious cases of causation by, 298, 301
and transitivity of causation, 198–199, 252
Accommodation, rule of, 405
Action at a distance
and causation at a distance, 85
and double prevention, 29, 184, 198, 242–243
as a far-fetched case, 38, 422
excluded from analyses of dependence and production, 226, 232, 258–259
and intrinsic character of causation, 240
in interaction diagrams, 439
and Lewis's treatment of early preemption, 24, 33, 373
and *Locality* thesis, 238, 242–243
and trumping preemption, 65–66, 215
Actual causation, 404, 410, 416
Agency, 60–61
Agency theory of causation, 449, 455
Albert, David, 8
Alterations of an event, 88–96, 99, 103–104, 146, 215–221, 345
Ancestral dependence maneuver
and backtracking, 234
and causation as influence, 51, 93, 95–96, 216–217
and the fragility strategy, 88

in Lewis's original analysis, 22, 39, 79, 121, 141–142, 206, 267, 310, 420, 445
and trumping preemption, 67–70
Armstrong, D. M., 13, 32, 48, 50, 59, 63–64, 319
Aronson, J., 456
Aspect analysis of causation, 43, 52–53, 186–189, 197, 205–222, 330, 345, 365
Australian rules football, 286

Background conditions, 52, 143–144, 146, 169, 172–178, 190, 403. *See also* Normal conditions
Backtracking
and aspect analysis of causation, 220
and contrastive causation, 352
and contrastive explanation, 149–150, 177
and *Dependence* thesis, 181, 200
and Lewis's original analysis, 17–19, 78, 141, 233–235, 445
and naive counterfactual analysis, 326
and neuron diagrams, 435
and production, 262
and similarity of worlds, 5–9, 165
and spurious causation, 163
and transitivity of causation, 247
Backup systems, 421–423, 428, 451
Backward causation, 6–12, 17, 38, 226, 232, 240, 258–259, 388, 390, 393, 400
Barker, Stephen, 401
Beebee, Helen, 25, 34–36, 48–50, 53, 401
Bennett, Jonathan, 20, 96, 130–131, 229–231, 253, 330, 335
Berkovitz, Joseph, 417
Biff, 53, 283–288, 448–449
Blocker. *See* Screener
Blueprint strategy. *See* Production
Bohm, David, 415
Byrne, Alex, 380

Canberra plan. *See* Causal functionalism
Carroll, John, 63–64
Cartwright, Nancy, 12, 158, 403
Causal
action (*see* Biff)
functionalism, 76, 279–287, 452–453
models, 158–166, 170–178
process theories (*see* Physical connection accounts of causation)
relevance, 359–380
relevance neutralizer (*see* Neutralizer)
tendencies, 404, 410, 416
Causation at a distance, 85, 240, 388. *See also* Action at a distance
Centering principle, 141, 162, 164, 166
Ceteris paribus conditional probabilities, 411
Ceteris paribus laws. *See* Laws

Index of Examples